Beyond Dispute Resolution

Nijhoff International Investment Law Series

VOLUME 28

The titles published in this series are listed at *brill.com/iils*

Beyond Dispute Resolution

Historical Investor-State Arbitration as Governance

By

Vladislav Djanic

BRILL | NIJHOFF

LEIDEN | BOSTON

Cover image: Construction Peace Palace – progress. Image courtesy of the Carnegie Foundation – Peace Palace.

Library of Congress Cataloging-in-Publication Data

Names: Djanic, Vladislav, author
Title: Beyond dispute resolution: historical investor-state arbitration as governance / by Vladislav Djanic.
Description: Boston, Massachusetts : Brill, 2025. | Series: Nijhoff international investment law series ; 28 | Includes bibliographical references and index.
Identifiers: LCCN 2025010137 (print) | LCCN 2025010138 (ebook) | ISBN 9789004733817 hardback | ISBN 9789004733824 ebook
Subjects: LCSH: International commercial arbitration–History | Arbitration and award–History | Dispute resolution (Law)–History | Investments, Foreign (International law) | Investments, Foreign–Law and legislation
Classification: LCC K2400 .B545 2025 (print) | LCC K2400 (ebook) | DDC 346/.092–dc23/eng/20250307
LC record available at https://lccn.loc.gov/2025010137
LC ebook record available at https://lccn.loc.gov/2025010138

Typeface for the Latin, Greek, and Cyrillic scripts: "Brill". See and download: brill.com/brill-typeface.

ISSN 2351-9542
ISBN 978-90-04-73381-7 (hardback)
ISBN 978-90-04-73382-4 (e-book)
DOI 10.1163/9789004733824

This book is printed on acid-free paper and produced in a sustainable manner.

Contents

Acknowledgments IX

1 **Introduction** 1
  1 Setting the Stage 1
  2 Rich Past Notwithstanding … A Field Lacking in History 3
  3 Aims of the Book 10
  4 Methodology 15
    4.1 *Historical Approach and Its Limitations* 15
    4.2 *Temporal Scope and (Lack of) Periodisation* 22
    4.3 *Conceptual Clarifications* 25
  5 The Structure of the Argument 27

2 **Historical Investor-State Arbitration as Private Dispute Settlement: A Breakdown** 32
  1 Introduction 32
  2 What Was at Stake in Historical Investor-State Arbitration? Beyond the Disputing Parties' Interests 37
    2.1 *The Nature of the Investor-State Relationships Underlying the Historical Investor-State Arbitrations* 38
    2.2 *The Anatomy of the Historical Investor-State Disputes* 43
  3 Legal Indeterminacy and the Room for Discretionary Decision-Making in Historical Investor-State Arbitration 48
  4 A Key Role for Private Actors in Historical Investor-State Arbitration 54
    4.1 *Private Party Control over Claims* 55
    4.2 *The Quest for Neutrality and the Externalisation of Decision-Making* 58
    4.3 *Auxiliary Private Actors* 67
  5 Similar in Dissimilarity: The Pervasiveness of Historical Investor-State Arbitration's Key Features 68
    5.1 *Cutting across the Different Legal Frameworks Underlying Historical Investor-State Arbitration* 68
    5.2 *Transcending the Private Law/Public Law Conceptual Chasm* 76
  6 Conclusions: The Breakdown of the Conception of Historical Investor-State Arbitration as (Just) Private Dispute Settlement 81

3 **Historical Investor-State Arbitration and the Cost of Governance** 84
1 Introduction 84
2 Deciding on Matters Relating to Public Debt 90
2.1 *Hambros and Lazard v Romanian Monopolies Institute* 92
2.2 *Peru v Peruvian Corporation* 102
3 Determining the Cost of State Appropriation of Investor Property 109
3.1 *Colombia v Cauca Company* 110
3.2 *The Grand Trunk Railway Arbitration* 118
3.3 *The Jaffa-Jerusalem Railway Arbitration* 131
4 Imposing Liability in Investor-State Relations for Breach of Obligations 138
4.1 *Duff Development Company v Government of Kelantan I and II* 140
4.2 *Sudan v Turriff* 152
5 Size Matters: Potential Ramifications and Governance Implications of Monetary Awards by Historical Investor-State Arbitral Tribunals 157
6 Conclusions 163

4 **Governing by Instruction: Directing State Conduct through Historical Investor-State Arbitration** 166
1 Introduction 166
2 Directing State Entity Conduct through Adjudicative (Arbitral) Review: *Czechoslovakian Administration v RCA* 170
2.1 *Radio Corporation of America: From Inception to Independence* 171
2.2 *The Establishment of RCA's Czechoslovakia Circuit: The First Direct US-Czechoslovakia Radio-Telegraphic Route* 174
2.3 *Trouble on the Horizon: Mackay Radio Sparks a Rift between the RCA and the Czechoslovakian Administration* 176
2.4 *The Arbitration* 180
2.5 *The Immediate (albeit Temporary) Fallout: Czechoslovakia Abstains from Opening an Additional Telegraphic Circuit with the US* 193
3 Directing State Conduct through Primary Decision-Making: The Post-World War I Peace Treaty Railway Arbitrations 198
3.1 *The Peace Treaties and the Need for Railway Reorganisation Following the Break-up of the Austro-Hungarian Empire* 200
3.2 *Sopron-Kőszeg Local Railway Company v Austria and Hungary* 207
3.3 *Zeltweg-Wolfsberg and Unterdrauburg-Woellan Railway Company v Austria and Yugoslavia* 212
3.4 *Barcs-Pakrac Railway Company, Ltd v Hungary and Yugoslavia* 224

3.5 *The Peace Treaty Railway Arbitrations and Historical Investor-State Arbitration as an Avenue for Directing State Conduct* 232
4 Historical Investor-State Arbitration as a Means of Directing State Conduct: A Recurring Theme 235
5 Conclusions 243

5 Developing the Law through Historical Investor-State Arbitration 246
1 Introduction 246
2 Developing the Law for the Disputing Parties: The Power and Traction Concession in Greece 249
2.1 *The Power and Traction Concession* 250
2.2 *The Arbitrations* 254
2.3 *The Implications of the Power and Traction Concession Cases – Governing an Investor-State Relationship through Arbitral Development of the Law* 278
3 Developing the Law for a Disputing Party's Relations with Third Parties: RCA *v China* 282
3.1 *The* RCA*'s Entrance into the Chinese Market amidst Uncertain Times* 283
3.2 *The* RCA*'s Troubles Spread to China: The Mukden Incident and China's Signing of a Contract with Mackay Radio* 286
3.3 *The Arbitral Proceedings* 294
3.4 *The Reverberations of the* RCA *v China Arbitration:* RCA*'s Recalibration of Relations with Third Parties following the Tribunal's Decision* 312
4 Developing the Law beyond the Disputing Parties 323
4.1 *Into the Multiverse: The Gradual Shift toward the Reliance on Previous Case Law in Historical Investor-State Arbitration* 324
4.2 *Generating Normativity that Governed Investor-State Relations* 330
5 Conclusions 342

6 Historical Investor-State Arbitration as a Mode of Governance 347
1 A Recapitulation of Investor-State Arbitration's Historical Role in Governance 347
2 With an Eye to the Future: Toward a Comprehensive Understanding of Investor-State Arbitration's Role as a Mode of Governance 357

Bibliography 363
Index 396

Acknowledgments

The road to this book has been a long and winding one, having taken me through five different countries on two continents. Along this journey, I crossed paths with many people to whom I owe gratitude for helping me reach the desired destination and who have impacted me on either a personal or a professional level (or often on both).

First and foremost, I am forever indebted to my family members, who have provided immense support for my every personal and professional endeavour, and without whom I certainly would not be where I am today.

I also owe great thanks to my partner Bojana. Without you, this book perhaps could have been finished earlier – or, much more likely, may never have been finished at all. Maybe I could have done it without you, but I sure am glad I did not have to find out. I hope to be able to return the favour.

I am especially glad that I got to spend the best part of my PhD years that led to this book with amazing people at the Max Planck Institute for Comparative Public Law and International Law in Heidelberg, the University of Amsterdam and Columbia University. I am particularly grateful to my project-mates Katrine and Heather, my office-mate and Dutch 'host' Vincent, and my flatmate Sophie.

I am likewise indebted to Judge Stephen Schwebel for helping me locate a large amount of awards and related materials on the Greek arbitrations he had previously written on with Gillis Wetter, as well as to Lisa Sachs and George Bermann for sponsoring my stay at Columbia University, which proved to be highly inspiring. I also appreciate the effort of the wonderful staff who helped me during my many stays at the various archives that I visited while conducting the research for the book.

At the University of Novi Sad, I am thankful to Petar Đundić, Sanja Đajić and Maja Stanivuković, who were very influential in the early stages of my career and who nudged me along towards a career in international law and (investment) arbitration.

I owe much gratitude to Luke Eric Peterson and the team from *IAReporter*. Working with *IAReporter* has been a greatly rewarding experience and has played an important role in getting me to the finish line.

Of course, I am very grateful to the committee members for my PhD defence – Christoph Schreuer, Christian Tams, Catherine Brölmann, Yvonne Donders and Vid Prislan – for taking the time to read my work and provide the most insightful comments.

Many thanks to my co-supervisor Ingo Venzke for agreeing to jump in and take me on as one of his supervisees. Your writings were instrumental in shaping my thinking, and your comments and practical approach greatly contributed to the final product.

I would also like to acknowledge support by a European Council Starting Grant on 'Transnational Private-Public Arbitration as Global Regulatory Governance: Charting and Codifying the Lex Mercatoria Publica' (LexMercPub, Grant agreement no. 313355).

Lastly, but certainly not the least, I am immensely grateful to my supervisor, Stephan Schill. Thank you for your patience both before the start and towards the end of my PhD. You have set a great example with your dedication and relentless hard work, and your support during the various stages of this trying process was of course invaluable. I am grateful for the many professional opportunities that you have put in front of me and the doors that you have opened. The chance to work with you has certainly been a career highlight and a great learning experience.

CHAPTER 1

Introduction

> Who controls the past controls the future: who controls the present controls the past.

∴

1 Setting the Stage

In *1984*, George Orwell paints a grim account of a dystopian society that has fallen hostage to a totalitarian regime, embodied in the Party, which employs historical negationism in order to maintain its grip on power. The novel's main protagonist, Winston Smith, is employed in the Ministry of Truth, where he is tasked with altering historical records that no longer correspond to the Party's sanctioned version of past events. It is *inter alia* through this process of constant altering and (re)writing of historical records, through the reduction of the past to the (n)ever altering official version of events, that the Party maintains its authority; in other words, by controlling the past in the present, the Party controls the future. Despite his role in (re)writing the past so that it is up to date, Winston clandestinely holds deep resentment for the Party and does not clear his memory of the 'unsanctioned' past through doublethink (a process of 'holding two contradictory beliefs in one's mind simultaneously, and accepting both of them'). Yet even as he remains aware that the past is falsified, Winston himself questions whether the past has an unalterable existence or whether it is itself constituted through this very process, existing only in the present. When he eventually falls into the hands of the Thought Police, the latter appears more likely, as Winston is eventually forced to succumb to the Party and internalise its belief system.

Albeit without the same type of malign intentions, the history of investor-state arbitration (ISA) appears to have been constituted by, and controlled from, the present in a manner that betrays little interest in learning about the discipline's actual past. Certainly, it could hardly be said that there have been intentionally distortive attempts to (re)write ISA's past; quite to the contrary – ISA's past has barely even begun to be explored and written about. This, however, has not prevented the emergence of sweeping historical narratives

 | DOI:10.1163/9789004733824_002

about ISA that have largely been shaped not by what we might have tried to learn of its past, but by projecting onto its past what we in the present have, without having conducted much historical research, assumed that it had looked like. In so doing, this has for all intents and purposes in but a few strokes of the pen erased ISA's rich past with concerning past-altering reverberations, in turn influencing how we perceive and react to what is happening in the present, and potentially, also how we shape the future of ISA. Save efforts to provide accounts of the discipline's past that will be grounded in actual historical research, there is therefore a risk that our understanding of what ISA's past looked like will be shaped not by what we can to the best of our ability learn of it through historical research, but merely by what we in the present have imagined it to have been.

It is precisely the materialisation of this looming risk – the risk that knowledge of the past will be permanently supplanted by mere assumptions about it – that this book hopes to help obviate, in particular by offering an account that is grounded in a long overdue in-depth exploration of ISA's past. In doing so, the book recognises at the outset that, as is the case with any historical account, the account that is presented does not offer an unrestricted and unmediated view into ISA's past. To be sure, there is no historical account that perfectly corresponds to past events as they occurred. Yet, even if we can never hope to reconstruct past events with absolute accuracy, it does not follow that 'anything may go' or that objective knowledge about the past is unattainable. Indeed, as Mark Bevir has posited, '[o]bjectivity arises from criticizing and comparing rival webs of interpretations in terms of agreed facts'.[1] In other words, while historical facts may give rise to differing historical accounts, not all of these accounts will be able to lay an equal claim to being credible approximations of the past, as some of them will upon comparison prove more credible than others.

In particular, this means that it is possible, and indeed necessary, to differentiate between historical accounts that are grounded in extensive historical research, even if they may not represent immaculate reconstructions of past events, and accounts which, without actually being based on historical research, simply imagine what the past looked like. We do not, at least not as of yet, live in the world of *1984*; the past is not, and must not be, constituted merely by what the present says the past was, the past *actually was*. This necessarily implies that, just as they must not be based on what have come to be known as 'alternative facts', credible accounts of ISA's past must not consist

1 Mark Bevir, 'Objectivity in History' (1994) 33(3) History and Theory 328, 333–334.

of little more than unverified present-day assumptions about the past of the discipline. In order to purport to be credible, accounts of the past therefore at minimum need to be a culmination of proper historical research.

The present book is, to the best of my knowledge, based on by far the most comprehensive to date (albeit certainly not complete) exploration and overview of historical ISA. The review of the abundant historical material that has been carried out has invited the observation, which is the main argument advanced by the book, that, contrary to prevailing narratives of the discipline's past (or alleged lack thereof), ISA has historically played an important role in governance. This account, thus, not only helps improve upon existing accounts of ISA's past, but also challenges one of the fundamental premises that underpins our very understanding of ISA – that it has, until relatively recently, been little more than merely a private mechanism for settling disputes. In so doing, the account that the book presents therefore weaves together two threads of the discipline – history and theory – that have so far largely remained underexplored.[2]

2 Rich Past Notwithstanding … A Field Lacking in History

Speaking of arbitration in general, Lord Mustill once said that the discipline 'has a long *Past*, but scarcely any *History*'.[3] Even though his statement was not made specifically with ISA in mind, it does not lose any of its cogency when applied to this particular context. In spite of a historical record that shows an

2 That this has been the case is perhaps not surprising, considering that arbitration has long been perceived primarily as a practical discipline. Insofar as attention has been devoted to theoretical questions, such attention has, until relatively recently, rarely ventured beyond issues of direct practical importance to the actual outcome of disputes. See Stavros Brekoulakis, 'International Arbitration Scholarship and the Concept of Arbitration Law' (2013) 36(4) Fordham International Law Journal 745; Stephan W Schill, 'Conceptions of Legitimacy of International Arbitration' in David D Caron and others (eds), *Practising Virtue: Inside International Arbitration* (OUP 2015) 106, 109. There does, however, seem to be an ongoing shift in favour of deeper theoretical engagement with the discipline. See eg Jan Paulsson, *The Idea of Arbitration* (OUP 2013); Emmanuel Gaillard, *Legal Theory of International Arbitration* (Martinus Nijhoff 2010). A similar situation exists with the history of the discipline, which has likewise seldom been given much consideration and, even when it has, it has been approached mainly from a purely functional perspective, having in large part been limited to the use of prior cases to prop up arguments that are brought up in contemporary debates.

3 MJ Mustill, 'Foreword: Sources for the History of Arbitration' (1998) 14(3) Arbitration International 235. Emphasis added.

abundant and incredibly diverse use of ISA, spanning centuries back, historical research into ISA is still at an early, perhaps even embryonic, stage.

Thus, instances of what may be described as early antecedents of ISA are documented going at least as far back as the medieval period. The first such arbitration that I have come across occurred in the 12th century and was held between Katold of Harroz and the Order of St. John of Jerusalem over a dispute concerning a tract of land in what is now Vienna, Austria. The dispute was resolved by Duke Henry II of Bavaria, who rendered an award in 1156.[4] Several other arbitrations over concessions or other privately-held rights are recorded to have been held between the 12th and the 16th centuries.[5]

From the mid-19th century onwards, however, what may properly be termed ISAs took place at an increasingly frequent rate and are much better documented. By far the most extensive catalogue of this arbitral practice is given in what can perhaps be referred to as the 'bible' of ISA's history – AM Stuyt's *Survey of International Arbitrations*, which documents some 80 ISAs conducted from 1864 to 1989.[6] A cursory look at this catalogue reveals that, excluding the years lost to World War II, ISAs were held virtually on a yearly basis from the mid-1920s onwards, often with multiple awards being issued in a given year.[7] The catalogue offered by Stuyt's *Survey of International Arbitrations*, however, is by no means complete, and is more likely than not only the tip of the ice-berg.[8]

4 Peter Fischer (ed), *A Collection of International Concessions and Related Instruments*, vol I (Oceana 1976) 153.

5 See Peter Fischer (ed), *A Collection of International Concessions and Related Instruments*, vol III (Oceana 1976) 453 and 525 (documenting an arbitration between Nuremberg and the House of the Teutonic Order of the city over forest exploitation rights and an arbitration between the City of Bruges and a German merchant over claims against a landlady); Peter Fischer (ed), *A Collection of International Concessions and Related Instruments*, vol VIII (Oceana 1979) 105–107 (describing an arbitration between the Mining City of Biestritz and the Mining Enterprise of the Thurzos).

6 The first dispute documented in the *Survey of International Arbitrations* was between Egypt and the Suez Canal Company over a concession to construct the Suez Canal. See AM Stuyt (ed), *Survey of International Arbitrations: 1794–1989* (Martinus Nijhoff 1990) 471.

7 See ibid 471–561.

8 Instances of ISAs not documented in Stuyt (n 6) include, *inter alia*: *Oriental Railways Company v The Ottoman Empire* (1888 and 1903), *The Piraeus-Larissa Railway Arbitration* (1893), *The Cauca Company v The Republic of Colombia* (1897), *Duff Development Company v The Government of Kelantan* (1916 and 1921), *Grand Trunk v Canada* (1921), *Lake Copais Company v Greece* (1925), *Zeltweg-Wolfsberg and Unterdrauburg-Woellan Railway Company v Yugoslavia and Austria* (1934) (while this case is chronicled in Stuyt (n 6) it is classified among state-to-state arbitrations), *Batignolles v Yugoslavia* (1938), and *Societe Generale Hellenique, the Athens Piraeus Electricity Company and the Electric Transport Company v Greece* (1950).

These past arbitrations were remarkably diverse in terms of both the subject matter (see Chapter 2) and geographical distribution – they involved investors and states originating from more than 30 different countries or territories, spread over five continents. Moreover, the proceedings were organised both in *ad hoc* and institutional settings, with some of the most prestigious arbitral institutions taking part. For example, the International Chamber of Commerce (ICC) International Court of Arbitration had relatively early in its existence dealt with numerous investment disputes,[9] while the Permanent Court of Arbitration (PCA) had handled two ISAs – one in the 1930s and one in the late 1960s and early 1970s[10] – before its recent ISA-driven renaissance. In light of this substantial and varied body of arbitral practice, it would not be an overstatement to say that ISA has had a long-standing, consistent, and widespread historical presence.

Even with such a rich arbitral practice being well documented, research into the history of ISA has thus far been, to say the least, limited – indeed, despite the ever-growing literature, the abundant historical materials have barely even begun to be tapped. The relevant research that does exist has come not only from studies that are primarily historiographical, but also from enquiries that, despite not being historical research *per se*, still make use of historical arguments and references. While the existing writing on the history of ISA has also originated from non-legal historians whose area of interest intersected with certain questions relating to ISA, the preponderance of the interest in the history of ISA has nonetheless come from those specialising in ISA or related disciplines.[11] Yet, even within ISA historiography, disputes arbitrated directly between investors and states have hardly been the area of primary (or, for that matter, even significant) concern. The principal motivation behind the excursions into ISA's past has instead been the desire to elucidate the development

9 See Stuyt (n 6) 476; Karl-Heinz Böckstiegel, 'Arbitration of Disputes Between States and Private Enterprises in the International Chamber of Commerce' (1965) 59 AJIL 579.

10 *Radio Corporation of America v The National Government of the Republic of China* (1935) 3 RIAA 1621 and *Government of the Republic of the Sudan v Turriff Construction (Sudan) Limited*, Award (23 April 1970). In 1962, in an attempt to address the growing need for this type of arbitration, the PCA adopted arbitration rules created specifically for arbitrations in which only one party was a state. See The Permanent Court of Arbitration, 'Rules of Arbitration and Conciliation for Settlement of International Disputes Between Two Parties of Which Only One is a State' (1963) 57(2) AJIL 500.

11 See Stephan W Schill, Christian J Tams and Rainer Hofmann, 'International Investment Law and History: An Introduction' in Stephan W Schill, Christian J Tams and Rainer Hofmann (eds), *International Investment Law and History: Towards a Historiographical Turn* (Edward Elgar Publishing 2018) 3, 4–5.

and origins of substantive standards of investment protection,[12] of treaty-making practice,[13] or of the arbitral institutions that are focused on or have dealt with ISA, such as the International Centre for Settlement of Investment Disputes (ICSID)[14] or the PCA.[15] To the extent that there have been attempts to present broader narratives about the origins of the discipline and its development,[16] this literature for the most part entirely fails to engage with the historical ISA s.[17]

12 Martins Paparinskis, *The International Minimum Standard and Fair and Equitable Treatment* (OUP 2013); Todd Weiler, *The Interpretation of International Investment Law: Equality, Discrimination and Minimum Standards of Treatment in Historical Context* (Martinus Nijhoff 2013); Jean Ho, *State Responsibility for Breaches of Investment Contracts* (CUP 2018); Kathryn Greenman, *State Responsibility and Rebels: The History and Legacy of Protecting Investment Against Revolution* (CUP 2021); Andrew C Blandford, 'The History of Fair and Equitable Treatment before the Second World War' (2017) 32(2) ICSID Review – Foreign Investment Law Journal 287. See also Jan Paulsson, *Denial of Justice in International Law* (CUP 2005); Ivar Alvik, 'Protection of Private Property in the Early Law of Nations' (2018) 20 Journal of the History of International Law 217.

13 Kenneth J Vandevelde, 'A Brief History of International Investment Agreements' (2005) 12 UC-Davis Journal of International Law & Policy 157; Kenneth J Vandevelde, *The First Bilateral Investment Treaties: US Postwar Friendship, Commerce, and Navigation Treaties* (OUP 2017); Lauge N Skovgaard Poulsen, *Bounded Rationality and Economic Diplomacy: The Politics of Investment Treaties in Developing Countries* (CUP 2015); Eileen Denza and Lauge N Skovgaard Poulsen, 'The Euro – Arab Investment Treaty That Nearly Was' (2020) 69 ICLQ 267; Jarrod Hepburn and others, 'Investment Law before Arbitration' (2020) 23 JIEL 929; Ingo Venzke and Philipp Günther, 'International Investment Protection Made in Germany? On the Domestic and Foreign Policy Dynamics behind the First BIT s' (2022) 33(4) EJIL 1183; Filip Batsele, 'The Unknown Innovator: Switzerland and the Beginning of the Investment Treaty Regime' (2024) 34 Swiss Rev Int'l & Eur L 181; Jason Webb Yackee, 'The First French BIT' (2024) 35(3) EJIL 623.

14 Antonio R Parra, *The History of ICSID* (2nd ed, OUP 2017); Taylor St John, *The Rise of Investor-State Arbitration: Politics, Law, and Unintended Consequences* (OUP 2018); Juan Carlos Boue, 'Much More than a Footnote (or Three): Frank C Hendryx and an Untold Story of Petroleum Concessions and the Genesis of ICSID' (2022) 13(1) Journal of International Dispute Settlement 1.

15 Manuel Indlekofer, *International Arbitration and the Permanent Court of Arbitration* (Kluwer 2013) ch 1. See also P Hamilton and others (eds), *The Permanent Court of Arbitration: International Arbitration and Dispute Resolution: Summaries of Awards, Settlement Agreements and Reports* (Kluwer 1999) 145–148 and 164–169.

16 See eg St John (n 14); Nicolás M Perrone, *Investment Treaties and the Legal Imagination: How Foreign Investors Play By Their Own Rules* (OUP 2021); Joost Pauwelyn, 'At the Edge of Chaos? Foreign Investment Law as a Complex Adaptive System, How It Emerged and How It Can Be Reformed' (2014) 29(2) ICSID Review – Foreign Investment Law Journal 372.

17 There have of course also been critical legal histories that have purported to depict the supposed origins of IIL and ISA. See in particular Kate Miles, *The Origins of International Investment Law: Empire, Environment and the Safeguarding of Capital* (CUP 2013); Andrea

In addition to the international investment law (IIL) specific literature, general historical enquiries into certain events or regions have also occasionally devoted brief attention to ISAs.[18] Finally, there is likewise research into ISA which, while not historical *per se*, nonetheless deals with a considerable amount of historical case law.[19]

Instances of ISAs have, on the other hand, for the most part remained an afterthought within mainstream IIL literature, reduced to but a footnote, or perhaps to an occasional reference (or few), of the several cases that are commonly invoked as the 'usual suspects'.[20] For example, in its 15 page historical introduction, the seminal textbook by Dolzer, Kriebaum and Schreuer makes mention of only one relevant case from the early period (*Lena Goldfields v. USSR*), while at the same time noting that '(u)ntil the early 1990s, international

---

Leiter, *Making the World Safe for Investment: The Protection of Foreign Property 1922–1959* (CUP 2023). Unfortunately, such critical legal histories have to date been based on little to none original historical research, have been conceptually and factually unreliable (see eg ch 3 in relation to Leiter's work) and have been more interested in advocating for predetermined political positions than in genuinely discovering what the past was like. That is not to say, however, that the instrumentalisation of history for the purpose of pursuing political agendas has been reserved only for the critics of ISA. See Gary Born, 'The 1933 Directives on Arbitration of the German Reich: Echoes of the Past?' (2021) 38(4) Journal of International Arbitration 417.

18 See eg Amarjit Kaur, *Bridge and Barrier: Transport and Communications in Colonial Malaya 1870–1957* (OUP 1985) 69; Michael A Krysko, *American Radio in China: International Encounters with Technology and Communications, 1919–41* (Palgrave Macmillan 2011) 61–64; Ronn Pineo, *Ecuador and the United States: Useful Strangers* (University of Georgia Press 2007) 77; Harley Notter, *The Origins of the Foreign Policy of Woodrow Wilson* (Johns Hopkins Press 1937) 244.

19 See eg Karl-Heinz Böckstiegel, *Arbitration and State Enterprises: A Survey on the National and International State of Law and Practice* (Kluwer 1984) 97–100; Karl-Heinz Böckstiegel, *Der Staat als Vertragspartner ausländischer Privatunternehmen* (Athenäum Verlag 1971); Jerzy Makarczyk, *Principles of a New International Economic Order: A Study of International Law in the Making* (Springer 1988) 300–348. Similarly, writings by contemporary authors, while not themselves a result of historical research, are nonetheless an important source of knowledge on both the past ISAs and the issues that were topical contemporaneously. See eg only Martin Domke, 'The Settlement of International Investment Disputes' (1956–1957) 12 The Business Lawyer 264; Martin Domke, 'Foreign Nationalizations: Some Aspects of Contemporary International Law' (1961) 55 AJIL 585; Earl Snyder, 'Foreign Investment Protection: Is Institutional Arbitration an Answer?' (1961–1962) 40 NC L Rev 665; Earl Snyder, 'Foreign Investment Protection: A Proposed Arbitration Convention' (1962) 11 J Pub L 191; Earl Snyder, 'Foreign Investment Protection: The Dispute Solving Aspect' (1963–1964) 3 Colum J Transnat'l L 127.

20 These rather well-known cases that are typically referenced include eg *Lena Goldfields v USSR*, the two Radio Corporation of America arbitrations and the post-World War II Middle Eastern oil arbitrations.

investment law had not produced any significant case law'.[21] Newcombe and Paradell's *Law and Practice of Investment Treaties,* which gives probably the most thorough overview of the history of IIL, devotes but a paragraph to historical cases arbitrated directly between investors and host states, remarking (in what is a significant understatement) that there had been 'several direct investor-state arbitrations'.[22] While Sornarajah does stress the presence of a pre-bilateral investment treaty (BIT) investment protection system and shows awareness of the existence and relevance of pre-BIT arbitration between states and foreign investors,[23] the historical cases are nonetheless not given much mention within his treatise.

ISA is even more underrepresented in the conventional narrative about IIL's historical development, according to which the current system dominated by BITs was preceded by an era of diplomatic protection characterised by the individual's lack of standing to bring a claim in international law. Pursuant to this account, when faced with problems in its relations with the host state government, the investor in the pre-BIT era had little choice but to rely on its home government to espouse its claim and hope that it will be able to get redress by way of this indirect remedy.[24] This dominant account of IIL's past appears almost as a necessary externality that accompanies the fetishisation of the role of international law in investment protection – it is but an inevitable consequence of the investors' presumed lack of control over its own claim on the

21 Rudolf Dolzer, Ursula Kriebaum and Christoph Schreuer, *Principles of International Investment Law* (3rd edn, OUP 2022) 13.

22 Andrew Newcombe and Lluís Paradell, *Law and Practice of Investment Treaties: Standards of Treatment* (Kluwer 2009) 8. See also Flavia Marisi, *Rethinking Investor-State Arbitration* (Springer 2023) ch 2.

23 M Sornarajah, *The International Law on Foreign Investment* (3rd edn, CUP 2010) 276 and 286–289.

24 Christopher F Dugan and others, *Investor-State Arbitration* (OUP 2008) 42; Peter Muchlinski, 'The Diplomatic Protection of Foreign Investors: A Tale of Judicial Caution' in Christina Binder and others (eds), *International Investment Law for the 21st Century: Essays in Honour of Christoph Schreuer* (OUP 2009); Leon Trakman and Nicola Ranieri, 'Foreign Direct Investment: A Historical Perspective' in Leon Trakman and Nicola Ranieri (eds), *Regionalism in International Investment Law* (OUP 2013) 24; Barnali Choudhury, 'Recapturing Public Power: Is Investment Arbitration's Engagement of the Public Interest Contributing to the Democratic Deficit?' (2008) 41 Vand J Transnat'l L 775, 780–781; Asha Kaushal, 'Revisiting History: How the Past Matters for the Present Backlash against the Foreign Investment Regime' (2009) 50 Harvard International Law Journal 491, 498; Susan D Franck, 'The Legitimacy Crisis in Investment Treaty Arbitration: Privatizing Public International Law Through Inconsistent Decisions' (2005) 73 Fordham Law Review 1521, 1536–1538; Rodrigo Polanco, *The Return of the Home State to Investor-State Disputes: Bringing Back Diplomatic Protection?* (CUP 2019) 1–2, 5 and 22–23.

international plane. The perpetuation of this distorted, yet sweeping, narrative has only served to further the perception of ISA as historically insignificant.

The most noteworthy efforts aimed at remembering ISA's past have undoubtedly been the in-depth accounts of a few select individual investment disputes.[25] While these exhaustive analyses of particular cases have significantly contributed to preserving the memory of ISA's past, the information that such micro-histories provide – although undoubtedly useful[26] – is nonetheless only piecemeal. Even in the several instances where the enquiries have gone beyond the exploration of individual cases, chronicling instead a larger number of ISAs,[27] they still address only a markedly small fraction of past ISAs and tend to lack an overall perspective of the discipline's past.[28] Indeed, irrespective of its specific focus or breadth, one common trait that characterises all of

25 See Arthur Nussbaum, 'The Arbitration between Lena Goldfields Ltd and the Soviet Government' (1950) 36 Cornell Law Quarterly 31; VV Veeder, 'The *Lena Goldfields* Arbitration: The Historical Roots of Three Ideas' (1998) 47 ICLQ 747; Michael Reynolds, 'The Jaffa Jerusalem Railway Company Arbitration 1922' (1991) 6 Arab Law Quarterly 215; Shabtai Rosenne, 'The Jaffa-Jerusalem Railway Arbitration (1922)' in Shabtai Rosenne, *Essays on International Law and Practice* (Martinus Nijhoff 2007) 295; Jason Webb Yackee, 'The First Investor-State Arbitration: *The Suez Canal Company v Egypt* (1864)' (2016) 17 The Journal of World Investment and Trade 401; Maja Stanivuković and Sanja Đajić, 'From *Losinger* to *ATA v Jordan*: Retroactive Application of National Law to Arbitration Agreements' in Marianne Roth and Michael Geistlinger (eds), *Yearbook on International Arbitration and ADR* (Neuer Wissenschaftlicher Verlag 2019) 149; VV Veeder, 'Lloyd George, Lenin and Cannibals: The Harriman Arbitration – The 1999 Freshfields Lecture' (2000) 16 Arbitration International 115; Stephen D Fitch, 'The Harriman Manganese Concession in the Soviet Union: Lessons for Today' (1991) 9 Int'l Tax & Bus Law 209; Jason Yackee, 'Investor-State Dispute Settlement at the Dawn of International Investment Law: France, Mauritania, and the Nationalization of the MIFERMA Iron Ore Operations' (2019) 59(1) American Journal of Legal History 71.

26 See Yackee, 'Investor-State Dispute Settlement at the Dawn of International Investment Law' (n 25) 110.

27 See J Gillis Wetter and Stephen M Schwebel, 'Some Little-Known Cases on Concessions' (1964) 40 Brit YBIL 183; Jason Webb Yackee, 'Pacta Sunt Servanda and State Promises to Foreign Investors before Bilateral Investment Treaties: Myth and Reality' (2008–2009) 32 Fordham Int'l LJ 1550; Abolbashar Farmanfarma, 'The Oil Agreement Between Iran and the International Oil Consortium: the Law Controlling' (1955–1956) 34 Tex L Rev 259, 277ff; Böckstiegel, 'Arbitration of Disputes Between States and Private Enterprises in the International Chamber of Commerce' (n 9); Ivar Alvik, *Contracting with Sovereignty: State Contracts and International Arbitration* (Hart Publishing 2011) 30–41; Timothy G Nelson, '"History Ain't Changed": Why Investor-State Arbitration Will Survive the "New Revolution"' in Michael Waibel and others (eds), *The Backlash against Investment Arbitration: Perceptions and Reality* (Kluwer 2010) 555; Leiter (n 17) chs 2–4.

28 Compare only the ISAs referenced in the works cited in n 27 to the (still incomplete) listing of historical ISAs in Stuyt (n 6).

the aforementioned existing literature on the history of ISA is that it entirely overlooks the vast majority of direct historical ISA s or, at best, treats them with an occasional reference but without any systematic or in-depth analysis.

As this brief overview of existing research on the history of ISA illustrates, the exploration of the field's past is still nascent. While the tide does seem to be turning towards increased interest into the history of ISA with the 'historiographical turns' in both IIL specifically[29] and international law more generally,[30] the topic still largely remains unchartered territory. Thus, despite some of the pieces of the mosaic having been put in place, there is still much work to be done before the main contours of the overall composition that is ISA's past start to become discernible. It is in the hope of furthering this mosaic that the present book seeks to contribute to the better understanding of ISA's rich past.

3 Aims of the Book

In its effort to improve upon existing accounts of ISA's past, the book makes no attempt to chronicle every single ISA that has occurred throughout history, nor does it purport to offer a fully comprehensive, let alone definitive, account of the institution's past by telling *the history* of ISA. Such an endeavour, if at all feasible, is well beyond the confines of a single book. Instead, the book focuses on a rather specific, but nonetheless fundamental, aspect of the discipline's

29 See nn 11–17 and 25–27.

30 See only Alexander Orakhelashvili (ed), *Research Handbook on the Theory and History of International Law* (Edward Elgar Publishing 2011); Bardo Fassbender and Anne Peters (eds), *The Oxford Handbook of the History of International Law* (OUP 2012); Matthew Craven, Malgosia Fitzmaurice and Maria Vogiatzi (eds), *Time, History and International Law* (Martinus Nijhoff 2007); Pierre-Marie Dupuy and Vincent Chetail (eds), *The Roots of International Law/Les fondements du droit international: Liber Amicorum Peter Haggenmacher* (Brill 2014); George RB Galindo, 'Martti Koskenniemi and the Historiographical Turn in International Law' (2005) 16 European Journal of International Law 539; Matthew Craven, 'Theorizing the Turn to History in International Law' in Anne Orford and Florian Hoffmann (eds), *The Oxford Handbook of the Theory of International Law* (OUP 2016) 21; Martti Koskenniemi, *The Gentle Civilizer of Nations: The Rise and Fall of International Law 1870–1960* (CUP 2001); Martti Koskenniemi, 'Why History of International Law Today?' (2004) 4 Rechtsgeschichte 61; Ingo J Hueck, 'The Discipline of the History of International Law: New Trends and Methods on the History of International Law' (2001) 3 Journal of the History of International Law 194; Emmanuelle Tourme-Jouannet and Anne Peters, 'The Journal of the History of International Law: A Forum for New Research' (2014) 16 Journal of the History of International Law 1.

past, which represents a significant blind spot within the existing literature – the role that ISA has historically played as a mechanism of governance.

The curiosity toward this topic was sparked against the backdrop of ongoing debates that are challenging long-held beliefs about the very manner in which arbitration in general and the most conspicuous variant of ISA in particular – investment-treaty arbitration – are to be conceptualised. Namely, as an institution with an impressive pedigree, arbitration has roots that are usually traced back to various points in antiquity, including Mesopotamia, ancient Greece, Persia and Rome.[31] Over the course of history it has appeared in different shapes and forms, in a variety of settings, and in virtually all corners of the globe. It has been resorted to by states and private entities alike, within the backdrop of both private and public international law, as well as outside of any type of formal setting.[32] Yet, despite this diversity in form and underlying framework, for the most part, the quintessential understanding of what arbitration is has fundamentally remained the same – it predominantly has been, and still is, understood as (just) a dispute resolution mechanism. While there is considerable debate on how precisely to define arbitration, this conventional conception remains the primary guiding force behind such attempts. As noted by Gary Born:

> virtually all authorities accept that arbitration is – and *only is* – a process by which parties consensually *submit a dispute* to a non-governmental decision-maker, selected by or for the parties, *to render a binding decision resolving a dispute* in accordance with neutral, adjudicatory procedures affording each party to present its case.[33]

This sentiment is echoed in both public international law[34] and international commercial arbitration alike.[35] Recently, however, there has been a growing

31 See Gary B Born, *International Commercial Arbitration* (2nd edn, Kluwer 2014, vol I) 7–10 and 25–30.

32 See Paulsson, *The Idea of Arbitration* (n 2) 45–48.

33 Gary B Born, *International Arbitration: Law and Practice* (Kluwer 2012) 4. Emphases added.

34 See eg Malcolm N Shaw, *International Law* (6th edn, CUP 2008) 1048–49; John Collier and Vaughan Lowe, *The Settlement of Disputes in International Law: Institutions and Procedures* (OUP 1999) 31; Nii Lante Wallace-Bruce, *The Settlement of International Disputes: The Contribution of Australia and New Zealand* (Martinus Nijhoff 1998) 62.

35 For an overview of the various definitions of arbitration reflective of this view, see Born, *International Commercial Arbitration* (n 31) 247–249. See also Nigel Blackaby and others, *Redfern and Hunter on International Arbitration* (6th edn, OUP 2015) para 1.04 (noting that '[a]rbitration is essentially a very simple *method of resolving disputes*').

line of scholarship that has started to challenge this dominant conceptualisation, both in relation to arbitration in general,[36] and investment-treaty arbitration more specifically.[37] At least in relation to investment-treaty arbitration, it would appear that this once dominant conception has been all but eroded, with the discipline increasingly being likened to a form of (global) governance.[38]

Notably, however, because investment-treaty arbitration is predominantly seen as a relatively novel phenomenon,[39] this line of scholarship has

36 See eg Alec Stone Sweet, 'The New Lex Mercatoria and Transnational Governance' (2006) 13(5) Journal of European Public Policy 627; Christopher A Whytock, 'Private-Public Interaction in Global Governance: The Case of Transnational Commercial Arbitration' (2010) 12(3) Business and Politics 1; the contributions in Walter Mattli and Thomas Dietz (eds), *International Arbitration and Global Governance: Contending Theories and Evidence* (OUP 2014); Fabien Gélinas, 'Arbitration as Transnational Governance by Contract' (2016) 7(2) Transnational Legal Theory 181; Alec Stone Sweet and Florian Grisel, *The Evolution of International Arbitration: Judicialization, Governance, Legitimacy* (OUP 2017).

37 See eg Gus Van Harten, *Investment Treaty Arbitration and Public Law* (OUP 2007) ch 3; Stephan W Schill, 'International Investment Law and Comparative Public Law – an Introduction' in Stephan W Schill (ed), *International Investment Law and Comparative Public Law* (OUP 2010) 3, 3–4 and 18.

38 See Gus Van Harten, 'Private Authority and Transnational Governance: The Contours of the International System of Investor Protection' (2005) 12(4) Review of International Political Economy 600; Benedict Kingsbury and Stephan Schill, 'Investor-State Arbitration as Governance: Fair and Equitable Treatment, Proportionality, and the Emerging Global Administrative Law' in Albert Jan van den Berg (ed), *50 Years of the New York Convention* (Kluwer 2009) 5; Stephan W Schill, 'Crafting the International Economic Order: The Public Function of Investment Treaty Arbitration and Its Significance for the Role of the Arbitrator' (2010) 23 Leiden Journal of International Law 401, 413–418; Valentina Vadi, 'Global Cultural Governance by Investment Arbitral Tribunals: The Making of a *Lex Administrativa Culturalis*' (2015) 33 Boston University International Law Journal 101.

39 At the time when this governance discourse was gaining traction, investment-treaty arbitration was, and predominantly still is, characterised as being a 'new continent' that is 'dramatically different from anything previously known in the international sphere', a 'change in paradigm', 'revolutionary', 'exotic' and as being in its 'infancy'. See Jan Paulsson, 'Arbitration Without Privity' (1995) 10 ICSID Review – Foreign Investment Law Journal 232; Charles N Brower and Stephan W Schill, 'Is Arbitration a Threat or a Boon to the Legitimacy of International Investment Law?' (2009) 9(2) Chicago Journal of International Law 471, 477 (citing Christoph Schreuer); *International Thunderbird Gaming Corporation v United Mexican States*, UNCITRAL, Separate Opinion of Thomas Wälde (1 December 2005) para 14 (remarking that the introduction of direct investor-state arbitration has resulted in a 'discontinuity'); Van Harten, *Investment Treaty Arbitration and Public Law* (n 37) 4; Franck, 'The Legitimacy Crisis in Investment Treaty Arbitration' (n 24) 1523; Anthea Roberts, 'Clash of Paradigms: Actors and Analogies Shaping the Investment Treaty System' (2013) 107 AJIL 45, 49; International Law Commission, 'Fragmentation of International Law: Difficulties arising from the Diversification and Expansion of International Law – Report of the Study Group of the International Law Commission, finalized

overwhelmingly proceeded under the assumption that investment-treaty arbitration's aforesaid role as a mode of governance is equally as novel – even 'revolutionary'.[40] As a result, the turning of the tide in relation to how

---

by Mr Martti Koskenniemi' (13 April 2006) UN Doc A/CN4/L682 para 8; Velimir Živković, 'ISDS and Nazis or History Without Context: A Reply to Gary Born' (2022) 39(4) Journal of International Arbitration 575, 576 and 581–582. See, however, Barton Legum, 'The Innovation of Investor-State Arbitration Under NAFTA' (2002) 43 Harv Int'l LJ 531, 531 and 538–539; O Thomas Johnson and Jonathan Gimblett, 'From Gunboats to BITs: the Evolution of Modern International Investment Law' in Karl P Sauvant (ed), *Yearbook on International Investment Law and Policy 2010–2011* (OUP 2012) 649, 660–661; Jason Webb Yackee, 'Do We Really Need BITs – Toward a Return to Contract in International Investment Law' (2008) 3 Asian Journal of WTO and International Health Law and Policy 121, 122; Nelson, '"History Ain't Changed"' (n 27) 573–575; Heather L Bray, 'Understanding Change: Evolution from International Claims Commissions to Investment Treaty Arbitration' in Schill, Tams and Hofmann (n 11) 102; Richard Happ, 'Why Investment Arbitration Contributes to the Rule of Law: Without Knowing Where We Came from We Cannot Know Where We Are Heading' (2016) 1 EILA Rev 278; Yannick Radi, *Rules and Practices of International Investment Law and Arbitration* (CUP 2020) 8.

40 See in particular Van Harten, *Investment Treaty Arbitration and Public Law* (n 37) 4 (stating that '[t]he question at the heart of this book is what is the essential character and significance of this *new system*? In response, three claims are advanced. The first is that the advent of investment treaty arbitration is *a revolutionary development* in international adjudication. *The second is that the system's crucial importance is that – unlike any other form of international arbitration – it is a method of public law adjudication*, meaning that it is used to resolve regulatory disputes between individuals and the state as opposed to reciprocal disputes between private parties or between states'). Emphases added. Van Harten makes similar claims throughout his monograph ('individual investors can now, *rather suddenly in the historical context*, trigger the compulsory arbitration of international investment disputes'; 'the establishment of international arbitration as an adjudicative mechanism to resolve regulatory disputes between states and individuals is *a major departure from the conventional use of international arbitration* in the private sphere'; 'the transformation has been major in its scope and depth; *what makes it revolutionary is that private arbitrators are given the power to resolve regulatory disputes*'). See ibid 9, 47 and 120 (emphases added). See also Gus Van Harten and Martin Loughlin, 'Investment Treaty Arbitration as a Species of Global Administrative Law' (2006) 17(1) EJIL 121, 147 ('[h]istorically, international commercial arbitration was limited to disputes between private parties; this was true even when the arbitration involved a dispute between an investor and a state since the state, in agreeing to an arbitration clause in a contract, was acting in a private capacity. In these circumstances, *investment arbitration was confined to the transactions of private parties within the commercial sphere. By using a private model of adjudication to resolve what are quite clearly regulatory disputes, investment treaties have radically transformed how adjudication is used to review and control public authorities*'; emphasis added); Valentina Vadi and Lukasz Gruszczynski, 'Standards of Review in International Investment Law and Arbitration: Multilevel Governance and the Commonweal' (2013) 16(3) Journal of International Economic Law 613, 619 ('[a]djudication over a state's *acta jure imperii* implies a significant departure from the conventional use

present-day investment-treaty arbitration is understood has, as of yet, done little to spark interest into whether the remainder of ISA – investment-treaty arbitration being but one of its sub-variants – has historically been known to operate as a mode of governance; in fact, historical research into this topic has been virtually non-existent.

The main objective of the book is therefore to understand the extent to and manner in which governance was historically exercised through ISA, seen against the backdrop of its own time and for the sheer purpose of understanding this past phenomenon for what it was. As previously mentioned, and as the remainder of this book will show, the historical material that has for present purposes been analysed has invited the argument that ISA has in fact historically been an important vehicle of governance. This is an argument that stands in sharp contrast to the aforementioned prevailing narratives that see investment-treaty arbitration's governance role as a recent paradigmatical shift, and hence potentially carries with itself important implications for improving our understanding of the very nature of, not only investment-treaty arbitration, but also the remainder of ISA. Notwithstanding its primary interest in the past as it was,[41] the book is therefore not without important potential implications

---

of international arbitration in the commercial sphere'); Sophie Nappert, 'International Arbitration as a Tool of Global Governance: The Use (and Abuse) of Discretion' in Eric Brousseau, Jean-Michel Glachant and Jérôme Sgard (eds), *The Oxford Handbook of Institutions of International Economic Governance and Market Regulation* (online edn, Oxford Academic 2019) <https://doi.org/10.1093/oxfordhb/9780190900571.013.23> accessed 27 September 2024 (speaking of international arbitration in general, but with a strong focus on investment-treaty arbitration, Nappert notes that the 'modern characterization' of arbitration as governance 'challenges the process's historical and conceptual origins as an adjudicatory function that went no further than the four corners of the parties' dispute'; Santiago Montt, *State Liability in Investment Treaty Arbitration: Global Constitutionalism and Administrative Law in the BIT Generation* (Hart Publishing 2009) 139. But see Jan Paulsson, 'Public Interest in International Arbitration' (2012) 106 Proceedings of the Annual Meeting (American Society of International Law) 300.

41 Indeed, even though the interest in its theme may have emerged against the backdrop of contemporary debates, the first and foremost concern for the book remains not the usefulness of its findings for such present-day debates, but the attempt to contribute to and expand the existing knowledge about the history of ISA and its governance role. Moreover, in looking at the ISA's historical governance role, the book is not guided by the idea of showing that the past was akin to, or different from, the present, but instead acknowledges its uniqueness and self-standing character, along with all of its distinctive features for which there is no parallel in the present. Equally, it is demonstrably not the aim of the historical account presented by the book to legitimise the current practice of governance through ISA by providing it with a historical precursor, even if long-standing historical tradition certainly may potentially be viewed as a source of legitimacy. See eg Max Weber, *Economy and Society: A New Translation* (Keith Tribe ed and tr, Harvard Uni-

for present-day ISA, and hopes to ultimately contribute to the larger debates surrounding ISA, in particular those that concern the manner in which the discipline is to be conceptualised.

4 Methodology

4.1 *Historical Approach and Its Limitations*

Keeping in line with its theme, the book is a product of extensive historical research. While providing more thorough and more accurate accounts about the past of any phenomenon undoubtedly holds inherent value,[42] beyond this general usefulness of historical research there still remain certain additional advantages in looking at ISA through a historical lens in lieu of a contemporary analysis that are particularly pronounced with regard to the attempt to observe ISA's governance effects, from which the present book has benefited. The foremost of these relates to the accessibility of materials that, while crucial for understanding the functioning and ultimate impact of ISA, are simply not obtainable in relation to present-day ISA. Namely, despite the recent advances in transparency in investment-treaty arbitration, confidentiality, or more precisely, non-transparency, is still the name of the game when it comes to ISA. A considerable proportion of ISAs are thus still cloaked in obscurity and the resulting awards, let alone the complementary materials, are never made public. Even though such documents allow for a better understanding of how ISA operates by offering unique insight into the decision-making processes of arbitral tribunals, investors and governmental bodies alike, most of them tend to remain confidential for extended periods of time. It is only after they are made publicly available following the opening of government, personal or company archives that they can be accessed and analysed. Because a historical enquiry is able to look past this initial cloak of confidentiality, it

versity Press 2019) 341–342 and 354–374; Craig Matheson, 'Weber and the Classification of Forms of Legitimacy' 1987 (38) The British Journal of Sociology 199, 202; Thomas Franck, 'Legitimacy in the International System' (1988) 82 AJIL 705, 726–727; Patrick Norton, 'A Law of the Future or a Law of the Past? Modern Tribunals and the International Law of Expropriation' (1991) 85 AJIL 474, 499–500.

42 Jonathan Rose, 'Musing on Clio and Legal History: Why Study the Past, History, and Legal History' (2009) U Texas Law School Tarlton Library Legal History Series, 2009, 36–37 <https://papers.ssrn.com/sol3/papers.cfm?abstract_id=1411875> accessed 27 September 2024; William E Nelson, 'Standards of Criticism' (1982) 60 Tex L Rev 447, at 449; Louis Gottschalk, *Understanding History: A Primer of Historical Method* (Alfred A Knopf 1956) 86.

enables access to important categories of materials that are otherwise not available in relation to present-day ISAs (even those conducted according to best transparency practices), including, for example, correspondence between the disputing parties' themselves and their correspondence with the arbitrators, the arbitrators' personal files, diplomatic correspondence between states and previously confidential internal documents within both government and company structures. An illustration of the potential boon derived from accessing such documents is provided by the arbitration between The Administration of Posts and Telegraphs of the Republic of Czechoslovakia and the Radio Corporation of America (RCA), wherein the parties' correspondence revealed how The Administration reacted to, and indeed intended to adjust its behaviour because of, the tribunal's award.[43] Similarly, correspondence regarding the related *RCA v. China* arbitration reveals how the idea to have the arbitration administered by the PCA, which was the first such instance with respect to a dispute involving a non-state entity, came about.[44] As materials of this type are invaluable in assessing how the decisions of arbitral tribunals impacted policy-making and whether there was awareness on behalf of the arbitrators or other parties involved that these decisions would have such an effect, a historical analysis offers benefits that largely elude research restricted solely to contemporary events.

Moreover, in many instances it takes decades for a certain investor-state dispute to come full circle or for all of the consequences stemming from the ISA to fully materialise. This necessarily implies that a contemporary perspective is not always entirely adequate for properly understanding the dispute and the totality of its implications. For example, in the 1950s dispute between SEEE and Yugoslavia,[45] not only was the underlying concession signed in the 1930s, but the arbitration itself turned out to be far from the end of the matter, as enforcement issues lingered well into the 1980s, burdening Yugoslav-French diplomatic relations for an additional 30 years. Along similar lines, in *Lena Goldfields v. USSR*, the underlying concession was signed in the 1920s, the arbitration held in the early 1930s, a settlement agreement reached in the mid-1930s and then repudiated in the 1940s, while the definite conclusion of the saga came only in the early 1990s.[46] These underlying relationships and the resulting disputes spanned over at least half a century; any attempt to properly

---

43 See ch 4.

44 See ch 5.

45 *La Société Européenne d'Etudes et d'Entreprises* (SEEE) *v The Popular Federative Republic of Yugoslavia* (1959) 86 Journal du Droit International 1075.

46 See Veeder, 'The *Lena Goldfields* Arbitration' (n 25) 747.

grasp the cases and their implications thus necessarily must involve historical research. In addition, it is not always possible to tell straight away what significance a certain ISA may have – some of its (often important) repercussions are sometimes only manifested a considerable amount of time after the arbitration takes place. Reverting once more to *Lena Goldfields v. USSR* as an example, it was not until the relatively recent adoption of the 1996 Arbitration Act in the United Kingdom[47] and the discussions regarding transparency in investment-treaty arbitration[48] that the decision by the *Lena Goldfields v. USSR* tribunal to publish the award and the accompanying procedural orders in the London 'Times' due to the public interest involved became of particular interest. Other decisions have likewise sometimes taken decades to gain traction.[49] Viewing ISA through a historical lens, therefore, presents itself in this context not merely as beneficial, but as inevitable.

As for how this historical research was carried out, in following with the crucial importance of primary sources for historical research,[50] the present book is to a large extent based on primary materials created in relation to the various ISAs that have taken place throughout the examined period. While some of the relevant primary material (mostly published arbitral awards) is readily available, the majority of it is not, and is instead housed in various public and private archives scattered around the world. For this reason, the bulk of the primary material on which the book is based was obtained through original archival research, conducted at the following institutions: The National Archives of the UK,[51] the Commonwealth Office Pamphlet Collection at the University of Manchester Library Special Collections,[52] Foyle Special Collections Library

47 See ch 5.

48 See *Methanex Corporation v United States of America*, UNCITRAL (NAFTA), Decision of the Tribunal on Petitions from Third Persons to Intervene as 'amici curiae' (15 January 2001) para 44.

49 This was the case, for example, with the *Duff v Kelantan* arbitrations and the two RCA cases, which are only known to have been cited by other tribunals decades after they had taken place.

50 Jason Webb Yackee, 'The First Investor-State Arbitration? The Suez Canal Dispute of 1864 and Some Reflections on the Historiography of International Investment Law' in Schill, Tams and Hofmann (n 11) 70, 78–80; Susan Grigg, 'Archival Practice and the Foundations of Historical Method' (1991) 78 Journal of American History 228, 229.

51 Materials on the following cases were obtained at this archive: *Duff v Kelantan I and II*, *Jaffa v UK*, *Lake Copais v Greece*, *Peru v Peruvian Corporation*, *Petroleum Development v Qatar*, *Piraeus-Larissa Railway Arbitration*, *Sudan v Turriff Construction Company*, *Grand Trunk v Canada*, as well as the cases arising out of the Power and Traction Company concession in Greece.

52 Materials relating to the second arbitration between the Duff Development Company and Kelantan were retrieved from this archive.

at King's College London,[53] the National Archives of the Netherlands,[54] the Hagley Museum and Library,[55] the United Nations Archives at Geneva,[56] the International Labour Office (ILO) Archives,[57] the Archives of the Graduate Institute of International and Development Studies in Geneva,[58] the Archives of Yugoslavia[59] and the Diplomatic Archive of the Ministry of Foreign Affairs of the Republic of Serbia.[60] The archival research carried out at these institutions has yielded in excess of 17,000 pages of diverse material that has, to a large extent, not previously been analysed (or at least not within international legal literature).[61]

Of course, relying on primary sources is not in and of itself sufficient when doing historical research,[62] which is why the book has drawn heavily also on secondary sources, especially where those sources were themselves built upon extensive archival research by their authors.[63] Moreover, where original texts on relevant matters relating to historical ISAs could not be obtained, secondary

53 Materials relating to the first arbitration between the Duff Development Company and Kelantan were retrieved from this archive.

54 Materials regarding the following disputes were obtained from this archive: *Hambros Bank Limited and Lazard Brothers and Co Limited v Kingdom of Roumania Monopolies Institute*, *RCA v China*, *Sudan v Turriff Construction Company*, as well as information on two Dutch arbitrators who had acted in these ISAs: Joost Adriaan van Hamel (*RCA v China*) and Gijsbert Weijer Jan Bruins (*Hambros Bank Limited and Lazard Brothers and Co Limited v Kingdom of Roumania Monopolies Institute*).

55 Materials relating to the two RCA disputes were obtained from this archive.

56 Materials on the three railway arbitrations conducted pursuant to the World War I Peace Treaties, described in detail in ch 4, were obtained from this archive.

57 Materials on a series of arbitrations arising out of the Power and Traction Company's concession in Greece (see ch 5) were obtained from this archive.

58 Materials on the *Hedjaz Railway Line Arbitration* were obtained from this archive.

59 Materials on the following cases were obtained from this archive: *SEEE v Yugoslavia*, *Losinger v Yugoslavia*, *Barcs-Pakrac Railway Company v Yugoslavia and Hungary*, *Zeltweg-Wolfsberg and Unterdrauburg-Woellan Railway Company v Yugoslavia and Austria* and *Batignolles v Yugoslavia*.

60 Materials on *SEEE v Yugoslavia* were obtained from this archive.

61 All of the documents are on file with the author.

62 Martin S Flaherty, 'History "Lite" in Modern American Constitutionalism' (1995) 95 Colum L Rev 523, 552–553; John Tosh, *The Pursuit of History: Aims, Methods and New Directions in the Study of Modern History* (5th edn, Pearson 2010) 92; Larry D Kramer, 'When Lawyers Do History' (2003) 72 The George Washington Law Review 387, 390.

63 See eg generally Veeder, 'The *Lena Goldfields* Arbitration' (n 25); Böckstiegel, 'Arbitration of Disputes Between States and Private Enterprises in the International Chamber of Commerce' (n 9); Reynolds (n 25); Rosenne (n 25); Yackee, 'The First Investor-State Arbitration: *The Suez Canal Company v Egypt* (1864)' (n 25).

materials such as case reports,[64] scholarly work[65] and media reports[66] were invaluable in finding out the content, outcomes and fall-out from the disputes.

Notwithstanding the aforementioned advantages offered by historical research, the present book has also had to cope with its inherent limitations. Perhaps the most important of these limitations concerns a type of informational paradox that characterises the very historical record being analysed, which is somehow simultaneously both incomplete[67] and overly profuse.[68] Taken together, these two aspects – the concurrent incompleteness and overabundance of the historical record – mean that every historical research project proceeds with a considerable degree of informational indeterminacy, necessarily containing certain gaps in knowledge and blind spots. To the extent possible, this book has tried to alleviate these problems by combining a thorough exploration of select ISA s with a birds-eye view of the overall practice, thereby providing both a certain depth and width to its insight into ISA's past. It has moreover relied upon materials that originate from actors with vastly different perspectives (including those created by states at various stages of industrialisation, private companies, arbitrators and counsel), which are intended to provide sufficiently representative and/or relevant accounts. As many gaps nonetheless unavoidably remain, much like any attempt to reconstruct the past, the book where necessary relies on inferences, intuition and sometimes even imagination.[69]

A further key hurdle of historical research that the book has had to confront is the inevitable temporal distance that exists between the 'then' and the 'now', between the time when the past occurred and the time when the history of that past is being written. By default, any historical project entails a certain temporal detachment from its object of observation, introducing the risk that the past will be looked at through a present-day lens and that today's ideas, concepts and concerns will be projected onto past events. Such 'anachronistic' or 'presentist' accounts that see the past outside of the confines of its own time, and that are particularly pervasive in legal historiography, have been

64 See eg the report on *The Ditta Luigi Gallotti v The Somali Government* (1970) 40 ILR 158, 160.

65 Böckstiegel, 'Arbitration of Disputes Between States and Private Enterprises in the International Chamber of Commerce' (n 9); Wetter and Schwebel (n 27).

66 See eg 'RCA Units Enjoined on Foreign Claims' *The New York Times* (New York, 3 July 1935) 23.

67 Tosh (n 62) 180; Gottschalk (n 42) 45–46.

68 Tosh (n 62) 181 (noting that the preserved historical record consists of 'completely unmanageable quantities').

69 See Tosh (n 62) 185–186.

fervently decried by historians as 'sins'[70] or 'moral errors'[71] against history. The point is perhaps best illustrated by Lesaffer:

> This kind of historiography sins against the most basic rules of historical methodology, and the results are deplorable. This genealogic history from present to past leads to anachronistic interpretations of historical phenomena, clouds historical realities that bear no fruit in our own times and gives no information about the historical context of the phenomenon one claims to recognise. *It describes history in terms of similarities with or differences from the present, and not in terms of what it was.* It tries to understand the past for what it brought about and not for what it meant to the people living in it.[72]

While this reproach underlines a vital message regarding historical research – the critical need for the past to be approached with primarily the past, and not the present, in mind – the struggle against anachronism need not lead one to the extreme position that seeks to hermetically seal off the past from the present, denouncing entirely its usefulness to contemporary problems and debates.[73] The past is not a parallel universe that can be observed from a platform of seamless neutrality without being even in the slightest contaminated by the observer; much like in the physical world, so to in historical enquiries, all observation necessarily affects the very object of its examination. As much as it is a must to try to understand the past for what it was in its own time, barring the employment of techniques resembling Orwell's 'doublethink', one cannot simply approach a historical project as a *tabula rasa*, disremembering all previous knowledge and experiences. Indeed, the very reasons behind doing historical research, the way the research is brought into fruition and the contribution it seeks to make are, to a certain extent, rooted in one's own

---

70 Tosh (n 62) 9; Constantin Fasolt, *The Limits of History* (University of Chicago Press 2004) 6; Randall Lesaffer, 'International Law and its History: The Story of an Unrequited Love' in Craven, Fitzmaurice and Vogiatzi (n 30) 34.

71 Quentin Skinner, 'Meaning and Understanding in the History of Ideas' (1969) 8 History and Theory 3, 53.

72 Lesaffer (n 70) 34–35. Emphasis added.

73 See Skinner (n 71) 51. For a criticism of 'pure' contextualism, see Martti Koskenniemi, 'Histories of International Law: Significance and Problems for a Critical View' (2013) 27(2) Temple Int'l & Comp LJ 215, 229–232. On how this particular aspect of the contextual approach has been negatively received within the historian community, see also Mark Bevir, 'The Contextual Approach' in George Klosko (ed), *The Oxford Handbook of the History of Political Philosophy* (OUP 2011) 17–18.

subjective notions and pre-conceptions that are themselves inevitably influenced by contemporary considerations.[74] To a certain extent, then, 'the stories of the past we tell always reflect our present concerns (…) *every history is a history of the present*'.[75]

Anachronism, thus, is simply a fact of life in historical research;[76] while it therefore cannot be entirely eradicated, there are nonetheless ways to lessen its footprint. One such approach – which the present book follows – is suggested by Lesaffer, who proposes that the past should first, 'at least as far as this is humanly possible', be analysed and assessed on its own terms – as *past for the sake of the past*. According to Lesaffer, this is a process that mandates following 'the rudiments of classical historical methodology', which in turn amounts 'to what historians have been doing since the days of humanistic scholarship: the textual and contextual analysis of their written sources'. In other words, before attempting to make any useful comparisons or draw lessons for today, those venturing into historical research should at the least try to ensure that their sources are as authentic as possible, that those sources are read as the contemporaries of the authors would, and that they are read in light of the contexts and concerns of the authors.[77] With this in mind, the primary part of the book (Chapters 2 through 5) focuses simply on uncovering and examining how ISA affected governance in the past – it merely tries to understand historical ISA's governance role for what it was in the past. In doing so, the book recognises that the historical ISA s did not occur in a vacuum, but had rather taken place in vastly different geographical, cultural and temporal settings, as well as that, to properly gauge these historical ISA s and their effects, the various relevant primary and secondary sources need to be understood and analysed within the broader socio-economic and political context in which they were generated.[78] Accordingly, the book does not focus solely on primary and

---

74 Koskenniemi, 'Histories of International Law: Significance and Problems for a Critical View' (n 73) 230.

75 Ibid 232. Emphasis added.

76 Ibid 230.

77 Lesaffer (n 70) 37–40. For recent applications of this approach in legal historiography see Bray (n 39) 110–111 and Mona Pinchis-Paulsen, 'Resolving Challenges to Historical Research: Developing a Project to Define Fair and Equitable Treatment' in Schill, Tams and Hofmann (n 11) 179, 205–206.

78 Skinner (n 71); Tosh (n 62) 131–132; Flaherty (n 62) 553–554; Kramer (n 62) 394; Michael Lobban, 'Introduction: The Tools and the Tasks of the Legal Historian' in Andrew Lewis and Michael Lobban (eds), *Law and History: Current Legal Issues 2003 Volume 6* (OUP 2004) 3; Bardo Fassbender and Anne Peters, 'Introduction: Towards a Global History of International Law' in Fassbender and Peters, *The Oxford Handbook of the History of International Law* (n 30) 1, 14. Determining what constitutes the 'proper context', however, is

secondary materials created within or in relation to ISA, but also on sources that provide a deeper insight into the different actors involved, the socio-economic and political surrounding, as well as contemporary legal developments. Meanwhile, and only as a second step in the sequence, any potential insights as to the relevance of the past governance practices of ISA for contemporary debates are reserved for the concluding chapter.

4.2 *Temporal Scope and (Lack of) Periodisation*

With respect to the inevitable need to delimit the temporal scope of its examination,[79] the book places the starting point of its enquiry in the mid-19th century, as it is only from this point in time that I have managed to unearth the practice of ISA with some regularity. Of course, this does not purport to be an origins claim that would pinpoint *the beginning* of ISA; indeed, further research on the history of ISA very well may, and is perhaps even likely to, uncover earlier material on ISA. In contrast, the book does not choose a singular point in time as the juncture where the past ends and the present begins. Not only are such clear demarcation lines between the past and the present always somewhat arbitrary, in particular because the reality of life is never easily translated into neatly circumscribed categories,[80] but in this particular instance this task proved especially difficult against the relevant factual underpinnings, as reflected in the overlap between the relevant actors, the similarity of processes and the overall likeness of the continuing ISA practice. Accordingly, the book opts for a 'transitional period' between the then and the now, a sort of semi-permeable membrane that does not allow the present to supplant the past instantaneously, but only for it to gradually seep through. This transitional ending period is placed in the decades between the late 1950s and the 1980s. This is a period that is not only characterised by a progressive decrease in the accessibility to relevant archival materials (due to the required time periods for the release of classified materials not yet having lapsed), but throughout it several important developments, some of which were specific to

---

not an automatic exercise. See Anne Orford, 'On International Legal Method' (2013) 1 London Review of International Law 167, 173 (explaining that the relevant context is not necessarily that of temporal proximity) and Koskenniemi, 'Histories of International Law: Significance and Problems for a Critical View' (n 73) 232 (noting that context is a malleable concept, determined in large part by one's own choices and predispositions).

79 See Oliver Diggelmann, 'The Periodization of the History of International Law' in Fassbender and Peters, *The Oxford Handbook of the History of International Law* (n 30) 997; Pinchis-Paulsen, 'Resolving Challenges to Historical Research' (n 77) 184.

80 Pinchis-Paulsen, 'Resolving Challenges to Historical Research' (n 77) 185; Diggelmann (n 79) 1002–03; Gottschalk (n 42) 202–203.

ISA and some of which concern arbitration in general, incrementally led to a significantly different look for ISA.

Indeed, over the course of these few decades, ISA saw a substantial realignment of the legal, political and social framework through which it operates. This notably included the adoption of the New York Convention,[81] the European Convention on International Commercial Arbitration,[82] the PCA's 'Rules of Arbitration and Conciliation for Settlement of International Disputes Between Two Parties of Which Only One is a State',[83] the ICSID Convention,[84] the United Nations Commission on International Trade Law (UNCITRAL) Arbitration Rules[85] and the UNCITRAL Model Law.[86] Equally as important was the introduction of the BIT with the Germany-Pakistan BIT in 1959,[87] and crucially, the version of the BIT with direct investor-state dispute settlement in the late 1960s[88] (both of which were preceded by the 1959 Abs-Shawcross Draft Convention).[89] The number of concluded BITs grew steadily over this period (before finally exploding in the 1990s),[90] while their effective application was kicked-off in 1987 with the registration of the first known BIT case in *AAPL v. Sri Lanka*.[91] During this time, there was also a significant increase in the use of arbitration,[92] as well as a realignment of the power structure within the

---

81 Convention on the Recognition and Enforcement of Foreign Arbitral Awards (opened for signature 10 June 1958, entered into force 7 June 1959) 330 UNTS 38.

82 European Convention on International Commercial Arbitration (opened for signature 21 April 1961, entered into force 7 January 1964) 484 UNTS 349. In art II, the Convention explicitly authorises legal persons of public law to conclude valid arbitration agreements.

83 PCA (n 10).

84 Convention on the Settlement of Investment Disputes between States and Nationals of Other States (opened for signature 18 March 1965, entered into force 14 October 1966) 575 UNTS 159.

85 UNCITRAL Arbitration Rules (1976) 15 ILM 701.

86 UNCITRAL Model Law on International Commercial Arbitration (1985) 24 ILM 1302.

87 Treaty between the Federal Republic of Germany and Pakistan for the Promotion and Protection of Investments (signed 25 November 1959, entered into force 28 April 1962).

88 Agreement on Economic Cooperation (The Netherlands-Indonesia) (signed 7 July 1968, entered into force 17 July 1971).

89 'The Proposed Convention to Protect Private Foreign Investment – Introduction' (1960) 9 J Pub L 115.

90 See Jason Webb Yackee, 'Do Bilateral Investment Treaties Promote Foreign Direct Investment? Some Hints from Alternative Evidence' (2011) 51 Virginia Journal of International Law 397, 402.

91 *Asian Agricultural Products Ltd (AAPL) v Democratic Socialist Republic of Sri Lanka*, ICSID Case No ARB/87/3, Award (27 June 1990).

92 The world's leading arbitral institution, the ICC's International Court of Arbitration, has administered more than 20,000 cases since its inception in 1923, 17,000 of which were registered after 1980. See Stone Sweet and Griesel (n 36) 2.

system, reflected in a change in the type of actors that were at the heart of its operation.[93] While none of these developments could in and of themselves be dubbed as 'the end of history' of ISA, taken together they set up a markedly different backdrop for ISA going forward, even if they do not quite rise to the level of creating a true sense of discontinuity between the past and the present.

In focusing its attention on such a broad time frame, the book therefore adopts a type of *longue durée* approach to history, pursuant to which the study of history is undertaken by focusing on large time scales.[94] Unlike the typical *longue durée*, however, it does not do so in order to uncover enduring historical structures (although this ultimately appears inevitable), but rather in the hope of capturing the extent of ISA s historical governance potential. In accordance with this goal, the structure of the argument that is presented is non-linear and non-chronological – it does not purport to tell the story of how ISA got from point A in time to point B, which indeed hardly appears feasible in light of the rich and complex nature of the discipline's past. Instead of following a chronological trajectory, the book is thus organised thematically, according to how the various arbitrations fit under the different governance aspects that have been discerned from observing the historical ISA s.[95] Accordingly, the book is better understood as being concerned with providing a single long exposure photograph that attempts to map out ISA's historical track record in governance than as trying to assemble a series of snapshots into a motion picture that tells the story of ISA's journey through time. Consequently, many of the historical features of ISA that are discussed are false starts, dead ends, apparent quantum leaps or developments that occurred in parallel to one another but without any mutual interaction. For this very reason, the book likewise does

93 See ibid 9 (relying on work by Dezaley and Garth).

94 The *longue durée* was developed by the French Annales School. See Fernand Braudel, 'History and the Social Sciences: The *Longue Durée*' in Fernand Braudel, *On History* (Sarah Matthews tr, University of Chicago Press 1980); David Armitage and Jo Guldi, 'The Return of the *Longue Durée*: An Anglo-American Perspective' (2015) 70(2) Annales HSS (English edn) 219, 222–223. While the *longue durée* raises obvious concerns in terms of contextualisation, as Armitage shows, the two are not necessarily irreconcilable. See David Armitage, 'What's the Big Idea? Intellectual History and the Longue Durée' (2012) 38(4) History of European Ideas 493, 498–499 (arguing for 'serial contextualism', whereby ideas from different time periods are both each embedded within their own contexts and analyzed across time).

95 See sub-section 4.3 and section 5 below. Of course, the historical ISA s were not ideal types that fall perfectly under these categories, but were capable of exhibiting different governance features simultaneously. See ch 6. However, for the simplicity of analysis and narration, they are organised in such a manner that stories about particular ISA s are told one continuous episode at a time.

not adopt any further subdivision of the chosen timeframe into sub-periods, as the material that is analysed does not lend itself fittingly to such compartmentalisation in light of the constant temporal overlap between the different arbitrations and other significant contemporary events. At the same time, this lack of sub-periodisation does not mean that the temporal element is entirely disregarded. Where conducive to a better understanding of the governance implications of ISA, developments and changes that have occurred over time are duly taken into account.

4.3 *Conceptual Clarifications*

Finally, in furthering its main argument – that, historically, ISA was a recurring vehicle of governance – the book relies on two underlying concepts: multifunctionality and governance, each of which requires some additional clarification.

The former of these concepts concerns the manner in which the book perceives the function, or role, of arbitration. Rather than subscribe to the conventional view pursuant to which the function, or role, of arbitration is exhausted in dispute settlement, the book draws on approaches that view dispute settlement mechanisms as having a broader societal impact than their immediate goal – that of dispute settlement – would indicate, and see them instead as being *multifunctional*.[96] Pursuant to this conception, instead of being limited to the sole function of dispute settlement, the societal role of adjudication is thus seen as extending to a number of different functions, or roles.[97] In contrast to much of the previous literature that has adopted a multifunctional approach to adjudication, however, the focus here is not restricted

---

96 See Martin Shapiro, *Courts: A Comparative and Political Analysis* (University of Chicago Press 1981); David D Caron, 'Towards a Political Theory of International Courts and Tribunals' (2006) 24 Berkeley J Int'l Law 401; José E Alvarez, 'What are International Judges for? The Main Functions of International Adjudication' in Cesare PR Romano, Karen Alter and Yuval Shany (eds), *The Oxford Handbook of International Adjudication* (OUP 2013) 158; Armin von Bogdandy and Ingo Venzke, *In Whose Name?* (OUP 2014); Ingo Venzke, 'Investor-State Dispute Settlement in TTIP from the Perspective of a Public Law Theory of International Adjudication' (2016) 17 JWIT 274; Jason Webb Yackee, 'Controlling the International Investment Law Agency' (2012) 53(2) Harvard International Law Journal 391; Karen Alter, *The New Terrain of International Law: Courts, Politics, Rights* (Princeton University Press 2014).

97 There are seemingly as many approaches to the nomenclature of such functions as there are authors who adopt this approach. Thus, speaking of domestic courts, Shapiro (n 96) mentions (i) conflict resolution, (ii) social control and (iii) lawmaking, while at the international level Alvarez (n 96) identifies (i) complex dispute settlement, (ii) fact-finding, (iii) lawmaking and (iv) governance, and von Bogdandy and Venzke (n 96) speak of (i) dispute settlement, (ii) stabilising normative expectations, (iii) lawmaking and (iv) controlling and legitimating public authority. Referring specifically to IIL, Yackee,

to the functions, or roles, of the dispute settlement body itself but is rather more expansive and looks to the functions of a particular phenomenon – in this case ISA – as such.[98] Therefore, even though the primary emphasis is placed on the role played by tribunals, which remain at the centre of this process as the ultimate decision-makers, attention is also accorded to the part played by other relevant actors, such as the parties to the proceedings, the private party's home state or its counsel.

It would be possible to identify a range of different functions, or roles, with respect to any particular type of adjudication, ISA included, and the possibilities for their categorisation are, if not limitless, then at least plentiful.[99] The goal of the present endeavour, however, is not to catalogue the entirety of the possible functions, or roles, of ISA throughout history. Instead, the book focuses on a particular sub-group of functions, or roles, exercised historically through ISA – those that carried with themselves certain governance implications due to the involvement of states in the arbitral process.

Such a focus, in turn, raises the need to clarify what is understood by the term governance. *Governance* is a concept whose contours are all but clearly demarcated and that has often been used as a catchword without a precisely defined content.[100] Without going into a deep discussion as to the general meaning of the term, which exceeds the limits of this book,[101] it suffices to say that, for the purposes of this book, governance is understood as denoting the exertion, through a formalised process that presupposes the authority to issue binding decisions, of influence in law or in fact over how states or state entities exercise their official functions. Moreover, in addition to the actual exercise of such influence, this concept is understood to include also the very claim to its exercise, insofar as it originates from an actor that is not clearly and unmistakably acting beyond its mandate in making such a claim. Finally, guided by the idea that 'not all governance is created equal', the book further views this notion as not being homogenous. Instead, governance is seen as a multifarious concept, where it is possible to distinguish between various types

'Controlling the International Investment Law Agency' (n 96) points to (i) quasi-adjudicative, (ii) quasi-legislative and (iii) quasi-executive functions.

98 For a similar approach see Yackee, 'Controlling the International Investment Law Agency' (n 96) 401–407.

99 See n 97.

100 Jan Kooiman and Svein Jentoft, 'Meta-Governance: Values, Norms and Principles, and the Making of Hard Choices' (2009) 87(4) Public Administration 818, 819; Montt (n 40) 131.

101 For an overview of the different uses of the term governance, see Owen Hughes, 'Does Governance Exist?' in Stephen P Osborne (ed), *The New Public Governance: Emerging Perspectives on the Theory and Practice of Public Governance* (Routledge 2010) 87.

of governance that entail different implications and occur at different levels of interaction.

5 The Structure of the Argument

In presenting the account of how governance was historically exercised through ISA, the book proceeds as follows.

First, *Chapter 2* offers a birds-eye, analytical perspective on the historical ISA s, with the intent of providing a general overview of what these arbitrations were like. This overview is in particular aimed at examining how the basic features of historical ISA s compared to their nominal role, circumscribed in the mere resolution of disputes between the participating parties. With this in mind, the chapter asks three fundamental questions regarding these past arbitrations: the '*What*?', the '*How*?' and '*by Whom*?'. The first of these questions – the *What?* – is aimed at discerning the type of interests that were implicated in the disputes historically submitted to ISA, i.e. *what* the ISA s were about. In asking this question, the chapter looks at the nature of the relationship between the investors and the states that took part in these arbitrations, as well as at the specific issues ultimately submitted to tribunals. This examination reveals that, far from engaging merely the interests of the two directly disputing parties, the historical ISA s instead implicated the interests of a much broader spectre of stakeholders. The next question – the *How?* – looks at the decision-making process through which the historical ISA s were resolved; in other words, it examines *how* the decision-making process in historical ISA operated. What this examination uncovers is no mere mechanical exercise of subsuming factual circumstances under legal norms, but rather a process that was infused through and through with a significant degree of legal indeterminacy, which in turn left ample room for discretionary choices to the relevant decision-makers. The third question – *by Whom?* – examines who the key actors in this decision-making process that necessitated a creative element in matters involving such broad interests were. It reveals that a number of private actors, most prominently the arbitrators, partook in the externalisation of decision-making in these sensitive matters of broader public concern. As a final step, the chapter shows that the aforementioned characteristics were not idiosyncratic to specific legal settings or regimes in which the historical ISA s were perceived to operate. Instead, they are revealed as more general features of these past ISA s that transcended categories such as the international, the trans-/anational and the national, as well as the private law/public law conceptual divide. On the basis of this analysis, the chapter suggests the presence of a strong dissonance between the proclaimed nominal role of the historical ISAs and their basic features; in doing so, it paves the way for the chapters that follow to demonstrate through in-depth accounts how this dissonance materialised into a governance role for historical ISA.

Accordingly, each of the three following chapters focuses on a different aspect of historical ISA's role in governance. Thus, *Chapter 3* tracks the role of historical ISA in determining the cost of governance – i.e. the financial costs associated with states' governance choices, policies and conduct of official business; it reveals that decisions by historical ISA tribunals regularly affected the financial equilibrium of states' governance decisions. In particular, the chapter chronicles three main modalities through which historical ISA is observed to have factored into the cost of governance. The first of these comprises cases that centred on disputes regarding public debt, the second cases that concerned state takeover of private property, and the third cases where liability was imposed upon states for non-compliance with obligations for reasons that bore (at least an alleged) connection to, or were a direct result of, the implementation of certain governmental policies or behaviours. Crucially, a contextualisation of the cases chronicled in the chapter against the broader backdrop of comparable historical ISAs reveals that the substantial monetary awards handed down in the examined cases in relation to states' conduct of official business were not mere atypical outliers. What is more, as the chapter demonstrates, the historical record further suggests that the impact of these sizeable awards not only imposed a significant financial burden upon the affected states, but that it in certain instances even carried a potential to considerably impact their capacity to govern. Overall, then, the chapter reveals historical ISA to have been a recurrent component in determining the cost of governance in a manner that carried with itself significant potential implications for the states involved.

Chapter 4 aims to capture historical ISA's capacity to direct the conduct of states or state entities in their exercise of official functions. It does so primarily by offering two in-depth accounts of historical ISAs, with each of them being intended to shed light on a different modality through which historical ISA is observed to have purported to influence state or state entity conduct. The first of these modalities concerns historical ISA's capacity to direct the conduct of state entities by reviewing the legality of their actions, which is illustrated by recounting in-depth a 1930s arbitration between the RCA and The Administration of Posts and Telegraphs of the Republic of Czechoslovakia. The account of this historical ISA that is provided reveals how The Administration of Posts and Telegraphs of the Republic of Czechoslovakia was found by a historical tribunal not to have the right to open a new direct radio telegraphic circuit between Czechoslovakia and the US because this was deemed in conflict with its obligations toward the RCA – a decision which The Administration moreover viewed as an authoritative pronunciation on whether it was entitled to carry on with its intended conduct in offering this public utility service. The second modality concerns instances of historical ISA tribunals not merely reviewing whether certain conduct was permitted or not, but instead taking upon themselves to decide, as if a primary decision-maker that determines the initial course of action, what conduct states were to take in performing their official functions. This second modality is presented by offering a detailed account of a series of arbitrations held under the World War I Peace Treaties. The cluster of cases reveals how historical ISA tribunals, acting as primary decision-makers, determined (including by ordering states to, or not to, expropriate) how the relevant railway systems in the former Austro-Hungarian Empire were to be reorganised following the country's break-up. As a final step, the chapter then proceeds to demonstrate that these two in-depth accounts were far from isolated instances, in the process thus revealing that it was not uncommon for historical ISA tribunals to take upon themselves to direct through their decisions the conduct of states or state entities, including in particular in relation to how they were to exercise their official functions.

Chapter 5 takes a look at ISA's historical role in contributing to the development of the law that governs investor-state relations. The analysis it presents is premised on an understanding that views contributions to the law's development as not being restricted to the formal processes through which legally binding norms are generated in national parliaments or at the international level, but as also including the capacity by other actors to exert a certain degree of influence over the perceived content of legal norms. With this in mind, the chapter posits that historical ISA tribunals' role was not exhausted in subsuming sets of relevant facts under a pre-constructed normative architecture, but that they were instead an active ingredient in its very construction and development. The chapter observes this to have taken place at three different levels of generality, depending on the type of investor-state relationship a tribunal's normative influence was able to reach. At the narrowest level of generality, historical ISA's role in developing the law was restricted to just the two parties partaking in a particular dispute. This is illustrated through a detailed account of a cluster of arbitrations that arose out of an early 20th century Greek public services concession, wherein the tribunals are in a number of cases observed to have more or less overtly developed the underlying normative basis, in so doing setting out the normative parameters for the parties' continuing relationship. Extending beyond the normative frameworks that governed the relations between the particular disputing parties, the normative influence of the tribunals' decisions was, at the intermediate level of generality, known also to reach the relations between one of the parties to the dispute before the tribunal and a completely unrelated third party. A particularly apposite example of this is the *RCA v. China* arbitration, as an in-depth look at the dispute provided by the chapter reveals that the RCA had adjusted a number of its relationships with other telegraph administrations as a consequence of the tribunal's decision. Finally, the chapter looks to the broadest level of generality, revealing that decisions by historical ISA tribunals are known to have contributed to the development of norms governing investor-state relations of general application (i.e. norms that potentially applied to any investor-state relationship); notably, ISA tribunals' decisions are shown to have done so both with respect to norms that were relevant for assessing states' substantive conduct and with respect to norms relevant for the procedural conduct of ISA. A final, yet crucial, element of the argument presented in the chapter is that, in light of the nature of the underlying investor-state relationships, at all of the different levels of generality at which historical ISA is observed to have contributed to the development of the relevant normative structures, it did so in relation to norms that, *inter alia*, specifically concerned the behaviour of states in their conduct of official business. As such, having thus concerned how states were to govern, historical ISA's contribution to the development of the normative architecture that governs investor-state relations is distinguishable from similar phenomena that might concern only private parties.

Finally, *Chapter 6* offers a recapitulation of historical ISA's governance role, making a number of important observations about this well-established historical practice. The chapter thus reiterates that the governance implications that almost invariably accompanied historical ISA were not circumscribed to specific sets of historical circumstances and that they were known to manifest themselves through various modalities and sub-modalities – thus potentially giving rise to very different concerns as to their appropriateness. In light of the numerous avenues through which information about historical ISA was made publicly accessible, the chapter further posits that what took place in historical ISA was far from unknowable not only to those with the requisite specialised knowledge, but also to the general public. The overview of historical ISA's governance role that is presented by the chapter also emphasises the participation in historical ISA by individuals who were in their other professional capacities involved in governance. Finally, the chapter proceeds to situate the governance role of historical ISA within the broader context of how investor-state relations of the time were governed. In doing so, it reveals historical ISA to have been not an isolated mechanism of investor-state governance, but rather merely one of the many institutions of similar reach. With this in mind, the chapter posits that historical ISA is thus best understood as having formed part of a broader overarching structure through which investor-state relations of the time were governed. As a last step, and having regard to all of these previous findings, the chapter then posits that ISA's historical governance role points to a need for a comprehensive approach to and understanding of ISA's present-day governance role, which would focus not only on its investment-treaty variant, but on the discipline as a whole.

CHAPTER 2

Historical Investor-State Arbitration as Private Dispute Settlement: A Breakdown

1 Introduction

This Chapter provides a rudimentary overview of the historical investor-state arbitrations (ISAs), with a specific emphasis toward examining how the main features of the historical ISAs compared to their nominal role, circumscribed in the mere resolution of disputes between the participating parties. Unlike the subsequent chapters, this Chapter therefore does not offer in-depth accounts of individual historical ISAs. Instead, it presents a birds-eye, analytical perspective of the historical ISAs, so as to allow for an overall frame of reference of their underlying characteristics to be formed (inasmuch as such extrapolations may reasonably be made). The Chapter thus serves as a sort of prelude, or introductory sampling, to the more detailed analyses that follow by providing the reader, in broad strokes, with a better 'feel' of what the historical ISAs were like.

With that in mind, one may note as an initial observation that a cursory look at the process behind why and how the historical ISAs came about offers little indication that they had implications that went beyond the two opposing parties that were the official participants in the arbitrations and the particular disputes between them. Both in terms of by whom the arbitrations were set up and for which purpose, at face value, these past cases give out an impression of a mechanism principally established as between the private investor and the state, and with a mandate that is both very specific and limited in its scope. Thus, for instance, in terms of the driving force behind the historical ISAs, the choice to go to arbitration overwhelmingly found its roots in an agreement between the investor and the state. While there were some occasions where parties other than the two arbitrating parties were involved in the construction of the agreement to arbitrate,[1] such instances were rather the exception than

1 Several ISAs, described in detail in ch 4, were held pursuant to arbitration provisions included in the World War I Peace Treaties. See Treaty of Peace between the Allied and Associated Powers and Hungary (signed 4 June 1920, entered into force 26 July 1921) (1920) 10 UKTS Cmd 896 (hereinafter Treaty of Trianon) art 304 and Treaty of Peace between the Allied and Associated Powers and Austria (signed 10 September 1919, entered into force 16 July 1920)

 | DOI:10.1163/9789004733824_003

the norm. In any event, these extraordinary instances could at best only offer an indication that those particular historical ISAs might have been a matter of concern beyond the two disputing parties insofar as the parties who were privy to the arbitration agreement were concerned, but could not in and of themselves be understood as providing any type of general indication that this would be the case outside of this very limited context. Thus, at its foundation, the decision to go to arbitration remained one that involved a limited number of entities and could hardly be seen as indicative of any potential broader-reaching effects on behalf of the historical ISAs.

The mandate conferred by the disputing parties on the historical investor-state tribunals through such arbitration agreements was likewise nominally limited in its reach. The agreement to arbitrate typically took the form of either an arbitration clause, which allowed for arbitration in relation to a certain investor-state relationship concerning matters that may arise in the future, or of a *compromis* – a special agreement that provided for arbitration of already existing controversial issues.[2] The former, which was by far the more prevalent mechanism for establishing the historical ISA tribunals (especially in the later years), offered scant indication of ISA being anything but a mechanism for dispute resolution. In their most rudimentary iterations, such arbitration clauses, broadly speaking, merely provided that *any dispute* that could arise between two parties to a certain relationship would be resolved through arbitration.[3] The majority of the clauses on which the known historical cases were

(1919) 11 UKTS Cmd 400 (hereinafter Treaty of Saint-Germain) art 320. Likewise, there were instances where the decision to go to arbitration was reached between, not the two parties eventually going to arbitration, but rather the investor's home state and the state party to the arbitration. This was, for example, the case in *The Jaffa-Jerusalem Railway Arbitration*. See Michael Reynolds, 'The Jaffa Jerusalem Railway Company Arbitration 1922' (1991) 6 Arab Law Quarterly 215, 215–216; Shabtai Rosenne, 'The Jaffa-Jerusalem Railway Arbitration (1922)' in Shabtai Rosenne, *Essays on International Law and Practice* (Martinus Nijhoff 2007) 295. See also the Franco-Algerian arbitrations mentioned in nn 135–136.

2 Of course, these two methods were not necessarily mutually exclusive. See eg *Saudi Arabia v Arabian American Oil Company* (ARAMCO), Arbitration Agreement (1963) 27 ILR 229 (copies of both the agreement and the award are available in the Peace Palace Library in The Hague); J Gillis Wetter and Stephen M Schwebel, 'Some Little-Known Cases on Concessions' (1964) 40 Brit YBIL 183, 195 and 200. At the same time, there were also instances where the historical ISAs were based neither on contractual arbitration clauses nor on a *compromis* (see n 1).

3 This type of simplistic arbitration clause seems to have been particularly characteristic of Chinese practice. See the numerous contracts between foreign investors and China reproduced in John VA MacMurray (ed), *Treaties and Agreements With and Concerning China: 1894–1919* (OUP 1921, vol I) 135–145, 356–367, 462–476, 506–515 and 724–728. See also *The Ditta Luigi Gallotti v The Somali Government* (1970) 40 ILR 158, 160; *Martin Cowley Railway Construction Co, Limited and Alderton Construction (Westminster) Limited v The Higher Commit-*

based, however, were somewhat more expansive, and often specified that the disputes that would be subject to arbitration related to the interpretation and/or implementation of the agreement between the parties. An illustrative example of this type of arbitration clause is Article 90 (A) of the 1925 concession agreement between the Lena Goldfields Company Limited and the USSR, which provided that:

> All disputes and misunderstandings concerning the interpretation or performance of this agreement and all appendices thereto, on the declaration of either party, shall be examined and settled by an arbitration court.[4]

Many other agreements between investors and states, a number of which ended up giving rise to historical ISAs, contained similar arbitration clauses.[5]

---

tee for the Recommissioning of the Hedjaz Railway Line, Award (22 September 1972) 2 (a copy of the award can be found at the Archives of the Graduate Institute of International and Development Studies in Geneva, Reference code 1.7.5.HEI 2448).

4 The English translation of the arbitration clause is reproduced in Arthur Nussbaum, 'The Arbitration between Lena Goldfields Ltd and the Soviet Government' (1950) 36 Cornell Law Quarterly 31, 42 and in VV Veeder, 'The *Lena Goldfields* Arbitration: The Historical Roots of Three Ideas' (1998) 47 ICLQ 747, 790–792.

5 See eg Agreement in Regard to the Supply of Electricity and Transport Services between the Syndicat d'Etudes et Entreprises and the Power and Traction Finance Company Ltd and Greece (17 October 1925) art 49, reproduced in Wetter and Schwebel (n 2) 194–195; Agreement between the District of Pozarevac (Kingdom of Serbs, Croats and Slovenes, later Yugoslavia) and American Oriental Construction Syndicate (2 March 1929) art 16 (Archives of Yugoslavia: 70–288–535); Financial Agreement for the Carrying out of Reclamation Works on the Territory of the Dunav-Tamis Water Collective in Pancevo between the State Hypothecary Bank of the Kingdom of Serbs, Croats and Slovenes and Batignolles (18 May 1929) art 10 (Archives of Yugoslavia: 70–285–531); The Government of Kelantan and the Duff Development Company, Limited: Deed of Cancellation (15 July 1912) clause 21, reproduced in Shaharil Talib, *History of Kelantan: 1890–1940* (The Malaysian Branch of the Royal Asiatic Society 1995) 208–218; Financial Agreement for the Construction of the Veles-Prilep Railway between the Kingdom of Yugoslavia and the Société Européenne de Crédit Foncier et de Banque (later Société Européenne d'Etudes et d'Entreprises) (3 January 1932) art 17 (Archives of Yugoslavia: 70–288–536); Oil Concession Granted by the Shaikh of Qatar to the Anglo-Persian Oil Co, Ltd (17 May 1935) art 16 (available as part of the Qatar Digital Library at <https://www.qdl.qa/en/archive/81055/vdc_100000000833.0x000006> accessed 27 September 2024); Concession Agreement between the Government of the Union of Soviet Socialist Republics (USSR) and WA Harriman and Co Inc of New York Regarding the Manganese Deposits of Tchiatouri, Georgia (12 June 1925) sec 65, reproduced in Stephen D Fitch, 'The Harriman Manganese Concession in the Soviet Union: Lessons for Today' (1991) 9 Int'l Tax & Bus Law 209, 262–264; Concession Agreement between Junkers and the USSR (November 1922) art 56, reproduced in VV Veeder, 'Chancellor Wirth and the Mologales Concession 1923–1927:

At least at the outset, it is not readily apparent from the wording of such clauses that the task conveyed through the arbitration agreement implied much more than simple contractual interpretation and/or enforcement as between two contracting parties.

The first glimpses of historical ISAs potentially transcending the interests of the immediate disputing parties were given off by arbitration agreements concluded in the form of a *compromis*. Because *compromis* were only concluded once a contentious issue in the investor-state relationship had already arisen, unlike the generic arbitration clauses which provided little to no insight into the content of the arbitration, *compromis* tended to be much more detailed, and contained the specific questions that were to be discussed in the arbitration. Consequently, the questions that were submitted as part of the *compromis* were sometimes somewhat indicative of the fact that the arbitration could be of interest to actors that were not privy to the arbitration proceedings in the historical ISAs. Thus, for example, in the case of the 1864 arbitration between the Suez Canal Company and Egypt, one of the issues put forward by the two parties required the tribunal to decide on the nature of a 'regulation' that had been promulgated by Egypt's ruler regarding labour issues in relation to the

The German-Speaking Origins of the 1965 ICSID Convention' in Christina Binder and others (eds), *International Investment Law for the 21st Century: Essays in Honour of Christoph Schreuer* (OUP 2009) 387; Mologales Concession between the Gesellschaft für die wirtschaftlichen Beziehungen mit dem Osten GmbH and the USSR (11 September 1923) art 42, reproduced in Veeder, 'Chancellor Wirth and the Mologales Concession 1923–1927' (n 5) 400; Concession Agreement between the Government of His Imperial Majesty the Shah of Persia and William Knox D'Arcy (28 May 1901) art 17, reproduced in RW Ferrier, *The History of the British Petroleum Company: Volume I, the Developing Years 1901–1932* (CUP 1982) 640–643; Agreement Between the Imperial Government of Persia and the Anglo-Persian Oil Company, Limited (29 April 1933) art 22, reproduced in Alan W Ford, *The Anglo-Iranian Oil Dispute of 1951–1952: A Study of the Role of Law in the Relations of States* (University of California Press 1954) 233–247; Concession Agreement between the Shaikh of Kuwait and the Kuwait Oil Company Limited (23 December 1934) art 18, reproduced in Archibald HT Chisholm, *The First Kuwait Oil Concession Agreement: A Record of the Negotiations 1911–1934* (Frank Cass 1975) 242–246; Agreement between the National Iranian Oil Company and Sapphire Developments, Ltd (16 June 1958) (available at Columbia University Library) arts 39–41; Agreement between the National Iranian Oil Company and the Pan American Petroleum Corporation (24 April 1958) (available at Columbia University Library) arts 39–41; Agreement between the National Iranian Oil Company and La Societe AGIP Mineraria (24 August 1957) (available at Columbia University Library) art 44; Traffic Agreement between Radio Corporation of America and Administration of Posts and Telegraphs of the Republic of Czechoslovakia (10 November 1928) (The Hagley Museum and Library, records of MCI International, Inc (call number 2225, Series XV; hereinafter MCI International Archives), box 583, file 'Czechoslovakia: Correspondence and Agreements (1 of 6)') art 9 (hereinafter the Czechoslovakian Traffic Agreement). See also MacMurray (n 3) 782–784 and 785–787.

underlying concession.[6] Despite such occasional hints, *compromis* nonetheless formally remained instruments concluded between the two immediate disputing parties aimed at resolving the particular dispute being submitted to the tribunal.

As a general matter, then, the manner in which the historical ISAs were nominally intended to be structured gave out an impression of a mechanism that would appear to fit rather squarely within the conception of having been merely a means for resolving specific disagreements between the two disputing parties. The arbitrations owed their existence to the consent of the disputing parties, while the tribunals were set up individually for each singular dispute. The direct mandate conferred upon the arbitrators was restricted to resolving a particular controversy between the parties and, once this task had been fulfilled, the tribunals ceased their existence. Based on this, one could hardly be faulted for assuming, on a first impression basis, that historical ISA was nothing but a mode of resolving disputes between, and primarily of interest to, the two disputing parties.

In assessing how this first-impression perception of historical ISA compares against what actually took place – against the actual practice of historical ISA – this Chapter proceeds by breaking the historical ISAs down to their rudimentary features. It does so by asking three fundamental questions about the historical ISAs, each of which serves to highlight one of their quintessential traits: the '*What*?', the '*How*?' and the '*by Whom*?'. The idea behind the first of these questions is to provide a general understanding of *what* the historical ISAs were about, or in other words, what type of interests were implicated in the disputes historically submitted to ISA. (2). The second question purports to elucidate *how* decisions were made in historical ISA, and does so by examining the normative basis within which the decision-making process was embedded (3). The third question then looks at *who* the actors that were involved, and

6 See Jason Webb Yackee, 'The First Investor-State Arbitration: *The Suez Canal Company v Egypt* (1864)' (2016) 17 The Journal of World Investment and Trade 401, 427. For other examples of historical ISAs that were based on, or included, a *compromis*, see Saudi Arabia-ARAMCO Arbitration Agreement (n 2); Wetter and Schwebel (n 2) 185, 195, 200 and 222; Lambertus Erades, 'The Sudan Arbitration' (1970) 17(2) Netherlands International Law Review 200, 202–203; *Government of Peru v The Peruvian Corporation Limited*, English Translation of Memoire for the Peruvian Corporation Limited against the Peruvian Government (2–3 September 1908) (University College London Special Collections: PERUCORP C2/65B/1) 49–50; *Hambros Bank Limited and Lazard Brothers and Co Limited v Kingdom of Roumania Monopolies Institute*, Award (10 June 1937) (a copy of the award is available in the Nationaal Archief, Den Haag, Collection 341 Prof mr dr GWJ Bruins, Supplement 1981, 1929–1939, access number 2.21.191.02, inventory number 1) 1; *La Societe Rialet v The Government of Ethiopia* (1929) 8 Recueil des Décisions des Tribunaux Arbitraux Mixtes Institués par les Traités de Paix 742.

that played crucial roles, in this decision-making process in the historical ISAs were (4).

When tied together, this analysis reveals a practice that stood in stark contrast to the aforementioned initial impression given off by the nominal purpose that underlay the historical ISAs. It shows that historical ISAs revolved not only around the interests of the two directly participating disputing parties, but also implicated interests of a broader array of stakeholders. The analysis moreover reveals that the decision-making that took place in the historical ISAs over such interests was fraught with considerable legal indeterminacy and was thus necessarily infused with a certain dose of creative input on behalf of the decision-makers. Such creative decision-making in matters that were not only of concern to the two disputing parties, in turn, was undertaken through a process in which private actors, most notably arbitrators that comprised the tribunals, played a crucial role. In a final step, the Chapter then assesses whether the aforementioned characteristics were idiosyncratic to specific settings or regimes in which the historical ISAs operated or whether they were more general features of the historical ISAs. It does so by looking at the different underlying frameworks – the national, the international and the trans-/anational – in which the historical ISAs were embedded, as well as at the different conceptual framings through which they were approached (as epitomised in the private law/public law dichotomy). This cross-analysis reveals that the aforementioned features of the historical ISAs were in fact not unique to any specific underlying framework or conceptual approach in which these arbitrations operated, but rather seemed to have been their representative character traits (5). Ultimately, the picture that is painted by a deeper engagement with the practice of historical ISA is not one that is easily reconciled with it merely having been a mechanism for resolving disputes between two aggrieved parties, thus betraying a deeper underlying dissonance between what historical ISA might at face value appear to have been and what it actually was (6).

2 What Was at Stake in Historical Investor-State Arbitration? Beyond the Disputing Parties' Interests

Understanding *what* the historical ISAs were about and what type of interests they implicated is a two-pronged endeavour. To begin with, it requires looking at the general nature of the investor-state relationships from which the historical ISAs originated (2.1), which in turn invites a further exploration of the specific issues that were ultimately submitted to arbitration (2.2). As the examination that follows will attest, seemingly more often than not, the interests at play in the historical ISAs were not confined to the two disputing parties officially partaking in the arbitrations, but instead extended well beyond the confines of their mutual relationship.

2.1 *The Nature of the Investor-State Relationships Underlying the Historical Investor-State Arbitrations*

The first step in the endeavour to understand what the historical ISAs were about involves an evaluation of the underlying investor-state relationships, with the goal of grasping what these relationships were like and the area of activity in which they were forged. A wholesale assessment of the relationships underlying the historical ISAs reveals that they were in large part concluded in areas of activity that, in one way or another, involved interests of considerable public importance. These types of ventures were thus often of direct interest not only to the parties immediately privy to the investor-state relationships in question, but also to the constituencies of the relevant states, as well as in certain instances to other stakeholders. The four primary areas of activity of investor-state interaction from which the historical ISAs arose concerned (i) public infrastructure projects; (ii) natural resource exploitation; (iii) public debt; and (iv) activities related to state monopolies.

Public Infrastructure. The area of investor-state co-operation that was probably the most common source of the investor-state disputes from which the historical ISAs arose concerned important infrastructure projects. In such relationships, (foreign) investors were often endowed with the responsibility of constructing and/or operating important public utilities. In certain instances, the significance of these public utilities transcended the interests of the specific country in which they were to be constructed and had wider geo-strategic implications. This was the case, for example, with the Suez Canal or with the railways that were at the centre of the several arbitrations that arose under the World War I Peace Treaties (see Chapter 4). Indeed, in the latter instance, the tribunals that were eventually tasked with resolving the disputes that arose in relation to these railways openly recognised that the task put before them by the Peace Treaties was 'to restore the regular operation of the railways (…) *in the higher interests of the facility and freedom of international communication*'.[7] Likewise,

7 *Sopron-Köszeg Local Railway Company v Austria and Hungary* (1930) 24(1) AJIL 164, 170. See also *Zeltweg-Wolfsberg and Unterdrauburg-Woellan Railway Company v Austria and Yugoslavia* [1934] League of Nations Official Journal 1005, 1006 (*Zeltweg-Wolfsberg II*) (noting that the purpose of the provision providing for arbitration was, *inter alia*, 'the restoration of international communications').

the League of Nations' Permanent Legal Committee of the Communications and Transit Committee had opined that the provision upon which these arbitrations were based was inserted into the Peace Treaties in order 'to ensure the maintenance of railway communications *in the general interest*'.[8] The historical ISAs were particularly prevalent in the transport sector,[9] where the railway industry resorted to arbitration on a relatively frequent basis and was a source of a seemingly disproportionately large number of historical ISAs.[10] Other important public utilities where investor-state partnerships were concluded, and subsequently gave rise to historical ISAs, included telecommunications,[11] electrification projects,[12] water,[13] and gas supply,[14] as well as large construction and land reclamation projects.[15]

---

8 'Annex 1065*a*: Dispute Concerning the Sopron-Köszeg Local Railway' [1928] League of Nations Official Journal 1614, 1616. Emphasis added.

9 Apart from the aforementioned Suez Canal project and the railway arbitrations mentioned in n 10 below, there was also an arbitration that involved the operation of the Smyrna wharves. See *Societe des Quais de Smyrne v Greek Government* (1930) 37 Revue Générale de Droit International Public 335.

10 For example, this was the case in the following disputes: *The Guayaquil and Quito Railway v Ecuador, The Jaffa-Jerusalem Railway Arbitration, Sopron-Köszeg Local Railway Company v Austria and Hungary, SEEE v Yugoslavia, Losinger v Yugoslavia, Barcs-Pakrac Railway Company v Yugoslavia and Hungary, Zeltweg-Wolfsberg and Unterdrauburg-Woellan Railway Company v Yugoslavia and Austria, Oriental Railways Company v The Ottoman Empire, The Piraeus-Larissa Railway Arbitration, The Cauca Company v The Republic of Colombia, Duff Development Company v The Government of Kelantan, Canada v The Grand Trunk Railway Company, The Government of Greece v Sociéte Commerciale de Belgique (Socobelge)*, and the *Hedjaz Railway Arbitration.*

11 See eg *The Administration of Posts and Telegraphs of the Republic of Czechoslovakia v The Radio Corporation of America* (1936) 30 AJIL 523; *Radio Corporation of America v The National Government of the Republic of China* (1935) 3 RIAA 1621; *Greek Telephone Company v The Government of Greece*, Award (3 January 1935), reported in Wetter and Schwebel (n 2) 216.

12 See Wetter and Schwebel (n 2) 194.

13 See *The State of Lebanon and the Municipality of Beyrouth v La Compagnie des Eaux de Beyrouth*, Award (3 November 1953). A copy of the award (in French) is available in the Peace Palace Library. An extract from the award is reproduced in *'Électricité de Beyrouth' Company Case (France v Lebanon)* ICJ Pleadings 423.

14 *Société des Grands Travaux de Marseille v East Pakistan Industrial Development Corporation* (1984) 65 ILR 445.

15 *Government of the Republic of the Sudan v Turriff Construction (Sudan) Limited*, Award (23 April 1970); *La Société de Construction des Batignolles v Yugoslavia*, Award (5 February 1938) (*Batignolles v Yugoslavia I*) (Archives of Yugoslavia: 70–285–531); *La Société de Construction des Batignolles v Yugoslavia*, Award (8 July 1938) (*Batignolles v Yugoslavia II*) (Archives of Yugoslavia: 70–285–531). This was also the case in relation to the concession that gave rise to the arbitration between the Lake Copais Company and Greece. See

Natural Resources. Another area of investor-state co-operation that historically gave rise to a particularly high number of investor-state disputes was the exploitation of natural resources, which is unsurprising considering how closely knit the exploitation of natural resources was to questions of sovereignty and how much importance it held for the state to which such resources belonged. While there had been a significant tradition of investor-state co-operation in this sector in relation to various types of natural resources,[16] the sector particularly came to life, at least insofar as ISA was concerned, with the big oil arbitrations after World War II,[17] which accounted for a considerable proportion of the historical ISAs that took place in the natural resources sector.

Public Debt. One of the key areas of the investor-state partnerships that underlie historical ISAs was the financing of projects that were to be developed in the public interest through private funding. Throughout history, states have regularly borrowed money in order to finance their official activities, including from private entities. Unsurprisingly, these relationships frequently led to disputes[18] and, occasionally, also to ISA.[19] In addition, such financing activities

Ioanna Pepelasis Minoglou, 'The Greek State and The International Financial Community, 1922–1932: Demystifying the "Foreign Factor"' (PhD thesis, London School of Economics and Political Science 1993) 88 and 269 <http://etheses.lse.ac.uk/2590/> accessed 27 September 2024; Robert Graves, *Storm Centres of the Near East: Personal Memories, 1879–1929* (Hutchinson and Company Ltd 1933) 352–355 (Graves was one of the arbitrators in the arbitration).

16 Thus, for example, the Duff Development Company was granted extensive mining rights in Kelantan at the beginning of the 20th century, while the Lena Goldfields company had been involved in the mining of gold and other metals in Russia. See Agreement between the Raja of Kelantan and RW Duff (October 1900), reproduced in Talib (n 5) 194; Veeder, 'The *Lena Goldfields* Arbitration' (n 4) 756–757.

17 *Petroleum Development (Qatar) Ltd v Ruler of Qatar* (1951) 18 ILR 161; *Petroleum Development Ltd v The Sheikh of Abu Dhabi* (1951) 18 ILR 144; *Ruler of Qatar v International Marine Oil Company, Ltd* (1953) 20 ILR 534; *Saudi Arabia v ARAMCO* (1963) 27 ILR 117 (a copy of the award is available in the Peace Palace Library); *Sapphire International Petroleums Limited v National Iranian Oil Co (NIOC)* (1967) 35 ILR 136 (a copy of the award is available in the Peace Palace Library); *BP Exploration Company (Libya) Limited v The Government of the Libyan Arab Republic* (1979) 53 ILR 297; *Texaco Overseas Petroleum Company and California Asiatic Oil Company v The Government of the Libyan Arab Republic* (1978) 17 ILM 1 (a copy of the award, together with the Preliminary Award, is available in the Columbia University Library); *Libyan American Oil Company (LIAMCO) v The Government of the Libyan Arab Republic* (1981) 20(1) ILM 1.

18 See generally Michael Waibel, *Sovereign Defaults before International Courts and Tribunals* (CUP 2011).

19 This was the case eg in the *Peruvian Corporation v Peru* and *Hambros and Lazard v Roumania Monopolies Institute* disputes. See ch 3.

were often combined with other types of investor-state partnerships,[20] such as large infrastructure projects. In these types of arrangements, the private investor therefore appeared simultaneously as both the one carrying out the project and the one providing the financing.

Activities Relating to Monopolies in Public Services. There were also several instances where the historical ISAs were based on relationships that were closely related to the exploitation of monopolies for the provision of certain public services. Most notably, this was the case in *La Societe Rialet v. The Government of Ethiopia*,[21] where the company had been awarded a concessionary right to exploit a state monopoly relating to alcoholic beverages in Ethiopia, and in *The Alsing Trading Company, Ltd and Svenska Tändsticks Aktiebolaget v. Greece*,[22] where Alsing had been designated as the exclusive supplier for the Greek state's match monopoly.[23]

As this brief overview illustrates, the types of investor-state relationships that were at the root of the historical ISAs were hardly limited to purely commercial transactions whose relevance was strictly confined to the parties privy to this relationship. Instead, these types of partnerships were in large part concluded in spheres of activity that implicated interests of great importance not only to the constituencies of the states that participated in them, but also to stakeholders beyond them.[24] Moreover, in entering into these types of investor-state relationships, states often did so not in their private, or commercial, capacities, but rather in the exercise of their official public functions.[25]

---

20 The disputes in *Losinger v Yugoslavia*, SEEE *v Yugoslavia* and *Greece v Socobelge* arose from such combined contracts. Likewise, Ivar Kreuger, the controversial Swedish match magnate, often induced his match monopolies by offering foreign governments favourable loans. See Ulla Wikander, *Kreuger's Match Monopolies, 1925–1930: Case Studies in Market Control through Public Monopolies* (Julie Sundquist tr, LiberFörlag 1979) 264–269.

21 See n 6.

22 (1956) 23 ILR 633, 633–635 (a copy of the award can be found in the Peace Palace Library).

23 See also *Hellenic Electric Railways Ltd v The Greek State*, Award (23 December 1933) (ILO Archives: AR 1/26/10/1), which mentions a monopoly established in favour of the company in relation to the transport of passengers by rail along a certain route.

24 See nn 7–8.

25 This is, *inter alia*, evidenced by the fact that the agreements through which such relationships were concluded, and which often included arbitration clauses, were not infrequently ratified by the appropriate state institutions (including parliaments). See eg Veeder, 'The *Lena Goldfields* Arbitration' (n 4) 758; *Dominion of Canada v The Grand Trunk Railway Company of Canada*, Award (7 September 1921) 4 (see ch 3); *Batignolles v Yugoslavia II* (n 15) 56; 'Minister Fox to the Secretary of State' (29 September 1908) in *Papers Relating to the Foreign Relations of the United States, With the Annual Message of the President Transmitted to Congress December 8, 1908* (hereinafter FRUS) (US Government Printing Office 1912) 273 (in relation to *The Guayaquil and Quito Railway v Ecuador* dispute); *Losinger &*

Crucially, in so doing, they also frequently undertook certain limitations in terms of how they would exercise their public authority *vis-à-vis* the counterpart (foreign) investors, or in some instances even conferred upon them certain elements of such authority. In the most extreme examples, this went as far as granting to the investor certain rights that could be said to come close to including elements of sovereignty.

For instance, in discussing the *Compagnie du Katanga v. The Colony of the Belgian Congo* case, Wetter and Schwebel, when speaking of the scope of the rights that had been granted to the company by the underlying concession, observed that these rights 'were so extensive as to partake of *quasi-governmental powers* akin to those accorded the great trading companies of an earlier concessions era'.[26] Notably, the rights so granted extended over a third of Katanga's territory.[27] A claim to rights of similar scope in respect of a comparably sizeable proportion of a state's territory was advanced in relation to the initial iteration of the Duff concession in Kelantan, which was argued to had conferred administrative rights of such breadth that it had created fear of the company becoming 'a state within a state'.[28] Indeed, the aspirations behind the concession were described by the British Vice-Consul of Senggora in the following words:

> He obtained from the Rajah of Kelantan a territory of enormous area wherein he was to be allowed almost complete rights of sovereignty. The Company which he founded intended originally to carry out all the functions of a Government. They were to have had a complete set of Adminstra-tive Departments, a Police Force, a Gaol, etc. In fact, Mr. Duff probably pictured them as a sort of a Chartered Company ruling an independent territory.[29]

While examples such as these were no doubt somewhat exceptional extremes (at least within the time period covered by this book), and were seemingly primarily confined to arrangements stemming from the late 19th or the early

cie SA and 'Kompass' Allgemeine Kredit- und Garantie-Bank v The Kingdom of Yugoslavia, Award (31 October 1934) (*Losinger I*), reproduced in *The Losinger & Co Case (Switzerland v Yugoslavia)* PCIJ Rep Series C No 78 at 54, 61–62; *Sapphire v NIOC* (n 17) 143; *Saudi Arabia v ARAMCO* (n 17) 118; Original Bill of Complaint with Exhibits at iii, *Colombia v Cauca Co*, 106 Fed 337 (DW Va 1901) (available at Columbia University Library).

26 Wetter and Schwebel (n 2) 193. Emphasis added.

27 Ibid 184.

28 See ch 3.

29 Talib (n 5) 100–101.

20th century, there are numerous other, less extreme, instances that serve to illustrate the same point.

A notable case in point is a public utility concession in Greece that gave rise to a series of ISAs from the late 1920s onwards, which accorded the relevant concessionary companies wide 'financial and administrative independence'.[30] Likewise, a number of clauses frequently included in investor-state contracts of the period, such as those that eventually came to be known as stabilisation clauses[31] and clauses according tax and other fiscal benefits,[32] were of a similar character in that they restricted states' freedom in exercising their sovereign prerogatives. There were even instances where private enterprises were through such arrangements granted the right to expropriate.[33] It appears, thus, that the investor-state relationships from which the historical ISAs stemmed were not only known to be concerned with matters that transcended the interests of the two immediate disputing parties, but that they were moreover often set up so as to directly relate to, or even limit, how a state was to exercise its official functions. The power of contract, or better yet, the power (and willingness) of states that entered into these types of relationships to contract away important aspects of their official functions, is thus not to be understated. As might be expected, and as is illustrated in the following sub-section, this ultimately also reflected upon the nature of the disputes that would arise from such investor-state relationships.

2.2 *The Anatomy of the Historical Investor-State Disputes*

Bearing in mind these highly delicate domains in which the historical investor-state partnerships were formed, it was only natural that controversies that had arisen from them would carry a similar flavour. It is therefore not particularly surprising that the historical disputes that arose between investors, on the one

30 This clause was subsequently interpreted in a manner that was alleged to have severely restricted Greece's capacity to regulate the concessionary companies. See ch 5.

31 See eg Nussbaum (n 4) 46; *BP v Libya* (n 17) 322; *Texaco v Libya* (n 17) 4; *LIAMCO v Libya* (n 17) 31; *Sapphire v NIOC* (n 17) 140; Draft Agreement between the Government of Kelantan and the Duff Development Company (April 1905), reproduced in Talib (n 5) 201, 206; Persia-Anglo-Persian Oil Company Concession (n 5) art 21.

32 See eg Nussbaum (n 4) 45; Wetter and Schwebel (n 2) 201–203 and 208–210; Pozarevac-American Oriental Construction Syndicate Agreement (later assigned to Losinger) (n 5) art XI; Financial Agreement for the Construction of the Veles-Prilep Railway (n 5) art VII; *Hambros and Lazard v Roumania Monopolies Institute* (n 6) 10; Draft Agreement between Kelantan and the Duff Development Company (n 31) 206.

33 See eg Wetter and Schwebel (n 2) 206; Explanatory Document Sealed by the Raja of Kelantan and Signed by RW Duff (August 1903), reproduced in Talib (n 5) 198, 199; Draft Agreement between Kelantan and the Duff Development Company (n 31) 207.

hand, and states, on the other, regularly concerned issues closely tied in with some of the most fundamental aspects of the states' official functions.

By way of illustration, some of the questions that the parties sought to resolve through historical ISA directly concerned, or at least touched upon, ownership over land and water resources,[34] employee rights,[35] the extent of application of tax exemptions,[36] safety regulations,[37] organisation of public transport,[38] the state's obligation to transfer a part of its telecommunications network to a private company,[39] the effects of state succession or occupation on the operation of privately-held concessions,[40] the freedom of a government in selecting the course of a railway line and its obligation to construct road infrastructure,[41] alleged interference by a government in the exploitation of a natural resources concession,[42] the right of the state to establish a new radio telegraphic line,[43] the conditions under which a public loan was to be repaid,[44] the scope of application, territorial or otherwise, of concessions to exploit natural resources,[45] the termination of a concessionary right to exploit a state monopoly,[46] the duration of validity of a supply contract to

34 Wetter and Schwebel (n 2) 184–185; Yackee, 'The First Investor-State Arbitration' (n 6) 427–428.

35 Wetter and Schwebel (n 2) 197–198.

36 Ibid 201 and 208–209; *Societe generale Hellinique SA, Societe d'Electricite Athenes-Le Piree and Societe Electrique des Transports SA v The Greek State* (1951) 4 Revue Hellénique de Droit International 373, 375.

37 Wetter and Schwebel (n 2) 204.

38 Ibid 207–208.

39 Ibid 218.

40 See *Smyrne v Greece* (n 9) 335; *Sopron-Köszeg Local Railway Company v Austria and Hungary* (n 7); *Barcs-Pakrac Railway Company, Ltd v Hungary and Yugoslavia* (1935) 29(3) AJIL 523; *Zeltweg-Wolfsberg and Unterdrauburg-Woellan Railway Company v Austria and Yugoslavia* [1934] League of Nations Official Journal 1007 (*Zeltweg-Wolfsberg III*); *Compagnie du Katanga v The Colony of the Belgian Congo*, Award (11 December 1931), reported in Wetter and Schwebel (n 2) 184.

41 *The Duff Development Company Limited v The Government of Kelantan*, Award (31 March 1916) (*Duff v Kelantan I*). Copies of the award are available at the Foyle Special Collections Library at King's College London and the Foreign and Commonwealth Office Pamphlet Collection at the University of Manchester Library Special Collections.

42 *Lena Goldfields, Ltd v USSR*, Award (2 September 1930), reproduced in Nussbaum (n 4) 42, 42–43.

43 *Czechoslovakian Administration v RCA* (n 11); *RCA v China* (n 11).

44 *Hambros and Lazard v Roumania Monopolies Institute* (n 6) 1.

45 *Petroleum Development v Qatar* (n 17); *Petroleum Development v Abu Dhabi* (n 17); *Saudi Arabia v ARAMCO* (n 17) 230–231.

46 *Rialet v Ethiopia* (n 6) 742–743.

a public monopoly,[47] the implications of a government's refusal to issue visas to workers[48] and the power of a government to expropriate a concession for the exploitation of natural resources.[49] These disputes, then, were often not merely disputes that could just as equally have been between two private parties, but simply happened to involve a state. Quite to the contrary – in many an instance, they were disputes that could only have occurred precisely because one of the parties was a state, with all of the prerogatives that accompanied such status.

In light of this, it should perhaps further come as no surprise that many of the disputes submitted to historical investor-state tribunals required them, in order to discharge their mandate, to interpret, apply or rule on: mandatory norms that related to public policy,[50] legislative acts of (purported) general application,[51] international treaties,[52] the consequences of implementing or even the very alleged existence of particular governmental policies (including on matters relating to apartheid),[53] the implications arising from actions taken by the executive branch,[54] or whether certain governmental acts were contractual or unilateral/regulatory by nature.[55] Undoubtedly, the need for

47 *Alsing v Greece* (n 22) 633–634.

48 *Hedjaz Railway Arbitration* (n 3) 87–88 and 108–109.

49 *BP v Libya* (n 17); *Texaco v Libya* (n 17); *LIAMCO v Libya* (n 17).

50 *Hambros and Lazard v Roumania Monopolies Institute* (n 6) 23–25 (where the arbitrator was required to decide upon the effects of a US Congress joint resolution through which the US had renounced the gold standard); *Societe generale Hellinique, Societe d'Electricite Athenes-Le Piree and Societe Electrique des Transports v Greece* (n 36) 378. Likewise, in the two Radio Corporation of America arbitrations, the disputing parties debated whether Radio Corporation of America was in compliance with US anti-trust laws. See chs 4 and 5.

51 See *Societe generale Hellinique, Societe d'Electricite Athenes-Le Piree and Societe Electrique des Transports v Greece* (n 36) 373; Wetter and Schwebel (n 2) 195–200 and 201–204; *Sopron-Köszeg Local Railway Company v Austria and Hungary* (n 7) 172; *Katanga v Congo* (n 40) 184–185; *Losinger & cie SA v Kingdom of Yugoslavia*, Preliminary Award (11 October 1935) (*Losinger II*), reproduced in *The Losinger & Co Case (Switzerland v Yugoslavia)* PCIJ Rep Series C No 78 at 105, 109; *Rialet v Ethiopia* (n 6) 744–745.

52 See *Barcs-Pakrac Railway Company v Hungary and Yugoslavia* (n 40) 524ff; *Zeltweg-Wolfsberg II* (n 7) 1005–1006; *La Société Européenne d'Etudes et d'Entreprises (SEEE) v The Popular Federative Republic of Yugoslavia* (1959) 86 Journal du Droit International 1075, 1077; *Government of Peru v The Peruvian Corporation Limited* (1913) 50 Boletin del Ministerio de Relaciones Exteriores (Peru) 144, 146–147; *Smyrne v Greece* (n 9) 335; *Societe du Chemin de Fer Ottoman de Jaffa a Jerusalem et Prolongements v His Britannic Majesty's Government*, Preliminary Decision (29 May 1922), reproduced in Rosenne (n 1) 327, 332–334.

53 *Lena Goldfields v USSR* (n 42) 46–47; Erades (n 6) 203–204.

54 *GTM v East Pakistan IDC* (n 14) 445–446.

55 Yackee, 'The First Investor-State Arbitration' (n 6) 427–428; *Saudi Arabia v ARAMCO* (n 17) 140–141 and 228.

tribunals to deal with and decide these types of issues was to a certain extent a necessary corollary of the nature of the underlying disputes that were submitted to historical ISA, operating only to further add to the sensitivity of the subject matter under consideration. This, in turn, also meant that it was not out of the ordinary for the historical investor-state tribunals to be faced with, and be required to decide upon, arguments concerning the manner in which a state had wielded (or was to wield) its authority or had exercised its regulatory capacity. Indeed, in some instances, those types of arguments were even at the very core of the disputes before ISA tribunals. This was, for example, outright acknowledged by the *Saudi Arabia v. ARAMCO* tribunal, which observed that, throughout the proceedings, Saudi Arabia had:

> dwelt at great length upon its regulatory rights in respect of concessions and has invoked the notions of French administrative Law and international judicial decisions rendered in inter-State disputes. *These regulatory rights have even become the center of its whole argumentation.*[56]

A number of other historical ISAs saw similarly structured argumentation that put the states' regulatory powers at the forefront of considerations.[57] In light of such *problematique*, it appears that, in these instances, it was thus all but inevitable for the historical investor-state tribunals to engage with, and rule upon, matters that went to the very core of states' official functions. It would therefore seem that the characterisation made by the US Supreme Court at the dawn of the 20th century in relation to the *Colombia v. Cauca Company* arbitration (see Chapter 3) – to the effect that the arbitrators hearing the case were '*dealing with matters of public concern*'[58] – would be an apt description not only of this particular historical ISA, but also of the discipline's history more generally.

Yet, it was not only because of their *problematique* that the disputes underlying the historical ISAs can be said not to have been merely a matter of private concern to the disputing parties.[59] Since, as was previously mentioned,

56 *Saudi Arabia v ARAMCO* (n 17) 214.

57 See eg Wetter and Schwebel (n 2) 185–189, 197–200 and 204–205; Yackee, 'The First Investor-State Arbitration' (n 6) 403.

58 See ch 3. Emphasis added.

59 This is further exemplified, for instance, by a report published by an Ecuadorian newspaper on the basis of information provided by the Ministry of the Interior, wherein the Ecuadorian president is described as having characterised the open issues between Ecuador and The Guayaquil and Quito Railway Company as being 'among the most important that concern the public'. See 'The Chargé in Ecuador (Belt) to the Acting Secretary of

investor-state partnerships usually concerned projects or undertakings of considerable value, so too were the claims that were advanced in historical ISA often comparably large in magnitude. A good illustration of how much could potentially be at stake financially in the historical ISAs is provided by the 1921 *Grand Trunk Railway Arbitration*, where the majority's opinion was that shares in a major railway enterprise nationalised by Canada were essentially worthless, whereas the company-appointed arbitrator, former US president William Howard Taft, held in his dissenting opinion that the value of the railway stock under consideration was at the time at least $48 million (corresponding to approximately $668 million in present-day value).[60] Even when the arbitrations were solely concerned with contractual (non-)payments or the valuation of compensation or damages that were to be paid out to an investor from the public purse, the sheer size of the financial interest involved was therefore often sufficient to make the arbitration a matter of significant import to the broader public.

Thus, much like the very investor-state partnerships from which they arose, the potential implications of the disputes that were sought to be resolved through historical ISA were not limited in their reach only to the two parties taking part in the arbitration, but instead had the capacity to affect other stakeholders as well. Accordingly, both in terms of the nature of the implicated underlying investor-state partnerships more generally and the very issues that were submitted to historical ISA in particular, what was at stake in the historical ISAs transcended the relationship between the two disputing parties that nominally stood at their foundation. With this in mind, it becomes

---

State' (12 April 1919) in Joseph V Fuller (ed), *Papers Relating to the Foreign Relations of the United States, 1919* (US Government Printing Office 1934, vol II) 181, 182. Likewise, the agreement from which the dispute between the Cauca Company and Colombia arose provided explicitly that it was 'a work of public utility'. See Contract for the construction of the railway from Buenaventura to Manizales between the Government of Colombia and James L Cherry (27 August 1890) art 3. The concession is reproduced as part of Law 16 of 18 October 1890 through which it was ratified, which is contained in the record of the subsequent US court proceedings for the annulment of the award that can be found at Columbia University Library. See Original Bill of Complaint with Exhibits (Complainant's Exhibit No 4), *Colombia v Cauca Co*, 106 Fed 337 (n 25).

60 *Canada v Grand Trunk* (n 25), Reasons for dissent by the honourable William Howard Taft (7 September 1921) 58–62. The present-day value was estimated using Bank of Canada's Inflation Calculator at https://www.bankofcanada.ca/rates/related/inflation-calculator/. A copy of the award is available in The UK National Archives as part of the case materials in the *Jaffa-Jerusalem Railway Arbitration* (UK National Archives: TS 27/143–144). The *Grand Trunk Railway Arbitration* and other historical ISAs with similar financial ramifications are discussed in more detail in ch 3.

ever more important to understand how, or better yet, on what type of normative foundation, decisions on such matters were made in historical ISA.

3 Legal Indeterminacy and the Room for Discretionary Decision-Making in Historical Investor-State Arbitration

The next step in understanding what the past ISAs were like involves grasping the nature of the process through which decisions in these proceedings were made. On its surface, this decision-making process may have appeared as one that merely involved the interpretation and application of legal rules to the underlying factual basis; in reality, however, it left the door open for creative input by the relevant decision-makers. Namely, at least since the writings of Hans Kelsen in the 1920s, it has been recognised that, irrespective of the precision with which they are crafted, legal norms are never entirely determinate – they do not possess an inherent, entirely independent meaning that can be objectively ascertained.[61] This, in turn, means that no process of legal interpretation and application consists of automatic subsumption of facts under the relevant legal norm; it is never entirely predetermined, but instead necessarily implies a certain degree of discretionary input by the decision-maker. Without going any further into the general observations regarding the indeterminacy of legal norms, which have been much more eloquently developed elsewhere,[62] for present purposes it suffices to say that such considerations can without hesitation be said to have applied to historical ISA. This remains equally true even in relation to contracts that had been meticulously negotiated – a fact that arbitral tribunals on occasion openly recognised.[63]

More importantly, however, it was not only that historical ISA was not immune to such legal indeterminacy, but rather that there were still certain characteristics of historical ISA that amplified many times over these general indeterministic features of legal norms within the specific context of ISA. Thus,

61 Accordingly, every act of law-application is simultaneously also an act of law-creation. See Armin von Bogdandy and Ingo Venzke, *In Whose Name?: A Public Law Theory of International Adjudication* (OUP 2014) 103–104; Ingo Venzke, *How Interpretation Makes International Law: On Semantic Change and Normative Twists* (OUP 2012) 30–31.

62 See ibid.

63 See eg *Government of Greece v Hellenic Electric Railways Ltd and Electric Transport Company Ltd*, Award (5 June 1930), reported in Wetter and Schwebel (n 2) 204, 205; *BP v Libya* (n 17) 353 (holding in relation to the key issues in dispute that '[w]hile certain trends in the law are discernible, there are no precise and clear rules that provide an obvious answer to any of the issues').

first and foremost, in historical ISA it was often unclear even what the applicable law in a particular arbitration was supposed to be to begin with. Indeed, in many instances the parties to the historical ISAs had failed to instruct the respective tribunals upfront under which law the dispute was to be resolved.[64] This left the tribunals in question with the task of determining the applicable law on their own, for which they once again often had little to no guidance.[65] Essentially, in such scenarios, not only did the historical investor-state tribunals have to determine which law was to be applicable, but they also had to choose the basis upon which they would make the said determination, thus adding layer upon layer of indeterminacy to the already not perfectly determinate process of applying the relevant legal norms.

Even when the applicable law was provided by the disputing parties in advance, however, it was often an amalgamation of several different legal systems that were not necessarily easy to square with one another. For example, in the Libyan oil arbitrations, the concession contracts contained a clause on applicable law structured as follows:

> This concession shall be governed by and interpreted in accordance with the principles of the law of Libya common to the principles of international law and in the absence of such common principles then by and in accordance with the general principles of law, including such of those principles as may have been applied by international tribunals.[66]

---

64 See *Alsing v Greece* (n 22) 637; *Sapphire v NIOC* (n 17) 171; *Hambros and Lazard v Roumania Monopolies Institute* (n 6) 12; Abolbashar Farmanfarma, 'The Oil Agreement Between Iran and the International Oil Consortium: the Law Controlling' (1955) 34 Tex L Rev 259, 279–280; Yackee, 'The First Investor-State Arbitration' (n 6) 434; Veeder, 'The *Lena Goldfields* Arbitration' (n 4) 750. See also Wetter and Schwebel (n 2) 221. Likewise, in the *Jaffa-Jerusalem Railway Arbitration*, the counsel for the claimant company argued that 'the Tribunal [wa]s not bound by British or by any other law'. See Rosenne (n 1) 330. See also Treaty of Trianon (n 1) art 304 and Treaty of Saint-Germain (n 1) art 320, which served as the bases for the post-World War I railway arbitrations, described in detail in ch 4, and which did not provide for an applicable law.

65 For example, in *Hambros and Lazard v Roumania Monopolies Institute*, the arbitrator relied on the fluid concept of 'general principles of Conflict of Laws' while recognising that such principles were 'not clearly defined'. See *Hambros and Lazard v Roumania Monopolies Institute* (n 6) 12–13. See also *BP v Libya* (n 17) 326–327 and *LIAMCO v Libya* (n 17) 32–33.

66 See *BP v Libya* (n 17) 303. The remaining two Libyan oil arbitrations (*Texaco v Libya* and *LIAMCO v Libya*) were based on the same choice of law clause.

Another example of such a composite clause on applicable law was provided by the traffic agreement between the Radio Corporation of America (RCA) and The Administration of Posts and Telegraphs of the Republic of Czechoslovakia, which stated that:

> This agreement, as to the obligations or responsibilities hereunder of the Corporation and the Administration respectively, shall be construed, interpreted, and enforced according to the laws of the State of New York, United States of America, and of the Republic of Czechoslovakia respectively.[67]

Such composite clauses on applicable law hardly provided straightforward answers as to the law that the tribunals in these historical ISAs were supposed to apply. Indeed, it was by no means immediately obvious what the principles common to Libyan law and international law were (as was indeed evidenced by the tribunals' differing approaches when applying the clause),[68] or how a tribunal was to reconcile applying two vastly different systems of law to two parties in a relationship with reciprocal rights and obligations. The need for arbitral tribunals to make these choices and navigate within such unstructured normative settings, therefore, further compounded the legal uncertainty in which they were operating, thus increasing the potential for the arbitrators' discretionary decision-making.

To further complicate matters, the presence of a presumptive applicable law did not necessarily mean that the historical investor-state tribunals would actually go on and apply the said law. Instead, tribunals often found ways to, either openly or covertly, and sometimes with the help of the disputing parties, sidestep the law that they had ostensibly been supposed to apply, instead proceeding to rely on entirely different systems of law (usually ones with which the arbitrators were more familiar). One such example occurred in *Rialet v. Ethiopia*, where the tribunal found that, in light of the public law nature of the contract in dispute, the applicable law was under the normal course of events to be the administrative law of Ethiopia. However, having come to the conclusion that Ethiopia possessed no administrative law that could be applied, the

67 Czechoslovakian Traffic Agreement (n 5) art 11. An equivalent choice of law clause was provided in the RCA's agreement with China.

68 See Georges R Delaume, 'State Contracts and Transnational Arbitration' (1981) 75(4) AJIL 784, 797. The sole arbitrator in *BP v Libya* even overtly acknowledged that the provision generated practical difficulties. See *BP v Libya* (n 17) 327.

tribunal instead resorted to the law of European countries.[69] Lord Asquith of Bishopstone, the umpire in *Petroleum Development v. The Sheikh of Abu Dhabi*, infamously used similar reasoning to avoid applying the law of the state where the concession was located. While he had observed that the contract on which the arbitration was based was indeed most closely connected to Abu Dhabi, the umpire nonetheless held that Abu Dhabi possessed no law that could be applied,[70] and instead went on to apply what he termed 'a sort of "modern law of nature"' (including certain principles of English law which he found to be compatible with this concept).[71] Other historical ISA tribunals adopted similar approaches.[72] It was approaches such as these by the historical investor-state tribunals that prompted Farmanfarma to conclude in the 1950s that 'the procedure followed in these cases shows that *the element of foreseeability is almost nil*. The best that can be said is that the legal background of the future arbitrators tends to control.'[73]

An even broader element of legal indeterminacy was brought into the decision-making process underlying historical ISA by the fact that tribunals were often tasked with resolving, or chose to resolve, cases not solely pursuant to defined legal systems and precise legal norms, but instead by applying amorphous legal concepts such as 'general principles of law',[74] 'principles of right',[75] 'principle[s] of public international law',[76] 'general principles of justice and equity',[77] as well as 'general rule[s] of law' and 'general principle[s] of

69 *Rialet v Ethiopia* (n 6) 748–749. The tribunal's decision on this point appears to have been made with Ethiopia's acquiescence.

70 *Petroleum Development v Abu Dhabi* (n 17) 149.

71 Ibid.

72 See eg *Qatar v International Marine Oil* (n 17) 544–545; Erades (n 6) 221 (recounting the finding of the *Sudan v Turriff* tribunal to the effect that 'Sudanese law as to the matters in dispute is not materially different from English law').

73 Farmanfarma (n 64) 287 (emphasis added). Indeed, a number of historical ISAs are replete with references to the sole or presiding arbitrator's own legal system, despite it not having formed a part of the (nominally) applicable law. See eg *Alsing v Greece* (n 22) *passim*.

74 See eg the applicable law clause in the aforementioned Libyan oil arbitrations (n 17); Wetter and Schwebel (n 2) 190–191; *Lena Goldfields v USSR* (n 42) 50; *Rialet v Ethiopia* (n 6) 749; *Saudi Arabia v ARAMCO* (n 17) 158 and 168; *Sapphire v NIOC* (n 17) 170–175 and 182–183. See also *Czechoslovakian Administration v RCA* (n 11) (referring to 'ordinary principles of law') 532.

75 *Peru v Peruvian Corporation* (n 52) 148. The Spanish version of the award uses the term 'principios de derecho'; the English version of the Peruvian Corporation's memoire translated this term as 'principles of right'. See n 6.

76 *Zeltweg-Wolfsberg III* (n 40) 1006. See also *Sapphire v NIOC* (n 17) 140.

77 *The Ditta Luigi Gallotti v Somalia* (n 3) 159 and 163.

public law'.[78] In some instances, the arbitrators were even authorised to decide cases solely as *amiables compositeurs*, as was the case in *Société Européenne d'Etudes et d'Entreprises* (SEEE) *v. Yugoslavia*.[79] While these latter instances were admittedly rather the exception than the norm, it was nonetheless not uncommon for tribunals to at least partially base their decisions on nebulous concepts such as fairness and/or equity, irrespective of whether they had been instructed by the parties to do so.[80] Having to navigate such general and vague concepts only operated to further increase the manoeuvring space for making what were essentially (at least partially) discretionary decisions within the historical ISAs.

The space for discretionary decision-making in historical ISA that was created in the above described manner was furthermore in large part insulated from interference through a protective layer that was reflected in the limited oversight over the tribunals' decisions. As a matter of principle, decisions by the historical ISA tribunals were by and large intended by the parties to

78 *Greek Telephone Company v Greece* (n 11) 221.

79 *SEEE v Yugoslavia* (n 52) 1079–80. In at least two other instances, it was at certain points contended that the dispute was to be resolved under such an approach. See Yackee, 'The First Investor-State Arbitration' (n 6) 433; 'The Minister of Ecuador to the Secretary of State' (8 August 1913), 'The Secretary of State to the American Minister' (13 August 1913) and 'The Secretary of State to the Minister of Ecuador' (27 August 1913) in Joseph V Fuller (ed), *Papers Relating to the Foreign Relations of the United States, With the Address of the President to Congress December 2, 1913* (US Government Printing Office 1920) 495–497.

80 See Yackee, 'The First Investor-State Arbitration' (n 6) 434 (noting that the *Suez v Egypt* tribunal had partially based its considerations on equity); *The Ditta Luigi Gallotti v Somalia* (n 3) 159 and 163 (where the tribunal resorted to 'general principles of justice and equity' in making the valuation of the claim despite the arbitration clause providing that the tribunal was to decide according to law); *Rialet v Ethiopia* (n 6) 751 (where the tribunal invoked both law and equity when declaring its decision); *Smyrne v Greece* (n 9) 335–336 and 339–340; *LIAMCO v Libya* (n 17) 35–37, 76, 79–87; *Sopron-Köszeg Local Railway Company v Austria and Hungary* (n 7) 171–172; *Barcs-Pakrac Railway Company v Hungary and Yugoslavia* (n 40) 531–532; *Zeltweg-Wolfsberg III* (n 40) 1008–1009; *Qatar v International Marine Oil* (n 17) 541–547; *Hedjaz Railway Arbitration* (n 3) 122; *The Government of Greece v Sociéte Commerciale de Belgique* (*Socobelge*), Award (25 July 1936) (*Socobelge II*), reproduced in *The 'Société commerciale de Belgique'* (*Belgium v Greece*) PCIJ Rep Series C No 87 at 44, 48–49; *The Greek State v Hellenic Electric Railways*, Award (18 March 1930) (ILO Archives: AR 1/26/5/1) 23–24; *Greek Transport Company Ltd v The Greek State* (17 May 1956) (ILO Archives: AR 1–26–4–1) 7; Wetter and Schwebel (n 2) 190–191. See also Treaty of Peace between the Allied and Associated Powers and Turkey (signed 10 August 1920, never entered into force) (1921) 15 AJIL Supp 179, art 311. Even when tribunals explicitly declared that they would not decide according to equity, this did not necessarily mean that they did not in fact (at least partially) do so. See *Sapphire v NIOC* (n 17) 175 and 189–190.

be final and binding.[81] Thus, any conceivable recourse against the awards handed down in historical ISA was by nature limited in its reach. First of all, in a number of the historical ISAs, especially those from the earlier period[82] or those that were not entrenched within a particular national legal system,[83] it is doubtful whether recourse against the awards had at all even been available. Even where it was, however, as a matter of observed practice, it appears to have been resorted to relatively rarely. Finally, in the rare instances where one of the parties had sought to challenge an award that had been handed down in a historical ISA, the respective courts tasked with deciding upon such challenges viewed their roles as being fairly limited.[84] Accordingly, it can be inferred that, insofar as corrective mechanisms against the decisions by historical investor-state tribunals existed, such mechanisms were far from poised to entirely eliminate the room for discretionary decision-making enjoyed by historical investor-state tribunals.

As the above analysis suggests, the manner in which the historical ISAs were structured thus allowed for them to operate within a realm of considerable legal indeterminism, likely even more so than what would have been the norm in other types of contemporary adjudicatory processes (especially those

81 *Peru v Peruvian Corporation* (n 52) 144; *Losinger I* (n 25) 56; *The Government of Greece v Sociéte Commerciale de Belgique (Socobelge)*, Award (3 January 1936) (*Socobelge I*), reproduced in *The 'Société commerciale de Belgique' (Belgium v Greece)* PCIJ Rep Series C No 87 at 36; *Socobelge II* (n 80) 44; *Petroleum Development v Abu Dhabi* (n 17) 145; Saudi Arabia-Aramco Arbitration Agreement (n 2) art VIII; *The Ditta Luigi Gallotti v Somalia* (n 3) 159; *BP v Libya* (n 17) 302 (*Texaco v Libya* and *LIAMCO v Libya* were based on identical arbitration clauses); 'The American Chargé d'Affaires to the Secretary of State' (9 April 1913), 'The Minister of Ecuador to the Secretary of State' (8 August 1913), 'The Secretary of State to the American Minister' (13 August 1913), 'The Secretary of State to the Minister of Ecuador' (27 August 1913) and 'The Secretary of State to the American Minister' (14 November 1913) in Fuller, *FRUS 1913* (n 79) 492–493, 495–497 and 501–503; Stephen M Schwebel, 'The Alsing Case' (1959) 8 ICLQ 320, 323.

82 See n 142. See also 'The American Arbitrator to the Secretary of State' (5 March 1913), 'The American Chargé d'Affaires to the Secretary of State' (8 March 1913), 'The Minister of Ecuador to the Secretary of State' (8 August 1913), 'The Secretary of State to the American Minister' (13 August 1913), 'The Secretary of State to the Minister of Ecuador' (27 August 1913) and 'The Secretary of State to the American Minister' (14 November 1913) in Fuller, *FRUS 1913* (n 79) 480–484, 495–497 and 501–503.

83 See sub-section 5.1 below.

84 See *Colombia v Cauca Co*, 190 US 524 (1903) 530 (holding that, once the tribunal's powers were established, the court was 'not called upon to revise any finding that could have been made without going beyond the line which we lay down'); *Kelantan Government v Duff Development Company, Ltd* (1922–1923) 39 Times L Rep 337, 339–340 and 342–343 (holding that an error must appear 'on the face of the award' for it to be set aside).

anchored in concrete national legal systems).[85] As a result, the decisions that were being made in historical ISA could hardly be reduced to a simple mechanical process of logical deduction; instead, they involved a significant creative element, and often implied the need for balancing the different interests implicated in ISA – something that was on occasion even openly recognised by the historical ISA tribunals.[86] It was therefore precisely this indeterminate normative foundation that allowed for the exercise of discretionary decision-making within the historical ISAs. Consequently, every decision that was handed down in historical ISA, even when nominally declaratory or condemnatory, was at least to a certain extent, in fact, constitutive in nature; this is a characteristic of historical ISA that should be born in mind not only throughout the remainder of this Chapter but also in relation to the chapters that follow. Bearing in mind – as had been outlined in the previous section – the types of interests that were at stake in historical ISA, this meant that important areas of both domestic and international public policy were being shaped through historical ISA by way of a process that was infused through and through with the discretion of the relevant decision-makers.

4 A Key Role for Private Actors in Historical Investor-State Arbitration

In light of the broader public interests that were involved, as well as the considerable space for decision-making that included an ineluctable creative component, then, historical ISA proved to be a sphere where discretionary decisions in matters of significant public importance were forged. That being said, ISA was by no means the only historical adjudicatory process that could be described along such lines.[87]

85 Moreover, this lack of determinacy in the applicable legal norms further intersected with factual indeterminism. See eg *The Ditta Luigi Gallotti v Somalia* (n 3) 163 (noting that valuation was a matter that could not be determined with 'mathematical accuracy' and instead to a large extent remained 'a matter of opinion'); *Sapphire v NIOC* (n 17) 189–190.

86 See eg *Sopron-Köszeg Local Railway Company v Austria and Hungary* (n 7) 170; *Barcs-Pakrac Railway Company v Hungary and Yugoslavia* (n 40) 528–531; *Zeltweg-Wolfsberg III* (n 40) 1008; Wetter and Schwebel (n 2) 205. But see *Texaco v Libya* (n 17) 27. While the *Saudi Arabia v ARAMCO* tribunal proclaimed that its 'duty [wa]s to state the law' (and not to modify the parties' agreement), it also nonetheless said that '[t]he interpretation of contracts is not governed by rigid rules; it is rather an art, governed by principles of logic and common sense'. See *Saudi Arabia v ARAMCO* (n 17) 148 and 172.

87 Indeed, most public international law dispute resolution mechanisms could be said to be of the same ilk.

What gave this practice within historical ISA its distinctive flavour was the extensive role played within this process by a variety of different private actors. In this respect, the two groups of private actors with the most significant, and most direct, influence were undoubtedly the private individuals or companies that were the parties to the historical ISAs (4.1), and the arbitrators who were ultimately tasked with deciding upon the claims brought in historical ISA (4.2). Other auxiliary actors, such as counsel and experts, also had an important, albeit more subtle and indirect, influence (4.3).

4.1 *Private Party Control over Claims*

A distinctive feature of historical ISA was the ability of the investor to itself directly bring a claim (or, less frequently, defend one) against a state. As a result, unlike in instances of diplomatic protection, where the investor's home state ultimately had control over the decision of whether and how to pursue a case, in historical ISA it was directly the investor that was making the important procedural decisions and was thus able to pursue arbitration independently of, or even against, the will of its home state.[88] In light of the procedural equality of the participating arbitrating parties – a quintessential characteristic of the arbitral process, including in historical ISA – being made a direct participant in the proceedings formally put the investor on the same footing as its state counterpart, thus creating a stepping stone for it to take on a substantial role in determining how that very process was to be moulded.

Starting with the decision whether and when claims that potentially involved interests that transcended the two disputing parties would be brought to arbitration, all of the important decisions that could be made by a party to an arbitration were in the hands, whether exclusively or jointly with its counter-party, of the investor. Investors were thus able, either directly or through counsel, to make crucial choices throughout the arbitral process, such as deciding on the appointment of arbitrators that would participate in deciding the case,[89] framing how the relevant arguments were going to be presented,

---

88 See eg nn 94–96 below.

89 There were exceptions to this principle, however, as investors did not always have complete control over who would be appointed as arbitrator on their behalf. For instance, in *The Guayaquil and Quito Railway v Ecuador* case, the arbitrator, Henry L Janes, was appointed by the US but seemingly at the behest of the company. He was ultimately replaced following his resignation, which had been prompted by Ecuador's complaint that he was biased in favor of the company. See 'The Secretary of State to the American Chargé d'Affaires' (14 November 1912) in Joseph V Fuller (ed), *Papers Relating to the Foreign Relations of the United States, With the Annual Message of the President Transmitted to Congress December 3, 1912* (US Government Printing Office 1919) 421; 'The American Chargé

what issues were going to be raised, which sources invoked[90] and what type of remedies were ultimately going to be claimed. This last aspect was particularly important in terms of the potential influence that could be exerted by the involved private investors, as it allowed them to request not only monetary damages, but also, *inter alia*, for states to be instructed on how to, or how not to, act in the particular instance (including in relation to the carrying out of their official functions).[91] That choices such as these were in the hands of the private investors partaking in historical ISA meant that they were instrumental in determining both how the arbitral process was to unfold and the types of effects it was potentially to have.

Moreover, the capacity of private investors to exert their influence was not restricted to the arbitral process itself, but extended also to the pre- and post-arbitration stage. Thus, in some instances, the very fact, or even a mere threat, that an arbitration was about to be initiated was sufficient to alter the conduct of states in relation to how they went about their official business.[92] Similarly,

---

d'Affaires to the Secretary of State' (14 April 1913), 'The American Chargé d'Affaires to the Secretary of State' (18 April 1913) and 'The Chargé d'Affaires of Ecuador to the Secretary of State' (8 May 1913) in Fuller, *FRUS 1913* (n 79) 493–494; Ray Stannard Baker, *Woodrow Wilson: Life and Letters: President 1913–1914* (First Greenwood Printing 1968, vol IV) 431; Ronn Pineo, *Ecuador and the United States: Useful Strangers* (University of Georgia Press 2007) 79–80. See also reproduction in Rosenne (n 1) 342 of a Note from the French Embassy to the Foreign Office (20 July 1921) (UK National Archives: FO 371/6381) (showing that the arbitrator in the *Jaffa-Jerusalem Railway Arbitration* for the claimant was appointed by the French government).

90 Indeed, it was often the arbitrating parties themselves (or their counsel) that contributed significantly to the precedential value of previous awards by relying on them extensively during the proceedings and, in doing so, either made it easier for arbitrators to corroborate their decisions by relying on such precedent or exerted pressure on them to justify why they were departing from the reasoning of previous tribunals. See ch 5.

91 Thus, for example, an important prerequisite for René-Jean Dupuy's landmark decision to order *restitutio in integrum* against Libya (see *Texaco v Libya* (n 17) 37) was the claimants' decision to, instead of merely being content with monetary compensation, ask that Libya be ordered to perform the underlying concession. Requests such as these, which went to states' very freedom of action in specific instances, were not particularly uncommon in historical ISA; see ch 4, as well as *RCA v China* (n 11) 1623; Schwebel, 'The Alsing Case' (n 81) 324. Notably, it was also states themselves that were known to request that historical ISA tribunals rule on their freedom of action with respect to the exercise of their official functions. See eg ch 3 regarding the dispute between the Duff Development Company and Kelantan.

92 For example, fearing the potential financial implications of an adverse award, Kelantan essentially brought its work on a planned railway to a standstill once it became apparent that the Duff Development Company's grievances over the railway's planned route would be submitted to arbitration. See ch 3.

in instances where private investors were successful in their claims in the historical ISAs, they remained in control of the resulting awards beyond the arbitral process and were able to (insofar as such mechanisms were available at the time and in respect of the type of arbitral award that the private actors were in possession of)[93] make use of the enforcement mechanisms available for enforcing arbitral awards, even when this went against the will of their own governments. Where present, such enforcement mechanisms gave private investors an extremely powerful instrument through which to exert their influence. A prime example was *SEEE v. Yugoslavia*,[94] where SEEE had for more than 30 years made extensive efforts to enforce the six billion franc arbitral award it had obtained against Yugoslavia, even though the host and home state had as between them considered the claim to have been settled.[95] SEEE's tenaciousness in enforcing its award severely affected Franco-Yugoslav relations over the course of the 30-year period, with the relations between the two countries on the matter eventually reaching – once the award had definitely been found by the French courts to be enforceable – what was described at the time as a 'boiling point'.[96]

Thus, it was this very defining character trait of historical ISA – the fact that private investors were allowed directly to participate in, and have control over,

---

93 Arbitral awards became much more potent with the coming into force of the Convention on the Recognition and Enforcement of Foreign Arbitral Awards (opened for signature 10 June 1958, entered into force 7 June 1959) 330 UNTS 38. Prior to that, enforcing awards beyond the country of their origin was subject to a more complicated procedure known as 'double exequatur'. See Dana H Freyer and Hamid G Gharavi, 'Finality and Enforceability of Foreign Arbitral Awards: From "Double Exequatur" to the Enforcement of Annulled Awards: A Suggested Path to Uniformity Amidst Diversity' (1998) 13(1) ICSID Review – Foreign Investment Law Journal 101, 102–103.

94 *SEEE v Yugoslavia* (n 52).

95 See Georges R Delaume, 'SEEE v Yugoslavia: Epitaph or Interlude?' (1987) 4(3) Journal of International Arbitration 25, 25–26.

96 Yugoslavia had prepared severe counter-measures against France as a response. The situation was only diffused once France reached a settlement with SEEE against a 50 million franc payment. See Federal Secretariat for Foreign Affairs, 'Information on Consultations Held between the SFRY and French Departments for Foreign Affairs, Held 28 and 29 September 1987 in Belgrade' (30 September 1987) (Archives of Yugoslavia: 780–F10 (1971)); Vladimir Šitić, 'Note from an Interdepartmental Meeting Held at the Offices of International Legal Affairs on 1 September 1987' (4 September 1987) (Archives of Yugoslavia: 780–F10 (1971)); Note from the Federal Executive Council to the Federal Public Attorney's Office (15 January 1987) (Archives of Yugoslavia: 780–F10 (1971)); Branislav Stojaković, 'Official Note from a Meeting held at the Federal Public Attorney's Office on 16 December 1986' (Archives of Yugoslavia: 780–F10 (1971)); Note on the Talks between Deputy Federal Secretary B Loncar and the French Ambassador in Belgrade D Charpy, on 04 December 1986 (5 December 1986) (Archives of Yugoslavia: 780–F10 (1971)).

the arbitral process and its externalities – that provided investors with the tools through which they could exert significant influence in ultimately shaping the process through which matters whose importance transcended their individual interests were to be decided.

4.2 *The Quest for Neutrality and the Externalisation of Decision-Making*

For present purposes, private actors of equal, if not greater, importance as the private investors partaking in historical ISA were the arbitrators who were tasked with ultimately deciding upon the disputes. As the ultimate decision-makers, the arbitrators were given broad powers within the arbitral process, yet by and large remained (at least insofar as sole arbitrators or tribunal presidents or umpires were concerned) independent from the parties to the arbitrations. Through them, the decision-making process in highly sensitive matters that were under consideration in historical ISA was withdrawn, at least partially, from the exclusive domain of the states involved and externalised by being placed into the hands of private individuals.

As was previously set out, the relationships from which the historical ISAs arose were to a great extent forged in areas of activity that were in close proximity to some of the most important public functions of the involved states, and were moreover frequently of high monetary value.[97] As such, the relationships in question tended not to be merely ephemeral to the interests of the concerned states, but were instead tightly intertwined with their core interests. For this very reason, an intrinsic hazard that the involved states may be motivated to try to alter the equilibrium of the relationship unilaterally or to evade their obligations was, if not omnipresent, then at least often lurking. At the same time, in many an investor-state relationship that gave rise to the historical ISAs, the relevant states were also in a good position to in fact do so, as the investor had, upon entering into the investor-state relationship, to a considerable extent been subjected to the state's public authority.[98] Accordingly, states can be said to have more often than not been in a position to unilaterally influence the investor-state relationship through acts of public power, either by targeting their private counterpart directly (including potentially through

97 See section 2 above.

98 The historical investor-state relationships from which the disputes arose often concerned investment projects that required substantial initial investment of resources and were located within the territory falling under the state's jurisdiction. Once the investor had sunk in the initial cost, it was therefore committed to the project for the long-term if it was to have a likelihood of recouping its investment. Indeed, such risks to investors were recognised by several historical investor-state tribunals. See eg *Texaco v Libya* (n 17) 16–17; *Sapphire v NIOC* (n 17) 171.

the use of force) or even through acts of general application (or acts at least purporting to be of such character). Perhaps unsurprisingly, states did in fact on occasion avail themselves of such prerogatives, or were at least alleged to had done so, giving rise to historical ISAs.[99]

Once the private investor had committed its resources to an investor-state partnership, therefore, it had almost invariably been, and to a significant degree, exposed to the risk of public authority. For this very reason, it appears that one of the central tenets behind historical ISA was precisely the quest to externalise the decision-making process in relation to disputes arising from such sensitive activities, and put it beyond the reach of the state involved and its prerogatives of public power.[100] While this need for externalising decision-making can perhaps be said to be ubiquitous to all types of legal relationships, in light of the specific characteristics of investor-state relations outlined above, it appears to have been particularly pronounced in the case of historical ISA. An indispensable ingredient in achieving such externalisation, and consequently, one of the primary reasons why parties in historical ISA tended to decide to go to arbitration, was the need for a decision-maker who would be independent and impartial *vis-à-vis* the parties and the dispute.[101] The envisioned position of the arbitrators in the historical ISAs was thus ultimately in large part a reflection of one of the main driving ideas behind arbitration in general, and ISA in particular – the quest for neutrality.

In light of this need for externalised decision-making, it is therefore hardly surprising that the parties to the historical ISAs put considerable emphasis on the requirement that the arbitrators sitting in these arbitrations be truly independent, at least as it pertained to sole or presiding arbitrators, or umpires. Indeed, the parties often strived from the very beginning of their interaction to ensure that this need would be satisfied. For this reason, they often chose, or even designated in advance, individual or presiding arbitrators from countries

99 For example, the USSR secret police raided the offices of Lena Goldfields during the operation of its concession and arrested its staff. See Veeder, 'The *Lena Goldfields* Arbitration' (n 4) 762. See also generally nn 50–55 above.

100 See eg 'The American Chargé d'Affaires to the Secretary of State' (9 April 1913) in Fuller, *FRUS 1913* (n 79) 492–493.

101 For instance, when reporting back to his shareholders regarding the negotiation of a concession agreement with the USSR, Leslie Urquhart underlined that having in the agreement an arbitration clause that would ensure an 'unprejudiced arbitrator' was a 'vital necessity'. See VV Veeder, 'Lloyd George, Lenin and Cannibals: The Harriman Arbitration – The 1999 Freshfields Lecture' (2000) 16 Arbitration International 115, 123–124. This underlying motivation for opting for arbitration was also recognised by historical ISA tribunals. See eg *Saudi Arabia v ARAMCO* (n 17) 155, where the tribunal emphasised that the concessionaire had 'wished to secure the guarantee of a neutral judge'.

with perceived reputations for neutrality, such as Switzerland,[102] the Netherlands[103] or the Scandinavian countries.[104] In some instances, they went as far as to construct arbitration clauses with elaborate schemes that utilised several layers of different mechanisms in arbitrator appointment and relied on independent external appointing authorities, such as the Permanent Court of Arbitration, the Permanent Court of International Justice (later the International Court of Justice) or the president of the Swiss Federal Tribunal.[105] Indeed, on occasion, considerable effort was exerted on negotiating such clauses before an appropriate balance was struck, as well as in ensuring that the clauses that had been negotiated would ultimately give rise to an independent tribunal once the dispute arose.

In the negotiations over a mining concession between Leslie Urquhart and the USSR, for example, the arbitration clause proved to be one of the major contestation points – while the USSR had insisted for the president of the tribunal to be a Soviet citizen nominated by the Russian Academy of Science, Urquhart pushed for a presiding arbitrator whose neutrality would be beyond doubt.[106] The failure by the parties to agree on this point was one of the

102 It was not uncommon for arbitration clauses to stipulate that the umpire would be the president of the Swiss Federal Tribunal. See eg *Losinger II* (n 51) (where the umpire was Henri Thelin); *Alsing v Greece* (n 22) (Louis Python acting as umpire). Swiss nationals were the sole arbitrators or tribunal presidents in a number of other historical ISAs, including *Saudi Arabia v ARAMCO* (n 17) (where Georges Sauser-Hall was the 'referee'), *Sapphire v NIOC* (n 17) (Pierre Cavin sitting as sole arbitrator), as well as in a number of cases that arose under a utility concession in Greece (see AM Stuyt (ed), *Survey of International Arbitrations: 1794–1989* (Martinus Nijhoff 1990) 491, 507 and 538).

103 See eg *RCA v China* (n 11) (where the presiding arbitrator was Joost Adriaan van Hamel); *Hambros and Lazard v Roumania Monopolies Institute* (n 6) (where GWJ Bruins was the sole arbitrator); *Rialet v Ethiopia* (n 6) (where BCJ Loder was the presiding arbitrator); *Lebanon and the Municipality of Beyrouth v The Beyrouth Water Company* (n 13) (GJ Wiarda acting as tribunal president); *Sudan v Turriff* (n 15) (where Lambertus Erades was the presiding arbitrator).

104 See eg *Jaffa-Jerusalem Railway Arbitration* (n 52) (where FVN Beichmann (Norway) was tribunal president); *Czechoslovakian Administration v RCA* (n 11) (where Julius Möller (Denmark) was tribunal president); *Societe generale Hellinique, Societe d'Electricite Athenes-Le Piree and Societe Electrique des Transports v The Greek State* (n 36) (where Paal Berg (Norway) was tribunal president); *The Ditta Luigi Gallotti v Somalia* (n 3) (Gunnar Lagergren (Sweden) acting as president); *BP v Libya* (n 17) (Gunnar Lagergren (Sweden) acting as sole arbitrator).

105 Most notably and infamously, such a solution was provided in Anglo-Iranian Oil Company's concession with Iran (n 5) art 22. See also *The 'Societe Commerciale de Belgique' (Belgium v Greece)* PCIJ Rep Series A/B No 78 at 166.

106 Veeder, 'Lloyd George, Lenin and Cannibals' (n 101) 123–124.

primary causes for the initial break-down in the negotiations;[107] ultimately, however, the parties managed to reach a compromise by agreeing that, failing agreement on this point between the concessionaire and the USSR, the former would select an arbitrator from a list of six individuals proposed by the latter, who would all be 'of world wide or European fame as learned men, lawyers, engineers or public men'.[108]

The agreement between Urquhart and the USSR never became effective due to a lack of ratification by the USSR;[109] however, the manner in which arrangements of this type were put into action was demonstrated during the course of the dispute over the Lena Goldfields concession, which contained a similarly worded arbitration clause.[110] When the time to choose the chairman of the tribunal arrived, the initial step was made by Lena Goldfields, which proposed two candidates from neutral countries. These candidates, however, were rejected by the USSR. The USSR then countered by proposing another seemingly neutral candidate – none other than Albert Einstein – but this proposal likewise did not meet with the approval of the opposing side.[111] The parties then turned to the default mechanism provided for by the arbitral clause, pursuant to which the USSR – after, again, expending some effort on selecting the candidates it thought would be suitable neutral candidates – drew up a list of 6 professors from the Freiberg Mining Academy, out of which Lena would eventually chose the presiding arbitrator.[112] As these examples illustrate, then, the process through which the parties chose the people who would be the ultimate decision-makers in their matter was known to be rather extensive, and the parties often devoted considerable attention in determining how they would make their selection.

The arbitrating parties' sensitivity toward a perceived lack of neutrality on behalf of presiding arbitrators or umpires – even when based solely on nationality – was further highlighted in the somewhat unusual situation that arose in the dispute between Swiss firm Losinger and Yugoslavia. Namely, the underlying contract to which the dispute was related had originally been concluded between a local municipality in Yugoslavia and an American firm, and

107 Ibid 124.

108 Ibid 127.

109 Ibid.

110 See ibid 128 at fn 36.

111 Veeder suggests that the reason for refusal was probably simply unwillingness to give into the opposing party's proposal. See Veeder, 'The *Lena Goldfields* Arbitration' (n 4) 774.

112 The USSR's diligence, however, turned out to be in vain, as it had included on its list a candidate (eventually chosen by Lena as chairman) who had made statements critical of the ongoing situation in the USSR. See Veeder, 'The *Lena Goldfields* Arbitration' (n 4) 775.

had provided for the president of the Swiss Federal Tribunal to act as umpire in case of a dispute.[113] While such a solution was entirely understandable in the context of the initial contractual relationship, the default choice of a Swiss national, who was initially intended to be a personality of disinterested nationality, became controversial once Losinger was subrogated for the American firm.[114] Even though there appeared to be no indication that the umpire, Henri Thelin, was in any way connected to the claimant firm, Yugoslavia perceived the fact that he was of the same nationality as Losinger as sincerely troubling and felt that he could not be considered as sufficiently neutral.[115] Although this apprehension expressed by Yugoslavia toward presiding arbitrator nationality may not have been universally shared by parties partaking in historical ISAs,[116]

113 See the Agreement between the District of Pozarevac and American Oriental Construction Syndicate (n 5) art 16.

114 *Losinger I* (n 25) 56ff.

115 In an effort to remedy the issue, the Yugoslav side dispatched an envoy, Slavko Stojković, to meet with Thelin in Switzerland. Stojković proposed that the problem be resolved by expanding the tribunal with two additional neutral arbitrators. While Losinger seemed open to the proposal, the matter was eventually not followed through on. See Maja Stanivuković and Sanja Đajić, 'From *Losinger* to *ATA v Jordan*: Retroactive Application of National Law to Arbitration Agreements' in Marianne Roth and Michael Geistlinger (eds), *Yearbook on International Arbitration and ADR* (Neuer Wissenschaftlicher Verlag 2019) 149, 156. Although Yugoslavia appears to have formally raised an objection on this account before the umpire, this specific argument was not addressed in his decision. See *Losinger II* (n 51) 109 and 111–113. Whatever may have been the motivation behind Yugoslavia's sentiments regarding Thelin's nationality, the cogency of the argument in the particular instance was no doubt undermined by the fact that Thelin had already once acted as umpire in a dispute between Losinger and Yugoslavia, without such an objection having been raised. In internal discussions on the Yugoslav side in preparation for the PCIJ case that arose from the Losinger dispute, Stojković expressed the opinion that, irrespective of the oversight in relation to the contract, the need for the super-arbitrator to be a neutral personality was of 'higher principle'. See 'Minutes of the First Conference Held at the Transport Section of the Consular-Commercial Department on 12 December 1935, regarding the Application of the Swiss Government against the Kingdom of Yugoslavia before the Permanent Court of International Justice' (Archives of Yugoslavia: 338–45 (1935–1936)). The importance of the neutrality of presiding arbitrators was further highlighted by the *Lena Goldfields v USSR* arbitration, where the counsel for Lena Goldfields, Idelson, seems to have been of the opinion that the real reason behind the USSR's withdrawal from the arbitration was its dissatisfaction with certain uncomplimentary statements regarding the USSR that had been made by the presiding arbitrator. See Veeder, 'The *Lena Goldfields* Arbitration' (n 4) 777.

116 There were numerous instances where the presiding arbitrator or umpire, or even the entire tribunal, were of the same nationality as one of the parties to the dispute without this undoubtedly less than ideal solution seemingly having been cause for much concern. See eg Yackee, 'The First Investor-State Arbitration' (n 6) 402 (in relation to the French

it was hardly uncommon,[117] and is certainly illustrative of the broader concerns that existed regarding requisite arbitrator neutrality.

While the party-appointed arbitrators in the historical ISAs were not as uniformly detached from the parties that had appointed them as were sole arbitrators, umpires or tribunal presidents,[118] and had in certain instances even

Emperor Napoleon III deciding the *Suez v Egypt* case); *Duff v Kelantan I* (n 41); *The Duff Development Company, Ltd v The Government of Kelantan*, Award (17 November 1921) (*Duff v Kelantan II*) (a copy of the award is available in the UK National Archives: TS 36/216); *Batignolles v Yugoslavia I* (n 15) 1; *Batignolles v Yugoslavia II* (n 15) 1; *Canada v Grand Trunk* (n 25) 37 (where the presiding arbitrator, Sir Walter Cassels, was not only a Canadian national, but also a sitting judge on the Exchequer Court of Canada); Original Bill of Complaint with Exhibits (Complainant's Exhibit No 15), *Colombia v Cauca Co*, 106 Fed 337 (n 25); *Greek Telephone Company v Greece* (n 11) 216.

117 Indeed, several arbitration agreements or clauses pursuant to which historical ISAs were conducted envisaged that the presiding arbitrator would be of a different nationality than either of the disputing parties. See Saudi Arabia-Aramco Arbitration Agreement (n 2) art I(2); *Sapphire v NIOC* (n 17) 140–141; *BP v Libya* (n 17) 302–303; Anglo-Iranian Oil Company's concession in Iran (n 5) art 22. Moreover, in *RCA v China*, the two party-appointed arbitrators had, when discussing the identity of the presiding arbitrator, agreed that he was to be of a different nationality than the parties' counsel (although China's subsequent choice of counsel ultimately undermined these considerations). See ch 5.

118 Thus, for example, in the first of a series of arbitrations that would arise between Greece and a number of related companies under a utility concession (see ch 5), the arbitrator nominated by the interested company, Percy Horsfall, vacillated about whether to accept the appointment in light of his business interests in the underlying concession. Namely, while Horsfall had no direct financial interest in the company that had nominated him, he was 'substantially interested' in the other companies operating under the same concession (two of which he was a director of), and which he deemed were 'liable to be directly affected' by the tribunal's decision. As there would in any event be a neutral chairman, Horsfall ultimately decided to take up the nomination. In so doing, he highlighted that it appeared 'customary' for the two remaining tribunal members to be 'quite frankly partisan' and that Greece had not hesitated to appoint one of its own officials. See Letter from Horsfall to H B Butler (18 October 1927) (International Labour Office (ILO) Archives: AR 1/26/2). Likewise, a Greek lawyer, Alexandre Wamwetzos, had transitioned from acting as counsel for the concessionary companies into an arbitrator role, all in cases under the same concession. Compare Stuyt (n 102) 491 and ILO Archives: AR 1/26/2/1, AR 1/26/3/1, AR 1/26/4/1, AR 1/26/5/1, AR 1/26/10/1 and AR 1/26/11/1. It appears moreover that it was not uncommon for states to appoint as arbitrators current or former government officials. In addition to the aforementioned utility concession cases, Greece took this approach in disputes with Socobelge (appointing its minister plenipotentiary in France) and Alsing (appointing a legal counsellor to the Ministry of Finance). See *Socobelge I* (n 81) 36; Schwebel, 'The Alsing Case' (n 81) 324. Similarly, in the arbitrations arising from the dispute between Ecuador and The Guayaquil and Quito Railway Company, both arbitrators appointed by Ecuador held public office. The first, Cesar Borja, was appointed to the post of minister of public instruction while still serving as arbitrator; while he resigned his ministerial post within months, since a question of 'legality' of him holding these two

taken on more of a role of party advocate than of a truly independent decision-maker (especially where the arbitrations were structured in a manner so that the dispute was first submitted to the two party-appointed arbitrators, and only in case of their lack of agreement to an umpire),[119] they were nonetheless

posts simultaneously had arisen, he was given a second appointment as arbitrator by the Ecuadorian president so as to 'cure any defect'. See 'Minister Fox to the Secretary of State' (29 September 1908) (n 25) 274. In the second arbitration, Ecuador appointed senate president Alfredo Baquerizo Moreno. See 'The American Chargé d'Affaires to the Secretary of State' in Fuller, *FRUS 1912* (n 89) 422. Likewise, the opposing side appointed officials from the US diplomatic service, one of which, Williams C Fox, was the US minister plenipotentiary to Ecuador (the appointee in the second arbitration, Henry L Janes, was eventually replaced by a US judge). See 'The Acting Secretary of State to Minister Fox' (11 July 1907) and 'Minister Fox to the Secretary of State' (7 October 1907) in *Papers Relating to the Foreign Relations of the United States, With the Annual Message of the President Transmitted to Congress December 3, 1907, (In two parts), Part I* (US Government Printing Office 1910) 389–390; 'The Secretary of State to the American Chargé d'Affaires' (n 89); 'The American Chargé d'Affaires to the Secretary of State' (14 April 1913), 'The American Chargé d'Affaires to the Secretary of State' (18 April 1913) and 'The Chargé d'Affaires of Ecuador to the Secretary of State' (8 May 1913) in Fuller, *FRUS 1913* (n 79) 493–494. Notably, Janes is known to have communicated and consulted with the US government in relation to the case. See eg 'The American Chargé d'Affaires to the Secretary of State' (22 February 1913), 'The American Arbitrator to the Secretary of State' (5 March 1913) and 'The American Chargé d'Affaires to the Secretary of State' (11 March 1913) in Fuller, *FRUS 1913* (n 79) 479–484. A similar practice, indicating even more conspicuous partisanship, can be observed from the first arbitration between SEEE and Yugoslavia, where Yugoslavia's appointee to the tribunal, Slavko Stojković, was in constant communication with the Yugoslavian government. Stojković, who at the time was the secretary to Yugoslavia's permanent delegation to the League of Nations and an advisor in the Losinger dispute (see n 115), saw himself more as a party representative than an independent arbitrator, and was actively involved in moulding Yugoslavia's strategy and arguments in the case. See Copy of Letter from S Stojković to the Assistant Minister of Transport (December 1934) (Archives of Yugoslavia: 70–288–536); Copy of Telegram from Spalajković to the Minister of Transport (24 January 1935) (Archives of Yugoslavia: 70–288–536); Copy of Letter from Slavko Stojković to the Ministry of Transport (2 February 1935) (Archives of Yugoslavia: 70–288–536); Copy of Letter from S Stojković to the Assistant Minister of Transport Zdravko Vasković (9 February 1935) (Archives of Yugoslavia: 70–288–536); Letter from Stojković to the Ministry of Finance (18 March 1935) (Archives of Yugoslavia: 70–288–536); Maja Stanivuković and Sanja Đajić, 'Hommage jednom zastupniku pred međunarodnim sudovima – profesor dr Slavko Stojković' (2020) 2(2) Revija Kopaoničke škole prirodnog prava 197, 200. Yugoslavia likewise saw it appropriate to 'order' Stojković which course of action to take in his arbitrator role and expected him to act in accordance with the government's interests. See Letter from the Minister of Finance to the Minister of Transport (31 January 1935) (Archives of Yugoslavia: 70–288–536). Finally, see also Veeder, 'The *Lena Goldfields* Arbitration' (n 4) 781.

119 See eg *Colombia v Cauca Co*, 106 Fed 337 (n 25) 347, where the circuit judge hearing Colombia's annulment request stated that, unlike the presiding arbitrator, the party-appointed

on occasion also seen as needing to possess sufficient levels of neutrality. For instance, during the negotiations for the establishment of the tribunal in the *Jaffa-Jerusalem Railway Arbitration*, the British government – in what it termed 'the usual practice in international arbitration cases' – expressed its expectation that the two party-appointed arbitrators would act solely in their capacity as arbitrators and would not be advancing the interests of the respective parties that had appointed them.[120] The same underlying sentiment was perhaps most eruditely captured by Ecuador's minister of foreign affairs, who, in striving to fight off diplomatic intervention by the US in relation to its dispute with The Guayaquil and Quito Railway Company, noted that:

> The arbitrators, in this case, as in every other, are nothing more than judges who are to exercise the functions of such, whether in accordance with law or equity – *judges, who, once appointed, do not represent those who appointed them*; nor are they to pronounce sentence in representation thereof. Therefore, the participation of the Presidents is no more than a procedure to bring about the designation of the judges, who, once designated, cause the participation of those who elected them to cease.[121]

In similar vein, when contemplating who to appoint as arbitrator in their dispute with The Administration of Posts and Telegraphs of the Republic of Czechoslovakia, the representatives of the RCA felt that, irrespective of possible legal constraints, the best course of action was to appoint a person who would not be connected to the company.[122] As these examples illustrate, then, the quest

arbitrators were 'avowedly favorable to the contentions of those respectively designating them'. Notably, in the proceedings before the US courts, the company acknowledged that the arbitrator appointed by it had an interest in its affairs, although it was submitted that Colombia had had full knowledge of this circumstance. See Record Filed February 28, 1902 at 26, *Colombia v Cauca Co*, 190 US 524 (n 84) (available at Columbia University Library). See also *Petroleum Development v Qatar* (n 17) 161 (wherein the party-appointed arbitrators are referred to as 'Arbitrator-Advocates'); *Hedjaz Railway Arbitration* (n 3) 2 (where the underlying arbitration clause provided that the disputing parties would appoint arbitrators 'to represent them').

120 See reproduction in Rosenne (n 1) 349 of a Note from the Foreign Office to the French Embassy (21 December 1921) (UK National Archives: FO 371/6381).

121 'The Minister in Ecuador (Hartman) to the Secretary of State' (22 January 1918) in Joseph V Fuller (ed), *Papers Relating to the Foreign Relations of the United States, 1918* (US Government Printing Office 1930) 401, 403. Emphasis added. See also 'The American Chargé d'Affaires to the Secretary of State' (3 April 1913) in Fuller, *FRUS 1913* (n 79) 486, 489.

122 In the dispute, the RCA understood its choice of arbitrator to be governed by New York law, which required arbitrators to be impartial. However, even if this were not the case, the general sentiment was that choosing a person who was not impartial would have

for neutral decision-makers in historical ISA, albeit admittedly imperfectly and not ubiquitously so, went beyond the sole or the presiding arbitrator.

It therefore appears that the perceived neutrality of the ultimate decision-maker(s), even if by no means immaculate (especially when judged against present-day standards),[123] was a quintessential feature of the historical ISAs. As a consequence, independent (and for the most part) private[124] actors, who were decoupled from the influence of the disputing parties, were interposed into the historical ISAs and accorded with the final say on the eventual outcomes of the process. Such externalisation of the ultimate decision-making in relation to the sensitive matters considered in historical ISA thus removed these matters from the exclusive decision-making purview of the states involved.

---

been a policy misjudgment. Consequently, the RCA decided against appointing its traffic manager as arbitrator, which had initially been considered as an option. See Memo from Manton Davis to Winterbottom (telephoned to Miss MacInnis) (22 June 1931) (MCI International Archives, box 583, file 'Czechoslovakia: Correspondence and Agreements (3 of 6)'); Copy of Letter from Robert T Swaine to Colonel Davis (3 July 1931) (MCI International Archives, box 583, file 'Czechoslovakia: Correspondence and Agreements (3 of 6)'); Copy of Letter from Manton Davis to Winterbottom (9 July 1931) (MCI International Archives, box 583, file 'Czechoslovakia: Correspondence and Agreements (3 of 6)').

123 It must be born in mind that the concept of what was considered as 'neutral', 'impartial' or 'independent' with respect to the historical ISAs did not necessarily correspond to the present-day understanding of these notions. Thus, while in the abovementioned examples (see nn 120 and 122) both the British government and the RCA had in principle considered the arbitrators they had appointed to be independent, in practice the situation was less than ideal. Namely, the Britain-appointed arbitrator, Henry Osborne Mance, was still a member of the British Army, for which he received remuneration. See Copy of Letter from BB Cubitt to the Under Secretary of State, Colonial Office (22 November 1921) (UK National Archives: TS 27/143); Copy of Letter from Lancelot Oliphant to the Under Secretary of State, Colonial Office (15 December 1921) (UK National Archives: TS 27/143); Copy of Letter from JE Shuckburgh to the War Office (5 December 1921) (UK National Archives: TS 27/143); Copy of Letter from JE Shuckburgh to the War Office (21 October 1921) (UK National Archives: TS 27/143); Letter (unsigned) to the Under Secretary of State, Foreign Office (17 December 1921) (UK National Archives: TS 27/143). Similarly, the RCA expressed its expectation that, while neutral, its arbitrator would be someone who at least would be sympathetic to its position and then went on to maintain a channel of communication with the arbitrator during the proceedings (see ch 4 and 5). See also nn 116, 118 and 119.

124 Many of the arbitrators (both party-appointed and presiding) did nonetheless hold public office; in fact, some of them were even appointed precisely because of this fact (eg because they were a judge of the highest court of a certain country). However, in discharging their duties as arbitrators, they did not act in their official capacities.

4.3 *Auxiliary Private Actors*

While the arbitrators and the investors that were parties to the arbitrations were by far the two categories of private actors that had the most immediate impact on shaping the historical ISAs and their eventual upshots, they were nonetheless not the only ones capable of exerting such influence. Indeed, other, less conspicuous, categories of private actors, such as counsel, advisors or experts, on occasion managed, albeit in a more subtle manner, to have a similar type of influence. Even though these auxiliary private actors did not necessarily have a formal role within the historical ISAs, in certain instances their impact was at least comparable to those private actors that had a more prominent formal role. A particularly notable example of such intrinsic involvement and influence of this type of auxiliary actors is the 19th century *Suez v. Egypt* arbitration where, while it had nominally been Napoleon III that had acted as arbitrator, in actuality it was a five-member commission designated by him that had done the lion's share of the work.[125] There are other examples of a similar ilk to be found.[126]

Accordingly, it was not only the investors that were parties to the historical ISAs and the arbitrators, but also other private actors, that had an important role in shaping the entire process. In their totality, these private actors, whether they were the parties, arbitrators or influential auxiliary actors, played a crucial part in what was to unfold within, and as a consequence of, the historical ISAs. Thus, not only was historical ISA a process where important areas of public policy where moulded through discretionary decision-making, but this very process was, instead of being solely under the control of states, infused with a significant dose of, and in turn shaped by, private actor involvement.

---

125 See Yackee, 'The First Investor-State Arbitration' (n 6) 402, 426 and 448.

126 See eg *Socobelge I* (n 81) 41–43, and *Socobelge II* (n 80) *passim* (where an expert report commissioned by the tribunal in large part provided the basis for the tribunal's eventual decision); 'Lake Copais Company' *The Times* (London, 27 October 1926) 23 (wherein the Chairman of the Lake Copais Company is quoted as stating that an arbitral award had settled many outstanding questions between the company and Greece, but had referred certain matters to commissions that were to be appointed by the parties); Yuliya Chernykh, 'The Gust of Wind: The Unknown Role of Sir Elihu Lauterpacht in the Drafting of the Abs-Shawcross Draft Convention' in Stephan W Schill, Christian J Tams and Rainer Hofmann (eds), *International Investment Law and History: Towards a Historiographical Turn* (Edward Elgar Publishing 2018) 241 (recounting the crucial role played by Elihu Lauterpacht in creating bilateral investment treaties with investor-state dispute settlement clauses).

5 Similar in Dissimilarity: The Pervasiveness of Historical Investor-State Arbitration's Key Features

The final component in elucidating historical ISA's key features presented above is the understanding of their perseverant nature throughout history, irrespective of the vastly different *milieus* in which the arbitrations unravelled. Indeed, these features were present not merely as incidental occurrences or historical curiosities that were confined to a set of very specific circumstances or settings, but rather as pervasive characteristics that appear to have been inherent to historical ISA. Namely, as this section will illustrate, the historical ISAs took place within a number of different types of underlying legal frameworks and were approached through directly contrasting conceptualisations. Yet, these differing backdrops against which historical ISA operated – while not necessarily entirely irrelevant for this purpose – do not appear to have been determinative for the presence of the aforementioned features. As a matter of fact, not only were the boundaries delimiting the different underlying frameworks in which historical ISA operated not as clear as it may initially appear, but the previously highlighted features of historical ISA were still present irrespective of the different procedural legal frameworks in which the ISAs took place (5.1). The same holds true for the tribunals' conceptualisations of the historical investor-state disputes – whether the disputes were approached from a private or a public law conceptual perspective (or irrespective of such conceptualisation), these key features remained (5.2).

5.1 *Cutting across the Different Legal Frameworks Underlying Historical Investor-State Arbitration*

By almost all parameters, the historical ISAs were incredibly diverse. While there are many different aspects through which this diversity manifested itself,[127] in the present context, the most important one is the difference in the underlying legal frameworks within which the arbitrations were perceived to operate. The legal framework within which an arbitration is conducted is perhaps one of its most (if not *the* most) important features, significantly affecting how the arbitration unfolds and what powers, as well as the limits in their exercise, its participants have. In this respect, the historical ISAs exhibited considerable diversity – not only did they ostensibly operate within the backdrop of both national systems of law and public international law, but also seemingly independently of any particular underlying legal framework.

127 See ch 1.

Perhaps the most easily anticipated setting for the historical ISAs was that of being anchored within a particular *national system of law*. Such arbitrations were typically based on contracts concluded between the investor and the state, which sometimes provided either explicitly or implicitly which national system the arbitration would be tied to.[128] Where this was not the case, and where the parties had not subsequently made such a choice,[129] it was often the arbitrators who played a key part in embedding the arbitration within a particular national system.[130] The fact that these arbitrations were entrenched into specific national legal systems of course entailed that the manner in which they were to be conducted was dictated by that very system, while the arbitrations were made subject to the control of that national system's courts.[131] At the same time, in light of the significant differences between the various national systems within which the arbitrations took place, this necessarily also implied that this category of historical ISAs were themselves far from a perfectly homogenous group.

Another relatively frequent setting for the historical ISAs was *public international law*. Perhaps the most notable examples of historical ISAs that can ostensibly best be described as having been based on, and administered according to, public international law, are the several railway arbitrations held after World War I in relation to the re-organisation of railway lines that had been affected by the redistribution of territories and the emergence of new states after the

128 For instance, the arbitrations between French firm Batignolles and Yugoslavia were based on a specific agreement which provided that the tribunal would be seated in Belgrade and that the proceedings would follow Yugoslavia's rules of civil procedure. The entrenchment of the awards within Yugoslavia's legal system was symbolically reflected in the somewhat curious fact that the awards were pronounced 'In the Name of His Majesty the King'. See Annex to the Technical Agreement of 30 April 1929 for the Carrying out of Reclamation Works on the Territory of the Dunav-Tamis Water Collective in Pancevo between the Kingdom of Yugoslavia and Batignolles (Arbitration Agreement) (12 September 1936) (Archives of Yugoslavia: 70–285–531) arts 1.a and 1.f. Likewise, the concession agreement that served as the basis for the *Duff v Kelantan* arbitrations specifically invoked the English Arbitration Act of 1889, while the arbitration clause in the contract between the Ditta Luigi Gallotti and Somalia simultaneously referred to the Italian Civil Code and provided that the tribunal was to 'reside' in Mogadishu. See respectively Duff Kelantan Deed of Cancellation (n 5) clause 21; *The Ditta Luigi Gallotti v Somalia* (n 3) 160.

129 See *GTM v East Pakistan IDC* (n 14) 446.

130 See eg *BP v Libya* (n 17) 308–311. The arbitrator, Judge Lagergren, did nonetheless observe that he was 'not competent to establish conclusively the nationality of its Award, for this can only be decided by the courts of Denmark and of other jurisdictions in which enforcement of the Award may be sought'. See also *Sapphire v NIOC* (n 17) 168–169; *Alsing v Greece* (n 22) 639.

131 See eg *Kelantan v Duff Development Company* (n 84); *GTM v East Pakistan IDC* (n 14) 450.

war.[132] While these historical ISAs also revolved around concession contracts, they were not based on the concession contracts as such. Instead, the bases for these arbitrations were to be found directly in instruments of public international law, and in particular the Peace Treaties with Austria and Hungary (which accorded the companies a direct right to seek arbitration against the respective states),[133] while the League of Nations itself played a significant role in the conduct of the arbitrations.[134] Some half a century later (but several years before the adoption of first bilateral investment treaties with investor-state dispute settlement clauses), several Franco-Algerian agreements arising out of Algerian independence provided direct recourse against the Algerian state through arbitration for companies operating in the hydrocarbons sector.[135] A number of cases are known to have arisen under these agreements.[136] A further significant instance of a tribunal procedurally internationalising an arbitration was *Saudi Arabia v. ARAMCO*[137] – an example that was later explicitly followed in *Texaco v. Libya*.[138] In addition, there were also other historical ISAs where, while the arbitration itself had been held as between an investor and a state, the agreement to arbitrate had been set up directly by the two

---

132 See *Sopron-Köszeg Local Railway Company v Austria and Hungary* (n 7); *Barcs-Pakrac Railway Company v Hungary and Yugoslavia* (n 40); *Zeltweg-Wolfsberg III* (n 40).

133 See Treaty of Trianon (n 1) art 304; Treaty of Saint-Germain (n 1) art 320. While the legal regime in which the tribunals were operating was not explicitly addressed by the respective tribunals, at least one of them (consisting of at least two of the three arbitrators that had sat on the two remaining tribunals) compared its competencies to that of 'an international judge'. See *Zeltweg-Wolfsberg II* (n 7) 1006.

134 For example, the arbitrator appointments were made through resolutions of the Council of the League of Nations. See *Sopron-Köszeg Local Railway Company v Austria and Hungary* (n 7) 164; *Barcs-Pakrac Railway Company v Hungary and Yugoslavia* (n 40) 523; *Zeltweg-Wolfsberg II* (n 7) 1005. See also ch 4.

135 Agreements Relating to Algerian Independence (Algeria-France) (signed 18 March 1962) (1962) 1 ILM 214, 230; Agreement on Arbitration of Disputes between Algeria and France Regarding Exploitation of the Saharan Subsoil (signed 26 June 1963) (1963) 2 ILM 1025 and Algeria-France Oil Accord (signed 29 July 1965) (1965) 4 ILM 809, 841–843, 906 and 908–912. Under the agreements, the tribunals' awards were self-executing in both France and Algeria, as well as abroad. The tribunals had unusually wide powers, including the authority to annul contested measures and issue injunctive relief.

136 See Stuyt (n 102) 537 and 540–542.

137 *Saudi Arabia v ARAMCO* (n 17) 154–156.

138 *Texaco v Libya* (n 17) paras 11–16.

concerned states.[139] As these and other examples illustrate,[140] arbitrations embedded in public international law, therefore, were not a particularly unusual occurrence in historical ISA.

Finally, there were also historical ISAs that seemingly were not entrenched within any particular legal framework, operating instead primarily, if not exclusively, within the confines, and on the basis, of the parties' agreement. Such arbitrations were not subject to the constraints of either a specific national system of law or of public international law, and could thus most appropriately be characterised as being *anational* or *transnational* in character. A prime example of this type of historical ISA was the (in)famous *SEEE v. Yugoslavia* case,[141] which is often referred to as one of the emblematic instances of anational arbitration. Even though the award in this historical ISA was handed down in Lausanne, the Swiss courts ultimately refused to register it as a Canton of Vaud arbitration award in light of its incompatibilities with the procedural requirements under local law. At the same time, however, the Swiss courts also

139 This was, for example, the case in the *Jaffa-Jerusalem Railway Arbitration*, where the original agreement to arbitrate was arrived at by France and the UK. However, it eventually turned out that the company (rather than France itself) would be the direct participant in the proceedings, to which the British government (with Winston Churchill being the one to give the final blessing) assented. See ch 3.

140 Whether the arbitral process was to be deemed 'international' or subject to Ecuador's laws and courts was a point of some controversy during the dispute between The Guayaquil and Quito Railway Company and Ecuador, wherein the American side advocated for the former option, while Ecuador insisted on the latter. See 'Minister Fox to the Secretary of State' (29 September 1908) (n 25) 274; 'The American Arbitrator to the Secretary of State' (5 March 1913) and 'The American Chargé d'Affaires to the Secretary of State' (9 April 1913) in Fuller, *FRUS 1913* (n 79) 480–482 and 492–493; 'Minister Hartman to the Secretary of State' (12 August 1914), 'Minister Hartman to the Secretary of State' (8 February 1914) and 'The American Arbitrator to the Secretary of State' (13 February 1914) in Joseph V Fuller (ed), *Papers Relating to the Foreign Relations of the United States, With the Address of the President to Congress December 8, 1914* (US Government Printing Office 1922) 265–267 and 275–276; 'The Minister in Ecuador (Hartman) to the Secretary of State' (22 January 1918) (n 121) 403. An intriguing example of an envisioned procedural internationalisation of a historical investment dispute, perhaps inadvertently so, is also provided by the contract between Batignolles and Yugoslavia, which provided that all disputes were to be submitted to the 'Permanent Court of International Justice in the Hague'. See Technical Agreement for the Carrying out of Reclamation Works on the Territory of the Dunav-Tamis Water Collective in Pancevo between the Kingdom of Serbs, Croats and Slovenes and Batignolles (30 April 1929) (Archives of Yugoslavia: 70–285–531) art 64. Unfortunately, this unconventional (and almost certainly pathological) dispute resolution clause was never put into motion, as it was replaced by a different agreement once a dispute arose. See n 128. See also n 145.

141 *SEEE v Yugoslavia* (n 52).

refused to set the award aside, holding that the parties had never intended for their arbitration to be subject to the requirements of the procedural law of the Canton of Vaud,[142] thus abstaining from negating the award's validity despite its detachment from the legal system of its place of arbitration.

The procedural backdrop within which the historical ISAs took place thus demonstrated considerable diversity, oscillating between the national, the international and the a- or transnational. Yet, despite such heterogeneity, the aforementioned key features of the historical ISAs remained, if not omnipresent, than at least pervasive. In large part, this can probably be explained by the fact that the underlying framework within which a particular historical ISA was to be conducted was not a corollary of some inherent characteristic of a particular type of investor-state relationship or dispute that would have preordained arbitrations arising from them to by necessity be handled within a particular legal framework. Rather, the legal framework was primarily a matter of choice, or sometimes, even chance. As a result, in many instances it was not possible to discern in advance within which underlying framework an arbitration would unfold – it was often only during the very arbitration proceedings, or sometimes even subsequent to them, that the backdrop within which the arbitration was to operate, or was deemed to have operated, became apparent.

The trifecta of cases that arose out of Libya's nationalisation of its oil fields in the 1970s provide an illustrative example. Even though the cases all stemmed from essentially the same set of circumstances and were based on identical arbitration clauses, the arbitrators hearing the cases came to diametrically opposing conclusions regarding the legal settings that underlay the

142 See Delaume, 'SEEE v Yugoslavia' (n 95) 27. In many instances, of course, it is not easy to say with certainty whether a historical ISA truly was conducted as an a- or transnational one, as the underlying framework was often not addressed explicitly by the parties and the tribunal, nor was there any need for the involvement of national courts. As a result, the underlying frameworks thus often operated in the background, without ever concretising into any of their possible definitive forms. This was seemingly particularly pronounced with the older historical ISAs that took place in the late 19th and early 20th century, in which the participants had less of a legalistic approach and appeared to be less centered on placing the relevant issues within clearly demarcated legal categories. One case that could possibly represent such an example is *Suez v Egypt*. Although the issue does not seem to have been raised during the arbitration and the award does not appear to have ever been remitted to any national court, the arbitration looks to have been conducted solely on the basis of the agreement between the parties; and even though the award was delivered in France, it seems highly questionable whether an arbitration where the arbitrator was nominally the French emperor would be subject to the control of the French courts. On the difficulty of categorising the *Suez v Egypt* award (albeit in a somewhat different context), see Yackee, 'The First Investor-State Arbitration' (n 6) 459.

arbitrations. Thus, while Judge Gunnar Lagergren, sitting in *BP v. Libya*, held that the arbitration in which he was acting as sole arbitrator was subject to the regime of the country where the tribunal was seated,[143] his counterpart in *Texaco v. Libya*, René-Jean Dupuy, decided that the arbitration was to take place in the arena of international law.[144] The arbitrator in the remaining case, *LIAMCO v. Libya*, was somewhat ambiguous on the issue, designating Geneva as the seat of the arbitration, while holding that the procedure would be guided 'by the general principles contained in the Draft Convention on Arbitral Procedure elaborated by the International Law Commission of the United Nations in 1958'.[145] As the concessions on which the arbitrations were based did not provide any guidance on the issue, the matter had been up in the air until it was decided by the arbitrators, whose decisions could hardly be characterised as having been foregone conclusions. Similarly, in the previously mentioned *SEEE v. Yugoslavia* case,[146] the eventual anational character of the arbitration had by no means been self-evident from the outset. Indeed, it was not until after the arbitration had concluded and the decision of the Swiss courts to the

143 *BP v Libya* (n 17) 308–311. Judge Lagergren's decision on this point seems to have been based not so much on the understanding that the arbitration *had* to be entrenched within a particular national system as it was on his view that this would be more effective and convenient. Unpredictability in this respect was further compounded by the fact that, in many instances, there was no upfront choice of the seat or place of arbitration, thus leaving to the tribunal, through its choice of the seat of arbitration, not only the decision of whether the arbitration would be embedded in a particular national system, but also, if so, in which one. See ibid 303; *Sapphire v NIOC* (n 17) 168–169.

144 *Texaco v Libya* (n 17) paras 11–16.

145 See *LIAMCO v Libya* (n 17) 5. Ultimately, however, the award seems to have been treated in subsequent court proceedings as a Swiss award, pursuant to the seat chosen by the arbitrator. See David D Caron, 'The Nature of the Iran-United States Claims Tribunal and the Evolving Structure of International Dispute Resolution' (1990) 84 AJIL 104, 120 and 123; Zachary Douglas, *The International Law of Investment Claims* (CUP 2009) 112–113. See also, however, William T Lake and Jane Tucker Dana, 'Judicial Review of Awards of the Iran-United States Claims Tribunal: Are the Tribunal's Awards Dutch' (1984) 16 Law & Pol'y Int'l Bus 755, 803–805. An eerily similar approach to that in *LIAMCO v Libya* was taken by the tribunal in the earlier *Hedjaz Railway Arbitration*, which likewise chose Geneva as the seat of the tribunal, but held that its procedure would be 'guided by the principles of the draft on Arbitral Procedure elaborated by the International Law Commission in 1958'. Notably, the arbitration clause on which the *Hedjaz Railway Arbitration* was based had explicitly provided that the tribunal's award 'shall not be subject to the provisions of any laws on procedure'. See *Hedjaz Railway Arbitration* (n 3) 4–5. Sobhi Mahmassani, the sole arbitrator in *LIAMCO v Libya*, also sat on the *Hedjaz Railway Arbitration* tribunal, so it is very much possible that his decision in the subsequent *LIAMCO v Libya* case was based on the approach adopted by the tribunal in that arbitration.

146 See nn 141–142.

effect that the rendered award was not a Canton of Vaud award was handed down that this aspect of the arbitration became apparent. Given this relative lack of preordination in terms of the legal backdrop in which the historical ISAs were deemed to have operated, the fact that the features that were outlined in the preceding sections were not restricted to any particular 'archetype' of historical ISA, or to historical ISA's operating within a certain type of framework, is thus, perhaps, unsurprising.

That is not to say that the underlying framework within which a particular historical ISA was set was completely agnostic *vis-à-vis* such features of the historical ISAs – certain underlying characteristics of the different applicable frameworks did indeed have the potential to influence how these arbitrations would proceed and the ultimate impact they would (or could) have. For instance, in light of the oversight to which they were subjected by the courts of the country of their seat, the tribunals entrenched within a particular national system would have been under more stringent limitations with respect to which powers, and how, could be wielded by the arbitrators. As a result, the tribunals operating in such settings were likely to have had significantly less leeway in their decision-making in comparison to tribunals sitting in public international law or anational settings, which did not have to face the same prospects of their decisions potentially being reviewed, and possibly set aside, due to a possible over-step of authority. At the same time, however, parties from the historical ISAs that belonged to a particular national system could call upon more effective enforcement mechanisms (especially after the adoption of the New York Convention), giving the tribunals' decisions significantly more potential 'bite'.[147] Other subtle differences between the different

147 *BP v Libya* (n 17) 309; *Texaco v Libya* (n 17) 7–8. This does not mean, however, that tribunals from other frameworks were absolutely excluded from making use of such mechanisms. See eg *SEEE v Yugoslavia* (n 52), where the anational arbitral decision was ultimately allowed enforcement by French courts. The position of a prevailing party in such an arbitration was, nonetheless, significantly more complex. See Delaume, 'State Contracts and Transnational Arbitration' (n 68) 813; Robert B von Mehren and P Nicholas Kourides, 'International Arbitrations between States and Foreign Private Parties: The Libyan Nationalization Cases' (1981) 75 AJIL 476, 508 (citing J Gillis Wetter). Likewise, in the aftermath of the *Barcs-Pakrac Railway Company v Hungary and Yugoslavia* (n 40) case, the claimant company sought to enforce the award against Yugoslavia before Yugoslavian courts. Enforcement was allowed by the court of first instance, but this decision was later overturned. Notably, however, the reason for ultimately refusing enforcement was a then existing moratorium in Yugoslavia on payments to Hungarian subjects for debts arising under the Peace Treaties and related agreements, and not that the award, having been handed down pursuant to an international treaty, was as such not capable of being enforced. See *Barcs-Pakrac Railway Company v Estate of the Kingdom of Yugoslavia,*

underlying frameworks were also capable of having a potential impact on how the aforementioned key features of historical ISA would materialise in any specific instance.

For present purposes, however, it is sufficient to observe that at least some, if not many, of the historical ISAs unfolding under each of the underlying frameworks possessed the abovementioned key features, even if they may have been somewhat differently aligned and accentuated under each framework. Irrespective of these idiosyncrasies, then, all of the previously outlined elements remained present in the historical ISAs that unfolded within the various backdrops. Thus, disputes that involved interests that transcended the two disputing parties were hardly constrained to historical ISAs arbitrated under a particular framework. Instead, owing in part to the fact that the same types of issues could be reformulated so as to be capable of being brought under the different underlying frameworks,[148] the disputes involving highly sensitive issues showed up across the board.[149] The same can be said of the room for the arbitrators' discretionary decision-making, as its prerequisite – the indeterminacy of the legal norms interpreted and applied by the tribunals – was likewise not specific to a particular legal framework in which the historical ISAs operated. While it is arguable that the degree of such indeterminacy might have fluctuated depending on the underlying legal framework,[150] as a phenomenon it was nonetheless essentially ubiquitous in the historical ISAs, opening the door for the arbitrators' discretionary decision-making. Finally, even if perhaps not identical in the various backdrops in which the historical ISAs operated, the role of private actors (their capacity to shape how the process was to unfold

---

Decision of the Table of Seven (at the time the highest court instance for Croatia, then part of Yugoslavia) (19 November 1937) (Archives of Yugoslavia: 70–292–542).

148 See eg the example of the Libyan oil concession cases (n 17), where virtually identical disputes were resolved under different frameworks; Yackee, 'The First Investor-State Arbitration' (n 6) 403 (noting how an 1864 claim brought by the Suez Canal Company might be qualified differently today).

149 Compare only eg *Duff v Kelantan I* (n 41); *Sopron-Köszeg Local Railway Company v Austria and Hungary* (n 7) and *SEEE v Yugoslavia* (n 52). In fact, there does not even seem to have been much of a correlation or certain tendency in this respect, as both the most sensitive types of disputes that go to the very core of certain sovereign interests and disputes that are the least connected to the aforesaid interests, such as eg those concerning simple valuation of property or amount of compensation, can be found across the different frameworks.

150 For example, it could be said that, in light of the decentralised nature of certain underlying frameworks, in particular those of public international law or of the anational, legal norms within such frameworks were less likely to be clearly defined and were therefore particularly susceptible to giving way to creative decision-making.

included), was nonetheless significant in all of them.[151] While the different settings in which the historical ISAs materialised might have therefore influenced *how* and to which degree certain features would manifest themselves, they nonetheless did not influence *whether* they would be present within the historical ISAs. Consequently, rather independently of the underlying framework in which they were set, the historical ISAs thus remained processes where private actors were able to significantly affect how discretionary decisions in areas of great public importance would be shaped.

5.2 *Transcending the Private Law/Public Law Conceptual Chasm*

As different as the underlying procedural frameworks in which the historical ISAs operated were, their variance was far exceeded by that of the applicable law according to which the disputes were resolved. In fact, the chosen applicable laws, and all the utilised amalgamations thereof (see section 3), were so vastly dissimilar that any meaningful analysis of the key features of historical ISA across cases conducted pursuant to such applicable laws seems both elusive and futile. This variance in applicable law notwithstanding, there nonetheless appears to have been a recurring, although by no means universal, common conceptual theme underlying the historical ISAs, reflected in the *private law/ public law* dichotomy. Indeed, irrespective of the applicable law pursuant to which a particular historical ISA was proceeding, instances were abound where the discussion before the tribunal was centred on whether the relationship between the parties was one of private (civil) or public law (in large part reflected through the French notion of *contrat administratif*).[152] Rather than

151 Indeed, in all of the different underlying frameworks in which the historical ISAs operated, arbitrators, counsel and other key participants were predominantly private actors.

152 See eg *Greek State v Hellenic Electric Railways* (n 80) 21–22; Wetter and Schwebel (n 2) 220–221; *Czechoslovakian Administration v RCA* (n 11) 530–532; *RCA v China* (n 11) 1626–1627; *Alsing v Greece* (n 22) 640–642; *Saudi Arabia v ARAMCO* (n 17) 157–165, 192–194 and 215–216; *Sapphire v NIOC* (n 17) 171, 173 and 183–184; *Hedjaz Railway Arbitration* (n 3) 92–93; *Rialet v Ethiopia* (n 6) 748; *BP v Libya* (n 17) 324 and 327; *Texaco v Libya* (n 17) 19–21; *LIAMCO v Libya* (n 17) 29–30. See also Yackee, 'The First Investor-State Arbitration' (n 6) 453; Veeder, 'The *Lena Goldfields* Arbitration' (n 4) 771–772. In light of this, it is perhaps not particularly surprising that administrative law sources and scholars were not infrequently cited in historical ISA; this includes prominent French administrative law specialist, Gaston Jeze (who even acted as counsel in at least two historical ISAs, *Rialet v Ethiopia* (n 6) and *Hambros and Lazard v Roumania Monopolies Institute* (n 6)). See eg *Batignolles v Yugoslavia I* (n 15) 44–45; *Alsing v Greece* (n 22) 656; *Saudi Arabia v ARAMCO* (n 17) 159; *LIAMCO v Libya* (n 17) 62; Wetter and Schwebel (n 2) 220–221. Interestingly, contrary to what one might intuitively have expected, it was not always the state that was insisting that its relationship with a private investor was one falling under public law when the matter was under discussion. See 'Minister Hartman to the Secretary of State' (27 March

the seemingly unsurmountable variance in the governing law, it is thus this iterative conceptual theme whose interaction with the key features of historical ISA provides fertile ground for analysis. This analysis, once more, leads to an outcome eerily similar to that arrived at in the previous sub-section – the private law/public law conceptual dichotomy, while not without potential relevance for how the disputes would be approached (and ultimately resolved) by historical ISA tribunals, certainly does not invalidate the main contours of historical ISA that were previously outlined in sections 2–4.

This is perhaps most clearly epitomised by the two RCA arbitrations – two cases that arose out of fundamentally identical factual bases, were based on very similarly constructed arbitration clauses and were decided by tribunals composed of the same types of actors (i.e. private individuals).[153] Essentially, both disputes centred on whether the state entity with whom the RCA was operating a direct radio-telegraphic circuit was entitled to open a parallel direct circuit along the same route with another company. In both disputes, the question of how the contractual relationship between the RCA and the corresponding state entity was to be understood was essential, and the two tribunals took diametrically opposing conceptual approaches when addressing it. In assessing whether the underlying agreement was to be judged under civil or under public law, the *Czechoslovakian Administration v. RCA* tribunal opted for the former, ultimately holding that The Czechoslovakian Administration was prohibited from establishing a parallel route.[154] While the issue was not couched in as explicit terms in the *RCA v. China* case, the tribunal nonetheless put great emphasis on the fact that one party to the contract was a sovereign entity.[155] This lead the tribunal to the eventual conclusion that '[c]ontracts affecting the public interest are to be construed liberally in favour of the public', from which a finding against the RCA followed.[156]

As can be seen, the conceptual approach by the two tribunals could hardly have been more divergent, and this was undoubtedly, as is evidenced by the eventual outcomes, quite relevant for how the cases were decided. Crucially,

---

1917) in Joseph V Fuller (ed), *Papers Relating to the Foreign Relations of the United States, With the Address of the President to Congress December 4, 1917* (US Government Printing Office 1926) 739, 742; Record Filed February 28, 1902 at 67, *Colombia v Cauca Co*, 190 US 524 (n 84); Brief for Appellees at 45–50, *Colombia v Cauca Co*, 190 US 524 (n 84).

153 For in-depth accounts of the two cases, see chs 4 and 5.

154 *Czechoslovakian Administration v RCA* (n 11) 530–532 and 534.

155 Notably, the tribunal pointedly refuted the notion that a difference was in this respect to be drawn between a government and a mere governmental administration. See *RCA v China* (n 11) 1627.

156 Ibid 1626–1627 and 1636.

however, this conceptual framing demonstrably was not relevant for *whether* the cases involving this type of dispute would be decided upon by a tribunal consisting of private individuals. Indeed, the consequence that flowed from the more public-law-oriented approach chosen by the *RCA v. China* tribunal was not that the tribunal did not deem itself competent to rule on China's right to establish a new direct radio telegraphic route, but merely that a different degree of deference would be accorded to China in determining whether China had undertaken an obligation not to do so. The tribunal's ultimate finding, thus, was not based on a principled stance that the nature of the contract made it inappropriate for the tribunal to carry out an assessment of the kind requested by the RCA, but rather on the simple fact that the tribunal did not think that China had by virtue of its contract with the RCA imposed upon itself a limitation of the sort that would deprive it of the right to operate a parallel radio telegraphic route. Had the underlying agreement been more explicit in this respect, the tribunal was adamant that it would have deemed China's actions that had given rise to the arbitration as illegal.[157] A similar sentiment was echoed by the *Czechoslovakian Administration v. RCA* tribunal, according to which qualifying the agreement in question as a public law contract would not have, in any event, put it beyond the tribunal's purview. Among other things, the tribunal's position was based on the understanding that a public law approach did not negate the principle of *pacta sunt servanda* and that the circumstances of the case were not such as to allow The Czechoslovakian Administration, even under the rules of public law, to cancel or alter the contract.[158]

As significant as it initially may seem, the difference in conceptual approach between the two RCA tribunals was thus not so much a question of *whether* the arbitrators were competent to decide the question put before them as it was a question of *how* they would decide it. While choosing one or the other – whether the relationships were to be viewed through a private law or a public law lens – may therefore have affected how this task was to be carried out by the tribunals, it did not in the arbitrators' eyes call into question the underlying principle that a decision dictating how a public communications service was to be offered to the citizens of the state entity involved in the arbitration was capable of being handed down by a tribunal comprised of private individuals. For this reason, despite their contrasting conceptual approaches, the *Czechoslovakian Administration v. RCA* and the *RCA v. China* decisions – at least insofar as ISA's characteristic of being a mechanism in which matters of public concern are decided upon by private individuals through discretionary

157 Ibid 1627.

158 *Czechoslovakian Administration v RCA* (n 11) 531–532.

decision-making – stand not so much in opposition to each other as they do as one another's reinforcement.

This takeaway from the two RCA arbitrations is further fortified by similar dynamics discernible from the Libyan oil arbitrations. As seems to have been tradition with this trifecta of cases, there was again a lack of unanimity by the tribunals on how the underlying investor-state relationship was to be conceptualised. Thus, whereas in *BP v. Libya* Judge Lagergren, without elaboration, accepted the claimant's contention that the concession was an administrative contract,[159] in *Texaco v. Libya* arbitrator Dupuy explicitly rejected such a characterisation.[160] For his part, the arbitrator in *LIAMCO v. Libya*, Sobhi Mahmassani, held that the concessions were 'of mixed public and private legal character', but that they were 'generally governed by the principles of the private law of contracts'.[161] Yet, despite this difference in how each of the arbitrators approached the underlying investor-state relationship, notably, neither of them deemed himself unable to rule on the dispute submitted to him. Again, then, while the manner in which the underlying relationship was conceptualised may have been of relevance for *how* the cases would be decided,[162] in each of the cases, the arbitrators' capacity to rule upon the claims before them decidedly remained unaffected.[163]

The contours of the pattern that is starting to emerge are only made more easily discernible by the 1930s *Ten Lepta Charge Case*. Whereas Greece had in this case argued that the relationship between the parties was based not on an ordinary contract of civil law but on a public utility concession, and that its legislative sovereignty (entailing the right to modify the concession through general and impartial legislation) thus remained unaffected, the tribunal was indifferent to this distinction drawn by Greece. In the tribunal's view, it did not matter how the contract was conceptualised – whether it was one of civil law or a public utility concession, it contained *bona fide* obligations that had to

159 *BP v Libya* (n 17) 324 and 327.

160 *Texaco v Libya* (n 17) 19–21.

161 *LIAMCO v Libya* (n 17) 29–30. A number of other tribunals also pointed to the mixed character of the underlying contractual relationship. See eg *Saudi Arabia v ARAMCO* (n 17) 169; *Sapphire v NIOC* (n 17) 171.

162 Thus, for example, in *Texaco v Libya* it was alluded that ordering *restitutio in integrum* as a remedy might have been excluded had the contracts in dispute been understood as administrative contracts. See *Texaco v Libya* (n 17) 32.

163 Somewhat similarly, the arbitrators sitting in *Alsing v Greece* and the *Hedjaz Railway Arbitration* were not perturbed by the possibility of a matter that fell under administrative and/or public law being submitted to arbitration. See *Alsing v Greece* (n 22) 641; *Hedjaz Railway Arbitration* (n 3) 92.

be respected.[164] A similar line of reasoning was followed by the *Saudi Arabia v. ARAMCO* tribunal when determining the nature of the concession between the parties, as the tribunal held that Islamic (or Moslem, as it was referred to in the award) law did 'not distinguish between a treaty, a contract of public or administrative law and a contract of civil or commercial law' – all were pacts that had to be observed.[165]

As this brief overview illustrates, the historical ISAs were capable of being, and were indeed, approached through starkly contrasting conceptualisations. This included viewing them not only through the lenses of both private and public law, but also without taking this dichotomy that may be of second nature to the legal mind into consideration. Yet, the variance in conceptual framing decidedly did not serve to negate, and perhaps even reinforced, what have been described in this Chapter as the key characteristics of historical ISA. To this, there can hardly be a better testament than the fact that the variance in conceptual approach between factually virtually indistinguishable historical ISAs was not always explainable through any sort of objectively observable attributes, but was rather a matter of choice, or even mere preference, on behalf of the parties or arbitrators. The nature of the dispute at hand, as it would follow, was thus not necessarily determinative of the conceptual framework a historical ISA would be subsumed under; at the same time, whatever conceptual framing may eventually have been chosen did not seem to have been deemed by the historical ISA tribunals as an obstacle for deciding upon the matters before them. Indeed, it would appear that, on balance, the nature of the underlying historical investor-state dispute was no more predictive of the eventual choice of conceptual approach than the choice of said conceptual approach was prohibitive for that dispute to be resolved by arbitrators who were private individuals.

If at all, then, the conceptual approach a particular historical ISA was subsumed under – whichever side of the private law/public law conceptual chasm it fell on – was relevant for *how*, but not *if*, a tribunal was to exercise its powers in deciding a dispute that had been submitted to it. Such variance in conceptual framing, however, did not take away from historical ISA being an undertaking where private individuals were able to shape matters of broader public concern through a discretionary decision-making process.

164 *Greek State v Hellenic Electric Railways* (n 80) 21–22. See ch 5.

165 *Saudi Arabia v ARAMCO* (n 17) 163–165.

6 Conclusions: The Breakdown of the Conception of Historical Investor-State Arbitration as (Just) Private Dispute Settlement

Getting acquainted with historical ISA at the very outset invites two distinct initial impressions. The first is the realisation of just how seemingly heterogeneous and uncategorisable these past arbitrations were, having unravelled in different geographical and temporal spaces, within different legal frameworks and conceptualisations, and with the participation of various actors with vastly differing backgrounds. Second, it would equally appear upon first impression (but only upon first impression, as this Chapter has shown) that historical ISA squarely fits the mould of being nothing more than a private dispute resolution mechanism. In light of this, it is somewhat unexpected, and perhaps even ironic, that it would be the former of these initial impressions that would ultimately prove quintessential in confuting the latter. Yet this is nonetheless the exact inevitable inference one is drawn to, as it is precisely because the traits of historical ISA that this Chapter has highlighted – traits which, when taken together, are difficult to square with historical ISA being nothing more than a private dispute resolution mechanism – are recognisable across the discipline's initial apparent randomness that they can be considered ostensibly intrinsic to historical ISA. In other words, it is because the traits that challenge the conception of historical ISA as 'just dispute settlement' can be observed across the various settings in which historical ISA is known to have operated that one can infer that they were not mere circumstance-dependent idiosyncrasies.

The first step in eroding the impression that historical ISA was nothing more than a private dispute resolution mechanism has been the exploration of the nature of the interests that were at the heart of the historical ISAs. This exercise revealed that the historical ISAs in large part stemmed from investor-state relationships the importance of which exceeded the two parties directly privy to them, including, but not solely, because the implicated state, when entering such relationships, often acted in the exercise of prerogatives associated with its official functions. An expected, and perhaps necessary, corollary to this was the fact that the types of disputes that arose from such relationships were likewise hardly of concern only to the two disputing parties. Simply put, the matters implicated in historical ISA were not of interest solely to the parties privy to the dispute, but also to a broader array of stakeholders.

The initial apparent randomness of historical ISA likewise ultimately betrays a pattern with respect to the process through which decisions within historical ISA were made, as the lack of determinacy in the normative foundation underlying this decision-making process looks to have been particularly marked and ubiquitous, even more so than what might have been the case in other contemporary adjudicatory processes. Indeed, whether it was because the disputing parties had not bestowed the tribunals with pre-ordained normative bases, or because such pre-ordained normative bases were amalgamations of different legal systems that were susceptible to vastly differing interpretations, or because the chosen normative bases included nebulous concepts capable of seemingly infinite expansion, or even because the historical ISA tribunals found ways to eschew the normative bases upon which they were intended to operate, the fact remains that the decisions that were made in historical ISA were rarely, if ever, reducible to a mere mechanical process of subsuming the relevant facts under clearly defined legal norms. Instead, whatever may have been decided in historical ISA, it was done so through a process that necessarily implied creative input on behalf of the relevant decision-makers.

A further recurrent, even omnipresent, characteristic of historical ISA was the prominent role that several categories of private actors had in the historical ISAs. Thus, not only were the private investors that were parties to the disputes able to make numerous decisions that were crucial for how the entire process was to unfold, but the ultimate decision-making was externalised and placed into the hands of (predominantly) private individuals – the arbitrators, who were, at least for the most part, independent of either disputing party. Taken together with certain auxiliary actors that were on occasion also known to play an important, even if less conspicuous, role in the underlying processes, this meant that historical ISAs, as well as their eventual reverberations, were in large part shaped by private actors.

These observations notwithstanding, inferring any broader extrapolations from these noted character traits of historical ISA would have been difficult, if not impossible, without accounting for the aforementioned variability of the examined arbitrations. It is this very overarching trait – this variability – that proves to be the connecting tissue that permeates and ties together all of the said traits of historical ISA, as their contours remain recognisable irrespective of the change in scenery that may accompany the various historical ISAs. Indeed, while the historical ISAs were both capable of being embedded within different procedural legal frameworks (or even eluded such embedding altogether) and susceptible to differing legal conceptualisations, neither of these backdrops were determinative, or indeed even indicative, of the presence of what have been described here as historical ISA's character traits. Thus, regardless of how dissimilar certain individual historical ISAs may have been, there was nonetheless a certain 'similarity to their dissimilarity' in that these traits were equally capable of manifesting themselves irrespective of underlying legal framework or conceptualisation. It would appear, then, that the aforementioned features of historical ISA were not constrained to sets of certain specific historical circumstances but were rather seemingly interwoven into the very fabric of historical ISA as an institution.

At face value, one could hardly be faulted for being tempted to assume that historical ISA was nothing more than a private bi-party dispute resolution mechanism. After all, the historical ISAs were nominally almost exclusively established by the two disputing parties, while the tribunals had a mandate restricted to resolving a particular dispute and were disassembled once this narrow objective had been fulfilled. First impressions notwithstanding, the historical record examined herein suggests that the role of historical ISA went well beyond what such a limited understanding of this institution would have suggested. Indeed, by breaking down the historical ISAs to their core structural elements, this Chapter also ineluctably invited the symbolical breaking down of the notion that historical ISA was nothing more than a private dispute resolution mechanism. In consequence, historical ISA was instead revealed as an institution that is best understood in its historical context not as a dyadic mode of dispute resolution, but rather as an institution through which private actors were able to significantly shape a process in which value judgments and policy choices were made in matters whose importance transcended the interests of the two arbitrating parties. How exactly this took place, and the full implications that arose thereof, is explored in detail in the chapters that follow.

CHAPTER 3

Historical Investor-State Arbitration and the Cost of Governance

1 Introduction

That the exploration of investor-state arbitration's (ISA'S) past would reveal that the decisions handed down in historical ISA would have had potential financial implications for the disputing parties, including the states involved, can hardly be characterised as surprising. To be sure, issuing monetary awards is one of the main, if not the main, *modus operandi* for arbitral tribunals; that historical ISA would have had some sort of imprint on the public purse was thus more or less a given. What is, on the other hand, at face value certainly far less obvious is the full extent of this capacity by historical ISA tribunals to influence the financial balance of investor-state relationships and, in particular, whether this capacity extended also to matters that stemmed from, or related to, states' conduct of their official business – to how they governed. It is precisely this nexus between the manner in which states governed and the capacity by historical ISA tribunals to impose financial consequences upon the disputing parties before them that the present Chapter explores.

That it was certainly not unprecedented for historical ISA to have influenced the cost of states' policy choices may already be apparent from one of the more fabled historical ISAs, which concerned the Soviet Union's reversal of a policy that was at the very foundation of its society at the time. Namely, toward the end of the 1920s, the Soviet Union adopted its First Five Year Plan, ushering in a shift to a fully centrally planned economy according to socialist principles.[1] The First Five Year Plan was a departure from the Soviet Union's previous policy – the New Economic Policy (NEP), which had been more conciliatory toward the market economy and capitalistic enterprise.[2] The shift in policy from

1 The Royal Institute of International Affairs, 'The National Economy of the USSR: the Five-Year Plan' (1930) 7(4) Bulletin of International News 3, 8; David R Shearer, 'Stalinism, 1928–1940' in Ronald Grigor Suny (ed), *The Cambridge History of Russia*, vol III (CUP 2006) 192, 198; Peter Gatrell, 'Economic and Demographic Change: Russia's Age of Economic Extremes' in Suny (n 1) 383, 394–395.

2 Henry Somerville, 'The Soviet Five Year Plan' (1930) 19 Studies: An Irish Quarterly Review 624, 625; Robert C North, 'The NEP and the New Democracy' (1951) 24(1) Pacific Affairs 52, 53–54; Royal Institute of International Affairs (n 1) 7; Jonathan J Bean, 'Nikolai Bukharin and

 | DOI:10.1163/9789004733824_004

the NEP to the First Five Year Plan was, to say the least, significant, and has perhaps been more accurately described as 'a radical break'.[3] The magnitude of the alteration to the Soviet Union's social fabric brought about through this change in policy has been most vividly captured, in his 1931 speech at London's Chatham House, by Hubert Renfro Knickerbocker, an American journalist who was awarded the Pulitzer Prize for a series of articles on the practical operation of the Five Year Plan:

> The changes that had taken place from 1927 to the end of 1930 were astonishing. One used to date all events in Russia from the Revolution, and time was reckoned as ante-revolutionary and post-revolutionary. To-day one dates time in the Soviet Union from before and after the beginning of the Five-Year Plan.[4]

The abandonment of the NEP in favour of the First Five Year Plan was by the very nature of the two polices to have a profound effect on the operation of private market actors within the Soviet Union. Indeed, unlike the NEP, which had been tolerant, and even inviting, of foreign investment,[5] with the adoption of the First Five Year Plan this invitation was soon set to expire. There is hardly a better illustration of this shifting landscape than the fact that, of the many foreign concessionaries that had been operating in the Soviet Union when the First Five Year Plan was adopted, at the outset of World War II there were none left.[6] In the words of Knickerbocker, the concessionaries were 'very effectively induced to leave'.[7]

One of the many foreign concessionaires whose fortunes in the Soviet Union would change with the change in policy from the NEP to the First Five

---

the New Economic Policy: *A Middle Way?*' (1997) 2(1) The Independent Review 79, 80; V N Bandera, 'The New Economic Policy (NEP) as an Economic System' (1963) 71(3) Journal of Political Economy 265, 267–268; Mark Harrison, 'Why Did NEP Fail?' (1980) 16(2) Economics of Planning 57; Gatrell (n 1) 390–391.

3 Shearer (n 1) 199.

4 H R Knickerbocker, 'The Soviet Five-Year Plan' (1931) 10(4) International Affairs (Royal Institute of International Affairs 1931–1939) 433.

5 Ibid 451; John P McKay, 'Foreign Enterprise in Russian and Soviet Industry: A Long Term Perspective' (1974) 48(3) The Business History Review 336, 350; Jon Lundesgaard and Victoria V Tevlina, 'Profit under the Soviets: Timber Concessions, Western Interests and the Monetary Reforms under NEP' (2021) 34(1) Revolutionary Russia 71; Bean (n 2) 80–81.

6 See Arthur Nussbaum, 'The Arbitration between Lena Goldfields Ltd and the Soviet Government' (1950) 36 Cornell Law Quarterly 31, 32; VV Veeder, 'The *Lena Goldfields* Arbitration: The Historical Roots of Three Ideas' (1998) 47 ICLQ 747, 761.

7 Knickerbocker (n 4) 457.

Year Plan was the Lena Goldfields company. Lena Goldfields was an English enterprise that had operated on Soviet Union soil since the beginning of the 20th century.[8] After having had its mining properties expropriated following the October Revolution, Lena returned to the country during the NEP and was awarded a comprehensive long-term mining concession (as part of which it had to forego its compensation claims toward the Soviet government for the post-revolution expropriations), which has been described as 'the most important foreign concession granted by the Soviet Union'.[9] While the workings of Lena Goldfields in the USSR were not without difficulty during the NEP, the company had in its first three years of operating the concession turned a profit. With the adoption of the First Five Year Plan, however, the company's position became increasingly difficult, as it was exposed to harassment from the government, including the raiding of its offices by secret police and the detainment of its staff. Eventually, Lena Goldfields deemed its position untenable and decided to make use of the arbitration clause contained in the concession. Notably, when doing so, Lena Goldfields informed the USSR government that it would submit to the tribunal the question of whether '*changes of legislation and economic policy* and administrative practice and the attitude of the government have created for Lena Goldfields undue difficulties and interference and in fact the impossibility as regards performing its part of the concession agreement', as well as of the compensation that it was due as a result.[10] From the outset, then, the mandate for the tribunal, as formulated by Lena Goldfields, was to assess whether the Soviet Union's change in policy, and the implementation thereof, was to be accompanied by compensation to the company. This is a task that the tribunal (or at least what remained of it following the withdrawal of the Soviet Union's arbitrator)[11] did not shy away from.

In its award, the tribunal discussed the Soviet Union's shift in policy from the NEP to the First Five Year Plan, as well as the resulting consequences for Lena Goldfields' operations, at length:

> In the year 1925, when Lena entered into the Concession Agreement, the policy of the Russian Government was to encourage the entrance into Russia of commercial and industrial enterprises conducted on ordinary individualistic lines as so-called "capitalist" concerns, in order

8 Veeder (n 6) 756–762.

9 Ibid 748.

10 Evsey S Rashba, 'Settlement of Disputes in Commercial Dealings with the Soviet Union' (1945) 45(4) Columbia Law Review 530, 539. Emphasis added.

11 See Veeder (n 6) 773–780.

to encourage development and promote employment in the U.S.S.R. This was what was then known as "the New Economic Policy."

Lena was a concern of the kind; and *the Court finds as a fact that if this policy had been continued* and if the Concession Agreement had been carried out by the Government in accordance with its true meaning – which inter alia implied and demanded a continuance of that policy, at least towards Lena – *the company would have encountered no insuperable difficulties up to the present time*, would have had credit to obtain all necessary financial assistance in the great money centres of the world and would in fact have been by now far advanced on the road to very great prosperity.

(...)

But by the autumn of 1929 a radically different policy had been adopted by the Government – the so-called "Five-Year Plan" – which meant the development of the U.S.S.R. and of all its industries, commerce, banking, agriculture, transport, and indeed its whole economic life on purely Communistic principles, and brought with it a bitter class war against capitalistic enterprise and everyone connected with such enterprise. With the "Five-Year Plan" a capitalistic concern like Lena, conducting its manifold enterprises on ordinary commercial and individualist lines, was radically incongruous, however obedient it might be to the laws of the U.S.S.R., or however purely commercial and non-political it might be in its behaviour, as the Court finds that Lena in fact was.

(...)

This complete reversal in 1929 of the official policy of 1925 towards Lena necessarily meant, when measured in terms of contractual obligation, *the breach by the Government of many of the fundamental provisions*, express and implied, *of the Concession Agreement*. Open markets ceased to exist. The Government became the only buyer of the company's production. The Government became the only seller of the company's supplies – and Lena had under the contract inter alia to feed and clothe all its employees and workmen. Difficulties with labour organizations and authorities became incessant and overpowering, and Lena's workmen became in the words of its counsel "untouchables." Banking and exchange facilities were denied it. Difficulties with Government departments and local authorities multiplied in intensity. *The end was inevitable* (...).[12]

---

12 *Lena Goldfields, Ltd v USSR*, Award (2 September 1930), reproduced in Nussbaum (n 6) 42, 46–47. Emphases added.

Not only, thus, did the tribunal feel comfortable discussing the policy choices of the Soviet government, but it went as far as to hold that, because of the underlying policy framework existing at the time when the concession was concluded and the concession's true meaning as understood by the tribunal, the Soviet Union had been obliged to continue the NEP toward (at least) Lena Goldfields. The reversal of this policy that followed instead, for the tribunal necessarily implied a breach of the concession, the end of which the tribunal deemed inevitable once the Soviet Union had forgone (the relatively) peaceful co-existence between socialism and the market economy in favour of the unbridled supremacy of socialism. After then recounting the manner in which this policy shift materialised into concrete breaches of the concession by the Soviet government, the tribunal awarded Lena just short of £13 million (present-day value of between approximately £800 million and £6 billion[13]) as compensation.[14] Through the tribunal's award, the Soviet Union's choice to govern by pursuing a purer brand of socialism was thus coupled with steep financial consequences; in other words, the tribunal's award purported to, if not wholly determine, then at least influence to a non-negligible extent, the policy cost of the Soviet Union's aforementioned departure from the NEP in favour of the First Five Year Plan.

The *Lena Goldfields v. USSR* arbitration is one of the best remembered and most influential historical ISAs, and indeed one that carries with itself the most symbolic value. In his incredibly vivid and thorough account of the arbitration, VV Veeder has hailed the *Lena Goldfields v. USSR* arbitration as 'unusual by any measures' and innovative in many respects.[15] It might thus be tempting, indeed even intuitive, to extrapolate such characterisations of the *Lena Goldfields v. USSR* arbitration so as to include also the tribunal's aforementioned engagement with the Soviet Union's policy choices, as well as its consequential influence on the costs associated with such choices, and assume that the *Lena Goldfields v. USSR* award was a pioneer in this respect as well. As Chapter 2 already might have foreshadowed, however, this was hardly so. Indeed, what perhaps stands out the most about the *Lena Goldfields v. USSR* award in terms of its interaction with the cost of governance is just how this particular aspect of the award does *not* stand out within the broader context of other historical ISAs, both those that preceded it and those that followed. This, of course, serves not as an indictment against the *Lena Goldfields v. USSR* arbitration or its well-deserved stature among the most recognisable historical ISAs, but rather

13 On why the present-day value is expressed through such a broad range, see n 17 below.
14 *Lena Goldfields v USSR* (n 12) 52.
15 Veeder (n 6) 747–749.

as an illustration of historical ISA's deeply rooted intertwinement with the process of determining the cost of governance.

In fact, the historical record is so profuse with examples of ISA tribunals influencing through their awards the costs of states' governance decisions, that it would be impossible to recount all of them in much detail in a single chapter. For this reason, the focus throughout the Chapter is on the historical ISAs that have thus far remained underexplored yet which still faithfully convey the *zeitgeist* of such practice. Even though all of these cases advance the same overall argument – that historical ISA was a recurring component in determining the cost of governance – they each tell their own unique stories that help elucidate different aspects of the phenomenon.

Without implying that such a categorisation is exhaustive, the Chapter groups the seven cases that are discussed in-depth into three categories according to the observed modalities through which they operated to influence the cost of governance. The first subset of cases comprises historical ISAs that revolved around disputes relating to public debt, and which resultantly played an important role in determining the cost of the underlying borrowing by states (2). The next grouping consist of a line of cases that highlight how historical ISA was utilised as an instrument for determining the ultimate cost of states' takeover of investor property and, by association, also of the underlying governance choices (3). The final category of cases concerns historical ISAs in which liability was imposed upon states for non-compliance with obligations for reasons that bore (at least an alleged) connection to, or were a direct result of, the implementation of certain governmental policies (4). This portrayal of the modalities through which historical ISA was involved in establishing the cost of governance is then complemented by a contextualisation of the depicted cases against the broader backdrop of historical ISAs of similar ilk. What this exercise reveals is that the substantial monetary awards that were handed down in the examined cases in relation to the states' conduct of official business were not atypical outliers. The historical record moreover suggests that the impact of these sizeable awards was often such that it not only posed a significant financial burden for the affected states, but that it even carried with itself the potential to considerably impact their capacity to conduct their official business (5). As a result, through whichever aforementioned modality this may have been expressed, historical ISA thus reveals itself as a recurrent component in determining the cost of governance in a manner that entailed significant potential implications for the states involved (6).

Before proceeding, however, a minor clarification is in order regarding the methodology through which the monetary sums referred to throughout the Chapter (and the remainder of the book) are converted to present-day value. Namely, as the Chapter deals with monetary awards that span more than a century, referencing just the absolute amount contained in any given award would fail to properly convey its true value and would in most instances even be grossly misleading – indeed, many of the awards, especially those dating back to the 19th or early 20th century, might at face value appear to the present-day reader as trivial in terms of monetary value. In their time, however, they were anything but. In order to properly express the relative value of these historical awards in terms of present-day value, the Chapter relies on a tool for comparing the relative worth of money over time – MeasuringWorth.com[16] – that has been developed by academics engaged with economic history at reputable institutions. Notably, because the true relative worth of money depends on numerous economic variables, the tool does not provide a singular answer when comparing worth over time,[17] but rather offers a number of different values that might best fit different factual contexts. Because of the context-specific character of these values, the present-day relative worth of the historical monetary awards is not expressed in the Chapter through any singular amount, but rather through a range of possible values delimited by the lowest and highest of the arrived at values (which may, and often do, diverge significantly). While these ranges might not convey historical monetary value with the exactitude that one would ideally prefer, they nonetheless for present purposes suffice to situate the historical monetary awards within the appropriate referential system for the present-day reader.

2 Deciding on Matters Relating to Public Debt

One manner in which historical ISA played an important part in determining the financial implications of states' conduct of governance was by deciding on matters involving public debt. Historically, states have regularly resorted to borrowing from private lenders in order to finance projects of public importance or implement policy decisions. As early as the late 19th century, and with increased frequency in the first part of the 20th century, such borrowing arrangements between states and private lenders are known to have included

---

16 See <https://www.measuringworth.com/aboutus.php> accessed 27 September 2024.

17 For an explanation of the methodology employed by the tool, see Samuel H Williamson and Louis P Cain, 'Defining Measures of Worth: Most are Better than the CPI' (*Measuring-Worth*, 2022) <www.measuringworth.com/defining_measures_of_worth.php> accessed 27 September 2024.

arbitration clauses.[18] The presence of arbitration clauses in public debt instruments notwithstanding, it appears that the historical record is less profuse with actual public-debt-related ISAs from the period; this has prompted some, like Weidemaier, to hypothesise that arbitration clauses were included in public debt instruments not so much out of the expectation that they would materialise into a meaningful remedy in case of dispute, but rather as a signal that the borrowers' home state might intervene, or even as an inducement for it to do so.[19] Irrespective of the credence that this hypothesis may hold, historical ISAs relating to public debt are known to have in fact occurred (which was undoubtedly the case also because the presence of an arbitration clause was not a *conditio sine qua non* for an ISA to take place).

A number of the better documented such historical ISAs – *Losinger v. Yugoslavia*,[20] *Greece v. Socobelge*[21] and SEEE *v. Yugoslavia*[22] – concerned disputes over public debt that was not of a general issuance, but which had instead been tied in with particular infrastructural projects through the issuance of debt instruments to the specifically concerned investors. Records can also be found, although much less detailed, of at least several other historical ISAs involving public debt.[23] To the aforementioned can be added also the two cases that are

---

18 Michael Waibel, *Sovereign Defaults before International Courts and Tribunals* (CUP 2011) 157–162; W Mark C Weidemaier, 'Contracting for State Intervention: The Origins of Sovereign Debt Arbitration' (2010) 73 Law & Contemp Probs 335, 342–344; Edwin Borchard, *State Insolvency and Foreign Bondholders: General Principles*, vol 1 (Beard Books 2000) 36–41. See also G R Delaume, 'Jurisdiction of Courts and International Loans: A Study of Lenders' Practice' (1957) 6 The American Journal of Comparative Law 189, 192.

19 Weidemaier (n 18) 345–355.

20 *Losinger & cie SA and 'Kompass' Allgemeine Kredit- und Garantie-Bank v The Kingdom of Yugoslavia*, Award (31 October 1934) (*Losinger I*), reproduced in *The Losinger & Co Case (Switzerland v Yugoslavia)* PCIJ Rep Series C No 78 at 54.

21 *The Government of Greece v Sociéte Commerciale de Belgique (Socobelge)*, Award (3 January 1936) (*Socobelge I*), reproduced in *The 'Société commerciale de Belgique' (Belgium v Greece)* PCIJ Rep Series C No 87 at 36; *The Government of Greece v Sociéte Commerciale de Belgique (Socobelge)*, Award (25 July 1936) (*Socobelge II*), reproduced in *The 'Société commerciale de Belgique' (Belgium v Greece)* PCIJ Rep Series C No 87 at 44.

22 *La Société Européenne d'Etudes et d'Entreprises* (SEEE) *v The Popular Federative Republic of Yugoslavia* (1959) 86 Journal du Droit International 1075.

23 See eg League of Nations, 'Report of the Committee for the Study of International Loan Contracts' (12 May 1939) Official No C.145.M.93.1939.II.A. para 86 (describing a 1930s arbitration of a dispute between Bulgaria and the trustees of the 1928 Bulgarian Stabilisation Loan; the arbitrator's award is housed at the United Nations Archives at Geneva: R4585/10C/27028/2055); Corporation of Foreign Bondholders, 'Twelfth Annual General Report of the Council of the Corporation of Foreign Bondholders' (Wertheimer, Lea & Co 1885) 123–125 (mentioning a dispute between Romania and the trustees of the Romanian government iron bridges certificates decided by a 'Court of Arbitrage'); Corporation of

discussed in the remainder of this section, *Hambros and Lazard v. Romanian Monopolies Institute* and *Peru v. Peruvian Corporation*, both of which appear to have remained underexplored despite their existence being well documented.

Although it may be difficult to discern with exactitude how frequently historical ISAs relating to public debt occurred, what is certain is that they did occur; and when they did occur, they were an important ingredient in determining the actual cost of the underlying public borrowing. The reason for this was the fact that, while the cost of the decision to issue public debt may in principle have been determined beforehand either solely by the state involved or through the joint will of the two sides participating in the investor-state relationship, once disagreement arose over the interpretation of the underlying terms under which the funds were borrowed, or problems with compliance occurred, such envisioned cost necessitated concretisation. Historical ISA was known to facilitate such concretisation, thus indirectly also playing a part in ascertaining the ultimate cost of public borrowing.

The remainder of the section tells the stories of two historical ISAs that illustrate the point. The first is a 1930s arbitration that concerned the conditions for the performance of payment obligations under a large stabilisation loan taken out by the Romanian Monopolies Institute (2.1). The second dates back even further – to the early 20th century, and involves the interpretation of an important agreement for the cancellation of Peru's outstanding public debt (2.2).

2.1 *Hambros and Lazard v Romanian Monopolies Institute*

The *Hambros and Lazard v. Romanian Monopolies Institute* arbitration arose out of a dispute relating to the Romanian Stabilisation Loan of 1929. While the arbitration itself was held shortly before World War II, its backstory dates back to the 1920s, when the Romanian economy was still looking to regain its footing

Foreign Bondholders, 'Twenty-Eight Annual General Report of the Council of the Corporation of Foreign Bondholders' (Wertheimer, Lea & Co 1901) 404 (referencing a dispute between the Ottoman Council of the Debt and the Cretan government referred to the ambassadors of the four mediating powers for arbitration); Corporation of Foreign Bondholders, 'Thirtieth Annual General Report of the Council of the Corporation of Foreign Bondholders' (Wertheimer, Lea & Co 1903) 16 and 361–364 (describing a dispute over the increase of a bond interest rate between Turkey and the Ottoman Debt Council referred to arbitration and eventually to the Lord Chief Justice of England as umpire); Corporation of Foreign Bondholders, 'Fifty-Fourth Annual General Report of the Council of the Corporation of Foreign Bondholders' (Williams, Lea & Co) 18 and 133 (referring to a dispute between Colombia and the Council concerning Colombia's consolidated external debt of 1896 that was resolved by arbitration).

following World War I.[24] A particularly problematic aspect in this endeavour was Romania's national currency, the leu, which had been rather volatile and had lost considerable value during the first post-war decade.[25] Romania ultimately decided to stabilize the leu, which was to be achieved by taking out a loan on the international markets. For this purpose, and with the help of fiscal agents from the US, the UK and France, bonds were issued in three currencies (the US dollar, the pound sterling and the French franc), with a total value of more than $100 million (present-day value between more than $1 billion and almost $20 billion).[26]

Notably, the bonds for the loan were issued not by the Romanian government itself, but by the Kingdom of Romania Monopolies Institute, an autonomous institution created specifically for this purpose,[27] which was then to turn over the proceeds from the loan to the Romanian government as part of the compensation for the granting to it by the state of a number of state monopolies.[28] The Government of Romania, however, did appear as guarantor for the

---

24 Elisabeta Blejan, Brîndușa Costache and Adriana Aloman, 'The National Bank of Romania during The Great Depression: 1929–1933' (Fourth Conference of Southeast Europe Monetary History Network (SEEMHN), Belgrade, 27–28 March 2009) 2–3 <https://www.nbs.rs/export/sites/NBS_site/documents/publikacije/konferencije/seemhn_conf/SEEMHN_14_Rumunija.pdf> accessed 27 September 2024; Raphael Chiappini and others, 'Romania's Unsustainable Stabilization: 1929–1933' (66th Annual Congress of the French Economic Association, Nice, 19–21 June 2017) 3–4 <https://afse2017.sciencesconf.org/143369/chiappini_costache_torre_tosi_20feb.pdf> accessed 27 September 2024; Dominique Torre and Elise Tosi, 'Charles Rist and the French Missions in Romania 1929–1933: Why the "Money Doctors" Failed?' (Fourth Conference of Southeast Europe Monetary History Network (SEEMHN), Belgrade, 27–28 March 2009) 3–5 <https://www.nbs.rs/export/sites/NBS_site/documents/publikacije/konferencije/seemhn_conf/SEEMHN_5_Torre_Tosi.pdf> accessed 27 September 2024.

25 Chiappini and others (n 24) 3.

26 Ibid 6; Torre and Tosi (n 24) 5; Blejan, Costache and Aloman (n 24) 3–4; Rudolf Nötel, 'International Capital Movements and Finance in Eastern Europe 1919–1949' (1974) 61(1) VSWG: Vierteljahrschrift für Sozial- und Wirtschaftsgeschichte 65, 83. All documents relating to the loan are available in a booklet published by the Romanian Ministry of Finance titled 'I: The Monetary Law. II: A Law for Creating the Kingdom of Roumania Autonomous Monopoly Institute' (Government Press 1929) (hereinafter: The Loan Documents), which can be found in the personal archives of the sole arbitrator in the arbitration, GWJ Bruins. See Nationaal Archief, Den Haag, Collection 341 Prof mr dr GWJ Bruins, Supplement 1981, 1929–1939, access number 2.21.191.02, inventory number 4.

27 See A Law for Creating the Kingdom of Roumania Autonomous Monopolies Institute, Schedule A: Statutes of Kingdom of Roumania Monopolies Institute (Created by the Law of February 7, 1929) art 2 in The Loan Documents (n 26) 47.

28 Monetary Law, Schedule A: Program of the Roumanian Government for Monetary Stabilization and Economic Development in The Loan Documents (n 26) 20–21; A Law for

loan – and did so 'absolutely and unconditionally' in the capacity of 'a primary obligor and not as a surety merely'.[29] In addition to stabilising the leu, the loan was also to be used for other public-interest-related purposes, such as the reorganisation of the National Bank of Romania and its liquidity, the maintaining of a budgetary equilibrium and the reorganisation and modernisation of the country's railways.[30]

For a brief period following the loan, the stabilisation programme was an apparent success;[31] the situation, however, soon took a turn for the worse for Romania. Prompted by both external[32] and internal forces,[33] before long the Romanian economy found itself in a significant slump, resulting not only in a sizeable economic downturn[34] but also in the depletion of the country's foreign exchange reserves.[35] As a consequence, servicing the repayment of the Stabilisation Loan of 1929 (as well as Romania's other outstanding public debts) became increasingly difficult. While considerable efforts were made in order to ensure that the foreign currency needed for servicing the external debt could be obtained, these efforts were ultimately unsuccessful as problems only accumulated.[36] Eventually, in the summer of 1933, it became apparent that the debt could no longer be serviced under existing conditions and payments under the Stabilisation Loan of 1929 were ceased. A series of renegotiations

---

Creating the Kingdom of Roumania Autonomous Monopolies Institute art 2 in The Loan Documents (n 26) 41.

29 See specimen of Monopolies Institute £100 bond (NL-HaNA, Bruins suppl, 2.21.191.02, inv. nr. 4); A Law for Creating the Kingdom of Roumania Autonomous Monopolies Institute, Schedule F: Guarantee Contract of February 2nd 1929 in The Loan Documents (n 26) 109; *Hambros Bank Limited and Lazard Brothers and Co Limited v Kingdom of Roumania Monopolies Institute*, Award (10 June 1937) (NL-HaNA, Bruins suppl, 2.21.191.02, inv.nr. 1) 11.

30 Program for Monetary Stabilization and Economic Development (n 28). See also Chiappini and others (n 24) 6.

31 Chiappini and others (n 24) 6.

32 Torre and Tosi (n 24) 3 and 12–13; Kim Oosterlinck and Loredana Ureche-Rangau, 'Interwar Romanian Sovereign Bonds: the Impact of Diplomacy, Politics and the Economy' (2012) 19(2) Financial History Review 219, 230; George Virgil Stoenescu and others, 'Foreign Exchange Regime in Romania between 1929 and 1939' in Peter Mooslechner and Ernest Gnan (eds), *Proceedings of OeNB Workshops No 13: The Experience of Exchange Rate Regimes in Southeastern Europe in a Historical and Comparative Perspective: Second Conference of the South-Eastern European Monetary History Network* (Oesterreichische Nationalbank 2008) 244, 245–247; Blejan, Costache and Aloman (n 24) 5, 19–26.

33 Blejan, Costache and Aloman (n 24) 5; Chiappini and others (n 24) 10–11; Torre and Tosi (n 24) 9–12.

34 The country's public revenue was reduced by almost 40% within a few years. See Blejan, Costache and Aloman (n 24) 25.

35 Ibid 11–13.

36 Ibid 16–18; Stoenescu and others (n 32) 247–253.

with creditors and the partial servicing of the loans ensued, only for the break-out of World War II to lead to a definite suspension of payments.[37]

It was against this background that the dispute between Hambros Bank Ltd and Lazard Brothers and Co Ltd, the fiscal agents for the UK tranche of the Stabilisation Loan of 1929, and the Monopolies Institute arose. The difference in opinion between the two sides came about in the wake of currency fluctuations that occurred after the abandonment of the gold standard following the Great Depression. Namely, under the conditions of the loan, the UK bonds were payable in either pound sterling in London or US gold coin in New York at a fixed rate.[38] Following the UK's departure from the gold standard in 1931,[39] the UK fiscal agents requested the Monopolies Institute to allow for the bondholders to receive payment as if they had presented the bonds in New York but to receive payment in the pound sterling equivalent. Arguing that such coupons were likely entirely to be presented for payment in dollars due to the devaluation of the UK currency, the fiscal agents felt that this solution would be much more convenient yet would not compromise the Institute's financial interests.[40] While the Monopolies Institute complied with the request, it explicitly noted that, in so doing, it was not creating a precedent.[41] This arrangement then continued until the US government also abandoned the gold standard with respect to the dollar,[42] which expectedly led to a disagreement over how the next payment was going to be effected. As the US dollars obtained in advance by the Monopolies Institute were no longer sufficient to cover the gold value of the coupons, the Monopolies Institute was only prepared to pay the paper (and not the gold) dollar value;[43] for their part,

37 Torre and Tosi (n 24) 7; Nötel (n 26) 94; Elisabeta Blejan, Brîndușa Costache and Adriana Iarovici, 'International Reserves of the National Bank of Romania 1920–1944' (December 2006) 9 <https://bnro.ro/Studies-3215.aspx> accessed 27 September 2024; Oosterlinck and Ureche-Rangau (n 32) 230–231; Blejan, Costache and Aloman (n 24) 18.

38 *Hambros and Lazard v Roumania Monopolies Institute* (n 29) 9–10. For the original bond, see n 29.

39 Blejan, Costache and Iarovici (n 37) 10; Blejan, Costache and Aloman (n 24) 11.

40 Letter (unsigned) to Direction Generale, Caisse Autonome des Monopoles du Royaume de Roumanie (22 December 1931) (NL-HaNA, Bruins suppl, 2.21.191.02, inv.nr. 4).

41 Copy of Letter from Caisse Autonome des Monopoles du Royaume de Roumanie to Lazard Brothers and Co Ltd (16 January 1932) (NL-HaNA, Bruins suppl, 2.21.191.02, inv.nr. 4).

42 *Hambros and Lazard v Roumania Monopolies Institute* (n 29) 18–19; Blejan, Costache and Iarovici (n 37) 10; Blejan, Costache and Aloman (n 24) 11.

43 'Copy of Wire Received From Casa Monopol Statescu, Bucarest' (21 June 1933) (NL-HaNA, Bruins suppl, 2.21.191.02, inv.nr. 4); Translation of 'Notice' by the Monopolies Institute (NL-HaNA, Bruins suppl, 2.21.191.02, inv.nr. 4).

the fiscal agents maintained that the obligation under the loan was to pay in gold dollars.[44]

Since the two sides could not resolve the stand-off, in the summer of 1934 they agreed to refer the matter to arbitration.[45] Per the terms of their agreement to submit the dispute to arbitration, the arbitrator was to be chosen jointly by the governors of the Bank of England and the National Bank of Romania.[46] The two governors selected Dutch financial expert Gijsbert Weijer Jan Bruins, who accepted the appointment.[47] Bruins, whose diverse professional background included not only experience in academia and banking, but also giving economics lessons to Queen Wilhelmina, was at the time a royal commissioner at the Dutch central bank (De Nederlandsche Bank); after World War II, he would go on to take up a position with the International Monetary Fund.[48]

Prior to delving into the proceedings before the arbitrator, however, an explanation is in order as to why the arbitration between the UK fiscal agents and the Monopolies Institute is treated here as an ISA. Namely, the law by which the Monopolies Institute was created explicitly provided that it was 'a legally independent institution, enjoying full civil personality and financial autonomy', while its operations were to be deemed 'commercial' and it was to 'enjoy all the rights and powers of commercial companies'.[49] Indeed, it was on this account that the arbitrator himself, while acknowledging the close relationship between the Monopolies Institute and the Romanian state, when arriving at the conclusion to disregard Romanian law, had in his award taken the position that the Stabilisation Loan of 1929 was not a 'direct Government loan'.[50] Be that as it may, the same law that created the Monopolies

44 'Copy of Wire Sent to "Bancanat" Bucarest' (16 June 1933) (NL-HaNA, Bruins suppl, 2.21.191.02, inv.nr. 4); 'Copy of Wire Sent to Caisse Monopoles, Bucarest' (23 June 1933) (NL-HaNA, Bruins suppl, 2.21.191.02, inv.nr. 4).

45 Letter (unsigned) to MC Norman (6 September 1934) (NL-HaNA, Bruins suppl, 2.21.191.02, inv.nr. 4).

46 Ibid.

47 Letter from Norman to GWJ Bruins (2 October 1934) (NL-HaNA, Bruins suppl, 2.21.191.02, inv.nr. 3); Letter (unsigned) to Montagu C Norman (5 October 1934) (NL-HaNA, Bruins suppl, 2.21.191.02, inv.nr. 3); Letter from Norman to GWJ Bruins (10 October 1934) (NL-HaNA, Bruins suppl, 2.21.191.02, inv.nr. 3); Copy of Letter from M Norman to Hambros Bank Ltd and Lazard Bros and Co Ltd (10 October 1934) (NL-HaNA, Bruins suppl, 2.21.191.02, inv. nr. 4).

48 MHJ Dullaart, 'Bruins, Gijsbert Weijer Jan (1883–1948)' (*Biografisch Woordenboek van Nederland*, 12 November 2013) <http://resources.huygens.knaw.nl/bwn1880-2000/lemmata/bwn2/bruins> accessed 27 September 2024.

49 See A Law for Creating the Monopolies Institute (n 28) art 1.

50 See *Hambros and Lazard v Roumania Monopolies Institute* (n 29) 14–15.

Institute nonetheless also provided that the Monopolies Institute was created in 'the interest of the monetary stabilisation and the economic development of the State' and that its bonds were to 'enjoy all the privileges and exemptions of public loans of the State'.[51] In addition, the Monopolies Institute's governing body was almost entirely either directly appointed by, or chosen on the proposal of, state organs.[52] Finally, and perhaps most importantly, as the Romanian state had guaranteed the loan 'absolutely and unconditionally' as 'a primary obligor' (see n 29), it was also ultimately directly concerned with the potential (non-)repayment of the loan. Thus, both the rationale behind the loan and the control over the body that had formally taken it out and that was a party to the arbitration, as well as the ultimate financial responsibility, were inextricably linked to the Romanian state; therefore, the Monopolies Institute seems to have in actuality acted merely as an agent, or surrogate, for the Romanian state in taking out the loan, rather than being a truly independent entity. For these reasons, and notwithstanding the fact that it was only the Monopolies Institute that was formally a party to the arbitration or the arbitrator's abovementioned comments (which, in any event, were made in the specific context of determining the applicable law), this arbitration is for present purposes treated as an ISA.[53]

As for the arbitration itself, it centred on a question of principled interpretation of the manner in which the obligations under the loan were to be performed rather than on any specific claims submitted by each side, and the arbitrator's decision, as is discussed more comprehensively below, was intended by the parties to serve as instructive guidance in their future relationship. The question that the UK fiscal agents and the Monopolies Institute jointly submitted to Bruins was formulated as follows:

> Are principal of and interest on the sterling tranche of the Stabilization Loan 1929 (as regards interest, as from the coupon due on February 1st 1934) to be paid on a gold basis in view of the devaluation of the pound sterling and of the United States dollar and taking into account the terms of the documents of the loan?[54]

---

51 See A Law for Creating the Monopolies Institute (n 28) arts 1 and 8; Statutes of the Monopolies Institute (n 27) art 1.

52 See Statutes of the Monopolies Institute (n 27) art 4.

53 See also Blejan, Costache and Aloman (n 24) 4 (describing the Stabilisation Loan of 1929 as having been taken by the Romanian government through the agency of the Monopolies Institute).

54 *Hambros and Lazard v Roumania Monopolies Institute* (n 29) 1.

During the proceedings,[55] which included hearings at the Peace Palace in The Hague,[56] the UK fiscal agents argued that the loan contract was governed by English law and that the conditions of the loan were such that the Monopolies Institute was obliged to repay it in sterling on a gold basis (despite there being no mention of gold in the loan with respect to the pound sterling). The applicants further submitted that the payment option in dollars in New York contained a gold value clause, so that the bondholders were entitled at the time to payment of an amount equivalent at that time to the number of gold dollars specified in the coupon in question. In their view, the situation would not have been any different even if the arbitrator opted for American law as being applicable.[57]

On the other hand, the Monopolies Institute insisted that its relationship with the bondholders was governed by the loan prospectus and that neither this document nor the loan contract itself had contained a gold clause with respect to either pounds sterling or US dollars. Alternatively, the Monopolies Institute argued that the payment option in New York was in any event governed by American law, pursuant to which such an option would have been invalidated.[58]

Bruins handed down his award in The Hague suburb of Wassenaar on 10 June 1937. His decision is perhaps above all characterised by a meticulous private international law (or conflict of laws) analysis as to the proper law(s) applicable to the parties' relations, which permeates the award throughout. Of equal, indeed critical, importance was the manner in which Bruins interpreted, and eventually gave effect to, mandatory norms of US law relating to the country's

---

55 Notably, the Monopolies Institute was represented in the arbitration by Professor Gaston Jeze, who had been an important contributor to Romania's stabilisation programme. See Torre and Tosi (n 24) 5; Chiappini and others (n 24) 6. In addition to having had his work cited in several historical ISA awards, Jeze is known to have acted as counsel in at least one other historical ISA – *Rialet v Ethiopia* (see ch 2). Meanwhile, the UK fiscal agents were, amongst others, represented by the law firm Slaughter and May, which appears to be the first instance of a major law firm (if it could then have been described as such) taking part in an ISA. See *Hambros and Lazard v Roumania Monopolies Institute* (n 29) 2.

56 Copy of Letter from G Bruins to Hambros Bank Ltd and Lazard Brothers and Co Ltd (24 February 1937) (NL-HaNA, Bruins suppl, 2.21.191.02, inv.nr. 3); Copy of Letter from G Bruins to JPA Francois (16 February 1937) (NL-HaNA, Bruins suppl, 2.21.191.02, inv.nr. 3); Letter from JPA Francois to GWJ Bruins (23 February 1937) (NL-HaNA, Bruins suppl, 2.21.191.02, inv.nr. 3); Copy of Letter from G Bruins to JPA Francois (30 June 1937) (NL-HaNA, Bruins suppl, 2.21.191.02, inv.nr. 3).

57 *Hambros and Lazard v Roumania Monopolies Institute* (n 29) 2–3.

58 Ibid 3. The parties' full argumentation in the proceedings is available in NL-HaNA, Bruins suppl, 2.21.191.02, inv.nr. 2.

monetary policy. Notably, in dealing with this matter, Bruins analysed not only how the central issue of the (in)validity of the gold clause with respect to the dollar had been dealt with by US courts, but also by the decisions of a number of courts of other countries that the parties had invoked during the proceedings. As is explained below, the manner in which Bruins addressed these two pivotal issues ultimately led him to rule in favour of the Monopolies Institute.

In the award, Bruins first addressed the question – the law applicable to the loan contract between the Monopolies Institute and the bondholders – the determination of which would channel the analysis that followed in the remainder of the award. As the parties to the loan contract had made no direct or indirect choice of law, Bruins turned to what he termed as 'general principles of Conflict of Laws'. Since these principles were, in his view, in the end part and parcel of a certain national law, the law of the country to which they alluded as the law governing the contract needed itself to confirm the result arrived at. The arbitrator also noted that not all parts of the contract needed necessarily to be governed by the same law. As the overwhelming majority of aspects of the loan had strong connections to England,[59] he concluded that the proper law of the loan contract as such was English law, which was also in his view confirmed by English law itself. With respect to the option to request payment in New York in US dollars, however, the arbitrator felt that the *lex loci solutionis* principle mandated that this aspect be first and foremost examined pursuant to American law, although he felt obliged to address this matter under English law as well.[60]

Having so found, Bruins then turned to examine the principal obligation under the bonds – payment in sterling in London. None of the documents relating to the loan had any mention of gold insofar payment in sterling was concerned; in the arbitrator's opinion, this was not unintentional, as other currencies mentioned in the loan had been defined as gold currencies. While the applicants had argued that, irrespective of that fact, the circumstances of concluding the loan had been such that the underlying intention had been to contract in gold also in respect of the sterling bonds, the arbitrator was not prepared to read such an important clause into the loan solely based on surrounding circumstances, especially considering that such a clause had been expressly included in the definition of other currencies under the loan.

59 Including that the bonds were called sterling bonds, that they were drawn up in English in the form of typical English bonds and according to the requirements of the London Stock Exchange, and that the principal obligation under the bonds was expressed in sterling and was to be performed in London.

60 *Hambros and Lazard v Roumania Monopolies Institute* (n 29) 12–14.

Accordingly, Bruins concluded that the principal obligation of payment in sterling in London was not to be done on a gold basis.[61]

With respect to the option for payment in dollars in New York, however, the arbitrator's conclusion was different, despite the documents relating to the loan being contradictory on this point – while the loan contract and the offer for sale had made no mention of a gold clause, the coupons attached to the bond and the Loan Agreement (not to be confused with the loan contract)[62] did contain references to gold currency, albeit each in a slightly different manner. As in this particular instance the loan contract had explicitly stipulated that it was subject to the Loan Agreement, the Loan Agreement was to have priority, thus entitling the bondholders to the benefits of its provisions. As a result, Bruins held that the option to pay in dollars in New York did in fact contain a gold clause.[63]

With that in mind, Bruins then – in order to analyse whether such a clause was valid – returned to the question of the law applicable to the option for payment in dollars in New York, assessing the matter according to both American and English law.[64] He arrived at the conclusion that, according to the former, it was American law that governed the option for payment in dollars in New York (without necessarily affecting the law applicable to the loan contract as a whole). The more pressing question, however, was whether the gold clause had remained valid under American law. Namely, following the conclusion of the loan, the US Congress had on 5 June 1933 passed a Joint Resolution that declared all provisions that entitled creditors to request payment in (or on the basis of) gold to be against public policy and provided that such obligations could be discharged through the payment of the nominal amount of the currency valid at the time of payment.[65] As the arbitrator found that, pursuant to American law, the Joint Resolution was applicable even where both of the interested parties were foreign entities and had the effect of rendering gold clauses invalid, he concluded that under American law the option for payment in dollars in New York could be 'discharged dollar for dollar, in any currency

---

61 Ibid 16–19.

62 While the loan contract regulated the relationship between the Monopolies Institute and the bondholders and was reproduced on the bond, the Loan Agreement was concluded between the Monopolies Institute and the fiscal agents for the respective tranches of the loan. For the text of the Loan Agreement, see The Loan Documents (n 26) 59.

63 *Hambros and Lazard v Roumania Monopolies Institute* (n 29) 19–22.

64 See n 60.

65 For the relevant extract from the Joint Resolution, see Arthur Nussbaum, 'Comparative and International Aspects of American Gold Clause Abrogation' (1934) 44(1) The Yale Law Journal 53.

which at the time of payment is legal tender'.[66] After an extensive review of English case law, Bruins found that English law would have led to the same outcome.[67]

Based on the above analysis, Bruins thus answered the question put before him by the parties in the negative – the principal of and the interest on the sterling tranche of the loan was not to be paid on a gold basis.[68]

In so deciding, Bruins assigned a definitive cost, at least in legal terms, to a major policy project of public importance that had been carried out in Romania and that had been financed through a public loan. As World War II soon intervened and led to a definite suspension of loan repayments by Romania,[69] it is not entirely clear whether and to which extent the arbitrator's decision then also translated into actual impact on the cost of the project for Romania. Nonetheless, the parties had at least indicated to the arbitrator that his decision would be treated as authoritative on the matter and complied with – it had been agreed that the Monopolies Institute was to fund the sterling coupons of the loan on a gold basis if the arbitrator's decision was to that effect and the parties were eager to find out his decision as the negotiations on the repayment of the loan had at the time reached a critical juncture.[70] The envisioned effect of the arbitration was thus one that would have had a sizeable impact on the ultimate cost of the loan (and by correlation, on the policies for which the loan was acquired). The potential ramifications in this respect were made all the more consequential not only by the immense size of the underlying loan, but perhaps even more so by the financial situation faced at the time by Romania, which had been forced to default on its debt only a few years prior. Accordingly, irrespective of whether the award was ever acted upon, the *Hambros and Lazard v. Romanian Monopolies Institute* arbitration remains

66 *Hambros and Lazard v Roumania Monopolies Institute* (n 29) 22–29.

67 Ibid 35–46.

68 Ibid 46–47.

69 See n 37. It appears that Romania's outstanding debt from this period was mostly settled through inter-state settlements. See Silviu Cerna, 'Romanian Stabilisation in the 1920s and the Missing Gold Reserves' (conference titled Facing the Crisis and Depression Discussions on Economic Policy and Reforms in Europe during the Interwar Period, Amiens, 21–22 September 2017) 12 <https://www.researchgate.net/publication/320077223_Romanian_Stabilization_at_the_20thies_and_the_missing_gold_reserves_Conferinta_Facing_the_Crisis_and_Depression_Discussions_on_Economic_Policcy_and_Reforms_in_Europe_during_the_Interwar_period_Unversi> accessed 27 September 2024.

70 Letter from R M Kindersley to GWJ Bruins (27 April 1937) (NL-HaNA, Bruins suppl, 2.21.191.02, inv.nr. 3); Letter from Slaughter and May to GWJ Bruins (31 May 1937) (NL-HaNA, Bruins suppl, 2.21.191.02, inv.nr. 3).

illustrative of historical ISA's considerable capacity to influence the cost of governance, both in general and more specifically in relation to public debt.

Yet, gauging the full gravitas of arbitrator Bruins' role in determining the ultimate cost of Romania's governance choices would not be done justice without the proper appreciation of the process that allowed him to do so. Several factors necessitate accentuation in making such an assessment. First, notwithstanding that Bruins' award is characterised by a tenacious legal analysis, the normative framework, both procedural and substantive, within which this analysis was embedded was hardly one that facilitated the precise application of legal categories. As to the procedural side of things, in light of the loan contract being silent regarding the forum to which disputes were to be submitted, Bruins felt that by referring the matter to arbitration the parties had 'not submitted themselves to the forum of a specific country'.[71] The situation was not much different on the substantive front – the parties not having chosen any applicable law(s), and with no forum with rules that would guide him on how to make the choice in the absence of the parties' agreement, Bruins resorted to the vague concept of 'general principles of Conflict of Laws'. By his own account, these were principles that were 'not clearly defined'.[72] Thus, despite the award's intense legalistic flavour, the process through which Bruins arrived at his decision was anything but the mere precise application of the relevant legal categories, instead necessitating choices by Bruins for which the underlying legal framework offered little to no guidance. Equally as important, in arriving at his decision, Bruins went on to interpret and apply mandatory norms of US law relating to monetary public policy – the Joint Resolution of the US Congress – and in doing so appeared to have little hesitation in terms of his capacity to do exactly that. Thus, the *Hambros and Lazard v. Romanian Monopolies Institute* arbitration stands not only as an example of a historical ISA tribunal partaking in the determination of the costs of governance, but as one where this was done through a process wherein the arbitrator, all the while applying mandatory norms of public policy, was allowed considerable manoeuvring space in arriving at his decision.

2.2 *Peru v Peruvian Corporation*

The arbitration over the Romanian Stabilisation Loan was preceded by some three decades by another public-debt-related arbitration, involving a country on the different side of the globe. Unlike the Romanian Stabilisation Loan dispute, however, the *Peru v. Peruvian Corporation* arbitration was tied to public

---

71 *Hambros and Lazard v Roumania Monopolies Institute* (n 29) 13.

72 Ibid.

debt less directly – it did not arise outright out of a dispute over the terms of a public debt contract, but had rather centred around the interpretation of an agreement that had cancelled Peru's outstanding debt toward certain foreign bondholders.

The dispute finds its roots in an extensive period of Peru's sovereign borrowing in the second half of the 19th century. During this time of Peru's newfound economic resurgence fuelled by the country's guano boom, Peru *inter alia* made several bond issues in foreign markets in order to finance the building of railways.[73] The repayment of the bonds was guaranteed by Peru's rich guano deposits, which were at the time perceived as a highly credible form of security.[74] In light of the subsequent decrease in revenues from guano exploitation, however, the debt that had in 1875 swollen to as much as 40% of government revenue had soon proved too much for Peru to service, and the country defaulted on its entire foreign debt in January of 1876.[75] The situation was made all the more complicated by The War of the Pacific that had broken out several years following Peru's default, primarily because Chile had during the war occupied parts of Peruvian territory that had contained most of the guano deposits that were supposed to act as collateral for the servicing of the debt. This territory was later ceded by Peru to Chile through the Treaty of Ancon, which was concluded between the two countries in 1883, ending the war.[76] As a consequence, Chile was also brought into the fold as an interested party.

Following complex and drawn out negotiations that lasted more than a decade (mostly due to Chile's opposition to any agreement between Peru and its creditors that would not absolve Chile of responsibility *vis-à-vis* the bondholders),[77] an agreement was eventually reached between Peru and the holders of bonds to three of the loans (made in 1869, 1870, and 1872). The agreement, which came to be known as The Grace Contract (named after a key figure in the contract negotiations, American merchant with business interests

73 See Rory Miller, 'The Making of the Grace Contract: British Bondholders and the Peruvian Government, 1885–1890' (1976) 8(1) Journal of Latin American Studies 73, 75; Catalina Vizcarra, 'Guano, Credible Commitments, and Sovereign Debt Repayment in Nineteenth-Century Peru' (2009) 69(2) The Journal of Economic History 358, 361–363.

74 Vizcarra (n 73) 373–378.

75 Ibid 365 and 381–383. See also Miller, 'The Making of the Grace Contract' (n 73) 75.

76 Miller, 'The Making of the Grace Contract' (n 73) 77–79.

77 *Government of Peru v The Peruvian Corporation Limited*, English Translation of Memoire for the Peruvian Corporation Limited against the Peruvian Government (2–3 September 1908) (University College London Special Collections: PERUCORP C2/65B/1) 69–70. See also Miller, 'The Making of the Grace Contract' (n 73) 84.

in Peru, Michael P. Grace),[78] restructured the relationship between Peru and the bondholders. Pursuant to the new arrangement, in return for the cancellation of the bonds, Peru had granted the bondholders several concessions, including the right to exploit guano to the amount of up to three million tons.[79] These concessions were to be exploited through a newly established company that was to be incorporated by the bondholders in London – the Peruvian Corporation.[80] The Peruvian Corporation was 'the first main foreign company with a direct involvement in the Peruvian economy'; in the City of London, it was viewed as 'the principal British company operating in Peru', while in Peru it gave rise to criticism from early on.[81] Despite its symbolic importance, however, overall the company was not particularly successful, especially in its early years, in which it appears to have been plagued by poor management.[82]

The signing of The Grace Contract and the incorporation of the Peruvian Corporation had nonetheless failed to put a definitive end to all of the open issues between all of the interested parties,[83] and a number of supplementary arrangements were needed in order to take care of loose ends.[84] The Grace Contract was in consequence eventually put into operation (albeit with imperfect performance on both ends);[85] the relationship between Peru and the Peruvian Corporation, however, remained strained, with various contentious issues arising between the two sides over the years.[86] While the majority of these

78 See Miller, 'The Making of the Grace Contract' (n 73) *passim*. According to Miller, it was ultimately neither Peru nor the bondholders who were the main beneficiaries of the contract, but none other than Michael Grace. See ibid 99–100.

79 See Article 21 of The Grace Contract, reproduced in Memoire for the Peruvian Corporation (n 77) 21–22.

80 For a detailed account on how The Grace Contract came to be, see generally Miller, 'The Making of the Grace Contract' (n 73). The parts of The Grace Contract relevant to the dispute are reproduced in the Memoire for the Peruvian Corporation (n 77) 20–24. See also 'The Grace Contract: The Peruvian Bondholders Claims against Chili' *The New York Times* (New York, 14 January 1890) 2.

81 Rory Miller, 'The Grace Contract, the Peruvian Corporation, and Peruvian History' (1983) 9 Ibero-amerikanisches Archiv 319, 331–333 and 344. While both its proponents and its opponents have compared the Peruvian Corporation to the East India Company, Miller discards such comparisons as unwarranted. See ibid 331.

82 See ibid 335–339 and Miller, 'The Making of the Grace Contract' (n 73) 97–99.

83 Additional problems had arisen due to protests by Peru's other creditors, whose claims had not formed part of the settlement. See Memoire for the Peruvian Corporation (n 77) 36–38.

84 Ibid 38–47.

85 Miller, 'The Grace Contract, the Peruvian Corporation, and Peruvian History' (n 81) 332–333.

86 Ibid 326 and 329.

outstanding issues were, at least for the time being, put to rest by way of a comprehensive agreement between Peru and the Peruvian Corporation in 1907,[87] one of them could not be resolved. In order to settle this remaining issue, the parties concluded a separate agreement, arranging for the matter to be submitted to arbitration.[88] Under the arbitration agreement, the arbitrator was to be the president of the French Court of Cassation, who was to settle the dispute by applying 'the principles of right'.[89] His decision was to be without appeal and was to have the effect of a '*chose jugée*' (i.e. *res judicata*).

Pursuant to the arbitration agreement, the issue in dispute concerned Article 21(2) of The Grace Contract, which had provided that:

> The Government of Peru likewise cedes to the Bondholders the surplus of the 50% of the guano of the Lobos Islands which comes to it, according to the Treaty of Ancon after covering with the proceeds of the said 50%, what Peru owes to Chili for obligations contracted and advances received by the Iglesias administration, and the amount of which, subject to liquidation, shall not exceed 2 million soles.[90]

The controversy between the parties to The Grace Contract regarding this provision stemmed from the fact that, by virtue of the agreements supplementary to The Grace Contract, Chile had, in return for the bondholders denouncing any claims they might have possessed against it, among other things returned the Lobos Islands mentioned in Article 21(2) of The Grace Contract[91] to Peru,[92] so that the exploitation of the guano deposits contained therein could be

87 See ibid 334; Memoire for the Peruvian Corporation (n 77) 48.

88 Memoire for the Peruvian Corporation (n 77) 49.

89 Ibid. While the English translation provided by the Peruvian Corporation used the term 'the principles of right', the Spanish version of the award refers to 'principios de derecho'. See *Government of Peru v The Peruvian Corporation Limited* (1913) 50 Boletin del Ministerio de Relaciones Exteriores (Peru) 144, 148.

90 Reproduced in Memoire for the Peruvian Corporation (n 77) 23. On the background to the Iglesias debt, see *Government of Peru v The Peruvian Corporation Limited*, English Translation of Memoire of the Peruvian Government against the Peruvian Corporation Limited (31 July 1908) (University College London Special Collections: PERUCORP C2/65A) 11–12.

91 Pursuant to the Treaty of Ancon, the Lobos Islands were to be administered by Chile until one million tons of guano had been exploited, upon which they were to be returned to Peru; the proceeds from the exploitation of the islands were to be divided up in equal shares between Peru and its creditors. See Treaty of Ancon Articles IV, IX and X, reproduced in Memoire for the Peruvian Corporation (n 77) 10–11.

92 Protocol of 8 January 1890 between Chile and Peru, reproduced in ibid 27.

passed on to the Peruvian Corporation.[93] The regime established pursuant to the supplementary agreements and the Peruvian Corporation's exploitation of the deposits arising thereunder had seemingly persisted for more than a decade without objection from Peru. The situation, however, ultimately became a contentious matter, as Peru eventually raised a claim that, pursuant to Article 21(2) of The Grace Contract, it was owed money by the Peruvian Corporation on account of the company's exploitation of the Lobos Islands guano deposits.[94] Since the two sides were not able to iron out their disagreement over this issue, it was ultimately designated that an arbitrator was to rule on 'the interpretation and effects of the second part of article 21 of the Contract between the Supreme Government and the Bondholders'.[95] As framed in the arbitration agreement, the matter put before the arbitrator was thus not only one of principle, but also of the practical implications arising under such an interpretation.

In the arbitral proceedings that followed, Peru took the position that, pursuant to Article 21(2) of The Grace Contract, it was entitled to half of the proceeds of the Lobos Islands guano for the purpose of cancelling the Iglesias debt. Peru also averred that, as a consequence, the Peruvian Corporation should put up to two million soles at its disposal.[96] For its part, the Peruvian Corporation maintained that, in light of the return of the Lobos Islands to Peru, Article 21(2) of The Grace Contract had as of that date ceased to produce effects for the future. The argument of the Peruvian Corporation was that, instead, from that point onwards the Lobos Islands fell under the Peruvian Corporation's general right under The Grace Contract to exploit Peruvian guano deposits; the proceeds from their exploitation thus no more derived from the Treaty of Ancon and were, consequently, no longer tied to the repayment of Peru's debt to Chile.[97]

Following the exchange of memorials between the Peruvian Corporation and Peru, the arbitrator, first president of the French Court of Cassation Alexis Ballot-Beaupré, handed down his award on 24 July 1909 in Paris. The award is

93 Protocol of 10 January 1890 between Peru and the English Committee of Bondholders, reproduced in ibid 29.

94 See *Peru v Peruvian Corporation* (n 89) 157. See also *Government of Peru v The Peruvian Corporation Limited*, English Translation of Response of the Peruvian Corporation Limited to the Government of Peru (14–15 May 1909) (University College London Special Collections: PERUCORP C2/65C/1–2) 6–7.

95 Memoire for the Peruvian Corporation (n 77) 49.

96 See Memoire of the Peruvian Government (n 90) 1–2.

97 See Memoire for the Peruvian Corporation (n 77) 73–78; Response of the Peruvian Corporation (n 94) 4–5, 23–35 and 74–76.

slightly more than 15 pages long and is, not unusually for ISA awards of the period, relatively minimalist in terms of legal analysis. Indeed, the award consists primarily of Ballot-Beaupré's own interpretations of the relevant legal instruments and the underlying facts, which do not appear to stem from, or bear a connection to, any broader legal principles or categories.

Ultimately, Ballot-Beaupré adjudicated the matter in favour of the Peruvian Corporation.[98] A key aspect of his decision was the finding that Article 21(2) of The Grace Contract had not encumbered the bondholders with paying off the Iglesias debt directly, but had merely provided that they were to tolerate that the proceeds accruing to Peru under the Treaty of Ancon be used for a set-off against the Iglesias debt before the bondholders could lay claim to the said proceeds.[99] Since the return of the Lobos Islands to Peru had meant that there were no longer any such proceeds to which Peru was entitled to, the arbitrator considered that Article 21(2) of The Grace Contract had lost its applicability.[100] In consequence, Ballot-Beaupré held that, as of the date of the return of the Lobos Islands to Peru, the Peruvian Corporation was entitled to exploit the guano found in the islands without the proceeds of such exploitation being subject to any kind of set-off against the Iglesias debt.[101] Ballot-Beaupré found further confirmation for such a conclusion in the fact that the Lobos Islands guano deposits had been handed to the Peruvian Corporation and exploited by the company for 12 years without Peru (or, for that matter, Chile) voicing any claim that the proceeds so obtained should be used for settling the Iglesias debt.[102]

Accordingly, Ballot-Beaupré held that Peru's claims in the arbitration were unfounded and that the Peruvian Corporation was not obliged to put up to two millions soles at its disposal.[103] He did, nonetheless, confirm that the Peruvian Corporation only had right to Peru's half of the proceeds from the guano extracted from the Lobos Islands from the date of the Treaty of Ancon's ratification until the supplementary agreements had handed the islands back to Peru[104] insofar as there remained a surplus after the said proceeds had

98 See *Peru v Peruvian Corporation* (n 89).
99 Ibid 151–152, 156 and 159.
100 Ibid 152, 154 and 158–159.
101 Ibid 152, 154 and 159.
102 Ibid 157.
103 Ibid 159.
104 See nn 92–93.

been used to set off the Iglesias debt pursuant to Article 21(2) of The Grace Contract.[105]

The final say on the legal interpretation of a contentious provision of an agreement by which Peru's outstanding public debt had been cancelled, then, was had by the arbitrator appointed by the parties to settle their dispute. While Ballot-Beaupré's decision may not have determined the final value of Peru's borrowing in a formal sense – that had, strictly speaking, been done by the parties to The Grace Contract themselves – it did nonetheless indirectly, through his interpretation of The Grace Contract, have such an effect. Namely, as the arbitrator's findings were of consequence for the ultimate balance of the cancellation of the debt, the definitive cost for Peru's borrowing from the bondholders in order to finance the construction of its railway system was, if not directly determined, then at least influenced, by the arbitrator's decision. The importance of the arbitrator's decision in this respect is only further underlined by the sheer size of the defaulted debt to which The Grace Contract had pertained.[106]

Even though it took a different road to get there, ultimately, the impact of the *Peru v. Peruvian Corporation* arbitration on determining the cost of governance was thus comparable to that of the *Hambros and Lazard v. Romanian Monopolies Institute* arbitration. To still go further – not only are the two arbitrations comparable in terms of their ultimate impact, but so too in terms of the decision-making freedom accorded to the two arbitrators along their respective paths to such outcomes. And while the extent of this latitude within which the arbitrator both needed, and was allowed, to manoeuvre, was in the *Hambros and Lazard v. Romanian Monopolies Institute* arbitration less readily apparent owing to the thick layer of legal analysis permeating the award, in the *Peru v. Peruvian Corporation* arbitration the view was unrestricted. Indeed, from a formal standpoint, Ballot-Beaupré was only constrained in his decision-making by the parties' instruction to apply 'the principles of right'; in practice, his decision bore little in terms of legal analysis and was instead reduced to his own interpretations of the relevant legal instruments and assessment of the facts.

---

105 In this respect, the arbitrator declared that the rights of the Peruvian Corporation were to be held above all other in case the record produced by Peru showed that not all of Peru's half of the proceeds had been used for servicing the Iglesias debt. See *Peru v Peruvian Corporation* (n 89) 159.

106 The Grace Contract has been highlighted by some historians as 'one of the milestones of Peruvian economic history' and 'a major landmark'. See Miller, 'The Grace Contract, the Peruvian Corporation, and Peruvian History' (n 81) 319–320. Conversely, Miller describes it as having had more of a symbolic value. See ibid 344.

Together with the *Hambros and Lazard v. Romanian Monopolies Institute* arbitration, then, the *Peru v. Peruvian Corporation* arbitration stands as an example of historical ISA not only playing a role in assigning a cost to states' governance decisions by deciding on matters relating to public debt, but of doing so in a manner that implied little circumscription upon the arbitrator's freedom of action in exercising this role.

3 Determining the Cost of State Appropriation of Investor Property

The role of historical ISA in ascertaining the cost of governance was not, however, exhausted in the above described practice of tribunals deciding on public-debt-related matters. An equally important aspect of this feature of historical ISA, and one which serves to further illustrate both its prevalence and breath of spectrum, was the part played by historical ISA in determining the cost of states' appropriation of investor property. Irrespective of the form it took – whether it was undertaken unilaterally or with the sanction of the affected private enterprise – a state's decision to acquire investor property was often, if not by necessity, a corollary of its broader governance choices or policies. This was especially so when the property in question concerned private interests or enterprises of strategic importance, such as, for example, those relating to public infrastructure. And while, in such instances, the very decision to acquire investor property may have remained within the purview of the state in question (whether arrived at one-sidedly or in concert with the interested investor), the same did not necessarily apply to the costs associated with it. Indeed, when those costs could not be ascertained to the mutual satisfaction of both the state and the investor involved, historical ISA was on many an occasion leaned upon to help facilitate a solution.

Thus, as much as the history of investor-state interaction may be fraught with examples of states' uncompensated appropriation of property – indeed, this is perhaps one of the most frequently recurring themes underpinning the history of international relations – so too did it give rise to situations where the cost of such appropriation was ascertained through historical ISA. The remainder of this section illustrates the point by recounting three such instances, all of which are rooted in the acquirement by states of important railway enterprises. The first of these concerns the taking over of a railway concession by Colombia in the twilight of the 19th century (3.1). The second relates to Canada's acquisition in the early 1920s of one of its major railway enterprises as part of its policy to establish a national railway company (3.2). The third, and final, is based on the takeover of a railway in post-World War I Palestine (3.3). This trifecta of cases, together with other documented instances where historical ISA served a similar purpose,[107] attests not only that historical ISA operated to help ascertain the cost of states' appropriation of investor property – and through this more broadly the cost of governance – but also that it did so recurrently.

3.1 *Colombia v Cauca Company*

An early example of ISA being utilised for determining the cost of state appropriation of investor property was the late 19th century case between the Cauca Company and Colombia. The dispute arose out of a concession to construct and operate a railway between the Colombian cities of Buenaventura and Manizales that had in 1890 been obtained for a period of 70 years by a US citizen, James L. Cherry. The concession was awarded pursuant to a contract concluded between Colombia and Cherry, which was subsequently ratified by the Colombian congress.[108] Under the concession, the first section of the railway (from Buenaventura to Cali) was to be constructed within the 'peremptory' period of four years following the start of construction (which was to commence within four months from the date of the execution of the contract).[109] The failure to finish the section within the prescribed period incurred the possibility of the concession being forfeited to the Colombian government.[110] The concession also envisaged that it could be assigned by the concessionary to third parties (but only of private character), subject to the Colombian government being notified of the assignment[111] – a possibility of which Cherry made

107 See eg *The Ditta Luigi Gallotti v The Somali Government* (1970) 40 ILR 158, where the tribunal was tasked with determining the compensation payable by Somalia for the take-over of equipment belonging to a port concession operator following its cancellation (as had been contractually provided). See likewise *Libyan American Oil Company (LIAMCO) v The Government of the Libyan Arab Republic* (1981) 20(1) ILM 1, where the arbitrator held that it was within Libya's rights to nationalise the concession in question and then proceeded to determine the amount of compensation owed to the company.

108 Contract for the construction of the railway from Buenaventura to Manizales between the Government of Colombia and James L Cherry (27 August 1890). The concession is reproduced as part of Law 16 of 18 October 1890 through which it was ratified, which is contained in the record of the subsequent US court proceedings for the annulment of the award that can be found at Columbia University Library. See Original Bill of Complaint with Exhibits (Complainant's Exhibit No 4), *Colombia v Cauca Co*, 106 Fed 337 (DW Va 1901).

109 Ibid art 4.

110 Ibid art 39.

111 Ibid art 34.

use, transferring his rights in the concession to the Cauca Company, which had been established for this very purpose.[112]

Despite the work on the concession having been begun on time, it proceeded slowly and was not completed within the envisioned time frame. Almost two years prior to the expiration of the deadline, the company had reached an agreement with the Colombian minister of public works for the extension of the deadline for an additional two years on the account of construction having been delayed by causes beyond the company's control.[113] Following the expiration of the original deadline, however, the Colombian congress refuted the minister's power to conclude such an agreement and instead declared the concession to have been forfeited.[114] Under the concession, the available remedy in case of Colombia's declaration of the concession to have been forfeited was arbitration.[115] Despite the company's apparent desire to make use of the availability of arbitration under the concession, for reasons that remained disputed between the parties,[116] little progress was initially made on this front. In fact, it was not until after the US had intervened through diplomatic channels that the two sides agreed on how to proceed.[117]

---

112 Agreement between James L Cherry and the Cauca Company (29 November 1890), reproduced in Original Bill of Complaint with Exhibits (Complainant's Exhibit No 7), *Colombia v Cauca Co*, 106 Fed 337 (n 108). Cherry then assigned his contract with the Cauca Company to the Colombian Construction and Improvement Company, which was the sole shareholder in the Cauca Company. See Agreement between James L Cherry and the Colombian Construction and Improvement Company (29 November 1890), reproduced in Original Bill of Complaint with Exhibits (Complainant's Exhibit No 8), *Colombia v Cauca Co*, 106 Fed 337 (n 108). The involvement of the latter company was controversial, as Colombia had argued when challenging the award before US courts that it had never been notified of this assignment, as had been required under the concession, and as a result protested to the expenses of the latter company being included in the compensation that Colombia was required to pay for taking over the railway. These objections were, however, dismissed by the US courts. See *Colombia v Cauca Co*, 190 US 524, 530–531 (1903).

113 *Colombia v Cauca Co*, 106 Fed 337 (n 108) 341.

114 Law 60 of 16 November 1894, reproduced in Original Bill of Complaint with Exhibits (Complainant's Exhibit No 10), *Colombia v Cauca Co*, 106 Fed 337 (n 108).

115 The Cherry Concession (n 108) art 37.

116 Original Bill of Complaint with Exhibits at vii, *Colombia v Cauca Co*, 106 Fed 337 (n 108); Record Filed February 28, 1902 at 22–23 and 60–61, *Colombia v Cauca Co*, 190 US 524 (n 112); Brief for Appellees at 9–12, *Colombia v Cauca Co*, 190 US 524 (n 112); Brief for the Republic of Colombia at 16–18, *Colombia v Cauca Co*, 190 US 524 (n 112). The record of the proceedings and the parties' pleadings from US Supreme Court case 190 US 524 can be found at Columbia University Library.

117 Original Bill of Complaint with Exhibits at vii-viii, *Colombia v Cauca Co*, 106 Fed 337 (n 108); Record Filed February 28, 1902 at 22–23, 47–48 and 61, *Colombia v Cauca Co*, 190 US

The foundation for an agreement between Colombia and the company was laid by a law passed by the Colombian congress on 20 October 1896, which authorised the Colombian executive branch to compromise with the concessionary, albeit under the condition that the franchise and railroad were in any event to be handed over to Colombia.[118] In case no agreement could be reached, the law instructed the executive to 'proceed to carry out whatever may be required for constituting the Court of Arbitration, in accordance with the contract'.[119] On the basis of this law, Colombia and Cauca then concluded a settlement, pursuant to which the company was to surrender the concession and turn the railway over to Colombia against the payment of 'a just indemnity for all the works constructed by the Company' (as well as for the rolling stock and other items imported by the company).[120] The settlement envisioned that the exact amount of compensation to be paid was to be determined by a three member commission.[121] Under the settlement, Colombia had also agreed to in any event pay $200,000 (between $5.3 million and $250 million in present-day value) in advance on account of its estimation of the costs expended by the company on its work on the railway (which was then to be deducted from the amount determined by the commission).[122] While the decision to cancel

524 (n 112); Brief for Appellees at 12–16, *Colombia v Cauca Co*, 190 US 524 (n 112); *Colombia v Cauca Co*, 106 Fed 337 (n 108) 341–342.

118 Law 41 of 20 October 1896 art 1, reproduced in Original Bill of Complaint with Exhibits (Complainant's Exhibit No 11), *Colombia v Cauca Co*, 106 Fed 337 (n 108).

119 Ibid art 2. The law further provided that, in case the tribunal could not be constituted or could not complete its task in time, the attorney general was to institute 'whatever judicial proceedings may be necessary' for the contract's fulfilment.

120 Agreement of January 4, 1897, for the Submission to Arbitration of the Claims of the Cauca Company against Colombia art II, reproduced in Original Bill of Complaint with Exhibits (Complainant's Exhibit No 12), *Colombia v Cauca Co*, 106 Fed 337 (n 108).

121 Ibid art IV. The use of this terminology, which designated the decision-makers as 'commissioners', rather than as 'arbitrators', was possibly not merely an issue of semantics. Namely, in subsequent proceedings before the US Supreme Court, when making the argument that a majority vote was sufficient for the award's validity because the matter was one of 'public contention', the company tried to draw a strict conceptual distinction between the role of commissioners and that of arbitrators. According to the company, while the former were entrusted with a public service, the latter had the role of private judges. The company thus argued that '[t]he fact that the members of the board were designated Commissioners and not arbitrators seems of itself to fix their character as public officials, and the public character of the matter submitted'. See Brief for Appellees at 45–50, *Colombia v Cauca Co*, 190 US 524 (n 112). Although it adopted the same characterisation of the matter that the commission had been tasked to deal with, the Supreme Court did not address the relevance of this terminological difference. See *Colombia v Cauca Co*, 190 US 524 (n 112) 530.

122 Agreement of January 4, 1897 (n 120) art X.

the contract and take possession of the railway remained that of the Colombian congress, the ultimate determination of the full cost associated with such action was thus to belong to the commissioners.

In light of the prevalence of the Calvo doctrine among South American countries at the time,[123] such course of action was certainly an interesting choice. Colombia's eventual agreement to submit the matter to the three member commission appears to have been strongly induced, and can thus likely be explained, by diplomatic intervention by the US;[124] the reasons behind the initial inclusion of an arbitration clause in the concession, however, are less clear from the available material. In any event, it is notable that the availability of arbitration for instances where the concession was declared forfeited was a narrowly circumscribed exception to the general approach adopted in the concession, pursuant to which, in reflection of the Calvo doctrine, all differences arising in relation to the concession were otherwise to be resolved before Colombian courts and pursuant to Colombian law, to the exclusion of diplomatic protection.[125]

Soon after the two sides had agreed to submit the matter to the commission's consideration, the three commissioners were appointed. While Colombia chose a certain Manuel H. Peña,[126] on whom little information is available apart from the fact that he appears to have been an engineer,[127] Cauca

123 The Calvo doctrine, the development of which is perhaps incorrectly attributed to Argentinian lawyer Carlos Calvo, whose name it carries, was formulated in the second part of the 19th century. The doctrine sought to bring an end to the practice wherein foreigners were accorded a higher level of legal protection than domestic citizens. A corollary to the doctrine was the Calvo clause, which was often included in concession contracts between South American states and foreigners, and which provided that, to the exclusion of diplomatic protection, all disputes were to be resolved by domestic courts and pursuant to domestic law. See Santiago Montt, *State Liability in Investment Treaty Arbitration: Global Constitutionalism and Administrative Law in the BIT Generation* (Hart Publishing 2009) 38–48.

124 See n 117. Further possible motivation for Colombia opting for arbitration was alluded to by the company in subsequent US court proceedings, as it claimed that the Colombian president had acknowledged that arbitration was a less favourable option for Colombia than paying a gross sum, but that the former was preferred in order to 'satisfy the felling of the Colombian people', which could then 'not find fault with him'. See Brief for Appellees at 73–74, *Colombia v Cauca Co*, 190 US 524 (n 112).

125 The Cherry Concession (n 108) art 37.

126 Original Bill of Complaint with Exhibits (Complainant's Exhibit No 13), *Colombia v Cauca Co*, 106 Fed 337 (n 108).

127 See Sociedad Colombiana de Ingenieros, 'Historia' <https://sci.org.co/historia/> accessed 29 September 2024. It appears that Peña had previously acted as an arbitrator, having been appointed by Colombia, in another arbitration between Colombia and a different

appointed an individual, Christian F. Schrame, who was closely affiliated with the company and who had even participated as a company representative in the negotiations that preceded the commission's formation.[128] The third member, Philadelphia civil engineer Lewis M. Haupt, was chosen jointly by the US Secretary of State and the Colombian *chargé d'affaires* at Washington.[129]

Before delving into the commission's findings, it is worth pausing for a moment in order to lament, and properly appreciate, the breadth of the undertaking that was carried out by its members, as this undertaking was not confined to merely attaching a value to clearly specified items that related to the work done by the company in constructing the railway. Instead, the commission first had to deal with the question of the very scope of the task that had been put before it, thus making the impact of its undertaking on the eventual cost of the Colombian government's decision to take over the concession that more sizeable. Namely, during the proceedings, Colombia had taken the position that the commission's competence was restricted to merely assessing the immediate costs associated with the physical construction of the railway, while the company had, conversely, insisted that the commission was empowered to include in its award all legitimate costs more broadly related to the project,[130] and asked for more than $960,000 (between $25.7 million and $1.2 billion in present-day value) in compensation.[131] The commission decided this preliminary matter in the company's favour (albeit with the dissent from Colombia's appointee, Manuel H. Peña),[132] thus allowing for a significantly higher number

---

private party, Francisco J Cisneros, regarding the same railroad. Ironically enough, Cisneros would then also go on to represent Colombia in its dispute with the Cauca Company. See Record Filed February 28, 1902 at 25–26 and 40–41, *Colombia v Cauca Co*, 190 US 524 (n 112).

128 Original Bill of Complaint with Exhibits (Complainant's Exhibit No 14), *Colombia v Cauca Co*, 106 Fed 337 (n 108); Record Filed February 28, 1902 at 26, *Colombia v Cauca Co*, 190 US 524 (n 112); Brief for Appellees at 13, *Colombia v Cauca Co*, 190 US 524 (n 112).

129 Original Bill of Complaint with Exhibits (Complainant's Exhibit No 15), *Colombia v Cauca Co*, 106 Fed 337 (n 108).

130 See Brief for Appellees at 20, *Colombia v Cauca Co*, 190 US 524 (n 112); Brief for the Republic of Colombia at 47–50, *Colombia v Cauca Co*, 190 US 524 (n 112). The divide between the parties on this point had been caused by the ambiguity of certain wording used in the original Spanish version of the submission to arbitration. See *Colombia v Cauca Co*, 106 Fed 337 (n 108) 349.

131 'The Cauca Company's Claim: Arbitrators Make Their Award, Fixing the Amount Colombia Must Pay at $452,048.93' *The New York Times* (New York, 24 October 1897) 5.

132 Brief for Appellees at 20–23, *Colombia v Cauca Co*, 190 US 524 (n 112).

of items to be included in its valuation of the company's expenses than would have otherwise been the case.[133]

Pursuant to such an understanding of the task before it, the commission proceeded to examine the compensable expenses incurred by the company in constructing the railway and, following more than 30 sessions that spanned over more than 200 days, finally issued its award on 22 October 1897, in New York. Before the commission could do so, however, the Colombia-appointed commissioner had, in an apparent attempt to undercut the commission's authority to issue the award, resigned from the commission on the account that the two remaining commissioners were, in his view, awarding compensation to the company for items beyond the scope of the parties' submission.[134] In a short and essentially unreasoned award that spanned no more than two pages and merely gave a brief overview of the procedure before the commission, as well as its eventual findings, the two remaining commissioners awarded the company, in addition to the $200,000 advance that had already been paid by

133 Among the items included, in addition to the cost of the physical construction of the railway, were those costs pertaining to the salaries of the company's executive officers, the cost of acquiring the concession through assignment, the travelling expenses of the company's officers, additional traveling expenses for procuring the settlement of the dispute, the expenses of the company's New York office and other incidental expenses, as well as interest on the physical construction of the railway, the cost of the concession and the original amount paid in by the company's bondholders. A number of the said items (the cost of the concession, the expenses of obtaining the settlement and the awarded interest) were later disallowed by US courts following Colombia's challenge to the award. Interestingly, the amount awarded for legal representation before the tribunal was also disallowed. See *Colombia v Cauca Co*, 106 Fed 337 (n 108) 349–353; *Colombia v Cauca Co*, 190 US 524 (n 112) 529–531.

134 The translation of the resignation letter is reproduced in *Colombia v Cauca Co*, 106 Fed 337 (n 108) 345. The resignation was made mere days before the commission's mandate, which had been limited to a maximum of 210 days, was set to expire. While the arbitration agreement had provided that in such an instance the resigning commissioner was to be replaced within 30 days through a new appointment by the party which had appointed the resigning commissioner, faced with the commission's expiring mandate, the two remaining commissioners decided not to wait for the appointment of a replacement but to instead proceed with issuing the award. In their view, such action was warranted by the fact that all matters had been deliberated upon and decided prior to the resignation, leaving only the announcement of the commission's decision. Colombia expectedly argued that the two remaining commissioners did not have the power to take such a step, as it took the position, when challenging the award, that the resignation of a commissioner had deprived the commission of its capacity to act until it was reconstituted. The US Supreme Court, however, ultimately held that the two remaining commissioners were, considering that there had hardly been anything left to do in the case, allowed to issue the award by majority vote in order to safeguard the proceedings. See *Colombia v Cauca Co*, 190 US 524 (n 112) 527–528.

Colombia, a total of $452,048.93 (present-day value between $12.1 million and $568 million).[135]

This capacity by the commission to have, at least within the confines of its competence, final say on the price tag that was to accompany Colombia's decision to take over the railway was all the more consequential in light of the fact that it was subsequently given credence, even if not without circumscription, by US courts (the Supreme Court included). Namely, soon after it was handed down, Colombia challenged the commission's award before US courts by initiating a suit in equity,[136] basing jurisdiction on account of Colombia being a sovereign state that was involved in a controversy with US citizens (i.e. US-registered companies).[137] While the sum that had been awarded by the commission was eventually more than halved in these proceedings, it having been found by the lower courts and the US Supreme Court that a number of items which had been included in the commission's valuation of the compensation had been so included improperly,[138] the commission's decision-making prerogatives were nonetheless affirmed in principle. Most notably, when handing down its final say on the matter within the US legal system, the US Supreme Court made it a point to emphasise that it only had the power to examine whether the commission had acted within the scope of the parties' submission and not to in any manner revise its findings insofar as they were made

135 *Colombia v Cauca Company*, Award (22 October 1897), reproduced in *Colombia v Cauca Co*, 106 Fed 337 (n 108) 346–347.

136 Original Bill of Complaint with Exhibits, *Colombia v Cauca Co*, 106 Fed 337 (n 108).

137 Brief for the Republic of Colombia at 32, *Colombia v Cauca Co*, 190 US 524 (n 112); Brief for Appellant in Opposition to Motion to Dismiss at 3, *Colombia v Cauca Co*, 190 US 524 (n 112). The US Constitution expressly provides that, irrespective of the subject matter, the judicial power of its courts extends also to cases between citizens of one of its states and foreign states. See *The Sapphire*, 78 US 164, 167 (1870). Rather interestingly, at one point in the court proceedings, the companies argued want of jurisdiction on account that the commission's decision was an 'international award' handed down by a body constituted by Colombia 'in its sovereign capacity through an act of congress' for the purposes of settling claims made by the US through diplomatic channels. See Record Filed February 28, 1902 at 43, *Colombia v Cauca Co*, 190 US 524 (n 112). The Circuit Court did not address this argument directly, but merely held that it was well settled that courts of equity had jurisdiction over bills that aimed to set aside awards. See *Colombia v Cauca Co*, 106 Fed 337 (n 108) 339–340. Notably, while the commission's award was handed down in New York, this does not seem to have been invoked as a possible jurisdictional basis before US courts (the suit was initiated in West Virginia, where the respondent companies were incorporated).

138 See n 133.

within the confines of the said scope.[139] While the powers of the commissioners in assigning a cost to the Colombian government's decision to cancel the concession and take possession of the railway were thus not perceived by the US Supreme Court as being limitless, the commissioners having been required to act within the boundaries of the authority that had been bestowed upon them, within those confines determining the said cost was left up to the commissioners.

That the Supreme Court gave such leeway to the commission's findings is still more noteworthy when accounting for how the court understood the commission's role with respect to the valuation of the appropriated railway. Namely, when dealing with the matter, the Supreme Court reflected on the nature of the commission's work, observing that the commission:

> was constituted after, if not as the result of, diplomatic discussion in pursuance of a public statute of Colombia. It was to decide between a sovereign state and a railroad, declared by a law of Colombia to be a work of public utility. In short, it was *dealing with matters of public concern.*[140]

Thus, not only had the US Supreme Court felt obliged to restrain itself from interfering with the commission's exercise of the powers that had been accorded to it, but it had done so while fully cognizant that such powers had been exercised in relation to a matter of public concern. As a matter of fact, apart from finding that it made a unanimous award unlikely and that an award by majority was thus entirely valid, it does not appear that the Supreme Court even contemplated the possibility that such nature of the matter before the commission would affect, and in particular diminish, the commission's capacity to exercise the prerogatives bestowed upon it.

The importance of the *Colombia v. Cauca Company* arbitration appears almost inversely proportional to the length of the award handed down in the case; indeed, for having taken place in the late 19th century, the arbitration contained a number of interesting yet deeply relevant procedural wrinkles, such as the commission deciding on the extent of its own mandate – its competence – and opting to proceed despite the resignation of one of its members.[141]

---

139 *Colombia v Cauca Co*, 190 US 524 (n 112) 530. A similar position was taken by the circuit judge. See *Colombia v Cauca Co*, 106 Fed 337 (n 108) 350–351.

140 *Colombia v Cauca Co*, 190 US 524 (n 112) 528. Emphasis added. A corresponding approach was taken by the Circuit Court, which held that the matter before the commission was 'in the nature of a public contention'. See *Colombia v Cauca Co*, 106 Fed 337 (n 108) 348.

141 To put things into perspective, in his account of the *Lena Goldfields v USSR* arbitration, which took place more than thirty years after *Colombia v Cauca Co*, Veeder described the

For present purposes even more consequentially, within the broader context of historical ISA's role in determining the cost of governance, the *Colombia v. Cauca Company* arbitration stands relevant not only as one of the earlier recorded examples of tribunals in ISA doing so by deciding on the financial costs that would be associated with a state's appropriation of the property of a private enterprise, but perhaps even more so for the validation that its taking on of this role received from the US Supreme Court. Indeed, while the US Supreme Court did hold the commission's prerogatives to some limitations – in particular the need to operate within the confines of its mandate as understood by the Supreme Court – it deemed itself unable, even with full cognizance of the public interest involved in the matter, to interfere with how the commissionaires exercised their authority within such confines. Accordingly, not only is it the embodiment of the practice itself, but the *Colombia v. Cauca Company* arbitration stands also as a testament to the fact that the recognition of the validity of historical ISA's role in determining the cost of governance by national courts, including those of the US Supreme Court's stature, dates at least as far back as the early 20th century.

3.2 *The Grand Trunk Railway Arbitration*

A further befitting illustration of historical ISA's role in establishing the costs of states' governance decisions, as well as of the magnitude of the potential implications arising thereunder, is the *Grand Trunk Railway Arbitration*,[142] which concerned the valuation of one of Canada's largest railway enterprises upon its takeover by the Canadian government.

At the tail end of World War I, the situation in the Canadian railway industry was grim. While the period at the beginning of the 20th century had been one of great enthusiasm that had prompted ambitious expansion of Canada's railway network,[143] in the long run, these optimistic plans had proved overzealous for a country of Canada's size and population. As a result, two of Canada's major railway companies, the Grand Trunk Railway and the Canadian

Lena Goldfields v USSR tribunal's decision to proceed despite a truncated tribunal and to decide upon its own competence as 'innovative'. See Veeder (n 6) 747–748.

142 *Dominion of Canada v The Grand Trunk Railway Company of Canada*, Award (7 September 1921). A copy of the award is available in the UK National Archives as part of the documents on the *Jaffa-Jerusalem Railway Arbitration* (UK National Archives: TS 27/143–144). The award and the records of the proceedings can also be found at the Library and Archives Canada.

143 See G P de T Glazebrook, *A History of Transportation in Canada* (originally published by Ryerson Press 1938, Greenwood Press 1969) 313–341.

Northern Railway, found themselves in dire circumstances.[144] Faced with a potential break-down of its railway industry, and after pondering the different available options, the Canadian government ultimately opted to take over the flailing companies and establish a national railway enterprise – a policy choice in which ISA would play a prominent role.[145]

The first step in this process was the acquisition of the remainder of the shares of the already partially government-owned Canadian Northern Railway. For this purpose, legislation was passed authorising the government to enter into an agreement with the shareholders, and providing that the value of the said shares was to be determined through arbitration.[146] The tribunal that was set up as a result was presided by Sir William Meredith, chief justice of Ontario, while the two remaining arbitrators were former Supreme Court justice Wallace Nesbitt and Robert E. Harris, justice of the Supreme Court of Nova Scotia.[147] Despite the fact that a government appointed commission had previously found the shares to be of no value,[148] the arbitrators proceeded to put on them a price of $10.8 million (present-day value of approximately $170 million).[149]

The status of the Grand Trunk Railway took a bit longer to resolve than that of the Canadian Northern Railway, as its situation was more complex.[150] Nonetheless, after protracted negotiations between the representatives of the government and the company, the two sides finally agreed on Canada's acquisition of the Grand Trunk Railway.[151] Nominally, this transaction was indisputably a voluntary one, as the takeover had been consented to by the company's

144 See ibid 342–350.

145 On the nationalisation of Canada's railways, see ibid 342–376.

146 An Act providing for the acquisition by His Majesty of the capital stock of the Canadian Northern Railway Company, SC 1916–17, ch 24.

147 Glazebrook (n 143) 352; Rae Bruce Fleming, *Railway King of Canada: Sir William MacKenzie, 1849–1923* (UBC Press 1991) 230.

148 Glazebrook (n 143) 359.

149 The tribunal's award could unfortunately not be accessed. According to Glazebrook, a copy of the award is contained in the records of Canada's department of railways and canals. See Glazebrook (n 143) 360. Interestingly, the amount that was awarded went slightly above the $10 million threshold that had been set as the maximum that could be awarded by the tribunal. On the nationalisation of the Canadian Northern Railway see ibid 350–361. For a more detailed account of the related arbitration proceedings, see Fleming (n 147) 230–235.

150 Glazebrook (n 143) 361. For detailed accounts of the nationalisation of the Grand Trunk Railway, see ibid 361–371; John A Eagle, 'Monopoly or Competition: the Nationalization of the Grand Trunk Railway' (1981) 62(1) The Canadian Historical Review 3.

151 On the negotiations, see Eagle (n 150) 17–24; Glazebrook (n 143) 362–364; AW Currie, *The Grand Trunk Railway of Canada* (University of Toronto Press 1957) 444–457.

leadership. This nominal character of the transaction notwithstanding, the company's financial situation was nonetheless such that its leadership ultimately had little alternative but to come to some sort of an agreement with the Canadian government on the acquisition.[152] This aspect was all the more significant when one accounts for the fact that the company's poor financial standing seems in large part to have been intertwined with, if not a corollary of, Canada's (non-)adoption of certain measures affecting the business of the Grand Trunk Railway and its subsidiaries.[153] At the same time, it should likewise not be overlooked that the Canadian government had also explored the option of invoking the War Measures Act in order to take over the railway through coercive measures in case no agreement could be reached.[154] It is thus hard to avoid the conclusion that the nature of the transaction through which Canada acquired the Grand Trunk Railway was, to say the least, much more complex than its nominal form would indicate. More importantly for present purposes, however, irrespective of how the underlying transaction is characterised, it was nonetheless undoubtedly a direct implementation, and foundational element, of Canada's policy to nationalise two of its major railway systems and establish a national railway enterprise.

The terms of the arrangement between Canada and the company were such that, for its acquisition of the majority of the Grand Trunk Railway stock, the Canadian government was to pay an annual interest for certain guaranteed and debenture stock; meanwhile, the value of the preferential and common stock that was to be acquired, and on which interest was likewise to be paid, was to be determined through arbitration.[155] The idea to submit the outstanding issues to arbitration originated with the Canadian government as an alternative

152 See Currie (n 151) 459–460; Eagle (n 150) 23–24.

153 The most important course of action by Canada in this respect was likely to merely withhold from the company the financial aid that had on previous occasions been forthcoming. Nonetheless, Eagle notes that the company's 'financial difficulties were caused mainly by the government's refusal to use the War Measures Act to permit freight rate increases commensurate with increased costs', while also pointing out that the government had unilaterally modified the terms of a loan that had been extended to the troubled subsidiary of the Grand Trunk Railway, the Grand Trunk Pacific Railway, in order to exert pressure over the company. In what is perhaps an overly harsh characterisation, Eagle describes Canada's measures that were aimed at bringing about an agreement over the acquisition of the Grand Trunk Railway as a 'policy of coercion' and 'rigorous, even ruthless'. See Eagle (n 150) 14–24.

154 See Eagle (n 150) 19–22; Currie (n 151) 451. A compulsory takeover of the railway by the Canadian government was made difficult by the fact that a significant mileage of the Grand Trunk Railway system was located in the United States.

155 Glazebrook (n 143) 363–364; Eagle (n 150) 24–25; Currie (n 151) 456–457.

proposal to its cash offer to the company.[156] Initially, the arbitration proposal was intended to relate to the value of the entirety of the company's stock,[157] but was later limited to the common and preferential stock after the government had, in a move intended to induce the company to accede to arbitration, agreed to treat the company's guaranteed stock the same as its bonds.[158] As is often the case, recourse to arbitration was thus in this instance a creature of necessity, brought about by mere desire to avoid a deadlock in the negotiations. Indeed, in addressing the parliament over the issue, Canada's then minister of the interior and soon to be prime minister, Arthur Meighen, who was a 'dominant' figure in Canada's acquisition of the Grand Trunk Railway,[159] indicated that the parties' turn to arbitration was 'compelled (…) for the simple reason that we cannot agree'.[160] While the company had initially been cautious about the idea of arbitrating the value of the preferential and common stock,[161] it eventually had little choice but to compromise on the government's alternative offer that included arbitration. Notably, the decision by the company's leadership to agree to arbitration has been described as a 'major breakthrough' in its negotiations with the government.[162]

After the two sides had reached an agreement, the Canadian parliament was notified of the arrangement in October of 1919.[163] Both the government's decision to acquire the Grand Trunk Railway and, more specifically, its decision to submit the valuation of its preferential and common stock to arbitration, were met with significant opposition in parliament. The underlying anxiety was in large part fuelled by Canada's earlier unpleasant experience with the Canadian Northern arbitration.[164] Meighen's response to concerns about going to

156 Glazebrook (n 143) 363; Eagle (n 150) 18; Currie (n 151) 447–448 and 450.

157 Canada. Parliament. House of Commons. Debates, 13th Parliament, 3rd Session, 1919, vol 140 (Ottawa: J de Labroquerie Taché 1920) 1051.

158 Eagle (n 150) 18. See also House of Commons. Debates, vol 140 (n 157) 1051.

159 Eagle (n 150) 6.

160 House of Commons. Debates, vol 140 (n 157) 1274.

161 See Currie (n 151) 447 and 450.

162 Eagle (n 150) 23–24.

163 Canada. Parliament. House of Commons. Debates, 13th Parliament, 3rd Session, 1919, vol 139 (Ottawa: J de Labroquerie Taché 1920) 977.

164 See eg House of Commons. Debates, vol 140 (n 157) 1073–1074, 1126–1127, 1215–1216, 1241, 1267, 1321–1322, 1513, 1672–1673, 1685 and 1711. One of the main requests by the opposition, voiced repeatedly, was for the arbitrators' award to be submitted to the Canadian parliament for ratification before it would become binding. See House of Commons. Debates, vol 140 (n 157) 1074, 1089, 1156, 1172, 1213, 1267, 1280, 1306, 1330, 1409, 1510, 1514, 1705, 1711 and 1740–1741. Such a possibility was rejected by Meighen as impracticable for numerous reasons, including that it was contrary to the very principle of arbitration, that 'it gets us nowhere and we have no agreement when we are all through' and that parliament

arbitration, directed in the particular occasion at a prominent opposition parliamentarian, offered a defence of the role of arbitration in instances such as the one for which it was to be deployed in relation to the takeover of the Grand Trunk Railway that was perhaps as fervent as could have been ideated:

> what plan does he suggest to get at the value when we cannot agree upon it? He is afraid of arbitration. Arbitration is not only the method employed in the past in similar transactions, one of which he referred to, but it is the method embedded in the legislation of this country everywhere in the case of acquirement of land or property. *It is universally and historically recognized as the best, fairest and the only way for determining disputed claims.*[165]

After intense discussions in parliament that lasted several weeks, and following a brief detour to the senate,[166] the bill for the acquisition of the Grand Trunk Railway was passed,[167] paving the way for the government and the company to proceed with concluding a formal agreement. That agreement was then subsequently again submitted to parliament, where it was confirmed.[168] Under the final version of the arrangement, the railway's preferential and common stock

---

would be 'in no position to review intelligently the judgment which an independent judicial tribunal after hearing the evidence and seeing the witnesses had rendered'. House of Commons. Debates, vol 140 (n 157) 1511–1512. At one juncture, Meighen even decried this proposal as 'Bolshevism itself'. See House of Commons. Debates, vol 140 (n 157) 1519–1520. To this, the opposition responded by arguing that their proposal was 'not Bolshevism but that it is the exercise of the power of democracy by the people and in Parliament through their representatives'. See House of Commons. Debates, vol 140 (n 157) 1721. Another interesting objection was to the effect that there was no reason why the matter could not be submitted to Canadian courts. See House of Commons. Debates, vol 140 (n 157) 1522–1523 and 1685–1686.

165 House of Commons. Debates, vol 140 (n 157) 1085. Emphasis added.

166 See Eagle (n 150) 26–28; Currie (n 151) 458–459. The bill faced strong opposition in the senate, but was passed after an amendment limiting the maximum amount of the award was introduced. Although he ultimately proposed that the amendment be approved, Meighen was highly critical of it, going as far as to state that the other party to the arbitration might 'regard a maximum fixed by the one side as taking away from the arbitration the very essence of arbitration itself'. See House of Commons. Debates, vol 140 (n 157) 1926–1927.

167 The Grand Trunk Railway Acquisition Act, 1919, SC 1919 (3d Sess), ch 17.

168 An Act to confirm the Agreement dated the eighth day of March, 1920, between His Majesty The King and the Grand Trunk Railway Company of Canada for the acquisition by His Majesty of the capital stock of the said Grand Trunk Railway Company, except the four per cent guaranteed stock, SC 1920, ch 13. The agreement was appended to the Act as a Schedule.

(but not the guaranteed stock, on which the government had already agreed to pay interest, as noted above) was to be taken over by the Canadian government at a value that was to be determined through arbitration. For this purpose, the tribunal had been authorised to go as high as $64,166,666.66 (present-day value of $957.7 million); the value arrived at by the tribunal within these confines was then to serve as the basis for determining the annual interest that was to be paid by the Canadian government.

The tribunal that was set up was presided by a judge of the Exchequer Court of Canada, Sir Walter Cassels. The choice of Cassels had been explicitly envisioned in the enabling legislation that had authorised the takeover of the Grand Trunk Railway.[169] In explaining the choice of Cassels to parliament, Meighen argued that it was 'peculiarly desirable that he should be selected for the reason that he is the head of the court that determine [sic] all values as between the country and individual citizens', as well as for his experience and 'reputation for the highest integrity and ability'.[170] The two remaining tribunal members were Canada's appointee Sir Thomas White (who had previously been heavily involved in the matter as the then minister of finance)[171] and the company's appointee, then already former US president and soon to be US Supreme Court judge, William Howard Taft, who had had some previous experience with the railway and transportation industries.[172]

Following an in-depth investigation of the matter that involved more than seventy days of hearings,[173] the tribunal arrived at its decision in September of 1921. While all of the arbitrators had been in agreement on the fact that the appropriate basis for the valuation of the railway was its earning capacity,[174]

169 The Grand Trunk Railway Acquisition Act (n 167) s 6. Notably, however, the initial arrangement between Canada and the Grand Trunk Railway did not specifically designate Cassels as the third arbitrator, but had instead provided as a primary solution for the tribunal president to be chosen by the two party-appointed arbitrators. It was only through a subsequent amendment that Cassels was designated. See nn 191–194.

170 House of Commons. Debates, vol 140 (n 157) 1522.

171 See Eagle (n 150) *passim*; Currie (n 151) 441–456, 471 and 478. White was later, with some temporal overlap with his involvement with the *Grand Trunk Railway Arbitration*, also an arbitrator in the *Toronto Railway Arbitration*. See Fleming (n 147) 239.

172 See Eagle (n 150) 29; Currie (n 151) 461. Taft had been informed of his appointment to the US Supreme Court as the arbitration was unfolding. See 'Ex-President Taft Succeeds White as Chief Justice' *The New York Times* (New York, 1 July 1921) 1. Rather curiously, prior to his appointment to the tribunal by the company, Taft had been rumored as Canada's preferred choice for its tribunal appointee. See 'Canada Asks Taft to Represent Her' *The New York Times* (New York, 15 June 1920) 1.

173 Eagle (n 150) 28.

174 *Canada v Grand Trunk* (n 142) 20–21 (opinion of Cassels).

their views as to what this capacity actually was could hardly have been more diametrically opposed. At least in part, this divergence in views seems to have derived from the arbitrators' difference of opinion on whether evidence as to the reproductive value of the railway should have been allowed into the record; while the majority had deemed such evidence inadmissible, Taft felt that it should have been allowed, not as directly determinative of the value of the Grand Trunk Railway, but as nonetheless relevant for estimating its future earning capacity.[175] Ultimately, the tribunal majority, consisting of Cassels and White, found the Grand Trunk Railway's preferential and common stock to be entirely worthless.[176] Their findings were based primarily on the fact that the railway's books had been tampered with by the company's management, resulting in dividends having been paid in the past when the company's earnings had not warranted it, and insufficient resources having been invested in the maintenance of the system. White also put emphasis on the company's obligations as guarantor for the debts which its subsidiary, the Grand Trunk Pacific Railway, was unable to service. All of this had in their view left the Grand Trunk Railway in a poor financial state but with significant requirements for capital in the upcoming period, leading the two majority arbitrators to conclude that the Grand Trunk Railway did not have sufficient earning capacity to finance these expenditures. Cassels and White therefore concluded that the Grand Trunk Railway had no prospects of producing profits going forward.

At the other end of the spectrum was former president Taft, already appointed to the US Supreme Court when the award was handed down,[177] who valued the same stock at no less than $48 million (present-day value of approximately $640 million).[178] While Taft had acknowledged the company's financial difficulties and was certainly critical of the management's indiscretions and oversights, he was nonetheless much more optimistic about the railway's future prospects than the two remaining arbitrators. In his view, the problems with the maintenance of the Grand Trunk Railway's infrastructure had been overstated, as the condition of the company's system was, while by no means pristine, at least satisfactory for operating purposes. Taft was rather impressed with the Grand Trunk Railway's past track record of profitable operation and felt that its current troubles could largely be ascribed to the abnormal situation

175 Ibid 44–45 (Taft Dissenting Opinion).

176 Ibid 5–23 (opinion of Cassels) and 23–36 (opinion of White).

177 Taft had taken the oath on 11 July 1921. See Supreme Court of the United States, 'Justices 1789 to Present' <https://www.supremecourt.gov/about/members_text.aspx> accessed 27 September 2024.

178 *Canada v Grand Trunk* (n 142) 36–62 (Taft Dissenting Opinion).

of the war and post-war years, which was soon expected to revert to normality. As a result, he considered that the railway would have returned to its profitable ways in the upcoming years.

What is pertinent for present purposes is not so much whether it was Taft or the tribunal majority who were in the right when valuing the Grand Trunk Railway's stock (the subsequent development of events, at least, does not seem to indicate that Cassels and White were incorrect in their assessment).[179] Rather, it is the fact that, on its face, the position adopted by Taft does not read as unreasonable, and could have thus very possibly, had the underlying circumstances been slightly different, ended up as the dominant one. The figure which Taft had proposed as the appropriate valuation was certainly well within the range within which the tribunal had been mandated to operate.[180] While the figure in question was no doubt substantial, it must not be overlooked that, despite the government's claims that the stock was likely valueless, there was at the time considerable apprehension by members of Canada's parliament of a substantial award in favour of the company;[181] the outcome of the arbitration, then, had hardly been a foregone conclusion prior to the fact.

There was also the question of Canada's (non-)adoption of certain measures prior to the arbitration, some of which had been aimed at inducing the Grand Trunk Railway to reach an agreement with the government and/or which may have contributed to its poor financial outlook.[182] This fact appears to further give at least some credence to Taft's assumptions at the time that the financial position of the Grand Trunk Railway was not as dire as it had appeared to the tribunal majority and that the railway would have, once in the hands of the Canadian government, possibly returned to its profitable ways relatively swiftly.

To be sure, the question whether Taft had been entirely independent in his assessment of the matter is certainly also a valid one, considering that reports from the period note that he had 'represented' the shareholders in the arbitration and that he had received compensation for his role in the arbitration directly from them.[183] Yet similar concerns could also be raised, perhaps even

179 Glazebrook (n 143) 55.

180 See n 168.

181 See House of Commons. Debates, vol 140 (n 157) 1074, 1200, 1242–1243, 1672–1673, 1927, and 1930.

182 See n 153.

183 See 'Grand Trunk Names Taft: Appoints Him on Board to Fix Price to be Paid by the Dominion' *The New York Times* (New York, 13 July 1920) 14; 'GTR Paid Taft $75,000: Canadian Railway Shareholders Bore Charge for Arbitration' *The New York Times* (New York, 16 March 1923) 31.

more so, with respect to the two remaining arbitrators, both of whom were Canadian citizens and had been, either previously or at the time of the arbitration, public officials. This is perhaps not surprising in relation to Canada's appointee to the tribunal, as it appears that, at least in the discussions in the Canadian parliament, little was expected in terms of impartiality from the party-appointed arbitrators.[184] Possibly in line with such expectations, Canada's appointee, Sir Thomas White, was a former minister of finance[185] who had in that capacity been heavily involved with both the development of the policy that had led to the take-over of the Grand Trunk Railway and the subsequent negotiations as to the conditions under which this was to take place.[186] Moreover, as the then minister of finance, White had also been the architect of some of Canada's policies and measures that were aimed at inducing the Grand Trunk Railway into entering into the agreement for the takeover of its stock.[187] During his time in office, White was furthermore quoted as saying that the company was 'clearly bankrupt and should take what Government will offer',[188] and had even advocated for the nationalisation of the railway under the War Measures Act.[189]

Even though not in as conspicuous a manner as with respect to White, Cassels' ability to approach the matter in arbitration entirely impartially was not incontrovertible. Namely, in addition to being an active judge in the Canadian judiciary, Cassels had also been the law partner to the senior counsel of the, at the time of the arbitration already government-owned, Canadian Northern Railway. Indeed, it had been following advice by none other than that same law partner of Cassels that the government had decided to acquire ownership of the Grand Trunk Railway stock (rather than merely leasing it long term, which had been the initial intention).[190] The matter, to say the least, was not aided by the fact that the original agreement between Canada and the company had, as a primary solution, provided for the third tribunal member to be appointed

184 See eg House of Commons. Debates, vol 140 (n 157) 1523–1524 and 1685–1686.

185 White also remained a member of Canada's parliament as the arbitration was ongoing, resigning only in April of 1921. See 'The Right Hon Sir William Thomas White, PC, KCMG, MP' <https://lop.parl.ca/sites/ParlInfo/default/en_CA/People/Profile?personId=1380> accessed 27 September 2024.

186 See n 171.

187 Eagle (n 150) 20–23. See also n 153.

188 Cited in Eagle (n 150) 19 and Currie (n 151) 451.

189 Eagle (n 150) 19. For further circumstances that raise doubts as to White's impartiality on the matter, see Currie (n 151) 471.

190 Eagle (n 150) 25 and 29.

by agreement of the two party-appointed arbitrators.[191] It was only during the legislative process in Canadian parliament that the enabling legislation that was based on the parties' agreement, and pursuant to which the formal agreement between Canada and the Grand Trunk Railway was later concluded, was amended by the Canadian government so as to specifically designate Cassels as the third arbitrator.[192] The magnitude of this change did not escape the Canadian government, for when explaining the alteration to parliament on behalf of the government, Meighen noted that the change was being made in order to avoid 'leaving to any chance at all the appointment of the third arbitrator', which was understood to be 'one of the most vital factors in the whole solution of the problem'.[193] Unfortunately for the company, it was hardly in a position to cry foul after the fact, as its chairman had given a resounding endorsement to Cassels when explaining the situation to the company's shareholders, describing him as 'a man of ability, high character, and great reputation', and his choice as fortunate for the company.[194]

The point here, however, is not so much whether Cassels was entirely objective in his assessment (that, in any event, can only be the subject of speculation from this temporal distance) nor whether his designation was fair toward the company. The point, rather, is that, had the third arbitrator been chosen by the two party-appointed arbitrators, as had originally been envisioned as the primary solution, it is far from obvious that the outcome of the entire process would have been the same. Indeed, it is not at all inconceivable that this original procedure for choosing the third arbitrator would have yielded a candidate more sympathetic toward the Grand Trunk Railway, and thus more inclined to subscribe to Taft's view than was Cassels. The mere possibility that this could have been so, which would have made a difference in valuation to the tune of $48 million ($660 million in present-day value), is illustrative of the gravity of ISAs capacity to affect the cost of the Canadian government's decision to take over the Grand Trunk Railway.

Setting the 'What ifs?' aside, that the decision that was ultimately handed down by the tribunal came as an unpleasant shock to the Grand Trunk Railway's

191 See House of Commons. Debates, vol 139 (n 163) 978–979 and 983. Failing agreement, the third arbitrator was to be appointed jointly by several judges holding highest judicial office in Canada.

192 House of Commons. Debates, vol 140 (n 157) 1295–1296 and 1522–1526. See also Eagle (n 150) 28–29.

193 House of Commons. Debates, vol 140 (n 157) 1522.

194 See Currie (n 151) 459.

shareholders, was hardly surprising.[195] The shares of the Grand Trunk Railway that were at the centre of the arbitration had a nominal value of some $180 million (present-day value of almost $2.5 billion) and had at the time had a market value of around $31 million (present-day value of $426 million)[196] (it had, however, been the unanimous opinion of all three arbitrators that market value was not a relevant factor in determining the true value of the railway). In fact, the market value of the stocks had even been trending up in the expectation of a favourable award.[197]

Owing to Taft's dissenting opinion, which was thus not merely of symbolic, but also of practical significance, the shareholders were nonetheless given one last chance to salvage the situation by appealing to the Privy Council. Namely, pursuant to the parties' agreement and the relevant confirming legislation, although appeal against a unanimous award was not allowed, appeal was possible in case the award was not unanimous (as had been the case by virtue of Taft's dissenting opinion).[198] Even though the shareholders were granted leave to appeal, this effort was likewise ultimately to no avail, as the appeal, which mostly turned on matters of evidence, was dismissed by the Privy Council.[199] What is particularly notable regarding the Privy Council's decision, however, perhaps even more so than the outcome, is the restrained approach that the Privy Council adopted in assessing the award. This approach was very much reminiscent of that by the US Supreme Court in the *Colombia v. Cauca Company* case discussed previously, and is perhaps best conveyed through the Privy Council's own words:

---

195 At the time, the New York Times reported that the award had caused a 'sensation' on the London Stock Exchange not seen in years. See 'Grand Trunk Stocks Tumble in London as Arbitrators Declare Them Valueless' *The New York Times* (New York, 9 September 1921) 1. See also Glazebrook (n 143) 369–370; Currie (n 151) 468–473.

196 Eagle (n 150) 28.

197 See 'Grand Trunk Stocks Tumble in London' (n 195).

198 The agreement between Canada and the Grand Trunk Railway (see n 168) provided that:

'The unanimous award of the arbitrators shall be final, but should the award not be unanimous, and should notice of appeal be given by either party to the other within thirty days after the making of the award, an appeal therefrom, upon any question of law, shall lie to the Supreme Court of Canada and or to the Judicial Committee of the Privy Council, if leave be granted by the said Committee'.

199 *The Grand Trunk Railway Company of Canada v The King* [1923] AC 150. See also Eagle (n 150) 30; Glazebrook (n 143) 369–370; Currie (n 151) 468; 'Birkenhead Explains Grand Trunk Award: He Upholds the Majority Arbitrators' Decision, to Which Justice Taft Dissented' *The New York Times* (New York, 11 November 1922) 6.

> their Lordships have *neither the right nor the duty to enquire into the merits of the award made by the arbitrators*. Under the statute which confirms the agreement, they have only jurisdiction to deal with the points of law raised before them and to determine whether the arbitrators so erred in law that their award should be set aside.[200]

Having definitely lost the legal battle, as a last resort, the shareholders made an appeal to the compassion and sense of fairness of the Canadian government, but once more without any success.[201]

In the end, as part of Canada's policy to restructure its railway system and establish a national railway carrier – the Canadian National Railway, the majority of the Grand Trunk Railway stock was, by virtue of the tribunal's decision, taken over by the Canadian government against no compensation to the holders of the preferential and common stock. The tribunal's decision, of course, had no bearing on the very policy of the Canadian government to take over the Grand Trunk Railway, as that course of action had already been decided before the tribunal had been established. The tribunal did, however, have the capacity to determine, and to do so to a significant extent, the cost of implementing the said policy – a one (seemingly quite plausible) vote swing could have been the difference between the preferential and common stock that was being taken over being valued at $0 and it being valued at $48 million ($660 million in present-day value). This valuation was, in turn, determinative of the annuity that was to be paid by the Canadian government to the shareholders, reflecting a difference between the government paying nothing or potentially being obliged to pay the shareholders annually tens of millions of dollars in present-day value.

Not only, however, were the arbitrators given the capacity to have a significant say in determining the cost of Canada's decision to take over the Grand Trunk Railway, but they were, by design, envisioned to exercise such capacity with as little constraint as possible. Namely, one of the proposals that was put forward during parliamentary debates in the hope of reducing the risk of an unfavourable award was for the tribunal to at least be given direction on the basis on which the valuation of the relevant stock was to be carried out. This proposal, however, was not met favourably by the government, which deemed it unwise to impose such strictures upon the tribunal.[202] The government's position on this point is perhaps best reflected by Meighen's statement that the

---

200 *Grand Trunk Railway v King* (n 199) 167. Emphasis added.

201 Eagle (n 150) 30; Glazebrook (n 143) 369–370; Currie (n 151) 468–473.

202 House of Commons. Debates, vol 140 (n 157) 1105–1106, 1507–1508, 1570–1571, 1706 and 1714.

tribunal was in this respect to have 'carte blanche'.[203] As was mentioned above, the thus created significant leeway for the tribunal in its decision-making was later endorsed also by the Privy Council.[204]

When the Grand Trunk Railway was eventually absorbed into the Canadian national railway enterprise,[205] the costs associated with this important policy decision were thus, to a significant extent and with considerable freedom in decision-making for the arbitrators by virtue of the Canadian government's own preference, determined through ISA. Accordingly, during the nationalisation of Canada's railways in the early 20th century, ISA was an integral component of, if not policy-making itself, then at least of the pricing that accompanied it.

This conclusion, however, does not exhaust the contribution of the *Grand Trunk Railway Arbitration* with regard to historical ISA's role in determining the cost of governance through appropriating investor property. Perhaps equally as important as the tribunal's very exercise of this role is the fact that its authority to do so, and do so with some degree of discretion, was validated by the Privy Council. This decision by the Privy Council serves as yet another very early example – adding to the abovementioned decision of the US Supreme Court in *Colombia v. Cauca Company* – of a highly respected judicial institution from an important arbitral jurisdiction confirming the capacity of historical ISA to decide on the cost of governance. Yet even more important than such validation is the unique insight that is offered by the debates in the Canadian parliament that accompanied the decision to submit the valuation of the Grand Trunk Railway's stock to arbitration. These parliamentary debates reveal that the appropriateness of leaving the decision on the ultimate cost of Canada's decision to take over the Grand Trunk Railway to ISA was, even in the early 20th century, very much questioned by, and a source of anxiety for, Canadian parliamentarians – even if primarily those from the opposition. While aware of such apprehensions, the Canadian government was not only insistent that submitting the matter to arbitration with the company was the best available course of action, but also wished to impose as little strictures as possible on the arbitrators in their exercise of the mandate that had been entrusted to them. This shows that the tribunal's role in ascertaining the costs of Canada's governance decisions was very much something that was thoroughly and very consciously considered, and ultimately approved, by the relevant branches of

203 Ibid 1508. This is not to be understood as if the tribunal was to operate beyond any confines whatsoever, as Meighen later clarified that the arbitrators would in any event be bound by 'the principles of equity and law'. See ibid 1714.

204 *Grand Trunk Railway v King* (n 199) 165–167.

205 Glazebrook (n 143) 372–373.

the Canadian government – on this particular occasion, no doubt with an outcome that was to the government's satisfaction.

3.3 *The Jaffa-Jerusalem Railway Arbitration*

Just as the *Grand Trunk Railway Arbitration* was winding down, a similar one, involving the takeover of the Jaffa-Jerusalem railway, was picking up steam, albeit in a very different setting. In a sense, *The Jaffa-Jerusalem Railway Arbitration* was somewhat of a *post scriptum* to the *Grand Trunk Railway Arbitration*, both because of the general similarity of certain pivotal issues and because the *Grand Trunk Railway Arbitration* award was actually relied upon by one of the parties in *The Jaffa-Jerusalem Railway Arbitration* – the UK – when formulating its position in this latter arbitration. In many respects, it was also one of the more fascinating historical ISAs, not least because of the involvement with the case of Sir Winston Churchill, at the time the Secretary of State for the Colonies,[206] and Sir Cecil Hurst, a renowned international lawyer, then a legal advisor to the Foreign Office, who would not long thereafter go on to serve as a judge (and eventually president) of the Permanent Court of International Justice (PCIJ).[207] In light of the fact that *The Jaffa-Jerusalem Railway Arbitration* has already been chronicled elsewhere in some detail,[208] it is presented here only in a relatively succinct manner, primarily so in order to illustrate the tribunal's central role in facilitating the parties' eventual settlement regarding the compensation that was to be paid for the appropriation of the railway.

The Jaffa-Jerusalem railway, which was at the root of the underlying dispute, was located in Palestine, and was constructed pursuant to a concession awarded in the 19th century.[209] The concession to construct and operate the railway was awarded, Palestine being at the time under Ottoman control, by the Ottoman government to one of its subjects, Youssouf Navon Effendi; it was subsequently transferred to the would-be-claimant French company, the

206 'Churchill's Political Offices, 1906–1955' (14 October 2008) <https://winstonchurchill.org/resources/reference/churchills-political-offices-1906-1955/> accessed 27 September 2024.

207 Lord McNair, 'Sir Cecil James Barrington Hurst, GCMG, KCB, QC, LLD' (1962) 38 Brit YBIL 400, 402.

208 See Shabtai Rosenne, 'The Jaffa-Jerusalem Railway Arbitration (1922)' in Shabtai Rosenne, *Essays on International Law and Practice* (Martinus Nijhoff 2007) 295; Michael Reynolds, 'The Jaffa Jerusalem Railway Company Arbitration 1922' (1991) 6 Arab Law Quarterly 215; J Gillis Wetter and Stephen M Schwebel, 'Some Little-Known Cases on Concessions' (1964) 40 Brit YBIL 183, 222.

209 Rosenne (n 208) 297. A copy of the concession (in French) is available as an appendix to the company's General Statement of Claim that is, together with the remaining documents from the arbitration, held at the UK National Archives. See UK National Archives: TS 27/144.

Société du Chemin de Fer Ottoman de Jaffa à Jérusalem et Prolongements.[210] The concession was envisaged to run for 71 years; after the expiration of this period, the fixed property of the railway was to be handed over by the concessionaire without compensation.[211]

During World War I, the railway fell into the hands of UK armed forces as they advanced into Palestine; contrary to the company's wishes, however, it was seemingly never formally requisitioned.[212] After World War I ended, Turkey's armistice and relations with the Allied Powers were intended to be regulated by the Treaty of Sevres. Among other things, the Treaty of Sevres provided that Palestine was to be placed under the administration of a mandatory that was to be selected by the principal Allied Powers.[213] In addition, the Treaty of Sevres envisioned in Article 311 that, subject to the right of the concessionaires to have the concession adapted to 'the new economic conditions', all concessions controlled by Allied nationals in territories that were to be detached from Turkey and placed under Allied administration were, in principle, to continue as before.[214] At the same time, the same article also stated that the Allied Power controlling the territory was, subject to the payment of adequate compensation (based on both equitable and legal considerations), allowed to buy out the concession if it deemed the concession 'contrary to the public interests'.[215]

The Treaty of Sevres, however, never came into force;[216] instead, in replacement of the previous military administration, a civil administration was installed by the UK in Palestine in 1920,[217] although the UK's formal mandate over Palestine was only approved by the League of Nations in 1922.[218] The Treaty of Sevres' lack of entry into force notwithstanding, possession of the railway was handed over to this newly established administration, which in turn

210 Rosenne (n 208) 297.

211 Ibid.

212 Ibid 298–299.

213 Treaty of Peace between the Allied and Associated Powers and Turkey (signed 10 August 1920, never entered into force) (1921) 15 AJIL Supp 179, art 95.

214 Ibid art 311.

215 Ibid.

216 Because of this, Palestine was at the time still technically Turkish territory under belligerent occupation. See Rosenne (n 208) 295–296.

217 Norman Bentwich, 'Mandated Territories: Palestine and Mesopotamia (Iraq)' (1921–1922) 2 Brit YBIL 48, 50.

218 Matthijs de Blois, 'The Unique Character of the Mandate for Palestine' (2016) 49 Isr L Rev 365, 368. The groundwork for the UK's mandate over Palestine, however, was laid down at the San Remo Conference, which was an extension of the 1919 Paris Peace Conference, and where the major Allied Powers had agreed that the mandate over Palestine would be awarded to the UK. See ibid.

decided to buy out the concession from the French company.[219] The matter of the compensation owed to the company, however, could not be settled through negotiations; this resulted in France and the UK ultimately deciding to make use of the mechanism for settling disputes that had been envisioned in Article 311 of the Treaty of Sevres in order to determine the compensation that was to be paid to the French company.[220] Article 311 provided that:

> If the parties cannot agree on the amount of such compensation, it will be determined by Arbitral Tribunals composed of three members, one designated by the State of which the concessionaire or the holders of the majority of the capital in the case of a company is or are nationals, one by the Government exercising authority in the territory in question, and the third designated, failing agreement between the parties, by the Council of the League of Nations.
>
> The Tribunal shall take into account, from both the legal and equitable standpoint all relevant matters, on the basis of the maintenance of the contract adapted as indicated in the following paragraph.[221]

Because the Treaty of Sevres had not entered into force, France and the UK did not invoke Article 311 as such, but instead subsequently independently agreed to submit the dispute to arbitration pursuant to the terms of Article 311.[222]

---

219 Rosenne (n 208) 299–300.

220 Ibid 300. See also Reynolds (n 208) 215–216.

221 Treaty of Sevres (n 213) art 311.

222 Indeed, the diplomatic correspondence between the UK and France reproduced in Rosenne (n 208) 341–343 shows clearly that both governments were very much cognizant that the Treaty of Sevres was not in force, yet nonetheless respectively proceeded to propose, and accept, that the dispute be settled through arbitration; 'though not yet in force' art 311 was merely said by the UK government to provide 'a procedure designed to meet cases of this nature'. In light of this explicit agreement between France and the UK, which was external to the Treaty of Serves, Andrea Leiter's curious argument that 'the arbitration was based on a document that lacked a legal basis' and that it was therefore somehow '*self-authorised*' is manifestly incorrect. See Andrea Leiter, *Making the World Safe for Investment: The Protection of Foreign Property 1922–1959* (CUP 2023) 29–37 (emphasis in the original). While Leiter acknowledges this subsequent agreement between France and the UK, she fails to appreciate the jurisdictional implications arising therefrom, according this subsequent agreement no jurisdictional significance whatsoever. Instead, Leiter focuses solely on the (undisputed and quite obvious) fact that the Treaty of Sevres had never entered into force, which is for reasons that remain unclear treated as some sort of irredeemable 'formal flaw' for the arbitration. In doing so, Leiter overlooks the fact that the consent to arbitrate in this particular instance was not, and need not necessarily have been, contained in Article 311, but was rather independently contained in this

While the arbitration agreement was concluded between the two governments, France and the UK, an interesting (and, for present purposes, decisive) wrinkle was added to the story when the company sought to interpose itself into the arbitration in place of the French government. Although this request initially caused a sense of bewilderment among those involved on the

---

separate subsequent agreement between the two governments. This latter fact was not only obvious to the tribunal itself, but also to all of those who have since commented on the case. See *Societe du Chemin de Fer Ottoman de Jaffa a Jerusalem et Prolongements v His Britannic Majesty's Government*, Award (4 October 1922), reproduced in Rosenne (n 208) 313, 314 (observing at the very beginning of the decision that the tribunal was constituted '[b]y agreement between the British and French Governments'); *Societe du Chemin de Fer Ottoman de Jaffa a Jerusalem et Prolongements v His Britannic Majesty's Government*, Preliminary Decision (29 May 1922), reproduced in Rosenne (n 208) 327, 328 and 334 (noting at the outset that '*The British and French Governments have concluded an agreement to constitute an Arbitration Tribunal* for the purpose of determining the equitable compensation which *would* be due (...) under the terms of article 311 of the Treaty of Peace with Turkey', as well as later on that 'article 311 of the Treaty of Sevres (...), *as a result of the agreement arrived at*, is to form the basis of its decision'. Emphases added.); Wetter and Schwebel (n 208) 222 (noting that '[t]he Palestine Railway arbitration took place pursuant to a *compromis* between the British and French Governments entered into in accordance with the Treaty of Sevres' and that '[t]he Treaty had not been ratified at the time when the *compromis* was signed'. Emphases in the original.); Rosenne (n 208) 295 and 300–301; Reynolds (n 208) 215–216. This conclusion is further confirmed by a letter from Cecil Hurst to the UK's agent in the arbitration, in which Hurst advises that a certain potential ambiguity in art 311 with respect to the body to which disputes were to be referred was 'not of importance at the present juncture because France and Great Britain have agreed to the reference of the question to an arbitral tribunal'. See Letter from Cecil Hurst to Orme Clarke (10 February 1922) (UK National Archives: TS 27/143); Letter from HA Payne to Cecil Hurst (with enclosed memorandum by Fountain) (9 February 1922) (UK National Archives: TS 27/143). The arbitration, then, was not '*self-authorised*', but was based, as innumerable an international arbitration before and after, on the explicit authorisation of two states, France and the UK. In other words, the authorisation and the jurisdictional basis for the arbitration did not stem from Article 311, which was undoubtedly not in force, but from the two governments' subsequent independent agreement to submit a dispute to arbitration. This remained unchanged by the fact that the two governments had agreed to arbitrate by delineating the scope of the tribunal's task through a reference to art 311. Whether or not such consent to arbitration by France and the UK could be deemed to have been validly given in light of the interests of other states or entities that may have been implicated in the matter in dispute, which are rightly highlighted by Leiter, is a valid question; that, however, is a different discussion altogether. It suffices to say at this juncture that the tribunal was both aware and wary of these potentially problematic aspects. See *Jaffa-Jerusalem Railway Arbitration*, Preliminary Decision (n 222) 332 (noting that 'in constituting the Tribunal the British and French Governments decided to apply 6.s [sic] between themselves the stipulations of article 311 of the Treaty of Sevres, notwithstanding that this treaty has not yet been ratified. *It is evident that the rights of others who may ultimately be interested are reserved*.' Emphasis added.)

UK side,[223] the company's solicitation for direct participation was eventually explicitly granted under the directions of none other than Churchill,[224] thus rendering the arbitration an ISA.

The tribunal that was established in order to deal with the matter was presided by Norwegian jurist and civil servant, Frederik Valdemar Nikolai Beichmann. At the time, Beichmann was president of the Superior Court of Trondheim and a deputy-judge of the PCIJ. He was also a member of the Permanent Court of Arbitration (PCA) and would later go on to become the president of the Institute of International Law.[225] Beichmann moreover remains notable as the person responsible for the only ever Nobel peace prize nominations for both the PCA and the PCIJ.[226] Interestingly, Beichmann was not the first name considered for the role, as both Chilean jurist Alejandro Alvarez, a judge-to-be of the International Court of Justice (ICJ), and Max Huber, then

---

223 'Jaffa Jerusalem Railway. Interview' (20 March 1922) (UK National Archives: TS 27/143); 'Extract from Societe du Chemin de Fer Ottoman de Jaffa a Jerusalem et Prolongements' letter dated Paris, 17th March 1922 addressed to Colonel AJ Barry' (UK National Archives: TS 27/143); Letter from AJ Barry to Colonel Orme Clarke (20 March 1922) (UK National Archives: TS 27/143); Letter (unsigned) to Colonel AJ Barry (22 March 1922) (UK National Archives: TS 27/143).

224 See Letter from (signature illegible) to Orme B Clarke (31 March 1922) (UK National Archives: TS 27/143); Letter (unsigned) to Colonel AJ Barry (5 April 1922) (UK National Archives: TS 27/143). Under the instructions of Churchill, the letter that resolved the matter, sent from the Colonial Office to the UK's agent in the arbitration, explicitly notes that 'His Majesty's Government *have decided to recognise this Company as the other party to the arbitration*'. Emphasis added. Rather curiously, in his account of the arbitration, Rosenne does mention that there was 'some question as to the identity of the parties to this arbitration proceeding' and that the company's attempt to interpose itself into the proceeding was described by the UK representatives as not being 'in conformity with their instructions'. However, despite having had access to the records in which this correspondence is contained, for unknown reasons, he does not discuss the documentation that explicitly addresses the UK's recognition of the company as a party to the arbitration. See Rosenne (n 208) 304–305. In her account of the arbitration, Leiter, who appears not to have reviewed the archival material relevant for this point independently, repeats Rosenne's oversight, and goes on to incorrectly claim that '[t]he official party to the arbitration on part of the claimant was the French government'. See Leiter (n 222) 39.

225 See Dag Michalsen, 'Frederik Beichmann' (*Norsk biografisk leksikon*) <https://nbl.snl.no/Frederik_Beichmann> accessed 27 September 2024.

226 See NobelPrize.org, 'Nomination Archive' <https://www.nobelprize.org/nomination/archive/show.php?id=7391> and NobelPrize.org, 'Nomination Archive: Permanent Court of International Justice (Cour permanente de justice internat.)' <https://www.nobelprize.org/nomination/archive/show_people.php?id=7124> both accessed 27 September 2024.

judge at the PCIJ, were considered before him.[227] The two party-appointed arbitrators, H. Osborne Mance and Ferdinand Mayer, were both engineers.[228]

The tribunal so composed was once more to determine the eventual cost of a policy decision – that to take over the Jaffa-Jerusalem railway – that had already been taken in the name of public interests. Ultimately, the tribunal did not end up having to decide the matter, as the parties had managed to settle the dispute amicably before the tribunal could issue its final say; the tribunal's award was thus merely a recording of the parties' will.[229] That is not to say, however, that the tribunal did not play an integral part in the process of establishing the amount of compensation that was to be paid for the takeover of the railway. Namely, the parties' settlement was preceded, and was very likely induced, by a preliminary decision by the tribunal on the legal principles according to which compensation was to be determined, with the tribunal finding that it was the railway's potential to earn profits during the life of the concession, and not the reproduction cost of the railway, that was relevant for valuation.[230]

The tribunal's decision on this point was prompted by a request for a preliminary ruling by the UK's agent in the arbitration, Orme Clarke.[231] The request by Clarke came in response to the company's statement of claim,[232] wherein the largest individual item related to the 'physical value of the railway calculated at the present cost of constructing and equipping the line'.[233] As the available documentary record shows, the decision to request the preliminary ruling on this matter had indeed been influenced by the earlier award in the *Grand Trunk Railway Arbitration*, which had deemed evidence relating to the reproduction cost of the railway inadmissible when valuating the relevant railway stock.[234] Following the same approach, Clarke argued that the tribunal's task was not to

227 Rosenne (n 208) 304–305.

228 Ibid 303–304.

229 *Jaffa-Jerusalem Railway Arbitration*, Award (n 222).

230 *Jaffa-Jerusalem Railway Arbitration*, Preliminary Decision (n 222).

231 Ibid 328.

232 Societe du Chemin de Fer Ottoman de Jaffa a Jerusalem et Prolongements, 'Purchase of the Concession by the Palestine Government: General Statement of Claim on Behalf of the Railway Company' (UK National Archives: TS 27/144).

233 *Jaffa-Jerusalem Railway Arbitration*, Preliminary Decision (n 222) 328.

234 Letter (unsigned) to Norman Bentwich (16 March 1922) (UK National Archives: TS 27/144); Letter from (signature illegible) to the Under-Secretary of State, Colonial Office (27 February 1922) (UK National Archives: TS 27/143). From the reviewed materials, it remains unclear whether Clarke explicitly invoked the *Grand Trunk Railway Arbitration* before the tribunal, although the case was at least mentioned in one of the supporting expert opinions attached to the UK's memorial. See 'In the Matter of an Arbitration between The

assess the value of any property as such, but rather to assess compensation for the revocation of the concession – which he submitted could not be done on the basis of the reproduction value of the railway.[235]

Having heard each side's arguments both in writing and orally,[236] the tribunal agreed with Clarke. In coming to its decision, the tribunal deemed it necessary to consider the position in which the company would have found itself if the railway had not been taken over.[237] Because the terms of the concession had envisioned that, following its termination, the company was to hand over the railway line with the accompanying fixed properties without compensation, the tribunal was convinced that the company 'would have only been entitled to the profits which could be earned by the operation of the line for the duration of the concession'.[238] Since the tribunal did not think that such profits depended on the reproduction value of the railway, it held that this value could not factor into the assessment of the compensation owed to the company. As Rosenne has observed, in coming to this decision, the tribunal 'effectively determined in favour of the British Government one of the principal legal issues arising out of the Company's claims'.[239] In so doing, the tribunal thus put a serious dent into the company's case, decreasing the gap between the respective positions of the two sides and making it easier for them to ultimately find common ground.[240]

On the face of it, the role of the tribunal in the *Jaffa-Jerusalem Railway Arbitration* in attaching a cost to the Palestinian civil administration's decision to take over the railway might appear trivial; indeed, from a formal perspective, the tribunal's eventual award was but a recording of the disputing parties' agreement. Yet, according such little weight to the tribunal's role would hardly do justice to its actual influence. Even if it was not the final say in the matter, by eliminating the possibility that the compensation due may be determined according to the reproduction cost of the railway, the tribunal's preliminary

Jaffa-Jerusalem Railway Company and the British Government: Opinion of Mr R Newton Crane, KC' (19 May 1922) (UK National Archives: TS 27/144).

235 *Jaffa-Jerusalem Railway Arbitration*, 'Memorial in Support of the Contentions of the Respondents Set out in an Application to the Tribunal Dated 19th April, 1922' (6 May 1922) (UK National Archives: TS 27/144) 3.

236 Ibid; 'Claim of the Jaffa Jerusalem Railway: Arbitration Tribunal: Sitting of 26th May 1922' (UK National Archives: TS 27/144); *Jaffa-Jerusalem Railway Arbitration*, 'Answer of the Claimants to the Memorial of the Respondents, dated the 6th May 1922' (18 May 1922) (UK National Archives: TS 27/144).

237 *Jaffa-Jerusalem Railway Arbitration*, Preliminary Decision (n 222) 334–336.

238 Ibid 336.

239 Rosenne (n 208) 308.

240 On the settlement, see Rosenne (n 208) 307–309; Reynolds (n 208) 222–223.

decision was pivotal in reducing the plausible divergence between the parties' positions. In so doing, the tribunal's preliminary decision thus laid the groundwork for the parties' eventual settlement (which was no doubt further facilitated by the tribunal's looming assignment of a definitive cost to the takeover of the railway in case a settlement was not forthcoming). Accordingly, it would not be an overstatement to say that the *Jaffa-Jerusalem Railway Arbitration* was integral, even if indirectly so, to the process of determining the cost of the appropriation of the Jaffa-Jerusalem Railway. In fact, by highlighting how historical ISA operated to influence the cost of state appropriation of investor property in situations other than when this was achieved directly through a tribunal's decision, the *Jaffa-Jerusalem Railway Arbitration* stands as a complement to the *Colombia v. Cauca Company* and *Grand Trunk Railway Arbitration* cases in painting a fuller picture of historical ISA's role in determining such cost.

4 Imposing Liability in Investor-State Relations for Breach of Obligations

An account about historical ISA's role in determining the cost of governance would hardly be complete without addressing perhaps its most distinctive manifestation – the capacity to impose liability upon parties in the investor-state relationship for lack of compliance with their obligations and to, in turn, encumber them with an accompanying obligation to pay indemnification. By shedding light on this facet of its past, this section thus complements, and expands upon, the modalities of historical ISA's role in ascertaining the cost of governance explored in the preceding sections.

That historical ISA, having been an adjudicative process, would have taken on the role of holding parties to a contract accountable for non-compliance is hardly surprising. What made this otherwise routine adjudicative role stand out when implemented in historical ISA was the involvement of states in the process. This is because the presence of states as disputing parties implied that a historical ISA tribunal's assessment of the parties' compliance with obligations was often predicated upon the need to review whether the conduct of public officials, or even certain governmental policies themselves (or their implementation), were in line with the states' obligations.[241] The requirement

241 Certainly, instances where a private investor was the one being held accountable through a monetary award were not unknown in historical ISA, although such occasions for obvious reasons appear to have been far less common than the reverse situation. One such

for tribunals to make this type of assessment created significant room for historical ISA to influence the cost of a state's conduct of official business. Ample examples of historical ISA taking on this role can be found. Many of these cases – such as e.g. *Suez v. Egypt*,[242] the abovementioned *Lena Goldfields v. USSR*[243] and *Sapphire v. National Iranian Oil Company* (*NIOC*)[244] – are among the more fabled, and well chronicled, historical ISAs; others, including those analysed in the remainder of this section, have either remained obscure or have received comparatively little attention, despite being able to offer significant insight into historical ISA's capacity to impose costs upon states for how they governed.[245]

In an attempt to simultaneously both remedy the hitherto overlooking, and unwarrantedly so, of some of these past ISAs and to faithfully convey the essence of such practice, this section analyses two underexplored instances of historical ISA influencing the cost of governance by imposing liability upon states. The first of these concerns an early 20th century dispute over an alleged breach of undertaking by a government in Southeast Asia due to a failure to construct certain infrastructural projects (4.1). The second looks at a decision from the second part of the 20th century that imposed significant pecuniary liability on a penurious African country, Sudan, in response to its cancellation of an investment contract. The decision is of particular interest in terms of historical ISA's capacity to affect the cost of governance as Sudan alleged that the cancellation of the contract had been carried out due to the investor's non-compliance with Sudan's policy at the time, adopted in response to South

example is provided by the late 19th century arbitration between the Oriental Railways and the Ottoman Empire, where the former was obliged to pay to the latter more than 26 million francs (against which 12 million was to be set off on account of the Ottoman Empire's debt to the company). See Kurt Grunwald, *Turkenhirsch: A Study of Baron Maurice de Hirsch, Entrepreneur and Philanthropist* (Israel Program for Scientific Translations 1966) 58–59.

242 See Jason Webb Yackee, 'The First Investor-State Arbitration: *The Suez Canal Company v Egypt* (1864)' (2016) 17 The Journal of World Investment and Trade 401.

243 *Lena Goldfields v USSR* (n 12).

244 *Sapphire International Petroleums Limited v National Iranian Oil Co* (*NIOC*) (1967) 35 ILR 136. See also *BP Exploration Company* (*Libya*) *Limited v The Government of the Libyan Arab Republic* (1979) 53 ILR 297, where the arbitrator found that Libya had breached its obligations towards the claimant under a concession and was in principle liable to pay damages. The dispute was settled before the tribunal could rule on the amount of damages.

245 In addition to the arbitrations analysed in this section, see also *Martin Cowley Railway Construction Co, Limited and Alderton Construction* (*Westminster*) *Limited v The Higher Committee for the Recommissioning of the Hedjaz Railway Line*, Award (22 September 1972) 2. A copy of the award can be found at the Archives of the Graduate Institute of International and Development Studies in Geneva, Reference code 1.7.5.HEI 2448.

Africa's apartheid regime, of not entering into commercial dealings with South Africa or its citizens (4.2).

4.1 *Duff Development Company v Government of Kelantan I and II*

A particularly apposite example of an ISA tribunal imposing liability upon a government for its policy choices concerns a pair of arbitration proceedings that involved Kelantan – a territory now forming part of Malaysia, but whose status prior to and during the arbitrations was rather complex.[246] While the two arbitrations constitute two inextricably linked chapters of a continuous and drawn out dispute, as is expounded upon below, each of them sheds light on different aspects of historical ISA's role in determining the cost of governance.

246 When the Duff concession was obtained, Kelantan was in 'vague and loosely defined tributary relations' with Siam, leading to a dispute, resolved only in 1902, over whether there was a need for Siam to ratify the concession. See Kobkua Suwannathat-Pian, 'The 1902 Siamese-Kelantan Treaty: An End to the Traditional Relations' (1984) 72 Journal of the Siam Society 95, 95–97; Ernest LeVos, 'Robert W Duff: a British Seigneur in Kelantan, 1892–1932' (1997) 70(1) Journal of the Malaysian Branch of the Royal Asiatic Society 1, 6–7; Leslie Ratnasingam Robert, 'The Duff Syndicate in Kelantan 1900–1902' (1972) 45(1) Journal of the Malaysian Branch of the Royal Asiatic Society 81, 104–105. In 1909, Siamese rights over Kelantan were transferred by treaty to the UK, with Kelantan becoming a protectorate of the latter. See Treaty and Notes between Great Britain and Siam regarding the Cession and Boundaries of the Siamese Malay States, the Jurisdiction of the Siamese Courts and the Non-cession etc of Siamese Territory (signed 10 March 1909) (1909) 208 CTS 367 art 1; Agreement between Great Britain and Kelantan respecting Administration (signed 22 October 1910) (1910) 212 CTS 276; Alfred P Rubin, *Piracy, Paramountcy and Protectorates* (Penerbit Universiti Malaya 1974) 140; Lawrence Collins, 'Captain Duff, the Sultan of Kelantan and Their Legacy in the Law of State Immunity and International Arbitration' (2021) 37 Arbitration International 463, 465; David Baillargeon, '"Imperium in Imperio": The Corporation, Mining, and Governance in British Southeast Asia, 1900–1930' (2022) 23(2) Enterprise & Society 325, 348. Interestingly, during enforcement proceedings before UK courts stemming from the second arbitration between the Duff Development Company and the Government of Kelantan, the then Secretary of State for the Colonies (none other than Winston Churchill) took the position on behalf of the UK that Kelantan was an independent state. See *Duff Development Co Ltd v Government of Kelantan* [1924] AC 797, 806–807 (HL). For the reasons stated above, the mentions made to the Government of Kelantan and its decisions or positions on certain matters should be taken with some reservation, as there was, to say the least, 'a strong influence' (or even control, as it was claimed in some instances) by UK government officials over the Government of Kelantan in these respects. See eg *Kelantan Government v Duff Development Company, Limited* [1922–1923] 39 Times L Rep 337, 339 and 341 (HL) (Viscount Cave, Lord Chancellor, remarking that the Colonial Office 'controlled' the Kelantan government or that its operations were carried out under the Colonial Office's directions). Such considerations, however, go beyond the scope of this book.

The disputes giving rise to the arbitrations spanned several decades, and arose in relation to a concession to exploit a large area in Kelantan obtained in the twilight of the 19th century by a former colonial police officer stationed in the Malay Peninsula, Robert W. Duff.[247] Upon his retirement from service, Duff formed a syndicate of British interests (the Duff Syndicate, which later evolved into the Duff Development Company) and managed to obtain from the ruler of Kelantan an extremely comprehensive concession, both in terms of the territory that it covered (estimated to had been between a third and a half of Kelantan's entire territory)[248] and the privileges that had been granted.[249] The concession had awarded Duff extensive and exclusive rights to work the land granted to him for forty years, including with respect to minerals and timber, as well as 'every other kind of work in whatever manner he pleases'.[250] The scope of the concession – which had arguably transferred to the concessionaire considerable administrative powers within the territory of the concession[251] – was a source of friction from the outset, and there followed a series of attempts to scale back the authority that had been granted to the company, with the

247 For Duff's background prior to his endeavors with the Kelantan concession, see LeVos (n 246) 3–4; Collins (n 246) 463–464.

248 Robert (n 246) 94–95; Amarjit Kaur, *Bridge and Barrier: Transport and Communications in Colonial Malaya 1870–1957* (OUP 1985) 60; Rubin (n 246) 98. See also 'Memorandum: History of the Affairs of the Duff Development Company: 1900 – March, 1923' (10 April 1923) (UK National Archives: CO 1073/133) para 6.

249 Agreement between the Raja of Kelantan and RW Duff (October 1900), reproduced in Shaharil Talib, *History of Kelantan: 1890–1940* (The Malaysian Branch of the Royal Asiatic Society 1995) 194. On how the concession came to be, see Robert (n 246); Talib (n 249) 20–21; Rubin (n 246) 92–133; Baillargeon (n 246) 344 and 348.

250 1900 Agreement Between the Raja and RW Duff (n 249) art 1 para 2.

251 Such powers at various junctures included, amongst others, the rights of taxation, the exercise of judicial authority and vetoing legislation. See Robert (n 246) 94; WA Graham, *Kelantan: A State of The Malay Peninsula: A Handbook of Information* (James Maclehose and Sons 1908) 110; Talib (n 249) 65, 79, 93 and 100–101; Kaur (n 248) 60; Rubin (n 246) 143. See also the terms of the various iterations of the concession reproduced in Talib (n 249) 194–207. While the Kelantan government disputed in the first arbitration that the company had ever been granted rights of an administrative or executive character, UK government sources used similar epithets in describing the rights held by the company. Compare *The Duff Development Company Limited v The Government of Kelantan*, Defence (20 September 1915) (*Duff v Kelantan I*) (Foyle Special Collections Library at King's College London: FCDO Historical Coll, FOL DS598.K3 DUF) 1–2 with W Langham-Carter, *Kelantan Administration Report for the Year 1912* (FMS Government Printing Office 1913) (UK National Archives: CO 827/1) 12; 'Memorandum: History of the Affairs of the Duff Development Company' (n 248) para 30 (noting that the company had been informed that it was in possession of rights that 'ought only to be exercised by Government'); Baillargeon (n 246) 348; Collins (n 246) 465.

goal of preventing it from becoming 'a state within a state' (or 'imperium in imperio').[252] After a few modifications,[253] the concession was ultimately cancelled in 1912 by a Deed of Cancellation that was supposed to finally resolve all of the open issues between Kelantan and the company. As part of this settlement, in exchange for cash considerations, the company received a more moderate set of rights over a considerably smaller part of territory.[254] Notably, and rather consequentially, as it would prove to be the case, the Deed of Cancellation also contained a comprehensive arbitration clause.[255]

The hopes that the Deed of Cancellation would be a turning point in the relations between the company and the Kelantan government, however, proved futile, as frictions between the two sides resumed almost immediately, this time regarding the construction of a railway through territory that had under the concession belonged to the company. Namely, under the previous iterations of the concession, the Duff Development Company had held the exclusive right of communication by rail within the ambit of the concession.[256] While the company had under the Deed of Cancellation given up this right (which had been its strongest bargaining chip in the negotiations leading up to the Deed, so much so that it was accused of 'holding the Government up to ransom'),[257] in return the said Deed nonetheless noted the Kelantan government's 'intention' to build a railway through the company's concession and made the exercise of certain rights granted to the company under the Deed of

252 LeVos (n 246) 13; Langham-Carter (n 251) 12; Collins (n 246) 465; Baillargeon (n 246) 348–349.

253 See Explanatory Document Sealed by the Raja of Kelantan and Signed by RW Duff (August 1903), reproduced in Talib (n 249) 198; Draft Agreement between the Government of Kelantan and the Duff Development Company (April 1905), reproduced in Talib (n 249) 201.

254 The Government of Kelantan and the Duff Development Company, Limited: Deed of Cancellation (15 July 1912), reproduced in Talib (n 249) 208.

255 Ibid art 21. The arbitration clause read:

"Any and every dispute differences or questions which shall at any time arise between the parties hereto touching the construction, meaning or effect of these presents or of any clause or thing herein contained or the rights or liabilities of the parties hereunder or otherwise howsoever relating to the premises shall be referred to the arbitration of a sole Arbitrator to be agreed upon between the parties or failing agreement to be nominated by the Secretary of State for the Colonies for the time being and thus shall be deemed a submission to arbitration within the Arbitration Act 1889 or any statutory modification or re-enactment thereof for the time being in force the provisions whereof shall apply so far as applicable".

256 See 1905 Draft Agreement (n 253) clause 3.

257 'Memorandum: History of the Affairs of the Duff Development Company' (n 248) para 34. See also Talib (n 249) 150–152; Rubin (n 246) 146; Baillargeon (n 246) 349.

Cancellation dependent on the government's obligation to provide the company with the proposed railway route.[258] Once it became apparent that the Kelantan government would not go through with the railway according to the route that had allegedly been promised to the company (and which the company deemed key for its continued economic development), the company and the Kelantan government once more found themselves in disagreement.[259] Making use of the arbitration clause in the Deed of Cancellation, the two sides submitted the matter to a jointly selected arbitrator, former Chief Justice of the Colony of Ceylon, Sir Alfred George Lascelles.[260]

The Duff Development Company's claim in the arbitration was that the Deed of Cancellation had been conditional upon the government's performance of its alleged representations that the railway would be constructed according to a certain route; accordingly, the company requested a declaration to the effect that it was entitled to set the Deed aside in case the Kelantan government failed to meet this requirement. If this were to be the case, the company further requested declarations to the effect that, in this event, the Deed will never have been valid, operative or binding and that the parties were to be restored to their previous positions, as well as that the company would be entitled, *ex tunc*, to its rights under the concession that had preceded the Deed of Cancellation.[261] The Kelantan government, on the other hand, asked the arbitrator to affirm that the government had not yet set the general route for the railway and that it was entitled to do so in a manner it thought appropriate. In addition, the government also wanted the arbitrator to declare that it was only obliged to deliver to the company a definitive plan for the railway after the route had been chosen, as well as that, once delivered, it was entitled to make any such deviations from the said plan as it saw fit.[262]

The oral proceedings before the arbitrator lasted ten days,[263] and resulted in a short and essentially unreasoned award, handed down on 31 March 1916,[264]

---

258 Deed of Cancellation (n 254), preamble and clause 4.

259 Kaur (n 248) 67–72.

260 *Duff v Kelantan I* (n 251), Copy of Submission to Arbitration (2 June 1915) (UK National Archives: FCO 141/16706).

261 Ibid.

262 Ibid.

263 The government's defence (see n 251) and the transcripts of the oral hearings in the first arbitration are available at the Foyle Special Collections Library at King's College London (FCDO Historical Coll, FOL DS598.K3 DUF).

264 *Duff v Kelantan I* (n 251), Award (31 March 1916). Copies of the award are available at the Foreign and Commonwealth Office Pamphlet Collection at the University of Manchester Library Special Collections and the Foyle Special Collections Library at King's College London (FCDO Historical Coll, FOL DS598.K3 DUF).

wherein the arbitrator's ultimate conclusions and findings were preceded only by his brief recounting of the documentary and procedural basis for the arbitration, the parties' claims, and the relevant procedural steps. In his award, Lascelles sided entirely with the Kelantan government, as he found that no representations had been made to the Duff Development Company on behalf of the Kelantan government to the effect that the railway would be built along a specific route. In fact, the arbitrator held that the persons alleged to have made such representations were at the relevant time aware both that the government had not yet decided the railway route and that it had not even been in a position to do so. The company was, according to the arbitrator's finding, thus not induced into entering into the Deed of Cancellation through such alleged representations nor was it ever understood between the negotiating parties that their fulfilment was the basis or a condition for the Deed of Cancellation's validity or effectiveness. In consequence, the arbitrator held that the Duff Development Company was not entitled to the requested declarations, dismissing its claim in its entirety.[265]

Lascelles also proceeded to rule on the relief requested by the Kelantan government, holding that the said railway route had, as of the time of the arbitrator's award, not yet been chosen, as well as that the government did have the right to choose the general route for the railway as it best thought appropriate (but with the added restriction that such route needed to be 'in accordance with the Deed of Cancellation').[266] This aspect of the arbitrator's decision is rather remarkable, as Lascelles took upon himself to provide in the award explicit authorisation to the government for performing a task such as building a railway along a preferred route.[267] As noteworthy as it may be, that Lascelles felt empowered to do so is nonetheless perhaps not entirely surprising under the circumstances, considering that his decision on this point was taken at the behest of the government itself, which appears before the fact to have viewed the arbitrator's eventual findings as controlling on the matter. Indeed, once it became evident that the dispute would be going to arbitration, in anticipation of the arbitrator's award, the government issued an order to halt the work on the railway that had already begun (along the course to which

265 Ibid 3–4.

266 Ibid 4. The arbitrator did not decide the government's two remaining claims, as its counsel did not insist on them being in the award in case the company's claims were rejected.

267 In this respect, the arbitrator's award goes along the same lines as the decisions discussed in ch 4.

the company had objected), as there was fear that, if the work was continued, an award in favour of the company might prove too costly.[268]

Lascelles' decision to dismiss the company's claim, however, once more failed to definitively relieve the strain from the relations between the Duff Development Company and the Kelantan government. While the parties had accepted the arbitrator's decision regarding the validity of the Deed of Cancellation, they nonetheless proceeded to quarrel as to the content of the obligations incurred by the government under the said (now undoubtedly valid) Deed and whether those obligations had been observed. The matter was once more submitted to arbitration; this time, however, the parties were unable to agree on an arbitrator, so the appointment was (in line with the Deed of Cancellation) referred to the Colonial Secretary, who in 1919 appointed Sir Edwin Arney Speed, the former Chief Justice of Nigeria.[269] The parties agreed that this second arbitration was to proceed in two stages: the arbitrator was first to decide questions of liability and then, if need be, questions of damages in a second stage.[270]

Unlike in the first arbitration, where the company's claim was founded upon certain representations allegedly made to it, in its second bite at the cherry the Duff Development Company grounded its claim on the Deed of Cancellation itself. The company's submission was that it had suffered substantial losses due to a significantly higher cost of doing business resulting from the Kelantan government's failure to perform its obligations under the Deed – that is, to build a cart road and railway along a certain route.[271] In this respect, the company relied on clause 18 of the Deed of Cancellation, which had expressly

268 *The Duff Development Company Limited v The Government of Kelantan,* Transcript Days 1–5 (24–28 October 1921) (*Duff v Kelantan II*) (Foreign and Commonwealth Office Pamphlet Collection at the University of Manchester Library Special Collections) 39–41, 100–105, 173–174 and 180–187. It appears that, owing to technical reasons, the work on the railway was not altogether suspended but merely slackened. See ibid 104 and 181. See also 'Memorandum: History of the Affairs of the Duff Development Company' (n 248) paras 38 and 44.

269 *Duff v Kelantan II* (n 268), Transcript 15 and 52; *Kelantan v Duff Development Company* (n 246) 338. The Duff Development Company was opposed to Speed's appointment on account of his connections to the colonial administration. See 'Memorandum: History of the Affairs of the Duff Development Company' (n 248) para 71. Rather ironically, after his decisions were handed down, it would be not the company, but its opponents, who would be complaining about Speed. See 'Notes of a Meeting Held at Bel Retiro, Penang Hills, on Sunday, January the 6th at 9.30 AM' (UK National Archives: FCO 141/16715); Letter from AFR to Hall (1 July 1923) (UK National Archives FCO 141/16714); Copy of Letter from Devonshire (unaddressed) (30 July 1923) (UK National Archives FCO 141/16705).

270 *Duff v Kelantan II* (n 268), Transcript 52–53.

271 Ibid 2, 15 and 53–56.

provided that the Kelantan government was to build a cart road within the company's concession within four years.[272] Based on the fact that one of the terminal points of the road was to be the said railway (as well as on certain other rights granted to the company under the Deed of Cancellation being dependent on the existence of the railway), the Duff Development Company also argued that, in addition to the road itself, the Deed of Cancellation had contained an implied obligation to construct a railway that would serve the road in question.[273]

Despite the cart road admittedly not having been built (whereas the railway had, following the decision by Lascelles in the first arbitration, proceeded along a route that differed from the one preferred by the company),[274] the Kelantan government denied that it had breached the Deed of Cancellation. As for the railway, the Kelantan government argued that it had been under no obligation at all to build a railway, as there had been no express provision to that effect in the Deed of Cancellation; in its view, an obligation of such importance and financial magnitude could not be implied from the few side references to the railway contained in certain provisions of the Deed.[275] While the counsel for Kelantan had acknowledged the express nature of clause 18 concerning the cart road, he nonetheless maintained that the provision was not sufficiently specific (in terms of its route, quality, maintenance, etc …). Accordingly, considering the government's discretionary rights in terms of how it was to proceed with the construction of a road that was going to be for public use and the various interests it needed to take into account in this respect, this provision could at best give rise only to a right to nominal damages, as there was no guarantee that the road would be of any substantial benefit to the company.[276] Finally, Kelantan also put forward a defence that, by virtue of its position that aimed to void the Deed of Cancellation and that had subsequently led to the

272 For the company's argumentation on this point, see *Duff v Kelantan II* (n 268), Transcript 53–55 and 203–209.

273 *Duff v Kelantan II* (n 268), Transcript 55, 209–216 and 220–223.

274 See ibid 198. Following the conclusion of the first arbitration, however, the government expressed its desire to construct the road and even enquired with the company about the preferred route, but the company refused to give its opinion beyond stating that the road was to be built in accordance with the Deed of Cancellation. See ibid 43, 112 and 192–193. As the matter dragged on with no road being built, the company eventually took the position that the government was no longer entitled to construct the road, arguing that doing so would have caused significant damage to the company in light of the land that the company would be required to give up and the possibility that the government might enlist the company's workforce for this purpose. See ibid 49–50, 113–114 and 194–195.

275 Ibid 136–152.

276 Ibid 152–172.

first arbitration, the company had hindered the performance of the government's obligations under the Deed of Cancellation and that it could therefore not bring a claim against the government on this account.[277]

In yet another short award, handed down on 17 November 1921, arbitrator Speed found entirely in favour of the Duff Development Company.[278] As far as the government's alleged implied obligation to build a railway was concerned, Speed's award was based on principles deduced from two UK Court of Appeal cases. The first of these had held that an implication of a contractual term should only be made where necessary so as to give the transaction the efficacy intended by both sides and to prevent a failure of consideration that could not have been contemplated by either side. Whether such an implication should be made in a particular instance was dependent on the particular facts of the case. According to the second case, in all of the cases of implied covenants, the law raised an implication from the parties' presumed intention with the goal of conferring upon the transaction the efficacy intended by both parties.

In line with these principles, any attempt to construe the Deed of Cancellation, in Speed's view, required taking into account the natural features of the country where the parties' obligations were to be performed, as well as the parties' positions and the circumstances present during the preliminary negotiations and the agreement's conclusion. It was deemed that an approach to the contrary would have resulted in a construction that involved a failure of consideration not contemplated by either party and depriving the transaction of its intended efficacy. Having considered the evidence available on these points and the company's claim, Speed concluded that the Kelantan government was,

277 Ibid 172–198. According to the government, as the two had been interconnected, this defence applied to both the railway (which was the subject of the company's objections at the time of the arbitration) and, by extension, to the road. As was previously mentioned (n 268), the work on the railway had been suspended while the first arbitration was ongoing and the arbitration was completed only months before the four year deadline under the Deed of Cancellation was set to expire. The time that was left, in Kelantan's view, was insufficient to carry out the works that the company argued were required under the Deed of Cancellation (and the company had also rejected the government's request to move back the deadline due to the arbitration).

278 *Duff v Kelantan II* (n 268), Award (17 November 1921). A copy of the award is available as an appendix contained in the documents relating to the House of Lords proceedings that resulted from attempts to enforce the arbitrator's award as to costs. See UK National Archives: TS 36/216. See also 'Duff Development Co: Arbitrator's Decree Against Kelantan Government' *The Straits Times* (Singapore, 29 November 1921) 12; 'The Duff Development Company, Limited: Kelantan Government's Breach of Contract: Important Bearing of Arbitrator's Award' *The Times* (London, 21 December 1921) 20; Rubin (n 246) 148; Viscount Maugham, *At the End of the Day* (Heinemann 1954) 72.

pursuant to the Deed of Cancellation, under an explicit obligation to construct within the concession a cart road from a certain point and within a four year period. In addition, the arbitrator held that it were implied contractual terms that the said road was to proceed according to a certain route and terminate on the railway line within the concession, as well as that the railway in question was to be constructed within the time period for the construction of the road and in a manner that would allow for the construction of such road. Speed decided that the Kelantan government had failed to fulfil these contractual terms and that it had, by doing so, caused damage to the company; the nature and amount of such damage was directed for further inquiry. At the same time, the arbitrator also rejected Kelantan's defence to the effect that it was the company's own conduct that had given rise to the failure to construct the road and railway, as he saw no evidence of either act or omission on behalf of the company that would have disentitled it to damages for breach of contract.

Speed's award, which established Kelantan's liability for breach of contract, was followed, in anticipation of the damages phase of the arbitration, by the parties' negotiations aimed at settling the dispute. While the parties appeared at one point to have been close to reaching a settlement, these negotiations nonetheless ultimately proved unsuccessful.[279] The damages phase was also preceded by a panoply of proceedings before UK courts in relation to the award; these included the (ultimately unsuccessful) attempts by Kelantan to have the award set aside and by the company to enforce the arbitrator's award in relation to costs, both of which ended up before the House of Lords.[280] Once the court proceedings were concluded, the matter was referred back to Speed for his decision on the amount of damages to be paid by Kelantan. The protracted examination as to the various items of damage alleged by the Duff Development Company,[281] valued by the company as being worth in excess

279 On the negotiations, see generally UK National Archives: FCO 141/16704-16705 and FCO 141/16711.

280 For an overview of these various proceedings, see *Kelantan v Duff Development Company* (n 246) 339; *Duff v Kelantan* [1924] AC 797 (n 246) 798–799; Maugham (n 278) 72–74; Rubin (n 246) 148–153; Collins (n 246) 466–468 and 469–473. Viscount Maugham had been counsel for the Duff Development Company in the proceedings. As mentioned in n 278, documents relating to the latter of the proceedings before the House of Lords are available in UK National Archives: TS 36/216.

281 The company alleged four items of damage: timber rights, undeveloped land, cultivated lands, and dredging and mining rights. See *Duff v Kelantan II* (n 268), Particulars of Damage (1 November 1923) (UK National Archives: FCO 141/16715). On the complex nature and duration of this part of the arbitration, which lasted from June until November of 1924, see Maugham (n 278) 73–74. The transcripts of the hearings in the damages phase are unfortunately only partially preserved in UK National Archives: FCO 141/16701-16703.

of £1 million (present-day value between £61.2 million and £558.5 million), culminated with the arbitrator finally awarding the company £378,000 (present-day value between £21.2 million and £187.3 million) in compensation for the government's failure to comply with its obligations under the Deed of Cancellation.[282]

Arbitrator Speed's decision that the Kelantan government had failed to fulfil its obligations *vis-à-vis* the Duff Development Company was thus coupled with steep financial consequences, in the process altering the ultimate cost of the government's choices and policies with respect to infrastructure projects of considerable magnitude. These financial consequences, as is explained in more detail in section 5 below, were significantly beyond Kelantan's financial capacity at the time. In light of Kelantan's unquestionable inability to comply with Speed's award, an arrangement was made for Kelantan to receive financial assistance from the Federated Malay States and the Straits Settlements,[283] allowing it to reach a settlement with the Duff Development Company. While the settlement was thus concluded with the company in 1926,[284] and the award paid out,[285] Kelantan was nonetheless left with a significant public

282 G E Shaw, *Kelantan Administration Report for the Year 1925* (Government Printing Office Singapore 1926) (UK National Archives: CO 827/1) 14; Maugham (n 278) 74; Rubin (n 246) 154; LeVos (n 246) 15. Unfortunately, the arbitrator's award of 27 November 1925 could not be located. However, an excerpt from the award's *dispositif* is contained in a speech given by the Governor of the Straits Settlements and High Commissioner for the Federated Malay States, Sir Laurence Guillemard, before the Legislative Council of the Straits Settlements. See 'Straits Settlements: Legislative Council: Monday, 11th October, 1926' (UK National Archives: CO 717/53/12) 4. Together with costs, the award was worth approximately £440,000 (present-day value between £24.7 million and £218.1 million). See 'FMS and Kelantan: Chief Secretary's Assurance to the Public: Extraordinarily Sound Position' *Malay Mail* (Kuala Lumpur, 12 October 1926) (UK National Archives CO: 717/53/12).

283 'Straits Settlements: Legislative Council' (n 282) 3–5; FMS and Kelantan: Chief Secretary's Assurance to the Public (n 282). According to these arrangements, Kelantan was to receive a loan of $4.25 million, free of interest for five years, from the Straits Settlements, while the Federated Malay States wrote off an earlier £300,000 loan (made also on account of Kelantan's dealings with the Duff Development Company) and agreed to repay to Kelantan the interest that had already been paid on that loan (amounting to almost $1 million).

284 See Deed of Settlement between the Government of Kelantan and the Duff Development Company Limited (27 November 1926) (UK National Archives FCO: 141/16840). Under the deed, in consideration for the government's payment of the award, several clauses of a previous Deed of Surrender of 21 July 1921 were cancelled, and all of the company's claims against the government in relation to the Deed of Cancellation were deemed completely settled.

285 Letter from WAF Wickhart to the Under Secretary of State, Colonial Office (1 December 1926) (UK National Archives: CO 717/53/12); Letter from WAF Wickhart to the Colonial Secretary, Straits Settlements (9 December 1926) (UK National Archives: CO 717/53/12);

debt burden, mostly consisting of the loan taken out on account of the Duff arbitration.[286]

Although the 1926 settlement was supposed to resolve all of the contentious issues between Kelantan and the Duff Development Company once and for all, this again proved not to be the case. This time, the controversy arose over certain lands that were still to be granted to the company, as it became disputed which lands precisely the company was entitled to; another point of contention was the fact that the Federated Malay States Railways had at certain points trespassed on the company's selection area.[287] During the negotiations, Duff once more raised the possibility of taking the matter to arbitration. Although Kelantan's representatives were seemingly reasonably confident in the strength of their case, they were apprehensive of arbitration from previous experience in litigating against the company and opted for settling the matter instead of once more facing the risk inherent in arbitration.[288] Accordingly, another deed was signed in 1930, which finally cancelled all of the previous deeds and released the government from any claims or obligations in relation to them in exchange for another £140,000 payment (present-day value between £8.7 million and £64.6 million), once more obtained with the support of the Federated Malay States and the Straits Settlements.[289] Notably, this time the deed no longer contained an arbitration clause in case of possible disputes;[290]

W M Millington, *Kelantan Administration Report for the Year 1926* (Government Printing Office Singapore 1927) 3 and 15.

286 See Millington (n 285) 20. The debt incurred on account of the payment of the Duff award was twice the size of Kelantan's yearly revenue in 1926. See ibid 3.

287 For materials on this dispute, see generally UK National Archives: CO 717/73/16.

288 See Letter from the High Commissioner for the Malay States to Lord Passfield (22 May 1930) (UK National Archives: CO 717/73/16) and C Clementi, 'Memorandum to the Hon'ble Unofficial Members of the Legislative and Federal Councils: Financial Assistance to Kelantan' (11 May 1930) (UK National Archives: CO 717/73/16). Another prominent reason for agreeing to the settlement was the wish to avoid the anticipated public criticism that accompanied the previous arbitration.

289 Deed Dated the 7th of June 1930 Between His Highness the Sultan of Kelantan (for and on Behalf of the Kelantan Government) the Chief Secretary to Government Federated Malay States (for and on Behalf of the Government of the Federated Malay States and of the Railway Administration) and the Duff Development Company Limited (UK National Archives CO 717/73/16). See also Copy of Telegram from the High Commissioner for the Federated Malay States to the Secretary of State for the Colonies (7 June 1930) (UK National Archives CO 717/73/16).

290 The 1926 Deed of Settlement had already provided for arbitration only insofar as a supreme court, which was to be the primary forum for dispute settlement under that deed, was not yet established in Kelantan. See 1926 Deed of Settlement (n 284) clause 6. It appears that the reason behind the establishment of the supreme court was the need to

with this, the 'bogey of arbitration' (as it was referred to by one high-ranking colonial administrator) was laid forever and the company was put in the same position as any other land holder in Kelantan.[291] Soon thereafter, the company went into liquidation, but was then reorganised and continued operations under the same name.[292]

So came an end to a several decade long saga that plagued Kelantan for much of the first part of the 20th century, a saga at the root of which was the capacity of historical ISA to impose liability upon a government over how it discharged its official functions. The two arbitrations between the Duff Development Company and Kelantan thus serve to highlight historical ISA's role in ascertaining the costs of governance choices that were perceived to be in contravention to a government's obligations, although each arbitration does so from a slightly different vantage point.

Even though it resulted in no monetary consequences, by the mere fact of its existence, the first arbitration instilled such apprehension in the Kelantan authorities of the financial consequences that may follow that they changed their approach to the construction of the railway in dispute and decided to slacken the works until the arbitration was completed. The first arbitration thus stands as a testament to the fact that, even in the early 20th century, governments were known to alter the manner in which they governed due to the fear of financial sanctions that might be imposed through ISA. As is further elaborated in section 5, similar behaviour by the Kelantan authorities was likewise observed in anticipation of the award in the second arbitration. When the award in the second arbitration was handed down, the Kelantan authorities' fear of having to pay compensation finally materialised, as the arbitrator imposed potentially crippling liability upon Kelantan for its perceived failure to comply with its obligations, including those that were only implied in the contractual terms. Indeed, as is discussed in detail below, when compared to Kelantan's financial capabilities at the time, the size of the arbitrator's award was such that one can hardly imagine a more suitable paragon for the potential gravity of historical ISA's role in determining the cost of governance than the *Duff v. Kelantan II* arbitration.

---

provide a less expensive method than arbitration for settling potential disputes between the company and Kelantan. See 'Company Meetings: Duff Development Company' *The Times* (London, 22 October 1926) 25.

291 Clementi (n 288).

292 Rubin (n 246) 154–155; LeVos (n 246) 15.

4.2 *Sudan v Turriff*

The dispute between Turriff Construction (Sudan) Limited and Sudan, which arose in the 1960s and culminated with the tribunal's award on 23 April 1970, was the second ever arbitration that involved a non-state entity as one of the disputing parties to be administered by the PCA (the first being the 1930s *Radio Corporation of America v. China* case discussed in Chapter 5).[293] Without a doubt, the arbitration is one of the more fascinating historical ISAs, not least, as is relevant for present purposes, due to the tribunal's role in imposing significant liability upon Sudan for its perceived failure to comply with its contractual obligations, irrespective of Sudan's assertions that the contract was contrary to its public policy. While the award's contents have in most part (but certainly not in full) entered the public domain through a number of reports on the arbitration, the full text of the award, which is preserved at the National Archives of the Netherlands after being deposited with The Hague district court following the arbitration,[294] is not known to have ever been published.

The underlying controversy arose in relation to the construction of a large housing project needed for the relocation of a considerable number of people following the building of the Aswan High Dam on the Nile.[295] After a drawn-out tender process, the contract was handed out to Turriff in late 1962; because the tender process had taken so long, the company was in a time constraint to finish virtually from the inception of its work on the project. Unsurprisingly under such circumstances, problems between the contractor and the Sudanese government arose practically immediately, with each side accusing the other for the delays – while Sudan argued that Turriff was working too slowly, the company claimed that it could not proceed according to plan due to the government's own behaviour. Soon thereafter, the Sudanese government informed Turriff that, in light of the company's alleged failure to comply with its contractual obligations, it was bringing in other contractors to complete

---

293 See 'Sudan v Turriff Construction Company' in P Hamilton and others (eds), *The Permanent Court of Arbitration: International Arbitration and Dispute Resolution: Summaries of Awards, Settlement Agreements and Reports* (Kluwer 1999) 164.

294 See 'Rapport du Conseil Administratif de la Cour Permanente d'Arbitrage sur les travaux de la Cour, sur le fonctionnement des services administratifs et sur les depenses de l'exercice 1970' (Bureau International de la Cour Permanente d'Arbitrage 1971) 5. The award can be found in the Nationaal Archief, Den Haag, Arrondissementsrechtbank Den Haag 1960–1979, access number 3.03.79, inventory number 4903.

295 On the factual background to the dispute, see 'Sudan v Turriff Construction Company' (n 293) 165; Lambertus Erades, 'The Sudan Arbitration' (1970) 17(2) Netherlands International Law Review 200; Fath El Rahman Abdalla El Sheikh, *The Legal Regime of Foreign Private Investment in Sudan and Saudi Arabia* (2nd ed, CUP 2003) 341–342.

some of the work initially envisioned to be carried out by Turriff. To this Turriff objected, taking it to mean that Sudan was repudiating the contract (to which supposed repudiation Turriff assented). In the end, on 21 October 1966, at the Peace Palace in The Hague, the parties signed a submission to arbitration.[296]

The tribunal that heard the parties' dispute had one of the more complex procedural backgrounds in historical ISA. As initially constituted, the tribunal was presided by a Canadian judge, Charles A. Cameron, while the two remaining arbitrators were a member of the Sudanese judiciary, Sayed Mohammed Yussif Mudawi, and English Q.C. Roger J. Parker (who would later go on to become Lord Justice of Appeal).[297] Before the end of the proceedings, however, only one of the original members would remain on the tribunal. Namely, prior to the scheduled hearings, Cameron resigned his post, and was through the parties' agreement replaced by Dutch judge and the vice-president of the District Court of Rotterdam, Lambertus Erades.[298] The second reconstitution of the tribunal came after the arbitrator appointed by Sudan, Mudawi, had, following Sudan's withdrawal from the arbitration (see nn 306–308 below), first requested postponement of the hearings due to his inability to attend and then ultimately stopped communicating with the remaining participants in the arbitration.[299] Mudawi's unresponsiveness prompted the conclusion that a vacancy had occurred on the tribunal; as Sudan had not named another arbitrator within the prescribed deadline, in accordance with the submission to arbitration, his replacement was appointed by the president of the ICJ.[300] Mudawi's replacement was another African lawyer – Ghanaian born, but (in addition to his schooling in Ghana) Oxford and Harvard educated,

296 Erades (n 295) 202; 'Sudan v Turriff Construction Company' (n 293) 164; AM Stuyt, 'Dr Erades, Chairman of Two International Arbitral Tribunals' in TMC Asser Instituut, *Essays on International & Comparative Law* (Springer 1983) 178, 180; El Sheikh (n 295) 403. It is not entirely clear whether the submission to arbitration was the only basis for the arbitration, or whether the underlying contract also contained an arbitration clause. While the contract could unfortunately not be located, the latter certainly seems plausible, as El Sheikh states that the parties agreed to submit the dispute to arbitration '[p]ursuant to clause 70 of the contract'. See El Sheikh (n 295) 342.

297 Erades (n 295) 202; Stuyt (n 296) 180; El Sheikh (n 295) 403.

298 Erades (n 295) 205; Stuyt (n 296) 180. Erades also had an extensive background in international law, diplomatic experience in the United Nations and was editor in chief of the Netherlands International Law Review. See 'Gut Dam Case (Canada/United State of America)' in Cairo AR Robb (ed), *International Environmental Law Reports, Volume 1: Early Decisions* (CUP 1999) 386, 411.

299 Erades (n 295) 212–215.

300 Erades (n 295) 215; Stuyt (n 296) 180.

Kwamena Bentsi-Enchill, who was the dean of the University of Zambia law school.[301]

While the *Sudan v. Turriff* arbitration is an interesting one for many reasons, not least because of the procedural issues raised by Sudan's eventual withdrawal from the arbitration and the permutations in the tribunal's composition, of particular interest for present purposes is the so-called 'South African issue' that arose during the course of the ensuing proceedings. Namely, as the arbitration developed, in the first part of 1967, Sudan in its pleadings came forward with an allegation that Turriff possessed previously undisclosed connections to South African capital, which had been contrary to Sudan's policy at the time of not entering into commercial relations with South Africa or its citizens.[302] Notably, this policy had been adopted by Sudan as a response to the apartheid that was at the time on-going in South Africa, in line with a request by the United Nations (UN) General Assembly for countries to take measures that would bring about the abandonment of South Africa's racist policies.[303]

While there had been indications of such South African connections prior to the signing of the contract, Sudan alleged in the proceedings that it had at the time been reassured by the then UK Ambassador in Khartoum that Turriff had no connection to South Africa.[304] On this account, Sudan raised a defence in the arbitration that the contract had been void, or at least voidable, and that Turriff was in any event not entitled to bring a claim under the contract due to its fraudulent behaviour.[305] The defence rested on a number of presuppositions – that the declared position had in fact been the policy of Sudan at

301 See 'Curriculum Vitae of Kwamena Bentsi-Enchill' (UK National Archives: FCO 39/505).

302 Erades (n 295) 203–204; 'Turriff Arbitration: Note to the British Ambassador, Khartoum' (8 May 1969) (UK National Archives: FCO 39/710). The note is reproduced in its entirety in Erades (n 295) 207–209. According to Sudan, half of Turriff's shares had at all relevant times been indirectly beneficially owned by a South African construction company, Roberts Construction Holdings Ltd. During the proceedings, Turriff admitted that it was in part indirectly owned by a South African enterprise, but denied the said enterprise's involvement in the contract. See Erades (n 295) 203.

303 Sudan's South Africa Boycott Act of 1963 is reproduced in UN Security Council 'Report by the Secretary-General in Pursuance of the Resolution Adopted by the Security Council at its 1056th Meeting on 7 August 1963 (S/5386)' (11 October 1963) UN Doc S/5438 at 23. See also UN General Assembly Resolution 1761 (XVII) (6 November 1962) UN Doc A/RES/1761(XVII); UNSC 'Report of the Special Committee on the Policies of Apartheid of the Government of the Republic of South Africa' (26 September 1963) UN Doc S/5426/Add 1 at 144.

304 Note to the British Ambassador (n 302).

305 See Erades (n 295) 203–204, 206 and 219–220; 'Sudan v Turriff Construction Company' (n 293) 166–167; 'Answer by the Government to the Claim by Turriff' (UK National Archives: FCO 39/505). While Sudan initially only claimed that it had entered into the

all relevant times, that Sudan had concluded the contract without knowing that it was not in line with the said policy and that Turriff was fully aware of the position of the Sudanese government. The ultimate effect of the defence, according to Sudan, was that the contract could not be enforced against it, with the consequence that Sudan would only be liable for the costs actually incurred by Turriff in relation to the project, but not for any payments under the contract or potential damages for repudiation.

In addition to serving as Sudan's defence against Turriff's claim, the 'South Africa issue' had another important implication for the proceedings. According to Sudan, the said issue had gained increased importance during the course of the arbitration, resulting in the matter in dispute assuming 'a wholly different character' in comparison to the 'purely commercial dispute which was originally submitted to arbitration'.[306] Besides the issue in consequence raising serious questions of public policy for Sudan, it also implied that the matters that would need to be considered by the tribunal would be considerably more delicate. Namely, Turriff had in its arguments alleged that former high ranking Sudanese officials had been aware of, and had acquiesced to, the South African connection to the contract, as well as that Sudan had carried out considerable trade with South Africa and its companies, or at least that it had allowed such trade to be carried out.[307] Sudan felt that the raising of these matters necessitated a debate in the arbitration of both the content and the implementation of Sudan's policy towards South Africa, as well as that it required testimony of former senior Sudanese government officials. In Sudan's view, it was 'not appropriate for issues of this kind to be debated in a commercial arbitration and submitted for decision to a tribunal which had been appointed by the parties originally solely in their capacity as contracting parties', leading Sudan to withdraw from the arbitration and attempt to recall the mandate of the arbitrator it had appointed to the tribunal.[308]

---

contract under mistaken pretenses, it later developed its argument in a manner that implied that Sudan was induced to enter into the contract by Turriff's misrepresentations.

306 Note to the British Ambassador (n 302).

307 See Erades (n 295) 207.

308 Note to the British Ambassador (n 302); Stuyt (n 296) 182. Although Mudawi was eventually replaced on the tribunal for reasons described in nn 299–301, the tribunal did not consider that the Sudanese government had the power to revoke his appointment as arbitrator. See Erades (n 295) 215.

Despite Sudan's withdrawal, the reconstituted tribunal[309] decided to proceed with the arbitration, having considered the withdrawal unjustified.[310] The tribunal noted in this respect that the initial position of both parties had been that the contract was a valid one and that it was Sudan itself that had subsequently introduced into the arbitration the relevance of the 'South Africa issue' in relation to the validity of the contract; it was further noted that, despite Turriff's initial objection to the tribunal's competence to deal with Sudan's objection as to the validity of the contract, the parties had subsequently explicitly agreed that the tribunal was to rule on the matter and that Sudan had, even after learning of the relevant facts, for a while proceeded under the assumption that the 'South Africa issue' was properly before the arbitrators. Accordingly, the tribunal took the position that, having itself brought up the 'South Africa issue', it was not open to Sudan to then later use the fact that this issue would be discussed before the tribunal as a justification for its withdrawal from the proceedings – that the former would be the case was merely the inevitable consequence of Sudan's own free decision to raise the matter in the arbitration.[311]

In terms of the merits of the 'South Africa issue', while the tribunal could have merely dismissed the defence based on Sudan's failure to argue its case, it having been up to Sudan to positively prove its case regarding this defence, the tribunal, upon Turriff's invitation, instead actively engaged with the matter. Having examined the merits of Sudan's allegation on this point, the tribunal decided not only that Sudan's case could not be supported, but that it had in fact been positively disproven.[312] As it had also found against Sudan on the other relevant points, the tribunal proceeded to make an award in Turriff's favour to the effect of almost £6.2 million (present-day value between approximately £81 million and £233.2 million).[313]

The tribunal's decision thus imposed a more than significant financial burden on Sudan for failing to live up to its contract with Turriff, especially

309 See nn 299–301 above.

310 Under the submission to arbitration, the tribunal was only allowed to go ahead with the proceedings in the absence of a party if the said party had not demonstrated a valid reason for being absent. See Erades (n 295) 216.

311 See ibid 216–218.

312 Ibid 220; 'Sudan v Turriff Construction Company' (n 293) 167.

313 See Erades (n 295) 220–222. The award substantially exceeded even the expectations of the company's counsel. See Copy of Letter from MS Green to PLV Mallet (26 January 1970) (UK National Archives: FCO 39/710). See also Copy of Letter from RC Hope-Jones to PLV Mallet (25 September 1970) (UK National Archives: FCO 39/710), which notes that the company regarded the award as 'highly favourable' and considered this a consequence of Sudan's failure to appear before the tribunal.

when accounting for the country's financial standing at the time (see section 5 below). This fact allows for the *Sudan v. Turriff* arbitration to be placed squarely within the line of decisions wherein historical ISA tribunals influenced the cost of governance by imposing liability on states for acting contrary to their legal obligations; what makes the tribunal's decision stand out within this cluster, however, is the fact that the tribunal did so in a manner that presupposed that the arbitrators pass judgment on whether the contract was in line with Sudan's public policy on a matter as sensitive as racial discrimination. Indeed, neither Sudan's mere raising of the objection that such policy issues could not be debated in what it termed 'a commercial arbitration' nor its claim that the contract had contravened Sudan's policy on this matter were determinative of the issue; instead, the tribunal proceeded to make its own independent assessment, finding that it was neither precluded from considering the issue nor that Sudan's objections were justified.[314] With this in mind, the *Sudan v. Turriff* arbitration thus remains not only yet another example where historical ISA played a role in assigning the ultimate cost to a project of public significance by imposing liability for a state's failure to live up to its obligations,[315] but also one where the tribunal did so while fully engaging with sensitive questions of public policy.

5 Size Matters: Potential Ramifications and Governance Implications of Monetary Awards by Historical Investor-State Arbitral Tribunals

The previous sections have offered portrayals of how historical ISA operated to tie in a vast array of governance-related decisions by states – whether concerning public debt, state appropriation of investor property or (non-)compliance

314 A similar approach was taken in *Saudi Arabia v ARAMCO*. The issue in that historical ISA was whether an agreement that Saudi Arabia had concluded with a third party (the so-called Onassis Agreement) went against the rights granted to ARAMCO under its concession. The Saudi Arabian government had in large part based its case on the argument that the Onassis Agreement, having been ratified by a royal decree, had the character of a government regulation with which ARAMCO had to comply. Paralleling the approach from *Sudan v Turriff*, the tribunal did not simply accept Saudi Arabia's characterisation to the effect that the Onassis Agreement was a government regulation, but rather independently proceeded to examine its character and determined that, being contractual in nature, it could not be considered as such. See *Saudi Arabia v Arabian American Oil Company* (ARAMCO) (1963) 27 ILR 117, 140–141 and 214–219.

315 While Sudan refused to comply with the award, the matter was in the end settled amicably a few years later, with Sudan agreeing to pay £3.3 million in instalments (between £43.2 million and £117.2 million in present day value). See El Sheikh (n 295) 355.

with legal obligations – with substantial financial implications. As interesting as these previously largely untold individual narratives may be, one could hardly be faulted for questioning whether awards with such steep financial implications were merely occasional atypical outliers, rather than a representative illustration of historical ISA in this respect. In answering this question, this section contextualises the awards analysed in the previous sections against the backdrop of other historical ISAs that saw monetary awards handed down under similar circumstances. This exercise reveals that extremely large financial awards were not isolated instances in historical ISA, but were instead part of a more broadly present pattern. In an additional step, the section also illustrates the extent of the impact that awards of such magnitude were capable of having on states and their respective fiscal capacities. In doing so, it reveals that the footprints of monetary awards handed down in historical ISA were such that they not only affected the cost of specific governance decisions, but also potentially more broadly the capability of states to exercise their official functions – their very capacity to govern.

Turning first to the sheer monetary size of the awards, it is necessary at the outset to reiterate that – as was more fully elaborated above (see nn 16-17) – the absolute values of historical awards cannot simply be compared across time as the value of money has not remained constant. In order to put the awards from different time periods into proper perspective, Table 1 converts nine awards, spanning more than a century, to their equivalents in present-day approximated value. Because the conversion tool that is used is limited in terms of the currencies for which comparison of historical value is possible, it could only be applied to awards that were expressed in UK pounds or US dollars; however, awards of comparable magnitude were made in other currencies in numerous other historical ISAs. Moreover, for reasons that were explained above, the present-day value of the awards is expressed through a range, rather than an exact value; for present purposes, however, this is sufficient to provide a frame of reference through which the historical values can be properly contextualised.

As the data from Table 1 indicates, the examined awards by historical ISA tribunals were worth at least millions of pounds or dollars in present-day value virtually as a matter of course, and extended not infrequently into the tens or hundreds of millions, or even into the billions. It is therefore not just the case that decidedly hefty monetary awards were not an unknown for historical ISAs, but rather that they appear to have been more or less part of the norm.

TABLE 1 Representation of present-day approximated monetary values of historical ISA awards

	Year	Case	Amount awarded	Present-day approximated value
1.	1864	*Suez v. Egypt*[a]	£3.36 million	£320 million to £7.5 billion
2.	1897	*Colombia v. Cauca Company*[b]	$452,048	$12.1 million to $568 million
3.	1922	*Jaffa-Jerusalem Railway Company v. British Government*[c]	£565,000	£28.4 million to £274.4 million
4.	1925	*Duff v. Kelantan II (Damages Award)*[d]	£378,000	£21 million to £181.5 million
5.	1930	*Lena Goldfields v. USSR*[e]	£12.965 million	£800 million to £6 billion
6.	1936	*Greece v. Socobelge*[f]	$6.77 million	$78.5 million to $1.5 billion
7.	1963	*Sapphire v. NIOC*[g]	$3 million	$19.2 million to $96.5 million
8.	1970	*Sudan v. Turriff*[h]	£6.186 million	£81 million to £233.2 million
9.	1977	*LIAMCO v. Libya*[i]	$79.88 million	$264 million to $786 million

a Yackee (n 242) 458.
b *Colombia v Cauca Co*, Award (n 135).
c *Jaffa-Jerusalem Railway Arbitration*, Award (n 222) 324.
d See Rubin (n 246) 154.
e *Lena Goldfields v USSR* (n 12) 52.
f *Socobelge II* (n 21) 53.
g *Sapphire v NIOC* (n 244) 191.
h See n 313.
i *LIAMCO v Libya* (n 107) 171.

Awards handed down in ISA throughout history are therefore of the kind that would have posed a significant burden to virtually any state. In some instances, in fact, it is difficult to overstate just how substantial the potential repercussions for the finances of the involved states were. This is particularly fittingly illustrated by the abovementioned *Sudan v. Turriff* arbitration,[316] where all of those involved were fully aware that the award was well beyond Sudan's financial capabilities at the time – not only did Sudan claim that it lacked the resources to comply with the nearly £6.2 million award (£81 million to £233.2 million in present-day value),[317] but this fact was readily

316 See sub-section 4.2.

317 Telegram (no 459) from Etherington-Smith to Foreign and Commonwealth Office (22 July 1970) (UK National Archives: FCO 39/710).

acknowledged by both Turriff itself[318] and the UK government.[319] The sentiments of the members of the UK embassy in Sudan, who during settlement negotiations repeatedly expressed their scepticism that Sudan could conjure up the funds to meet even the significantly reduced amounts being discussed as part of Sudan's settlement proposal, let alone the award in full, particularly stand out in this respect. Sudan's capacity to pay at the time was perhaps best captured by the words of the then UK ambassador to Sudan, who, when asked how much Sudan could be expected to pay and when, retorted with a deeply pessimistic 'Not very much, and in driblets'.[320]

An ever more acute example is provided by the aftermath of the monetary award handed down in the *Duff v. Kelantan II* arbitration.[321] At the time of the arbitration, various contemporary accounts described Kelantan as having a 'precarious' financial outlook[322] or being for 'all intents and purposes (…) bankrupt';[323] likewise, it was anticipated that an award allowing the company's claim would leave Kelantan in an 'embarrassing financial position' and would 'permanently cripple the State'.[324] As it turned out, such projections were not far off. When it was eventually handed down in 1925, arbitrator Speed's award was approximately double the amount of Kelantan's annual revenue for that year – which had been its largest to date.[325] An additional problem for Kelantan was that its existing outstanding excess of liabilities already exceeded its annual revenue by more than a factor of two.[326] As a matter of fact, it was not only the award by Speed that went beyond what Kelantan could handle – even the burden of the legal costs of either of the two arbitrations against the Duff Development Company was a difficult one for Kelantan.[327] The Duff

318 Letter from HSK Peppiatt of Freshfields to RC Hope-Jones (21 August 1970) (UK National Archives: FCO 39/710).

319 Telegram (no 473) from Etherington-Smith to Foreign and Commonwealth Office (3 August 1970) (UK National Archives: FCO 39/710); Letter from PLV Mallet to MS Green (15 August 1970) (UK National Archives: FCO 39/710); Copy of Letter from RGA Etherington-Smith to Hope-Jones (3 September 1970) (UK National Archives: FCO 39/710).

320 Letter from Etherington-Smith to Hope-Jones (3 September 1970) (n 319).

321 See n 282.

322 'Memorandum to Hon'ble Members of the Legislative and Federal Councils: Financial Assistance to Kelantan' (UK National Archives FCO 141/16704 and FCO 141/16709).

323 See Letter from Devonshire (30 July 1923) (n 269).

324 See nn 322 and 323.

325 Compare the converted amount of the award as mentioned in FMS and Kelantan: Chief Secretary's Assurance to the Public (n 282) with Shaw (n 282) 3.

326 See Shaw (n 282) 18.

327 See Letter from Devonshire (30 July 1923) (n 269) and R J Farrer, *Kelantan Administration Report for the Year 1916* (Federated Malay States Government Printing Office 1917) 11 (UK National Archives: CO 827/1).

Development Company itself acknowledged the fact that Kelantan simply did not have the money to meet its obligations toward the company.[328]

As was outlined above, the inevitable outcome was that Kelantan was forced into heavy borrowing so that it would be able to pay the award, which is all the more significant considering that the state was at the time not in 'a position to borrow any more money without seriously impairing its resources or imposing oppressive taxation on its people'.[329] Kelantan's position was ultimately considerably alleviated by the fact that its outstanding debt to the Federate Malay States was written off as part of this arrangement; as a result, its (already high) overall indebtedness was thus ultimately not significantly altered.[330] When making the plea before the Straits Settlements Legislative Council for a loan to be granted to Kelantan for the purpose of settling the award, the Governor of the Straits Settlements and High Commissioner for the Federated Malay States, Sir Laurence Guillemard, not only stated that the award was one Kelantan 'cannot possibly pay', but also remarked that the state had 'been placed in a humiliating and invidious position and incurred undeserved obloquy'.[331]

By no means were the *Sudan v. Turriff* and *Duff v. Kelantan II* arbitrations the only instances in historical ISA where tribunals' awards were beyond the financial capacities of the states involved.[332] Indeed, as much as direct evidence of this phenomenon may be hard to come across, there are at least some indications that the financial ramifications of certain historical ISAs were such that they were potentially capable of having a substantial effect not only on

328 'Company Meetings: Duff Development Company' (n 290).

329 'Memorandum: History of the Affairs of the Duff Development Company' (n 248) para 113.

330 See nn 283–286 and compare Shaw (n 282) 18 with Millington (n 285) 20.

331 'Straits Settlements: Legislative Council' (n 282) 5.

332 For example, in relation to the *Lena Goldfields v USSR* arbitration, Veeder has commented that 'the Soviet Union was probably too weak financially to pay the award in full'. See Veeder (n 6) 787. Rather intriguingly, when discussing the financial implications of the *Suez v Egypt* award – possibly the largest, relatively speaking, of the historical ISA awards – Jason Yackee, while acknowledging that the award was 'not insignificant', nonetheless concludes that its payment 'should have been quite manageable'. See Yackee (n 242) 455–459. Yackee arrives at this conclusion despite noting that the award equated to approximately 1.5% of the Egypt government's estimated total spending over a seventeen year period. This would imply that the award would on average be equal to approximately one quarter of the total yearly government spending by Egypt in any given year during the said period. Without getting into whether the magnitude of the award was justified under the circumstances, and irrespective of whether Egypt had the financial capacity at the time to comply with the award, it appears hard to avoid the conclusion that the award was in any event a monumental drain on public finances. For illustrative purposes, an award amounting to a similar proportion of the US government's budget for 2023 would equal approximately $1.5 trillion.

the cost of particular policy decisions by states, but also more broadly on the general financial capacity of the said states and, as a corollary, on their capacity to conduct their official business. Although made in a slightly different context, a remark by the UK ambassador to Sudan when commenting on the *Sudan v. Turriff* dispute – 'There is only one lemon. The more juice you squeeze into one glass, the less there will be for anyone else'[333] – once more seems particularly apt. As this section has demonstrated, justifiably or not, historical ISA was known to 'squeeze' quite a bit of juice from the public purse into a single glass, thus inevitably leaving less of it for other matters of public concern. At least one instance that can offer a befitting illustration of what this had the potential to lead to has been documented; it is yet again provided by the example of Kelantan where, in anticipation of a possible sizeable adverse award in the second Duff arbitration, public expenditure had been kept as low as possible to such an extent that it became 'impossible to starve public services without running the risk of stunting the development of the State'.[334] It was only following the removal of uncertainty over Kelantan's financial position that came with the settlement of the Duff award that plans for 'overdue public works' (such as the construction of serviceable main roads and essential public buildings) were resumed.[335] On this occasion, then, the apprehension of the impending financial implications from the arbitration against the Duff Development Company was such that it affected the Kelantan government's perception of its financial capacity to govern, and thus also in fact the manner in which it did so. The circumstances in which some of the other abovementioned arbitrations took place – with a number of them having occurred shortly after sovereign debt defaults[336] – at least suggest that this may not have been an isolated occurrence.

What is in any event apparent, is that, from a historical perspective, ISA was a recurrent instrument of determining the cost of governance. In many an

333 Letter from Etherington-Smith to Hope-Jones (3 September 1970) (n 319).

334 Shaw (n 282) 3. See also RJB Clayton, *Kelantan Administration Report for the Year 1927* (Government Printing Office Singapore 1928) (UK National Archives: CO 827/1) 15; 'Straits Settlements: Legislative Council' (n 282) 5; Clementi (n 288); 'Memorandum to Hon'ble Unofficial Members of the Legislative and Federal Councils' (n 322).

335 Millington (n 285) 15. See also Clayton (n 334) 15. Some of the public works carried out in the year after the settlement of the award included the construction of roads and bridges, hospital wards, an electric power house and an installation of an electric light supply in the state capital.

336 See eg the *Hambros and Lazard v Roumania Monopolies Institute* arbitration discussed in sub-section 2.1 above; *Socobelge I* (n 21).

instance, the monetary awards handed down in historical ISA as part of this exercise were such that the imposed costs represented, to say the least, a significant burden for the states involved; in at least some instances, historical ISA was known to starve the public purse to such an extent – or at least threaten to do so – so as to compromise the affected states' financial capacity to govern.[337]

6 Conclusions

Awards imposing financial obligations upon parties to investor-state relationships, and more specifically, upon states, are plenty to be found scattered throughout ISA's past. Indeed, as the historical ISAs that this Chapter has recounted attest, whether it was through deciding on matters of public debt, through providing valuation for states' appropriation of investor property, through imposing liability upon parties to investor-state partnerships for non-compliance with their obligations, or through whatever other modality of decision-making that had comparable financial implications, there was no paucity of historical ISAs that were central in ascertaining the cost of governance. What is more – be it South America in the late 19th and early 20th century, North America, Europe, and Southeast Asia in the interwar period, or Africa in the 1960s – historical ISA's taking on of such a role can be traced back to different temporal and geographical settings. Thus, it is safe to say that historical ISA's capacity to influence the cost of governance was one of its most enduring and deeply entrenched features.

Yet, the contribution of this Chapter is not exhausted in merely conveying the existence and magnitude of historical ISA's role in determining the cost of governance, but extends also to capturing a number of its features that help explain the underlying process. While this task was certainly not aided by

337 Admittedly, the sizeable monetary awards handed down by historical ISA tribunals did not necessarily translate directly into a difference in the public purse, as the awards were sometimes, perhaps even too often, not complied with. This, however, does not negate historical ISA's footprint on the cost of governance, for two primary reasons. First, such instances of non-compliance do not detract from the ample occasions where the awards were respected. Second, even when the awards themselves were not complied with, this did not necessarily imply that they were without any effect, as a refusal to comply with a large outstanding monetary award certainly affected the position of the party against whom it was made. Thus, for example, while Sudan was adamant that it lacked the resources to satisfy the *Turriff* award, it was nonetheless motivated to work towards an amicable settlement as it was wary of the negative reputational costs of non-compliance. See Telegram from Etherington-Smith to Foreign and Commonwealth Office (22 July 1970) (n 317).

the minimalistic character of some of the awards, especially many of the earlier ones that are but a few pages long and contain little to no legal or factual assessment, a number of the analysed historical ISAs were able to offer a window into the decision-making process through which historical ISA partook in determining the cost of governance. What these historical ISAs – such as *Hambros and Lazard v. Romanian Monopolies Institute*, *Peru v. Peruvian Corporation* and the *Grand Trunk Railway Arbitration* – betray is a decision-making process that often, if not by default, lacked rooting in a well-defined normative frame of reference, allowing instead, and even necessitating, for the arbitrators to make decisions that were imbued with a little inhibited dose of discretion. In light of this significant leeway that was accorded to decision-makers by such lack of clear normative guidance and strictures, historical ISA was not merely a process that facilitated the crystallisation of the cost of certain governance decisions through precise legal categories, but rather one which was in essence constitutive of it.

Equally relevant is the realisation that the capacity of historical ISA to have a central role in determining the cost of governance, and do so in the above described manner, did not remain unnoticed or entirely unchallenged. As is exemplified by, once more, the *Grand Trunk Railway Arbitration*, concerns against the appropriateness of historical ISA tribunals wielding such authority were repeatedly voiced in the Canadian parliament in preparation for the arbitration, but were met with a forcible rebuttal, and strong endorsement in favour of the arbitrators taking on this role, from the Canadian government. As follows from the *Colombia v. Cauca Company* and *Grand Trunk Railway Arbitration* cases, validation was likewise provided by the judicial branch, with highly reputable judicial institutions of the highest instance on more than one occasion not only sanctioning historical ISA's role in ascertaining the cost of governance, but according it a considerable degree of deference when exercising this role. This suggests that, at least in these instances, historical ISA's partaking in determining the cost of governance was not merely a *de facto* occurrence, but something that received careful and conscious deliberation – and eventual stamp of approval – from different branches of the democratic machinery, both before and after the event.

Finally, another unavoidable and lasting impression that emanates from the historical ISAs recounted in this Chapter concerns the gravity of the impact that the tribunals' capacity to influence the cost of certain governance choices was capable of having on the public purse of the involved states. Indeed, in essentially all of the reviewed historical ISAs, the awards that were handed down were such as to be capable of creating a significant dent in the finances of the states involved; in some instances, such as *Sudan v. Turriff* and the arbitrations between the Duff Development Company and Kelantan, it was even readily recognised by all of the parties involved that the awards were simply beyond the fiscal capacity of the respective states. Further, on occasion, the potential impact on public finances was even such that there are recorded instances, as was the case in Kelantan, of governments adjusting the manner in which they governed so as to accommodate a prospective adverse award from a historical ISA. Accordingly, it can be surmised that historical ISA was not only recurrently instrumental in determining the cost of governance, but that it also was, as a result, known to alter the very manner in which governance was exercised (a topic that is discussed in depth in the following chapter).

CHAPTER 4

Governing by Instruction: Directing State Conduct through Historical Investor-State Arbitration

1 Introduction

Chapter 3 was devoted to tracing one manner in which historical investor-state arbitration (ISA) interacted with how states governed – by being an important and recurring element in the determination of the costs associated with their governance choices. The present Chapter continues the exploration of historical ISA's governance footprint by in turn looking at how historical ISA more immediately not only purported to influence, but in some instances in fact influenced, the very manner in which states were to discharge their official functions.

This is a discussion in which most international lawyers would no doubt expect for what is certainly the most emblematic and (in)famous historical ISA award in this respect – the award handed down by French academic René-Jean Dupuy in *Texaco v. Libya*[1] – to feature prominently. The present Chapter, however, is hardly centred around Dupuy's award, although the award does indeed provide an appropriate starting point for the discussion that is to follow.

Dupuy handed down the Award on the Merits in *Texaco v. Libya* on 19 January 1977 in Geneva; ever since, his award has captured the imagination of generations of international legal scholars, remaining as controversial as it is revered. Without doubt one of the award's more controversial aspects has been precisely Dupuy's willingness to not only hold Libya accountable for a breach of the claimants' concessions through the adoption of nationalisation measures, but to also decide that Libya was obliged to continue its compliance with the concessions. Libya's nationalisation measures notwithstanding, Dupuy said, the Libyan Government was 'legally bound to perform these contracts and to give them full effect'.[2]

At the outset, Dupuy's decision to order a government to specifically perform the concessions that it had sought to nationalise through an exercise of

1 *Texaco Overseas Petroleum Company and California Asiatic Oil Company v The Government of the Libyan Arab Republic* (1978) 17 ILM 1.

2 Ibid 37.

 | DOI:10.1163/9789004733824_005

its sovereign powers caused unease in many a quarter,[3] and this unease hardly appears to have since subsided.[4] There can be little doubt that the reception, and perception, of Dupuy's decision was in large part shaped through its juxtaposition against the decisions of his contemporaries who had heard the parallel cases that arose from the Libyan oil nationalisations. In both the *BP v. Libya* and LIAMCO *v. Libya* awards, the former having been issued before and the latter after *Texaco v. Libya*, the arbitrators refused to order specific performance as a recourse, limiting instead the available remedies to monetary damages.[5] And in both instances, the respective arbitrators raised concerns as to the appropriateness of a tribunal ordering a remedy that contradicted a state's sovereign act, such as nationalisation.[6]

Yet, if the critics of Dupuy's *Texaco v. Libya* award were sceptical as to whether his approach to allow *restitutio in integrum* accurately reflected the then existing position in international law, it was the specific context in which it was applied – in relations between a private investor and a sovereign government – to which they seemed particularly to have taken exception. This objection against Dupuy's decision was perhaps most concisely, yet eloquently, formulated by a Greek academic who would latter go on to sit on several ICSID tribunals and annulment committees, Arghyrios Fatouros – '[s]urely, if the imposition of the strict remedy of *restitutio* might possibly be justified in some cases, as between states, *it is much harder to defend such a limitation on a state's freedom of action within its territory for the benefit of private persons*.'[7]

3 See eg AA Fatouros, 'International Law and the Internationalized Contract' (1980) 74(1) AJIL 134, 137–139; Robin CA White, 'Expropriation of the Libyan Oil Concessions: Two Conflicting International Arbitrations' (1981) 30(1) The International and Comparative Law Quarterly 1, 16–17.

4 See eg Anna De Luca, 'Non-Pecuniary Remedies Under the Energy Charter Treaty' (2015) Energy Charter Secretariat Knowledge Centre Occasional Paper, 2 <https://ssrn.com/abstract=2589428> accessed 27 September 2024 (remarking that *Texaco v Libya* has 'limited value as legal authority, since it is not consistent with both previous and successive case-law'); Alan Redfern and others, *Law and Practice of International Commercial Arbitration* (4th edn, Sweet & Maxwell 2004) 360.

5 *BP Exploration Company (Libya) Limited v The Government of the Libyan Arab Republic* (1979) 53 ILR 297, 329–357; *Libyan American Oil Company (LIAMCO) v The Government of the Libyan Arab Republic* (1981) 20(1) ILM 1, 62–64 and 84–87.

6 *BP v Libya* (n 5) 353–354; *LIAMCO v Libya* (n 5) 63–64.

7 Fatouros (n 3) 139. Emphasis added. Similar sensitivity toward applying *restitutio in integrum* specifically to investor-state relations was expressed already by Judge Lagergren in *BP v Libya*. See *BP v Libya* (n 5) 349 and 352 (noting that '*the fact that the State is the respondent party is one which cannot be overlooked*', and that there exists 'no uniform general principle of law pursuant to which specific performance is a remedy available at the option of an innocent party, *especially not a private party acting under a contract with a Government*'). Emphases added.

Such scepticism, aimed in particular toward Libya being instructed in the *Texaco v. Libya* award to specifically perform its obligations *vis-à-vis* a private investor (rather than a state), appeared particularly apt in light of Dupuy's lack of reference in the award, despite his fairly extensive discussion of international case law on the matter, to any precedent wherein such a remedy had been ordered in arbitration proceedings conducted directly between a state and a private enterprise. Dupuy's failure to ground his decision in previous practice in ISA was all the more accentuated by the fact that, in the *BP v. Libya* award that had preceded it, Judge Lagergren had, although speaking within the narrow context of the very particular issues that were before him, framed these issues as 'novel in character and scope in that they have not previously been scrutinised judicially.'[8] Lagergren came to such a conclusion after an extensive survey of, *inter alia*, historical ISAs that could have in his view possibly served as precedents for ordering specific performance, ultimately remarking that:

> [t]he survey of cases and other relevant materials presented above demonstrates that there is no explicit support for the proposition that specific performance, and even less so *restitutio in integrum*, are remedies of public international law available at the option of a party suffering a wrongful breach by a co-contracting party.[9]

Thus, from its inception, the *Texaco v. Libya* award was welcomed into jurisprudential existence by a kindred, yet starkly contrasting, award that had framed this particular issue as one of first impression, had assessed what it perceived as plausible precedents from earlier ISAs, and had found no support for ordering specific performance. Dupuy himself had done little to change the tide, addressing in his award neither Judge Lagergren's award nor any of the earlier ISAs referred to therein that could have served as precedents for his decision. For good measure, Dupuy also failed to invoke any other historical ISAs when justifying his decision to order Libya to perform the contracts.

Against this backdrop, that Dupuy's *Texaco v. Libya* award has been described as 'audacious' (even if not primarily for its finding regarding specific performance)[10] or that his approach of providing for *restitutio in integrum* as a

8 *BP v Libya* (n 5) 353. See also ibid 351.

9 Ibid 347.

10 Julien Cantegreil, 'The Audacity of the Texaco/Calasiatic Award: René-Jean Dupuy and the Internationalization of Foreign Investment Law' (2011) 22(2) EJIL 441.

remedy has frequently been labelled as an 'exception',[11] is far from surprising. Indeed, one could hardly be faulted for inferring that the *Texaco v. Libya* award was treading on uncharted territory and deeming it as a progenitor of the practice wherein arbitrators in ISA instruct states on how they should go about their official business. In fact, at face value, such a conclusion would appear almost ineluctable. If Chapters 2 and 3 have been any indication, however, face value appearances tend to be deceiving when it comes to historical ISA. This remains no less true with respect to *Texaco v. Libya's* standing within the genealogy of historical ISA awards purporting to direct state conduct – against ISA's broader historical record, Dupuy's approach in *Texaco v. Libya* appears not so much as the progenitor of such practice as it does as merely one of the many instalments in a series of comparable episodes.

It is this seemingly hitherto overlooked practice of historical ISA tribunals purporting to influence, and in some instances in fact influencing, state conduct that the remainder of this Chapter is devoted to rediscovering. As it is impossible to recount all such instances within a single chapter in much detail, the Chapter offers two in-depth accounts, each of which sheds light on the different modalities through which historical ISA is observed to have purported to influence state conduct. The Chapter first recounts the 1930s arbitration between Radio Corporation of America (RCA) and The Administration of Posts and Telegraphs of the Republic of Czechoslovakia (The Czechoslovakian Administration), which exemplifies the role of historical ISA tribunals in reviewing, as a secondary decision-maker, the permissibility of state entity conduct. The significance of this arbitration for the purposes of illustrating historical ISA's capacity to influence state entity conduct lies not only in the fact that the tribunal was asked to rule, and eventually did rule, that The Czechoslovakian Administration was not allowed to open an additional public utility service, but perhaps even more so in the fact that The Czechoslovakian Administration itself appears to have perceived the tribunal's decision on this matter as controlling (2). The second detailed account that is presented consists of a series of arbitrations held under the World War I Peace Treaties with respect to the reorganisation of the railway system of the former Austro-Hungarian Empire. In contrast to the *RCA v. The Czechoslovakian Administration* arbitration, the tribunals belonging to this cluster of cases were not limited to reviewing whether certain action intended by states was permitted or not. Instead, they proceeded to actively engage, as primary decision-makers determining the initial course of action, with how the relevant railway systems were to be

11 Jan Paulsson, *Denial of Justice in International Law* (CUP 2005) 215; Redfern and others (n 4) 360.

reorganised, including by obliging states to, or not to, expropriate (3). Any room for scepticism as to the representative value of these two individual in-depth accounts of historical ISA operating to influence state conduct is dissipated by situating them against the backdrop of other historical ISAs of comparable reach. This analysis reveals that the two in-depth accounts examined in detail in the Chapter were, much like *Texaco v. Libya*, hardly the only, or even the earliest, such examples (4). With that, historical ISA thus reveals itself as an institution wherein it was far from uncommon for arbitrators to direct the conduct of states through their decisions, including in relation to how they exercised their official functions – how they governed (5).

2 Directing State Entity Conduct through Adjudicative (Arbitral) Review: *Czechoslovakian Administration v RCA*

The arbitration between the RCA and The Czechoslovakian Administration took place in the early 1930s and was the first instalment in an arbitral diptych that was completed by the RCA's subsequent arbitration against the National Government of the Republic of China.[12] Together, these two arbitrations in many respects represent extraordinary examples of historical ISA, not least because the latter was the first ever arbitration administered by the Permanent Court of Arbitration (PCA) where one of the parties was not a state (this arbitration, together with the accidental origin of the PCA's involvement with ISA, is chronicled in depth in Chapter 5). For present purposes, however, the most interesting aspect of the two arbitrations was the fact that in both cases the arbitrators were asked to review the permissibility of the conduct of the

12 The two arbitrations are inextricably linked, not so much because the underlying traffic agreements were forged on the same day, which was but a fortuitous coincidence, but primarily due to the similarity of circumstances under which they arose and the involvement of one and the same party in both disputes. Copies of both traffic agreements can be found in the records of MCI International, Inc (which acquired RCA Global Communications Inc in 1987) at The Hagley Museum and Library in Wilmington, Delaware (US) (call number 2225 (Series XV); hereinafter MCI International Archives). See Traffic Agreement between Radio Corporation of America and Administration of Posts and Telegraphs of the Republic of Czechoslovakia (10 November 1928) (MCI International Archives, box 583, file 'Czechoslovakia: Correspondence and Agreements (1 of 6)'); Traffic Agreement between the Radio Corporation of America and the National Council of Reconstruction (10 November 1928) (MCI International Archives, box 581, file 'China: Chinese Arbitration Correspondence (2 of 13)'); Copy of Letter from George Shecklen to the Chinese Minister of Communications (18 June 1932) (MCI International Archives, box 581, file 'China: Chinese Arbitration Correspondence (5 of 13)').

involved states or state entities in operating the public utilities within their purview. And it was in the *Czechoslovakian Administration v.* RCA arbitration that the tribunal, upon exercising such adjudicative, or to be more precise, arbitral review, found that The Czechoslovakian Administration was not permitted to open a new radio telegraphic circuit with the United States (US). This decision by the *Czechoslovakian Administration v.* RCA tribunal to direct a state entity tasked with operating an important public utility service on how to go about exercising its competencies held all the more gravitas considering that The Czechoslovakian Administration had, even if ultimately only temporarily, in fact abstained from opening the envisioned new route because of the tribunal's decision. As such, the *Czechoslovakian Administration v.* RCA arbitration stands as one of the most compelling attestations of historical ISA's capacity to influence state entity conduct.

The story of how the *Czechoslovakian Administration v.* RCA arbitration came to influence the operation of the Czechoslovakia-US radio telegraphic route is recounted as follows. First, the section contextualises the underlying dispute by providing a brief background to the origins and early development of the RCA all the way up until its emergence as an independent company (2.1), before discussing the establishment of the RCA's radio-telegraphic route with Czechoslovakia (2.2). The section then chronicles the origins of the dispute between the RCA and The Czechoslovakian Administration (2.3), following which it delves into the arbitration proceedings and the tribunal's award (2.4). The section concludes by discussing the influence of the tribunal's award upon The Czechoslovakian Administration's operation of the Czechoslovakia-US radio telegraphic route (2.5).

2.1 *Radio Corporation of America: From Inception to Independence*

Now defunct, the RCA was one of the leading players in the technology sector throughout the better part of the 20th century. The company was birthed as part of an attempt to bring overseas radio communications under the control of American interests in the aftermath of World War I. Namely, in the lead up to the war, the US radio communication industry had been dominated by the Marconi Wireless Telegraph Company of America (American Marconi), which was the partially owned subsidiary of Marconi Wireless Telegraph (British Marconi) – a British company that was the global leader in wireless communication.[13] However, over the course of the United States' participation in the

13 See Robert Sobel, *RCA* (Stein and Day 1986) 21; Alejandro Casasempere García and Antonio Pérez Yuste, 'The Role of the White House in the Establishment of a Governmental Radio Monopoly in the United States. The Case of the Radio Corporation of America'

war, the US Navy had temporarily taken over control of wireless communication in the country and had during this time come to realize both the potency of the technology and the possible security concerns that it raised.[14] As the operation of the radio services that had been taken over was set to be returned to the private sector following the conclusion of the war,[15] the notion of such a sensitive industry being placed under foreign control started increasingly to be seen with significant unease in US government circles. Despite the fact that British Marconi only held a minority interest in American Marconi and that the majority of the executives controlling American Marconi were US citizens,[16] the company was still quintessentially seen as a British enterprise; consequently, having it return to its pre-war position was considered unacceptable.[17] Accordingly, a decision was made to establish a new, American, company that would take over the interests of American Marconi. Thus, on 17 October 1919, the RCA was incorporated.[18] A significant role in the formation of the RCA was played by the General Electric Company (GE),[19] which would soon be joined in the ownership of the RCA by other key players in the US radio industry – the American Telephone and Telegraph Company (AT&T), the Westinghouse Electric & Manufacturing Company and the United Fruit Company.[20]

At the time of its establishment, the RCA's primary area of operation was international telecommunications.[21] The newly formed company sent its inaugural messages over its England circuit on 1 March 1920[22] and had during its first year of operation established circuits with a number of additional countries.[23] While the RCA continued to expand its radio-telegraphic network

---

(2010 Second Region 8 IEEE Conference on the History of Communications, Madrid, 3–5 November 2010) 1 <https://ieeexplore.ieee.org/document/5735292> accessed 27 September 2024; Gleason L Archer, *Big Business and Radio* (The American Historical Society 1939) 5.

14 Sobel, *RCA* (n 13) 20–21; García and Yuste (n 13) 2–3; Archer, *Big Business and Radio* (n 13) 5.

15 Sobel, *RCA* (n 13) 28.

16 See Sobel, *RCA* (n 13) 21 and 25. Nonetheless, American Marconi was unable to prove in 1919 that a majority of its stock was held by American citizens. See García and Yuste (n 13) 1.

17 See Sobel, *RCA* (n 13) 23–30.

18 Gleason L Archer, *History of Radio to 1926* (The American Historical Society 1938) 177.

19 On the formation of the RCA and the crucial role played therein by GE, see Sobel, *RCA* (n 13) 22–30 and Archer, *History of Radio to 1926* (n 18) 176–189.

20 See Sobel, *RCA* (n 13) 31–35 and Archer, *Big Business and Radio* (n 13) 6–8.

21 Sobel, *RCA* (n 13) 31; J C Warner, 'A History of Radio Corporation of America – The Years to 1938' (1957) 3(1) RCA Engineer 3, 4.

22 Archer, *History of Radio to 1926* (n 18) 188.

23 See Warner (n 21) 4.

in the following years,[24] the company soon branched out into other areas of activity, such as broadcasting, merchandising, entertainment and, eventually, manufacturing.[25]

By the end of the 1920s, it would become apparent to the RCA's leadership that international telecommunications would not be the primary focus of the RCA's business going forward.[26] As a result, plans were made to offload this aspect of the RCA's operations, with the intended target being International Telephone & Telegraph (IT&T). IT&T had recently acquired the Mackay Radio and Telegraph Company (Mackay Radio), a significant yet stumbling telecommunications company,[27] and was looking to position itself as precisely the type of concern that the RCA had been envisioned to be – a leader in international communications.[28] In order to better facilitate the envisioned arrangement, the RCA's entire foreign business was placed into the hands of a newly formed subsidiary, RCA Communications, which was then intended to be taken over by IT&T in exchange for IT&T stock.[29] Although the discussions regarding the takeover of the RCA's telecommunications business had been on-going for some time and the sale had at one point been on the cusp of being consummated,[30] the deal ultimately fell through. Consequently, instead of having their interests in the international telecommunications industry aligned,[31] the RCA and IT&T would find themselves in competition. The following years would thus see IT&T (through its subsidiary, Mackay Radio) challenge the RCA's international contracts in several jurisdictions, including in Czechoslovakia and China,[32] eventually giving rise to arbitrations in relation to the RCA's traffic agreements concerning those two countries.

As the struggle for the overseas communications market with IT&T was on-going, the RCA was simultaneously engulfed in an even more important battle domestically – together with its affiliated companies, it was embroiled in an

24 By the early 1930s, the RCA had established radio-telegraphic routes with over thirty countries. See Copy of Letter from Samuel Reber to the Minister of Posts and Telegraphs of the Republic of Czechoslovakia (25 April 1930) (MCI International Archives, box 583, file 'Czechoslovakia: Correspondence and Agreements (2 of 6)').

25 See Warner (n 21) 4–8.

26 See Robert Sobel, *ITT: The Management of Opportunity* (Truman Talley Books 1982) 62.

27 Ibid 58–60.

28 Ibid 61–63; Sobel, *RCA* (n 13) 88–89.

29 Sobel, *ITT* (n 26) 63–64.

30 Indeed, at one point, The New York Times even published a front-page article announcing the sale of RCA Communications to IT&T. See ibid 64.

31 The proposed sale would have made the RCA the largest IT&T stockholder. See ibid.

32 See Letter from Manton Davis to David Sarnoff (25 January 1933) (MCI International Archives, box 581, file 'China: Chinese Arbitration Correspondence (5 of 13)').

anti-trust controversy with the US government. Namely, the US government had, in May of 1930, brought an anti-trust suit against the RCA and its related companies under the proposition that they had unlawfully restrained competition in the radio industry.[33] At the heart of the controversy were certain cross-licensing agreements into which the RCA and its parent companies had entered upon the RCA's establishment in order to avoid patent impasses that would have hindered the successful operation of the newly formed company.[34] The dispute was eventually resolved with the two opposing sides entering into a consent decree by which the cross-licensing structure had been rearranged and the RCA's parent companies obliged to divest their interest in the RCA.[35] As a result, the RCA would, for the first time, emerge out of the anti-trust litigation as a fully independent company, separated from the corporate giants that had brought it into existence.[36]

One issue that had not been resolved by the consent decree, however, was the status of the RCA's overseas contracts, which had also been targeted by the government's suit; this issue was deemed too difficult at the time and its definite resolution was consequently put off for another two and a half years.[37] It was precisely the nature of one of these overseas contracts that would be at the crux of the RCA's arbitration against The Czechoslovakian Administration, as the tribunal would be tasked with deciding – and would answer the question in the positive – whether the RCA's contract with The Czechoslovakian Administration prevented the latter from opening a new direct radio telegraphic route to the US.

2.2 *The Establishment of RCA's Czechoslovakia Circuit: The First Direct US-Czechoslovakia Radio-Telegraphic Route*

The RCA and The Czechoslovakian Administration entered into a traffic agreement on 10 November 1928 (the Czechoslovakian Traffic Agreement), providing for the establishment and operation of a direct radio telegraphic circuit for the purpose of furnishing commercial radio communication services between

33 Archer, *Big Business and Radio* (n 13) 349.

34 Sobel, *RCA* (n 13) 94; Archer, *Big Business and Radio* (n 13) 349.

35 See Archer, *Big Business and Radio* (n 13) 378ff.

36 Arguably, the RCA had gotten out of the anti-trust controversy as the winner. The RCA's president David Sarnoff was quoted as saying: '(t)he Department of Justice handed me a lemon and I made lemonade out of it'. See Archer, *Big Business and Radio* (n 13) 386; Sobel, *RCA* (n 13) 98.

37 'Decree Dissolving Radio Group Under Anti-Trust Law' *The New York Times* (New York, 22 November 1932) 17.

Czechoslovakia and the US.[38] While there had already been a number of telegraphic routes in existence between Czechoslovakia and the US, unlike the newly envisioned RCA route, none of them had provided for a direct radio telegraphic circuit between the two countries.[39] The RCA circuit was therefore to become the first direct radio circuit between the US and Czechoslovakia.

The Czechoslovakian Traffic Agreement was similar (but not entirely identical) to the traffic agreements the RCA had concluded with several other countries.[40] Pursuant to its provisions, the two sides were to make use of their respective radio stations in order to enable the transmission and reception of radio messages between the two countries.[41] For this purpose, each of them would 'transmit *exclusively* over the said circuit (...) every available message within its control destined to' Czechoslovakia or the US '*unless routed otherwise by the sender*'.[42] The radio communications services were to be conducted in accordance with the Regulations of the International Telegraph Conventions,[43] while each party had generally undertaken to cooperate with the other in ensuring the successful and remunerative operation of the joint circuit.[44] The Czechoslovakian Traffic Agreement also contained a rather interesting provision on the governing law, which provided that the obligations and responsibilities of the RCA and The Czechoslovakian Administration would be governed by the laws of the State of New York and of the Republic of Czechoslovakia, respectively.[45] Finally, the Czechoslovakian Traffic Agreement included a dispute resolution clause whereby both sides agreed, insofar an amicable solution could not be reached, to submit all disputes regarding the performance of the agreement to arbitration.[46] The RCA-Czechoslovakia route was officially inaugurated on 1 December 1930, some two years following the signing of the Czechoslovakian Traffic Agreement.[47]

---

38 See Czechoslovakian Traffic Agreement (n 12).

39 All of the alternative routes were either *via* cable or were indirect radio routes. See *Czechoslovakian Administration v RCA*, Statement of the Radio Corporation of America (23 November 1931) (MCI International Archives, box 581, file 'China: Chinese Arbitration Correspondence (2 of 13)') 5–6.

40 Letter from Reber to the Czechoslovakian Minister (25 April 1930) (n 24).

41 Czechoslovakian Traffic Agreement (n 12) art 1.

42 Ibid art 2. Emphases added.

43 Ibid art 3.

44 Ibid art 7.

45 Ibid art 11.

46 Ibid art 9.

47 See Letter from Secretary to Colonel Mitchell (25 September 1944) (MCI International Archives, box 583, file 'Czechoslovakia: Correspondence and Agreements (6 of 6)').

2.3 *Trouble on the Horizon: Mackay Radio Sparks a Rift between the RCA and the Czechoslovakian Administration*

It did not take long for the first cracks in the relationship between the RCA and The Czechoslovakian Administration to appear. In fact, already before the RCA-Czechoslovakia circuit had been put into operation, The Czechoslovakian Administration wrote to the RCA, requesting an interpretation of Article 2 of the Czechoslovakian Traffic Agreement. Specifically, The Czechoslovakian Administration asked for permission to interpret the exception under Article 2 – which allowed the parties, at the behest of the sender, to route a message that would normally be sent over the RCA-Czechoslovakia circuit over a different circuit – as likewise being applicable to instances where cable companies possessed not only cable routes but also radio-telegraphic connections between the US and Czechoslovakia; under such an interpretation, the message could thus be transmitted from The Czechoslovakian Administration's station in Prague to the cable company's station in the US via direct radio.[48] While the question was framed as a hypothetical one, it was later revealed that the request for interpretation was made after The Czechoslovakian Administration had already been approached by the Commercial Cable Company – an IT&T subsidiary – with a view on establishing such a direct route.[49]

The initial response by the RCA was straightforward – the RCA 'vigorously protested' the interpretation suggested by The Czechoslovakian Administration as one that was not possible and would undercut the very spirit of the Traffic Agreement.[50] Emphasising the significant expenditures that the RCA was making in developing the joint circuit, the company had pointed out that, had The Czechoslovakian Administration been allowed to enter into cooperation with other radio stations located in the US, the obligations under Article 2 would have been rendered entirely meaningless.[51] The Czechoslovakian Administration, however, was neither convinced nor satisfied by the

48 Copy of Letter from the Minister of Posts and Telegraphs of the Republic of Czechoslovakia to the Radio Corporation of America (11 October 1929) (MCI International Archives, box 583, file 'Czechoslovakia: Correspondence and Agreements (2 of 6)').

49 See *Czechoslovakian Administration v RCA*, Statement by the Administration of Posts and Telegraphs of the Republic of Czechoslovakia (23 November 1931) (MCI International Archives, box 581, file 'China: Chinese Arbitration Correspondence (2 of 13)') 2–3. (Note: the records of the proceedings from the Czechoslovakian arbitration are contained in the archival files relating to the Chinese arbitration.)

50 Copy of Letter from H L Roosevelt to the Ministry of Posts and Telegraphs of the Republic of Czechoslovakia (24 October 1929) (MCI International Archives, box 583, file 'Czechoslovakia: Correspondence and Agreements (2 of 6)').

51 Ibid.

RCA's response and continued to insist upon its interpretation. The parties subsequently exchanged a pair of letters where each side adhered adamantly to its initial position.[52] Ultimately, as the two sides had reached an apparent deadlock, The Czechoslovakian Administration suggested that the contentious issue be resolved by arbitration, as provided for by Article 9 of the Czechoslovakian Traffic Agreement.[53]

The RCA, to say the least, was not enthused about this proposal; the sentiment within company circles was that a potential arbitration would put the RCA in a precarious position, with neither of the possible outcomes being particularly favourable. It was feared that, if the arbitration was to turn out negatively for the RCA, the 'effect on [their] traffic agreements might be disastrous' and 'would advertise internationally that [RCA's] agreements were of no value'.[54] And there was indeed doubt within the company whether the RCA would prevail in a potential arbitration.[55] On the other hand, were the RCA to prevail in the proceeding, it was feared that this fact would be used against it back home in order to show that the RCA's overseas contracts were monopolistic in nature, thus undermining its position in its highly important anti-trust litigation against the US government.[56] The position of the RCA was made all the more difficult by the fact that the company had previously, during hearings before the Senate Interstate Commerce Commission, denied that its foreign traffic agreements were exclusive and would thus prevent other companies from concluding traffic agreements with the same administrations.[57] With these circumstances in mind, it is unsurprising that the RCA was reluctant to proceed to arbitration, especially over a matter that was as of yet (or so the RCA had thought) only of theoretical relevance.

52 See Translation of Letter from Minister of Posts and Telegraphs of the Republic of Czechoslovakia to the Radio Corporation of America (4 December 1929) (MCI International Archives, box 583, file 'Czechoslovakia: Correspondence and Agreements (2 of 6)'); Letter from Reber to the Czechoslovakian Minister (25 April 1930) (n 24).

53 See Copy of Letter from the Ministry of Posts and Telegraphs of Czechoslovakia to the RCA (5 June 1930) (MCI International Archives, box 583, file 'Czechoslovakia: Correspondence and Agreements (2 of 6)').

54 Letter (unsigned) to Winterbottom (3 July 1930) (MCI International Archives, box 583, file 'Czechoslovakia: Correspondence and Agreements (3 of 6)').

55 Copy of Letter from Samuel Reber to Brown (7 July 1930) (MCI International Archives, box 583, file 'Czechoslovakia: Correspondence and Agreements (3 of 6)'). In the letter, Reber states that he is 'very much afraid that any arbitrators selected from European communication administrations would rule against our contention.'

56 Letter to Winterbottom (3 July 1930) (n 54).

57 Letter from Reber to Brown (7 July 1930) (n 55).

While the RCA had also considered other options, such as breaking off their mutual cooperation if The Czechoslovakian Administration did not adhere to the RCA's position,[58] ultimately it was decided that the best course of action would be for the company to try to avoid arbitration by seemingly receding from its original position. Accordingly, on 22 July 1930, the RCA sent a letter to The Czechoslovakian Administration, informing it that the RCA had decided to 'refrain from insisting upon [its] interpretation of the *purely technical matter*' that had arisen between them.[59] The RCA explained this change in course by the apparent assurances that had been given by the Czechoslovakian side regarding their efforts towards making the joint circuit a successful enterprise.[60] The letter was drafted carefully so as to, while giving out the impression that The Czechoslovakian Administration had been given the requested concession, not preclude the RCA from again invoking its original position should circumstance so require.[61]

As it would turn out, the RCA's letter of 22 July 1930 had indeed put the controversial issue between the parties at rest only temporarily. Namely, already at the beginning of the following year, The Czechoslovakian Administration had approached the RCA in order to inform the company that it was unsatisfied with the volume of traffic that the RCA-Czechoslovakia circuit had generated upon its inauguration in the direction from the US towards Czechoslovakia, requesting the RCA to up its efforts in order to increase traffic.[62] Less than a month thereafter, invoking the alleged insufficiency of traffic and relying upon the RCA's letter of 22 July 1930, The Czechoslovakian Administration notified the RCA that it was planning to conclude a traffic agreement with Mackay Radio for the opening of another direct radio-telegraphic route between the US and Czechoslovakia.[63]

58 Letter to Winterbottom (3 July 1930) (n 54).

59 Copy of Letter from Samuel Reber to the Minister of Posts and Telegraphs of the Republic of Czechoslovakia (22 July 1930) (MCI International Archives, box 583, file 'Czechoslovakia: Arbitration (1 of 3)'). Emphasis added.

60 Ibid.

61 See Copy of Letter from William Brown to Samuel Reber (21 July 1930) (MCI International Archives, box 583, file 'Czechoslovakia: Correspondence and Agreements (3 of 6)').

62 Copy of Letter from Czechoslovakia to the RCA (27 March 1931) (MCI International Archives, box 583, file 'Czechoslovakia: Correspondence and Agreements (3 of 6)').

63 Copy of Telegram from the Czechoslovak Postministry to Radio Corporation of America (21 April 1931) (MCI International Archives, box 583, file 'Czechoslovakia: Correspondence and Agreements (3 of 6)').

The RCA responded by noting that it would consider the proposed opening of another direct circuit as a violation of the Czechoslovakian Traffic Agreement[64] and denied that its letter of 22 July 1930 could be interpreted as giving The Czechoslovakian Administration any indication that it had the right to establish an additional direct radio route. While the RCA did not question the rights of the sender to indicate according to which routing the message was to be sent, it maintained that this was an altogether different thing from The Czechoslovakian Administration itself participating in the establishment of additional circuits that would allow senders to divert their messages from the RCA-Czechoslovakia circuit.

The parties exchanged one more round of correspondence,[65] but, as each side had stuck to its position, once again found themselves at an impasse; it would once more be The Czechoslovakian Administration that would be the first to bring up arbitration.[66] While the RCA tried to defer resolving the issue as much as possible, this time arbitration appeared inevitable. Following several reminders[67] and an eventual ultimatum from The Czechoslovakian Administration that it would immediately appoint its arbitrator if the

64 Copy of Telegram from Radio Corporation of America to the Ministry of Posts and Telegraphs of Czechoslovakia (21 April 1931) (MCI International Archives, box 583, file 'Czechoslovakia: Correspondence and Agreements (2 of 6)'). In addition to expressing its disapproval to The Czechoslovakian Administration, the RCA also protested to Mackay Radio's parent company, IT&T. See Letter from J G Harbord to Colonel Sosthenes Behn (21 April 1921) (MCI International Archives, box 583, file 'Czechoslovakia: Arbitration (1 of 3)').

65 See Telegram from the Czechoslovak Postministry to the Radio Corporation of America (25 April 1931) (MCI International Archives, box 583, file 'Czechoslovakia: Arbitration (1 of 3)'); Telegram from Radio Corporation of America to the Minister of Posts and Telegraphs of the Republic of Czechoslovakia (4 May 1931) (MCI International Archives, box 583, file 'Czechoslovakia: Arbitration (1 of 3)').

66 Translation of Telegram from the Ministry of Posts and Telegraphs of the Republic of Czechoslovakia to Radio Corporation of America (27 May 1931) (MCI International Archives, box 583, file 'Czechoslovakia: Arbitration (1 of 3)').

67 Copy of Telegram from the Ministry of Posts and Telegraphs of the Republic of Czechoslovakia to Radio Corporation of America (16 June 1931) (MCI International Archives, box 583, file 'Czechoslovakia: Correspondence and Agreements (3 of 6)'); Copy of Telegram from the Ministry of Posts and Telegraphs of the Republic of Czechoslovakia to Radio Corporation of America (17 June 1931) (MCI International Archives, box 583, file 'Czechoslovakia: Correspondence and Agreements (3 of 6)'); Copy of Telegram from Radio Corporation of America to the Ministry of Posts and Telegraphs of the Republic of Czechoslovakia (17 June 1931) (MCI International Archives, box 583, file 'Czechoslovakia: Correspondence and Agreements (3 of 6)').

RCA did not respond to its request for arbitration,[68] the RCA finally acceded to arbitration.[69]

2.4 *The Arbitration*

2.4.1 The Constitution of the Tribunal

Pursuant to the Czechoslovakian Traffic Agreement, each side was to appoint an arbitrator, the two of whom were then to select the tribunal's president.[70] The RCA had started contemplating the best candidate for its appointee even before it had notified The Czechoslovakian Administration of its acceptance to proceed to arbitration.[71] In making the selection, the RCA was initially inclined to look toward someone from its own ranks or at least a person with connections to the company.[72] However, it was soon concluded that the position of arbitrator required someone who would 'be disinterested and must not be the representative or the champion of either party'.[73] From a policy perspective, this was perceived as the optimal way to proceed even if The Czechoslovakian Administration were to appoint an arbitrator who would not be impartial.[74] Despite these aspirations toward neutrality, the person that was to be chosen

---

68 Copy of Telegram from the Ministry of Posts and Telegraphs of the Republic of Czechoslovakia to Radio Corporation of America (30 June 1931) (MCI International Archives, box 583, file 'Czechoslovakia: Correspondence and Agreements (3 of 6)'). The RCA would then have had 10 days to appoint its arbitrator. See Czechoslovakian Traffic Agreement (n 12) art 9.

69 Copy of Telegram from Radio Corporation of America to the Ministry of Posts and Telegraphs of the Republic of Czechoslovakia (2 July 1931) (MCI International Archives, box 583, file 'Czechoslovakia: Correspondence and Agreements (3 of 6)').

70 Czechoslovakian Traffic Agreement (n 12) art 9.

71 Memo from Manton Davis to Winterbottom (telephoned to Miss MacInnis) (22 June 1931) (MCI International Archives, box 583, file 'Czechoslovakia: Correspondence and Agreements (3 of 6)').

72 The two options considered by the RCA were either its own traffic manager or Otto Arendt from the German Reichspost. Arendt was then to be invited to America to discuss the controversy between the RCA and The Czechoslovakian Administration, for which he was to have his expenses covered and accorded a reasonable fee. Both options were soon discarded as inappropriate. See ibid; Letter from the RCA (unsigned) to Otto Arendt (29 June 1931) (MCI International Archives, box 583, file 'Czechoslovakia: Arbitration (1 of 3)'); Copy of Letter from Robert T Swaine to Colonel Davis (3 July 1931) (MCI International Archives, box 583, file 'Czechoslovakia: Correspondence and Agreements (3 of 6)'); Copy of Letter from Manton Davis to Winterbottom (9 July 1931) (MCI International Archives, box 583, file 'Czechoslovakia: Correspondence and Agreements (3 of 6)').

73 Memo from Davis to Winterbottom (22 June 1931) (n 71).

74 Letter from Swaine to Davis (3 July 1931) (n 72); Letter from Davis to Winterbottom (9 July 1931) (n 72).

was nonetheless still expected to be 'sympathetically inclined toward [the RCA's] point of view'.[75]

75 Letter from Davis to Winterbottom (9 July 1931) (n 72). Moreover, the professed desire for the impartiality of all of the arbitrators is not to be taken without serious reservations, especially when compared to present-day standards. In both arbitrations, the RCA throughout the proceedings maintained continuous contact with the arbitrators appointed by it, seemingly even discussing the merits of the case with them and receiving apparent feedback on its arguments. See eg Letter from W A Winterbottom to Colonel Davis (14 August 1931) (MCI International Archives, box 583, file 'Czechoslovakia: Correspondence and Agreements (3 of 6)'); Telegram from Judge Woodward to Colonel Manton Davis (14 October 1931) (MCI International Archives, box 583, file 'Czechoslovakia: Arbitration (2 of 3)'); Letter from Manton Davis to Schuloff (8 October 1934) (MCI International Archives, box 581, file 'China: Chinese Arbitration Correspondence (11 of 13)'); Copy of Letter from A Hubert to Colonel Davis (22 May 1933) (MCI International Archives, box 581, file 'China: Chinese Arbitration Correspondence (5 of 13)'); Letter (unsigned) to Schuloff (12 June 1933) (MCI International Archives, box 581, file 'China: Chinese Arbitration Correspondence (6 of 13)'); Letter from Manton Davis to Schuloff (21 June 1933) (MCI International Archives, box 581, file 'China: Chinese Arbitration Correspondence (7 of 13)'); Letter from Manton Davis to A Hubert (14 July 1933) (MCI International Archives, box 581, file 'China: Chinese Arbitration Correspondence (7 of 13)'); Letter (unsigned) to A Hubert (17 August 1933) (MCI International Archives, box 581, file 'China: Chinese Arbitration Correspondence (9 of 13)'); Copy of Letter from A Hubert to Morton (20 April 1933) (MCI International Archives, box 581, file 'China: Chinese Arbitration Correspondence (10 of 13)'); Letter from Manton Davis to A Hubert (6 July 1934) (MCI International Archives, box 581, file 'China: Chinese Arbitration Correspondence (11 of 13)'). Whitmore, the RCA-appointed arbitrator in the case against The Czechoslovakian Administration, had also apparently disclosed his opinion on the merits of the case to the RCA president David Sarnoff already in August of 1931, although he had, when doing so, noted that, had he so thought, he would not have hesitated to say that the RCA had been in the wrong. See Letter from Whitmore to W A Winterbottom (26 April 1932) (MCI International Archives, box 583, file 'Czechoslovakia: Arbitration (3 of 3)'). Hubert, the RCA-appointed arbitrator in the China arbitration, had done the same even prior to his appointment, as he had, upon going through the documents regarding the Chinese arbitration that had been sent to him by the RCA, revealed to Winterbottom that his first impression was that the RCA's 'view of the matter [wa]s completely justified.' See Letter from A Hubert to Winterbottom (10 May 1933) (MCI International Archives, box 581, file 'China: Chinese Arbitration Correspondence (5 of 13)'). Moreover, while he was unable to once more serve as the RCA's arbitrator in the China arbitration due to conflicting commitments, Whitmore was nonetheless seemingly 'anxious' to help the RCA with the case in any way possible. See Telegram from Kellaway to Sarnoff (3 January 1933) (MCI International Archives, box 581, file 'China: Chinese Arbitration Correspondence (10 of 13)'); Letter (unsigned) to Colonel Manton Davis (21 July 1933) (MCI International Archives, box 581, file 'China: Chinese Arbitration Correspondence (7 of 13)'). In a letter following the Czechoslovakian arbitration, Whitmore also disclosed that he would have been happy to assist the RCA in any way within his power in light of the 'pleasant relations, both business and personal' that he had had with RCA personnel over 'so many years'. See Letter from Whitmore to Winterbot-

The RCA's fears that the Czechoslovakian side would appoint one of its officials as arbitrator, however, proved to be unfounded, as on 24 July 1931, The Czechoslovakian Administration informed the RCA that it had appointed Reinhold Furrer, the Director General of the Swiss Postal and Telegraph Administration, as its arbitrator in the proceeding.[76] As for the RCA, the choice ultimately came down to G S Whitmore, the Controller of Telegraph Services at Imperial and International Communications Limited of London.[77]

The two party-appointed arbitrators then proceeded to search for an appropriate candidate for the presiding arbitrator. Within RCA circles, the feeling was that the presiding arbitrator should be a 'high class neutral lawyer', preferably from Belgium or the Netherlands, or perhaps even 'a member of the International Court'.[78] While several candidates were considered,[79] the search was eventually narrowed down to members of the Danish judiciary. Eventually, the decision was made to appoint Judge Julius Möller, who was a judge at the High Court of Justice in Denmark.[80] With the tribunal in place, the arbitration was ready to begin.

---

tom (26 April 1932) (MCI International Archives, box 583, file 'Czechoslovakia: Arbitration (3 of 3)'). It would seem, therefore, that the role of the party-appointed arbitrator in the two arbitrations was in reality somewhere in between a truly independent third party and a party representative to the tribunal (and was perhaps even leaning toward the latter).

76 Copy of Letter from the Telegraph Administration of Czechoslovakia to Radio Corporation of America (24 July 1931) (MCI International Archives, box 583, file 'Czechoslovakia: Correspondence and Agreements (3 of 6)').

77 Telegram from Sarnoff to Kellaway (13 August 1932) (MCI International Archives, box 583, file 'Czechoslovakia: Correspondence and Agreements (3 of 6)'); Letter from W A Winterbottom to the Minister of Posts and Telegraphs of the Republic of Czechoslovakia (14 August 1931) (MCI International Archives, box 583, file 'Czechoslovakia: Correspondence and Agreements (3 of 6)'); Letter from the RCA (unsigned) to Whitmore (18 August 1931) (MCI International Archives, box 583, file 'Czechoslovakia: Correspondence and Agreements (3 of 6)').

78 Letter from Winterbottom to Davis (14 August 1931) (n 75).

79 See Letter from J M Woodward to David Sarnoff (24 August 1931) (MCI International Archives, box 583, file 'Czechoslovakia: Correspondence and Agreements (3 of 6)'); Memorandum by J M Woodward (26 August 1931) (MCI International Archives, box 583, file 'Czechoslovakia: Correspondence and Agreements (3 of 6)').

80 Letter from Whitmore and Furrer to RCA President (14 September 1931) (MCI International Archives, box 583, file 'Czechoslovakia: Arbitration (1 of 3)'); Letter from Whitmore and Furrer to Julius Möller (14 September 1931) (MCI International Archives, box 583, file 'Czechoslovakia: Arbitration (1 of 3)'). On the selection of Judge Möller, see Letter from Whitmore to John B Rostron (5 October 1931) (MCI International Archives, box 583, file 'Czechoslovakia: Arbitration (2 of 3)').

2.4.2 The Order of Proceedings and the Parties' Arguments: The Nature of RCA's Agreement with the Czechoslovakian Administration Takes Centre Stage

Once constituted, the first matter that the tribunal sought to address were the rules of procedure pursuant to which the arbitration was to proceed. The initial proposal in this respect was made by the presiding arbitrator, Judge Möller,[81] and gave rise to a controversial issue right from the outset. Namely, the president's proposal presupposed that it was to be determined which party would be the claimant in the arbitration; this, as was pointed out by the arbitrator appointed by The Czechoslovakian Administration, was 'a delicate question'.[82] The RCA's general counsel, Colonel Manton Davis, was initially of the opinion that The Czechoslovakian Administration ought to present the case first, as the case had been brought upon its insistence.[83] Ultimately, however, it was decided that the arbitration would be organised so that there would be no need to determine explicitly which side was the claimant.[84] Both parties accordingly submitted their initial memoranda and subsequent responses simultaneously.[85] The parties submitted several rounds of written pleadings, after which an oral hearing was held in The Hague at the end of March of 1932.[86]

The main arguments put forward by each party during the written proceedings are integral not only for understanding the case itself but also its eventual outcome. As would ultimately prove to be pivotal, in their pleadings, the parties had put at least as much emphasis on their understanding of the proper conceptualisation of the relationship between the RCA and The Czechoslovakian Administration as they did on the very terms of the Czechoslovakian Traffic Agreement.

Of course, a significant part of the parties' arguments focused on the wording of the Czechoslovakian Traffic Agreement itself, with two of the agreement's clauses drawing the preponderance of the attention: Article 2 and Article 7.

81 Copy of Letter from Julius Möller to Whitmore (2 October 1931) (MCI International Archives, box 583, file 'Czechoslovakia: Arbitration (2 of 3)').

82 Telegram from Whitmore to the RCA (9 October 1931) (MCI International Archives, box 583, file 'Czechoslovakia: Arbitration (2 of 3)').

83 Copy of Telegram from Manton Davis to Judge Woodward (9 October 1931) (MCI International Archives, box 583, file 'Czechoslovakia: Arbitration (2 of 3)').

84 Copy of Telegram from Manton Davis to Hubert (12 June 1933) (MCI International Archives, box 581, file 'China: Chinese Arbitration Correspondence (10 of 13)').

85 For an overview of the parties' submissions in the proceedings, see Letter from Manton Davis to F Eldred Boland (26 December 1933) (MCI International Archives, box 581, file 'China: Chinese Arbitration Correspondence (8 of 13)').

86 See 'Minutes' of the oral hearing (MCI International Archives, box 581, file 'China: Chinese Arbitration Correspondence (2 of 13)').

The Czechoslovakian Administration maintained that it had always intended to reserve for itself the right to establish additional circuits with the US and saw the wording of Article 2, which provided that 'the Administration shall transmit exclusively over the said circuit (…) every message within its control destined to the United States of America (…) unless routed otherwise by the sender'[87] as providing support for this argument. During the proceedings, the Czechoslovakian side in particular emphasised the phrase 'unless routed otherwise by the sender', interpreting this as putting telegrams so routed beyond the reach of the Czechoslovakian Traffic Agreement. In its view, this applied not only to routes already established, but included also the possibility of instituting new ones.[88] Conversely, for the RCA, this wording merely reflected the already existing obligation of The Czechoslovakian Administration under international telegraph conventions to respect the routing prescribed by the sender; it thus pertained only to existing routes and did not establish any rights for The Czechoslovakian Administration which otherwise would not have existed.[89] The RCA instead preferred to accentuate the part of Article 2 which, barring the aforementioned exception, prescribed for the 'exclusive' transmission of messages over the joint circuit.

The RCA furthermore put considerable emphasis on Article 7, which provided that '[g]enerally, each party hereto [was to] cooperate with the other to secure the successful and remunerative working of the jointly operated circuit.'[90] According to the RCA, this provision implied that neither party was to take action which could cause the joint circuit to be less successful – as, it was argued, would have been the case if The Czechoslovakian Administration

87 See n 42.

88 See The Czechoslovakian Administration's Statement (n 49) 2 and 8–11; *Czechoslovakian Administration v RCA*, Reply of the Administration of Posts and Telegraphs of the Republic of Czechoslovakia to the Expose of the Radio Corporation of America (5 January 1932) (MCI International Archives, box 581, file 'China: Chinese Arbitration Correspondence (2 of 13)') 7ff; *Czechoslovakian Administration v RCA*, Reply of the Administration of Posts and Telegraphs of the Republic of Czechoslovakia to the Rejoinder of the Radio Corporation of America of January 5th 1931 (25 February 1932) (MCI International Archives, box 581, file 'China: Chinese Arbitration Correspondence (2 of 13)') 2 and 5–6. (The reference to 5 January 1931 in title of The Czechoslovakian Administration's last memorandum is a clerical error. The correct date was 5 January 1932).

89 See RCA's Statement (n 39) 11–13; *Czechoslovakian Administration v RCA*, Reply of the Radio Corporation of America (5 January 1932) (MCI International Archives, box 581, file 'China: Chinese Arbitration Correspondence (2 of 13)') 3–4 and 6; *Czechoslovakian Administration v RCA*, Rejoinder of the Radio Corporation of America (26 February 1932) (MCI International Archives, box 581, file 'China: Chinese Arbitration Correspondence (2 of 13)') 49–52.

90 See n 44.

were to establish a parallel circuit with Mackay Radio.[91] The Czechoslovakian Administration, meanwhile, sought to downplay the importance of this clause by pointing to its general nature and corresponding lack of concrete obligations. The Czechoslovakian side also underlined all of the positive efforts it had made in making the joint circuit with the RCA successful, while simultaneously disputing the RCA's contentions that the RCA-Czechoslovakia circuit would in fact be put at a disadvantage due to the Mackay circuit.[92]

The RCA's argument that The Czechoslovakian Administration was precluded from establishing the direct circuit with Mackay Radio, however, was not based solely on the specific text of the Czechoslovakian Traffic Agreement; the crux of its argument instead related more broadly to the very nature of the agreement itself and the resulting underlying relationship between the parties. Namely, according to the RCA, as the two sides had joined both property and efforts in order to achieve mutual profit in establishing the joint circuit, a community for mutual profit (*Erwerbsgesellschaft* under paragraph 1175 of the Common Civil Code) – the equivalent of a joint venture under US law – had been established between the parties pursuant to the Czechoslovakian law applicable to The Czechoslovakian Administration's obligations.[93] The RCA further argued that under the relevant law neither side participating in such a community was permitted to partake in activities that would be prejudicial to the community's interests (as opening the Mackay circuit would arguably have been).[94] For its part, The Czechoslovakian Administration disagreed with such a characterisation of the Czechoslovakian Traffic Agreement, disputing that the aim behind the agreement was the pursuit of (joint) profit and arguing that – at least on the Czechoslovakian side – much broader interests than just financial ones were at the forefront of considerations at the time of the agreement's conclusion. Consequently, the agreement was much more appropriately to be classified as an innominate or *sui generis* one.[95]

91 See RCA's Statement (n 39) 13–15; RCA's Reply (n 89) 7–8; RCA's Rejoinder (n 89) 48–49. According to the RCA, the existing circuit had already been sufficient to handle the existing traffic between Czechoslovakia and the US.

92 See The Czechoslovakian Administration's Statement (n 49) 11–13; The Czechoslovakian Administration's Reply (25 February 1932) (n 88) 13 and 15.

93 The Czechoslovakian Administration translated the term *Erwerbsgesellschaft* as 'cooperative association'. See The Czechoslovakian Administration's Reply (5 January 1932) (n 88) 21.

94 See RCA's Statement (n 39) 16–23; RCA's Reply (n 89) 6–7; RCA's Rejoinder (n 89) 42–49.

95 See The Czechoslovakian Administration's Reply (5 January 1932) (n 88) 21–26; The Czechoslovakian Administration's Reply (25 February 1932) (n 88) 8–9.

The Czechoslovakian Administration's key argument in relation to the nature of the contract, however, went much further – it disputed the very fact that the Traffic Agreement was at all a contract of civil law, designating it instead as a public law contract or *contrat administratif*. The Czechoslovakian Administration's position was that the operation of telegraphic services was an essential function of the state[96] and that, in concluding the Czechoslovakian Traffic Agreement, The Czechoslovakian Administration itself was a public institution acting for the benefit of the public, with more than just monetary interests in mind. Accordingly, it was argued that the Czechoslovakian Traffic Agreement could not be interpreted in a manner that would restrict The Czechoslovakian Administration's capacity, as well as obligation, to act in the best interests of Czechoslovakian citizens by introducing an additional radio-telegraphic route.[97] The RCA, on the other hand, disputed the notion that the Czechoslovakian Traffic Agreement could be treated as anything but an ordinary contract under civil law. For the RCA, the question of the nature of the Czechoslovakian Traffic Agreement was not to be answered in the abstract, but could instead only be resolved on a case-by-case basis pursuant to the positive laws of a specific state. The RCA then proceeded to analyse the provisions of Czechoslovakian law pertaining to The Czechoslovakian Administration in-depth, putting particular emphasis on the fact that it had been designated by governmental decree as an enterprise that was to be administered according to principles of commercial policy.[98] The RCA took this to mean that, while the very organisation of The Czechoslovakian Administration may have been subject to public law, the contracts concluded by it were not, but were instead governed by ordinary rules of civil law.[99]

As can be seen, then, the matter of the proper conceptualisation of the underlying agreement proved rather controversial in the proceedings – it was

96 See The Czechoslovakian Administration's Reply (5 January 1932) (n 88) 16 ('the exploitation of the postal and telegraphic traffic, as generally in Europe, so also in Czechoslovakia forms one of the principal tasks of the State. The state proceeds here, at the present time, as administrator of public interests and acts therefore as subject of the Public-law').

97 Ibid 16–20.

98 RCA's Rejoinder (n 89) 20–42.

99 The RCA also maintained that, even if the Czechoslovakian Traffic Agreement were categorised as a public law contract, this would have no bearing on the dispute. Namely, the RCA argued that even under public law contracts parties could not simply refuse to comply with contractual obligations because they thought that the public interest would be better served in that way than if the contract was carried out, as well as that The Czechoslovakian Administration had failed to actually explain why the public interest demanded the establishment of a second direct radio-telegraphic route between Czechoslovakia and the US. See ibid 40–41.

extensively debated between the parties, with the two opposing sides devoting significant portions of their written pleadings to it and going into fine detail on both the organisational structure of The Czechoslovakian Administration and the nature of its relations with the Czechoslovakian public. The effort that the two sides expended in arguing the matter was not in vain, for the issue of the proper conceptualisation of the underlying agreement – as the analysis of the tribunal's decision in the following sub-section will show – would eventually also feature prominently in the tribunal's reasoning.

Finally, the two sides also touched upon the question of whether the RCA's interpretation of the agreement, if accepted, would create a monopolistic position for the RCA. Namely, The Czechoslovakian Administration had argued that, since it was the only entity allowed under Czechoslovakian law to establish radio-telegraphic circuits, a prohibition for it to operate additional circuits towards the US would result in an effective monopoly for the RCA on this route, which was prohibited under US anti-trust law.[100] The RCA, for its part, denied that it was seeking to establish such a monopolistic position – its claim was not that The Czechoslovakian Administration was prohibited from establishing new circuits in the absolute terms, but rather only those circuits that could potentially harm the jointly operated circuit.[101] This issue would unfortunately not feature in the tribunal's considerations.

2.4.3 The Tribunal's Decision: The Czechoslovakian Administration is Prohibited from Opening a New Radio Telegraphic Circuit with the US

The tribunal rendered its decision in The Hague, on 1 April 1932.[102] The decision was handed down immediately after the oral hearings and was not unanimous, but was adopted by a majority of votes.[103]

The decision centred not so much on the wording of the specific clauses of the underlying agreement as it did on the tribunal's conceptualisation of the very nature of the parties' relationship. Crucial in this respect – and for the eventual outcome of the case – was the tribunal's finding that the underlying agreement had created a co-partnership between the RCA and The Czechoslovakian Administration, which obliged both parties to act in the furtherance of

100 See The Czechoslovakian Administration's Reply (25 February 1932) (n 88) 10–12.

101 See RCA's Reply (n 89) 7–8.

102 *The Administration of Posts and Telegraphs of the Republic of Czechoslovakia v The Radio Corporation of America* (1936) 30 AJIL 523.

103 While the decision itself does not indicate how the votes were split, there can be little doubt that the dissenting vote came from Furrer.

their joint interests. For present purposes, equally, if not more, relevant was how the tribunal framed the relationship between the RCA and The Czechoslovakian Administration; not only did the tribunal characterise this relationship as falling within the purview of ordinary civil law, but the arbitrators stressed that their decision would not have differed even if the problem had been approached from a public law perspective. Thus, at least in this particular instance, this possible divergence in conceptual approach was not determinative for the tribunal's eventual finding on The Czechoslovakian Administration's capacity to open a new direct radio telegraphic route.

As a preliminary matter, the tribunal first clarified the exact question that it had been called upon to resolve. Namely, during the written phase of the proceedings, there had been some controversy between the parties as to what precisely the task of the tribunal in the arbitration was. While the RCA had asked the tribunal to rule on The Czechoslovakian Administration's right to establish an additional radio-telegraphic circuit with the US,[104] The Czechoslovakian Administration had formulated its request to the tribunal in a somewhat different manner;[105] a manner that – at least in the view of the RCA – had presupposed that The Czechoslovakian Administration's right to establish such a circuit was undisputed, leaving as the only open question the extent to which the circuit could be utilised.[106] Although the tribunal did not address the parties' arguments and opposing positions on this point explicitly, it adopted a position that essentially reflected that of the RCA. Thus, in what perhaps foreshadowed that the tribunal would have little doubt of its own capacity to direct The Czechoslovakian Administration's conduct on the matter, the tribunal defined its task in the arbitration as having to determine:

> whether the traffic agreement, agreed upon by both parties on November 10, 1928, debars the Administration from establishing a second direct radio-telegraphic service between Czechoslovakia and USA via Mackay Radio for telegrams marked by sender via Mackay Radio.[107]

One of the central points of the decision was the status of the Czechoslovakian Traffic Agreement – i.e. whether it was to be understood as a regular civil law contract or one that was subject to public law. The tribunal opted for the former approach. In coming to this conclusion, the tribunal initially observed

104 See RCA's Statement (n 39) 28–29.
105 See The Czechoslovakian Administration's Statement (n 49) 13.
106 See RCA's Reply (n 89) 15.
107 *Czechoslovakian Administration v RCA* (n 102) 529.

that the status of agreements involving state entities was a highly disputed matter; however, the tribunal ultimately echoed the opinion of Hans Kelsen that, once states enter into concrete legal obligations, they do not hold a different status than any other party.[108] With a view on the specific dispute at hand, the tribunal added that:

> this must especially apply in a case like the present, where the private contracting party was at perfect liberty to decide whether or no he would enter upon an agreement like the one under discussion, and where any possibility of compulsory administrative action was absent. At the same time it may be added that also in public law there is room for the principle of liberty in concluding contracts, both as regards whether an agreement should be entered upon at all and what contents it should contain, and in public law the sentence *pacta sunt servanda* will also apply, just as public interest requires stability as regards any arrangement legally agreed upon.[109]

The tribunal's reasons for refusing to treat the agreement as belonging to public law were, however, not limited to general observations regarding this category of contracts. Instead, they were also rooted more specifically in how the tribunal perceived the concrete agreement that the parties had concluded, which perception was primarily shaped by the tribunal's understanding that the agreement was not one that by default needed to be concluded by a public authority. Thus, while the tribunal acknowledged that in the majority of countries, including Czechoslovakia, telegraphy was a state-operated business, it simultaneously seized upon the fact that a sizeable share of the industry was run by private companies. Accordingly, the tribunal noted that an agreement identical to the one between the RCA and The Czechoslovakian Administration could just as easily have been concluded between two private parties; there was little doubt for the tribunal that in such a case the agreement would have been governed by ordinary civil law. Invoking Austrian law, which had not

108 Ibid 530–531.

109 Ibid 531. Emphasis in the original. The tribunal moreover went on to emphasise that, even in relation to public law contracts, public authorities could not simply introduce modifications without consequence. Thus, the tribunal pointed out that, irrespective of any impact that a possible adjustment of a public law contract in safeguarding the public interest might have on its validity, 'any alteration or cancellation of an agreement on this basis as a rule *should only be possible subject to compensation to the other party*.' Emphasis added.

been proved to differ from Czechoslovakian law on this point,[110] the tribunal concluded that the simple fact that one of the parties to the agreement was a public authority was insufficient reason to deviate from its determination as to the types of norms the agreement would fall under – whether those of ordinary civil law or of public law.

While a proper understanding of the tribunal's decision necessitates understanding also the tribunal's conceptual approach to the Czechoslovakian Traffic Agreement, it is equally important to appreciate that the tribunal's treatment of this question was not outcome determinative. Indeed, even if the tribunal had held that the Czechoslovakian Traffic Agreement was not subject to ordinary rules of civil law but to public law, its ultimate conclusion would not have been any different, as the tribunal established a high bar for cancelling such public law contracts. In the words of the tribunal:

> even if this agreement should really be considered a public law agreement, it must at any rate be a condition for allowing the State to repudiate the responsibilities which such agreement might contain, and which the private party would be forced to respect, that *the State would be able to show that public interests of vital importance would suffer if the agreement should be upheld under the rules of ordinary civil law*.[111]

The tribunal thus circumscribed the possibility of modifying even public law agreements only to instances where this was dictated by 'public interests of vital importance'. The tribunal was unconvinced that this had been the case in the dispute before it. The tribunal justified such a conclusion by stressing that The Czechoslovakian Administration was an enterprise run on commercial terms and that – seemingly by The Czechoslovakian Administration's own admission[112] – the driving motivation behind its desire to establish an additional radio telegraphic service was its dissatisfaction with the number of telegrams transmitted over its joint circuit with the RCA. Conversely, there had been no indications that there were any technical problems with the existing circuit or that its capacity was inadequate. Under such circumstances, the tribunal found that letting The Czechoslovakian Administration out of its

110 Ibid. Austrian civil law remained applicable in Czechoslovakia following its independence after the dissolution of the Austro-Hungarian Empire. See David Falada, 'Codification of Private Law in the Czech Republic' (2009) 15(1) Fundamina: A Journal of Legal History 38, 52–53.

111 *Czechoslovakian Administration v RCA* (n 102) 531. Emphasis added.

112 See ibid 531–532.

contractual obligations due to its appeals to the public law nature of the agreement would have been unjustified.

The tribunal's decision on the ordinary civil law nature of the Czechoslovakian Traffic Agreement set the stage for its ruling on the fundamental question underpinning the entire dispute – whether The Czechoslovakian Administration was prohibited from entering into an agreement with Mackay Radio for the purpose of establishing another radio telegraphic circuit. Ultimately, this question would turn not on the specific wording of the Czechoslovakian Traffic Agreement, but on the tribunal's overall understanding of the agreement. Thus, while the tribunal's view was that the Czechoslovakian Traffic Agreement did not explicitly prohibit such a course of action by The Czechoslovakian Administration, it held that the 'very nature of the agreement' – which was found to have established a co-partnership of interest between the two sides in operating the joint circuit – prevented it from doing so. The precise nature of this co-partnership – a matter that had been subject to some debate between the parties[113] – was in the end deemed immaterial by the tribunal, as it found that the same regime would have applied either way.

As a result, the tribunal's position was that each party to the Czechoslovakian Traffic Agreement had been obliged to try to further the interests of the co-partnership as much as possible.[114] The tribunal perceived this obligation as incompatible with the desire to establish an additional radio telegraphic circuit between Czechoslovakia and the US, on condition that two further qualifiers were met. The first pertained to the absence of possibility that another provision of the Czechoslovakian Traffic Agreement explicitly allowed for an activity of the type envisioned by The Czechoslovakian Administration. The second qualifier related to the likelihood that the joint undertaking would suffer as a result of the competition resulting from a party's efforts to establish the second circuit. The tribunal deemed both of these additional requirements to have been met.[115]

---

113 See sub-section 2.4.2.

114 The tribunal found these interests to be reflected in art 2 (providing that 'each party shall transmit exclusively over the jointly operated circuit every available message within its control') and art 7 (providing that 'each party shall cooperate with the other to secure the successful and remunerative working' of the circuit) of the Traffic Agreement. See nn 42 and 44.

115 Regarding the first qualifier, The Czechoslovakian Administration relied on art 2 of the Traffic Agreement, which provided that the parties were obliged to send all messages over the joint circuit, but only 'unless routed otherwise by the sender.' The tribunal, however, did not see this provision as giving the parties the freedom that The Czechoslovakian Administration was seeking to ascribe to itself, as it considered the provision a simple

The final issue of significance dealt with by the tribunal concerned The Czechoslovakian Administration's argument that it was inappropriate to deem its relationship with the RCA as a community for mutual profit or joint venture (*Erwerbsgesellschaft*), because, unlike such a community or joint venture, which was motivated solely by the pursuit of profit, the state needed to have broader considerations in mind. The tribunal, however, was not convinced by this position, emphasising instead that:

> (w)hen a public institution enters into an agreement with a private person or a private company, it must be assumed that the institution has intended by this agreement to benefit its citizens. *But that this expectation sometimes proves to fail in not giving the country as large a profit as was expected, cannot be considered sufficient reason for releasing that public institution from its obligations as signatory of said agreement.*[116]

The inevitable outcome from the arbitrators' foregoing findings was that the tribunal decided the dispute in favour of the RCA. Crucially, in so doing, the tribunal did not merely provide for compensation for the RCA in case the Czechoslovakian side proceeded with its intention of establishing an additional circuit; this, after all, had not been asked of it. Instead, the tribunal outright decided, as the RCA had requested, that The Czechoslovakian Administration did not have the right to establish the additional circuit. The tribunal's *dispositif* thus reads as clear a direction to a state entity on its conduct as could have been articulated by a historical ISA tribunal:

> The Administration of Posts and Telegraphs of the Republic of Czechoslovakia *has not the right to establish a second direct radio-telegraphic service between Czechoslovakia and the USA* via Mackay Radio for telegrams marked by sender "Via Mackay Radio."[117]

---

reflection of the obligations that the parties would have anyway incurred under the International Telegraph Regulations in preserving the rights of telegram senders. In the tribunal's view, not only had an exception sought by The Czechoslovakian Administration not been expressly provided for in the Czechoslovakian Traffic Agreement, but it would have actually been in direct contravention to its other provisions. While the tribunal recognised that the second qualifier depended on the specific factual circumstances, in this instance, it deemed that an additional direct radio telegraphic service between Czechoslovakia and the US was 'certain' to give rise to a danger of such direct competition. See *Czechoslovakian Administration v RCA* (n 102) 532–534.

116 Ibid 534. Emphasis added.

117 Ibid 534. Emphasis added.

By so deciding, the tribunal pronounced upon, and ultimately restricted, The Czechoslovakian Administration's very freedom of action in carrying out its activities. With this, the tribunal thus effectively dictated the manner in which a state entity – and, as a matter of fact, the only entity in Czechoslovakia authorised to do so – would offer an important communications public utility, such as radio telegraphic services, to its citizens.

2.5 *The Immediate (albeit Temporary) Fallout: Czechoslovakia Abstains from Opening an Additional Telegraphic Circuit with the US*

The news of the outcome of the arbitration was quick to flow out of The Hague.[118] Upon learning of the tribunal's decision, the spirits within RCA circles were, unsurprisingly, high.[119] The RCA promptly sent a celebratory yet reconciliatory message to The Czechoslovakian Administration, noting that, despite being happy with the outcome of the arbitration, the American company was nonetheless devoted to improving its services and promised to undertake all the efforts required to make the joint circuit effective and profitable for both sides.[120] The mood within RCA quarters, however, would not stay positive for long, as the response that was forthcoming from the Czechoslovakian side would, to say the least, come as an unpleasant surprise. In its reply, The Czechoslovakian Administration alleged that, contrary to what had been promised by the RCA during the negotiations for the conclusion of the Czechoslovakian Traffic Agreement, the division of tolls for the RCA-Czechoslovakia circuit had been less favourable to the Czechoslovakian side than what some of the RCA's other partners had received.[121] Accordingly, The Czechoslovakian Administration requested to be credited with the loss in revenue that it had supposedly suffered.

---

118 See Telegram from J B Rostron to Winterbottom (4 April 1932) (MCI International Archives, box 583, file 'Czechoslovakia: Arbitration (3 of 3)'); Telegram from Judge Woodward to Manton Davis (5 April 1932) (MCI International Archives, box 583, file 'Czechoslovakia: Arbitration (3 of 3)').

119 The internal messages exchanged after the pronouncement of the award were expectedly filled with praise for all of those involved. See Telegram from Manton Davis to Judge Woodward (5 April 1932) (MCI International Archives, box 583, file 'Czechoslovakia: Arbitration (3 of 3)'); Letter from J M Woodward to William A Winterbottom (27 April 1932) (MCI International Archives, box 583, file 'Czechoslovakia: Arbitration (3 of 3)').

120 Telegram from W A Winterbottom to the Administration of Posts and Telegraphs of the Republic of Czechoslovakia (12 April 1932) (MCI International Archives, box 583, file 'Czechoslovakia: Arbitration (3 of 3)').

121 See Letter by the Ministry of Posts and Telegraphs of the Republic of Czechoslovakia to the RCA (18 April 1932) (MCI International Archives, box 583, file 'Czechoslovakia: Arbitration (3 of 3)').

The RCA's leadership was in disbelief with the reaction received from The Czechoslovakian Administration. For example, William Winterbottom, the vice-president and general manager of RCA Communications, described the Czechoslovakian side as having 'plenty of nerve', while Colonel Manton Davis, vice-president and general counsel, remarked that he had 'never had a letter so difficult politely to answer', characterised the opposing side as 'poor losers' and described his initial reaction as wanting to 'tell them if they didn't like our service to take their traffic and go wherever they darned pleased'.[122]

Despite being taken aback by The Czechoslovakian Administration's somewhat audacious response to losing the arbitration, the RCA was nonetheless inclined to entertain further negotiations regarding possible revisions to the Czechoslovakian Traffic Agreement. The RCA's willingness to compromise with the Czechoslovakian side was primarily prompted by the uneasy situation in which it had found itself back home. Namely, as previously mentioned, the matter of the RCA's foreign contracts had not been resolved by the consent decree that had been entered into in the US government's anti-trust suit against the RCA; instead, the RCA was given an additional two and a half years to renegotiate, in a manner satisfactory to US authorities, the contracts that had contained exclusivity clauses.[123] The RCA was therefore highly motivated to come to an arrangement with The Czechoslovakian Administration that would be agreeable to both sides, which fact could then be reported to the US government in relation to the on-going anti-trust suit.[124]

In light of these circumstances, the two sides tried to find common ground for revising the Czechoslovakian Traffic Agreement. In order to renegotiate the agreement, The Czechoslovakian Administration, again rather audaciously, had requested not only the adjustment of the manner in which the proceeds from the joint circuit were to be divided, but also for the RCA to reimburse its costs from the arbitration that the RCA had won.[125] While the

---

122 See Letter from W A Winterbottom to Colonel Davis (4 May 1932) (MCI International Archives, box 583, file 'Czechoslovakia: Arbitration (3 of 3)'); Letter from Manton Davis to W A Winterbottom (13 May 1932) (MCI International Archives, box 583, file 'Czechoslovakia: Arbitration (3 of 3)').

123 'Decree Dissolving Radio Group Under Anti-Trust Law' (n 37).

124 See Letter from Manton Davis to W A Winterbottom (21 August 1933) (MCI International Archives, box 583, file 'Czechoslovakia: Correspondence and Agreements (5 of 6)'), where it is stated that '[i]t would be helpful if we reported on the 21st day of November, 1933, when we must make a report, that we have negotiated a new traffic contract with Czechoslovakia with which they expressed satisfaction.'

125 Copy of Letter from Otto Kucera to Winterbottom (29 June 1933) (MCI International Archives, box 583, file 'Czechoslovakia: Correspondence and Agreements (5 of 6)').

RCA, unsurprisingly, did not even seriously entertain the latter request, it was more than willing to renegotiate the division of tolls, and, after some back and forth, made The Czechoslovakian Administration an offer that was expected to seal the deal.[126] Despite this seemingly promising offer, The Czechoslovakian side would rather curiously stay silent for more than a year; by the time its (affirmative) response finally arrived,[127] the circumstances had changed considerably and the RCA was no longer willing to proceed on the same terms.[128] Consequently, the attempts at renegotiating the Traffic Agreement eventually dwindled out.

For present purposes, however, more important than the fate of the renegotiation efforts is the attitude that The Czechoslovakian Administration had adopted toward the tribunal's decision. Namely, by way of a letter sent on 24 January 1935, the Czechoslovakian authorities had enquired with the RCA whether it was still persisting in 'its monopolist point of view' and noted that they were suffering 'heavy losses' because of the inability to install a second radio telegraphic circuit, which resulted in many telegrams being transmitted from the US to Czechoslovakia by wire.[129] This indicates that The Czechoslovakian Administration had taken the tribunal's determination as an authoritative pronunciation as to its capacity to open an additional radio telegraphic circuit with the US and had accordingly refrained, for several years, from concluding a contract with Mackay Radio, despite having perceived such a situation as severely damaging to its interests.[130] Even though this would eventually only turn out to be a temporary state of affairs, at the time the situation in the relations between the RCA and The Czechoslovakian Administration was therefore

126 See Copy of Letter from RCA Communications (unsigned) to Otto Kucera (21 September 1933) (MCI International Archives, box 583, file 'Czechoslovakia: Correspondence and Agreements (5 of 6)').

127 Letter from the Ministry of Posts and Telegraphs of the Republic of Czechoslovakia to RCA Communications, Inc (8 December 1934) (MCI International Archives, box 583, file 'Czechoslovakia: Correspondence and Agreements (5 of 6)').

128 Letter from the RCA (unsigned) to the Ministry of Posts and Telegraphs of the Republic of Czechoslovakia (2 January 1935) (MCI International Archives, box 583, file 'Czechoslovakia: Correspondence and Agreements (5 of 6)').

129 Letter from the Ministry of Posts and Telegraphs of the Republic of Czechoslovakia to RCA Communications, Inc (24 January 1935) (MCI International Archives, box 583, file 'Czechoslovakia: Correspondence and Agreements (5 of 6)').

130 The tribunal's award, however, might not have been the only reason for such a course of action by The Czechoslovakian Administration, as shortly after the legal obstacles to the opening of the parallel circuit were removed, the Czechoslovakian side notified the RCA that it would for the time being not proceed with the Mackay Radio circuit due to a lack of technical capacities. See ch 5.

such that, owing to the tribunal's decision, no efforts were being exerted towards the establishment of a second radio telegraphic circuit between Czechoslovakia and the US. The tribunal's decision, thus, was no mere claim to authority to instruct The Czechoslovakian Administration on how it must (not) carry out its functions that remained unheeded by its addressee, but seemingly had a tangible impact on how The Czechoslovakian Administration would, for years to come, offer an important public utility service to Czechoslovakian citizens.

Interestingly, the final chapter in the battle over Czechoslovakia's second radio telegraphic circuit with the US would be written following a decision in a different, even if related, historical ISA – *RCA v. China*. As is described in detail in Chapter 5, the tribunal in that case was faced with essentially the same circumstances as the tribunal in the *Czechoslovakian Administration v. RCA* arbitration, yet came to an opposing conclusion – that China's operation of a parallel radio telegraphic circuit was not in violation of its agreement with the RCA – ultimately prompting the RCA to give up on its favoured interpretation also in relation to its agreement with The Czechoslovakian Administration. As contradictory as this may seem at face value, however, the *RCA v. China* decision does not undermine the *Czechoslovakian Administration v. RCA* arbitration's exemplification of the capacity of historical ISA to direct state entity conduct, but rather buttresses it. This is because, as was discussed in Chapter 2, irrespective of the *RCA v. China* tribunal's public law conceptualisation of the relationship underlying the dispute before it, the tribunal in that case did not consider that it was inappropriate for it to decide upon China's right to establish a new direct radio telegraphic route. To the contrary – the arbitrators were adamant that they were prepared to find China's actions in operating a parallel circuit to have been illegal had there been a more explicit prohibition of such behaviour in the underlying agreement. Insofar as the capacity of historical investor-state tribunals to review, and ultimately direct, state entity conduct is concerned, the *RCA v. China* decision thus follows in the footsteps of, and serves to further reinforce the findings by, the *Czechoslovakian Administration v. RCA* tribunal.[131]

Most importantly, however, and irrespective of what came after, even on its own, the *Czechoslovakian Administration v. RCA* arbitration stands as an

131 That the approach by the *Czechoslovakian Administration v RCA* tribunal was not necessarily predicated on its conceptualisation of the underlying relationship as one of ordinary civil law is further attested to by the examples of other historical ISA tribunals that similarly proceeded to direct state conduct, despite having approached the issue from a public-law, rather than a private-law, perspective. See section 4.

exemplification more than capable of appropriately conveying historical ISA's role in directing, in particular through adjudicative (arbitral) review, state entity conduct. In fact, in light of not only what the tribunal ultimately decided, but also how it arrived at its decision and how the said decision was perceived by its addressees, the arbitration manages to capture a number of different yet similarly important facets of this phenomenon. Nominally, what the tribunal was asked to do, like innumerable an adjudicator that came before and after, was to review, as a secondary decision-maker, whether the intended conduct of a disputing party (the primary decision-maker) was in line with its contractual obligations. That in this instance the prospective conduct to be reviewed was that of a state entity made no difference to the tribunal in terms of its capacity to exercise such adjudicative (arbitral) review. And not only that, but the tribunal then proceeded to review the permissibility of The Czechoslovakian Administration's conduct pursuant to rules of ordinary civil law, having found no reason to treat the underlying relationship between the RCA and The Czechoslovakian Administration as not falling under their purview (but the purview of public law). Rather notably, the tribunal arrived at this conclusion with full cognizance and proper consideration of the nature and potential public importance of the activities performed by The Czechoslovakian Administration; by the tribunal's own admission, these activities were at the time a service undertaken by the state not only in Czechoslovakia, but also in the majority of other countries.

Nonetheless, the tribunal's award is characterised not only by the fact that the tribunal came to its decision while treating the agreement between the RCA and The Czechoslovakian Administration as one of ordinary civil law, but equally so by the tribunal's indication that a public law inspired approach would not have yielded a different outcome. By doing so, the tribunal thus clearly communicated an understanding that its capacity to review a state entity's conduct operated within a gamut that exceeded just the specific circumstances of the particular dispute or the ordinary civil law framework in which the tribunal had situated it. Crucially, the tribunal completed its review of the permissibility of The Czechoslovakian Administration's envisaged conduct not merely by coupling its potential non-compliance with the underlying agreement with a monetary sanction, but by coupling it instead with a categorical finding that The Czechoslovakian Administration was not permitted to proceed as intended. With this, then, what had nominally comprised of adjudicative review of a party's compliance with its contractual obligations, had in the end effectively amounted to the tribunal dictating how a state entity involved in the arbitration would offer a public communications service to Czechoslovakian citizens.

Finally, the aspect brought to light by the *Czechoslovakian Administration v. RCA* arbitration that offers perhaps the most important insight into historical ISA's capacity to direct state entity conduct, if only because of the difficulty of obtaining the requisite evidence, is the fact that the tribunal's assertion of authority to conclusively determine The Czechoslovakian Administration's course of conduct was given validation by The Czechoslovakian Administration itself. Even if The Czechoslovakian Administration's abstention from opening a second direct radio-telegraphic circuit to the US may have been short-lived, its decision to treat the tribunal's pronunciation as determinative of its competency to do so remains a lasting testament to historical ISA's capacity not only to purport to, but also to actually alter the course of state entity conduct through adjudicative (arbitral) review.

3 Directing State Conduct through Primary Decision-Making: The Post-World War I Peace Treaty Railway Arbitrations

The trifecta of arbitrations recounted in this section both complement, as well as contrast, the depiction of historical ISA's role in directing state conduct that was advanced through the portrayal of the *Czechoslovakian Administration v. RCA* arbitration in the preceding section. The three arbitrations, which dealt with the reorganisation of the railway system of the former Austro-Hungarian Empire, were held throughout the late 1920s and the 1930s pursuant to the World War I Peace Treaties. In many respects, the three Peace Treaty railway arbitrations represent truly unique examples of historical ISAs. Most notably, they possibly represent the first known instance where states had by way of international treaties given their (advance) agreement to arbitrate disputes with private enterprises; that the treaties that served as the bases for the arbitrations were none other than the multilateral World War I Peace Treaties perhaps only serves to further augment their relevance in this respect.[132] The three cases are moreover distinguishable for their three-party character, as the arbitrations were conducted between the concessionary companies, on the one side, and the two territorially interested states, each representing their own distinct interests, on the other. This three-party character of the arbitrations was preserved even in instances where two of the parties to the arbitration appeared to be in agreement that no dispute existed between them. Yet another interesting characteristic of the arbitrations was the prominent

132 The reach of the relevant treaty provisions was admittedly limited in scope to a predefined set of circumstances from which such disputes could arise.

involvement of the Council of the League of Nations, which, despite a role that under the Peace Treaties nominally extended merely to arbitrator appointment, had a significant influence in streamlining the entire process and even made overtures into defining the very task of the tribunals it was appointing.[133]

Not to be overlooked in this overflow of thought-provoking features, however, is that the arbitrations also stand out as one of the most unequivocal representations of historical ISA's role in directing state conduct. Much like in the *Czechoslovakian Administration v. RCA* arbitration, the tribunals handed down decisions that purported to instruct states on their future behaviour; this, most notably, included ordering the states whether or not they could (or had to) expropriate, thus reaching into spheres of activity that are normally reserved for the exclusive purview of states. In this, the tribunals' decisions complement, and serve to further expand, the illustration of historical ISA's role in directing state entity conduct that flows from the *Czechoslovakian Administration v. RCA* arbitration. Conversely, where the three arbitrations contrast the *Czechoslovakian Administration v. RCA* arbitration is in terms of *how* the tribunals went about this – i.e. in terms of the manner in which they proceeded to direct state conduct. Thus, unlike in the *Czechoslovakian Administration v. RCA* arbitration, the tribunals' roles in directing state conduct were not consummated merely in reviewing, as a secondary decision-maker, whether a state entity's intended conduct was permissible; instead, the tribunals in the Peace Treaty railway arbitrations operated to fill an existing decision-making vacuum and proceeded to decide matters of prospective state conduct as if a primary decision-maker would, i.e. by determining in the first instance the course of conduct that was to be taken. In this, as compared to the *Czechoslovakian Administration v. RCA* arbitration, the three arbitrations thus offer a

133 See eg nn 186 and 221. Nonetheless, the role of the League of Nations in relation to the disputes was subsequently represented as strictly being limited to arbitrator appointment, and understood not to give rise to possible financial obligations for the League regarding expenses or an interest for it in the enforcement of the tribunals' awards. See Letter from McKinnon Wood to the Treasurer and Secretary General (23 January 1934) (United Nations Archives at Geneva: R4277/9D/1199/309/Jacket1); Letter from McKinnon Wood to the Financial Section (2 August 1935) (United Nations Archives at Geneva: R4278/9D/3801/309/Jacket3); Letter from McKinnon Wood to Metternich, Loveday and the Secretary General (17 April 1935) (United Nations Archives at Geneva: R4278/9D/3801/309/Jacket3). See, however, Letter from the Director of the Financial Section and Economic Intelligence Service to the Secretary General (9 April 1935) (United Nations Archives at Geneva: R4278/9D/3801/309/Jacket3); Note from the Director of the Financial Section and Economic Intelligence Service to the Secretary General (3 May 1935) (United Nations Archives at Geneva: R4278/9D/3801/309/Jacket3).

depiction of yet another, alternative, mode of directing state conduct through historical ISA.

In recounting the Peace Treaty railway arbitrations, the section proceeds as follows. At the outset, it offers a brief description of the need for railway reorganisation that had arisen following the break-up of the former Austro-Hungarian Empire, as well as of the relevant provisions of the Peace Treaties, which were meant to address this situation and which ultimately served as the bases for the arbitrations (3.1). The section then discusses the three arbitrations – *Sopron-Köszeg Local Railway Company v. Austria and Hungary* (3.2), *Zeltweg-Wolfsberg and Unterdrauburg-Woellan Railway Company v. Austria and Yugoslavia* (3.3) and *Barcs-Pakrac Railway Company, Ltd v. Hungary and Yugoslavia* (3.4) – illustrating along the way how the relevant tribunals proceeded through their decisions to direct the conduct of the involved states. Finally, the section assesses the significance of the Peace Treaty railway arbitrations for historical ISA's role in directing state conduct (3.5).

3.1 *The Peace Treaties and the Need for Railway Reorganisation Following the Break-up of the Austro-Hungarian Empire*

The end of World War I had brought about significant changes to the European political landscape. One of the foremost of these was undoubtedly the disintegration of the Austro-Hungarian Empire, which had been one of the dominant powers in the preceding period, as well as one of the key protagonists in the war itself. Over the course of its existence, the dual monarchy had been a heterogeneous empire, with many different ethnic groups, in addition to the titular Austrian and Hungarian ones, living under its rule. As World War I was drawing to an end, however, the country crumbled under the mounting pressure for the independence of the minorities living within its boundaries and ultimately fell apart. As a result, the territory of the former empire was carved up into smaller pieces, some of which emerged as newly formed successor states while others were joined to already existing ones, the new boundaries being finalised by the Peace Treaties with the now separate states of Austria[134] and Hungary.[135]

134 Treaty of Peace between the Allied and Associated Powers and Austria (signed 10 September 1919, entered into force 16 July 1920) (1919) 11 UKTS Cmd 400 (hereinafter Treaty of Saint-Germain) pt II.

135 Treaty of Peace between the Allied and Associated Powers and Hungary (signed 4 June 1920, entered into force 26 July 1921) (1920) 10 UKTS Cmd 896 (hereinafter Treaty of Trianon) pt II.

One of the many implications of the territorial reorganisation that accompanied the dissolution of the Austro-Hungarian Empire was the fact that the newly drawn borders sliced, sometimes multiple times with respect to the same railway line, across the existing railway network of the former Empire. That this was the case was hardly surprising, as the railway network in the Austro-Hungarian Empire had obviously not been designed with the newly drawn-up borders in mind. The very Peace Treaties that had set the new boundaries had anticipated that such a situation could potentially create significant problems for the operation of the railways; accordingly, they both contained identical provisions (Articles 304 and 320 of the respective treaties) that were envisaged to deal with the issue, and which provided that:

> With the object of ensuring regular utilisation of the railroads of the former Austro-Hungarian Monarchy owned by private companies which, as a result of the stipulations of the present Treaty, will be situated in the territory of several States, the administrative and technical reorganisation of the said lines shall be regulated in each instance by an agreement between the owning company and the States territorially concerned.
>
> *Any differences on which agreement is not reached, including questions relating to the interpretation of contracts concerning the expropriation of the lines, shall be submitted to arbitrators designated by the Council of the League of Nations.*
>
> This arbitration may, as regards the South Austrian Railway Company, be required either by the Board of Management or by the Committee representing the bondholders.[136]

Therefore, according to the Peace Treaties with Austria and Hungary, the reorganisation of the railways that had been left situated in more than one country by the border changes stemming from the dissolution of the Austro-Hungarian Empire was first and foremost to be achieved by negotiation between the

136 Treaty of Trianon (n 135) art 304 and Treaty of Saint-Germain (n 134) art 320. Emphasis added. The two Peace Treaties thus represent early examples wherein companies were accorded the right to arbitrate future disputes with a state by way of (multilateral) international treaties, even if this right was of a limited reach, as the disputes that could potentially fall under the scope of the provisions were clearly circumscribed and pertained to already existing investor-state relationships. A somewhat similar provision, although arguably providing for state-state arbitration, rather than ISA, was included in the Treaty of Sevres (which, however, never entered into force). See ch 3 and Treaty of Peace between the Allied and Associated Powers and Turkey (signed 10 August 1920, never entered into force) (1921) 15 AJIL Supp 179, art 311.

companies and the interested states. Failing this, the matter was to be submitted to a tribunal appointed by the Council of the League of Nations. Notably, the respective Peace Treaties provisions did not indicate the law, or even the legal system, pursuant to which the arbitrators were to decide the matters submitted to them.

Many railways in the former Austro-Hungarian Empire had in fact been affected by the newly established boundaries.[137] An appeal to the Council of the League of Nations was not necessary in all such instances, as some disputes were resolved through direct negotiation with the territorially concerned states.[138] Nonetheless, there was still a considerable number of instances where the railway companies were unable to reach an agreement with the relevant states and had consequently requested the Council of the League of Nations to appoint arbitrators pursuant to Articles 304 or 320 of the respective Peace Treaties.[139]

---

137 For example, Yugoslavia had 15 such railways. See Gojko Mudrinic, 'The Creation and Function of Vicinal Railways' (January 1924) (Archives of Yugoslavia: 70–292–542).

138 By way of illustration, Yugoslavia had reached agreements with several of the affected railways. Compare ibid with Copy of Report by the Minister of Transport and the Minister of Finance to the President of the Ministerial Council (28 February 1931) (Archives of Yugoslavia: 70–292–542).

139 Apart from the three cases discussed below, see eg also 'Minutes of the Thirty-Fifth Session of the Council: Seventeenth Meeting (Public and Then Private)' [1925] League of Nations Official Journal 1395, 1403 (on the request by the Maramarosi Sovasut Reszveny railway company); 'Minutes of the Seventieth Session of the Council: First Meeting (Private, Then Public)' [1933] League of Nations Official Journal 180, 181 (on the request by the Radkersburg-Luttenberg Local Railway Company); 'Minutes of the Seventy-Sixth Session of the Council (Part 1): First Meeting (Private, Then Public)' [1933] League of Nations Official Journal 1300 (on the request by the Noskovci-Slatine-Nasice Local Railway Company); 'Minutes of the Forty-Third Session of the Council: First Meeting (Private, Then Public)' [1927] League of Nations Official Journal 114 (on the request by the Debreczen-Nagyvarad and Szatmar-Fehergyarmat Private Railway Companies); 'Annex 1076: Dispute Concerning the Boldva Valley Local Railway' [1928] League of Nations Official Journal 1763; 'Minutes of the Fifty-Sixth Session of the Council: First Meeting (Private, Then Public)' [1929] League of Nations Official Journal 1442, 1442–1443 (on the requests by the Nagykikinda-Aradi-Helyierdekű Local Railway Company and the South-West Hungary Local Railway Company); 'Minutes of the Fifty-Fourth Session of the Council: First Meeting (Private, Then Public)' [1929] League of Nations Official Journal 502 (on the requests by the Sopron-Pozsony Railway Company); 'Minutes of the Fifty-Ninth Session of the Council: First Meeting (Private, Then Public)' [1930] League of Nations Official Journal 496, 497 (on the request by the Gyula Local Railway Company); 'Minutes of the Seventy-Third Session of the Council (Part 1): First Meeting (Private, Then Public)' [1933] League of Nations Official Journal 798, 799 (on the request by the Torontál Local Railway Company at Budapest). It seems that in certain instances the railway companies not only requested the appointment of arbitrators by the Council of the League of Nations but also turned to

Not all of the cases in which the railway companies had requested the appointment of arbitrators, however, materialised into actual arbitrations; in fact, hardly any did. This was likely because the Peace Treaty articles were interpreted by the Council of the League of Nations in such a manner that the request of a claimant company was not deemed to automatically trigger an appointment of arbitrators by the Council. Namely, while it was generally regarded that the Council was indeed bound to appoint a tribunal whenever the conditions laid out in Articles 304 and 320 of the respective Peace Treaties were satisfied,[140] the determination of the very fact whether those conditions had in fact been met was not left to the claiming companies themselves.[141] Making this determination involved not only ascertaining that the dispute fell within the scope of the respective Peace Treaties' provisions, but also whether there had been serious attempts at an amicable settlement that had proved to be unsuccessful.[142] Neither of these questions were mere formalities – while the former sometimes involved complicated questions of a legal nature,[143] the bar for satisfying the latter was set rather high and steps in various stages of the process were often postponed if it was felt that a negotiated agreement remained possible[144] – thus effectively leaving considerable independent

the Mixed Arbitral Tribunals established under the Peace Treaties regarding the same disputes. See 'Minutes of the Sixty-Second Session of the Council: Sixth Meeting (Public, Then Private)' [1931] League of Nations Official Journal 194, 203 (on the application from the Local Railway Company of the Gyula District).

140 See eg 'Annex 1065*a*: Dispute Concerning the Sopron-Köszeg Local Railway' [1928] League of Nations Official Journal 1614; 'Annex 1487: Petition from the Barcs-Pakrac Railway Company, Limited, Budapest' [1934] League of Nations Official Journal 183, 184; 'Annex 1488: Petition from the Radkersburg-Luttenberg Railway Company Limited Vienna' [1934] League of Nations Official Journal 185, 186; 'Communications and Transit' [1930] League of Nations Official Journal 324, 336–341.

141 The claiming company was, nonetheless, expected to 'clearly' satisfy the burden of showing that these conditions had been met. See eg 'Minutes of the Sixty-Sixth Session of the Council: First Meeting (Private, Then Public)' [1932] League of Nations Official Journal 438, 439 (regarding the petition of the Zeltweg-Wolfsberg and Unterdrauburg-Woellan Railway Company), as well as the sources mentioned in n 139.

142 See eg 'Annex 1065*a*: Dispute Concerning the Sopron-Köszeg Local Railway' (n 140) 1614; 'Annex 1487: Petition from the Barcs-Pakrac Railway Company' (n 140) 184; 'Annex 1488: Petition from the Radkersburg-Luttenberg Railway Company Limited Vienna' (n 140) 186.

143 See eg 'Annex 1510: Petition of the Radkersburg-Luttenberg Railway Company, Ltd, Vienna' [1934] League of Nations Official Journal 1397; 'Annex 1065*a*: Dispute Concerning the Sopron-Köszeg Local Railway' (n 140) 1615–1616.

144 For example, the Council would refuse to act on an application until all of the concerned states had fully expressed their position regarding it, a matter would not be included in the Council's agenda or a question not dealt with by the relevant committee as long as an amicable settlement was considered possible, and the Council would in certain instances

decision-making power to the Council in deciding whether or not to appoint a tribunal in a particular case.[145]

While the majority of the cases where the appointment of arbitrators under articles 304 and 320 was requested were eventually settled amicably,[146] no doubt in part due to the Council's hands-on approach, three of them proceeded to arbitration and resulted in awards. These three cases were all based on similar circumstances and were resolved by similarly constituted tribunals, which appears to have been a matter of the Council's preference rather than a coincidence.[147]

---

even appoint the tribunal with a delayed starting date in order to allow for a negotiated solution. See eg 'Minutes of the Sixty-Sixth Session of the Council: First Meeting' (n 141) 439; 'Advisory and Technical Committee for Communications and Transit' [1928] League of Nations Official Journal 720; 'Minutes of the Fifty-Fourth Session of the Council: Seventh Meeting (Public, Then Private)' [1929] League of Nations Official Journal 553, 560–561 (regarding the application from the Local Railway Company of the Boldva Valley); 'Minutes of the Thirty-Fifth Session of the Council: Seventeenth Meeting' (n 139) 1404 (regarding the request by the Maramarosi Sovasut Reszveny railway company); 'Minutes of the Fifty-Fourth Session of the Council: First Meeting' (n 139) 502 (regarding the request by the Sopron-Pozsony Railway Company).

145 The procedure in appointing a tribunal under Articles 304 and/or 320 of the respective Peace Treaties typically went as follows: once a party would request the appointment of arbitrators, the Council would refer the question of the applicability to the matter of the said articles to the Advisory and Technical Committee for Communications and Transit, which would then itself further refer the question to either its own Bureau, the Permanent Committee on Transport by Rail or to an expert committee. Only once these bodies had reported back to the Council would a final decision regarding the potential arbitrator appointment be made. Thus, despite the Peace Treaties only, without offering any further information regarding its competences in this respect, providing that the Council was to appoint the arbitrators, the Council (as well as other organs of the League from which the Council sought assistance) played an important role in streamlining the entire process, deciding which cases, under which conditions and at which point in time were to be submitted to arbitration under Articles 304 and 320. See 'Annex 1603: Constitution, Procedure and Practice of Committees of the League of Nations' [1936] League of Nations Official Journal 725, 736.

146 Ibid. Some of the cases were even settled after the Council had appointed the arbitrators. See ibid. The existence of the threat of arbitration and the Council's approach, which strongly encouraged amicable settlements, seem to have contributed to the high rate of settlements.

147 Thus, already in the case of the Local Railway Company of the Boldva Valley it was indicated that the arbitrators should be the same as those appointed in *Sopron-Köszeg Local Railway Company v Austria and Hungary*. See 'Minutes of the Fifty-Fourth Session of the Council: Seventh Meeting' (n 144) 560. Following this, identical tribunals were appointed in subsequent cases up until one of the arbitrators was incapable of participating due to a conflicting appointment. See 'Minutes of the Sixty-Second Session of the Council: Sixth Meeting' (n 139) 201–202; 'Minutes of the Seventy-Third Session of the Council (Part 1):

All of the appointed arbitrators were, or had previously been, members of the League's Advisory and Technical Committee for Communications and Transit or of the Permanent Committee on Transport by Rail of the Communications and Transit Committee; sometimes, they had even been directly involved in this capacity with the work on the cases under Articles 304 or 320, including the ones in which they latter sat as arbitrators.[148] Each of the tribunals included Salvadoran diplomat and jurist José Gustavo Guerrero. Guerrero had been the minister for foreign affairs of El Salvador and the president of the Assembly of the League of Nations, although he is certainly best remembered as a long tenured judge on both the Permanent Court of International Justice (PCIJ) and the International Court of Justice (ICJ).[149] Indeed, there is perhaps no better embodiment of the continuity between the PCIJ and the ICJ than Guerrero,[150] not only because he holds the unique honour of having been the last president of the former court and the first president of the latter, but also due to Guerrero's personal and, without exaggeration, heroic role

Fourth Meeting (Private, Then Public)' [1933] League of Nations Official Journal 823, 828–829 (regarding the petition of the Zeltweg-Wolfsberg and Unterdrauberg-Woellan Railway Company); 'Minutes of the Seventy-Third Session of the Council (Part 1): Sixth Meeting (Public)' [1933] League of Nations Official Journal 838, 844 (regarding the petition of the Zeltweg-Wolfsberg and Unterdrauberg-Woellan Railway Company). Moreover, when proposing the arbitrators that were to be appointed in *Barcs-Pakrac Railway Company, Ltd v Hungary and Yugoslavia*, the rapporteur argued that the proposed candidates were 'eminently qualified to be nominated as arbitrators' in light of their previous service in similar cases. See 'Minutes of the Seventy-Eighth Session of the Council (Part 1): Second Meeting (Private, Then Public)' [1934] League of Nations Official Journal 111, 124. It is therefore quite probable that the tribunal constitution in all of the cases would have been identical had one of the arbitrators from the initially appointed tribunal not been prevented from serving in the latter cases.

148 See eg 'Minutes of the Forty-Third Session of the Council: Sixth Meeting (Private, Then Public)' [1927] League of Nations Official Journal 160, 163 (regarding the requests of the Arad-Csanad Railways, Maramarosi Railways and the Local Railway Companies of Szatmár-Mátészalka and Nagykaroly-Mátészalka-Csap); 'Minutes of the Forty-Fourth Session of the Council: Third Meeting (Public)' [1927] League of Nations Official Journal 373, 375 (regarding the request of the Maramarosi-Sovasut Reszveny-Tarsasag Railway Company); 'Minutes of the Fifty-First Session of the Council: Seventh Meeting (Public, Then Private)' [1928] League of Nations Official Journal 1483, 1484 (regarding the application from the Sopron-Köszeg Local Railway Company).

149 International Court of Justice, 'Tribute to José Gustavo Guerrero, first President of the International Court of Justice' (23 October 2018) 2 <https://www.icj-cij.org/public/files/press-releases/0/000-20181023-PRE-01-00-EN.pdf> accessed 27 September 2024.

150 See ibid 1 (former ICJ registrar, Philippe Couvreur, remarking that 'Judge Guerrero personified the continuity between the Permanent Court … and the International Court of Justice').

in defending the PCIJ from Nazi destruction during World War II.[151] Namely, following the German invasion of the Netherlands, fearing the arrest of the local personnel, Guerrero was the last judge that remained at the Peace Palace in The Hague. Guerrero met the German military upon its arrival in front of the Peace Palace, telling those in charge that the court and its personnel were inviolable, and that the armed troops could enter the premises '[o]nly over [his] dead body'.[152] Guerrero's bold exploit yielded the desired result – even though the Peace Palace was ordered to be evacuated for military reasons, the German Ministry of Foreign Affairs informed Guerrero that the court's and the personnel's sanctity would be preserved; Guerrero and the staff then loaded the court's archives onto a train to Geneva, where an improvised location for the court was set up. For this, among other things, Guerrero was nominated for the Nobel Peace Prize in 1948 and 1949.[153] At the time of the Peace Treaty railway arbitrations, Guerrero was, in one instance, a future and, in two of the instances, a sitting judge of the PCIJ.

Alongside Guerrero, all three tribunals featured Rene Mayer, honorary *Maître des Requêtes* on the French *Conseil d'État* and future French statesman (having later held several ministerial posts and very briefly the post of the prime minister of France).[154] Notably, Mayer also had extensive experience in railway administration, as did the third members of each of the tribunals, both of whom had served as directors of national railways.[155]

In light of both the overlapping constitution of the respective tribunals and the likeness of the underlying disputes, the three arbitrations can best be described as having formed a closely related batch of jurisprudence on the post-World War I reorganisation of the railway system of the former Austro-Hungarian Empire. As is discussed in more detail below, one of the stand-out

151 Liliana Obregón, 'The Third World Judges: Neutrality, Bias or Activism at the Permanent Court of International Justice and International Court of Justice?' in William A Schabas and Shannonbrooke Murphy (eds), *Research Handbook on International Courts and Tribunals* (Edward Elgar Publishing 2017) 181, 193.

152 Guerrero's statement deserves quoting in full: 'the Court and its personnel, according to the contract signed with the Dutch Government and customary rules of diplomatic law, are inviolable. Only over my dead body can armed troops come into the Palace'. See ibid.

153 See NobelPrize.org, 'Nomination Archive: José Gustavo Guerrero' <https://www.nobelprize.org/nomination/archive/show_people.php?id=3703> accessed 27 September 2024.

154 See 'Mayer, René (1895–1972)' <https://www.siv.archives-nationales.culture.gouv.fr/siv/rechercheconsultation/consultation/producteur/consultationProducteur.action?notProdId=FRAN_NP_050262> accessed 27 September 2024.

155 The two other arbitrators in the three cases were Jacob Adriaan Kalff, the General Director of the Netherlands Railways (and subsequent Dutch minister of water management), and Athanase Politis, former Director of the Greek Railways. See nn 167 and 186.

features of this batch of jurisprudence is the tribunals' role, while reorganising the relevant railways systems, in directing the conduct of the territorially concerned states.

3.2 *Sopron-Köszeg Local Railway Company v Austria and Hungary*

The first case to be heard by a tribunal appointed by the Council of the League of Nations pursuant to the Peace Treaties was *Sopron-Köszeg Local Railway Company v. Austria and Hungary*.[156] The applicant was a Hungarian company that had obtained a ninety year concession from the Hungarian government for a railway from Sopron to Köszeg.[157] Following the Paris Peace Conference, however, as well as some minor further modifications to their joint border by Austria and Hungary, the company found its railway line intersected by the new border not once, but twice.[158] Soon after the new borders were established, the company reached an agreement with the Hungarian government.[159] It was, however, unable to find a workable solution with the Austrian side and consequently filed a petition for the appointment of arbitrators under Article 304 of the Treaty of Trianon and Article 320 of the Treaty of Saint-Germain.[160] In the petition, the company claimed that its concession was still valid but that the Austrian government had made no payments under it since taking over the operation of the line; as a result, the company requested that the arbitrators regulate the administrative and technical reorganisation of the line, recognise the validity of the company's concession and corresponding working contract and indemnify the company for the losses it had incurred due to the lack of payments from the Austrian side.[161]

Austria initially opposed the appointment of a tribunal, arguing that the Treaty of Saint-Germain was inapplicable to the Sopron-Köszeg Local Railway Company on account that Hungary was not a party to it and that a Hungarian company could not make use of the Treaty's provisions.[162] However, once the

156 *Sopron-Köszeg Local Railway Company v Austria and Hungary* (1930) 24(1) AJIL 164. The original award (in French) is housed at the United Nations Archives at Geneva: CRID134/343/160/2.

157 Ibid 165.

158 Thus, while the majority of the line was situated in Austria, both ends of the line ended up in Hungary. See ibid 166; 'Annex 1065: Dispute Concerning the Sopron-Köszeg Local Railway' [1928] League of Nations Official Journal 1609.

159 Ibid 1610.

160 See generally ibid.

161 Ibid 1610–1611.

162 Ibid 1612; 'Annex 1065*a*: Dispute Concerning the Sopron-Köszeg Local Railway' (n 140) 1615.

Permanent Legal Committee of the Communications and Transit Committee had found Austria's arguments on this point invalid and suggested that the Council proceed with the appointment of arbitrators,[163] Austria acquiesced to the arbitration and joined in with the company's request.[164] For its part, Hungary supported the company's application, although it insisted that it was not the one that had made the arbitration necessary, as it had previously settled its own relationship with the company.[165] Under these circumstances, the Council proceeded with appointing the tribunal. Rather interestingly, although both Austria and Hungary had made clear a preference for a single arbitrator to be appointed in order to keep the costs of the arbitration down, the case rapporteur noted that this request may not be easy to satisfy as it might prove difficult to find a single arbitrator who would be an expert in both the legal and the other questions that may arise in the case.[166] Ultimately, the Council appointed a three person tribunal.[167]

The tribunal handed down its award in Paris, on 18 June 1929. The award reads as one that was grounded primarily, if not exclusively, in the arbitrators' own understanding of the Peace Treaty provisions pursuant to which the tribunal was constituted. Much like the relevant Peace Treaty provisions themselves, the tribunal's award contains no explicit mention of the law governing the underlying investor-State relations, although at least a part of the tribunal's reasoning seems to have been guided, even if without reference to any specific sources, by international law. The tribunal's decision is dominated by the arbitrators' understanding of their role as being to modify, seemingly with little external constrains, the pre-existing relations between the participants in the arbitration when reorganising the Sopron-Köszeg railway. Indeed, it was precisely this perceived freedom to modify the parties' underlying legal positions that allowed the tribunal to proceed with directing the prospective conduct of the involved states, including by ordering them to take over the railway from the concessionary company.

---

163 'Annex 1065*a*: Dispute Concerning the Sopron-Köszeg Local Railway' (n 140) 1615–1616.

164 While Austria had maintained its legal position, it preferred to avoid protracted legal proceedings in light of its poor post-war economic situation and was therefore ultimately in favour of arbitration as the most expedient way of resolving the dispute. See 'Minutes of the Fifty-First Session of the Council: Seventh Meeting' (n 148) 1485–1486.

165 Ibid 1486.

166 See ibid.

167 See 'Minutes of the Fifty-Second Session of the Council: Sixth Meeting (Public, Then Private)' [1928] League of Nations Official Journal 1664, 1679. The appointed arbitrators were J G Guerrero, at the time still only future judge at the Permanent Court of International Justice (PCIJ), J A Kalff (see n 155), and R Mayer.

The framing for the discussion that would follow in the remainder of the award was laid out already in the tribunal's particularisation of the issue before it. Namely, the tribunal had perceived its task to be to ensure through its award 'a final and general settlement of the questions raised in the company's request to the Council of the League of Nations.'[168] This was deemed by the arbitrators to require not only for the tribunal to define the company's rights *vis-à-vis* Austria up to the date of its award and with respect to both Austria and Hungary for the future, but also to 'lay the foundation of the administrative and technical reorganisation of the Sopron-Köszeg Railway'.[169] In understanding, and defining, its own mandate to be as comprehensive, if not all-embracing, in scope, the tribunal set the tone for a decision that would be equally far-reaching in character.

The first question relating to the company's claim that the tribunal addressed – concerning the validity of the company's concession and the accompanying contractual arrangements *vis-à-vis* Austria – was perhaps also the most important one, as it served as the basis for the remainder of the tribunal's findings. The tribunal held that a company's concession rights were, in principle, not affected by the change of the nationality of the territory to which the concession pertained. Even if only implicitly, this was a rare instance where the arbitrators referred to external legal authorities in arriving at their conclusion, as the tribunal supported its finding with the observation that this was a view taken by 'most authorities and the international judgments which conform most nearly to modern views of international law'.[170] The tribunal found further support for this conclusion in the Peace Treaties themselves. Namely, the tribunal considered that Articles 304 and 320 had been inserted into the Treaty of Trianon and the Treaty of Saint-Germain, respectively, with a dual purpose – first, to serve the interests of the population of the territory in which the railway operated and, second, to benefit the railway companies, which would have, absent such treaty clauses, been unable to enforce their rights under the concessions. The tribunal therefore concluded that the Peace Treaties had intended to recognise concessionary rights such as those of the Sopron-Köszeg Local Railway Company in relation to states on whose territories their railways were now situated.[171] The tribunal further extended the same status to the working contract for the operation of the Sopron-Köszeg railway; while the tribunal held that states in whose territory railway lines came to be

168 *Sopron-Köszeg Local Railway Company v Austria and Hungary* (n 156) 167.
169 Ibid.
170 Ibid.
171 Ibid.

situated through territorial changes were generally not bound by the concessionaire's contracts with third parties, in this instance it was considered appropriate to make an exception. This was because the company had, under the then applicable Hungarian law and practice, been effectively obliged to conclude a working contract transferring the operation of the railway line to the Hungarian State Railways, which contract had thus formed an integral part of the concession.[172]

Crucially, however, the tribunal's principled endorsement of the validity of the concession came with significant caveats – caveats that would ultimately allow the tribunal to step into the underlying investor-state relationships in the capacity of a decision-maker determining the course of state conduct. Namely, while the tribunal had endorsed the company's contention that its rights under the concession as existing prior to the territorial changes were to be respected in their 'general features', the tribunal nonetheless held that these rights were 'not [to] be enforced literally.'[173] In the tribunal's view, doing so would not only have disregarded the consequences stemming from World War I and the Peace Treaties (including their respective Articles 304 and 320), but also the very competence of the tribunal itself (the tribunal's intervention having been envisioned by the aforementioned Peace Treaty provisions). This was because the tribunal considered the very existence of these Peace Treaty provisions to imply that the treaty parties expected the envisaged difficulties with the reorganisation of the Austro-Hungarian railway system to be resolved by new agreements that would take into account the new political and economic climate. Since arbitration was the fall back solution in case the anticipated agreements could not be reached, the tribunal deemed that this invited the conclusion that such arbitration – and this was critical for how the tribunal would come to understand the nature and extent of its mandate – could not amount to merely enforcing the existing contractual terms, but rather required their 'extensive modification'.[174] With this, the tribunal thus freed itself of the strictures imposed by the legal instruments that had defined the underlying investor-state relationship, and instead positioned itself as a decision-maker that could operate outside of such normative limitations – a decision-maker that was determining the initial course of conduct rather than merely reviewing the permissibility of the conduct envisioned by a state under pre-existing normative frameworks.

172 Ibid 168–169.
173 Ibid 169.
174 Ibid.

In doing so, the tribunal adopted the position that the company's pre-war contracts could 'be pronounced neither wholly invalidated by the change of sovereignty affecting the territories on which its undertaking [wa]s situated, nor indeed wholly valid and enforceable.'[175] In the absence of an agreement between the interested parties, the arbitrators considered that it was instead up to them to adapt the contracts to the change of circumstances that had occurred since the contracts had been concluded. Since the tribunal had earlier freed itself of the strictures of the pre-existing legal instruments, little remained to guide, or constrain, the tribunal in making this adaption. Indeed, the arbitrators themselves merely observed that, in performing this task, they needed to consider both the 'legitimate interests involved in the public-utility undertaking concerned' and the need, as provided for in the Peace Treaties, 'to restore the regular operation of the railways of the former Austro-Hungarian Monarchy in the higher interests of the facility and freedom of international communication'.[176]

It is against this background, and with such understanding of its own powers in modifying the existing relationships between the parties, that the tribunal proceeded with, at least for present purposes, the most important aspect of its decision – setting out the administrative and technical reorganisation of the Sopron-Köszeg railway. The extent of the tribunal's endeavour that followed certainly was foreshadowed by its earlier findings. The tribunal considered that the administrative and technical reorganisation of the railway required handing over the operation of the entire line to one administration. The tribunal's task in this respect had been made somewhat easier by the fact that Austria and Hungary had already previously concluded a protocol which provided the grounds for entrusting the entire line to the Austrian Railways, a goal which the tribunal thought would best be achieved through Austria's acquisition of the entirety of the company's rights to the railway. Notably, in facilitating this solution, the tribunal went as far as to pronounce certain Hungarian laws inoperative, citing the 'peculiar circumstances' of the acquisition as a justification.[177] In a critical step, the tribunal then proceeded to order both Austria and Hungary to repurchase from the company the sections of the railway that were located on each of their territories, following which Hungary was to transfer to Austria its rights over the sections of the railway situated in Hungary (the price for the purchase of the Hungarian section, accordingly, was to be paid by Austria). As a result of the tribunal's orders, therefore, the ownership over

175 Ibid.
176 Ibid 170.
177 Ibid.

the railway was to be transferred to Austria, which was to become the sole owner of the entire line. As a final order of business, the tribunal determined the compensation that was to be paid by Austria for taking over the railway.[178]

To say that it is no easy task to discern where the tribunal in *Sopron-Köszeg Local Railway Company v. Austria and Hungary* perceived the limits of its powers to lie would certainly be an understatement. If anything, it appears that the tribunal was guided, and thought itself constrained, by little apart from its own construction of the mandate that had been conferred upon it by the Peace Treaty provisions pursuant to which it was constituted. What is certain, however, is that the tribunal undoubtedly deemed itself competent to instruct the states involved – Austria and Hungary – to take ownership of the railway (in Hungary's case only as an intermediary) that was at the root of the arbitration, and did so while declaring relevant national laws inoperative. Yet it was not just that the tribunal directed the involved states on their prospective conduct; it was equally so that the tribunal did this not merely through trying, as a secondary decision-maker, to ensure compliance with previously undertaken legal obligations, but rather as a decision-maker, unbound from pre-existing normative strictures, that was determining the initial course of conduct that was to be undertaken. As the following two sub-sections reveal, in this the tribunal would soon be joined by other similarly composed tribunals established under the Peace Treaties.

3.3 *Zeltweg-Wolfsberg and Unterdrauburg-Woellan Railway Company v Austria and Yugoslavia*

The *Zeltweg-Wolfsberg and Unterdrauburg-Woellan Railway Company v. Austria and Yugoslavia* case was the second case that was heard by a tribunal appointed by the Council under the Peace Treaties, but also the last one to come to a definitive conclusion. The case was brought by an Austrian company, which had at the end of the 19th century obtained a ninety year concession for two railway lines (Zeltweg-Wolfsberg and Unterdrauburg-Woellan) in the Austro-Hungarian Empire. Following the territorial changes after World War I, the Zeltweg-Wolfsberg section of the line remained in Austria, while the Unterdrauburg-Woellan section came to be situated in Yugoslavia (in what is now Slovenia) and had its operation taken over by the Yugoslav government.[179] The company had reached an agreement with the Austrian government regarding the future

178 Ibid 171–173. The railway company was also awarded compensation for the period during which Austria had operated the part of the railway located on its territory without giving the company a share from the receipts.

179 'Minutes of the Sixty-Sixth Session of the Council: First Meeting' (n 141) 439.

operation of the section situated in Austria,[180] but was not able to do the same with respect to the section in Yugoslavian territory; as a consequence, it turned to the Council of the League of Nations.

While Austria was supportive of the company's request, Yugoslavia objected to the appointment of arbitrators on the account that Article 320 of the Treaty of Saint-Germain was inapplicable to the company, arguing that the two lines that were situated in the two countries were independent of one another and that neither of them had been intersected by the new border.[181] In line with its usual practice, before dealing with the request, the Council asked for a report on the matter from the Advisory and Technical Committee for Communications and Transit,[182] which in turn referred the question to a committee of experts. While the committee of experts opined that the two lines had in reality formed part of a single system that had previously been jointly operated and that the case therefore fell under Article 320, it nonetheless felt that an agreed settlement in the case was still possible.[183] For its part, the Advisory and Technical Committee felt unable to take a position on whether Article 320 was applicable, but it did associate itself with the proposals of the committee of experts under the understanding that the applicability of Article 320 was a question to be resolved by the tribunal, should it be appointed.[184] In light of these findings, the Council initially deferred the decision on arbitrator appointment for six months in the hope of a friendly settlement,[185] but eventually proceeded to appoint a tribunal after it had not been informed of any such agreement within the prescribed period. In doing so, the Council set out that the tribunal was first to answer the preliminary question of the applicability of Article 320; only if it found the said article applicable was the tribunal to move on to resolve the remaining open question between the parties.[186]

---

180 *Zeltweg-Wolfsberg and Unterdrauburg-Woellan Railway Company v Austria and Yugoslavia* [1934] League of Nations Official Journal 1007, 1008 (*Zeltweg-Wolfsberg III*). The original award (in French) is housed at the United Nations Archives at Geneva: CRID134/343/163/1.

181 'Minutes of the Sixty-Sixth Session of the Council: First Meeting' (n 141) 439.

182 Ibid.

183 League of Nations Advisory and Technical Committee for Communications and Transit, 'Records of the Work of the Seventeenth Session, Held at Geneva from June 1st to 4th, 1932 (Annex 7: Report of the Committee of Experts Appointed to Study a Question Connected with the Petition Submitted to the Council by the Zeltweg-Wolfsberg and Unterdrauburg-Wöllan Railway Company, Vienna)' (23 June 1932) Official No C.531.M.265.1932.VIII 47.

184 'Communications and Transit' [1932] League of Nations Official Journal 1493, 1494.

185 'Minutes of the Sixty-Eighth Session of the Council: Third Meeting (Public)' [1932] League of Nations Official Journal 1736, 1737–1738.

186 'Minutes of the Seventy-Third Session of the Council (Part I): Fourth Meeting' (n 147) 828–829. Guerrero (then PCIJ vice-president and PCIJ president at the time of his appoint-

The tribunal rendered a total of four decisions regarding the application of the Zeltweg-Wolfsberg and Unterdrauburg-Woellan Railway Company. The first two decisions dealt with a pair of preliminary issues, both of which were found not to represent obstacles for the tribunal to proceed with deciding the substance of the dispute. The first of these preliminary issues concerned the aforementioned applicability of Article 320 of the Treaty of Saint-Germain (3.3.1). The second preliminary decision, which centred on the effect on the company's claim of an international agreement concluded between Austria and, *inter alia*, Yugoslavia, offered an important window into how the tribunal conceived of the powers conferred upon it by Article 320 of the Treaty of Saint-Germain (3.3.2). The substance of the dispute was then decided in the tribunal's third award, with the tribunal once more proceeding to direct the conduct of the involved states, including by ordering them to expropriate railway lines situated on their respective territories (3.3.3). The last decision, which came several years later, concerned an attempt to settle certain lingering differences between the company and Austria in the interpretation of the tribunal's third award (3.3.4).

3.3.1 The Preliminary Award on the Applicability of Article 320 of the Treaty of Saint-Germain

In accordance with the mandate set out for it in the Council's resolution through which the arbitrators were appointed, the tribunal first dealt with the applicability of Article 320 of the Treaty of Saint-Germain.[187] Much like the *Sopron-Köszeg Local Railway Company v. Austria and Hungary* tribunal, this tribunal too found Article 320 to serve a dual purpose: on the one hand, the normal operation of the railway system of the former Austro-Hungarian Empire for the benefit of the population of the areas affected by the territorial changes and, on the other, the protection of the interests of the private concession holders, who otherwise would have been left without recourse for the protection of their rights after finding themselves simultaneously under the authority of two states. Regarding the latter aspect, the tribunal saw the Treaty of Saint-Germain as giving official recognition to the position of the concession holders for the railways now situated in the territories of the successor states to

ment in the resubmitted case) and Mayer were once more tribunal members, while Kalff was replaced by Athanase Politis, former Director of the Greek Railways and Technical Adviser of the Greek Legation in Paris.

187 *Zeltweg-Wolfsberg and Unterdrauburg-Woellan Railway Company v Austria and Yugoslavia* [1934] League of Nations Official Journal 84 (*Zeltweg-Wolfsberg I*). The original award (in French) is housed at the United Nations Archives at Geneva: CRID134/343/163/4.

Austria *vis-à-vis* those states. The only condition for the application of Article 320 under the terms of that provision was, in the tribunal's view, the need for a railway to have found itself in the territory of more than one state following the territorial changes after World War I; there was no need for the new boundaries to have specifically crossed the railway line.

Accordingly, the tribunal's task in deciding on the applicability of Article 320 came down to determining whether the two lines owned by the applicant company had prior to the war formed 'a system' for the purposes of Article 320.[188] As the arbitrators were convinced that this had been the case,[189] the tribunal held that Article 320 of the Treaty of Saint-Germain was applicable to the Zeltweg-Wolfsberg and Unterdrauburg-Woellan Railway Company.[190]

3.3.2 The Preliminary Award on the Effect of the Hague Agreement of 20 January 1930 on the Applicant Company's Claims

Before the tribunal could address the substance of the dispute, however, it was forced to deal with another preliminary objection subsequently raised by Yugoslavia.[191] Namely, Yugoslavia had invoked the provisions of an agreement concluded between Austria and its creditor powers, including Yugoslavia (hereinafter The Hague Agreement), pursuant to which 'all outstanding claims and counter-claims arising under the Treaty of St. Germain (…) between Austrian nationals and the said Powers (…) [were thereby] reciprocally waived.'[192] In Yugoslavia's view, this meant that the claims the applicant company had invoked before the tribunal had been waived by Austria and that, since such waiver was binding on the company in light of its Austrian seat, its claim was to be dismissed. As an alternative argument in relation to The Hague Agreement, Yugoslavia had also submitted that the tribunal was at least to withhold from ruling on the request until the tribunal envisioned by The Hague Agreement's

188 Ibid 85.

189 The tribunal on this point relied on the fact that the concession for the two lines had been conferred on the applicant company with a single deed, while the lines themselves had been constructed at the same time and in reality represented extensions of the Unterdrauburg-Wolfsberg line that had already been in operation by the Austrian State Railways. Moreover, the tribunal found particularly convincing the fact that the operation of the two lines was indivisible from a financial standpoint. Ibid 85–86.

190 Ibid 86.

191 See *Zeltweg-Wolfsberg and Unterdrauburg-Woellan Railway Company v Austria and Yugoslavia* [1934] League of Nations Official Journal 1005 (*Zeltweg-Wolfsberg II*). The original award (in French) is housed at the United Nations Archives at Geneva: CRID134/343/163/2.

192 See Agreement Regarding the Final Discharge of the Financial Obligations of Austria (signed 20 January 1930, entered into force 28 June 1930) 104 LNTS 413, art III (Hague Agreement).

own dispute resolution clause could give its ruling on the applicability of the relevant provision to the company's claims.[193]

The tribunal's award on the second preliminary issue, albeit as short as its award on the first one, was considerably more layered. Several aspects of the award dealt with issues of broader conceptual relevance, such as the tribunal's capacity to rule on its own jurisdiction, its powers in relation to other international agreements and whether Article 320 of the Treaty of Saint-Germain had created novel rights for the applicant company. Most importantly, however, the award offers a window into the arbitrators' own conceptualisation of both their roles and the extent of the powers that the Peace Treaties had conferred upon them. Considering the overlapping constitution of the tribunals in the three Peace Treaty railway arbitrations, this provides crucial insight not only for understanding what the tribunal would subsequently set out to do in the *Zeltweg-Wolfsberg and Unterdrauburg-Woellan Railway Company v. Austria and Yugoslavia* case, but also for properly situating the decisions handed down in the two remaining Peace Treaty railway arbitrations.

The first issue dealt with by the tribunal in the award was the arbitrators' capacity to decide upon their own jurisdiction. In a statement that, despite its brevity, leaves plenty to unpack, the tribunal held that it was 'an accepted principle that an international judge has the right to decide as to his own jurisdiction'.[194] The more obvious observation that this statement invites is certainly that the tribunal offered a resounding endorsement of the *Kompetenz-Kompetenz* principle and applied it in the context of a historical ISA; yet perhaps the more salient one is that the tribunal considered itself an 'international judge'. That the tribunal would have viewed itself as operating at the level of international law is perhaps not particularly surprising considering that it was constituted pursuant to an international treaty and that two states had (in addition to the claimant company) participated in the arbitration. While such an understanding by the tribunals in the Peace Treaty arbitrations had at various points been implicitly hinted at through references to international law or international judicial precedent, nowhere was it so clearly articulated as here.

A further important observation by the tribunal regarding the breadth of its own jurisdiction related to its capacity to look beyond the Treaty of Saint-Germain, pursuant to which it was constituted. Of this, the tribunal had little doubt, as it stated that it had the competence to interpret, in addition to the Treaty of Saint-Germain, any other international agreement so long as such

193 *Zeltweg-Wolfsberg II* (n 191) 1005–1006. See Hague Agreement (n 192) art VIII. It appears that no such proceeding was ever initiated.

194 *Zeltweg-Wolfsberg II* (n 191) 1006.

interpretation was 'incidental to a decision on a point in regard to which it has jurisdiction'.[195] In what was a signalling of how expansively the arbitrators would come to understand their role, the tribunal found this especially to be the case with respect to an 'arbitral tribunal to which *so comprehensive and far-reaching a mission has been entrusted* (...) as that which is given by Article 320 of the Treaty of St. Germain to the arbitrators appointed by the Council of the League of Nations'.[196] Although the tribunal admitted an exception to the rule concerning the interpretation of other international agreements insofar a specific agreement foresaw that a particular jurisdiction was to deal with disputes regarding the interpretation of its provisions, it equally held that this exception was to be interpreted restrictively and was not to cause tribunals to fail to rule on questions put before them unless the incidental agreement that needed interpretation was unclear.

As for Article 320 of the Treaty of Saint-Germain itself, the tribunal perceived it as having a dual purpose; on the one hand, restoring international communications, and, on the other, the regular utilisation of the railways now located in several states. For the tribunal, the latter did not imply just technical measures that would allow the local populations to make use of the railways, but also the administrative and financial measures that would 'regularise' the position of the private concessionaires. In this respect, the tribunal deemed that Article 320 merely reflected the principle that the rights of private concession holders could not be altered solely by the change of the nationality of the territory to which they related. The tribunal characterised this as 'a principle of public international law' that had been recognised by 'previous legal practice';[197] even though the tribunal did not specify the 'previous legal practice' it was invoking, the similarity in both approach and tribunal constitution imply that this was most likely a reference, at least *inter alia*, to the award previously handed down in *Sopron-Köszeg Local Railway Company v. Austria and Hungary*.[198] The tribunal's next observation – that Article 320 had envisaged recourse to the arbitrators appointed by the Council of the League of Nations in case no agreement was reached by the concessionary companies and the territorially concerned states – was a critical premise for how the arbitrators would come to understand their own role.[199] That such a part had been envisaged for arbitration in

195 Ibid.
196 Ibid. Emphasis added.
197 Ibid.
198 See n 170.
199 See ibid.

the process regulated by Article 320 prompted the tribunal to conceive of its own role in the following, seemingly unconstrained, terms:

> *the Treaty of Peace thus conferred on the said arbitrators the widest administrative and judicial powers*, since their awards are to replace detailed agreements between the States and the companies, these powers, as also appears from previous legal practice, *going so far as to allow them to call upon the States to expropriate the lines, while adjusting the conditions to which this expropriation was made subject in the original concessions.*[200]

By framing its own perception of the powers that had been conferred upon it in this manner, the tribunal simultaneously both put what two of its members had done as part of the tribunal in the *Sopron-Köszeg Local Railway Company v. Austria and Hungary* case in clearer conceptual terms and foreshadowed how the tribunal itself would subsequently concretise powers so understood when deciding the substance of the dispute.

A final, and particularly interesting, prong in the tribunal's reasoning was its treatment of the issue of whether Article 320 had created any new rights for the applicant company. The tribunal's understanding that no such new right had been created was rooted in a lack of distinction between the substance of the rights held by the concessionary companies and the mechanism for their enforcement. Namely, the tribunal considered that Article 320 had merely confirmed the already existing rights of the concessionary companies; in the arbitrators' understanding, Article 320 had simply 'confined itself, without conferring any new right on the said companies, to instituting an exceptional and special procedure to enable them to avail themselves of the rights which they held under their previous concessions',[201] but which they would have otherwise been unable to have recognised by some of the territorially concerned states. This new procedural avenue created by Article 320 was thus not recognised by the tribunal as a right with an existence independent from the already existing substantive rights. The tribunal's negation that the procedural recourse available under Article 320 was a self-standing right invited the conclusion that the company's claim before the tribunal could not be characterised as 'a claim arising under the treaty of St. Germain' so that it would fall under The Hague Agreement.[202] As a consequence, Yugoslavia's objection

200 Ibid. Emphasis added.
201 Ibid.
202 Ibid.

based on The Hague Agreement was dismissed,[203] and the tribunal was free to proceed with the administrative and technical reorganisation of the Zeltweg-Wolfsberg and Unterdrauburg-Woellan Railway.

3.3.3 The Award on Substance

Shortly after dismissing Yugoslavia's second preliminary objection, the tribunal issued its award on substance on 12 May 1934 in Geneva.[204] Considering the overlapping constitution of the tribunals, it should not come as a surprise that the tribunal's chosen course of action to a significant extent mirrored the approach from *Sopron-Köszeg Local Railway Company v. Austria and Hungary*. Likewise, in light of the manner in which the tribunal had conceived of its role, as discussed in the previous sub-section, it should equally not come as a surprise that this approach included also the tribunal directing the conduct of the involved states, in particular by ordering them to expropriate the relevant railway lines.

In terms of the arbitrators' understanding of the breadth of their powers, the tribunal's award on substance continued right where its award on the second preliminary issue had left off. Yet another clue toward offering a fuller picture of the arbitrators' approach was the tribunal's observation that Article 320 of the Treaty of Saint-Germain had, if the matter could not be resolved by negotiated settlement, referred to the arbitrators 'the general settlement of the legal, financial, and technical position of the railway systems of the former Austro-Hungarian Monarchy' that had ended up in more than one state as the result of the territorial changes. After reiterating the finding from its earlier preliminary award to the effect that, in such an instance, the tribunal's award was to stand in for the envisioned party agreement, the tribunal held that this implied resolving 'all questions arising out of the administrative and technical reorganisation of the system in the several countries'.[205] An interesting twist, and a further indication that the tribunal conceived of its powers as being circumscribed by little, if anything, was the tribunal's proposition that the arbitrators were, not merely empowered, but seemingly also obliged to assess whether the provisional or partial agreements that may have been concluded by the interested parties were in line with the future solution envisaged by the tribunal. The tribunal was moreover to ensure that the interests of all of the parties involved, and in particular of the companies' bondholders, were to be given 'equitable treatment'; rather curiously (as such an interpretation does not

203 Ibid 1006–1007.

204 *Zeltweg-Wolfsberg III* (n 180).

205 Ibid 1007–1008.

appear to follow immediately from the treaty text), the arbitrators added that the treaty parties had in Article 320 provided that 'they cannot approve tacit or explicit agreements which do not take sufficient account of the rights of bondholders'.[206] This led the tribunal to the conclusion that, should the circumstances so require, it was up to the arbitrators to resettle the questions on which such provisional or partial agreements were not to be upheld. With this, the tribunal thus allocated to itself, not merely the power to decide issues on which the parties had failed to agree, but, absent an all-encompassing agreement between them, also the power to re-decide the issues on which partial or provisional agreement may have existed.

This was precisely what the tribunal would then proceed to do, as it held that the proceedings had shown that it would be best to reorganise the entire railway system from a legal, financial and technical standpoint, despite the applicant company and Austria being in agreement that there was no dispute as in between them. In light of the changes resulting from the war, the tribunal thought that the most 'expedient and reasonable solution' was for each state to expropriate the part of the company's railway that came to be on its territory.[207] Since Yugoslavia and the applicant company appeared to be in agreement on this point regarding the part of the line situated in Yugoslavia, the tribunal felt that there was no reason to decide differently with respect to the part of the line located in Austria (which was, in any event, operated by the Austrian Federal Railways rather than the company itself). The tribunal thus ordered that, on 1 January 1935, Yugoslavia was to expropriate the Unterdrauburg-Woellan section of the railway, while Austria was to expropriate the Zeltweg-Wolfsberg section.[208] The tribunal's solution, hence, albeit expressed through a slightly different modality, was parallel to that adopted in *Sopron-Köszeg Local Railway Company v. Austria and Hungary*, and included directing the involved states to take over the relevant railway systems.

The tribunal then proceeded to determine the compensation that was to be paid by Yugoslavia and Austria; following payment, Yugoslavia and Austria were, by way of the tribunal's decision, to become the respective owners of the two lines.[209] Notably, when determining compensation, the tribunal made another vague, yet unmistakable, reference to the findings in *Sopron-Köszeg Local Railway Company v. Austria and Hungary*. Namely, although the tribunal merely made a reference to 'former legal precedents', it essentially echoed the

206 Ibid 1008.
207 Ibid.
208 Ibid.
209 Ibid 1008–1009.

findings of the earlier similarly composed tribunal, to the effect that the pre-war contractual provisions were to be treated neither as wholly valid nor as wholly invalid due to the post-war territorial changes.[210] Instead, it was again up to the tribunal to adjust the contractual situation to the unforeseeable circumstances that had arisen since its conclusion.

A further symbolic illustration of just how broad the tribunal had perceived its powers to be was the arbitrators' solution for the distribution of compensation funds amongst the priority bondholders. Namely, the tribunal proceeded to establish a fund into which the annual payments were to be made and provided for this fund to be managed by a trustee.[211] In performing this task, the trustee was required, if the circumstances called for, to conclude an agreement with the railway company before its liquidation on a new loan redemption schedule and its own remuneration. Rather remarkably, in case the two sides were unable to reach the envisioned agreement, the tribunal decided that the differences between the trustee and the company were to be resolved by an arbitrator, thus effectively providing for arbitration independently of the will of its envisioned participants.[212] In order to see through the enforcement of these provisions regarding the distribution of the funds to the bondholders, the tribunal even empowered the tribunal president to take 'any measures which may be found necessary in [their] execution'.[213] Although this part of the

---

210 Ibid 1008. See n 173.

211 This aspect of the award turned out to be problematic and, ultimately, inoperative. The tribunal had provided for the trustee to be the Bank for International Settlements or, in the case of its inability to act, another competent entity appointed by the Financial Committee of the League of Nations. See *Zeltweg-Wolfsberg III* (n 180) 1009. As the Bank for International Settlements was indeed incapable of taking on the trustee role due to a conflict of interest, Société de Banque Suisse was eventually appointed. The Société de Banque Suisse would, however, soon itself ask to be relieved of this function as certain matters arose regarding the interpretation of the award that could not be resolved. See 'Annex 1512: Appointment of a Trustee for the Priority Bonds Fund of the Zeltweg-Wolfsberg and Unterdrauburg-Woellan Railway Company' [1934] League of Nations Official Journal 1411; League of Nations Financial Committee, 'Report to the Council on the Work of the Fifty-Fifth Session of the Committee (*Geneva, September 3rd-10th, 1934*)' (10 September 1934) Official No C.393.M.177.1934.II.A.; 'Minutes of the Eighty-Sixth Session of the Council: Second Meeting (Private, Then Public)' [1935] League of Nations Official Journal 599, 614; Letter from the Director of the Financial Section and Economic Intelligence Service to the Secretary General (9 April 1935) (n 133); Annex II ('Difficulties in Regard to the Trustee's Functions') to the Letter from McKinnon Wood to the Financial Section (2 August 1935) (n 133).

212 See *Zeltweg-Wolfsberg III* (n 180) 1009–1010.

213 Ibid 1010. While the provision seemed to confer very wide powers on the tribunal president, when called upon to act under this clause, Guerrero interpreted his powers rather

tribunal's award was not directed at, or of direct concern to, the states involved in the arbitration, the course of action adopted by the tribunal is nonetheless consistent with, and illustrative of, its overall, seemingly little constrained, understanding of its own competencies.

As a final step, the tribunal also dealt with the hypothecary guarantee that existed on the two lines of the railway. Insofar as the Zeltweg-Wolfsberg section was concerned, the guarantee was to be maintained, while for the Unterdrauburg-Woellan line the tribunal provided that the guarantee was to be re-registered in the name of the priority bondholders pursuant to Yugoslav law.[214]

At the time, it had appeared that the tribunal had with this disposed of the matter concerning the Zeltweg-Wolfsberg and Unterdrauburg-Woellan Railway Company; an additional brief episode, however, soon followed.

3.3.4 The Resubmitted Case[215]

As it would turn out, the tribunal's award on substance was plagued with several practical difficulties[216] and did not put the matter definitively to rest. Shortly after the tribunal had issued the award on substance, a disagreement over its interpretation arose, rooted in Austria's assertion that it had a right to deduct claims that it alleged to have had against the company under a guarantee from the compensation owed to the company for the expropriation of its lines, resulting in a lack of compliance with this aspect of the award. As the company disputed Austria's claim to such deduction, just over a year after the award on substance was handed down, the League of Nations received, from a committee appointed by the company specifically in order to oversee the award's enforcement, a request for the reappointment of the tribunal, so that it would clarify the matter.[217]

---

restrictively, refusing to confirm the agreement concluded between the trustee and the company or to provide an interpretation of a contentious aspect of the award. See 'Difficulties in Regard to the Trustee's Functions' (n 211); Letter from McKinnon Wood to Metternich, Loveday and the Secretary General (17 April 1935) (n 133); Letter from the Director of the Financial Section and Economic Intelligence Service to the Secretary General (9 April 1935) (n 133).

214 *Zeltweg-Wolfsberg III* (n 180) 1010.

215 *Zeltweg-Wolfsberg and Unterdrauburg-Woellan Railway Company v Austria and Yugoslavia* [1938] League of Nations Official Journal 1172 (*Zeltweg-Wolfsberg IV*). The original award (in French) is housed at the United Nations Archives at Geneva: CRID134/343/163/5.

216 See nn 211 and 213.

217 'Annex 1683: Petition by the Zeltweg-Wolfsberg and Unterdrauburg Woellan Railway Company, Vienna' [1937] League of Nations Official Journal 1273.

Following some complications due to a challenge to the validity of this new request from the company's board of directors,[218] the Council eventually referred the question to the Permanent Legal Committee of the Communications and Transit Committee,[219] which ultimately found the request for the appointment of arbitrators to have been validly made.[220] Accordingly, the Council proceeded to reappoint the tribunal as it had been originally constituted. In doing so, the Council tasked the thus reappointed tribunal with deciding all unresolved issues still existing between the parties for which they found themselves competent, which was to take the form of giving an authentic interpretation of the award, supplementing it, or adapting it to the new circumstances.[221]

Ultimately, however, there would be little for the reappointed tribunal to decide, as the request was withdrawn by the petitioner before the tribunal could give its ruling.[222] All that remained for the tribunal was to confirm that the withdrawal had been validly given and that it had been accepted by the other litigants.[223] One interesting matter that the tribunal did have to deal with, however, was the requests for intervention that had been submitted on behalf of several groups of bondholders. In principle, the tribunal was receptive to such intervention, as it recognised that the bondholders' legal rights were independent from those of the applicant company itself or of the two territorially concerned states. Nonetheless, the company's withdrawal of its request meant that there was no dispute, and thus no proceedings, in which to intervene. Accordingly, the intervention requests were dismissed.[224]

With this, the tribunal's fourth award finally brought the arbitration proceedings regarding the dispute over the Zeltweg-Wolfsberg and Unterdrauburg-Woellan Railway to an end. For an ISA set in the 1930s, this dispute gave rise to

218 See ibid 1276–1279.

219 'Minutes of the Ninety-Fourth Session of the Council: Fourth Meeting (Private)' [1936] League of Nations Official Journal 1194, 1196.

220 'Annex 1683: Petition by the Zeltweg-Wolfsberg and Unterdrauburg Woellan Railway Company' (n 217) 1283–1286.

221 'Minutes of the Ninety-Ninth Session of the Council: First Meeting (Private, Then Public)' [1937] League of Nations Official Journal 922, 933.

222 *Zeltweg-Wolfsberg IV* (n 215) 1173. The unexpected turn of events seems to have been brought about by Austria's acquisition, having already been the company's largest shareholder, of a sufficient amount of additional shares so as to take over full control of the company and disband the special committee that had requested renewed proceedings. See Letter (unsigned) to Mehmed Spaho, the Minister of Transport (15 July 1938) (Archives of Yugoslavia: 338–33 (1931–1938)).

223 See *Zeltweg-Wolfsberg IV* (n 215) 1173.

224 Ibid.

several extremely interesting yet complex issues, especially from a procedural standpoint. Among other things, the tribunal addressed both its capacity to rule on its own jurisdiction and to interpret international agreements other than the one pursuant to which it was established, the (in)separability of the procedural rights provided for in Article 320 of the Treaty of Saint-Germain from the substantive rights for the enforcement of which they were introduced, as well as the right of interested third parties to intervene into the arbitration. Yet perhaps the most distinguishable characteristic of this historical ISA is the tribunal's detailed explication on the nature and extent of its mandate, which in many respects complemented, and provided additional elaboration of, the much less conspicuous conceptual underpinnings of the earlier *Sopron-Köszeg Local Railway Company v. Austria and Hungary* case, with which it shared two of the three arbitrators. Under both the tribunal's given rationalisation and its eventual actions, the arbitrators' perception of their own powers appeared to have seen little limit to what the tribunal could do in fulfilling the mandate conferred upon it by the Treaty of Saint-Germain.

For present purposes, the most important manifestation of such, seemingly little constrained, powers was certainly the tribunal's decision to order each of the concerned states to take over the applicant company's railway lines situated in their respective territories. While this was a solution equivalent to that adopted in *Sopron-Köszeg Local Railway Company v. Austria and Hungary*, a notable symbolic difference was that the tribunal's instruction to the states was this time around couched in terminology – 'expropriation' rather than 'purchase' – that was better representative of the true nature of the tribunal's instruction. Despite this difference in terminology, considering the overlapping constitution of the two tribunals and the latter tribunal's interchangeable use of the two terms, there should be little doubt that both tribunals had the same instruction for the concerned states in mind – for them to appropriate, irrespective of volition, a private enterprise. If any lingering doubt remained as to whether this had been the arbitrators' understanding of what they were doing, one only needs to look to the findings of the tribunal in the third Peace Treaty railway arbitration, which once more consisted of the same overlapping arbitrators and which, once again, adopted a comparable solution.

3.4 *Barcs-Pakrac Railway Company, Ltd v Hungary and Yugoslavia*

Finally, a tribunal appointed by the Council of the League of Nations under the Peace Treaties also dealt with the case of the Barcs-Pakrac Railway Company.[225]

225 *Barcs-Pakrac Railway Company, Ltd v Hungary and Yugoslavia* (1935) 29(3) AJIL 523. The original award (in French) is housed at the United Nations Archives at Geneva: CRID134/343/162.

The factual basis underpinning this dispute was, expectedly, largely analogous to the two preceding Peace Treaty railway arbitrations – the Budapest-based company had at the end of the 19th century obtained a ninety year concession to construct and operate, together with the accompanying branch lines, a local railway from Barcs to Pakrac; the actual operation of the line was then entrusted to the South Austrian Railway Company (the Südbahn Company). Following the post-war territorial changes, the vast majority of the railway line ended up in Yugoslavia, with only a minor section remaining in Hungary.[226] The operation of the railway by the South Austrian Railway Company, however, continued until 1923, at which point it was taken over by Yugoslavia in line with an agreement concluded between the company and the four territorially concerned states that sought to reorganise the South Austrian Railway Company (hereinafter the Rome Agreement).[227] As no friendly solution could be found between the Barcs-Pakrac Railway Company and Yugoslavia regarding the financial arrangements pertaining to the railway, the company appealed to the Council of the League of Nations under Article 304 of the Treaty of Trianon, and a tribunal was eventually appointed by the Council to resolve the dispute.[228]

In the proceedings before the arbitrators, the applicant company requested the tribunal to, when proceeding with the administrative and technical reorganisation of its railway system, fully validate the binding effect of the company's arrangements with the South Austrian Railway Company on Yugoslavia. The company further asked to be paid sums, calculated on a gold basis, owed to it by Yugoslavia under the operating contract since Yugoslavia's takeover of the railway, as well as for the arbitrators to set out the rules that would ensure that Yugoslavia and Hungary comply with their obligations as successors to the South Austrian Railway Company under the Rome Agreement.[229] Meanwhile,

---

226 'Minutes of the Seventieth Session of the Council: First Meeting' (n 139) 181. A map of the railways following the territorial changes is available at the United Nations Archives at Geneva: S492/11/6.

227 Agreement Between the Republic of Austria, the Kingdom of Hungary, the Kingdom of Italy, the Kingdom of the Serbs, Croats and Slovenes and the Southern Railway Company (Sudbahn), Drawn Up with the Concurrence of the Committee Representing the Holders of Bonds Issued by the Above Company with a View to the Administrative and Technical Re-organisation of the Southern Railway Company's System (Signed 29 March 1923) 23 LNTS 336. While Hungary had taken over its portion of the operation of the Southern Railway Company network in 1932, this did not affect the Barcs-Pakrac line. See *Barcs-Pakrac Railway Company v Hungary and Yugoslavia* (n 225) 526.

228 'Minutes of the Seventy-Eighth Session of the Council (Part 1): Second Meeting' (n 147) 123–124. See also 'Annex 1487: Petition from the Barcs-Pakrac Railway Company' (n 140) 183–185. The tribunal composition was the same as in *Zeltweg-Wolfsberg*. See n 186.

229 *Barcs-Pakrac Railway Company v Hungary and Yugoslavia* (n 225) 526.

Yugoslavia argued that, considering the change in circumstances caused by the war, the existing contract could not be applied without modification and that the company could not be compensated on a gold basis due to the significant decrease in the value of the railway and the simultaneous increase in operation costs. Instead, Yugoslavia asked the tribunal to retroactively reformulate the financial relations between itself and the company.[230] For its part, Hungary in principle supported the position of the applicant company, although it argued that in reality Hungary had no interest in the claim, having never actually taken part in operating the railway.[231]

The tribunal issued its award on 5 October 1934, in Paris. Unsurprisingly, the tribunal's award in many respects followed in the footsteps of the two tribunals that had preceded it. This perhaps above all applied to the tribunal's understanding of the breadth and extent of its own powers, including more specifically in relation to its capacity to direct the conduct of the disputing parties, including the concerned states. Accordingly, just like in the two cases that came before it, the tribunal once more instructed the two states involved on the actions they were to take in terms of the expropriation of the railway company, only this time its instructions went in the opposite direction – with both Yugoslavia and Hungary being prohibited by the tribunal from carrying out expropriation.

Already at the outset, the manner in which the arbitrators had conceived of their task felt familiar against the background of their earlier decisions – once more, the tribunal was to provide a 'final and comprehensive settlement' of the dispute before it. In this particular instance, this was understood to entail three things: first, ruling on the company's claims concerning the period after the operation of the railway had been taken over by Yugoslavia up until the year of the tribunal's award; second, determining the rights of the concessionaire and the state operating the railway going forward, as well as the steps that may be required for the railway's administrative and technical reorganisation; and third, interpreting the contractual provisions relating to expropriation and laying out how such expropriation, if found to be necessary, was to be carried out.[232]

The first question addressed by the tribunal was the interpretation of the relevant provision of the Rome Agreement and of the provisions of the operating contract; how the tribunal would proceed to deal with this question once again served to highlight the arbitrators' perceived power to modify the parties'

230 Ibid 526–527.
231 Ibid 527.
232 Ibid.

pre-existing relationships, as well as its leeway in so doing. The tribunal recognised the dual nature of the status Yugoslavia had attained *vis-à-vis* the applicant company – not only had Yugoslavia become the concessionary state to the claimant company by virtue of the post-war territorial changes, but it had also, pursuant to the Rome Agreement, succeeded to the position of the South Austrian Railway Company under the operating contract, which was a legal relationship entirely distinct from the concession. The tribunal considered that the concession's existence could not result in Yugoslavia being obliged to perform the operating contract in '[its] entirety and without modification'. The tribunal's position on this point was the same one that had been well established in the two preceding Peace Treaty railway arbitrations[233] – while the main features of this contractual relationship, as existing before the war, were indeed to be maintained, it could not be expected that that they would be enforced literally, as doing so would have ignored the political and economic changes resulting from the war that Article 304 of the Treaty of Trianon had reflected.[234] And not only that, but, in what was a reminder of just how broadly the arbitrators had understood their own powers, the tribunal considered that such literal enforcement of the contractual provisions would have also misunderstood the extent of the powers that had been conferred upon the arbitrators by Article 304. That the tribunal would have this perception is hardly surprising when taking into account what the arbitrators understood these power to entail – they felt themselves not merely empowered, but indeed 'required', to modify the underlying contractual relationship so as to take into account the unforeseen circumstances brought about by the war.[235] The arbitrators in the three Peace Treaty railway arbitrations, thus, were nothing if not consistent in terms of how broadly they understood their competencies.

A particularly interesting aspect of the tribunal's award, especially from the specific vantage point of ISA, was the significance that the arbitrators had accorded to the fact that a state had taken over the operation of the railway. Namely, while the tribunal had found that Article 11(2) of the Rome Agreement had ensured to the applicant company the continuation of all provisions of the operating contract that (after revision) were not in conflict with the situation brought about by the consequences of the war, the Peace Treaties or the Rome Agreement itself, it also felt that it could not be disregarded that the railway was no longer operated by a private company but by a state. Instead, the arbitrators felt obliged to take into consideration this fact when proceeding with

233 See nn 173 and 210.

234 *Barcs-Pakrac Railway Company v Hungary and Yugoslavia* (n 225) 528.

235 Ibid.

the technical and administrative reorganisation of the railway. For the tribunal, in what was an analogous solution to that contained in the Rome Agreement, the fact that Yugoslavia had thus found itself as both the concessionary state and the operator of the railway implied that it was to compensate the Barcs-Pakrac Railway Company by paying royalties for the use of the railway. The manner and amount of such royalties, however, was not to be determined by the provisions of the operating contract regulating this issue, but rather by the arbitrators themselves.[236]

At the same time, the tribunal concluded that Yugoslavia had, by taking over the South Austrian Railway Company's operating contract with the applicant company, incurred an obligation not to fully incorporate the Barcs-Pakrac Railway into its railway system, but was instead to maintain a separate operating account and submit annual statements. Ultimately, the tribunal felt that the pre-war contractual terms needed revising from two perspectives. The first concerned the modifications that were needed because of the unforeseen developments from the preceding period, while the second related to the need to take into account the railway's continued operation 'as a separate line belonging to a third party'. It was with respect to this second set of modifications where the tribunal once more put special emphasis on the fact that a state had entered the frame, as it held that this was to include also 'adjusting the rules laid down for that purpose so as to allow for the fact that operation has passed from private hands into the hands of a State which has taken over such operation as being accessory to the direct management by its own State Railways of the Yugoslav lines of the former' South Austrian Railway Company.[237] The involvement of a state in the underlying relationship, then, was a specific consideration that the tribunal had taken into account when deciding on the principles according to which it would modify the parties' pre-existing contractual terms.

By laying out its principled approach as to the validity of the operating contract, the tribunal had paved the way for its preferred solutions to a number of relevant specific issues. The tribunal thus determined the compensation that the applicant company was owed for the period following Yugoslavia's takeover of the operation of the railway up until the year of the tribunal's award.[238] The tribunal's regulation of the parties' future relationship, meanwhile, was a bit more layered. As for the administrative and technical reorganisation of the Barcs-Pakrac Railway, the tribunal's solution had undeniably been as practical

236 Ibid 528–529.
237 Ibid 529.
238 Ibid 530–531.

as it probably could have been. Namely, considering the lack of indications that Yugoslavia's operation of the entire Barcs-Pakrac line, the minor part situated in Hungarian territory included, had caused problems, the tribunal held that the best solution was for the operation of the railway to continue on the same basis.[239]

In terms of the future payments that were to be made to the applicant company for Yugoslavia's operation of the railway, the tribunal laid out how both the relevant tariffs and the royalties were to be determined.[240] Interestingly, the tribunal then took the additional step of making sure to insulate the determined royalty against potential changes of transport taxes by Yugoslavia, by providing that the royalty's ratio to the total receipts would remain unaffected in case the tax was changed.[241]

Finally, and most importantly for present purposes, the tribunal also dealt with the question of the expropriation of the Barcs-Pakrac Railway.[242] Rather expectedly, in doing so, the tribunal followed the same pattern as the tribunals in the two preceding Peace Treaty railway arbitrations, considering itself at liberty to direct the involved states on their future conduct, albeit while adding certain additional wrinkles of its own. Having not deemed the expropriation of the railway necessary for its technical and administrative reorganisation, the tribunal decided to echo the solution contained in the Rome Agreement, pursuant to which the railways of the South Austrian Railway Company were not to be repurchased while that agreement was in force.[243] Consequently, the tribunal prohibited both Yugoslavia and Hungary from expropriating the Barcs-Pakrac Railway before 31 December 1968 (until when the Rome Agreement was to remain in force). This solution by the tribunal, while equally representative of the arbitrators' propensity to direct state conduct, was thus aimed at an opposite result as compared to the decisions in the two preceding Peace Treaty railway arbitrations – rather than ordering the involved states

---

239 Ibid 531–532. Accordingly, the tribunal reserved Hungary's rights in case of the expropriation of the railway (see below) and provided that Yugoslavia was, during the concession's validity, not to force the applicant company into taking over the operation of the railway. At the same time, were Yugoslavia to exercise its right under the Rome Agreement and hand back the operation of the railway to the successor company of the South Austrian Railway Company, the said company was to take Yugoslavia's place both in terms of the operation of the railway and with respect to the royalties owed to the Barcs-Pakrac Railway Company for such operation.

240 See ibid 532.

241 Ibid 533.

242 Ibid 533–534.

243 Rome Agreement (n 227) art 2(2).

to expropriate, the tribunal prohibited them from doing so. That is not to say that there was no place in the tribunal's decision also for the former variant of directing the conduct of the territorially interested states. Namely, as the applicant company's concession ran for an additional seven years following 1968, the tribunal further provided that, in case Yugoslavia was to expropriate the part of the railway located in its territory during this latter period, Hungary would be obliged to do the same regarding the part of the railway located in its territory (which was then to be transferred to Yugoslavia).[244]

While the tribunal's mandate was thus accomplished, the enforcement of its award, at least with respect to its monetary aspects, was not exactly a smooth affair, as Yugoslavia refused to comply with its payment obligations under the award. Importantly, however, the reason behind this refusal was not open disregard for the tribunal's decision. Instead, Yugoslavia's stance was part of its broader position regarding payments owed to Hungary or its subjects and was related to a moratorium that had previously been introduced on Hungarian war reparations due to the country's dire financial situation. Namely, while Yugoslavia had signed off on the temporary moratorium on Hungarian reparations at the 1932 Lausanne Conference, it did so only under a declaration that it too would, while the moratorium was in place, withhold its payments owed to Hungary or its subjects arising from the Peace Treaties and related agreements.[245] Despite this unfavourable stance by Yugoslavia, the

244 The tribunal also set out the parameters pursuant to which the compensation was to be calculated in case this were to happen, finding itself unconstrained when so doing by either Hungarian pre-war laws or the company's original concession. See *Barcs-Pakrac Railway Company v Hungary and Yugoslavia* (n 225) 534.

245 Yugoslavia's position was subsequently also published in the Yugoslav Official Gazette. See the reproduction of the decision by the Royal government on the postponement of payments of reparations for the duration of the Lausanne Moratorium from the Yugoslav Official Gazette No 172/33 (1 August 1933) (Archives of Yugoslavia: 70–292–542). The Yugoslav position was based more on the impact of the moratorium on its general financial situation than on the legal effects of its declaration at the Lausanne Conference as such. See Clerk to the Minister of Transport, 'Minutes of a Meeting Held at the Ministry of Foreign Affairs on 31 December 1934 Regarding the Question of Compliance with the Award Handed Down in the Dispute between Yugoslavia and the Barcs-Pakrac Local Railway Company' (2 January 1935) (Archives of Yugoslavia: 70–292–542). Namely, as part of an earlier package aimed at easing the financial hit on Hungary, a special fund (Fund B) had been established by Great Britain, France and Italy in the name of several Eastern European countries, including Yugoslavia, in order to contribute to their efforts to satisfy the decisions obtained against them from the Mixed Arbitral Tribunals established under the Peace Treaties by Hungarian nationals. See Agreement between France, Great Britain, Italy, Roumania, Czechoslovakia and Yugoslavia Concerning the Constitution of a Special Fund Entitled 'Fund B' (signed 28 April 1930) (1931) 30 UKTS Cmd 3910. Once Hungary

company did nonetheless try to have the decision of the tribunal honoured, even going so far as to try to enforce it before Yugoslav courts, but its efforts in this respect were ultimately unsuccessful.[246] As a result, the impasse continued for some time; eventually, the company was finally forced to let up and significantly decrease its claims, leading to an apparent settlement being concluded between the company and Yugoslavia, albeit for a considerably lower value than that awarded by the tribunal and with the company relinquishing its rights *vis-à-vis* Yugoslavia under the award.[247]

The tribunal's overall approach in *Barcs-Pakrac Railway Company v. Hungary and Yugoslavia* thus bears much resemblance to those of the tribunals of overlapping constitution from the two preceding Peace Treaty railway arbitrations. To be sure, the case was not without certain idiosyncrasies of its own, such as those that arose due to the relevance for the case of the Rome Agreement. Another idiosyncrasy was the fact that the tribunal did not, unlike in the preceding cases, order the territorially interested states to expropriate the relevant railway lines,[248] but instead prohibited them from doing so. This choice by the tribunal of a contrasting solution as compared to its predecessors was, however, ultimately merely a different manifestation of one and the same broader principle regarding the tribunal's capacity to instruct the parties, and in this particular instance states, on their future conduct. In this, then, the tribunal's decision stands as a complement to the decisions from the two preceding Peace Treaty railway arbitrations with respect to the arbitrators' powers to direct state conduct. What further stands out from the tribunal's decision in this respect is that, as is evidenced by the fact that the award only

---

ceased its reparations payments, however, the sponsoring states also ceased their contributions to the fund, leaving Yugoslavia considerably worse off with respect to its obligations under the Peace Treaties towards Hungarian subjects. While Yugoslavia had invoked this development as a justification for not complying with the award obtained by the Barcs-Pakrac Railway Company, Yugoslav officials were aware that this was only a temporary defence and therefore saw it primarily as a tactical move aimed at ultimately making the Barcs-Pakrac Railway Company reduce its claim. See Minutes of Meeting at Ministry of Foreign Affairs (n 245).

246 *Barcs-Pakrac Railway Company v Estate of the Kingdom of Yugoslavia*, Decision of the Table of Seven (at the time the highest court instance for Croatia, then part of Yugoslavia) (19 November 1937) (Archives of Yugoslavia: 70–292–542).

247 Letter from the Minister of Transport to the Ministerial Council (November 1940) (Archives of Yugoslavia: 138–6–32); Agreement Concluded between the Kingdom of Yugoslavia and the Barcs-Pakrac Railway Company Concerning the Purchase of the Barcs-Pakrac, Suhopolje-Podravska Slatina and Bastaji-Zdenci Railway (Archives of Yugoslavia: 138–6–32).

248 At least not unconditionally. See n 244.

contemplates the possibility of Yugoslavia expropriating the railways after the moratorium imposed by the tribunal had passed, the arbitrators hardly appear to have expected the involved states not to respect their prohibition against the railway's expropriation. Thus, it seems that, at least in the arbitrators' own eyes, the tribunal's instructions to the two territorially concerned states were nothing if not intended as imperative.

3.5 *The Peace Treaty Railway Arbitrations and Historical Investor-State Arbitration as an Avenue for Directing State Conduct*

One would likely be hard pressed to find a historical ISA, and even more so a set of historical ISAs, more worthy of being remembered than the Peace Treaty railway arbitrations. Indeed, there is a palette of reasons that one could point to in order to underline why the Peace Treaty railway arbitrations remain one of the more significant, and unique (if not necessarily hitherto influential), historical ISAs. These reasons include the fact that the three arbitrations were quite possibly the first-known ISAs where states had given their (advance) agreement to arbitrate with private enterprises by way of international treaty, the tribunals' consideration of a number of, especially for their time, interesting procedural issues,[249] as well as the extensive involvement of the Council of the League of Nations in the arbitral process. Moreover, while the awards appear to have above all been characterised by pragmatism and the tribunals not overly concerned about framing their findings in strictly defined legal terms or conceptual categories, the arbitrators did appear to consider themselves entrenched in public international law.[250] The latter is perhaps not all too surprising when considering that the arbitrations were based on international treaties, that they involved sovereign states, that they were conducted under the auspices of the League of Nations, and, perhaps most importantly, the presence on the tribunals by a judge (either to be or sitting) of the PCIJ, Judge Guerrero.

But the aspect that probably stands out the most is just how broad, indeed seemingly unconstrained, an understanding the tribunals had of their own mandate, and how intrusive, or far reaching, their decisions were as a consequence. While each of the three Peace Treaty railway arbitrations was a separate case and each certainly had its own idiosyncrasies, considering the

---

249 Such as, as discussed above, a tribunal's capacity to rule on its own jurisdiction and to interpret international agreements other than the one pursuant to which it was established, the (in)separability of a party's substantive and procedural rights, or a third party's right to intervene into arbitration proceedings.

250 See nn 170, 194 and 197.

overlap in the tribunals' constitutions, that this common thread permeated all three arbitrations is hardly surprising. Thus, all of the tribunals in question saw as their task to provide for the comprehensive reorganisation of the railway systems of the applicant companies, as well as to (re)define their relations with the states on whose territory the railways were located. In so doing, the tribunals openly recognised that their role was not merely restricted to the simple application of a pre-existing normative structure to the relevant facts, but instead equally necessitated a certain creative element and involved the need to balance the different interests involved, both public and private. As a result, the tribunals repeatedly found themselves not to be bound by the strictures of the existing concessions or operating contracts, certain national laws or decisions by government officials, while the determinations of the payable compensation were made primarily (if not exclusively) on the basis of equitable considerations.

Although such an understanding by the tribunals' of their mission was perhaps not an implausible interpretation of the Peace Treaty provisions pursuant to which they were constituted, it was equally not necessarily a foregone conclusion that the said provisions called for such an extensive mandate. Namely, as was mentioned above,[251] the relevant Peace Treaty provisions merely provided that the arbitrators were to resolve *any differences* with respect to the technical and administrative reorganisation of railways that came to be situated in more than one country following World War I on which the interested parties could not reach agreement (including those regarding the interpretation of contracts concerning the expropriation of the lines). Although the open-ended nature of this provision certainly allowed for a broad interpretation in terms of the disputes that could be subsumed under it, it can at the same time by no means be said to have unequivocally established, through its sheer wording, a mandate as broad as the one envisioned by the tribunals – that required an additional interpretative, and certainly not inevitable, step.[252]

Irrespective of whether one considers the tribunals to have been justified in interpreting their mandate as they did, the fact remains that they did understand it in such an exceptionally broad manner and acted accordingly. As has been highlighted throughout this section, one of the primary manifestations

251 See sub-section 3.1.

252 In contrast, a similar provision contained in the Treaty of Sevres was a bit more explicit regarding the powers of a tribunal that could be established under it, as it had provided that a holder of a concession that would be maintained could 'demand the adaptation of his contract to the new economic conditions, and in the absence of agreement direct with the Government concerned the decision shall be referred to the Arbitral Commission provided for above'. See Treaty of Sevres (n 136) art 311.

of the arbitrators conceiving of their own powers to be as extensive was that they deemed themselves competent to direct the future conduct of the disputing parties. Crucially, when doing so, unlike the tribunal in the *Czechoslovakian Administration v.* RCA arbitration, the tribunals did not merely rule on whether certain intended conduct was in compliance with a pre-existing normative structure, but instead unbound themselves of such strictures and stepped into the role of a decision-maker dictating the initial course of action. While acting in the capacity of such a primary decision-maker, the tribunals proceeded, *inter alia*, to order the involved sovereign states to expropriate (while also prescribing the underlying conditions for the expropriations), or prohibited them from doing so. Thus, not only did the tribunals take upon themselves to direct the conduct of the states involved, but they did so regarding a domain – the right to take private property irrespective of volition – that is normally reserved for states in their conduct of official business.

Yet, in order to properly appreciate this aspect of the three Peace Treaty railway arbitrations, one must not overlook the fact that these three arbitrations very easily could have been, and were perhaps even envisioned to have been, but a small fraction of a much larger cluster of historical ISAs. Indeed, had the Council of the League of Nations not put such strong emphasis, perhaps inappropriately so, and in excess of its mandate under the Peace Treaties, on settling the disputes in question amicably, the true reach of Article 304 of the Treaty of Trianon and Article 320 of the Treaty of Saint-Germain could have been – as is evidenced by the number of applications initially submitted to the Council[253] – far greater than the number of arbitrations ultimately held pursuant to the two articles. There is little doubt that these arbitrations that never materialised would have involved similar issues, that they most likely would have been, in light of the Council's propensity to appoint one and the same arbitrators, decided by similarly constituted tribunals, and that they would have, as a result, featured both similar conceptual approaches and similar practical solutions. Thus, although this section has recounted three historical ISAs that saw arbitrators direct state conduct while acting as primary decisions makers, had circumstances been a little different, there very likely could have been plenty more, perhaps even dozens of, such instances. While the three Peace Treaty railway arbitrations thus remain exceptional testaments to the capacity of historical ISA tribunals to direct state conduct by acting as primary decision-makers, they therefore provide but a taste of the

253 See n 139.

true potential carried in this respect by the provisions providing for ISA under the World War I Peace Treaties.

4 Historical Investor-State Arbitration as a Means of Directing State Conduct: A Recurring Theme

As the preceding discussion of the *Czechoslovakian Administration v. RCA* case and the Peace Treaty railway arbitrations would thus indicate, at the time when Dupuy's decision in *Texaco v. Libya* was handed down in the 1970s, it had, at the least, hardly been unprecedented for tribunals in historical ISA to take upon themselves to direct state conduct. One could, of course, nonetheless still legitimately question whether these antecedent cases were themselves but mere early progenitors of such practice, likewise exceptional in their nature. An examination of historical ISA's track record suggests otherwise, as one does not have to look very far to come across several other historical ISAs with a similar pattern.

One such instance is certainly the late 1920s *Rialet v. Ethiopia* arbitration.[254] The underlying dispute concerned the operation of a concession for the exploitation of an alcohol monopoly in Ethiopia that had been granted to Rialet in the mid-1920s. Under the concession, Rialet had acquired, for a fifty-year period, the right to manufacture, distil, import and export alcohol on behalf of Ethiopia's State Liquor Board. While the parties' relations had been troublesome from the outset, the straw that broke the camel's back was the passing by Ethiopia, in response to the perceived insufficient production of alcohol by Rialet, of a regulation that opened up the import of alcohol to the public and halved excise duties. In response, convinced that such measures violated its contractual rights and made its operations unviable, Rialet ceased the operation of the monopoly and liquidated its stock. By a *comporomis* signed in May of 1928,[255] the matter was submitted to a five-member tribunal chaired by another former president of, and at the time sitting judge at, the PCIJ, BCJ Loder, with both sides asking the tribunal to assign the blame for the failure of the concession to the opposing party and order damages accordingly.[256]

254 *La Societe Rialet v The Government of Ethiopia* (1929) 8 Recueil des Décisions des Tribunaux Arbitraux Mixtes Institués par les Traités de Paix 742.

255 It appears that the underlying agreements also contained an arbitration clause. See ibid 749.

256 Ibid 742–745 and 747–748. The remaining arbitrators were: Belgian lawyer, statesman and at the time governor of the National Bank of Belgium, Louis Franck; French law professor and former president of the Institute of International Law (as had been Loder and Poli-

The tribunal's award was delivered in Paris on 15 January 1929. While relatively short, the award was anything but unremarkable. Among the award's most distinguishable features were the tribunal's classification of the parties' underlying relationship as one of public, rather than private law, as well as its undisguised circumvention of Ethiopian law. More pertinently for present purposes, especially in light of the tribunal's aforementioned conceptualisation of the parties' relationship as one of public law, an equally interesting aspect of the award was the arbitrators' choice, in what was yet another instance of a historical ISA tribunal directing state conduct, to order Ethiopia to take over the company's property.

In dealing with the matter submitted to it, the tribunal's first step was to determine the nature of the parties' legal relationship and the corresponding applicable law. While Rialet had argued that the concession was a regular contract of private law, the tribunal disagreed; in its view, a state monopoly was by nature a public service and the fact that its exploitation had been entrusted to a private party did not change its character. Accordingly, the tribunal declared that the contract was to be deemed a public service concession. While the tribunal noted that, in such circumstances, it would ordinarily be the administrative law of the country of the monopoly which would govern the concession, in this particular instance it was 'European public law' ('le droit public européen') that came to be applied. The tribunal drew such a conclusion, which allowed it to eschew the application of Ethiopian law, from what it described as the parties' common wish, in light of the recognition by the Ethiopian Government that administrative law had not yet been developed in Ethiopia, to comply with the law and practice of the European countries regarding public services concessions.[257]

Regarding Rialet's claim that its alleged exclusive right to import alcohol had been violated, the tribunal disagreed that the concession had granted such a right to the company. In the tribunal's view, the said right had (among others) been reserved by Ethiopian regulations for the State Liquor Board and could not be diminished beyond the limitations imposed by explicit exceptions. While such exceptions could have been included in the concession, the tribunal deemed that this had not been the case. Accordingly, the tribunal concluded that the granting of the right of importation to other traders did not

---

tis), Charles Lyon-Caen; Greek law professor and diplomat, Nikolaos Politis; and French law professor Georges Ripert (who had later sat as arbitrator also in *La Société Européenne d'Etudes et d'Entreprises* (SEEE) *v The Popular Federative Republic of Yugoslavia*).

257 Ultimately, however, this was of secondary importance to the tribunal, as the contract was, per its own terms, based on 'generally accepted principles of law'. See ibid 748–749.

violate the concession and could thus not serve as a justification for Rialet's cessation of the exploitation of the monopoly.[258]

For the tribunal, the more important aspect was the decision to reduce the rate of the excise duties for imported spirits. The tribunal acknowledged that the state had freedom of action in this respect, irrespective of Rialet's position on the matter; however, even had this not been the case, as a concessionaire for the exploitation of a public monopoly, Rialet would in any event not have been entitled to stop its operation so suddenly (especially since the contract had provided for arbitration in case of potential disputes). That being said, the tribunal also considered that the State Liquor Board had not fully accounted for the fact that the effects of its decision would make it impossible for Rialet to operate on a commercial basis in light of the heightened competition that resulted from increased importation. The tribunal therefore held that, even if the State Liquor Board was entitled to adopt the disputed measure, the measure was nonetheless to be deemed an abuse of rights, thus depriving Ethiopia of the right to request damages. The tribunal similarly considered Rialet's damages claim unfounded.[259]

Overall, the tribunal concluded that the failure of the enterprise was the fault of both sides[260] and that the termination of their contractual relationship (as both sides had requested) was inevitable considering the lack of joint co-operation needed for its proper functioning. Accordingly, the tribunal declared the contractual arrangements relating to the concession terminated. Crucially, as a result of this decision, the tribunal then decided that Ethiopia was, as had apparently been envisioned by the concession upon its expiration, to take over all of Rialet's property in Ethiopia, as well as the assets that had previously been expropriated (in Rialet's favour) for the purpose of the monopoly.[261] Rialet, for its part, was ordered to transfer the property in question to Ethiopia.

Much like the tribunals in the Peace Treaty railway arbitrations, then, the arbitrators in *Rialet v. Ethiopia* had instructed a state to take over the property of a private enterprise, irrespective of volition. That the tribunal opted for this course of action perhaps leaves an even deeper imprint considering that it had explicitly rejected Rialet's contention that the parties' underlying relationship was merely one of private law, characterising it instead as a public service concession. What in any event remains certain, is that, in proceeding to instruct Ethiopia's conduct in this manner, the tribunal's decision further enhances the

---

258 Ibid 749.
259 Ibid 749–750.
260 See ibid 744–745.
261 See ibid 750–751.

image conveyed by the historical ISAs previously discussed in this Chapter – that of historical ISA tribunals taking upon themselves to direct state conduct.

Yet another case illustrative of this propensity by historical ISA is the 1930s *Greek Telephone Company Case.*[262] In what was a highly sensitive issue with potentially significant repercussions for the organisation of the Greek telephone network, the problem that was put before the arbitrators in this case required them to decide whether a foreign private company was entitled to have an important public utility transferred to its operation, set to last almost a decade and a half. In deciding this question, once again, the tribunal seemed to have little doubt about its competence (although, as is discussed below, not without certain limitations) to impose upon the state instructions regarding the behaviour required of it.

The case arose from the (re)construction by a German company, Siemens & Halske AG, of a set of local and long-distance telephone networks in Greece, which were, following (re)construction, to be transferred to its local subsidiary for operation. While the local networks were constructed and transferred to the company as contractually envisioned, certain complications arose regarding the long-distance network. Namely, the contract pertaining to the long-distance network had provided that the concessionaire was to reconstruct a part of the existing network, as well as to construct certain new long-distance telephone lines. The exact lines to which these obligations pertained were to be specified by later agreement between the parties; once (re)constructed, the lines were then to be maintained and operated by the German company's local subsidiary for thirteen years.[263] Problems, however, ensued due to the fact that the Greek government had, upon its own request, itself (re)constructed parts of the long-distance network. When, following the completion of the works, the company requested that the long-distance network be transferred to it, Greece refused, arguing that the company was not entitled to have the whole network transferred. Eventually, the matter was submitted to arbitration under the relevant arbitration clause.

In the proceedings, the company maintained both that it was itself obligated to operate the entirety of Greece's long-distance network and that Greece was, for its part, required to transfer the said network to the company. The company moreover claimed a right to damages on account of the government's refusal to make the transfer. Greece, on the other hand, denied that it was under any

262 *Greek Telephone Company v The Government of Greece*, Award (3 January 1935), reported in J Gillis Wetter and Stephen M Schwebel, 'Some Little-Known Cases on Concessions' (1964) 40 Brit YBIL 183, 216.

263 For the relevant extracts from the concession, see ibid 217–218.

obligation to transfer the network, arguing not only that the contract was unclear and incomplete, but also that it was inoperable, as it would have led to the impracticable result of only a part of the network being transferred to the company. In terms of the existence of the company's alleged right to maintain and operate the long-distance network, Greece argued that the contract was not two-sided so that there would be mutually existing rights and obligations, but that, insofar as the maintenance and operation of the long-distance network was concerned, it merely operated in the government's favour.[264]

The tribunal, which consisted of three Greek nationals, handed down its award (in Greek) on 3 January 1935 in Athens.[265] The tribunal's decision, although described by Wetter and Schwebel as 'not the most lucid of awards', certainly is an intriguing one, not least because the tribunal, albeit without specifying the relevant applicable law, at several junctures in its interpretive process refers to 'a general rule of law' or a 'general principle of public law'.[266] For present purposes, however, it is the tribunal's ultimate decision, and the resulting instruction to the parties (i.e. Greece), rather than the process through which the tribunal arrived there, that is of primary interest.

In the award, the tribunal emphasised that the part of the network to be transferred to the company was to be defined in a special subsequent arrangement that was to be made pursuant to the contract. Accordingly, the tribunal saw no contractual basis for either Greece's contention that it could avoid transferring the network to the company on the account of the contract being an unequal one or for the company's argument that it was entitled to have the entire network transferred. The company's right to have at least a part of the network transferred to it, however, was unquestionable. With this in mind, the tribunal went on to assess if such a transfer would, nonetheless, be impossible. While the tribunal noted that, in principle, it was possible to have a telephone system operated by more than one operator, it acknowledged that transferring to the company only the parts of the network to which it was contractually entitled would be problematic, as these parts did not necessarily constitute independent units. An additional challenge was posed by the fact that some of the lines had in fact been constructed by the government instead of the company, which lines the tribunal was not certain that Greece was contractually obligated to transfer.

Based on these findings, the tribunal decided that only the country's main telephone lines, capable of being operated independently, and not the entire

264 Ibid 217–219.

265 See ibid 216.

266 Ibid 221.

long-distance network, were practicable to be transferred to the company. The Corinth-Athens-Thessaloniki line, which was the main and the most profitable line within the country, satisfied these criteria; it was thus deemed by the tribunal to provide sufficient satisfaction to the claimant company. Accordingly, the tribunal ordered Greece to transfer this line to the company. The tribunal moreover acknowledged that the company was entitled to have transferred to it all parts of the network which it had (re)constructed; however, in light of the aforementioned impracticability of such a solution, the arbitrators held that the company had the right to full compensation due to Greece's failure to transfer the said lines. While it appears to have been uncertain whether the company also had the right to have transferred to it the lines that had in reality been (re) constructed by the Government, in light of certain reservations that had been made by the company when this arrangement was made, the arbitrators found that the company was nonetheless entitled to 'reasonable' (in contrast to the aforementioned full) compensation for not having these lines transferred.[267]

A central element of the tribunal's decision, then, was its order for Greece to transfer the Corinth-Athens-Thessaloniki line, a public utility telecommunications line that was at the time the most important one in Greece, to the company. Although the tribunal admittedly held that Greece had the right, on account of important state interests, to refuse to transfer all parts of the long-distance network to the company (against, of course, the payment of proper compensation),[268] this in no way negates the conclusion that the tribunal deemed itself competent to instruct the state on its required conduct in a matter relating to the operation of public utilities. Even if the tribunal, giving recognition to the sovereign rights of one of the disputing parties, did allow for an alternative possibility in which Greece would refuse to make the transfer, the fact remains that its primary solution was to order Greece to transfer the line to the company. Accordingly, there can be no question that the *Greek Telephone Company Case* stands as yet another exemplification of the practice by historical ISA tribunals to direct state conduct.

---

267 The tribunal did not actually order compensation, as the company had indicated that the tribunal's recognition of its right to compensation would be sufficient. See ibid 221.

268 On this point, the tribunal (as quoted in ibid 220–221) unanimously noted that:

> "the State has the right to refuse a transfer of the maintenance and operation to the Company by virtue of the general principle of public law that under contracts concluded between a State and third parties, the State, in spite of being contractually bound, retains its superiority *vis-à-vis* the other party and is always entitled, when important State interests so demand, to renounce the contract, on the condition that it pay due compensation to the contracting party."

Another similar example of a tribunal in a historical ISA directing state conduct, likewise involving Greece, is offered by one of the numerous arbitrations that arose out of a 1925 Greek public utility concession (several of these cases, together with the underlying concession, are discussed in detail in Chapter 5). The underlying dispute arose between one of the local companies established pursuant to the concession, Hellenic Electric Railways Ltd, and Greece, over a dispute involving a social security scheme for the company's retired workers. Although very short – but a few pages long – the award handed down in this case nonetheless reinforces with equal vigour the account that has been advanced by the other historical ISAs recounted in this Chapter. In the 31 August 1935 award,[269] the tribunal, chaired by Belgian politician and former delegate to the League of Nations, Louis de Brouckere,[270] laid out a number of detailed instructions for the parties on how to secure funds for the social security scheme. In particular, the tribunal instructed Greece to give the required approval for the company to increase its ticket prices, as well as to introduce an equivalent tax on the tickets of private buses operating along the same route. The thus collected funds were, up to a certain amount, then to be paid into a special fund established in favour of the company's retired employees, upon which the collection of funds was to be ceased. In making the award, the tribunal thus not only instructed Greece on how to act in this particular instance, but did so in a manner that related to the giving of necessary government approval, as well as taxation matters, in the process determining the social security status of the company's retired workers. What is more, such a course of action by the tribunal can hardly be said to have been out of character for tribunals established under this particular public utility concession, as some of the other tribunals are known to have adopted decisions of comparable scope.[271] The practice by the tribunals established under this Greek public utility concession in directing state conduct thus fits squarely within, and further reinforces, the pattern described in this Chapter.

---

269 *Hellenic Electric Railways Ltd v The Greek State*, Award (31 August 1935). The award (in French), together with the related materials, is available in the International Labour Office (ILO) Archives: AR 1/26/11/1.

270 The two remaining arbitrators were Alexander Wamwetzos and Georges Mantas.

271 For example, another tribunal chaired by de Brouckere had previously in detail prescribed how a public transport route between Athens and Piraeus was to be operated (including by determining the maximum number of allowed buses and the minimum price of bus tickets that could be set by the competent Greek ministry). See *Hellenic Electric Railways Ltd v The Greek State*, Award (23 December 1933). The award (in French), together with related materials, is available in the ILO Archives: AR 1/26/10/1. See also ch 5 and Wetter and Schwebel (n 262) 194–210.

Finally, and rather importantly, the capacity of historical ISA tribunals to direct state conduct cannot be said to have merely been a construct of arbitral practice – this capacity was also known to have been given explicit sanction by states through international treaties. One notable example concerns the Franco-Algerian agreements that arose out of Algerian independence, and which provided for direct arbitral recourse against the Algerian state for companies operating in the hydrocarbons sector. These agreements conveyed extremely broad powers upon the tribunals that were to be set up to resolve potential disputes; crucially, this included the capacity by a tribunal to 'order the recision of any action inconsistent with applicable laws', to grant relief, in addition to monetary compensation, 'through any other means which it deems appropriate',[272] as well as to issue injunctive relief.[273] These provisions, which essentially left the arbitrators unconstrained in terms of the remedy they could order, undoubtedly provided the requisite normative framework that would allow the tribunals set up pursuant to them to direct the conduct of the states involved. Such powers bestowed upon the arbitrators were made all the more potent when considering that the tribunals' awards were made self-executory.[274] Although the awards that were handed down pursuant to these Franco-Algerian treaties could unfortunately not be located, several historical ISAs are known to have been held pursuant to these provisions.[275]

It would thus appear that, when viewed as examples of historical ISA tribunals directing state conduct, the *Czechoslovakian Administration v. RCA* case and the Peace Treaty railway arbitrations were hardly isolated instances. While it would, on the basis of the historical ISAs that have been recalled in this section,[276] perhaps be an overstatement to describe the practice of historical ISA tribunals directing state conduct as regular or commonplace, what does

---

272 Algeria-France Oil Accord (signed 29 July 1965) (1965) 4 ILM 809, 911 (art 174). See also Agreement on Arbitration of Disputes between Algeria and France Regarding Exploitation of the Saharan Subsoil (signed 26 June 1963) (1963) 2 ILM 1025, 1029 (Annex art 7).

273 Franco-Algerian Arbitration Agreement Regarding Exploitation of the Saharan Subsoil (n 272) 1028 (Annex art 5).

274 Algeria-France Oil Accord (n 272) 912 (art 178); Franco-Algerian Arbitration Agreement Regarding Exploitation of the Saharan Subsoil (n 272) 1025 (art 4).

275 AM Stuyt (ed), *Survey of International Arbitrations: 1794–1989* (Martinus Nijhoff 1990) 537 and 540–542.

276 To be sure, the cases discussed in this section by no means exhaust the list of historical ISAs where tribunals can be observed to have directed state conduct. One further such example is *Saudi Arabia v ARAMCO*, where the tribunal through its award *inter alia* determined which actions Saudi Arabia could or could not take in its relations with the concessionaire company. See *Saudi Arabia v Arabian American Oil Company (ARAMCO)* (1963) 27 ILR 117, 226–228. See also the *Duff v Kelantan I* arbitration discussed in ch 3,

appear certain is that, when viewed against the broader backdrop of historical ISA, these cases were hardly unprecedented, or even unorthodox. Moreover, not only were instances where historical ISA tribunals directed state conduct observed with relative frequency in practice, but their power to do so is also known to have been given formal sanction by states through international treaties. Against this background, the *Czechoslovakian Administration v. RCA* case and the Peace Treaty railway arbitrations, discussed in the previous sections, must thus be approached with the understanding that they were not mere historical eccentricities or aberrations, but rather part and parcel of a more recognisable and stable trend in historical ISA.

5 Conclusions

While it is perhaps inevitable that the accounts of the historical ISAs that this Chapter has offered will alter how the Libyan oil arbitrations discussed at the Chapter's very beginning are perceived within the context of the capacity of ISA tribunals to direct state conduct, the preceding pages were intended neither as a vindication of Dupuy's *Texaco v. Libya* award nor as a critique of Judge Lagergren's approach in *BP v. Libya*. Dupuy's reasoning, and in particular his lack of reference to relevant previous precedent from historical ISA in support of his finding, certainly left plenty to be desired. Meanwhile, Judge Lagergren's dismissal of the relevance of several (but by no means all) of the cases discussed within this Chapter for the matter before him can probably by and large be explained by the fact that his focus was narrowly aimed at the specific set of circumstances and questions that were required for his decision (such as e.g. whether one could deduce the existence of a principle of international law from the available practice). In the grand scheme of things, one must not lose sight of the fact that these arbitrators were primarily concerned with the specific factual matrices that had been put before them and that their reasoning very likely reflected, and was shaped by, the respective disputing parties' arguments.

For this reason, the emphasis here, rather than being on how these few prominent historical ISAs are to be viewed, is on how the capacity of historical ISA tribunals to direct state conduct should be perceived within the broader context of historical ISA. The crucial takeaway from this Chapter, thus, is that, contrary to the impression that the treatment of this question in the Libyan

---

where the arbitrator decided upon the right of the Kelantan government to construct a railway along a particular route.

oil arbitrations might have contributed to, the Libyan arbitrations were but a few of the many historical ISAs where this question was raised and decided. Indeed, as the ISAs recounted in depth in this Chapter have illustrated, historical ISA was far from unacquainted with the practice of arbitrators taking upon themselves to instruct states on how to conduct their official business. This, in particular, follows from the *Czechoslovakian Administration v. RCA* case and the Peace Treaty railway arbitrations, each of which have served to convey a different modality of historical ISA's propensity to direct state conduct. For its part, the *Czechoslovakian Administration v. RCA* arbitration encapsulated historical ISA's capacity to review, as a secondary decision-maker, the permissibility of, and ultimately as a result to restrain, the intended conduct of a state entity in relation to a public utility service. Meanwhile, while the tribunals in the Peace Treaty railway arbitrations similarly took upon themselves to instruct the conduct of the involved states regarding the reorganisation of railway systems, they did so not by merely pronouncing on the permissibility of their intended conduct, but rather as a decision-maker determining in the first place the chosen course of conduct instead of the said states. Notably, and rather importantly, as section 4 has illustrated, the *Czechoslovakian Administration v. RCA* case and the Peace Treaty railway arbitrations were by far not the only such examples in historical ISA. Thus, even if not necessarily something that took place with regular frequency, the phenomenon of tribunals directing states on their conduct at least constituted a body of jurisprudence that was both substantial and varied enough that it cannot be discounted as a mere historical curiosity or a one-off occurrence limited to a specific set of circumstances.

As important as it is to recognise the propensity of historical ISA tribunals to direct state conduct, however, it is perhaps even more crucial to properly appreciate the sphere of activity within which they did so. Whether it was deciding on if and how public utilities were to be installed and operated, how cross-border railways systems were to be reorganised, how social security schemes were to be operationalised, or whether or not expropriation was to be carried out, these were not matters in which states were acting as if they were no different from any other potential disputing party. Instead, they were matters that were either essential to how these state entities performed their official capacities or even matters that fell within their exclusive purview of competence. It was therefore not just that the historical ISA tribunals were known to have directed state conduct, but that they did so specifically with respect to how the states in question were to govern.

As a final matter, it is in this context equally relevant to underscore that historical ISA tribunals not only took upon themselves to direct state conduct in such governance-related matters, but also that their decisions are known to have in fact influenced the conduct of the state entities to which they were addressed. At least one instance where such validation of the tribunal's authority to direct the conduct of the involved state entity can be observed is the *Czechoslovakian Administration v. RCA* arbitration, where The Czechoslovakian Administration for several years abstained from opening a second direct radio-telegraphic circuit to the US in light of the tribunal's decision that such a course of action was not permitted. While this is obviously something on which evidence is particularly difficult to obtain, there are other examples that suggest that The Czechoslovakian Administration was not alone in treating a tribunal's pronunciation as to its freedom of action as determinative.[277] With this in mind, it is difficult to resist the conclusion that historical ISA tribunals' direction of state conduct was no mere unrecognised claim to such authority, but that it was, at least in some instances, actually capable of altering the manner in which the states concerned conducted their official business.

277 See, for example, Saudi Arabia's compliance with the *Saudi Arabia v ARAMCO* award, referred to in Robert B von Mehren and P Nicholas Kourides, 'International Arbitrations between States and Foreign Private Parties: The Libyan Nationalization Cases' (1981) 75 AJIL 476, 538. Likewise, as previously described in ch 3, in the *Duff v Kelantan I* arbitration, the Kelantan government appears to have considered the arbitrator's pronunciation as to its right to construct a railway along a particular route as controlling.

CHAPTER 5

Developing the Law through Historical Investor-State Arbitration

1 Introduction

If one were to attempt to convey in simple terms what took place in historical investor-state arbitration (ISA) – what it was that the historical ISA tribunals did – any given explanation would most likely center around the observation that these tribunals resolved disputes that had been submitted to them by applying the relevant legal norms. While not *per se* untrue, that such a description would equally be an oversimplification that falls considerably short of capturing the full gamut of what took place within historical ISA should have already been obvious from Chapter 2, which discussed the indeterminacy of the normative structures within which these historical tribunals operated. Indeed, as Chapter 2 indicated, reducing what occurred in historical ISA to the mere application of the law to the facts of a particular dispute fails to account for the fact that these historical tribunals also contributed to the development of the very legal norms that they (as well as subsequent tribunals) were applying. Indeed, historical ISA tribunals were not so much passive recipients of a pre-constructed normative architecture under which a set of relevant facts was to be subsumed as they were an active ingredient in its very construction and development. It is this role of historical ISA in contributing to the development of the law that governed investor-state relations that this Chapter explores.

Before proceeding, however, a brief explanation is in order as to what is for present purposes understood by historical ISA's contribution to developing the law. It should at the outset be noted that such 'development of the law' should not be understood as being equivalent to, nor should it be compared to, the type of formal legislative processes exercised by national parliaments or other bodies with such legislative prerogatives. Undoubtedly, historical ISA's contribution to developing the law was not of the direct normative effect that characterises legislation passed by national parliaments or similar legislative bodies, so that it could independently create or modify norms in a manner that was as such legally binding. Indeed, nominally, decisions by historical ISA tribunals did not have legally binding effect except for the parties to a particular dispute; and even then, that binding effect was limited to the specific matter in dispute and was ostensibly derived from the pre-existing content of the applicable legal

 | DOI:10.1163/9789004733824_006

norms. That being said, as is discussed below, in performing their formal role as dispute resolution bodies, these historical ISA tribunals were nonetheless undeniably not only the determinators of a preconceived meaning and content of legal norms, but were also the creators, or developers, of this very meaning and content; in other words, they exerted a certain degree of influence, referred to here as normative influence, over the content of legal norms. Such normative influence, in turn, was defined by the historical ISA tribunals' capacity to, through their decisions, affect how legal norms developed or came to be understood. It manifested itself through various modalities, whether it be by the tribunals' introduction of new precedent in the practice of historical ISA that was later adopted within more formalised processes of norm creation, by affecting through their decisions how certain legal norms came to be interpreted by the relevant actors, or by some other means. It is through such processes, then – processes that, albeit in and of themselves fell short of being independent sources of norm generation, nonetheless exerted a certain degree of normative influence over the content of such norms – that historical ISA is understood to have partaken in developing the law relevant to investor-state relations.

It is here further relevant to note that the manner in which historical ISA contributed to such development of the law governing the investor-state dynamic was not one-dimensional. Namely, just like the normative frameworks that governed historical ISA had operated on various levels of generality – ranging from contractual norms that specifically governed a particular investor-state relationship to norms of more general, if not universal, application – so too was the role of historical ISA in contributing to the development of such normative frameworks discernible at different levels of generality, even if it may not have followed an identical pattern. The Chapter identifies three such levels of generality at which historical ISA is observed to have contributed to developing the law, distinguishable depending on the type of investor-state relationship that a tribunal's normative influence was able to reach – whether it was just the disputing parties' relationship, the relationship between one of the disputing parties and a third party, or an investor-state relationship wholly unconnected to either of the disputing parties. These different levels of generality can best be visualised as corresponding to concentric circles, and the remainder of the Chapter is structured so as to follow this gradation, progressing from a historical ISA tribunal's normative influence that was closest to the tribunal itself and the disputing parties to that which was wholly unrelated to them.[1]

1 Although it does not draw upon it, this gradation may to an extent be reminiscent of the work by Alter, Helfer, and Madsen, who use the concept of concentric circles in their work on

At the *narrowest level of generality*, historical ISA's role in developing the law was of relevance just to the two disputing parties. It implied, as was discussed in Chapter 2, that the tribunals were not merely applying the legal rules relevant for resolving the particular dispute between these parties, but were also actively participating in giving them normative content – content that would then possibly go on to influence the future relations between the two disputing parties (if they were to continue following the arbitration). An illustrative example of the development of the law at this narrowest level of generality by historical ISA tribunals is provided through an in-depth account of a series of arbitrations that arose from a 1920s Greek public utility concession, which represent perhaps the clearest observed instance of such practice by historical ISA tribunals (2). At the *intermediate level of generality*, the tribunals' decisions were observed to exert influence over not only the normative frameworks governing the relations between the particular disputing parties, but also those normative frameworks governing the relations between one of the parties to the dispute before the tribunal and a completely unrelated third party. Here, the main conduit for spreading the tribunal's normative influence was one of the disputing parties, by way of its adoption of a tribunal's decision as an authoritative pronunciation on the meaning of norms regulating a particular matter and adjusting its other similar relationships accordingly. How historical ISA operated to contribute to the development of the law at this intermediate level of generality is demonstrated by recounting in detail the 1930s *Radio Corporation of America* (RCA) *v. China* arbitration, the fallout from which saw the RCA adjust a number of its relationships with third-party telegraph administrations (3). Finally, at the broadest level of generality, the decisions by historical ISA tribunals exhibited the capacity to contribute to the development of norms governing investor-state relations that were of *general application*, in that they potentially applied to any investor-state relationship. While this by

the authority of international courts. Alter, Helfer, and Madsen, however, recognise five types of *de facto* authority by international courts ('no authority', 'narrow authority', 'intermediate authority', 'extensive authority' and 'popular authority'), while their categorisation is based on somewhat different delineating factors than the present categorisation, which centres on whether the tribunals' role in contributing to the development of the law was observed in a relationship that included (one or both of) the disputing parties. Thus, categories that might at face value appear equivalent do not actually fully overlap under these two categorisations; for example, what Alter, Helfer, and Madsen describe as 'intermediate authority' would, because it concerns actors that need not necessarily be in a relationship with either of the disputing parties, in the present categorisation correspond not to the intermediate, but to the broadest level of generality. See Karen J Alter, Laurence R Helfer and Mikael Rask Madsen, 'How Context Shapes the Authority of International Courts' in Karen J Alter, Laurence R Helfer and Mikael Rask Madsen (eds), *International Court Authority* (OUP 2018) 24.

no means implied that these historical ISA awards had the weight of formally biding precedent that is accorded to judicial decisions in some legal systems, they did nonetheless exert a certain level of normative influence over how relevant third parties – primarily parties to subsequent investor-state disputes and investor-state tribunals tasked with resolving such disputes – came to understand and interpret norms governing investor-state relations, and thus also on how future investor-state disputes were to be resolved (4). These instances of historical ISA's extended normative influence, even if observable with varying frequency at each of the described levels of generality, when taken together reveal a consistent contribution by historical ISA to the development of the normative frameworks that governed investor-state relations. As such, they thus operate to further enhance the perception of historical ISA as a mechanism that influenced how investor-state relations were governed (5).

As a final preliminary remark, it is crucial to stress that, at all of these different levels of generality at which historical ISA contributed to the development of the law, the type of normativity being generated by the historical ISA tribunals was of a particular character. Namely, because the historical ISAs took place within the domain of investor-state interaction – and in light of the resulting types of issues and interests that were involved in arbitrations stemming from these kinds of interactions (see Chapter 2) – the development of the law which transpired in historical ISA was qualitatively distinguishable from that which might have occurred through arbitration that only involved private entities. Indeed, unlike in this latter instance, the normative influence being exerted through the decisions by historical ISA tribunals often, if not predominantly, concerned the behaviour of states in their conduct of official business – it concerned how they governed. Accordingly, the underlying argument in this Chapter regarding historical ISA's role in developing the law is two-pronged – that is, the argument is not just that historical ISA tribunals partook in the development of certain legal norms and rules, but also that they did so specifically with respect to legal norms and rules that were relevant for the future functioning of the investor-state dynamic, including in relation to how states were, within this context, to govern.

2 Developing the Law for the Disputing Parties: The Power and Traction Concession in Greece

This section explores the role of historical ISA in developing the law that occurred at the *narrowest level of generality* – for the disputing parties partaking in the particular arbitration. Its aim is not to explain *why* historical ISA tribunals should be understood to have had an active role in constructing the meaning of the very norms that they were applying in each particular instance instead of as merely having applied legal rules of an entirely pre-determined content to the relevant factual circumstances – that was discussed in Chapter 2. Rather, the aim of the section is to demonstrate in detail on a concrete historical example *how* exactly this took place, as well as, equally importantly, to show what this creative role by historical ISA tribunals implied when the relationship for which it was exercised was one between a private investor and a state. In pursuing these objectives, the remainder of the section examines in depth a series of arbitrations that arose under a 1920s Greek public utility concession.

2.1 *The Power and Traction Concession*

The concession in question was signed in 1925 (the 1925 Concession), during the dictatorship of General Theodoros Pangalos.[2] It provided the concessionaires, led by an English enterprise (the Power and Traction Company),[3] with comprehensive rights regarding certain public utilities in the Athens area, including the installation and operation of tram and bus lines and the supply of electric energy.[4] In order for the 1925 Concession to be realised, a number of local subsidiaries were created.[5]

Following General Pangalos' downfall, the 1925 Concession faced strong opposition. The legitimacy of the 1925 Concession, which had not been ratified

2 While the concession itself was signed during the rule of Pangalos, the underlying negotiations had already been underway. See William J Hausman, Peter Hertner and Mira Wilkins, *Global Electrification: Multinational Enterprise and International Finance in the History of Light and Power, 1878–2007* (CUP 2008) 163–164. The UK government played an important role in the granting of the concession and the British Treasury even provided a guarantee for the necessary £2 million loan. See ibid 164; Ioanna Pepelasis Minoglou, 'The Greek State and The International Financial Community, 1922–1932: Demystifying the "Foreign Factor"' (PhD thesis, London School of Economics and Political Science 1993) 88 <http://etheses.lse.ac.uk/2590/> accessed 27 September 2024; Margarita Dritsas, 'Foreign Capital and Greek Development in a Historical Perspective' (1993) Uppsala Papers in Economic History – Working Paper No 10, 20–21 <https://www.diva-portal.org/smash/get/diva2:128582/FULLTEXT01.pdf> accessed 27 September 2024. The text of the 1925 Concession is available in the International Labour Office (ILO) archives. See ILO Archives: AR 1–26–18.

3 The local participant in the project, the Syndicat d'Etudes et Entreprises, was included on the insistence of Power and Traction. See Minoglou (n 2) 219.

4 See Letter from (signature illegible) to His Majesty's Principal Secretary of State for Foreign Affairs (16 July 1950) (UK National Archives: FO 371/87759).

5 See J Gillis Wetter and Stephen M Schwebel, 'Some Little-Known Cases on Concessions' (1964) 40 Brit YBIL 183, 194.

by parliament (as the legislature had been suspended by General Pangalos),[6] was called into question both in parliament[7] and on the streets,[8] its terms having been perceived as 'scandalous'.[9] Despite protests by the general public and extensive criticism of the 1925 Concession during parliamentary debates (including on account that it would seriously harm certain industry sectors, result in an increase of railway ticket prices, and that the fiscal benefits granted to the company would incur significant losses for the Greek treasury),[10] the concession was nonetheless ultimately ratified with a strong majority by the Greek parliament, as the recently elected government staked its very survival on the approval of the 1925 Concession.[11] As an attempt to buy some good will for the concessionaires, the operation of the 1925 Concession was somewhat adjusted after ratification in order to better reflect the public interest.[12]

---

6 Minoglou (n 2) 154.

7 Telegram from HM representative in Athens (No 32) to FO (1 February 1927) (UK National Archives: FO 286/992); Copy of Letter from Percy Loraine to Sir Austen Chamberlain (5 February 1927) (UK National Archives: FO 286/992).

8 Telegram from HM representative in Athens (No 11) to Sir Austen Chamberlain (10 January 1927) (UK National Archives: FO 286/992); Telegram from HM representative in Athens (No 12) to Foreign Office (11 January 1927) (UK National Archives: FO 286/992); Telegram from HM representative to FO (1 February 1927) (n 7); Telegram from HM representative in Athens (No 43) to Sir Austen Chamberlain (8 February 1927) (UK National Archives: FO 286/992); Telegram from HM representative in Athens (No 47) to FO (9 February 1927) (UK National Archives: FO 286/992).

9 Minoglou (n 2) 154.

10 Letter from Loraine to Chamberlain (5 February 1927) (n 7).

11 Telegram from HM representative in Athens (No 50) to Sir Austen Chamberlain (11 February 1927) (UK National Archives: FO 286/992); Copy of Letter from Percy Loraine to Sir Austen Chamberlain (18 February 1927) (UK National Archives: FO 286/992). The majority with which the concession was ratified is somewhat deceptive, as the parliament was unanimous in its negative perception of the concession – all speakers, without exception, had characterised it as an 'evil' and the majority expressed their opinion that it should be eliminated. In light of this strong opposition, the British representative in Greece at one point felt compelled to intervene and remind the Greek government of the UK government's direct interest in the matter due the guarantee given by its treasury. See Copy of Letter from Percy Loraine to Monsieur Michalacopoulos, Minister for Foreign Affairs (9 February 1927) (UK National Archives: FO 286/992).

12 Copy of Letter from Societe Generale Hellenique, Hellenic Electric Railways, Societe Electrique de Production, Societe Electrique de Distrbution and Societe Electrique de Transports to the Minister of Communications (21 March 1927) (UK National Archives: FO 286/992); Copy of Letter from Minister I Metaxas to Societe Generale Hellenique, Hellenic Electric Railways, Societe Electrique de Production, Societe Electrique de Distrbution and Societe Electrique de Transports (22 March 1927) (UK National Archives: FO 286/992). This adjustment had already been envisioned prior to the concession's ratification and had even been used as an argument in parliament in order to ease the ratifica-

Despite this compromise on their part, however, the negative public perception of the concessionaires did not subside and the protests against them continued, sometimes even escalating to outbreaks of violence against their personnel.[13] Nor did, more importantly, the concessionaires' compromise prevent further problems with the operation of the 1925 Concession from arising before long.[14] Indeed, the years that ensued were marred by constant frictions between Greek authorities and the concessionaires on matters such as taxes and similar levies, the concessionaires' status under the 1925 Concession, safety regulations, etc.;[15] the most difficult of these numerous problems were eventually submitted to arbitration under the arbitration clause contained in the 1925 Concession.[16] While the arbitration clause did not state pursuant to which applicable law prospective disputes were to be resolved, it did, notably, provide that the tribunal chairman, should the party-appointed arbitrators fail to agree, would be 'the Director of the International Labour Office of the League of Nations or a person nominated by him'. Its seemingly limited scope notwithstanding, which merely provided for the Director of the International Labour Office (ILO) to act as tribunal chairman or appointing authority, this provision would in reality cause the ILO to become heavily involved with the disputes between Greece and the concessionaires in the coming years, essentially acting – in what was most probably a unique role for the international

tion process. The position of the British side, however, was that any discussion of possible alterations was only to be had following the concession's ratification, and that no changes were to be introduced into the text of the concession itself, but that additional arrangements were instead to be made as to how the concession was to be implemented. See Letter from Loraine to the Minister of Foreign Affairs (9 February 1927) (n 11); Letter from Loraine to Chamberlain (5 February 1927) (n 7).

13 See Dritsas (n 2) 21; Minoglou (n 2) 258 (describing that Power and Traction was often depicted in newspaper cartoons as 'a large beast'); Telegram (No 4) to Foreign Office (13 January 1934) (UK National Archives: FO 286/1123/190); Copy of Letter from Patrick Ramsay to Sir John Simon (23 March 1933) (UK National Archives: FO 286/1120/190); Note (signature illegible) to Morellet and Secretan (18 January 1935) (ILO Archives: AR 1/26/11).

14 See Copy of Letter from Percy Loraine to Monsieur Zaimis, President of the Council and Minister for Foreign Affairs, ad interim (2 December 1927) (UK National Archives: FO 286/992); 'Memorandum on Certain Differences Arising with the Greek Government Concerning the Interpretation and Fulfilment of the Power & Traction Concession of October 14th 1927' (1 December 1927) (UK National Archives: FO 286/992).

15 See the cases discussed in the remainder of this section, as well as in Wetter and Schwebel (n 5) 195–209. See also eg Copy of Letter from SP Waterlow to Sir John Simon (15 February 1934) (UK National Archives: FO 286/1123/190).

16 The 1925 Concession (n 2) art 49. An English translation of the arbitration clause is available in Wetter and Schwebel (n 5) 194–195.

organisation in its now century long existence – as the institution administering the arbitrations.[17]

The disputes between the Greek government and the concessionaires would, over the next several decades, result in more than a dozen arbitral awards.[18] Many of these awards provide some of the clearest historical examples of instances where ISA tribunals exercised an overtly creative role in relation to the relevant normative framework and are for this reason analyzed in more detail below. This role in developing the law for the parties in dispute taken on by the tribunals established under the 1925 Concession was all the more consequential considering that the arbitrations conducted on the basis of this concession gave rise, if not to an unprecedented, than certainly to an unusually high number of arbitral decisions between the same (or closely related) parties[19] over matters stemming from the same investor-state relationship. As such, this cluster of decisions provides invaluable insight into the impact that the role of ISA tribunals in developing the law can have on structuring an investor-state relationship, especially when the relationship in question is a continuing one and arbitration is not approached as an end-game to a relationship fractured beyond the point of no return.

17 Thus, hearings were regularly held, and awards handed down, at the ILO offices, while ILO staff assisted the tribunals in conducting the proceedings. The ILO's involvement was eventually scaled down so that it would continue to act as the appointing authority, but would no longer be involved in administering the arbitrations. See Letter from David L Pollock to David A Morse (25 June 1956) (ILO Archives: AR 1–26–6); Copy of Letter from Francis Wolf to David L Pollock (9 July 1956) (ILO Archives: AR 1–26–6); Copy of Note from Francis Wolf to The Director General (16 January 1958) (ILO Archives: AR 1–26–6); Note from Francis Wolf to Crosby (1 November 1956) (ILO Archives: AR 1–26–6).

18 Some of these awards were published by the Athens Piraeus Electricity Company Ltd in 1941 in a booklet titled *Arbitral Awards Issued in Application of Article 49 of the Agreement in Regard to the Supply of Electricity and Transport Services Dated 17 October 1925*. Summaries of these and some additional awards relating to the concession are given in Wetter and Schwebel (n 5) 194–210. The full text of several awards can be found in the ILO archives, which also contain what is most likely only a partially complete list of the arbitrations that arose under the concession. See 'Arbitrages Entre l'Etat Hellenique et des Compagnies Privees' (7 March 1958) (ILO Archives: AR 1–26).

19 While the concessionary companies that were parties to the arbitrations were nominally separate entities, considering that they were formed in order to carry out a single concession, which had in turn regulated the Greek state's potential disputes with all of the concessionaires through a single arbitration clause, it appears appropriate to treat all of the arbitrations arising under the 1925 Concession as belonging to a single cluster.

2.2 *The Arbitrations*

Five cases arbitrated under the 1925 Concession, two of which are analysed jointly as they concern closely related matters, are of particular interest for present purposes due to the tribunals' perspicuous role in developing the rules that would govern the disputing parties' future relations: the *Staff Regulations Case* (2.2.1), the *Truncated Tribunal Case* (2.2.2), the *Safety and Control Regulations Case* (2.2.3) and the *Social Contributions Cases* (2.2.4).

2.2.1 Staff Regulations Case

The first case of interest concerned an arbitration conducted in 1928 between Greece and one of the local companies established under the 1925 Concession, Hellenic Electric Railways Ltd, over a number of issues in relation to the company's administrative and financial independence regarding matters of employment.[20]

The company's administrative and financial independence had been rooted in Article 12 of the 1925 Concession, which provided that:

> [e]xcept as otherwise specifically provided in this concession *nothing in this concession shall be deemed to restrict the financial and administrative independence of the Company* or to restrict the right of the Company to carry on its undertaking until december 31st 1985 in the ordinary course of business.[21]

Simultaneously, however, a decree law through which the 1925 Concession had been ratified[22] envisioned that the concessionaires and their affiliated companies were to respect the existing obligations toward the staff of the companies that were being taken over pursuant to the 1925 Concession. Meanwhile, the company had also issued a letter to the Greek Ministry of Communications in order to explain and complete the obligations undertaken through the decree, in which it was stated that, in case of dismissal of a person currently employed, the concessionaires would undertake to either reemploy them in one of the

---

20 *The Greek State v Hellenic Electric Railways Ltd*, Award (6 March 1928) (*Staff Regulations Case*). The award is available in the ILO Archives: AR 1/26/2/1 and AR 1/26/11. ILO Archives: AR 1/26/2/1 contains the transcripts from the oral proceedings in the case. A summary of the award is available in Wetter and Schwebel (n 5) 195–200.

21 See *Staff Regulations Case* (n 20) 8. Emphasis added.

22 French and English versions of the decree law are available in ILO Archives: AR 1–26–18 and AR 1/26/2, respectively.

concessionaire companies or to compensate them for a certain minimum amount.[23]

The factual matrix that gave rise to the dispute was extremely complex and the dispute itself was not entirely clearly defined due to there being no formal *compromis*. The first signs of tension between the two sides came in October of 1926, when Greece's minister of communications informed the company that he was nominating three representatives to a staff council. The nomination was made based on a 1917 general staff regulation (the 1917 General Staff Regulation) that had been adopted pursuant to Greek legislation. In the company's view, however, this went against its administrative and financial independence guaranteed by the 1925 Concession, and the company indicated that it would soon be adopting its own staff regulations. The Greek minister of communications responded by claiming that, insofar as staff was concerned, the provision granting the company administrative and financial independence had been made inoperative by way of the decree law through which the 1925 Concession had been ratified (which had provided that all of the obligations of the existing companies *vis-à-vis* their Greek staff were to be observed once they were taken over by the concessionaries). While the company had in response maintained that the decree law pertained only to the contractual obligations of the predecessor companies, the minister of communications insisted that it covered all of their obligations toward their staff, including those based on the 1917 General Staff Regulation.[24]

Correspondence over the matter then temporarily ceased, and the issue was not mentioned during the negotiations on the implementation of the 1925 Concession that followed. At the end of these negotiations, the two sides exchanged letters, with the concessionaries asking the Greek state, and the Greek state accepting, to respect the letter and spirit of the 1925 Concession, particularly with respect to their administrative and financial independence, as well as to interpret it in a broad and conciliatory manner.[25]

It was not before long, however, that the rift between the two sides was reignited. The catalyst was a request by the Ministry of Communications, once more based on the 1917 General Staff Regulation, for the company to bring back an employee who had been released from military service. Unsurprisingly, the company again saw this as being incompatible with its administrative and financial independence, accepting the reinstatement only due to its proclaimed favourable stance towards former employees who were released

23 *Staff Regulations Case* (n 20) 8–9.

24 Ibid 7–9.

25 Ibid 9–10.

from military service. The ministry, meanwhile, took the position that the company was bound by all staff regulations that had the force of law and were applicable to all railway and tram companies in Greece. As the back-and-forth over the matter between the two sides was ongoing and with neither party yielding, Greece introduced a new point of contention – that the company had drawn up new staff regulations, but had not submitted them to the ministry for approval so that it could be determined whether they observed the workers' acquired rights under the 1925 decree law. In response, the company insisted that the new regulations were in line with the staff's acquired rights and implied that the question that could potentially be submitted for arbitration would be circumscribed to whether the employee's acquired rights had been respected. As Greece disagreed that the employees' acquired rights were unaffected, the arbitration was eventually initiated, with the ministry requesting that the new staff regulations not be applied until the arbitrators' award was issued.[26]

Rather fittingly, although perhaps also quite entirely coincidentally, the tribunal that was mandated with dealing with these sensitive issues of employee rights was presided by Albert Thomas, the director of an institution – the ILO – whose very founding purpose[27] was the concern for the conditions of labour.[28] Thomas was a French politician who had been the Director of the ILO from its inception until his untimely passing in 1932 (not long after awards in this and several other arbitrations under the 1925 Concession in which Thomas had acted as arbitrator were handed down).[29] Thomas' co-arbitrators were Percy Horsfall, an English banker with close connections to some of the concessionaire

26 Ibid 11–15.

27 See Treaty of Peace between the Allied and Associated Powers and Germany (signed 28 June 1919, entered into force 10 January 1920) (1919) 225 CTS 188 pt XIII, s 1. See also 'History of the ILO' <https://www.ilo.org/global/about-the-ilo/history/lang--en/index.htm> accessed 27 September 2024.

28 The concession provided that the role of chairman would, in case the parties could not agree, be assumed by the 'Director of the International Labour Office of the League of Nations or a person nominated by him'. See *Staff Regulations Case* (n 20) 1–2. It does not appear from the correspondence that lead to Thomas' appointment that his particular expertise, and its relation to the subject matter in dispute, was a relevant factor in the considerations regarding the choice of tribunal president. See Letter from Horsfall to H B Butler (18 October 1927) (ILO Archives: AR 1/26/2).

29 'Albert Thomas: Director of the International Labour Organization, 1919–1932' <https://www.ilo.org/global/about-the-ilo/how-the-ilo-works/ilo-director-general/former-directors-general/WCMS_192645/lang--en/index.htm> accessed 27 September 2024.

companies under the 1925 Concession (but not specifically Hellenic Electric Railways),[30] and a Greek railway inspector, Demetrios Schinas.

The tribunal's award is perhaps the most important, and interesting, of the awards handed down in the arbitrations held pursuant to the 1925 Concession. Not only did the award address several matters with broader societal implications, such as worker rights and the applicability of the Greek system of legislation to the company, but the tribunal openly recognised that, in deciding these issues, it was entering the arena of public law, appearing more than content to do so and even relying on what it termed 'general principles of public law' when deciding certain points. The relevance of the tribunal's award was only further augmented by the fact that the award was later invoked and relied upon as authoritative guidance in subsequent arbitrations under the 1925 Concession.[31] No less interesting an aspect of the tribunal's award, and one which serves as the main focus for present purposes, was the tribunal's role in not only applying to the case the relevant legal framework governing the parties' relations but also contributing to its development.

As the dispute had been submitted to the tribunal by the parties in a somewhat unclear manner, the tribunal's first order of business was to define exactly what was expected from it. The arbitrators set out the task before them as follows: to define the scope of the term 'acquired rights' of the staff and to determine the extent of the obligations falling on the company, all within the context of the 1925 decree law, the supplementary letter and the administrative and financial independence guaranteed to the company under the 1925 concession.[32]

As to acquired rights, the two disputing sides held starkly opposing views: while the company had understood the acquired rights of the existing staff as having been restricted to those set out in its letter to the government (more or less boiling down to the right of reemployment or proper compensation in case of dismissal), Greece maintained that they extended more broadly to essentially the entirety of the conditions of employment. The tribunal felt that there were good arguments in favour of the Greek government's position, as the 1925 decree law spoke of 'all' obligations towards existing staff, while the company's letter was not framed in a limiting manner; the implications of the 1925 decree law could thus not be restricted merely to those alleged by the company. In terms of Greece's argument that this meant that the company

30 For Horsfall's background, see 'Percy Horsfall: A Scholar in the City' (1965) 55 The Round Table 207. On how Horsfall's connections to the concessionary companies factored into his decision to accept (or not) the arbitrator appointment, see ch 2.

31 See in particular sub-section 2.2.4.

32 *Staff Regulations Case* (n 20) 15.

was bound by the 1917 General Staff Regulation, the tribunal observed that abstractly defining the meaning and scope of acquired rights, which had not been done by the interested parties, was a difficult task. On balance, the tribunal held that a broad interpretation of the term was justified and that the company's restrictive interpretation could thus not hold up; at the same time, this did not imply that Greece could ask the company to respect every provision of the 1917 General Staff Regulation based on acquired rights.[33]

The tribunal continued its analysis by turning to issues that carried broader implications for the company's overall status. Indeed, although the tribunal felt that it might have been possible to answer whether specific provisions of the 1917 General Staff Regulation were acquired rights, this was not put before the arbitrators; instead, the battleground had been expanded through the parties' arguments. Thus, the question ultimately became whether the administrative and financial independence guaranteed by the 1925 Concession allowed the company free reign, without the Greek government's intervention, in regulating its relations with its workers and their employment conditions (especially in light of the Greek government's letter that had acknowledged that the 1925 Concession was to be interpreted in a broad and conciliatory manner). Or, framed differently, whether the 1925 decree law obliged the company to respect the general regulations adopted pursuant to existing legislation, as well as, more specifically, whether it was under an obligation to submit its staff regulations for approval each time a new version was drawn up.[34]

The tribunal held that this was not merely an issue of acquired rights, but one that related more broadly, from a *public law perspective*, to the scope of the company's administrative and financial independence, and to its relation to Greek legislation as a whole. On this matter, the disputing parties' views had again fallen on two entirely different sides of the spectrum. For its part, the company had claimed that the 1925 Concession had allowed it complete liberty in regulating the status of its staff; meanwhile, Greece had argued that the company's independence under the 1925 Concession had in terms of working conditions been altered (if not entirely extinguished) by the 1925 decree

33 Ibid 16–21. The tribunal in particular differentiated between the provisions of the 1917 General Staff Regulation that were primarily in the workers' interest from those that were in the public interest or the interest of governmental control. Although the argument could thus be made that the company's refusal to recognise the workers' right to return to work following military service was a reduction of their acquired rights, the same could not be said regarding the provision allowing the government to appoint employees to staff councils.

34 Ibid 21–23.

law and that the company therefore had the obligation to comply fully with all of the relevant Greek laws and regulations. According to the Greek government, this was the case because, in Greece, the legislature had the right to add or replace an agreement's provisions when ratifying it; if a company did not renounce the agreement following such changes, they were to be considered as accepted.[35]

The tribunal accepted neither of these two diametrically opposing positions. Despite noting that the situation could be characterised as involving the imposition of unilateral changes by a state through the exercise of its public authority regarding obligations undertaken by the state as a contracting party, in this particular instance the tribunal found Greece's position unacceptable, as the 1925 decree law had provided that the provisions of the 1925 Concession had attained the force of law. The tribunal could thus not accept that two provisions having the force of law, and which had been adopted by the same organ on the same day, could directly contravene one another. Apart from the recognition of acquired rights, the 1925 decree law could therefore not be deemed to have imposed limitations of a general nature, as such limitations would have needed to have been clearly indicated by the legislator (particularly when considering the significance that the company had accorded to its administrative and financial independence during the negotiations).[36]

The tribunal also found the company's position untenable, deeming it unrealistic that a state would, without an explicit provision to that effect, entirely relinquish its right to regulate labour conditions in an important public utility service for a period as long as the company's 1925 Concession was intended to last (60 years).[37] Although the company tried to differentiate between laws of a general nature that applied regardless of industry from those that were applicable to only certain categories of industries, arguing that it was bound by the former but not by the latter, the tribunal did not deem it possible to distinguish between the two. Consequently, the tribunal held that the company could not be exempted from the legislation that provided that its staff regulations had to be submitted to Greek authorities for approval.[38]

Despite this finding, the tribunal was not entirely unreceptive to the company's position. Thus, while the tribunal maintained that the general principle

35 Ibid 23–25.

36 Ibid 24–25.

37 Indeed, considering the Hellenic tradition of intervention by public authorities into matters of worker rights in the name of security or public order, the tribunal was surprised that the company, if it wanted to escape the application of Greek laws and regulations, did not request specific exemptions in this regard. See ibid 25–26.

38 Ibid 26–27.

of the authority of public power and the need for uniform application of the law had to be preserved, it nonetheless equally stressed that Greece had by way of the 1925 Concession guaranteed the company financial and administrative independence. If the company was all the same to continue to be subject to laws of general application regulating all industry or the particular industry it was participating in, the question that presented itself was thus what such independence was to entail. No law, agreement or correspondence between the parties provided clarity in this respect; forced to rely on the parties' intention or explanations given during the proceedings, the tribunal deduced that it had been the apprehension of internal interference that seemed to have prompted the company to introduce the clause relating to administrative independence into the 1925 Concession. In light of this, the tribunal was nonetheless surprised that the company had never asked for further details on the matter, especially once the dispute had arisen. Although the tribunal found it plausible that the company had relied on Greece's assurance that its independence would be interpreted in a broad and conciliatory manner, the tribunal felt that this should have had the goal of establishing clearly defined rules inspired by the desire to observe and apply the relevant legislation in accordance with the spirit of the 1925 Concession.[39]

Such consensus on the matter, however, was lacking. This prompted the tribunal, in what is of foremost interest for present purposes, to proceed to formulate (relying on the text of the relevant legislation and the aforementioned principles, as well as the parties' negotiation history) certain principles which it thought would help resolve the issues between the parties. As a first matter of concern, the tribunal thus pointed out that, while the relevant Greek legislation in general continued to be applicable to the company, this did not necessarily imply that the company was, as Greece had argued, bound by every single provision of the 1917 General Staff Regulation. Although the tribunal acknowledged that many of the provisions of the 1917 General Staff Regulation were indeed concerned with the preservation of the workers' acquired rights, it was also apparent that others were not, but were rather aimed at ensuring state control, and were thus not in accordance with the company's administrative and financial independence. Therefore, while the company was under an obligation to submit its staff regulations for approval, the tribunal found that the government's claim that the 1917 General Staff Regulation was in all respects applicable to the company went against the spirit of the 1925 Concession; there

39 Ibid 27–29.

was therefore no need for the company's staff regulations to be identical to the 1917 General Staff Regulation (or any new general regulation).[40]

On the related matter of the manner in which the Greek ministry was to review the regulations submitted by the company, the tribunal emphasised that it would go against the 1925 Concession if the ministry were to arbitrarily introduce provisions not envisioned by laws of general application or by laws applicable to the whole railway or tramway industries. In light of the 1925 Concession, the tribunal deemed that the company was to be given considerable latitude regarding the matter, and that there was a limit to acquired rights. Thus, while Greece could insist that the company accept provisions that were in accordance with normal industry conditions or with general provisions imposed on other concessionaires, if it were to impose conditions differing from those imposed on all industries or a particular type of industry, it would by way of abuse of public authority run afoul of the company's independence under the 1925 Concession. According to the tribunal, the main purpose behind the ministry reviewing the regulations was to ensure that they were in compliance with general laws of public order or those in the interest of the community.[41]

Another aspect that particularly drew the tribunal's attention, and which the tribunal thought pointed to the reasons behind, and the scope of, the independence granted to the company under the 1925 Concession, was the company's resistance to the 1917 General Staff Regulation provisions on the appointment of a ministry representative to staff councils. Relying on its previous findings, the tribunal concluded that such an obligation could not be imposed upon the company, as it was only prescribed by the 1917 General Staff Regulation, but was not formally required under the relevant legislation. Although the tribunal saw some merit in the state's arguments that the presence of a ministry representative was intended to ensure that the approved staff regulations were being complied with and could thus be a guarantee for the workers, it also considered the company's fear of interference by the state's representative justified. The tribunal felt that this was an issue that the two sides should have resolved during their negotiations; crucially, in the absence of the parties' agreement on the matter, the arbitrators took it upon themselves to propose a solution. According to the tribunal, the two competing interests could best be reconciled through provisions that would guarantee to workers that the company would be impartial and would respect the staff regulations, while also ensuring that the state would not be tempted to interfere with the company's

40 Ibid 29–31.

41 Ibid 31–32.

administration as part of the implementation of the staff regulations. Absent turning to the courts for protection against arbitrary implementation of the staff regulations, the tribunal felt that the best solution would be to establish an independent appellate body that would consist of representatives of both the company and the workers, and that would deliberate with the help or chairmanship of an impartial third party appointed jointly by the company and the Greek state.[42]

The tribunal likewise observed that the company seemed to have ensured, having understood that this was in its best interest, that its new staff regulations complied with existing general regulations or even those that were simply deemed desirable by the administration. The tribunal stressed that it was in any event wise for the company to keep its staff regulations as close as possible to the provisions of general regulations or the conditions prevailing in Greece.[43]

Finally, the tribunal also addressed possible disputes that could arise between the state and the company regarding drafts submitted to the ministry, resulting in the state refusing approval to the proposed staff regulations. As the relevant Greek legislation envisioned a special procedure for settling such disputes, the tribunal did not think it possible to excuse the company from having to partake in the dispute resolution procedures provided therein without compromising the principles underlying its award; however, the tribunal had little doubt that, should the dispute persist even after the procedures envisioned by Greek legislation were exhausted, the matter was to be resolved through arbitration pursuant to the 1925 Concession.[44] The arbitrators believed that following this practical advice laid out by the tribunal would not only be in accordance with both Greek legislation and the company's interests, but would also allow the parties to overcome the difficulties that the tribunal had been engaged with.[45]

Having given the parties these recommendations, the tribunal then summed up its findings in the operative part of its decision. Crucially, even though the tribunal had framed the operative part as having been restricted to the legal decisions that flowed from the relevant texts, this hardly appears to have entirely been the case. On the question of acquired rights, the tribunal observed that there seemed to be no formal dispute that pertained to specific instances of alleged violations, and that the workers acquired rights had

42 Ibid 32–34.
43 Ibid 34.
44 Ibid 34–35.
45 Ibid 35.

in general been respected. In case Greece felt that the company's new staff regulations violated such rights, the tribunal pointed out that it could make use of the procedure for the approval of the new regulations provided for in the relevant legislation; should this not result in an agreement, recourse could be had to arbitration.[46]

The tribunal also reiterated its earlier finding that the company was subject to all laws of general application pertaining to all industries or to particular industries, and that it could thus not be exempted from the relevant legislation. Interestingly, the tribunal based this finding on both the 'general principles of public law' and the absence of any particular provision that would be contrary to the wording of the 1925 Concession or the decree law. Accordingly, the company was obliged to submit its new regulations to the Greek government for approval; at the same time, however, the 1917 General Staff Regulation (or any other general regulation adopted under the same regime) could not be imposed upon the company as such. The tribunal moreover emphasised that, when deciding whether to grant its approval to the new regulations, the Greek government could not introduce changes that would undermine the company's administrative and financial independence; its approval could thus only be conditioned by the requirement that the company had complied with Greek laws of a general nature (specifically those aimed at worker protection) and with the workers' acquired rights.[47] Notably, this last element, despite originally having been set out as part of the tribunal's 'practical recommendations' that had been framed as having been aimed at helping the parties resolve the issues between them, had thus found its way into the operative part of the tribunal's award.[48]

It is therefore apparent from the tribunal's ultimate award[49] that these practical recommendations formulated by the tribunal earlier in its decision with

46 Ibid 36–37.

47 The tribunal gave the company a one month deadline to deliver a draft of its new staff regulations to the Ministry of Communications, which was then to be applied provisionally until a definitive version was promulgated. Ibid 37–38.

48 See n 41.

49 Despite the best efforts of Thomas, the tribunal's decision was not unanimous. Indeed, both party-appointed arbitrators had certain reservations regarding the tribunal's decision. Although the company-appointed arbitrator, Percy Horsfall, on several points considered that the tribunal's decision did not fully accord with his own opinion, he nonetheless accepted the decision as a whole; conversely, the arbitrator appointed by Greece, Demetrios Schinas, issued a separate opinion. Thus, Schinas disagreed with the tribunal majority on the concern that the Ministry of Communications' representatives might interfere with the company's internal administration, as he pointed out that such representatives had previously limited their activity to strictly observing the implemen-

the intention of helping the parties' structure their relationship going forward had not remained entirely at the level of recommendations, but that some of them had in fact found their way into the operative part of the tribunal's decision. By blurring in this manner the lines between what were merely the tribunal's recommendations and what was mandated by the relevant legal texts, the tribunal thus played a central role not only in resolving a particular dispute between the parties according to the applicable legal regime, but also in itself setting out the rules pursuant to which their future relations were to be governed. This role by the tribunal in contributing to the development of the legal framework that governed the parties' relationship was all the more important as it related specifically to how the Greek state was to exercise its public authority in reviewing the staff regulations that were to govern the rights and obligations between the company and its workers.

2.2.2 Truncated Tribunal Case

Another of the tribunals set up under the 1925 Concession addressed matters that were more procedural in nature.[50] In particular, due to certain lacunas in the 1925 Concession, problems had subsequently arisen concerning the procedure that was to be followed for establishing a tribunal under the 1925 Concession. Perhaps somewhat paradoxically, the parties then turned to a tribunal established under the very same 1925 Concession in order to resolve these issues. The tribunal that was established for this purpose was once more presided by the Director of the ILO, Albert Thomas, who had been chosen

tation of the staff regulations and had done so without complaints of abuse. Schinas likewise considered that the participation of ministry representatives on staff councils was mandated both by the 1925 decree law and by the general principle, adopted by the tribunal unanimously, pursuant to which the company was obliged to observe laws of either general application or those relating to railways and tramways. Moreover, Schinas was convinced that the staff regulations adopted by the company violated the employees' acquired rights and that their application should therefore have been ceased, while the 1917 General Staff Regulation should have remained in force until the ministry approved the new regulations. According to Schinas, even if the 1917 General Staff Regulation had on certain points contravened the company's administrative and financial independence (which he did not believe to have been the case), this did not justify applying the regulation contrary to the state's laws. See *Staff Regulations Case* (n 20), Memoire de l'Arbitre le l'Etat Hellenique (6 March 1928) (in French) (ILO Archives: AR 1/26/2/1 and AR 1/26/11).

50 *The Greek State v The Hellenic Electric Railways Company*, Award (10 February 1930) (*Truncated Tribunal Case*). An English translation of the award can be found in the ILO Archives as an attachment to a Translation of a Note from Jacques Secretan to C W Jenks and The Director-General (ILO Archives: AR 1–26–3). A copy of the French version of the award is available in ILO Archives: AR 1–26–1. A summary of the award is also provided in Wetter and Schwebel (n 5) 200–201.

by the two party-appointed arbitrators, Andre Zakkas and Rene Besnard. Zakkas, who had been appointed by Greece, was a Greek lawyer and politician who at the time worked at the Greek Ministry of Labour,[51] while the company's appointee, Besnard, was a French lawyer and politician.[52] The tribunal's award was not particularly long and seems largely to have been facilitated by the parties eventually arriving at common positions regarding the disputed issues. The award, nonetheless, remains one of great interest for present purposes considering the tribunal's own acknowledgment that the solution that was eventually chosen was not entirely in conformity with the wording of the relevant provision of the 1925 Concession.

The tribunal was tasked by the parties with a two-fold request: to provide a solution for the situation where one of the parties fails to appoint an arbitrator within the time limit established by the 1925 Concession, and to determine the date from which the time for calculating the relevant time period for arbitrator appointment would run.[53] The first question had arisen because the 1925 Concession, while establishing a time limit for the nomination of arbitrators, did not mention, or provide a solution for, the possibility that one party may fail to nominate its arbitrator within this limit. The alternatives contemplated as possible solutions included the possibility of deeming that the defaulting party had recognised the claims of the other party by failing to appoint its arbitrator, that the tribunal was to consist just of the arbitrator nominated by the other party and the Director of the ILO, or that the arbitrator nominated by the other party and the Director of the ILO were by joint agreement to appoint the arbitrator on behalf of the defaulting party.[54] The parties, however, were not receptive to these solutions.[55]

The tribunal thus looked to the solution favoured by the parties themselves, pursuant to which the Director of the ILO would nominate an arbitrator on behalf of a defaulting party. In light of the 'special confidence' that both parties

51 See 'Ζάκκας Ανδρέας: 1892–1971' <https://greek-parliament-members.anavathmis.eu/%CE%B6%CE%AC%CE%BA%CE%BA%CE%B1%CF%82-%CE%B1%CE%BD%CE%B4%CF%81%CE%AD%CE%B1%CF%82/> accessed 18 March 2025.

52 See 'René Besnard: 1879–1952' <https://www2.assemblee-nationale.fr/sycomore/fiche/(num_dept)/749> accessed 27 September 2024.

53 *Truncated Tribunal Case* (n 50) 2–3. The English translation of the award found in the ILO Archives is paginated as part of the document to which it is attached; consequently, the page numbers as found on the award do not match the actual pages of the translated award. The page numbers indicated here refer to the actual pages of the English translation of the award and not to the numbers as indicated on the main document.

54 Ibid 4.

55 See ibid 5–6.

were said to place in the Director of the ILO, this option was accepted. Crucially, in accepting this solution, the tribunal acknowledged that:

> [s]*uch a procedure, of course, is not in complete conformity with the letter of paragraph 3 of Article 49 of the Agreement* but as the Greek State, on one hand, and the Hellenic Electric Railways Company, on the other hand, favour this solution it can be considered that they have thus reached an agreement concerning the interpretation of Article 49 of the Agreement and that they are simply seeking to have their interpretation endorsed and authenticated by a decision of the Arbitration Tribunal.[56]

Even if prompted by the parties' own favouring of the solution that was eventually adopted, the tribunal's award on this point should not be reduced to a mere recording of the parties' will – that the tribunal chose to treat the parties' preferences for the same solution as an agreement, while certainly a prudent course of action, does not necessarily mean that the arbitrators were bound to do so. Nor is there indication in the tribunal's award that such a definitive agreement between the parties had been formalised so as to have deprived the tribunal of any meaningful decision-making agency in the matter. The award, then, remains the tribunal's own, even if the chosen solution may have been rooted in the parties' preferences. And it is an award that, by the tribunal's own admission, was not restricted to merely applying the text of the 1925 Concession, but had instead introduced an innovative element into the procedural rules governing the disputing parties' relationship.

Perhaps more importantly, this novel solution introduced by the tribunal's award was not only intended by the parties to serve as a guidepost for their future relations, but this in fact subsequently seemingly proved to be the case, as the tribunal's award 'appears to have been accepted without question by both parties'.[57] Indeed, the company on numerous occasions of Greece's failure to appoint its arbitrator requested the Director of the ILO to either call upon Greece to do so or to appoint an arbitrator on its behalf, routinely citing the tribunal's award when so doing;[58] on at least one occasion, this was also

56 Ibid 6. Emphasis added.

57 See Note from C W Jenks to the Director-General (12 November 1948) (ILO Archives: AR 1–26–1).

58 See eg Letter from Societe Generale Hellenique SA, Athens Piraeus Electricity Company Ltd and Electric Transport Company Ltd to The Director of The International Labour Office (1 September 1948) (ILO Archives: AR 1–26–1); Note from Harding F Bancroft to the Director-General (12 March 1953) (ILO Archives: AR 1–26–2); Letter from the Athens Piraeus Electricity Company Limited and the Electric Transport Company Limited to The

done by the arbitrator appointed by the company.[59] Although those dealing with the arbitrations within the ILO were somewhat tentative in making use of the powers provided for in the award out of fear of causing resentment by the Greek government,[60] the award was ultimately viewed in a similar manner also within the ILO. It was thus recognised that it would be difficult for the Director of the ILO to 'repudiate' the tribunal's award,[61] and the Director proceeded in at least one instance, while explicitly invoking the tribunal's award, to appoint an arbitrator on Greece's behalf when the state had failed to do so.[62] The tribunal's award, then, was not just one that had introduced a novel normative element to the procedure that governed the parties' relationship, but this novel normative element was then in fact applied in practice in future arbitrations between the parties.

The second question put before the tribunal concerned uncertainty over the required form of the notification that a dispute had arisen between the parties and the means for communicating such a notification. Namely,

---

Director of The International Labour Office (27 March 1954) (ILO Archives: AR 1–26–3); Letter from the Athens Piraeus Electricity Company Ltd and the Electric Transport Company Ltd to The Director General of The International Labour Office (30 April 1957) (ILO Archives: AR 1–26–7); Copy of Letter from the Athens Piraeus Electricity Company Ltd and the Electric Transport Company Ltd to The Director General of The International Labour Office (17 August 1957) (ILO Archives AR: 1–26–7); Copy of Letter from H A Reid to The Director of The International Labour Office (25 May 1939) (ILO Archives: AR 1/26/8); Letter from the Managing Director of the Electric Transport Company Ltd to The Director General of The International Labour Office (30 April 1957) (ILO Archives AR: 1–26–8); Letter from the Chemins de fer Electriques Helleniques SA to The Director of The International Labour Office (26 March 1934) (ILO Archives: AR 1/26/11).

59 Note by Harding F Bancroft (19 May 1954) (ILO Archives: AR 1–26–2).

60 Note by Francis Wolf (29 August 1957) (ILO Archives: AR 11–26–7). See also Note by Bancroft (n 59). The ILO's general approach thus appears to have been not to appoint an arbitrator simply at the companies' request, but to first contact Greece in the hope that the government would eventually appoint an arbitrator itself. This cautious line of action sometimes resulted in significant delays in arbitrator appointment. See Letter from the Managing Director of the Electric Transport Company Limited to The Director of The International Labour Office (16 February 1940) (ILO Archives: AR 1/26/8) (urging the Director of the ILO to appoint an arbitrator on behalf of Greece as more than a year had passed since the company notified Greece of the dispute).

61 Note by Wolf (n 60). See also Note by Bancroft (n 59).

62 Letter on behalf of the Director of the International Labour Office (signature illegible) to the Societe Electrique de Transports SA (29 March 1940) (ILO Archives: AR 1/26/8); Letter on behalf of the Director of the International Labour Office (signature illegible) to the Minister of Labour in Athens (29 March 1940) (ILO Archives: AR 1/26/8); Letter on behalf of the Director of the International Labour Office (signature illegible) to Nicolas Phocas (29 March 1940) (ILO Archives: AR 1/26/8).

while the 1925 Concession had provided that the parties were to appoint their arbitrators 'within one month of the receipt of a notification in writing from the other party that a difference has arisen', the parties found this insufficiently precise wording to allow for ambiguities.[63] Indeed, in certain instances confusion had been caused by letters purporting to initiate the arbitrator nomination process that had not been sufficiently explicit, resulting in uncertainty over the date from which the one month deadline was to be calculated. The parties thus wanted the tribunal to '*lay down a definite procedure of communication* which would fix with certainty the date at which the [time] for nominating arbitrators would start running'.[64] As Greece and the company were in agreement that a notification that a dispute had arisen should be in the form of a writ served by a bailiff, the tribunal decided that the period for arbitrator appointment would start running from the day after such a writ had been served.[65]

On both points that had been put before it, then, the tribunal was invited by the parties to fill lacunas that existed within the normative framework of the 1925 Concession and that were of potential relevance for all subsequent arbitration proceedings that could arise under it in the future. The tribunal accepted this invitation and, in doing so (as grounded as its decision may have been in the parties' joint preferences), not merely applied, but in fact added to the normative framework that governed the procedural aspects of the parties' relationship. That this addition made through the tribunal's award was then also subsequently followed in practice only serves to further enhance the importance of the tribunal's contribution to the development of the normative framework underlying the parties' relationship.

2.2.3 Safety and Control Regulations Case

One more case that concerned the concessionaires' powers to regulate matters within the purview of the 1925 Concession was the 1930 *Greece v. the Hellenic Electric Railways Ltd and Electric Transport Company Ltd* case.[66] The tribunal's award handed down in this case could unfortunately not be located within the ILO Archives and could thus not be examined at first hand. Nonetheless, a summary of the award provided by Wetter and Schwebel[67] offers sufficient

63 *Truncated Tribunal Case* (n 50) 4–5.
64 Ibid 5. Emphasis added.
65 Ibid 6–7.
66 *Government of Greece v Hellenic Electric Railways Ltd and Electric Transport Company Ltd*, Award (5 June 1930), reported in Wetter and Schwebel (n 5) 204.
67 See n 66.

insight into the tribunal's reasoning so as to allow for the award to be recognised as one where the tribunal had taken on a distinctly creative role in relation to the normative framework underpinning the parties' relationship.

The underlying dispute was rooted in the fact that, under the 1925 Concession, the concessionary companies were obliged, in agreement with Greece's minister of communications, to implement certain necessary safety regulations. A problem arose when the Greek government withheld its required approval after the companies had put forward a draft of the regulations, and the two sides once more turned to arbitration.[68]

The tribunal's award is, above all, characterised by how broadly the arbitrators had understood their mandate. Namely, not only did the arbitrators view their task to be to pronounce upon the final wording of all of the 80 clauses of the draft regulations that had been under contestation but, even more importantly, as Wetter and Schwebel have conveyed, the tribunal '*did not feel bound to adopt either of the contradictory proposals advocated by the parties but considered itself at liberty to adopt*, if necessary, *a text of its own*'.[69] In other words, rather than merely assessing which of the opposing interpretations advanced by the parties was in accordance with the pre-existing normative framework, the tribunal appears to have deemed itself competent to draw up the safety regulations that would apply to the concessionaires' operations irrespective of either Greece's or the companies' position. As the number of disputed provisions of the regulations was rather large, the tribunal did not explain how it arrived at each particular wording, but instead merely set out the basic principles by which it was guided in doing so.[70]

While the starting point for the tribunal's decision-making process certainly was the 1925 Concession itself, the tribunal, despite the concessionaires' argument that their administrative and financial independence under the 1925 Concession would be undermined if the Greek government was allowed to interfere too much with the safety regulations,[71] considered that the concessionaires' rights under the 1925 Concession were to be understood restrictively. Accordingly, the tribunal deemed intervention by the Greek state inappropriate only insofar as the 1925 Concession explicitly provided for 'such limitations

68 Ibid. The arbitrators in the case were M Maison (tribunal president), N Politis and Rene Besnard. See also AM Stuyt (ed), *Survey of International Arbitrations: 1794–1989* (Martinus Nijhoff 1990) 486.

69 Wetter and Schwebel (n 5) 204. Emphasis added.

70 Ibid.

71 On the concessionaires' administrative independence, see the *Staff Regulations Case* discussed in sub-section 2.2.1.

upon its regulatory powers'.[72] If, conversely, there was any ambiguity within the text of the 1925 Concession, the situation was to be resolved by reconciling as much as possible the public interest with the companies' private interests.[73]

The tribunal's decision, then, represents yet another instance where a tribunal established under the 1925 Concession was not merely restricted to applying a pre-existing normative framework to the relevant factual matrix, but instead also contributed to the very development of that normative framework. In this particular instance, this creative role exercised by the tribunal was all the more accentuated by the fact that the tribunal did so not on the basis of precisely defined criteria that would have explained each adopted solution individually, but instead on the basis of certain broader principles that were said to have provided guidance to the tribunal. Moreover, the room for the tribunal's discretionary decision-making that was thus created was of considerable public import, since the normative framework to the development of which the tribunal contributed pertained to safety regulations applicable to the companies' operations and to how Greece was to exercise its regulatory powers within this domain. Indeed, this is something that had not gone unnoticed by the tribunal, as the arbitrators recognised that, where the 1925 Concession was ambiguous, their task would involve balancing public interest against those of the companies. In other words, not only did the tribunal contribute to the development of the normative framework that regulated the relationship between the concessionary companies and Greece, but it did so in relation to matters that touched upon Greece's regulatory powers and required the balancing between public and private interests.

2.2.4 Social Contributions Cases

Arbitral tribunals set up under the 1925 Concession also dealt with a pair of related cases involving social contributions in 1930 and 1933, respectively. Both of these cases further illustrate how tribunals established pursuant to the 1925 Concession contributed to the development of the normative framework that governed the relationship between Greece and the concessionary companies.

In the first arbitration, conducted between Greece and the Hellenic Electric Railways,[74] the question before the tribunal was whether an additional charge

72 Wetter and Schwebel (n 5) 205.

73 Ibid 204–205.

74 *The Greek State v Hellenic Electric Railways Ltd*, Award (18 March 1930) (*Ten Lepta Charge Case*). The award (in French) is available in the ILO Archives: AR 1/26/5/1, which contains also the parties' pleadings and the hearing transcripts. A summary of the award is available in Wetter and Schwebel (n 5) 201–204.

imposed by the government on railway tickets for the purpose of establishing a retirement fund for railway employees violated the 1925 Concession. The dispute arose after the Hellenic Electric Railways had, following the signing of the 1925 Concession, in April of 1926 taken over the operations of The Athens-Piraeus Railway Company. Under the legal regime applicable to The Athens-Piraeus Railway Company prior to the takeover, Greece was allowed to impose taxes and levies upon that company through charges exacted on railway tickets in an amount not exceeding five and a half per cent of the ticket price. In late 1925, shortly after the 1925 Concession was signed, but before the Athens-Piraeus Railway was taken over by the Hellenic Electric Railways, the Greek government, through a decree law, adopted a general measure for ensuring the functioning of a special purpose pension fund for retired railway workers. Under the decree law, for the purpose of the fund, charges imposed through railway tickets were added to ticket prices for various railway lines; this included a ten lepta charge for the line operated by The Athens-Piraeus Railway Company. In case of lack of compliance, the pension fund was authorised to collect the amounts owed in accordance with provisions applicable to the collection of public levies, as they were deemed fiscal obligations.[75]

Upon taking over the operation of the line in question, however, the Hellenic Electric Railways refused to add the ten leptas to its ticket prices. The company maintained that this charge went beyond the threshold set in the 1925 Concession, pursuant to which the government was not allowed to impose taxes on tickets totalling more than five per cent of the fare value.[76] Consequently, as of the date of the takeover, the company decided to charge on its tickets only the five per cent fee provided for in the 1925 Concession. Despite protests from the pension fund and the Greek Ministry of Agriculture, Trade and Industry, the company remained firm in its position.[77]

Although it had for about a year appeared that the differences between the company and Greece regarding this matter would subside, the dispute was reignited in 1927 when the Greek government passed yet another decree law. While the 1927 decree law essentially corresponded to the decree law of 1925, it contained one notable difference – it explicitly provided that the supplementary

75 *Ten Lepta Charge Case* (n 74) 7–8.

76 Art 25 para 2 of the 1925 Concession provided that:

"the State shall be entitled to impose taxation through the Company (…) on travellers as such on the Company's railway, tramway or omnibus routes Provided that the total of any taxes so imposed including the expenses of control shall at no time exceed five par centum (…) on fares (calculated before the addition of such tax)."

See ibid 10–11.

77 Ibid 9–13.

charge was a social contribution collected through the companies employing the beneficiaries of the insurance and not a tax collected by the government, as well as that the said contributions were to be paid into a special pension fund.[78] Despite the new decree law, the company, supported in its interpretation by Greece's Ministry of Communications, did not give up its previous position, insisting that it would not pay more than five per cent of the ticket fare and that it was not possible for Greece to outright undermine the company's rights under the 1925 Concession just by renaming the levy. Once the 1927 decree law was ratified by Law 3828 in 1929, the pension fund responsible for administering the funds turned to the company with a request for payment of the collected ten lepta charges. When the company refused, Greece's Ministry of Economy responded by stating that the matter will have to be submitted to arbitration if the company does not change its stance. Notably, in doing so, the ministry specifically invoked the decision handed down earlier in the *Staff Regulations Case*. According to the ministry, this decision, which had established that the company was subject to laws of a general nature regarding the protection of workers applicable to the industry as a whole or to an industry category, was *res judicata* as between the parties and was equally applicable to the matter at hand.[79]

The central issue before the tribunal was thus whether the ten lepta charge was by nature a tax or a different type of levy, and whether as such it was compatible with the 1925 Concession. The arbitrators appointed to the tribunal were the same as in the *Truncated Tribunal Case*,[80] with the Director of the ILO, Albert Thomas, again serving as tribunal president. As had been necessitated by the nature of the underlying dispute, the tribunal's award traversed a number of delicate issues, such as the distinction between taxes and other social contributions, the existence of a public purpose behind the disputed ten lepta charge, as well as whether a state's legislative powers could be utilised so as to unilaterally modify a public utility concession by adopting laws of general application. Not to be overshadowed by this inundation of the award's interesting aspects, however, is the fact that the tribunal did not conclude its examination once it determined whether the ten lepta charge was contrary to the 1925 Concession, but instead went on to discuss at length the applicability to the

78 An English translation of this legislative decree is available in the UK National Archives. See 'Translation No 47: Extract from Government Gazette of 9/11/27 (Issue No 243): Legislative Decree re: Creation of a Special Fund for Railway Pensioners' (UK National Archives: FO 286/992).

79 *Ten Lepta Charge Case* (n 74) 13–17. See the *Staff Regulations Case* discussed in sub-section 2.2.1.

80 See sub-section 2.2.2.

company of Greek general legislation on the protection of workers. Notably, it was precisely this additional analysis by the tribunal that then led to a seemingly conciliatory modification of stance by the applicant company, which in turn prompted a corresponding change of legislation by Greece.

The first matter that the tribunal addressed was the scope of the exemption established by Article 25 paragraph 2 of the 1925 Concession, pursuant to which the Greek state was empowered to impose through the company taxation upon passengers up to a limit of five per cent of the ticket fare. That this limit had not been overstepped before the ten lepta charge was undisputed; the key question was therefore whether the introduction of the ten lepta charge had crossed the five per cent threshold.[81]

The tribunal's analysis was situated within the broader historical backdrop of how taxes had been imposed upon the concessionaire company's predecessor. The tribunal underlined that the company that had been taken over by the Hellenic Electric Railways had likewise relied on a legal provision that guaranteed a certain upper limit on the taxes and other levies that could be imposed through tickets (in its case, five and a half per cent of the fare) so as to protect its tariffs from the legislator's tendency to impose public charges through ticket fares. There having been no change in the underlying circumstances, the tribunal found it only natural that the successor concessionaires would want the same type of guarantee introduced through the 1925 Concession. The arbitrators were thus not surprised that the company deemed that the ten lepta charge should be subject to the five percent limitation and refused to collect it from passengers. Meanwhile, Greece had argued that the ten lepta charge was not a tax, and was therefore not subject to the five per cent limit under the 1925 Concession. This argument was underpinned by Greece's contention that the funds gathered through the charge did not accrue to the public purse and were not meant to finance the state's general needs, but were instead intended for a special fund aimed at helping railway pensioners.[82]

Although its arguments gained some traction with the arbitrators, Greece was ultimately unsuccessful in swaying the tribunal. In arriving at its eventual decision, the tribunal withheld from expressing a general doctrine on this point, instead merely observing that the definition of what constituted a tax could vary significantly. The tribunal's decision was instead rooted in the specific characteristics of the ten lepta charge, which was deemed to have had the usual features of a tax in that it represented a pecuniary obligation without a corresponding counter-benefit, that it was collected involuntarily pursuant

81 *Ten Lepta Charge Case* (n 74) 17–18.

82 Ibid 18–19.

to an obligation established by law and through a legally prescribed process, and that it served a public purpose. This last element had been particularly contentious, as Greece had tried to dispute the public purpose of the ten lepta charge by pointing to its special purpose as a social contribution. The tribunal, however, did not think that this removed the public purpose behind the charge as it was obvious to the arbitrators that a social contribution was indeed in the public interest. The tribunal therefore concluded that, regardless of whether it was a tax in the strictest sense, the ten lepta charge was to be considered as such for purposes of the 1925 Concession (especially considering that the collection method had been the same as that envisaged by the 1925 Concession). The charge, which had exceeded the five per cent limit established by the 1925 Concession, was thus found to constitute a breach of the concession.[83]

A particularly interesting aspect of the tribunal's decision was the consideration (or, perhaps more accurately, the lack thereof) that was given to Greece's legislative powers. Namely, while the tribunal did not *per se* reject Greece's contention that the agreement, being a public utility concession, was open to unilateral modification through the exercise of the state's legislative powers by way of adopting impersonal laws of general application, it also saw no role in this particular instance for arguments rooted in legislative sovereignty. Without entering into a theoretical discussion on the importance of the principle of legislative sovereignty, the tribunal instead merely held that the distinction between public utility concessions and ordinary contracts of civil law invoked by Greece was under the circumstances immaterial. Irrespective of how the 1925 Concession was characterised, the commitments under the concession had in the tribunal's opinion been entered into in good faith and were therefore to be observed (or, at least, adequate compensation would be owed to the concessionaires in case of adverse legislative changes).[84] Thus, irrespective of any potential considerations as to Greece's legislative sovereignty, the exact nature of its obligations existing under the 1925 Concession was in any event to prevail.

What is for present purposes even more pertinent than the tribunal's approach to Greece's legislative sovereignty, however, is that the tribunal did not in its examination confine itself to merely concluding that the company was not obliged to collect the ten lepta charge, but instead felt the need to expound upon the implications that flowed therefrom. The tribunal thus observed that

---

83 Ibid 20–21. The arbitrator appointed by Greece disagreed with the tribunal majority on this point, and instead subscribed to Greece's position that the ten lepta charge was not a tax within the meaning of the 1925 Concession. See ibid 20.

84 Ibid 21–22.

the fact that a very precise provision of the 1925 Concession was found to be contrary to Law 3828 did not have broader connotations for the applicability of Greek legislation to the company, as the 1925 Concession was undoubtedly not intended to exempt the company from laws and regulations aimed at the social protection of workers. In this respect, the tribunal specifically reiterated the finding from the above-discussed *Staff Regulations Case* (which had also been chaired by Thomas and which Greece had invoked during the proceedings), where it was held that the company remained subject to all laws of a general nature pertaining to the protection of workers that were applicable to the industry as a whole or to a particular industry category.[85] Expenses stemming from a system of social insurance aimed at the protection of workers were in particular to be borne by the company. Even taking into account the fiscal immunity enjoyed by the company, the 1925 Concession could therefore not be interpreted as precluding Greece from applying its general legislation on social security to the company and thus absolving the company from participating in the system of social insurance by way of general contributions owed by employers.[86] The tribunal found such a solution to both be mandated by considerations of equity and in accordance with the 1925 Concession.

In the tribunal's view, Law 3828 was precisely the type of social insurance scheme in which the company was in principle to participate, as it was passed with the goal of ensuring that railway pensioners would have the minimum income needed to ensure their sustenance. This was particularly the case considering that the established fund was of a joint nature, providing equal coverage to pensioners of all of the Greek railway networks, and was therefore in line with the principle of solidarity entrenched in the concept of social insurance legislation. Thus, notwithstanding that the tribunal had found the ten lepta charge as established by Law 3828 inapplicable to the company, it nonetheless emphasised that the company in principle had to participate in the social insurance scheme established by that law due to its obligation to bear its fair share of social responsibilities imposed upon the community.[87]

That the tribunal, in order to ensure that a social insurance scheme for workers would not be undermined, went above and beyond what a strict application of the legal framework established by the 1925 Concession would have mandated is perhaps not particularly surprising considering that it was presided by the Director of the ILO, an organisation whose very *raison d'être*

85 See the *Staff Regulations Case* discussed in sub-section 2.2.1.

86 Ibid 22–23.

87 Ibid 23–24.

was the concern for labour standards.[88] Be that as it may, this intervention by the tribunal, inspired by equitable considerations and not strictly necessary in order to answer the question that had been put to the arbitrators, was not without its reverberations, as it was instrumental in helping the parties set out certain guidelines that were intended to be respected by both sides going forward.[89] In particular, the tribunal's findings regarding the impact of the 1925 Concession on Greece's capacity to regulate matters relating to social insurance ultimately prompted the company to submit to the tribunal a statement acknowledging that it was not exempted from participating in social security schemes of general application, and to put forward a plan that would allow it to do so in a meaningful way through a fare increase.[90] The tribunal took note of this statement, deeming it a satisfactory solution to the problem at hand (especially since earlier Greek legislation had already contained solutions comparable to the ones proposed by the company), and directed the parties to take the measures needed to implement this solution.[91] Crucially, in order to accommodate this compromise, Greece then adopted the necessary changes to its legislation.[92] Accordingly, as it would turn out, the tribunal's equity-inspired considerations would prove to be the impetus behind the changes introduced to Greece's legislation regulating social security matters.

The thus adopted solution directly led to the *Case Concerning the Collection of a Pension Fund Charge*,[93] some three years later. As previously mentioned, the scheme proposed by the company, acknowledged in the tribunal's award, had been enacted as law by the Greek government.[94] The key issue around

88 See n 27.

89 See Wetter and Schwebel (n 5) 203–204.

90 Under the proposed plan, the company was willing to increase the ticket price in a manner that would allow it to collect 2 million drachmas per year. Half of this sum would then be paid into the envisioned special fund, while the other half would go to the pension fund of the staff of the Hellenic Electric Railways. See *Ten Lepta Charge Case* (n 74) 24–25.

91 Ibid 25–27.

92 See n 94.

93 *Electric Transport Company Ltd and Athens-Piraeus Electricity Company Ltd v Greece*, Award (1 March 1933). Copies of the award in both French and English, along with the commentary by the companies' representative in the proceedings, are available in the UK National Archives; see DLJ Perkins, 'Notes on Arbitration Decision Dated 1st March 1933 on Dispute Regarding Tax on Tickets and on Electricity' (11 March 1933) together with 'Annexe No 15' (UK National Archives: FO 286/1120/190). A copy of the award (in French) is also available in ILO Archives: 1/26/6/1. A summary of the award is available in Wetter and Schwebel (n 5) 205–206.

94 *Electric Transport Company and Athens-Piraeus Electricity Company v Greece* (n 93) para 12.

which the new case revolved was whether the mechanism for collecting the charges under this scheme required the approval of the concessionaires.[95]

The tribunal that heard the case was presided by Belgian politician and former delegate to the League of Nations, Louis de Brouckere.[96] Once again, Greece appointed Andre Zakkas,[97] while the concessionaires nominated French lawyer Andre Mater.[98] In what was a very concise award, the tribunal at the outset recalled verbatim the findings by the *Ten Lepta Charge* tribunal to the effect that the tax exemption under the 1925 Concession should be interpreted strictly and not exceed five per cent of the ticket or electricity tariff, as well as that the companies should not be exempted from charges under employment laws of general application.[99] As for the very question submitted to it, the tribunal held that, from a purely legal point of view, it was not 'established by law' that the parties had to agree on the method of collection of the contributions and the possible corresponding adjustment of tariffs.

The tribunal's analysis, however, did not stop at what was strictly 'established by law', as the arbitrators proceeded instead to point out that it was nonetheless 'in equity, highly desirable' for the two sides to find common ground on the issue. Consequently, the tribunal instructed Greece and the concessionaires to start negotiations with this goal in mind.[100] Until such agreement was reached, the tribunal determined that the mechanism under the existing law would apply provisionally, with payments being made 'on account'.[101] Much

95 See Wetter and Schwebel (n 5) 205. The companies' position was that the relevant law was not a mere unilateral act by Greece but rather a ratification of an offer that had been made. See Notes on Arbitration Decision Dated 1st March (n 93) para 8.

96 'L de Brouckere, Belgian Socialist: Member of Council of State Dies at 81–Representative at League of Nations' *The New York Times* (New York, 5 June 1951) 31.

97 See n 51.

98 See 'Mater André' (*Comité des travaux historiques et scientifiques*, 21 January 2009) <https://cths.fr/an/savant.php?id=100895> accessed 27 September 2024.

99 *Electric Transport Company and Athens-Piraeus Electricity Company v Greece* (n 93) paras 10–11.

100 Ibid paras 13 and 15.

101 Ibid para 16. At the companies' request, the tribunal also formally acknowledged (but without expressing its own view and without prejudice to Greece's stance that the statement had been misinterpreted) a statement made by the Greek representative during the proceedings that was claimed to confirm the principle that the companies would be owed compensation if Greece unilaterally altered the financial balance of the 1925 Concession. See ibid para 17. Although he did not withhold his support to the tribunal's decision, the arbitrator appointed by the companies, Mater, made a declaration within the award of his positions on certain disputed points. According to Mater, no distinction was to be drawn between a direct or indirect levy denominated as a 'social charge', and a public duty denominated as a 'tax'. Likewise, Mater considered that the reference in the *Ten*

like in the *Ten Lepta Charge Case*, the tribunal thus, motivated by equitable considerations, did not confine itself to what the applicable legal framework would have *per se* mandated and proceeded instead to design an interim solution intended to allow the parties to find a commonly acceptable outcome.[102]

Taken together, the social contributions cases therefore further highlight the propensity of tribunals established under the 1925 Concession to, rather than operate within a static overarching normative structure, also contribute to its very development. Indeed, the tribunals in these cases did not merely apply the pre-existing legal norms to the facts as they were put before them; instead, inspired by equitable considerations, they also took an active role in devising solutions that were deemed desirable and that would, *inter alia*, eventually lead to changes in Greek legislation regulating the social status of retired railway workers. As a result, the extent to which Greek legislation on social security came to be applicable to the companies proved not to be an entirely fixed matter, but rather one that was ultimately equally, even if by no means entirely, shaped by the tribunals themselves.

2.3 *The Implications of the Power and Traction Concession Cases – Governing an Investor-State Relationship through Arbitral Development of the Law*

While each of the cases decided under the 1925 Concession is on its own merits undoubtedly capable of offering valuable insight into the workings of historical ISA, it is only when they are looked at in aggregation that their true significance can be properly appreciated. It is thus unsurprising that, as the arbitrations were ongoing, the ILO had attached particular relevance to the cases as a potential 'growing point' that could lead to the 'development of a possible international procedure for the adjustment of differences bearing on questions of social legislation between governments and foreign commercial interests', deeming the cases for this reason 'rather more important than their individual intrinsic importance'.[103] While the cases stemming from the 1925 Concession never attained such envisioned broader importance on a more

Lepta Charge decision to the companies' inability to escape a social insurance scheme of general application, and their own willingness to participate in such a scheme, could not be interpreted as anything but a confirmation of an agreement between the parties, as well as that the law subsequently passed by Greece can only be viewed as a ratification of that agreement. See ibid 14.

102 It appears, however, that no such compromise was reached, leading to another dispute between the concessionaires and Greece, in which a tribunal, also chaired by de Brouckere, then laid out how the social contributions were to be collected. See ch 4.

103 Note from C W Jenks to Bancroft (2 March 1953) (ILO Archives: AR 1–26–2).

universal scale, it is apparent that they did so operate insofar as the relations between the Greek state and the companies operating under the 1925 Concession were concerned.

This role by historical ISA in helping structure in the long term the relationship between the Greek state and the concessionaires only gains in importance when appreciated in conjunction with the fact that the tribunals' capacity in these arbitrations was, as the cases discussed have illustrated, not restricted to merely applying a pre-determined normative structure to the relevant factual matrices. Instead, the tribunals often took on more of a creative role, sometimes in a distinctly overt manner, and were in certain instances even required to balance between competing public and private interests when doing so or were in their decisions guided by equitable considerations. Not only was this proactive approach by the tribunals *vis-à-vis* the governing normative framework seemingly not objected to (and was perhaps even sanctioned) by the parties, but the arbitrators' decisions were on occasion (see e.g. sub-section 2.2.4) known to have (in)directly led to legislative changes being introduced by the Greek state.

In light of this, perhaps the most appropriate description of the cumulative effect of the arbitrations on the relationship between Greece and the concessionaires is found in the words of Wetter and Schwebel who, when discussing the arbitrations more than half a century ago, observed that:

> The foregoing cases are of great interest in their demonstration of the *central role arbitration can play not only in the settlement of disputes under an international concession contract, but also in the nourishment of the contractual relationship ex aequo et bono.* The Tribunals' decisions are significant: e.g., their definition of the meaning of a concessionaire's administrative independence and its relationship to legislative authority; their interpretation of the scope of a tax immunity; the need to interpret public-service concessions, like other contracts, in good faith; the limited right of legislative modification of concession rights with the consequent duty to pay compensation; the doctrine that contractual limitations upon the State's regulatory powers must be express. *Coupled with these holdings of law is a form of judicial legislation, either expressly invited by the parties or accepted by them. In this way the parties overcame a lacuna in their arbitral procedure by a ruling of the Tribunal.*[104]

104 Wetter and Schwebel (n 5) 209–210. Emphases added.

Accordingly, then, through this series of decisions, ISA effectively functioned as a mechanism that, over many decades, helped 'nourish' the relationship between the Greek state and private concessionaires operating an important public utility concession by, *inter alia*, calibrating and recalibrating the underlying normative framework. Yet, for the purposes of this Chapter, it is not just of key importance that this cluster of arbitrations contributed to the development of the normative framework that governed the parties' relationship through judicial – or better yet, arbitral – activism; rather, what is of equal importance is the kind of relationship that this normative framework was intended to, and did, regulate. Namely, as a corollary of the nature of the investment relationship that underpinned the arbitrations, the tribunals were tasked with deciding highly important matters that dealt with some of the most sensitive issues of public interest; this, in turn, meant that the tribunals' decisions had a direct impact on how various facets of Greek society regarding issues as important as workers' rights, safety regulations, social security schemes, and taxation were to unfold. This sentiment was echoed within the ILO, for example, where it was deemed that the first award, handed down by a tribunal presided by the Director of the ILO, Albert Thomas, 'had in fact *a real social importance* since it had a bearing on the acquired rights of the staff of the Hellenic Electric Railway Company'.[105] Indeed, it was precisely the social importance of the procedure envisioned by the 1925 Concession that had been one of the primary reasons behind Thomas' decision to accept the role envisioned for the Director of the ILO under the 1925 Concession. Thomas' motivation was described by Jacques Secretan, a legal advisor at the ILO who had served as secretary to several tribunals established pursuant to the 1925 Concession, in the following words:

> *Albert Thomas had accepted the functions indicated in Article 49 of the Agreement because of the social importance of such a procedure*, since, as a consequence of the Agreement and in practice, powerful foreign companies were given control of public services in the territory of a weaker State – the Greek State – and because he probably saw in such a procedure a means of increasing the prestige of the Office and of its Director.[106]

Consequently, then, by 'nourishing' the relationship between Greece and the concessionaires, including through contributing to the development of the underlying normative framework that governed it, the successive tribunals

105 Note from Secretan to Jenks and The Director-General (n 50). Emphasis added.
106 Ibid. Emphasis added.

established under the 1925 Concession effectively impacted how various central aspects of Greek public life – issues of 'real social importance', as they were described by Secretan – came to be regulated. What makes this governance aspect of the tribunals' decisions (which often operated in a concerted effort with the Greek government and the concessionaire companies) stand out even more in this instance is the relevance of the particular investment relationship to which they pertained, as the 1925 Concession was the most important British investment in Greece in the inter-war era.[107] Accordingly, insofar as Greece was concerned, the tribunals' decisions could hardly have 'nourished' – and for a period spanning several decades nonetheless – a more important investor-state relationship.

As a final remark on this matter, it is hard not to observe that it is both intriguing and indicative that, despite the general strong animosity toward the concessionaire companies that existed within Greek society,[108] the above described role of arbitration in (re)structuring their relationship with the Greek state and the resulting upshots did not, at least on the basis of the material reviewed for the purposes of this book, seem to have produced backlash. In fact, Greece later apparently doubled-down on this approach and made arbitration an even more integral part of structuring its relations with private investors.[109] As research by Dimolitsa indicates, starting from the 1950s, Greece passed a number of laws, intended to incentivise investment in the struggling Greek economy, which provided for arbitration between the Greek state and enterprises falling under the relevant legislation.[110] A similar scheme was provided in laws regulating the hydrocarbon industry.[111] Thus, it appears that, rather than being an isolated instance of such practice, the role played by arbitration in governing the relationship between the

107 Minoglou (n 2) 154.

108 See n 13.

109 This can perhaps be explained by the fact that arbitration has a particularly strong tradition in Greece, dating back to antiquity. See Gary B Born, *International Commercial Arbitration* (2nd edn, Kluwer 2014, vol 1) 7–10 and 25–30. Greece registered an unusually high number of historical ISA s, going back at least to the late 19th century and a dispute concerning the Piraeus Larissa Railway. Materials and the award from this dispute can be found in UK National Archives: FO 32/674–675 and FO 32/756.

110 Antonias Dimolitsa, 'Arbitration Agreements and Foreign Investments – The Greek State between Contractual Commitment and Sovereign Intervention' (1988) 5(4) Journal of International Arbitration 17, 18–24.

111 Writing in 1988, Dimolitsa mentions that some 50 awards had been handed down in arbitrations arising under two of the laws in question. See ibid 42. In many of these cases, tribunals were required to decide on matters, such as those relating to taxes and other similar charges, that touched upon the conduct of public administration.

concessionaires from the 1925 Concession and the Greek state was but an early step in arbitration having an important role in structuring investor-state relations in Greece.

3 Developing the Law for a Disputing Party's Relations with Third Parties: *RCA v China*

The next step along the gradation of historical ISA's role in developing the law, having in the previous section explored this role at its narrowest level of generality (i.e. affecting just the two disputing parties), is its assessment at the *intermediate level of generality*, wherein the normative influence of historical ISA tribunals was spread through one such disputing party acting as a conduit. Namely, for many a party that participated in historical ISA, be they states or private enterprises, the relationships that gave rise to historical ISAs were not the only investor-state partnership to which they were privy. One possible corollary of this was that, where decisions by historical ISA tribunals were taken by such disputing parties as authoritative pronunciations as to the content of certain applicable legal norms, this had the potential to then lead those disputing parties to adjust their understanding of the meaning of the same or similar legal norms that governed their other investor-state relationships. Where this occurred, the normative influence exerted by these historical ISA decisions thus extended not only to the parties partaking in an arbitration in which a particular decision was handed down, but also indirectly to their relations with entities in no way involved in that initial arbitration.

That a party participating in an arbitration might adjust its understanding of a particular legal norm following a tribunal's decision and adapt the remainder of its similarly-natured relationships accordingly perhaps may not, at face value, seem either entirely unexpected or particularly significant. Yet, considering the specific nature of investor-stare relations and the interests that were involved therein (see Chapter 2), the implications of parties to a historical ISA doing so proved to be substantially more consequential than might initially appear. What exactly such extended normative influence could entail in the context of investor-state relations is perhaps best captured by the *RCA v. China* arbitration and its ensuing fallout, to which the remainder of this section is devoted. As is discussed in detail below, the normative influence stemming from the tribunal's decision was in this case not circumscribed to the parties participating in the arbitration, but rather had a profound effect on several different layers of the RCA's relationships.

3.1 *The RCA's Entrance into the Chinese Market amidst Uncertain Times*

Before proceeding with an in-depth account of the RCA's dispute with China, it would be appropriate to first briefly recapitulate the company's dispute with The Administration of Posts and Telegraphs of the Republic of Czechoslovakia (The Czechoslovakian Administration) that had preceded it. As was discussed in Chapter 4, in the early 1930s, the RCA and The Czechoslovakian Administration had proceeded to arbitration after the latter indicated its intention to open a second direct radio telegraphic route to the United States in cooperation with Mackay Radio. The tribunal handed down its award in 1932, finding that The Czechoslovakian Administration was not allowed to open the planned route. The decision was primarily based on the arbitrators' understanding that the underlying agreement had created a co-partnership between the RCA and The Czechoslovakian Administration, pursuant to which the parties were under an obligation to act in the furtherance of their joint interests (which was deemed incompatible with The Czechoslovakian Administration's plans to open a parallel circuit). At the conceptual level, the tribunal had approached the disputing parties' relationship as falling under ordinary civil law, although the arbitrators had made clear that their decision would not have been different even if the problem had been approached from a public law perspective. In light of the tribunal's decision, The Czechoslovakian Administration had, rather begrudgingly, for the time being abstained from opening the planned parallel route. Consequently, things could hardly have looked more promising for the RCA in the immediate aftermath of its arbitration with The Czechoslovakian Administration.

Ultimately, however, there would be little time for the RCA to rejoice following its victory over The Czechoslovakian Administration. Namely, just as the RCA's arbitration with The Czechoslovakian Administration had been winding down, another crisis for the US company flared up half way around the globe – in China. At the time of the RCA's entry into the Chinese market in 1928, the country was undergoing significant political and societal change – it was in a situation that can be described, perhaps even somewhat euphemistically, as less than stable. The preceding period – known as the 'warlord era' – had been characterised by provincialism and fragmentation, wherein the country had been carved up into regional pockets of power ruled by local strongmen, referred to as warlords.[112] Although the country was eventually symbolically

112 On the warlord era, see Brantly Womack, 'Warlordism and Military Regionalism in China' in Richard H Yang and others (eds), *Chinese Regionalism: The Security Dimension* (Westview Press 1994) 22–30; James E Sheridan, 'The Warlord Era: Politics and Militarism Under

reunified following a military offensive known as the 'Northern Expedition', carried out by the Nationalist Party of China,[113] it would nonetheless take the new central government some time to properly solidify its control over the entire country; the following years would accordingly still be characterised by power-struggles with local warlords and in-fighting within the ruling party.[114]

It was within this turbulent atmosphere that the RCA ventured to establish its first telegraphic route with China. The traffic agreement was concluded with the North Eastern Radio and Long Distance Telephone Administration on 2 April 1928 and provided for the establishment of a direct radio-telegraph circuit between Mukden (now Shenyang) and San Francisco (the Mukden Traffic Agreement).[115] While the agreement had been concluded with a provincial telegraph authority, the provinces under the control of this administration were nonetheless under the rule of one of the aforementioned warlords – Zhang Zuolin (Chang Tso-lin) of Manchuria – who at the time also headed the internationally recognised government of China.[116] Mere months after the signing of the Mukden Traffic Agreement, however, an already complicated situation was seemingly made exponentially more complex for the RCA with Zhang

the Peking Government, 1916–28' in John K Fairbank (ed), *The Cambridge History of China*, vol XII (CUP 1983) 284.

113 See C Martin Wilbur, 'The Nationalist Revolution: from Canton to Nanking, 1923–28' in Fairbank (n 112) 527.

114 Ibid 719–720; Lloyd E Eastman, 'Nationalist China During the Nanking Decade 1927–1937' in John K Fairbank and Albert Feuerwerker (eds), *The Cambridge History of China*, vol XIII (CUP 1986) 116, 116–130 and 141–147; Womack (n 112) 29–30.

115 The archives of the RCA are kept as part of the records of MCI International, Inc (which acquired RCA Global Communications Inc in 1987) at The Hagley Museum and Library in Wilmington, Delaware (US) (call number 2225 (Series XV); hereinafter MCI International Archives). On the background to the Mukden Traffic Agreement, see 'Facts Re Mukden Traffic Agreement' (15 August 1933) (MCI International Archives, box 581, file 'China: Chinese Arbitration Correspondence (9 of 13)'); Copy of Letter from RCA's representative for China (unsigned) to W A Winterbottom (18 January 1934) (MCI International Archives, box 581, file 'China: Chinese Arbitration Legal Documents'). Pursuant to the agreement, the route was intended to be established between Tientsin (Tianjin) and San Francisco, but was temporarily removed to Mukden due to military operations; this however, in the end turned out to be more than temporary. See Copy of Letter from J M Regotazz to the Director of the North Eastern Radio and Long Distance Telephone Administration (2 April 1928) (MCI International Archives, box 581, file 'China: Chinese Arbitration Correspondence (9 of 13)').

116 Letter from RCA's representative for China to Winterbottom (18 January 1934) (n 115); Manton Davis, 'Notes Concerning the Mukden Station and the Mukden Traffic Contract and the Effect of These Upon the Chinese Administration' (5 June 1934) (MCI International Archives, box 581, file 'China: Chinese Arbitration Correspondence (3 of 13)').

Zuolin's downfall and subsequent assassination.[117] Despite the initial uncertainty regarding the future status of the Mukden Traffic Agreement amidst the changing power structure within China, the situation appeared to had played out well for the RCA – Zhang Zuolin's son and successor, Zhang Xueliang, had established good relations with the new nationalist government, which in turn eventually accepted the RCA's contract for the Mukden station.[118] Moreover, as the new nationalist government was eager to establish control over different facets of public life, including telecommunications, it likewise expressed interest in co-operating with the RCA in establishing the much more important radio-telegraphic route between Shanghai and San Francisco. As a result, the RCA's second traffic agreement for a direct radio-telegraphic route between the US and China – this time with the National Council of Reconstruction – was concluded on 10 November 1928 (the Shanghai Traffic Agreement).[119]

The Shanghai Traffic Agreement was very similar to the Czechoslovakian one (see Chapter 4), which is unsurprising considering that they were both based on the RCA's template. Much like the Czechoslovakian Traffic Agreement, it also provided for the establishment of a direct radio circuit,[120] ensured the co-operation between the two sides in maintaining the successful operation of the circuit[121] and included corresponding clauses on applicable law[122] and the resolution of disputes through arbitration.[123] The agreement did, however, also contain some notable differences. One such difference was reflected in the fact that, unlike in the Czechoslovakian Traffic Agreement, in the Shanghai Traffic Agreement there was no mention of the fact that all messages that had not been routed otherwise were to be transmitted to each other by the parties 'exclusively'.[124] The Shanghai Traffic Agreement also included an additional

117 Wilbur (n 113) 710. The RCA's officials seemed to have placed significant emphasis on the fact that the contract was concluded with an administration associated with what was at the time the internationally recognised government of China. See 'Notes Concerning the Mukden Station' (n 116); Copy of Letter from G F Shecklen to the Director of the Bureau of International Telegraphs (8 June 1932) (MCI International Archives, box 581, file 'China: Chinese Arbitration Legal Documents').

118 Michael A Krysko, *American Radio in China: International Encounters with Technology and Communications, 1919–41* (Palgrave Macmillan 2011) 51.

119 See Traffic Agreement between the Radio Corporation of America and the National Council of Reconstruction (10 November 1928) (MCI International Archives, box 581, file 'China: Chinese Arbitration Correspondence (2 of 13)').

120 Ibid art 1.

121 Ibid art 8.

122 Ibid art 13.

123 Ibid art 10.

124 Ibid arts 2 and 3.

clause, inserted at the behest of the Chinese side, which provided that, as long as the obligations regarding the transmission of messages under the Shanghai Traffic Agreement were observed, either side was free to conclude traffic agreements with any other nation or nations.[125]

By mid-1931, both the Shanghai and the Mukden circuits had been built and were ready to be put into operation.[126] With two circuits with China in place and good co-operation with the new nationalist government established, the RCA's position in China appeared very promising. To the RCA's misfortune, however, it would not be long before such an encouraging outlook for the company's operation in China would begin to deteriorate.

3.2 *The RCA's Troubles Spread to China: The Mukden Incident and China's Signing of a Contract with Mackay Radio*

The RCA's fortunes in China began to change courtesy of Japan and its territorial pretensions toward the Chinese region of Manchuria (where Mukden was located), in which Japan at the time had strong economic and strategic interests. Namely, during the night of 18 September 1931, the Japanese army launched an all-out offensive against Chinese positions at Mukden, purportedly as a response to an attack on the Japanese-controlled South Manchurian Railway. Immediately prior to the attack, an explosion close to Mukden, alleged to have been carried out by Chinese servicemen, had damaged a part of a railway line belonging to the company. As it would later be revealed, however, the explosion was merely a ploy orchestrated by a faction of the Japanese army in order to serve as a pretext for the takeover of Manchuria.[127] Since no significant resistance against the Japanese offensive was forthcoming, it was a matter of weeks before the Japanese army would effectively take control over most of Manchuria. Shortly thereafter, in March of 1932, an independent state

125 Ibid art 11. See Letter (unsigned) to Colonel Davis (27 June 1934) (MCI International Archives, box 581, file 'China: Chinese Arbitration Correspondence (3 of 13)') (noting that the clause did not appear in any of the other RCA contracts and that it was most likely introduced by China); Letter from Manton Davis to Heinrich Schuloff (6 July 1934) (MCI International Archives, box 581, file 'China: Chinese Arbitration Correspondence (11 of 13)').

126 See Letter from RCA's representative for China to Winterbottom (18 January 1934) (n 115).

127 On the Mukden incident, see Akira Iriye, 'Japanese Aggression and China's International Position 1931–1949' in Fairbank and Feuerwerker (n 114) 492, 499–504; Robert H Ferrell, 'The Mukden Incident: September 18–19, 1931' (1955) 27(1) The Journal of Modern History 66.

under the name of Manchukuo was proclaimed by a puppet government fully under the control of the Japanese army.[128]

As was to be expected, the Japanese military occupation of Manchuria had significant consequences also for the operation of the RCA's Mukden-San Francisco route. On the eve of the Mukden incident, Japanese forces had bombed the station used to operate the circuit;[129] San Francisco's communication with the Mukden station was thus discontinued, with the operators at the Mukden end of the circuit only managing to send out a short message – 'Japanese entering' – before transmission was interrupted.[130] Shortly thereafter, the RCA was informed by the administration operating the station that it was not possible to resume service at the time and that it would not assume responsibility for any loss of revenue or potential damage that the RCA may incur.[131] Thus, just a few months following its opening, the Mukden-San Francisco circuit was shut down, with its future operation up in the air.[132]

The station, however, would not stay inoperative for long, as it was soon repaired and put into service following the establishment of the Manchukuo puppet state. The reopening of the Mukden station had put the RCA at a crossroads – it had to decide whether it would be willing to cooperate with the newly installed puppet government in Manchuria, which had invited the RCA to continue the operation of the Mukden-San Francisco circuit. The RCA's position was hardly enviable. Namely, any co-operation with Manchukuo was undoubtedly to be perceived by the Chinese government as an unfriendly act, thus potentially endangering the RCA's existing and future interests in China. Meanwhile, a refusal to continue the circuit would have made it more difficult for the RCA to defend its position in Japan – one of its most important and profitable markets.[133] Stuck between a rock and a hard place, the RCA eventually chose to continue operating the Mukden circuit. In doing so, however, the RCA hoped to minimise the damage by insisting that a new traffic agreement

128 Iriye (n 127) 503.

129 Krysko (n 118) 52.

130 'Facts Re Mukden Traffic Agreement' (n 115).

131 Copy of Letter from the Director General of the Chinese Northeastern Telephone, Telegraph and Radio Administration to the RCA (27 October 1931) (MCI International Archives, box 581, file 'China: Chinese Arbitration Legal Documents').

132 When reporting on the situation in the fall of 1931, the RCA's China representative voiced fears that the Chinese would not be able to regain control of the station in the near future and that it was therefore probable that the station would be operated by the Japanese indefinitely. See Copy of Letter from G F Shecklen to J B Rostron (2 November 1931) (MCI International Archives, box 581, file 'China: Chinese Arbitration Correspondence (8 of 13)').

133 See Krysko (n 118) 53–54.

was not to be signed with the Manchukuo government, but that the route was to be operated under the terms of the existing Mukden Traffic Agreement and with a view of only providing the minimum necessary service.[134]

As was to be expected, the RCA's choice to reopen the Mukden circuit did not sit well with the Chinese authorities. Immediately after the rumours regarding the possible reopening of the Mukden station started to spread, Chinese officials wrote to the RCA seeking assurances that the activities towards that end, deemed inconsistent with the Shanghai Traffic Agreement, would be ceased.[135] The initial response from the RCA must have been encouraging to the Chinese authorities, as the RCA's representative for China, George Shecklen, wrote that he had no information about any such plans and provided assurance that the RCA would do nothing in contravention to the Shanghai Traffic Agreement.[136] However, talk about the impending reopening of the Mukden circuit persisted, drawing further enquiries from the Chinese side.[137] Eventually, the RCA conceded that the circuit would indeed be reopened; at the same time, the American company sought to downplay the importance of this fact by stressing that no new agreement would be signed and that the reopened circuit would operate at a capacity of only 'a few messages per day' on the basis of a verbal agreement to continue the existing Mukden Traffic Agreement.[138] Such a course of action was explained by the RCA with the need

134 Ibid 54. Copy of Letter from G F Shecklen to the Minister of Communications (26 April 1932) (MCI International Archives, box 581, file 'China: Chinese Arbitration Correspondence (8 of 13)').

135 Copy of the Letter from the Bureau of International Telegraphs to George F Shecklen (4 April 1932) (MCI International Archives, box 581, file 'China: Chinese Arbitration Correspondence (8 of 13)'). See also Copy of Letter from the North-Eastern Telegraph Administration to the RCA (3 April 1932) (MCI International Archives, box 581, file 'China: Chinese Arbitration Correspondence (8 of 13)').

136 Copy of Letter from G F Shecklen to the Bureau of International Telegraphs (5 April 1932) (MCI International Archives, box 581, file 'China: Chinese Arbitration Correspondence (8 of 13)').

137 Copy of Letter from the Director of the Bureau of International Telegraphs to George F Shecklen (18 April 1932) (MCI International Archives, box 581, file 'China: Chinese Arbitration Correspondence (8 of 13)').

138 Copy of Letter from G F Shecklen to the Director of the Bureau of International Telegraphs (21 April 1932) (MCI International Archives, box 581, file 'China: Chinese Arbitration Correspondence (8 of 13)'); Letter from Shecklen to the Minister of Communications (26 April 1932) (n 134); Copy of article from the 27 April 1932 edition of the Shanghai Evening Post and Mercury titled 'Radio Corporation of America Explains Manchukuo Situation' (MCI International Archives, box 581, file 'China: Chinese Arbitration Correspondence (8 of 13)').

to provide communication services for the benefit of the 'public good';[139] it was also simultaneously pointed out to the Chinese authorities that stations operated by the Chinese government had likewise been communicating with those operated by the Manchukuo.[140] The Chinese authorities, however, were far from impressed by such justifications. The RCA's co-operation with the hostile Manchukuo puppet government was seen as an unfriendly act that went against China's key strategic interest of keeping the Manchukuo government in international isolation.[141] As was to be expected, a strong protest by the Chinese administration was forthcoming, accompanied by claims alleging – somewhat ironically considering the later development of events – that the RCA's actions were a breach of Article 2 of the Shanghai Traffic Agreement.[142]

The reaction of the Chinese side to the reopening of the Mukden circuit was not, however, limited to protest. Not long after the Mukden circuit once more became operational, the RCA got word that the Chinese side was planning to sign a traffic agreement with Mackay Radio, which would provide for a direct radio-telegraphic circuit between Shanghai and San Francisco, in parallel to the existing RCA-China one. The RCA was quick to react and contacted all of the competent authorities within the Chinese administration in order to try to dissuade them from proceeding with such plans. The RCA centred these efforts on the recently obtained arbitral decision against The Czechoslovakian Administration, which was distributed to the various Chinese officials with the explanation that it was based on a virtually identical traffic agreement and circumstances as the present situation.[143] Instead of a reply from the Chinese authorities, however, the RCA soon received reports that the agreement had

139 Letter from Shecklen to the Director of the Bureau of International Telegraphs (21 April 1932) (n 138).

140 Copy of Letter from G F Shecklen to the North-eastern Telegraph Administration (20 May 1932) (MCI International Archives, box 581, file 'China: Chinese Arbitration Correspondence (8 of 13)').

141 Krysko (n 118) 55.

142 Copy of Letter from the Bureau of International Telegraphs to George F Shecklen (21 October 1932) (MCI International Archives, box 581, file 'China: Chinese Arbitration Correspondence (8 of 13)').

143 Copy of Letter from George F Shecklen to the Director General of Telegraphs and Telephones (18 June 1932) (MCI International Archives, box 581, file 'China: Chinese Arbitration Correspondence (5 of 13)'); Copy of Letter from George F Shecklen to the Minister of Communications (18 June 1932) (MCI International Archives, box 581, file 'China: Chinese Arbitration Correspondence (5 of 13)'); Copy of Letter from George F Shecklen to the Director of the Bureau of International Telegraphs (18 June 1932) (MCI International Archives, box 581, file 'China: Chinese Arbitration Correspondence (5 of 13)').

indeed been signed.[144] In response, the RCA immediately contacted the Chinese authorities in order to express its discontent against such a turn of events, as well as in the hope of receiving an official explanation of the situation;[145] even though it was confirmed that the rumours were indeed true, no other information regarding the particulars of the deal was forthcoming from the Chinese side.[146] Simultaneously, the signing of the Mackay agreement did make its way into the press, with the vice minister of communications, Chen Fu-mo, justifying the move primarily on the grounds of the RCA's co-operation with the Manchukuo puppet government.[147]

In the subsequent months, the RCA sent numerous letters of enquiry to the various Chinese authorities with competency in the matter in the hope of obtaining more details regarding the arrangement and getting a hold of the official text of the Mackay agreement.[148] Of particular interest in this respect

144 Copy of Radiogram from the Radio Corporation of America to the Minister of Communications (6 July 1932) (MCI International Archives, box 581, file 'China: Chinese Arbitration Correspondence (5 of 13)').

145 Translation of Telegram from Shecklen to the General Manager (15 July 1932) (MCI International Archives, box 581, file 'China: Chinese Arbitration Correspondence (4 of 13)'); Copy of Letter from George F Shecklen to the Minister of Communications (19 July 1932) (MCI International Archives, box 581, file 'China: Chinese Arbitration Correspondence (5 of 13)')).

146 Telegram from Shecklen to the General Manager (15 July 1932) (n 145); Letter from Shecklen to the Minister of Communications (19 July 1932) (n 145); Copy of Letter from George Shecklen to the Vice Minister of Communications (31 August 1932) (MCI International Archives, box 581, file 'China: Chinese Arbitration Correspondence (5 of 13)'); Copy of Letter from George F Shecklen to the Minister of Communications (21 September 1932) (MCI International Archives, box 581, file 'China: Chinese Arbitration Correspondence (5 of 13)').

147 See translation of article from the 17 July 1932 edition of The Shun Pao titled 'Detail of Negotiations with the Mackay Radio Company for Signing of Agreement' (MCI International Archives, box 581, file 'China: Chinese Arbitration Correspondence (1 of 13)'). The RCA, however, had its doubts as to whether the Mukden issue was really at the core of China's decision to turn to Mackay Radio. In particular, there had been indications that China was seriously considering an agreement with Mackay Radio even before the situation with the reopening of the Mukden circuit arose and there had even been certain hints of underlying dishonest dealings. See Copy of Letter from Shecklen to Colonel Samuel Reber (1 September 1932) (MCI International Archives, box 581, file 'China: Chinese Arbitration Correspondence (4 of 13)'); Letter from George F Shecklen to W A Winterbottom (22 August 1932) (MCI International Archives, box 581, file 'China: Chinese Arbitration Correspondence (4 of 13)').

148 On the attempts by the RCA to obtain from the Chinese authorities a clarification on the Mackay contract, see Copy of Letter from George F Shecklen to the Minister of Communications (26 November 1932) (MCI International Archives, box 581, file 'China: Chinese Arbitration Correspondence (5 of 13)').

was a letter of guarantee that had allegedly been provided to China by Mackay Radio by way of which China would be absolved of any liability if the agreement was not capable of being carried out due to a conflict with China's other agreements, while Mackay Radio would undertake to cover any litigation costs that may arise for China due to the signing of the agreement.[149] All such efforts to obtain further information, however, were to no avail, as no response from the Chinese authorities was forthcoming – the Chinese side had all of a sudden simply turned mute.[150] The reasons behind this silence seemed to lie in the fact that, following the signing of the Mackay agreement, the Ministry of Communications had been in a protracted state of flux and had thus been lacking the personnel with sufficient authority to tackle such a politically sensitive issue.[151] Namely, shortly after the agreement had been signed, the minister who had signed it had resigned;[152] while an acting minister was appointed to fill the thus created void, he had been away for most of his tenure and would soon himself offer his resignation.[153]

This limbo within the ministry would not be definitely resolved until the latter part of the year.[154] With the reshuffling within the Ministry of Communications eventually sorted out and the new cabinet in place, the time for tackling the question of the Mackay contract finally seemed ripe. The changes of personnel were perceived in a positive light by the RCA, as the incoming officials had seemed to acknowledge the problematic nature of the Mackay contract and had appeared to have had more understanding toward the RCA's positions

149 Telegram from Shecklen to the General Manager (28 July 1930) (MCI International Archives, box 581, file 'China: Chinese Arbitration Correspondence (4 of 13)').

150 An official acknowledgment of the RCA's numerous enquiries came only in early 1933. See Translation of the Letter from the Ministry of Communications to George F Shecklen (10 January 1933) (MCI International Archives, box 581, file 'China: Chinese Arbitration Correspondence (5 of 13)').

151 Letter from George F Shecklen to W A Winterbottom (16 September 1932) (MCI International Archives, box 581, file 'China: Chinese Arbitration Correspondence (4 of 13)'); Telegram from Shecklen to the General Manager (30 September 1932) (MCI International Archives, box 581, file 'China: Chinese Arbitration Correspondence (4 of 13)').

152 Letter from Shecklen to Winterbottom (16 September 1932) (n 151); translation of article from the 22 October 1932 edition of the China Times titled 'Chen Ming-Shu Again Resigning' (MCI International Archives, box 581, file 'China: Chinese Arbitration Correspondence (4 of 13)').

153 Letter from George F Shecklen to W A Winterbottom (24 September 1932) (MCI International Archives, box 581, file 'China: Chinese Arbitration Correspondence (4 of 13)').

154 Telegram from Shecklen to the General Manager (27 October 1932) (MCI International Archives, box 581, file 'China: Chinese Arbitration Correspondence (4 of 13)'); Telegram from Shecklen to the General Manager (7 November 1932) (MCI International Archives, box 581, file 'China: Chinese Arbitration Correspondence (4 of 13)').

than those who were on their way out.[155] Accordingly, the new administration engaged in what appear to have been earnest efforts at negotiating the cancellation of the agreement that had been signed with Mackay Radio.[156] With the momentum seemingly on its side, for a brief moment it looked like the RCA just might come out of the entire ordeal on top. Ultimately, however, Mackay Radio would not yield, and the new Chinese administration eventually estimated that its best option was to at least renegotiate the contract with Mackay Radio so as to be more favourable to Chinese interests.[157] As a result, an additional agreement revising the initial contract was signed with Mackay Radio in April of 1933, and the RCA was subsequently officially notified of both the original and the amended versions of the contract.[158]

This time around, it would be the RCA's turn to protest. The RCA immediately sent off a strongly worded objection to the signing of the agreements, stating that China's co-operation with Mackay Radio violated the Shanghai Traffic Agreement.[159] Despite the Chinese side's strong preference to avoid

155 Telegram from Shecklen to the General Manager (4 November 1932) (MCI International Archives, box 581, file 'China: Chinese Arbitration Correspondence (4 of 13)'); Telegram from Shecklen to the General Manager (15 November 1932) (MCI International Archives, box 581, file 'China: Chinese Arbitration Correspondence (4 of 13)'); Letter from George F Shecklen to W A Winterbottom (16 November 1932) (MCI International Archives, box 581, file 'China: Chinese Arbitration Correspondence (4 of 13)').

156 Telegram from Shecklen to the General Manager (6 December 1932) (MCI International Archives, box 581, file 'China: Chinese Arbitration Correspondence (5 of 13)'); translation of article from the 23 January 1933 edition of the Sin Wan Pao titled 'Adjustments of Communication Services by the Ministry of Communications, Revealed by Dr Chu Chia-hua' (MCI International Archives, box 581, file 'China: Chinese Arbitration Correspondence (10 of 13)'). Some factions within the Ministry of Communications seem to have been pushing for a cancellation of the agreement even before the restructuring within the ministry. See Letter from George F Shecklen to W A Winterbottom (31 August 1932) (MCI International Archives, box 581, file 'China: Chinese Arbitration Correspondence (4 of 13)'); Telegram from Shecklen to the General Manager (8 September 1932) (MCI International Archives, box 581, file 'China: Chinese Arbitration Correspondence (4 of 13)'); Letter from George F Shecklen to W A Winterbottom (16 September 1932) (MCI International Archives, box 581, file 'China: Chinese Arbitration Correspondence (4 of 13)').

157 Telegram from Shecklen to the General Manager (12 April 1933) (MCI International Archives, box 581, file 'China: Chinese Arbitration Correspondence (10 of 13)').

158 Telegram from Shecklen to the General Manager (10 April 1933) (MCI International Archives, box 581, file 'China: Chinese Arbitration Correspondence (10 of 13)').

159 Letter from RCA Communications, Inc (unsigned) to the Minister of Communications (13 April 1933) (MCI International Archives, box 581, file 'China: Chinese Arbitration Correspondence (10 of 13)').

arbitration,[160] at this point, it had become clear that such an outcome was inevitable. Thus, once the Chinese authorities followed through on the traffic agreement and officially inaugurated the direct circuit between Shanghai and San Francisco with Mackay Radio,[161] the RCA responded in the only way it could have under the circumstances – by immediately notifying Chinese authorities of arbitration under the Shanghai Traffic Agreement.[162]

With yet another arbitration over its traffic contracts imminent, it is easy to imagine how infuriating this whole ordeal with its Chinese operations must have been to the RCA leadership. The earlier victory over The Czechoslovakian Administration in the first arbitration was a significant achievement for the RCA and it was no doubt expected to help fend off similar future attacks against its contracts. In the end, however, there had been no time for the RCA to enjoy the moment, as the trouble in China had started brewing virtually immediately after the decision in the first arbitration was handed down. Just a year after securing victory against The Czechoslovakian Administration, then, the RCA once more found itself heading to arbitration over virtually the same issue. In contrast to its previous arbitration against The Czechoslovakian Administration,[163] however, this time the RCA went into the proceedings feeling confident about a positive outcome.[164] As it would turn out, to the RCA's

160 Telegram from Shecklen to the General Manager (12 April 1933) (MCI International Archives, box 581, file 'China: Chinese Arbitration Correspondence (10 of 13)'). One Chinese official was even quoted as having implied that China would, in case it did not fare well in the arbitration, break off co-operation with the RCA. See Translation of Message from Shecklen (24 May 1933) (MCI International Archives, box 581, file 'China: Chinese Arbitration Correspondence (5 of 13)').

161 See Telegram from the Traffic Manager to Beal (17 May 1932) (MCI International Archives, box 581, file 'China: Chinese Arbitration Correspondence (5 of 13)'); 'Mackay Service Opens Tomorrow: New Radio Connection with US Ready to Start' *The Shanghai Evening Post and Mercury* (Shanghai, 18 May 1933) (MCI International Archives, box 581, file 'China: Chinese Arbitration Correspondence (6 of 13)').

162 Copy of Letter from George F Shecklen to the Minister of Communications (18 May 1933) (MCI International Archives, box 581, file 'China: Chinese Arbitration Correspondence (6 of 13)').

163 See ch 4.

164 Letter from Manton Davis to Sarnoff (25 January 1933) (MCI International Archives, box 581, file 'China: Chinese Arbitration Correspondence (10 of 13)'). The RCA's general counsel, Colonel Manton Davis, was planning to use a potential favorable decision by the *RCA v China* tribunal to obtain an injunction from US courts that would have prevented Mackay Radio from attacking its contracts in the future. See ibid; Letter from Manton Davis to F Eldred Boland (26 December 1933) (MCI International Archives, box 581, file 'China: Chinese Arbitration Correspondence (8 of 13)').

misfortune, such optimism was severely misplaced – the outcome of the arbitration would not be to the American company's liking.

3.3 *The Arbitral Proceedings*

3.3.1 The Constitution of the Tribunal

On this occasion, the RCA wasted little time – the name of its nominee to the tribunal was in consideration well before it had become evident that arbitration would be inevitable; once the time to notify the Chinese side of the arbitration came, it was ready to be communicated to China. Perhaps unsurprisingly, the RCA's first choice for its appointee was again G S Whitmore, who had served – in the RCA's eyes, no doubt, quite satisfactorily – as the RCA-appointed arbitrator in the Czechoslovakia arbitration.[165] This time, however, Whitmore was unable to take up the post due to his company's close business ties to China at the time.[166] After a number of other prospective candidates were considered – including one who was deemed unsuitable due to having been perceived as 'a neutral character with no positive views and easily moved to change his opinions and views upon any subject'[167] – the choice eventually came down to Auguste Hubert of the Belgian Societe Anonyme Internationale de Telegraphie sans Fil, who promptly agreed to serve as arbitrator.[168]

165 Telegram from Sarnoff to F G Kellaway of Imperial and International Communications, Ltd (30 December 1932) (MCI International Archives, box 581, file 'China: Chinese Arbitration Correspondence (5 of 13)').

166 Telegram from Kellaway to Sarnoff (3 January 1933) (MCI International Archives, box 581, file 'China: Chinese Arbitration Correspondence (10 of 13)').

167 Letter from Samuel Reber to Winterbottom (21 January 1933) (MCI International Archives, box 581, file 'China: Chinese Arbitration Correspondence (10 of 13)'). See also Telegram from Winterbottom to Morton (20 January 1933) (MCI International Archives, box 581, file 'China: Chinese Arbitration Correspondence (10 of 13)'); Letter from Winterbottom (unsigned) to Alfred H Morton (25 January 1933) (MCI International Archives, box 581, file 'China: Chinese Arbitration Correspondence (10 of 13)'); Letter from Alfred H Morton to W A Winterbottom (6 February 1933) (MCI International Archives, box 581, file 'China: Chinese Arbitration Correspondence (10 of 13)').

168 See Letter from Winterbottom (unsigned) to Colonel Davis (15 February 1933) (MCI International Archives, box 581, file 'China: Chinese Arbitration Correspondence (10 of 13)'); Letter from Manton Davis to W A Winterbottom (16 February 1933) (MCI International Archives, box 581, file 'China: Chinese Arbitration Correspondence (10 of 13)'); Letter from Winterbottom (unsigned) to A Hubert (20 March 1933) (MCI International Archives, box 581, file 'China: Chinese Arbitration Correspondence (10 of 13)'); Letter from A Hubert to W A Winterbottom (31 March 1933) (MCI International Archives, box 581, file 'China: Chinese Arbitration Correspondence (10 of 13)'); Letter from Alfred H Morton to W A Winterbottom (12 April 1933) (MCI International Archives, box 581, file 'China: Chinese Arbitration Correspondence (10 of 13)'); Copy of Letter from Manton Davis and W A Winterbottom to A Hubert (20 May 1933) (MCI International Archives, box 581, file 'China:

With the RCA's tribunal nominee in place, it was now China's turn to appoint an arbitrator. Rather curiously, in making its selection, China too turned to an arbitrator from the Czechoslovakian case and, in spite of the RCA's success in the proceeding, chose the appointee of The Czechoslovakian Administration from that arbitration, Reinhold Furrer.[169] The propriety of such a repeat appointment was briefly discussed within RCA circles on account that Furrer had already made his opinions clear in the previous arbitration, but the idea of making any formal objections regarding his appointment never gained much traction.[170]

The two thus appointed arbitrators then turned to the final step in constituting the tribunal – appointing its president. At the outset, the RCA's officials had indicated to Hubert their inclinations regarding the qualifications of the presiding arbitrator – considering that the two party-appointed arbitrators were both telegraph officials, they envisioned the tribunal president as a highly qualified lawyer from a neutral European country.[171] Hubert and Furrer would proceed to discuss prospective nominees, with each of the arbitrators drawing up a list of several potentially deserving candidates.[172] Although the selection

Chinese Arbitration Correspondence (6 of 13)'); Letter from A Hubert to W A Winterbottom (22 May 1933) (MCI International Archives, box 581, file 'China: Chinese Arbitration Correspondence (5 of 13)').

169 Translation of Letter from the Ministry of Communications to George F Shecklen (7 June 1933) (MCI International Archives, box 581, file 'China: Chinese Arbitration Correspondence (7 of 13)'). The choice was indeed a strange one considering the outcome of the RCA's arbitration against The Czechoslovakian Administration. The RCA did try to uncover the motivation behind Furrer's nomination and whether perhaps there was some connection to Mackay Radio that was behind his repeat appointment. However, upon enquiry with the ministry by the RCA's representative in China for the rationale for selecting Furrer, the only forthcoming answer was that Furrer had 'lost the case for Czechoslovakia, did not he?'. See Telegram from Shecklen to the General Manager (13 June 1933) (MCI International Archives, box 581, file 'China: Chinese Arbitration Correspondence (6 of 13)').

170 Message of 12 June 1933 (Macinnis) (MCI International Archives, box 581, file 'China: Chinese Arbitration Correspondence (6 of 13)'); 'Memorandum of Interview with Dr Schuloff, Badgastein, Austria, June 10, 1933' (12 June 1933) (MCI International Archives, box 581, file 'China: Chinese Arbitration Correspondence (6 of 13)'). Any such protest by the RCA would have no doubt been highly hypocritical considering that the RCA's first pick for its appointee to the tribunal was Whitmore, whose position would have been equally as known from the first arbitration.

171 Copy of Letter from Manton Davis to A Hubert (12 June 1933) (MCI International Archives, box 581, file 'China: Chinese Arbitration Correspondence (6 of 13)'); Letter from Manton Davis to W A Winterbottom (23 June 1933) (MCI International Archives, box 581, file 'China: Chinese Arbitration Correspondence (7 of 13)').

172 See 'Propositions Dr Furrer' and 'Propositions Mr Hubert' (MCI International Archives, box 581, file 'China: Chinese Arbitration Correspondence (7 of 13)'). Both lists were com-

process over-stepped the time limits envisioned by the Traffic Agreement,[173] the two arbitrators eventually came to an agreement, choosing Joost Adriaan van Hamel.[174]

Van Hamel was a Dutch lawyer and the nephew of the inaugural president of the Permanent Court of International Justice (PCIJ), BCJ Loder (who had himself been an arbitrator in a historical ISA and in whose law office van Hamel had started his law career).[175] Although van Hamel had succeeded his father as a criminal law professor at the University of Amsterdam, his interests transcended his immediate area of expertise, which eventually led him to have a prominent international career. In 1919, van Hamel was appointed as the head of the legal department of the League of Nations Secretariat, following which he served as the High Commissioner of the League of Nations in the Free City of Danzig. Van Hamel later also acted as a neutral judge on the Hungaro-Yugoslav Mixed Arbitral Tribunal and appeared before the PCIJ on behalf of Bulgaria in *The Greco-Bulgarian 'Communities'* case (in which his uncle, Loder, was one of the judges).[176] Although he is not known to have served as an arbitrator in any other historical ISAs aside from *RCA v. China*, van Hamel left an imprint on ISA that can be matched by few historical figures, for, as is discussed in sub-section 4.2.2.1, it was none other than him who was responsible for the origination of the involvement of the Permanent Court of Arbitration (PCA) with ISA.[177]

An interesting wrinkle was soon added to the proceeding when China appointed as its representative in the arbitration a counsel of Dutch nationality, HAE Modderman.[178] Namely, when discussing the name of the presiding arbitrator, the two party-appointed arbitrators had agreed that he was to be

---

posed of the most eminent individuals, some of whom, such as Sir Leslie Scott (*Lena Goldfields v USSR*) and BCJ Loder (*Rialet v Ethiopia*), had previously acted as arbitrators in ISAs.

173 See Translation of Letter from A Hubert to Furrer (23 June 1933) (MCI International Archives, box 581, file 'China: Chinese Arbitration Correspondence (7 of 13)').

174 Translation of Letter from Furrer and Hubert (unsigned) to J A van Hamel (undated) (MCI International Archives, box 581, file 'China: Chinese Arbitration Correspondence (7 of 13)'); Translation of Letter from van Hamel to A Hubert (10 July 1933) (MCI International Archives, box 581, file 'China: Chinese Arbitration Correspondence (7 of 13)').

175 See n 172.

176 See *The Greco-Bulgarian 'Communities'* (Advisory Opinion) PCIJ Series B No 17 at 10.

177 For a short biography of van Hamel, see CG Roelofsen, 'Hamel, Joost Adriaan van (1880–1964)' (*Biografisch Woordenboek van Nederland*, 12 November 2013) <http://resources.huygens.knaw.nl/bwn1880-2000/lemmata/bwn1/hamelja> accessed 27 September 2024.

178 Telegram from Hubert to Davis (11 August 1933) (MCI International Archives, box 581, file 'China: Chinese Arbitration Correspondence (9 of 13)').

of a different nationality from the parties' counsel.[179] China's move to appoint Modderman thus came as somewhat of an unpleasant surprise to both Hubert and the RCA. Despite being initially taken aback by this development, the RCA ultimately chose not to protest China's choice (nor to appoint Dutch counsel itself) in the fear that this might prompt the presiding arbitrator to resign.[180] Instead, it was merely noted to van Hamel that China's appointment of counsel had come as a surprise to its counterparty in the arbitration in light of previous understandings on the matter.[181]

3.3.2 The Proceedings and the Parties' Arguments

Following the constitution of the tribunal, the proceedings, for the most part, developed along a pattern similar to the earlier Czechoslovakian arbitration, although at a considerably slower pace. The parties exchanged sets of written pleadings – with the important difference that this time the RCA was explicitly designated as the plaintiff[182] – subsequent to which an oral hearing was held at the Peace Palace in The Hague in mid-April of 1935.[183]

---

179 Ibid. Apparently, it was for this reason that an arbitrator of English nationality was discounted as a candidate, it having been assumed that China would appoint English counsel. See Translation of Letter from A Hubert to Schuloff (16 August 1933) (MCI International Archives, box 581, file 'China: Chinese Arbitration Correspondence (9 of 13)').

180 Telegram from Colonel Davis to Hubert (14 August 1933) (MCI International Archives, box 581, file 'China: Chinese Arbitration Correspondence (9 of 13)'). Any concerns that the RCA may have had regarding the appointment were obviated by van Hamel's statement that he only knew Modderman superficially and that he had no personal relationship with him. See Letter from Manton Davis to A Hubert (24 August 1933) (MCI International Archives, box 581, file 'China: Chinese Arbitration Correspondence (9 of 13)'); Translation of Letter from Heinrich Schuloff to Colonel Davis (18 August 1933) (MCI International Archives, box 581, file 'China: Chinese Arbitration Correspondence (9 of 13)'). It is nonetheless hard to imagine that the RCA would have been inclined to make too much of an issue out of Modderman's appointment, seeing how they themselves had been planning on engaging counsel of the same nationality as the presiding arbitrator in the Czechoslovakian arbitration. See Telegram from Judge Woodward to Colonel Manton Davis (10 October 1931) (MCI International Archives, box 583, file 'Czechoslovakia: Arbitration (2 of 3)').

181 Translation of Letter from A Hubert to J A van Hamel (21 August 1933) (MCI International Archives, box 581, file 'China: Chinese Arbitration Correspondence (9 of 13)'). See also Letter from Manton Davis to Heinrich Schuloff (1 March 1935) (MCI International Archives, box 581, file 'China: Chinese Arbitration Correspondence (9 of 13)'); Translation of Letter from Heinrich Schuloff to Colonel Davis (20 March 1935) (MCI International Archives, box 581, file 'China: Chinese Arbitration Correspondence (9 of 13)').

182 See Copy of Letter from Manton Davis to A Hubert (12 June 1933) (MCI International Archives, box 581, file 'China: Chinese Arbitration Correspondence (6 of 13)'). For an overview of the proceedings, see copy of 'Plan of Procedure' (MCI International Archives, box 581, file 'China: Chinese Arbitration Correspondence (9 of 13)').

183 See Translation of Letter from Heinrich Schuloff to Colonel Davis (13 February 1935) (MCI International Archives, box 581, file 'China: Chinese Arbitration Correspondence (13 of 13)').

Much like the procedural aspect of the arbitration, so too was the parties' argumentation eerily similar to that in the Czechoslovakian case. While some of the arguments were further refined, and others (such as those relating to Article 11, which was specific to the Shanghai Traffic Agreement) idiosyncratic to the *RCA v. China* dispute, the basic positions of the two sides essentially corresponded to those from the Czechoslovakian arbitration. Thus, the RCA once more argued that the nature of its relationship with its contracting partner (this time labelled under applicable Chinese law as a 'partnership')[184] was such that it excluded the possibility of China co-operating with the RCA's competitor on a parallel circuit. While the RCA again for this proposition mainly relied on Article 8 (under which the parties were to cooperate with each other in securing the successful working of the circuit),[185] it also invoked in its favour Article 11 (which had been specifically inserted in the Shanghai Traffic Agreement and which provided for the parties' right to conclude radio agreements with other nations).[186] China, for its part, denied that its obligation to co-operate with the RCA in making the joint circuit successful prohibited it from establishing the parallel Mackay circuit.[187] In so doing, China had (in an argument that paralleled that of The Czechoslovakian Administration) put great emphasis on the fact that it was a sovereign government and that the exercise of sovereign authority – which it contented the provision of telegraphy services was – could not be lightly presumed to have been contracted away.[188]

In response to this argument, the RCA made a slight adjustment to its position on the matter in comparison to the Czechoslovakian arbitration,[189]

184 *RCA v China*, Brief of the Radio Corporation of America (MCI International Archives, box 581, file 'China: Chinese Arbitration Legal Documents') 42–47; *RCA v China*, Reply Brief of Radio Corporation of America (MCI International Archives, box 581, file 'China: Chinese Arbitration Legal Documents') 40–44. All references to pages in relation to the briefs in the China arbitration pertain to the pages as enumerated in the copies of the briefs found in the RCA archives.

185 See RCA Brief (n 184) 24–29; RCA Reply Brief (n 184) 17–19. Due to a slight difference in numbering, art 7 of the Czechoslovakian Traffic Agreement corresponds to art 8 of the Shanghai Traffic Agreement. See also nn 222–223.

186 RCA Brief (n 184) 24; RCA Reply Brief (n 184) 9–12. In the RCA's view, since art 11 permitted China to conclude traffic agreements with other countries, it was also to be understood as preventing China from doing so with respect to parties from the same country as the RCA. See also n 230.

187 *RCA v China*, Reply Brief on Behalf of the National Government of the Republic of China (MCI International Archives, box 581, file 'China: Chinese Arbitration Legal Documents') 26–27.

188 Ibid 16–17.

189 In the arbitration against The Czechoslovakian Administration, the RCA had argued that The Czechoslovakian Administration was only allowed to permit the establishment of

drawing a nuanced yet important distinction between China's regulatory power as a state and the rights of the Chinese telegraph administration as an entity engaged in a commercial enterprise. Namely, while the RCA did not dispute that China as a state had the right to pass legislation cancelling the existing monopoly over telegraphy services and thus allowing other companies to establish direct circuits between China and the US, it challenged the right of its contracting partner – the Chinese telegraph administration – to take active participation in the establishment and operation of such competing routes.[190] China, meanwhile, attempted to frame this stance by the RCA as a 'vital admission' on its part that China was not absolutely prohibited from taking any action that might cause damage to their joint endeavour[191] – an argument that would ultimately gain traction with the tribunal despite the RCA's vehement denial as to its validity.

As was to be expected, an important aspect in this proceeding but not in the one involving The Czechoslovakian Administration – for the simple reason that it was not available to the parties in the first arbitration – was the very decision of the *Czechoslovakian Administration v. RCA* tribunal. Unsurprisingly, the RCA tried to underscore the importance of this earlier favourable decision as much as possible – it argued not only that the subject matter of the two cases was 'absolutely identical' but that, considering the involvement of Mackay Radio in both cases,[192] the parties to the dispute were also the same, at least in the material sense. Accordingly, the RCA maintained that the decision from the first arbitration was essentially a 'final adjudication' of the issue before the tribunal[193] and then proceeded to draw on it repeatedly throughout the proceedings.[194] Of course, China did not go along with this approach, and instead sought to distinguish the two cases and downplay the importance of the decision from the Czechoslovakian arbitration.[195]

new telegraphic routes insofar as such routes would not have an adverse effect on the RCA-Czechoslovakia circuit. See *Czechoslovakian Administration v RCA*, Reply of the Radio Corporation of America (5 January 1932) (MCI International Archives, box 581, file 'China: Chinese Arbitration Correspondence (2 of 13)') 7.

190 RCA Reply Brief (n 184) 12–17 and 39; *RCA v China*, Notes on China's Reply Brief (1 March 1935) (MCI International Archives, box 581, file 'China: Chinese Arbitration Legal Documents') 8–11.

191 China's Reply Brief (n 187) 6ff.

192 See RCA Brief (n 184) 23.

193 Ibid.

194 See ibid 51; RCA Reply Brief (n 184) 8–9 and 44; Notes on China's Reply Brief (n 190) 2 and 7–8.

195 China's Reply Brief (n 187) 7; RCA Reply Brief (n 184) 8.

Finally, an issue that received considerably more attention in this arbitration than in the Czechoslovakian one were the anti-trust implications that accompanied the RCA's claim that the Chinese Administration was not allowed to establish circuits parallel to the existing RCA-China one. Replying to China's argument that the parties' intention when concluding the Shanghai Traffic Agreement could not have been to create a monopolistic situation, as that would have been against existing US anti-trust regulation,[196] the RCA devoted almost half of its reply brief to a detailed explanation that outlined why its claim that China was not allowed to establish additional circuits with the US was not in breach of US anti-trust laws.[197] While the RCA put forward numerous submissions in support of its case, the essence of its position was reflected in the argument that the RCA was by no means seeking to prevent all potential competitors from establishing circuits with the US, but merely insisting that the RCA's contracting partners did not participate in such endeavours. That this might have in the particular instance resulted in a situation where the establishment of parallel circuits was *de facto* impossible due to the Chinese telegraph administration's monopoly over telegraphy in China was not to be attributed to the RCA, but to China itself.[198] Despite the parties' in-depth discussion of several different aspects of US anti-trust law, the tribunal ultimately did not engage with the topic, having deemed it unnecessary to do so in order to reach its decision.[199]

3.3.3 The Tribunal's Decision: No Prohibition for China to Operate Parallel Circuit

On 14 April 1935, news that the outcome of the arbitration would be in favour of China reached the RCA, as its general counsel, Colonel Manton Davis, telegraphed from The Hague a message that must have been as demoralising to the American company as it was short – 'decision(s) will be unfavourable'.[200] Although it was thus known that the overall outcome of the arbitration would

196 China's Reply Brief (n 187) 17–22.

197 RCA Reply Brief (n 184) 21–38. See also Notes on China's Reply Brief (n 190) 12–15.

198 RCA Reply Brief (n 184) 31–33.

199 Interestingly, the RCA did not question whether it would be appropriate for an arbitral tribunal to decide questions of US anti-trust law; an opinion to the effect that raising such an issue in the arbitration might have been inappropriate was brought up only in internal RCA correspondence. See Letter from Rostron to Winterbottom (25 July 1934) (MCI International Archives, box 581, file 'China: Chinese Arbitration Correspondence (11 of 13)').

200 Telegram from Colonel Manton Davis to Radio Corporation of America (14 April 1935) (MCI International Archives, box 581, file 'China: Chinese Arbitration Correspondence (12 of 13)').

not be favourable to the RCA, it soon became apparent that the tribunal's actual award would possibly not be nearly as negative for the American company as the initial report might have suggested. Namely, already the next day, the RCA received further details from The Hague, which indicated that the decision had not yet been formulated and that it would perhaps still be possible to limit the damage to the RCA's interests.[201] The tribunal would then proceed to conduct further consultations through correspondence and in person meetings for over a month in search for the final formulation of its position.

As this process was unravelling, the RCA was given additional reason to hope for a decision that would provide at least some satisfaction to its position, Colonel Davis having relayed from Europe the sentiment that there was 'further reason to expect lemonade'.[202] Colonel Davis subsequently reported that 'discussions have proceeded by correspondence and visits between chairman and Radio Corporation of America arbitrator' and that 'these discussions we believe are further tending towards a decision less harmful to us than first expected'.[203] This additional (re)consideration of the arbitrators' decision appears to have come about at the behest of the RCA-appointed arbitrator, Hubert, who seems to have viewed his role as more that of a representative of the RCA on the tribunal than as that of a truly independent arbitrator.[204] In

201 Telegram from Radio Corporation of America (London) to Radio Corporation of America (New York) (15 April 1935) (MCI International Archives, box 581, file 'China: Chinese Arbitration Correspondence (12 of 13)').

202 Telegram from Davis to Radio Corporation of America (26 April 1935) (MCI International Archives, box 581, file 'China: Chinese Arbitration Correspondence (12 of 13)').

203 Copy of telegram from Manton Davis to David Sarnoff (4 May 1935) (MCI International Archives, box 581, file 'China: Chinese Arbitration Correspondence (12 of 13)').

204 As discussed in ch 4, prior to his appointment, Hubert had, upon going through the documents sent to him by the RCA, revealed to RCA personnel that his first impression was that the RCA's 'view of the matter [wa]s completely justified.' See Letter from A Hubert to Winterbottom (10 May 1933) (MCI International Archives, box 581, file 'China: Chinese Arbitration Correspondence (5 of 13)'). Hubert had also throughout the proceedings maintained continuous contact with the RCA, seemingly even discussing the case merits with its personnel and giving them apparent feedback on arguments. See Letter from Manton Davis to Heinrich Schuloff (8 October 1934) (MCI International Archives, box 581, file 'China: Chinese Arbitration Correspondence (11 of 13)'); Copy of Letter from A Hubert to Colonel Manton Davis (22 May 1933) (MCI International Archives, box 581, file 'China: Chinese Arbitration Correspondence (5 of 13)'); Letter (unsigned) to Heinrich Schuloff (12 June 1933) (MCI International Archives, box 581, file 'China: Chinese Arbitration Correspondence (6 of 13)'); Letter from Manton Davis to Heinrich Schuloff (21 June 1933) (MCI International Archives, box 581, file 'China: Chinese Arbitration Correspondence (7 of 13)'); Letter from Manton Davis to A Hubert (14 July 1933) (MCI International Archives, box 581, file 'China: Chinese Arbitration Correspondence (7 of 13)'); Letter (unsigned) to A Hubert (17 August 1933) (MCI International Archives, box 581, file 'China: Chinese

fact, as the additional negotiations were progressing, Colonel Davis informed the RCA headquarters that he had spent the previous day in Brussels with Hubert, who he said had 'desire[d] to make one more effort [on] our behalf'.[205] It appears that Hubert had indeed succeeded in softening the tribunal's ultimate decision so as to provide at least some satisfaction to the position of the RCA, as is reflected in the tribunal's 'recommendations' on how China was to operate the parallel circuit with Mackay Radio, discussed below. The ultimate award, thus, would not be nearly as unpalatable for the RCA as it may have originally seemed.[206]

Nominally, the tribunal's award is dated 13 April 1935. However, considering the preceding discussion, there can be little doubt (as in fact the RCA itself had confirmed) that the award was antedated and that it was actually issued in late May, when it was communicated to the parties.[207] Although the award was certainly hardly to its liking, the RCA and its legal counsel were not dismissive of it; for example, while he obviously did not agree with the tribunal's ultimate conclusions, one of the RCA's counsel in the proceedings, Heinrich Schuloff, described the award as 'very exact and skilfully worded'.[208] The tribunal's award bore certain similarities but, more importantly, also some stark differences, as compared to the award previously handed down in the *Czechoslovakian*

Arbitration Correspondence (9 of 13)'); Copy of Letter from A Hubert to A H Morton (20 April 1933) (MCI International Archives, box 581, file 'China: Chinese Arbitration Correspondence (10 of 13)'); Letter from Manton Davis to A Hubert (6 July 1934) (MCI International Archives, box 581, file 'China: Chinese Arbitration Correspondence (11 of 13)'). As discussed in ch 2, such conduct by party-appointed arbitrators was hardly unheard of in historical ISA.

205 Telegram from Davis to Radio Corporation of America (9 May 1935) (MCI International Archives, box 581, file 'China: Chinese Arbitration Correspondence (12 of 13)').

206 Letter from the RCA (unsigned) to A Hubert (12 June 1935) (MCI International Archives, box 581, file 'China: Chinese Arbitration Correspondence (12 of 13)'); Translation of Letter from Heinrich Schuloff to Colonel Manton Davis (14 June 1935) (MCI International Archives, box 581, file 'China: Chinese Arbitration Correspondence (12 of 13)'). However, considering that China's need to separate its operation of the Mackay circuit from the RCA one would introduce an opportunity for IT&T subsidiaries to equip China with the equipment necessary for achieving such a goal, an internal letter to the RCA's president David Sarnoff opined that the decision 'could not [have been] more to the liking of the I.T. & T (…) if they had written it themselves'. See Letter (unsigned) to Sarnoff (11 June 1935) (MCI International Archives, box 581, file 'China: Chinese Arbitration Correspondence (12 of 13)').

207 See Letter from Radio Corporation of America and RCA Communications, Inc to the Administration of Posts and Telegraphs of the Republic of Czechoslovakia of 3 July 1935 (MCI International Archives, box 583, file 'Czechoslovakia: Correspondence and Agreements (6 of 6)').

208 Letter from Schuloff to Davis (14 June 1935) (n 206).

Administration v. RCA arbitration. Thus, just like in the Czechoslovakian arbitration, the tribunal was once again split in its decision, albeit this time only partially,[209] while the arbitrators similarly had (as was discussed in Chapter 4) little doubt as to their capacity to decide whether the RCA's contracting partner was entitled to establish a new direct radio telegraphic route. These similarities aside, the outcome of the arbitration could hardly have been more at odds with the *Czechoslovakian Administration v. RCA* arbitration, as the tribunal decided that China was not prohibited from operating a parallel circuit to the US with Mackay Radio. Crucially, as is explained below, this difference in outcome cannot merely be ascribed to the factual particularities underpinning each dispute – the tribunal's entire conceptual approach, as well as its understanding of the parties' underlying relationship, could hardly have differed more as compared to those of the tribunal in the preceding arbitration.

Despite the tribunal's ultimate finding that there was nothing in the Shanghai Traffic Agreement that prevented China from operating a parallel circuit with Mackay Radio, the tribunal's award was, as a matter of principle, very much open to such a possibility. In fact, the tribunal was adamant that it would have had little problem finding in favour of the RCA, not only if such a restriction had been imposed upon China in the agreement explicitly, but also implicitly. The tribunal, however, ultimately found neither to have been the case. In arriving at this conclusion, the tribunal first looked into whether China had undertaken an explicit obligation not to co-operate in the establishment and operation of a parallel direct radio circuit with the US – had this been the case, the tribunal would have deemed China's actions in operating the parallel circuit illegal and in breach of the Shanghai Traffic Agreement. The tribunal, however, failed to see that any such explicit constraint had been imposed upon China either by the very nature of the Shanghai Traffic Agreement, by its special character, or by any of its individual clauses.[210]

Before proceeding with a more detailed analysis on these specific points, however, the tribunal reflected also on the possibility that China had undertaken the obligation not to enter into agreements with third parties implicitly. The tribunal's considerations on this point were highly instructive of its overall approach to the issue before it and would, accordingly, set the tone for the

---

209 *Radio Corporation of America v The National Government of the Republic of China* (1935) 3 RIAA 1621, 1624. A copy of the award is also available in the RCA archives (MCI International Archives, box 581, file 'China: Chinese Arbitration Correspondence (12 of 13)'). The original version of the award, signed by van Hamel, appears to have been retained by the RCA's Austrian counsel, Heinrich Schuloff, and could not be located. See Letter from Schuloff to Davis (14 June 1935) (n 206).

210 *RCA v China* (n 209) 1626–1627.

remainder of its reasoning. Although, as previously mentioned, the tribunal was in principle entirely open to the possibility that China might have implicitly undertaken the limitations upon its freedom of action claimed by the RCA, the arbitrators' test for determining whether this had been the case was highly demanding – such limitations had to be 'very distinctly shown'. The tribunal emphasised this point as follows:

> *The Chinese Government can certainly sign away a part of its liberty of action,* and this also in the field of the establishment of international radio-telegraphic communications, and of its cooperation therein. *It can do so as well in an implicit manner,* if a reasonable construction of its undertakings leads up to that conclusion. It will, as any other party, be bound by law and by any obligations, legally accepted. *But as a sovereign government, on principle free in its action for the public interest as it sees it, it cannot be presumed to have accepted such restriction of its freedom of action, unless the acceptance of such restriction can be ascertained distinctly and beyond reasonable doubt.*[211]

Accordingly, the tribunal acknowledged that it was possible for a state entity – and the tribunal saw no distinction in this respect between a government discharging its sovereign rights and a governmental administration exercising its public function in the public interest[212] – to sign away a part of its freedom of action. The practical effectiveness of this statement by the tribunal, however, was severely circumscribed by the tribunal's understanding of when such signing away of governmental freedom of action can be deemed to have occurred. This was particularly so when considering the tribunal's approach to interpreting contracts that affected the public interest:

> It is a correct rule, known and recognized in common law as well as in international law, that *any restriction of a contracting Government's rights must be effected in a clear and distinct manner; 'Contracts affecting the public interest are to be construed liberally in favour of the public.'* The Plaintiff, dealing with a Government as its contracting party, will have born this point in mind, in negotiating the terms of the agreement.[213]

211 Ibid 1627. Emphases added.
212 Ibid. See nn 189–190
213 Ibid. Emphasis added.

In light of the law that was applicable to the parties' relationship under the Shanghai Traffic Agreement,[214] the tribunal's reference to international law appears both as unexpected and as puzzling; it can most likely only be explained by the extensive experience in international legal matters by the tribunal president, van Hamel. This notwithstanding, the important takeaway from the tribunal's interpretative approach is that any perceived lack of certainty in the Shanghai Traffic Agreement was bound to benefit China and work against the RCA. To say that such an approach was unlikely to yield the result the RCA was hoping for where there was no explicit imposition of restrictions upon China's freedom of action through the Shanghai Traffic Agreement would certainly have been an understatement. And, as already mentioned above, the tribunal indeed did not think that any such explicit restrictions had been imposed upon China.

In particular, insofar as the intrinsic nature of the Shanghai Traffic Agreement was concerned, the tribunal acknowledged that arrangements between public authorities and private parties could certainly be established as exclusive and would, as such, preclude any competitive behaviour. Simultaneously, the tribunal did not deem the establishment and operation of a radio circuit to be, by its very nature, such an exclusive activity, as it considered the establishment of parallel telegraph lines between two countries very much possible. This was something that, in the tribunal's view, was not only recognised as a possibility by the Shanghai Traffic Agreement, but also by the RCA in its submissions when it acknowledged that the Chinese government was allowed to grant a concession for a parallel China-US circuit (as long as the RCA's contracting partner did not itself participate in its establishment and operation).[215] The tribunal also recognised that the RCA had made a substantial contribution to the establishment and operationalisation of the RCA-China circuit, but ultimately found no circumstances that would have implied that this contribution was of such nature and magnitude that it would have necessarily been contingent on the Shanghai Traffic Agreement being exclusive in nature. Accordingly, the tribunal concluded that the Shanghai Traffic Agreement was not by its very nature an exclusive one.[216]

The tribunal was equally unconvinced that such a conclusion should follow from the alleged special character of the Shanghai Traffic Agreement,[217] as the RCA had argued. Perhaps the most interesting aspect of the tribunal's

214 See n 239.

215 See nn 189–191.

216 *RCA v China* (n 209) 1627–1628.

217 Ibid 1628–1630.

reasoning on this point – as contradictory as it may appear upon first impression, though it hardly was – was that the tribunal was both indifferent to, and highly appreciative of, the fact that one of the parties to the dispute was a state entity. Namely, at a broader conceptual level, the tribunal agreed with the RCA that a joint adventure or partnership agreement between the parties would indeed be of a special character and would therefore preclude China from concluding an agreement with Mackay Radio. The tribunal deemed the prohibition for parties to initiate joint activities on parallel lines with competing third parties as an essential feature of such a partnership – irrespective of whether such a prohibition was explicitly provided for or whether a government was a party to the agreement. The crucial question in this respect thus became whether the Shanghai Traffic Agreement could be deemed to have established such a partnership. If answered in the negative, the tribunal held that the interpretation of the agreement would as a result follow the principle 'that the Government cannot be held to have given up to the Radio Corporation a larger part of its freedom of action, than results beyond reasonable doubt from the very wording of the agreement.'[218]

Ultimately, the tribunal concluded that, despite bearing some similarities to such agreements, the Shanghai Traffic Agreement could not be classified as a partnership or joint adventure under either American or Chinese law. The arbitrators considered that the parties' intention when concluding the agreement was not to establish a common enterprise in order to pursue profit – an indispensable characteristic of a partnership agreement. It was here that the tribunal put specific emphasis on the fact that one of the parties to the agreement was a government, having found that no such profit-centred assumptions regarding the Chinese government's intentions when entering the agreement could be made. The tribunal instead described China's entering into the agreement with the RCA as follows:

> In making useful provisions for the working of a radio-telegraphic circuit between its territory and another country, *the Government envisages the establishment of a public service, in order to promote the interests of its people, to encourage their international communications* (business relations and personal relations), *and to make them enjoy the advantages of modern scientific development in this field*. It makes no difference that the Government will desire to make such a service pay, cover the expenses and, if possible, yield surplus advantages.[219]

218 Ibid 1629.

219 Ibid 1629. Emphasis added.

This perception by the tribunal of China's motivation for entering into the agreement was no mere cursory observation, as it was coupled with a corresponding approach as to the level of specificity that was expected of the parties in defining their relationship, as well as with the consequences accompanying any such lack of specificity. Thus, despite recognising that the RCA may have been motivated by other, more business oriented intentions, the tribunal underlined that, when contracting with a government, the RCA should have been aware that its counterparty was acting based on the aforementioned broader interests. Accordingly, any partnership or joint adventure to be concluded needed to be made clear 'beyond reasonable doubt'.[220] In the tribunal's words:

> If a party, like the Radio Corporation, wants to establish with the Government the entire complex of obligations and rights, included in the technical contract of partnership or joint adventure, they will have to see that this relation is clearly established, excluding every reasonable doubt on the subject. Otherwise, *the Government has only to be assumed to have entered into the rights and duties definitely established, and which it has judged advantageous to the general interests of which it is in charge.* It will be bound, of course, by the obligations which it is thereby duly accepting.[221]

With the tribunal's dismissal of both the very nature of the Shanghai Traffic Agreement and its alleged special character as reasons for precluding China from operating the parallel circuit with Mackay Radio, the last remaining avenue for success for the RCA were the specific clauses of the Shanghai Traffic Agreement. The tribunal examined the wording of three of the agreement's potentially relevant clauses in this respect – Articles 3, 8, and 11 – in order to determine whether China had undertaken an obligation not to introduce a circuit parallel to the RCA-China one, but found none of them sufficient to impose such a significant restriction on China.

Article 8, which provided that each party would in general 'cooperate with the other to secure the successful and remunerative working' of the joint circuit,[222] had served as the main prong of the RCA's claim. The tribunal understood this article as having created a general obligation of cooperation between the parties to the Shanghai Traffic Agreement; while the article had,

220 Ibid 1629–1630.

221 Ibid 1630. Emphasis added.

222 See art 8 of the Shanghai Traffic Agreement (n 119).

in the tribunal's view, thus imposed certain obligations upon the Chinese government, these did not go as far as to impose upon China *per se* a prohibition for the establishment of a parallel radio-telegraphic circuit. Consequently, although the tribunal recognised that the profitability of the RCA's operations in China would be somewhat reduced by the Mackay circuit, it did not deem that the mere establishment of such a parallel circuit would have made the successful operation of the RCA-China circuit impossible. The tribunal's position, instead, was that the operation of the China-Mackay circuit would have only become problematic under Article 8 if, as a result of its operation, the RCA-China circuit would have become a failure (which had not been argued by the RCA). For any stricter restriction to be imposed on a government, it needed – as the tribunal had previously stressed – to be imposed more explicitly.[223]

The tribunal was of the same opinion regarding Article 3,[224] which stipulated that China was to transmit over the circuit 'every message within its control destined to the United States of America or intended for transit through the United States unless routed otherwise by sender.'[225] The tribunal did not consider that the provision dealt with, or excluded, the establishment of new telegraphic lines, but simply accorded to the RCA the right to all of the radio traffic that was not being routed otherwise. The effect of the provision, according to the tribunal, was thus not to prohibit China from participating in the establishment of new circuits that would have diverted traffic from the RCA-China one,[226] but (merely) to establish for the RCA a privileged position, thus making it not the only but the '*main* direct radio-telegraph circuit between China and the United States.'[227] Such qualification by the tribunal of the parties' relationship under the Shanghai Traffic Agreement was, although it may not have been entirely satisfactory to the RCA, undoubtedly one of the tribunal's more important findings. In fact, not only did the tribunal particularly emphasise that China was expected to fully observe this privileged position for the RCA and later in the decision proceed to expound on what this might imply, but the RCA would itself subsequently come to rely on this aspect of the

223 See *RCA v China* (n 209) 1630–1632.

224 Ibid 1632–1633.

225 See art 3 of the Shanghai Traffic Agreement (n 119).

226 The tribunal was here again guided by the approach that had been a consistent theme throughout the decision – in order for the wording to preclude China from establishing additional radio-telegraphic circuits, such an intention should have been more clearly articulated. The tribunal, however, deemed the wording of art 3 agnostic on the matter – it neither accorded China the freedom of establishing additional radio-telegraphic circuits nor prohibited it from doing so.

227 *RCA v China* (n 209) 1632. Emphasis in the original.

tribunal's decision in numerous relationships with other telegraph administrations (see sub-section 3.4).

A particularly interesting aspect of the tribunal's decision in relation to Article 3 was the distinction that the tribunal drew between the wording of the Shanghai Traffic Agreement and the one that had been construed in the *Czechoslovakian Administration v. RCA* arbitration. Namely, while the Czechoslovakian Traffic Agreement had contained a clause extremely similar to Article 3 of the Shanghai Traffic Agreement, the relevant clause in the former agreement had in addition provided that such messages were to be transmitted 'exclusively' over the joint circuit.[228] Although neither party had, as the tribunal had itself acknowledged, accorded particular importance to this distinction, the tribunal nonetheless alluded that the opposite interpretations that had been reached by the tribunals in the two parallel arbitrations may be explained by this difference in language. Albeit with the caveat that it was not necessary for the arbitrators to interpret the Czechoslovakian Traffic Agreement, the tribunal thus emphasised that the lack of the term 'exclusive' in the Shanghai Traffic Agreement 'constitute[d] an interesting difference between the Chinese and the Czechoslovakian case; a difference which *might even lead to a more restrictive construction of the Czechoslovakian Traffic Agreement than of the Chinese one*'.[229] While this peculiar difference between the wordings of the two agreements highlighted by the tribunal is certainly noteworthy, it nonetheless hardly appears capable of explaining the differences between the two decisions. As is assessed in more detail in sub-section 3.4.1 below, the divergences between the two decisions were much more deeply rooted, including in relation to pivotal aspects of the tribunals' respective reasonings, for the difference in outcome to be ascribed to the presence (or not) of a single word in the underlying agreements.

The tribunal finally also analysed Article 11, which permitted the parties to conclude radio agreements with 'any other nation or nations',[230] finding it to be of no help to either party's cause, as it did not deal with restrictions that might have been imposed upon China in favour of the RCA. In the tribunal's view, the provision referred merely to the possibility of China concluding agreements with parties of a different nationality than the RCA and as such was of no importance for China's relationship with a party such as Mackay Radio, which was of the same (American) nationality.

---

228 See ch 4.

229 *RCA v China* (n 209) 1633. Emphasis added.

230 Ibid 1633–1634.

Having found no other provisions in the Shanghai Traffic Agreement that could have conceivably given the agreement the restrictive effect sought by the RCA, the tribunal thus concluded that China was, by virtue of its contract with the RCA, not prohibited from co-operating with Mackay Radio. Crucially, however, this was not the end of the tribunal's analysis. Namely, as previously mentioned,[231] the tribunal considered that China had, pursuant to the Shanghai Traffic Agreement, undertaken certain positive obligations *vis-à-vis* the RCA, and was thus not entirely unrestricted in its dealings with Mackay Radio. In light of this, the tribunal then, rather interestingly, decided to express itself on the parties' relationship beyond the confines of the specific mandate that had been conferred upon it by the parties. When doing so, the tribunal, by its own estimation, acknowledged that the parties had confined their request to the tribunal strictly to the principled legal question of the existence of a violation of the Shanghai Traffic Agreement due to China's conclusion of an agreement with Mackay Radio and their establishment of a joint circuit; any practical considerations as to the operation of such circuit had been addressed by the parties during the proceedings only tangentially and were thus to be left open. With this caveat in mind, the tribunal nonetheless expressed its desire to offer its interpretation of this matter 'at length', not only for the sake of 'complet[ing] the argumentation', but, more ambitiously, also in the hope that it could potentially '*serve as a guidance for the parties concerned*'.[232] After recalling its earlier finding that the Shanghai Traffic Agreement had established for the RCA a privileged position according to which the RCA circuit was to be the main direct circuit between China and the US, the tribunal then proceeded to offer a set of detailed 'recommendations' to the parties on how a potential parallel circuit was to be operated from a practical perspective.[233]

231 See nn 224–227.

232 *RCA v China* (n 209) 1634. Emphasis added.

233 Ibid 1635–1636. The tribunal's openly acknowledged creative role in this context was thus not dissimilar to that of the tribunals from the arbitrations discussed in section 2 above. One of the tribunal's observations on this point was that the initial version of the agreement between China and Mackay Radio exemplified a parallel circuit that would not have been compatible with the RCA's preferential status. More specifically, the tribunal *inter alia* opined that China could not participate in any canvassing activity for the parallel circuit, and that the technical and practical operation of the parallel circuit should in no way impair the RCA circuit. This ultimately led the tribunal to advise that '*the two services should be operated by the Chinese Government separately, by means of separate, properly equipped and staffed installations*'. According to the RCA's counsel, Heinrich Schuloff, this part of the tribunal's decision embraced 'all the points that [the RCA's representatives] desired to have stated'. See Letter from Schuloff to Davis (14 June 1935) (n 206).

Although these instructions were designated by the tribunal as 'recommendations', they were, curiously enough, referenced once more in the operative part of the tribunal's decision, albeit with the repeated caveat that the questions to which they related had not been specifically brought before the tribunal for decision.[234] Whether these recommendations by the tribunal would, in line with the tribunal's intentions, end up influencing the particular future relations between the RCA and China is not entirely clear. As is discussed in more detail below, the RCA would in its subsequent dealings with China, albeit with the acknowledgment that these were not formulated by the tribunal as strict requirements, rely on the tribunal's recommendations when discussing how their future relationship should be structured;[235] unfortunately, the archival materials obtained on the *RCA v. China* dispute do not reveal the position taken by China on the matter.[236]

In light of the foregoing, it appears that, perhaps somewhat ironically, it is the least because of the ultimate outcome that the decision of the *RCA v. China* tribunal remains one of great historical interest. Indeed, the tribunal's decision was characterised by a distinctly public-law-oriented approach, albeit one which, while certainly highly sensitised toward China's sovereign prerogatives, was not deemed by the arbitrators' to preclude the possibility that China might be restricted in how it exercised its sovereign capacities. Equally distinguishing was the tribunal's unmasked stepping outside of the strict confines of the mandate conferred upon it by the parties and the taking on of an overtly creative role in laying out a series of precise 'recommendations' that were intended to serve as guidance for the parties' future behaviour. And while there can be little doubt that the tribunal's decision will best be remembered for having been handed down in the first ever PCA arbitration where one of the parties was not a state (as is discussed in sub-section 4.2.2.1 below), for present purposes it is no less interesting that the decision would end up not only resolving the particular

234 The tribunal further stressed that such questions 'may, if they should arise, be subsequently submitted for arbitration by either party, if desired.' See *RCA v China* (n 209) 1636. The tribunal's exact motivation in referencing a possible future arbitration in this context is not readily apparent. Indeed, one of the RCA's counsel in the arbitration, Heinrich Schuloff, commented that it was unclear 'whether this part of the decision is of any substantial legal value', or 'whether the recommendations could be made binding through an eventual future arbitration'. See Letter from Schuloff to Davis (14 June 1935) (n 206). It appears that neither the RCA nor China ever followed through on the possibility of arbitrating these matters.

235 See sub-section 3.4.2 below.

236 There are, however, indications that at least some of the RCA's partner administrations had taken such recommendations to heart. See n 257.

dispute between the RCA and China but also, as is discussed in depth in the following sub-section, influencing how the rights and obligations underlying a number of the RCA's relations with third-party state entities would come to be understood.

3.4 *The Reverberations of the RCA v China Arbitration: RCA's Recalibration of Relations with Third Parties following the Tribunal's Decision*

The tribunal's decision in *RCA v. China* and the ensuing fallout are illustrative of historical ISA's capacity to exert extended normative influence on one of the disputing parties' relations with third parties, and to do so on multiple fronts. First of all, they reveal a reciprocal normative influence between the two RCA arbitrations, which culminated in the fact that the latter of the two awards (*RCA v. China*) would eventually come to govern how the relations underlying the *Czechoslovakian Administration v. RCA* arbitration would be structured (3.4.1). Moreover, not only did the *RCA v. China* award also influence how the RCA came to understand its relationship with other telegraph administrations in the numerous countries across the world in which it was operating at the time (3.4.2), but the RCA's corresponding adjustment of how it interpreted its international contracts was likewise a significant turning point in its anti-trust litigation with the US government (3.4.3).

3.4.1 The Mutual Interplay between the Two RCA Cases

At the forefront of such extended normative influence into which the *RCA v. China* arbitration offers insight was the strong reciprocal influence that the two RCA arbitrations had on one another.

Initially, it was the *Czechoslovakian Administration v. RCA* arbitration that exerted such influence on the subsequent *RCA v. China* case. Namely, following its victory in the first arbitration, the RCA had in the second arbitration relied heavily on the *Czechoslovakian Administration v. RCA* award, using it repeatedly as an argumentative tool and even attempting to present its effect as essentially being equivalent to that of *res judicata*.[237] The *RCA v. China* tribunal, however, obviously did not share the same view – despite such strong invocation by the RCA of the earlier decision and the obvious common legal and factual underpinnings of both cases, it decided the case before it differently.[238]

237 See RCA Brief (n 184) 21–23 and 51; RCA Reply Brief (n 184) 8–9 and 44; Notes on China's Reply Brief (n 190) 2 and 7–8. See also nn 192–194.

238 See ch 4.

Having reached this conclusion, the *RCA v. China* tribunal was, of course, by no means bound to engage whatsoever with the dispute between The Czechoslovakian Administration and the RCA; rather, it could have either simply ignored it or dismissed it as irrelevant under the pretext that it had concerned different parties and had been subject to a different applicable law.[239] Yet, the *RCA v. China* tribunal chose neither of these options. Instead, as was discussed in the previous sub-section, the tribunal tried to frame its finding as not necessarily being incongruous with that of the *Czechoslovakian Administration v. RCA* tribunal. What is particularly striking – and indicative of the extended normative influence of the *Czechoslovakian Administration v. RCA* award – is that the *RCA v. China* tribunal did so despite the obvious irreconcilability of the tribunals' respective approaches.

Namely, while there was undoubtedly a common denominator between the two decisions – in particular, that both tribunals had found that, in principle, a clear enough prohibition would have prevented the RCA's contractual counterpart from opening a parallel circuit – the manner in which the arbitrators had in the specific disputes before them arrived at opposing conclusions regarding whether this had in fact been the case could hardly have been more different. This is so because the two tribunals had both a fundamentally different understanding of the nature of the underlying relationship between the RCA and its respective contracting partners, and of how the contract between them was to be characterised and interpreted. Regarding the former, the *Czechoslovakian Administration v. RCA* tribunal had held that the Czechoslovakian Traffic Agreement had created a co-partnership between its parties,[240] whereas the *RCA v. China* tribunal did not see the Shanghai Traffic Agreement as having had such an effect (see sub-section 3.3.3 above). Likewise, on a conceptual level, while the *Czechoslovakian Administration v. RCA* tribunal had characterised the underlying traffic agreement as a civil law contract,[241] the *RCA v. China* tribunal viewed it as a public law contract (see sub-section 3.3.3 above). The tribunals' findings on both of these points were crucial in the respective cases and determinative for their eventual outcomes; the differences in the outcomes, thus, were deeply rooted in fundamentally disparate approaches by each tribunal and cannot be explained away by the textual dissimilarities between the two underlying traffic agreements (reflected in the fact that, unlike the Shanghai Traffic Agreement, the Czechoslovakian Traffic Agreement had contained

239 The applicable law in the two arbitrations was a composition of US law, on the one hand, and Czechoslovakian or Chinese law, respectively, on the other.

240 See ch 4.

241 See ibid.

the term 'exclusively'), as hinted at by the *RCA v. China* tribunal. This textual difference had, in any event, not served as the basis for the *Czechoslovakian Administration v. RCA* tribunal's finding, while one of the RCA's legal counsel had likewise himself indicated that the RCA had in the China dispute not really sought to justify its position based on the clause that had contained the said textual difference.[242] Therefore, at the conceptual level, squaring the two decisions was akin to squaring a circle – it just could not be done in a way that would truly fit. That, irrespective of this, the *RCA v. China* tribunal – perhaps inspired by the need to avoid the feeling of obvious unease that such an open conflict between two decisions with such strong common underlying features would have undoubtedly created – was willing to attempt to reconcile the irreconcilable by engaging with the dispute between The Czechoslovakian Administration and the RCA, only goes to show that the tribunal had, despite the opposing outcome, viewed the *Czechoslovakian Administration v. RCA* award as one that had exerted a certain degree of normative influence also on the dispute before it that simply could not be ignored. In other words, the *RCA v. China* tribunal had viewed the *Czechoslovakian Administration v. RCA* decision as one whose normative influence had extended beyond the relationship of the two parties participating in that particular dispute.

The subsequent normative influence of the *RCA v. China* decision in the reverse direction was even more pronounced, notwithstanding the fact that the *Czechoslovakian Administration v. RCA* dispute had previously been settled by a final award. Namely, following the conclusion of the *Czechoslovakian Administration v. RCA* arbitration, The Czechoslovakian Administration was – in compliance with the tribunal's decision – for the time being abstaining from opening an additional radio telegraphic circuit between Czechoslovakia and the US.[243] All of this, however, would change with the *RCA v. China* award, as this decision would cause the RCA to give up its stance on the meaning of its contracts that it had so successfully defended in the first arbitration. Indeed, not long after it had received the *RCA v. China* award, the RCA sent a letter to The Czechoslovakian Administration, informing it that, in light of the recently rendered *RCA v. China* award, the RCA would no longer insist on its earlier interpretation of the joint agreement. The RCA explained this change in its position, which had been prompted by the *RCA v. China* award, in the following manner:

242 Letter from Schuloff to Davis (14 June 1935) (n 206).

243 See ch 4 sub-section 2.5.

> The Arbitrators under our traffic contract with the National Government of the Republic of China have, by a decision dated April 13, 1935, but not actually rendered until May 27, 1935, decided that the National Government of the Republic of China did not violate its traffic contract with us by establishing a direct radio circuit with others in United States of America and transmitting by such other circuit messages that may be specially routed thereby by the sender.
>
> Previously, Arbitrators under our contract with the Czechoslovakian Republic had decided to the contrary with reference to the similar Czechoslovakian traffic contract with us.
>
> The foregoing results in a confused situation which might well give rise to further controversies on this same point. Such controversies are burdensome and disturbing to our correspondents, and we desire to put an end to them.
>
> Accordingly, we hereby agree that we shall not at any time hereafter assert or contend that any provisions of our present or future traffic contracts, arrangements or understandings, bind or shall bind any of our present or future correspondents not to establish or permit to be established, if they so desire, direct radio circuits with others in the United States for traffic specially routed there by the sender.[244]

At this juncture, it is critical to emphasise that there was no reason for the RCA to believe that the *RCA v. China* award would contribute to a 'confused situation', unless it understood the award's normative relevance not to be confined to the parties to that particular dispute but rather to extend also to the interpretation of its traffic agreements in general. This especially remains true regarding the RCA's rights and obligations arising under the Czechoslovakian Traffic Agreement, which had ostensibly already been definitively interpreted and decided upon by a final and binding award of the *Czechoslovakian Administration v. RCA* tribunal. Moreover, considering the *RCA v. China* tribunal's own distinguishing of the two underlying traffic agreements, it was likewise open to the RCA to take the position that, rather than a cause for a 'confused situation', the two seemingly conflicting awards were but a reflection of differing wordings in the agreements that they were tasked with interpreting. The RCA, thus, was by no means bound to reverse course following the *RCA v. China* award; that it chose to do so can only be indicative of the fact that it perceived the normative influence of the tribunal's award to go beyond the confines of just the

244 See Letter from RCA to The Czechoslovakian Administration (3 July 1935) (n 207).

relationship of the two parties privy to the *RCA v. China* arbitration and extend also to the remainder of the RCA's relationships that were based on similarly formulated contracts.

Interestingly enough, however, the relevance of the *RCA v. China* award for the relations between the RCA and The Czechoslovakian Administration was not restricted to the RCA's reversal of its earlier position regarding the proper interpretation of their underlying agreement. Instead, the RCA had in the letter that it had sent to The Czechoslovakian Administration also indicated that it would nonetheless expect its correspondents to 'operate such other circuits as to give effect to the preferential character of the service with us', as had been expressed in the *RCA v. China* award. Although it acknowledged that this had not been set out by the tribunal as a strict requirement and would therefore not be identical in every instance, the RCA then proceeded to quote heavily from the part of the tribunal's award that dealt with such preferential treatment and declared that it would be sending the full text of the award to The Czechoslovakian Administration.

Somewhat curiously, due to his having been away on holiday, this letter did not reach the RCA's main point of contact with the Czechoslovakian side, Otto Kucera, for some time, which prompted him to enquire with the RCA whether the decision in the China arbitration had induced a shift in the RCA's position on the matter.[245] It would not be long, however, before Kucera would learn of the RCA's new stance, to which he responded that he was 'very glad that our long controversies are *finished by the decision in the arbitration case between RCA and China*.'[246] It was thus not only the RCA, but also The Czechoslovakian Administration, that had perceived the *RCA v. China* decision as one that should have had a decisive influence on how norms governing their mutual relationship were to be understood. Crucially, the Czechoslovakian side's invocation of the *RCA v. China* award as a turning point in its relations with the RCA was not mere tokenism brought about due to the decision being favourable to its position, but instead appears to have been a true reflection of The Czechoslovakian Administration's genuine perception of the award as instructive for how its relations with the RCA were to be structured. This is evidenced by the fact

245 Translation of Letter from the Telegraph Administration of Czechoslovakia to RCA Communications, Inc (8 August 1935) (MCI International Archives, box 583, file 'Czechoslovakia: Correspondence and Agreements (6 of 6)'). Kucera had apparently found out the outcome of the *RCA v China* arbitration on his own.

246 Copy of Letter from the Ministry of Posts and Telegraphs of the Republic of Czechoslovakia to W A Winterbottom (13 September 1935) (MCI International Archives, box 583, file 'Czechoslovakia: Correspondence and Agreements (6 of 6)').

that Kucera had, during The Czechoslovakian Administration's preparation to conclude a contract with Mackay Radio for the purpose of opening a second direct circuit to the US, enquired with the RCA about the level of restriction that the RCA would insist upon in relation to the operation of such an additional circuit, pursuant to the decision in the Chinese arbitration.[247] Accordingly, The Czechoslovakian Administration appears to have viewed as authoritative pronunciations as to its own rights and obligations not only the elements of the *RCA v. China* award that were in its favour, but also the tribunal's overtly non-obligatory recommendations that were less favourable to its position.

It was the decision by the *RCA v. China* tribunal, then, rather than the very arbitration between the disputing parties, that had finally not only put the dispute between the RCA and The Czechoslovakian Administration to rest, but also determined how the normative framework for the parties' future relations (i.e. the Czechoslovakian Traffic Agreement) was to be interpreted. This was something that the RCA was by no means obliged to accept; regardless of its acknowledgment of the *RCA v. China* award as the guiding post for the remainder of its contracts,[248] its relationship with The Czechoslovakian Administration was distinguishable on the account that the matter had been finally adjudicated by a competent tribunal. Despite this fact, the normative influence of the *RCA v. China* decision was nonetheless extended by the RCA so as to restructure also the normative architecture of its relationship with The Czechoslovakian Administration.[249]

---

247 Letter from Loyd A Briggs to W A Winterbottom (27 November 1935) (MCI International Archives, box 583, file 'Czechoslovakia: Correspondence and Agreements (6 of 6)').

248 See sub-section 3.4.2 immediately below.

249 As is elaborated in the two sub-sections immediately below, the RCA's thinking in this respect was no doubt influenced by its ongoing anti-trust suit against the US government. Rather ironically, however, just as the RCA had withheld its objections to The Czechoslovakian Administration establishing such an additional circuit with Mackay Radio, word came from Czechoslovakia that they would, due to insufficient technical capabilities, not proceed with opening the second circuit, at least for the time being. See Copy of Letter from Otto Kucera to Loyd A Briggs (16 September 1935) (MCI International Archives, box 583, file 'Czechoslovakia: Correspondence and Agreements (6 of 6)'). The two sides then once more entered into negotiations regarding a possible adjustment to their relationship, which eventually proved futile, as The Czechoslovakian Administration definitely concluded the traffic agreement with Mackay Radio. See Letter from Loyd A Briggs to Otto Kucera (30 March 1936) (MCI International Archives, box 583, file 'Czechoslovakia: Correspondence and Agreements (6 of 6)').

3.4.2 RCA's Recalibration of Its Traffic Agreements on a World-Wide Scale

The RCA's relationship with The Czechoslovakian Administration was not the American company's only relationship with third parties that would be affected by the *RCA v. China* award. At the time of the two arbitrations, the RCA's communications business was a global undertaking, with the company possessing traffic agreements that allowed it to operate radio telegraphic circuits with dozens of countries.[250] Most of these contracts had been based on the RCA's model traffic agreement and, although not identical, were drafted similarly enough so that the RCA would view them as being closely related.[251] Accordingly, in what was already a foreshadowing of the extended normative influence that the RCA would eventually accord to the tribunals' decisions, the feeling within the RCA had from before the first arbitration against The Czechoslovakian Administration been that a decision in an arbitration involving one of those contracts could have potential repercussions for the greater part of its traffic agreements:

> If arbitration went against us *the effect on our traffic agreements with other countries might be disastrous*. If in our favour, it would be used by our antagonists here as conclusive evidence that we had set out to make exclusive traffic agreements and had always so regarded them. *Arbitration with the decision in favour of Czechoslovakia would advertise internationally that our agreements were of no value*.[252]

It is hardly shocking that the RCA maintained this position once it prevailed in the Czechoslovakian arbitration; it is perhaps more surprising that it stayed true to this stance even once the tables had turned with the unfavourable decision in *RCA v. China*.

Namely, shortly after the China arbitration, the RCA sent letters of identical content to the one it had sent to The Czechoslovakian Administration to all of its partnering administrations and informed them of the outcome of the case.[253] As was discussed in the previous sub-section, in the letter, the RCA

---

250 See Copy of Letter from Samuel Reber to the Minister of Posts and Telegraphs of the Republic of Czechoslovakia (25 April 1930) (MCI International Archives, box 583, file 'Czechoslovakia: Correspondence and Agreements (2 of 6)').

251 See ibid.

252 See Letter (unsigned) to Winterbottom (3 July 1930) (MCI International Archives, box 583, file 'Czechoslovakia: Correspondence and Agreements (3 of 6)'). Emphases added.

253 See Letter from RCA to The Czechoslovakian Administration (3 July 1935) (n 207); Letter from Radio Corporation of America and RCA Communications, Inc to the Ministry of

stated that, in light of the *RCA v. China* award, it would no longer object to its correspondents establishing additional direct radio telegraphic routes with the US.[254] The RCA's seemingly yielding acceptance of the *RCA v. China* award as controlling as to the meaning of all of its traffic agreements and lack of insistence that, out of the two conflicting interpretations given by the tribunals in the two arbitrations, the one to be followed was the one which was more favourable to its interests, was most likely made easier by the complicated situation the company faced back in the US in relation to an anti-trust suit that had been brought against it by the US government over its traffic agreements.[255] This, however, in no way detracts from the fact that the RCA's decision to recalibrate all of its global partnerships on a general basis was ultimately made as a direct consequence of the *RCA v. China* award.

It was based on the *RCA v. China* decision, then, that the RCA had ceased to insist upon its theretofore interpretation of its traffic agreements in the remaining jurisdictions in which it was operating. As was discussed in the previous sub-section, however, the RCA's reliance on the *RCA v. China* tribunal's decision did not end there, as the American company then invoked the tribunal's ruling in order to express its expectation that the correspondents with whom it had traffic agreements similar to the Chinese one would 'give effect to the preferential character of the service with us.'[256] The letter then proceeded to quote in full the 'recommendations' given by the RCA-China tribunal; while the RCA acknowledged in the letter that these were not set out by the tribunal as strict requirements, it nonetheless expressed its expectation that those administrations with whom such contracts existed would adhere to their preferential character. As was further noted above, that the RCA's expectations in this respect were indeed given at least some weight is evidenced by The Czechoslovakian Administration's stance to, when planning to open the second direct circuit to the US, enquire with the RCA about the level of restriction that the RCA would insist upon regarding the operation of such an additional

Communications of the Republic of China (3 July 1935) (MCI International Archives, box 581, file 'China: Correspondence (1 of 6)').

254 Letter from RCA to The Czechoslovakian Administration (3 July 1935) (n 207); Letter from RCA to China (3 July 1935) (n 253).

255 See ch 4 sub-section 2.1. Indeed, the letter that the RCA had sent out to all of its foreign correspondents was sent immediately the day after the company had entered into the consent decree with the US government (which was itself prompted by the *RCA v China* award, as is explained in sub-section 3.4.3 immediately below).

256 Letter from RCA to The Czechoslovakian Administration (3 July 1935) (n 207); Letter from RCA to China (3 July 1935) (n 253). See sub-section 3.4.1.

circuit.[257] It was thus not only the operative part of the *RCA v. China* tribunal's decision that would come to influence how a public utility service in other countries where the RCA operated would be structured, but also the tribunal's 'recommendations'.

3.4.3 The Impact of the Decision by the *RCA v China* Tribunal on the RCA's Anti-Trust Suit with the US Government

Perhaps the most curious aspect of the normative influence exerted by the *RCA v. China* decision on the RCA's relations with other public authorities is its effect on structuring the relationship between the RCA and the US government. Namely, as was explained in Chapter 4, the RCA and the US government were at the time of the RCA's arbitrations entangled in an important anti-trust suit. While an initial consent decree, entered into in 1932 by the two sides, had resolved the majority of the open issues on this matter, the allegedly monopolistic nature of the RCA's overseas traffic agreements – such as the one that was the subject of the *RCA v. China* arbitration – had been deemed too complicated to resolve at the time and had therefore been left to be settled at a future date.[258] As the moment when the matter needed finally to be resolved approached, it would turn out that it would be none other than the *RCA v. China* decision and its influence on how the remainder of the RCA's traffic agreements came to be interpreted that would provide the crucial spark for bringing the anti-trust suit to an end. That this would end up being the case was seemingly not at all unexpected for those involved. Namely, in light of the on-going anti-trust suit, the US government had been kept informed by the RCA about its arbitrations throughout the entire process.[259] During the discussions about the prospective arbitration against China, it had already been hinted to the Department of Justice that a potential loss for the RCA in the China arbitration may very well mean that there would be 'nothing for the Government to litigate about' regarding any of the RCA's contracts.[260]

---

257 See n 247.

258 'Decree Dissolving Radio Group Under Anti-Trust Law' *The New York Times* (New York, 22 November 1932) 17. See ch 4 for a more detailed discussion of the government's anti-trust suit and the initial consent decree.

259 See Aide Memoire titled 'An Arbitration Which China May Propose to RCA Communications, Inc Construing the Radio Traffic Contract between Them Executed in 1928' (7 January 1933) (MCI International Archives, box 581, file 'China: Chinese Arbitration Correspondence (10 of 13)'); Letter from Manton Davis to W A Winterbottom (6 May 1933) (MCI International Archives, box 581, file 'China: Chinese Arbitration Correspondence (10 of 13)'); 'Chinese Arbitration: Memorandum of Conference at the Department of Justice Monday, May 1, 1933' (MCI International Archives, box 581, file 'China: Chinese Arbitration Correspondence (10 of 13)').

260 Memorandum of Conference at the Department of Justice (n 259).

This prediction would indeed eventually prove to be true. After the *RCA v. China* award was issued, the US government was once again notified of the outcome and sent a copy of the decision. In response, the US government noted that it did not object to the preferential status of the RCA's contracts mentioned by the tribunal's decision,[261] pursuant to which the RCA's correspondents would be prevented from soliciting for its competitors, as long as this did not preclude the establishment and listing of such competitive routes.[262] As a result, on 2 July 1935, mere weeks after the conclusion of the *RCA v. China* arbitration, the RCA and the US government entered into a consent decree that would put a definite end to the government's anti-trust suit.

Much like in the case of the recalibration of the RCA's relationship with its overseas correspondents discussed earlier, the consent decree was thus made possible by the fact that – owing to the *RCA v. China* award – the RCA had altered its interpretation of its traffic agreements and given up on its previous insistence as to their exclusivity. Crucially, however, while this change in stance by the RCA as to the meaning of its traffic agreements was a necessary precondition for the consent decree, it was not in itself sufficient – the consent decree also required the acquiescence of the US government. Although the US government was, to be sure, by no means bound to accept the new interpretation that the RCA had adopted pursuant to the *RCA v. China* award, it nonetheless took the position that, under such an interpretation (including *vis-à-vis* the agreements' preferential status), the traffic agreements would no longer be objectionable. With this, the tribunal's decision therefore for all intents and purposes became the relevant benchmark for determining the meaning of the entirety of the RCA's traffic agreements also within the context of the RCA's anti-trust suit with the US government, thus paving the way for the consent decree. The critical role played by the tribunal's decision in this entire process was directly acknowledged by the RCA in a statement made immediately after entering into the decree, which statement explicitly credited the change in the company's stance that had led to the decree to the tribunal's decision. In the statement, reported in the New York Times, the RCA announced that:

> *The entry of the supplemental consent decree today followed decision by the RCA companies that they would no longer interpret the provisions of any of their traffic contracts with foreign correspondents as preventing those correspondents from establishing,* if they so desire, *direct radio circuits with*

261 See sub-sections 3.4.1 and 3.4.2.

262 Letter from RCA to The Czechoslovakian Administration (3 July 1935) (n 207); Letter from RCA to China (3 July 1935) (n 253).

> *others in the United States* to handle traffic specially routed by the sender via such circuits.
>
> *The RCA companies are so notifying all their foreign correspondents following the decision of the board in the recent arbitration between RCA and the Republic of China.*[263]

Accordingly, there can be no doubt that the *RCA v. China* decision played a major, perhaps even pivotal, role in putting to rest the last tail-ends of a several years-long dispute between a US company and its government – a dispute that had at the time been described by the New York Times as 'the greatest anti-trust action in the history of the nation.'[264] Once more, then, the decision of the *RCA v. China* tribunal, whose normative influence was not circumscribed to the two parties partaking in that particular dispute but also affected how the RCA's rights and obligations under the remainder of its traffic agreements would come to be understood, as a result affected the RCA's relations with a third-party public authority that was not a participant in the arbitration. Only this time, this third party was the RCA's own government and the relations affected were ones concerning anti-trust matters – an issue normally reserved for the domestic public regulatory domain.

Against this background, the interaction between the *RCA v. China* decision and the RCA's anti-trust suit with the US government only serves to further reinforce the impressions that flow from the previously explored instances of the impact had by the tribunal's decision on the RCA's relations with other telegraph administrations. Indeed, as has been demonstrated through these examples, the *RCA v. China* award, although nominally addressed only to the disputing parties and only obligatory as between them regarding that particular dispute, influenced not only how the provisions of the Shanghai Traffic Agreement were to be understood, but also the meaning that was to be attributed to the entirety of the RCA's overseas traffic agreements. Taken together, the three examples discussed above are thus illustrative of the influence that historical ISA tribunals were capable of exerting on the legal architecture that regulated a disputing party's relations with third-party public authorities.

Within the context of the investor-state dynamic, the implications that could follow from this – i.e. a disputing party that was a global enterprise operating a public utility viewing the decision of a historical ISA tribunal as an authoritative pronunciation as to its rights and obligations in a manner that

---

263 See 'RCA Units Enjoined on Foreign Claims' *The New York Times* (New York, 3 July 1935) 23. Emphasis added.

264 Ibid.

was not circumscribed to one particular dispute but was instead translatable to all of its comparable relations – can hardly be overstated. In the case of the RCA, because the nature of the company's operations was to offer an important public utility – such as telecommunications services, the norms over which the tribunal's decision was accorded this type of normative influence were ones that regulated the conditions under which the RCA would provide telecommunications services in various countries around the world. That the tribunal's normative influence over the interpretation of the totality of the RCA's overseas traffic agreements in addition resulted in the ending of the RCA's long-running anti-trust dispute with the US government only operates to further add to its gravity.

4 Developing the Law beyond the Disputing Parties

Sections 2 and 3 have explored historical ISA's tendencies to contribute to the development of the law governing investor-state interaction by exerting a level of normative influence over either the relations of the two parties privy to the particular arbitration or over the relations that a party to the arbitration had with another entity. In both of those instances, the tribunal's normative influence in question was of a limited generality, in that it was restricted to parties that were in one way or another connected to the dispute before the tribunal, either directly as participants or indirectly as entities with relations to such participants. In continuing to trace the gradation of historical ISA's role in developing the law governing investor-state relations, this section builds upon these findings by showing that the normative influence exerted by historical ISA tribunals was also capable of being *general in scope* – i.e. that it was capable of extending to instances where no such conduit, whether direct or indirect, through one of the original disputing parties existed. Accordingly, the section will recount how decisions by historical ISA tribunals operating in differing historical settings and under varied applicable laws contributed to the creation and development of the rules pursuant to which future wholly unrelated investor-state disputes were to be resolved.

Before proceeding, however, it is critical to once more underscore that it is not argued here that decisions by historical ISA tribunals had the capacity to directly and independently create or develop novel norms that would be obligatory for parties that participated in subsequent cases. That was clearly not the case – decisions by historical ISA tribunals did not have the status of binding precedent in the form of *stare decisis*. That being said, these decisions did nonetheless eventually come to be considered as holding certain persuasive value that influenced how subsequent ISA tribunals and other relevant actors would interpret the relevant legal norms and resolve disputes. As such, they were relied upon not only by the parties to the subsequent arbitrations in support of their arguments, but more importantly, also by the tribunals that decided such subsequent disputes in order to justify their findings, including on key points of the relevant awards. Moreover, they are equally similarly known to have influenced the decisions of other relevant actors, such as e.g. arbitral institutions or even national law-makers, in their adoption of norms regulating the arbitral process.

Upon first impression, that decisions handed down in historical ISA would carry such extended normative influence might not appear all that noteworthy; after all, it is not uncommon in adjudication, and is perhaps even standard, for previous case law to factor into subsequent decision-making processes. Be that as it may, whenever this did occur, it was nonetheless indicative of the fact that the said previous case law did contribute to the development of the overarching normative frameworks that determined how unrelated subsequent cases would unravel. Moreover, within the specific context of historical ISA, that this would take place is all the more notable considering that the existence of such practice was anything but a foregone conclusion in light of the significant dissimilarities that existed between the particular circumstances under which the various cases unfolded (including regarding the type of underlying investor-state relationship, applicable law, and geographical or temporal setting).[265]

In recounting the capacity of historical ISA tribunals to contribute to the development of the law that governed future investor-state disputes on such a general scale, this section proceeds as follows. The first sub-section retraces how the tendency to make use of decisions by previous tribunals as persuasive precedent developed from being virtually non-existent within historical ISA to becoming a relatively frequent occurrence (4.1). The next sub-section then analyses the character of the norms to whose development historical ISA contributed, finding that the significance of such practice was only further compounded by the fact that the normative influence exerted by historical ISA tribunals on such a general scale concerned norms that regulated the investor-state dynamic (4.2).

4.1 *Into the Multiverse: The Gradual Shift toward the Reliance on Previous Case Law in Historical Investor-State Arbitration*

For a long time, historical ISA awards seemingly had little to no impact on how subsequent unrelated investor-state disputes were to be resolved. These earlier

265 See sub-section 4.1 immediately below.

cases were often self-contained and the underlying disputes were frequently resolved simply within the 'four corners of a contract' (i.e. without reference to external legal sources);[266] the decisions were moreover often either minimally reasoned or lacked reasoning at all, and insofar as they relied on authorities, it were mostly decisions by national[267] and international courts,[268] or doctrine[269] that were cited. Based on the reviewed historical material, references to other ISAs appear to have in these awards in essence been non-existent – it was as if each award was set in its own universe.[270] From approximately the

---

266 See eg *Suez Canal Company v Egypt*, Award (6 July 1864), reproduced in Foreign Office, *British and Foreign State Papers: 1864–1865*, vol LV (William Ridgway 1870) 1004; *Colombia v Cauca Company*, Award (22 October 1897), reproduced in *Colombia v Cauca Co*, 106 Fed 337, 346–347 (DW Va 1901); *Government of Peru v The Peruvian Corporation Limited* (1913) 50 Boletin del Ministerio de Relaciones Exteriores (Peru) 144; *The Duff Development Company Limited v The Government of Kelantan*, Award (31 March 1916) (*Duff v Kelantan I*) (copies of the award are available at the Foreign and Commonwealth Office Pamphlet Collection at the University of Manchester Library Special Collections and the Foyle Special Collections Library at King's College London (FCDO Historical Coll, FOL DS598.K3 DUF)).

267 See eg *Dominion of Canada v The Grand Trunk Railway Company of Canada*, Award (7 September 1921) (a copy of the award is available in The UK National Archives as part of the case materials in the *Jaffa-Jerusalem Railway Arbitration*; see UK National Archives: TS 27/143–144); *Hambros Bank Limited and Lazard Brothers and Co Limited v Kingdom of Roumania Monopolies Institute*, Award (10 June 1937) (a copy of the award is available in the Nationaal Archief, Den Haag, Collection 341 Prof mr dr GWJ Bruins, Supplement 1981, 1929–1939, access number 2.21.191.02, inventory number 1); *Compagnie du Katanga v The Colony of the Belgian Congo*, Award (11 December 1931), reported in Wetter and Schwebel (n 5) 184; *The Duff Development Company Limited v The Government of Kelantan*, Award (17 November 1921) (*Duff v Kelantan II*) (a copy of the award is available in the UK National Archives: TS 36/216).

268 See eg *Hambros v Roumania Monopolies Institute* (n 267); *Zeltweg-Wolfsberg and Unterdrauburg-Woellan Railway Company v Austria and Yugoslavia* [1934] League of Nations Official Journal 1005 (*Zeltweg-Wolfsberg II*).

269 See eg *The Administration of Posts and Telegraphs of the Republic of Czechoslovakia v The Radio Corporation of America* (1936) 30 AJIL 523; *Losinger & cie SA and 'Kompass' Allgemeine Kredit- und Garantie-Bank v The Kingdom of Yugoslavia*, Award (31 October 1934) (*Losinger I*), reproduced in *The Losinger & Co Case (Switzerland v Yugoslavia)* PCIJ Rep Series C No 78 at 54; *Losinger & cie SA v Kingdom of Yugoslavia*, Preliminary Award (11 October 1935) (*Losinger II*), reproduced in *The Losinger & Co Case (Switzerland v Yugoslavia)* PCIJ Rep Series C No 78 at 105.

270 The only exceptions appear to have been instances of multiple arbitrations between the same sets of parties. See *Ministere du Commerce et des Travaux Publics – Chemins de fer Orientaux: Arbitrage de 1903 (Compromis, Proces-Verbaux, Sentences et Avis Separes)* (H Matteosian 1904) (wherein a series of subsequent awards contain multiple references to an earlier 1888 award between the same parties); *Duff v Kelantan II* (n 267), Transcript Days 1–5 (24–28 October 1921) (Foreign and Commonwealth Office Pamphlet Collection at the University of Manchester Library Special Collections).

1920s onwards, however, things appear to have slowly started to change, as these isolated universes began to expand and merge so as to include other ISA awards, albeit initially only in relation to arbitrations that shared a common connection through (at least) one of the parties.[271] This nascent practice of invoking decisions by previous ISA tribunals as authorities that supported the parties' arguments or the tribunals' findings was moreover initially not always easy to spot, as references to previous case law were often made only in an implicit or generalised manner, without citing a specific source.[272]

Following World War II, however, the reliance on precedent in historical ISA intensified and became more explicit, with more and more tribunals in historical ISA beginning to invoke rulings by earlier ISA tribunals in order to justify their own findings. Such a turn of events was perhaps foreshadowed by the words of Lord Asquith, the umpire in the *Petroleum Development v. The Sheikh of Abu Dhabi* arbitration. The decision by Lord Asquith was handed down only a year after Lord Radcliffe had dealt with a similar topic (the territorial application of a concession) in the *Petroleum Development (Qatar) Ltd. v. Ruler of Qatar* arbitration.[273] As Lord Radcliffe had not given a reasoned award, Lord Asquith could not draw on Lord Radcliffe's reasoning for the purposes of his own findings. Lord Asquith nonetheless indicated in his award that, despite certain factual differences between the two cases, he would have done so had he been given the opportunity:

> I would only add in conclusion a word about the Qatar Arbitration over which Lord Radcliffe presided. I have reached a result in this case which happens closely to correspond with that reached by Lord Radcliffe in that case, on other facts and a different Agreement. There is, in fact, little connection between the two Arbitrations if only because in the Qatar Agreement there was no allusion in the contract to 'sea waters' at all. *If Lord Radcliffe instead of merely recording his conclusions had expounded the*

---

271 See n 270, *Canada v Grand Trunk* (n 267) 45 (Taft Dissenting Opinion), as well as section 3.

272 Thus, for example, while the *Zeltweg-Wolfsberg and Unterdrauburg-Woellan Railway Company v Austria and Yugoslavia* tribunal did not mention any other ISA decisions by name, it supported its findings when interpreting the World War I Peace Treaties by invoking 'previous legal practice'. Upon closer analysis, it is clear that this previous legal practice refers, at least *inter alia*, to the *Sopron-Köszeg Local Railway Company v Austria and Hungary* award, whose conclusions on the relevant point are reproduced almost verbatim. Compare *Zeltweg-Wolfsberg II* (n 268) 1006 with *Sopron-Köszeg Local Railway Company v Austria and Hungary* (1930) 24(1) AJIL 164, 167.

273 *Petroleum Development (Qatar) Ltd v Ruler of Qatar* (1951) 18 ILR 161.

> *principles on which he had reached them, I should have derived invaluable and authoritative guidance from such an exposition.*[274]

Although there appears to be no reason to suspect that Lord Asquith's words were the catalyst for a change in direction, the principles contained therein certainly became more frequently followed in subsequent decisions.[275] This was especially the case with respect to the big Middle Eastern oil arbitrations, which almost invariably contained references to earlier historical ISA s. The first to adopt such an approach was the referee in *Ruler of Qatar v. International Marine Oil Company*, citing none other than the decision by Lord Asquith.[276] The *Saudi Arabia v. ARAMCO*[277] tribunal then further expanded on this by not only invoking five previous ISA awards when justifying its conclusions, but actually devoting several pages of its award to discussing a number of these decisions at length. Most notably, the *Saudi Arabia v. ARAMCO* tribunal prefaced one such discussion – a discussion that was to provide support for the important finding that it was necessary for the tribunal to resort to general principles of law when interpreting the parties' rights and obligations – by explicitly noting that it was 'rel[ying], by analogy, on the *precedent of the "Lena Goldfields Arbitration"*'.[278] By the time the three Libyan oil arbitrations of the 1970s,[279] which themselves relied heavily on previous ISA decisions, were concluded, more than two dozen historical ISAs had been cited – many of which multiple times. The most recurrent ones, such as e.g. *Lena Goldfields v. USSR* and *Petroleum Development v. The Sheikh of Abu Dhabi*, were in the later decisions cited almost as a matter of course.[280]

---

274 *Petroleum Development Ltd v The Sheikh of Abu Dhabi* (1951) 18 ILR 144. Emphasis added.

275 The shift was most likely facilitated by the ever increasing number of possible historical ISA s that could be referenced, by thoroughly reasoned decisions starting to become the norm within the discipline, as well as by their increased accessibility.

276 *Ruler of Qatar v International Marine Oil Company, Ltd* (1953) 20 ILR 534, 544.

277 See *Saudi Arabia v Arabian American Oil Company* (ARAMCO) (1963) 27 ILR 117. A copy of the award is available in the Peace Palace Library.

278 Quotation marks in the original, emphasis added. See ibid 168.

279 *BP Exploration Company (Libya) Limited v The Government of the Libyan Arab Republic* (1979) 53 ILR 297; *Texaco Overseas Petroleum Company and California Asiatic Oil Company v The Government of the Libyan Arab Republic* (1978) 17 ILM 1; *Libyan American Oil Company (LIAMCO) v The Government of the Libyan Arab Republic* (1981) 20(1) ILM 1.

280 This practice has continued in present-day ISA, as many of these awards are still invoked as relevant precedent. According to the Investor-State LawGuide database <https://new.investorstatelawguide.com/> (accessed 29 September 2024), the most cited historical case appears to be *Sapphire v NIOC*, with over fifty specific references.

It is critical to note that the aforementioned references to previous case law by historical ISA tribunals were mostly made without much, if any, consideration of the considerable differences that existed between the various ISAs being cited in terms of the type of investor-state relationship in question, the types of contract involved, applicable law (both procedural and substantive) or geographical or temporal setting. By way of illustration, in just a few pages of the *BP v. Libya* award one can find lumped together references to several 1950s Middle Eastern oil arbitrations, to cases concerning the operation of public utility concessions in Southern Europe from the 1930s, to a 1920s case concerning the exploitation of an alcohol monopoly in Africa, as well as to an arbitration over a comprehensive concession in Southeast Asia that took place during World War I.[281] Bearing these significant variations between the individual features of the historical ISAs in mind (see Chapter 2), the reliance on previous case law by subsequent ISA tribunals was by no means inevitable. Seeing, however, that this was how things played out, it is hard to avoid the conclusion that the historical ISAs, rather than each of them having been set in an entirely isolated universe, eventually came to inhabit a shared universe – a multiverse – within which they held potential value as persuasive precedent irrespective of the different settings and conditions under which they had occurred.[282]

Another related aspect that is important to highlight within this context is the apparent perception by ISA tribunals of fellow past ISA decisions as being of distinct significance in terms of their potential precedential value. Namely, while there was a wide range of sources referenced by historical ISA tribunals,[283] there seem to have been certain, albeit rather tentative, indications that decisions by fellow ISA tribunals were seen as being of more direct normative significance than other types of precedent. Thus, in *BP v. Libya*, when conducting an analysis of the relevant case law on one of the key points, Judge Lagergren observed that a 'category of cases, *which are of particular relevance in these proceedings, are international arbitral awards in disputes under contracts between States and aliens*.'[284] Likewise, at one point in its award, the

281 See *BP v Libya* (n 279) 343–345. See also the discussion in sub-section 4.2.1 below.

282 Even cases that have never been cited held (and still hold) such potential. Indeed, many seemingly forgotten cases were subsequently 'uncovered', sometimes many decades after they occurred.

283 It was not uncommon for tribunals to, in addition to other ISA decisions, also cite decisions from state-to-state disputes, claims commissions, national courts or national and international doctrine. See nn 267–269.

284 *BP v Libya* (n 279) 337. Emphasis added. It is true that Lagergren used the notion of 'international arbitral awards in disputes under contracts between States and aliens' in a sense that included not only ISAs but also state-to-state arbitrations. Regardless, his statement

Saudi Arabia v. ARAMCO tribunal, before proceeding to discuss at length the relevance of several previous ISA awards, dismissed the precedential value of several cases because they did not pertain specifically to the interpretation of concession contracts between states and private entities:

> The majority of the many judicial precedents which have been quoted by the Government in support of the opposite view *are irrelevant, for they concern the interpretation of rules of Public International Law or of interstate Treaties, and not of a concession between a State and a private corporation.* In the Law of Nations, the problem assumes a different character, for any limitation of the sovereignty of one State in favour of another entails on extension of the latter's sovereignty. *This cannot follow in the relations between a State and private individuals.*[285]

Accordingly, not only were previous historical ISAs seen as persuasive precedent, but they were potentially seen as persuasive precedent of the most immediate relevance.

That being said, it does need to be recognised that reliance by historical ISA tribunals on previous decisions had not become a uniform, or perhaps even prevalent, practice. Indeed, even following *Saudi Arabia v. ARAMCO* or the Libyan oil arbitrations, there remained both plenty of awards that had seemingly quietly disappeared into the annals of history without a single mention in subsequent case law or awards in which there had been no reference at all to previous ISAs.[286] Moreover, even in awards that were rife with references to earlier historical ISA decisions, there were on occasion instances where, on some key points, the discussion of certain previous precedent that would have been expected was conspicuous by its absence.[287] While these aspects certainly are relevant for assessing how prevalent this phenomenon was, they do not negate the fact that historical ISAs exerted a certain degree of normative influence, and did so on a considerable scale, over wholly unrelated ISAs

remains indicative of the position that ISAs were more directly relevant precedent than most (if not necessarily all) other types of cases, especially when considering that the vast majority of cases cited by him under this category were in fact ISAs. See ibid 342–345.

285 *Saudi Arabia v ARAMCO* (n 277) 192–193. Emphases added.

286 See eg *The Ditta Luigi Gallotti v The Somali Government* (1970) 40 ILR 158; *The Government of the State of Kuwait v The American Independent Oil Company* (AMINOIL) (1982) 21(5) ILM 976.

287 This can perhaps at least partially be explained by the fact that many of the historical ISA awards were only (if at all) published with a considerable delay, so that subsequent tribunals may not have been aware of them when issuing their own awards.

that followed. The fact thus remains that, despite a slow start in this respect, decisions by historical ISA tribunals, as well as the underlying reasons for their findings, eventually came to be used as significant building blocks with which the normative architecture of historical ISA would be constructed.

4.2 *Generating Normativity that Governed Investor-State Relations*

That decisions by historical ISA tribunals formed part of the normative foundation pursuant to which subsequent investor-state disputes that bore no connection to those arbitrations would be resolved is only half of the equation that captures the capacity of historical ISA to contribute to the development of the law on a general scale, as this trait is not in and of itself idiosyncratic to historical ISA. What instead makes historical ISA's contribution to developing the law particularly stand out in this context is the *type of norms* to whose development it contributed. Namely, as recounted at numerous previous junctures within this book, owing to the specific dynamic that underpinned the investor-state relationship and the type of interests that were implicated therein, these norms were of a different variety than those that might have been applied and developed in arbitrations that involved only private entities. More specifically, they on the one hand included rules for assessing the content of the rights and obligations within investor-state relations, as well as rules for assessing whether such obligations had been complied with and the potential consequences that may arise thereunder (4.2.1). On the other hand, they also concerned the procedural and jurisdictional conditions under which historical (and future) ISAs were to be conducted (4.2.2).

4.2.1 Rules for Assessing State Conduct

Perhaps the most distinguishable feature of historical ISA's contribution to developing the law on a general scale was the fact that the law being developed pertained to, *inter alia*, the assessment of how states conducted their official business. This follows from the fact that historical ISA tribunals were, among other things, tasked with determining the precise content of the rights and obligations contained in the investor-state relationship from which the disputes before them arose. In many an instance, they also as a result both evaluated whether the parties to the investor-state relationship (and in particular states) had acted in accordance with such rights and obligations, as well as provided for potential repercussions in case of their failure to do so. This further implied that, when decisions by historical ISA tribunals contributed to developing the law on a general scale, it was *inter alia* norms dealing with such matters to whose development they contributed – norms that would later be used for the same purpose of examining whether states had complied with their obligations arising pursuant to an investor-state relationship and for determining the consequences that might potentially arise thereunder.

As recounting in detail all instances of how historical ISA contributed to the development of these types of norms is unfortunately not possible within the confines of a single sub-section, what precisely this entailed in practice and how it transpired will be demonstrated through an illustrative example – crucially, however, one that will also be shown not to have been an isolated occurrence. Considering the familiarity with the two RCA arbitrations from the preceding discussion, perhaps the most appropriate candidate for such an illustrative example is the landmark *Saudi Arabia v. ARAMCO* arbitration, where the tribunal looked to the two RCA cases that took place some quarter of a century earlier when interpreting the obligations of Saudi Arabia under its concession agreement with ARAMCO.

The *Saudi Arabia v. ARAMCO* dispute arose out of circumstances that were in significant part comparable to those in the two RCA cases. Namely, ARAMCO had obtained an oil concession from Saudi Arabia under which it was granted the exclusive right to, *inter alia*, transport the oil that had been extracted pursuant to the concession. Notwithstanding this provision, Saudi Arabia subsequently concluded an agreement (later enacted as law) with shipping magnate Aristotle Onassis, granting him, through a Saudi-incorporated company, a right of priority for the transport of the oil extracted in Saudi Arabia for a 30-year period. ARAMCO refused to have Onassis transport its oil, claiming this to be in breach of its concession, and the matter was eventually submitted to arbitration.[288]

During the arbitration, the two opposing parties spent considerable time and effort, both in their memorials and their oral pleadings, arguing the two RCA awards and invoking them as relevant precedent that supported their respective cases.[289] They did so primarily in relation to the question of the manner in which the underlying ARAMCO concession was to be interpreted – a matter which was inevitably to be of relevance for how the parties' rights and

288 *Saudi Arabia v ARAMCO* (n 277) 118–130.

289 See *Saudi Arabia v ARAMCO* (n 277), Memorial of Arabian American Oil Company, Annex 16(e) (Opinion of Professor Henry P deVries) 424–425; *Saudi Arabia v ARAMCO* (n 277), Final Memorial of Arabian American Oil Company 290 and 312–316; *Saudi Arabia v ARAMCO* (n 277), Answering Memorial of Saudi Arabia 32–37 and 48; *Saudi Arabia v ARAMCO* (n 277), Sessions of the Tribunal (Vol I) 184–189; *Saudi Arabia v ARAMCO* (n 277), Sessions of the Tribunal (Vol II) 883–884, 951–953, 1072–1075 and 1088–1089; *Saudi Arabia v ARAMCO* (n 277), Sessions of the Tribunal (Vol III) 1827–1830, 1948–1949 and 2027–2028. All of the above case materials from *Saudi Arabia v ARAMCO* can be found at the Columbia University Library.

obligations under the concession, and thus also any possible restrictions upon Saudi Arabia's sovereignty, were to be understood. Taking into account the facts of the *Saudi Arabia v. ARAMCO* case and its analogous nature to the RCA disputes, it is not difficult to understand why the two diverging RCA decisions were appealing to the respective disputing parties. On the one hand, Saudi Arabia felt that a particularly apt comparator was the *RCA v. China* award, where the tribunal had found that the RCA's rights under the Shanghai Traffic Agreement could not restrict China from concluding an agreement with a third party.[290] In relying on the award, Saudi Arabia argued that the *RCA v. China* tribunal had applied what was termed as the 'principle of restrictive interpretation', pursuant to which any limitation on a government's sovereignty needed to be established clearly and beyond any reasonable doubt. According to Saudi Arabia, the *RCA v. China* case thus provided considerable support for applying the same interpretative approach in the *Saudi Arabia v. ARAMCO* arbitration. Conversely, ARAMCO denied that the *RCA v. China* award bolstered Saudi Arabia's contention as to the applicability of a 'principle of restrictive interpretation', arguing that the decision left no room for such an approach where the exclusive character of a relevant right had been explicitly established by the relevant agreement. Since ARAMCO considered that its concession had in fact established such exclusive rights, in light of the *RCA v. China* tribunal's principled preparedness to find China in breach under such circumstances (see sub-section 3.3.3), it submitted that this decision in actuality favoured its own position, rather than Saudi Arabia's. ARAMCO also expectedly relied on the *Czechoslovakian Administration v. RCA* decision, as the tribunal in that case had found that the RCA's rights under the Czechoslovakian Traffic Agreement prevented The Czechoslovakian Administration from concluding another traffic agreement that would have hampered the RCA's rights.[291] In ARAMCO's view, as its own situation under the concession was equivalent to that of the RCA *vis-à-vis* The Czechoslovakian Administration, the same approach was to be taken in its dispute with Saudi Arabia.

Following the cue given by the disputing parties, the tribunal did not fail to pick-up on the relevance of the two RCA arbitrations when addressing Saudi Arabia's contentions as to the applicability of the principle of restrictive interpretation to the concession. Unlike the case law stemming from state-to-state relations that the parties had cited, which the tribunal did not deem pertinent for this particular matter,[292] the tribunal did go on to discuss the two

290 See sub-section 3.3.3.
291 See ch 4.
292 See n 285.

RCA awards in depth as rare examples of ISA awards that had been invoked on this point, devoting some page and a half of its award to their analysis. While acknowledging that the *RCA v. China* tribunal had in fact decided that China's traffic agreement with Mackay Radio was not in breach of its original traffic agreement with the RCA, the tribunal reasoned that the rationale for the decision had been a perceived lack of an exclusive right in the first place rather than the restrictive interpretation of state contracts. Having thus (perhaps not entirely justifiably) undercut the usefulness of the *RCA v. China* decision for Saudi Arabia's position, the tribunal then went on to invoke favourably the *Czechoslovakian Administration v. RCA* award, which had found the second traffic agreement, establishing a circuit parallel to the one from the original traffic agreement, not to be permitted. In the tribunal's view, this decision, rather than interpreting the underlying concession restrictively, was a clear example of a tribunal recognising the exclusiveness of a company's right under a contract with a state when such right was expressly granted in the contract itself. The tribunal found this situation analogous to that in the dispute before it:

> *The resemblance of this latter case to that of Aramco is obvious.* This Company had also been granted expressly by the text of its concession an exclusive right which the State attempts to interpret restrictively, by alleging that it does not cover sea transport and that Aramco has so little need of this right that it never exercised it itself but always through third parties.[293]

The tribunal's analysis of the two RCA arbitrations was immediately followed (the tribunal having also summarily dismissed the notion that the principle of restrictive interpretation had been applied in *Petroleum Development v. The Sheikh of Abu Dhabi*) by the following finding:

> The Arbitration Tribunal comes therefore to the conclusion that *international tribunals, in disputes bearing a fairly close resemblance to the present one, have not applied the theory that, in case of doubt, a concession should be interpreted in favour of the State.*[294]

Ultimately, the tribunal would decide against applying the theory of restrictive interpretation to the concession and would conclude that ARAMCO's rights

293 *Saudi Arabia v ARAMCO* (n 277) 194. Emphasis added.

294 Ibid. Emphasis added.

under the concession were exclusive in character. To be sure, the tribunal's discussion of the two RCA awards did not represent the sole, or even the primary, basis for this latter conclusion.[295] Nonetheless, the two awards were an important factor in its interpretation of ARAMCO's concession and formed part of the tribunal's justification for refusing to make use of a legal norm of purported general application – the theory of restrictive interpretation of state contracts – advanced by Saudi Arabia. As such, the two RCA awards, or more precisely, the normative influence exerted by the tribunals' findings in those cases, were an important ingredient in determining how broadly Saudi Arabia's obligations under the concession – and thus also the potential restrictions upon its sovereign prerogatives – would eventually come to be understood.

On its face, such a course of action by the *Saudi Arabia v. ARAMCO* tribunal was hardly surprising – after all, that one tribunal would refer to earlier decisions in order to provide argumentative support for a certain finding is not exactly a ground-breaking development. Yet, despite the undeniable apparent parallels between the cases, reflected primarily in the analogous triangular relationship that had been created by a third party's imposition into an existing contractual relationship,[296] the relevance of the RCA awards for interpreting the ARAMCO concession was anything but axiomatic. Indeed, the two RCA arbitrations had involved different types of agreements than the ARAMCO concession,[297] had been subject to different applicable laws,[298] had concerned an entirely different industry and had taken place in different socio-economic and temporal *milieus*. In light of the lack of connection of the matter before it to any type of relationships involving the RCA, these differences were significant enough that the *Saudi Arabia v. ARAMCO* tribunal could have easily – much like it had done on that particular point with case law relating to state-to-state disputes – dismissed the two RCA awards as irrelevant for its decision. This was especially so when considering the significant emphasis that the

295 See ibid 172–202.

296 Ibid 193.

297 Whereas the RCA cases concerned traffic agreements, the *Saudi Arabia v ARAMCO* arbitration related to an oil concession.

298 See n 239 on the law applicable in the RCA arbitrations. The arbitration agreement between Saudi Arabia and ARAMCO likewise contained a composite applicable law clause, this time providing for the applicability of Saudi Arabian law or 'the law deemed by the Arbitration Tribunal to be applicable', depending on whether a matter was within the jurisdiction of Saudi Arabia or not. For the tribunal's interpretation of this clause, see *Saudi Arabia v ARAMCO* (n 277) 153–172.

tribunal had placed on distinguishing the legal nature of mining concessions such as ARAMCO's from public service concessions.[299]

The tribunal, however, did no such thing, opting instead to view the RCA awards as important (albeit not directly binding) precedent representative of certain broader principles that cut across these various significant differences between the cases. While the *Saudi Arabia v. ARAMCO* tribunal did admittedly have rather broad manoeuvring space at its disposal as the parties' arbitration agreement had merely stipulated that matters beyond the jurisdiction of Saudi Arabia were to be resolved according to the law that the tribunal deemed applicable,[300] it is nonetheless hard not to appreciate the fact that under its approach decisions by tribunals dealing with the operation of radiotelegraphic circuits in Czechoslovakia and China under agreements governed by different applicable laws ultimately became relevant precedent for deciding some quarter of a century later a dispute regarding the operation of an oil concession in Saudi Arabia. Owing to such an approach by the *Saudi Arabia v. ARAMCO* tribunal, the *Czechoslovakian Administration v. RCA* and *RCA v. China* decisions thus exhibited normative influence that went beyond the relationships involving one or both of the parties to those disputes, and instead also had an effect on the meaning that was to be accorded to the rights and obligations under another investor-state relationship that had no connection whatsoever to the two RCA disputes – that between ARAMCO and Saudi Arabia. Accordingly, in contrast to what was discussed in section 3, the norms to whose development the RCA tribunals in this instance contributed, and which were relevant for determining the extent of the restrictions that were to be imposed upon Saudi Arabia's sovereignty, were wholly unrelated to either of the disputing parties appearing before the tribunals – they were of a general application.

Crucially, the type of normative influence exerted by previous unrelated historical ISA tribunals over norms relevant for assessing state conduct, observable through the *Saudi Arabia v. ARAMCO* arbitration, was hardly exhausted in this one illustrative example. Indeed, similar patterns of tribunals' decisions contributing to the development of these types of legal norms of general application can also be observed in relation to other historical ISA awards. This includes, to name a few further examples, the *Lena Goldfields v. USSR* award, which is often referred to as an important precedent on compensation for unjust enrichment being a general principle of law,[301] the award in

299 Ibid 157–161 and 192.

300 See n 298.

301 VV Veeder, 'The *Lena Goldfields* Arbitration: The Historical Roots of Three Ideas' (1998) 47 ICLQ 747, 750.

Sapphire v. National Iranian Oil Company (NIOC), which is a relevant authority with respect to the standards of compensation,[302] and the *Texaco v. Libya* award, which is considered a landmark award for the internationalisation of state contracts.[303] These and other historical ISA awards that were relied upon in subsequent arbitrations thus contributed to the development of norms of general application that were of a particular character – they involved determining the content of the rights and/or obligations of states *vis-à-vis* private investors, how compliance with the said obligations was to be assessed, and what the consequences in case of non-compliance were to be. As a result, not only did the historical ISA tribunals take on a role in developing norms of a general scope of application, but they did so within an area of normativity that regulated state conduct with respect to their exercise of public authority.

4.2.2 Procedural Rules for Conducting Investor-State Arbitration

Yet, it was not only the rules that regulated the substantive relations between investors and states to whose development the historical ISA tribunals contributed, but also to those that regulated the procedure under which subsequent ISAs were to take place. While perhaps less conspicuously so, the importance of these latter rules – and, by association, also of historical ISA's contribution to their development – was not incomparable to that of the rules that regulated substantive aspects of the investor-state dynamic. This is because such procedural rules were relevant for determining the conditions under which states were to enter into ISA and how ISA was to function; as such, they left a significant imprint on how this entire process was to unfold. In consequence, and due to the fact that historical ISA was a mechanism whose operation entailed important governance implications, historical ISA's contribution to the development of such procedural rules was, albeit in less of a direct manner than with respect to rules substantively governing the investor-state dynamic, not without its own relevance for how the governance implications that accompanied historical ISA were to manifest themselves.

The remainder of this sub-section recounts a pair of instances in which historical ISA contributed to the development of the normative structure governing the procedural aspects of ISA. In particular, it looks at how decisions by historical ISA tribunals paved the way for the participation of non-state entities in arbitrations conducted under the auspices of the PCA (4.2.2.1), and at how they influenced the manner in which transparency of (investor-state)

302 *Sapphire International Petroleums Limited v National Iranian Oil Co* (NIOC) (1967) 35 ILR 136.

303 See *Texaco v Libya* (n 279) paras 22–52.

arbitral proceedings is regulated in one of the primary global arbitral jurisdictions (4.2.2.2).

4.2.2.1 *Joost Adriaan van Hamel and the Introduction of Investor-State Arbitration at the Permanent Court of Arbitration*

The first example of decisions taken in historical ISA that contributed to the development of norms regulating the procedural conduct of later ISAs that will be recounted pertains to the introduction of arbitration involving non-state parties at the PCA. As is well documented, the PCA was originally intended to operate only as a forum for inter-state dispute resolution;[304] such a state of things, however, would eventually change owing in large part to an impromptu procedural decision taken by the president of the *RCA v. China*[305] tribunal that was brought about more by chance and convenience than by any serious consideration of the expansion of the type of proceedings that would be administered by the PCA. Namely, much like the *Czechoslovakian Administration v. RCA* arbitration that had preceded it, the *RCA v. China* case was not originally intended to have a connection to the PCA. Neither the arbitration clause (which was identical to the one in the *Czechoslovakian Administration v. RCA* case)[306] nor the subsequently agreed upon rules of procedure[307] provided for such a solution. In fact, the arbitration had already been well on its way for more than a year before the possible involvement of the PCA would come up.

The idea to introduce the PCA to the case came about as a result of a minor logistical problem that had occurred during the proceedings. Namely, the presiding arbitrator, Joost Adriaan van Hamel, had in the summer of 1934 been

---

304 Both of the PCA's founding conventions provide that international arbitration has as its object 'the settlement of disputes [differences] between States', while consistently referring to possible disputing parties that would utilise the PCA's services as 'Powers'. See International Convention for the Pacific Settlement of International Disputes (adopted 29 July 1899, entered into force 4 September 1900) (1899) 187 CTS 410 art 15; Convention for the Pacific Settlement of International Disputes (adopted 18 October 1907; entered into force 26 January 1910) (1907) 205 CTS 233 art 37. See also James Crawford, 'The Permanent Court of Arbitration and Mixed Arbitration' (Celebration of the Centenary of the PCA, The Hague, 18 October 2007) 1–2 <https://docs.pca-cpa.org/2016/01/Reflections-on-the-Current-Relevance-of-the-PCA-Presentation-by-Professor-James-Crawford-SC.pdf> accessed 27 September 2024.

305 *RCA v China* (n 209).

306 Compare art 9 of the Traffic Agreement between Radio Corporation of America and Administration of Posts and Telegraphs of the Republic of Czechoslovakia (10 November 1928) (MCI International Archives, box 583, file 'Czechoslovakia: Correspondence and Agreements (1 of 6)') and art 10 of the Shanghai Traffic Agreement (n 119).

307 'Plan of Procedure' (n 182).

scheduled to receive the RCA's reply memorial; due to a deadline extension, however, the submission was likely to arrive at a period during which van Hamel was expecting to be away. While van Hamel's personal secretary would have under ordinary circumstances handled such a matter, on this occasion his secretary was also scheduled to be away on holiday. This situation prompted van Hamel to propose that the participants in the arbitration rely on the services of the PCA. As a result, van Hamel wrote to the RCA-appointed arbitrator, Hubert, stating the following:

> Mr. Schuloff's request makes me foresee the possibility that the answers to be sent in shortly in connection with the Arbitration case will arrive at a time when I shall be absent for a few weeks, whilst at the same time my secretary, who is accustomed to dealing with these matters will also be on holiday.
>
> In view of this eventuality, *I should like to come to an arrangement with the Secretariat of the International Arbitration Court which sits at La Hague* [sic] *and through whose intermediary the administrative side of the question could be dealt with.*
>
> I hope you will not see any objection to this arrangement which can only be of service in so far as concerns that part of the procedure still to be accomplished.[308]

Hubert replied promptly, stating no objections to van Hamel's proposal regarding the PCA's involvement (as had presumably, considering the subsequent development of events, the China-appointed arbitrator, although his correspondence on this matter is not contained in the RCA archives).[309] Van Hamel subsequently wrote to the Secretary General of the PCA with the request to have the PCA's administrative services put at the tribunal's disposal.[310] The Secretary General approved the request, receiving support for this decision from the PCA's Administrative Council,[311] and the arbitration was in consequence thereafter conducted with the benefit of the PCA's services.

---

308 Translation of Letter from J A van Hamel to A Hubert (2 July 1934) (MCI International Archives, box 581, file 'China: Chinese Arbitration Correspondence (11 of 13)'). Emphasis added.

309 Copy of Letter from A Hubert to J A van Hamel (6 July 1934) (MCI International Archives, box 581, file 'China: Chinese Arbitration Correspondence (11 of 13)').

310 Permanent Court of Arbitration, 'Circular Note of the Secretary General' (1960) 54 AJIL 933, 937.

311 Ibid 937.

What is crucial for present purposes is that the tribunal's decision to request the PCA's involvement in the arbitration did not influence just how the *RCA v. China* case was procedurally to be conducted, but also numerous ISAs thereafter. Indeed, in what was critical for the PCA's later transformation into one of the leading institutions for administering ISA, this impromptu procedural innovation that had been introduced through the *RCA v. China* case did not remain a one-off curious anomaly but was instead then further institutionalised and explicitly regulated. Namely, in 1939, only a few years after the *RCA v. China* arbitration, the PCA Secretary General invited the American Arbitration Association to publicise that the PCA was willing to make available its services for this category of disputes,[312] while in 1962 the PCA's administration of ISAs was given formal normative sanction with the adoption of the 'Rules of Arbitration and Conciliation for Settlement of International Disputes Between Two Parties of Which Only One Is a State'.[313] Although this development was far from instantaneous, the PCA would, as is all too well known, subsequently go on to become one of the pre-eminent arbitral institutions through which ISAs are administered.

The decision to allow the administration of ISA under the auspices of the PCA was an important procedural development in ISA and it would likely not be an overstatement to say that it has fundamentally altered the course of the PCA's history.[314] Yet, the origins of a procedural development of such magnitude lie not in the conscious legislative efforts aimed at bringing about such change, but rather in a precedent set in practice by the decision of the *RCA v. China* tribunal. Undoubtedly, one could hypothesise whether the norms that facilitated the conduct of ISA at the PCA would have, had the *RCA v. China* tribunal not requested the assistance of the PCA in its conduct of the arbitration, come about regardless.[315] That, however, remains beside the point – the

312 Ibid 937–938.

313 The Permanent Court of Arbitration, 'Rules of Arbitration and Conciliation for Settlement of International Disputes Between Two Parties of Which Only One is a State' (1963) 57(2) AJIL 500. The PCA would, however, not have its next arbitration involving a non-state party until the late 1960s dispute between Sudan and the Turriff Construction Company. See ch 3 and P Hamilton and others (eds), *The Permanent Court of Arbitration: International Arbitration and Dispute Resolution: Summaries of Awards, Settlement Agreements and Reports* (Kluwer 1999).

314 Indeed, the boom in investor-state arbitration is largely responsible for the PCA's renaissance in the preceding decades.

315 Ideas were floated at the time about allowing private parties to participate in arbitrations administered by the PCA. In fact, it was very possibly precisely these discussions that had sparked in van Hamel's mind the idea of involving the PCA in the *RCA v China* arbitration once the need had presented itself – as documents regarding one such proposal form part

matter of fact is that the actual course of historical events was such that the initial spark without which this development may never have occurred was none other than the procedural decision by the *RCA v. China* tribunal. In other words, the precedent set by the *RCA v. China* tribunal was the first step in a process that would eventually result in the development of a formal normative framework providing for the conduct of ISA under the auspices of the PCA. To be sure, such an initial step – the introduction of a new practice – needed to receive subsequent official institutional endorsement in order to be translated into norms that formally opened up this new procedural avenue for future ISAs. In no way, however, does the need for such institutional endorsement detract from the fact that, had it not been for the *RCA v. China* tribunal's innovative decision to ask for the PCA's involvement, this subsequent adoption of norms allowing for ISA at the PCA might never had occurred and, as a result, the procedural landscape of ISA might have looked very different today.

4.2.2.2 *Lena Goldfields v USSR and Exceptions to Privacy and Confidentiality in Arbitration*

Another instance where a precedent set by a historical ISA tribunal contributed to the shaping of the procedural framework regulating how future ISAs were to be conducted is provided by the *Lena Goldfields v. USSR* arbitration and its approach to the transparency of proceedings. Namely, when conducting the arbitration in 1930, the *Lena Goldfields v. USSR* tribunal had, in response to certain allegations made by one of the disputing parties, decided to open up its hearings to the media (but not to the public) and publish its award in the London Times.[316] As VV Veeder, who provided a detailed account of the arbitration almost 70 years later, has noted, this was an unusual step at the time for a tribunal operating from London:

---

of his personal archives, van Hamel would have certainly been aware of it. See Letter to James Brown Scott (unsigned) (26 May 1932) (Nationaal Archief, Den Haag, Collection 179 JA van Hamel, 1632–1964, access number 2.21.081, inventory number 62). However, similar creative proposals were hardly uncommon at the time, and there was little guarantee that any such proposal would have been successful – many comparable ideas had been, for example, advanced regarding the PCIJ without ever materialising. See Secretariat of the League of Nations, 'Memorandum on the Different Questions Arising in Connection with the Establishment of the Permanent Court of International Justice' in PCIJ Advisory Committee of Jurists, *Documents Presented to the Committee Relating to Existing Plans for the Establishment of a Permanent Court of International Justice* (HM Stationery Office Press 1920) 27–31.

316 Departmental Advisory Committee on Arbitration Law, '1996 Report on the Arbitration Bill' (1997) 13(3) Arbitration International 275, para 16; Veeder (n 301) 754.

> in opening the arbitration hearings to the press and publishing much of the award in the London Times, *the Lena tribunal established an important exception to the legal principle of privacy and confidentiality in commercial arbitration where transparency is required in the public interest.*[317]

Crucially, the exception thus established by the *Lena Goldfields v. USSR* tribunal would more than half a century later factor into the drafting process of the new arbitration act in the United Kingdom (UK), the country in which the *Lena Goldfields v. USSR* award was handed down. Namely, in its Report on the Arbitration Bill, the Departmental Advisory Committee on Arbitration Law (DAC), which had prepared the text of the new arbitration legislation,[318] and of which Veeder had been a member,[319] cited *Lena Goldfields v. USSR* as one of the 'important exceptions' to the principle of privacy in arbitration.[320] The existence of such exceptions, together with the concurrent lack of sufficient clarity as to their exact number or scope, in turn prompted the DAC to conclude that the matter of confidentiality and privacy in arbitration was unsettled in English law and was best left to evolve through common law.[321] As a result, the DAC ultimately took the view that 'no attempt should be made to codify English law on the privacy and confidentiality of English arbitration in the Bill';[322] this approach having been eventually adopted in the final version of the legislative text, the arbitration act in consequence remains silent on the question of confidentiality and privacy.[323]

---

317 Veeder (n 301) 754. Emphasis added.

318 See Bruce Harris, 'Report on the Arbitration Act 1996' (2007) 23(3) Arbitration International 437, 438.

319 Notably, Veeder also chaired the *Methanex v Mexico* tribunal – the first ISA tribunal known to have allowed *amicus curiae* briefs. In this landmark decision, the *Methanex* tribunal invoked the *Lena Goldfields v USSR* arbitration as relevant precedent on confidentiality of proceedings in English arbitration law, albeit on a point that the tribunal ultimately did not have to decide. See *Methanex Corporation v United States of America*, UNCITRAL (NAFTA), Decision of the Tribunal on Petitions from Third Persons to Intervene as 'amici curiae' (15 January 2001) para 44.

320 DAC Report (n 316) para 16.

321 Ibid para 10. Notably, the DAC report at no point questions the existence of the principles of confidentiality and privacy in English arbitration, but merely their boundaries.

322 Ibid para 17.

323 Following the second reading of the bill, during which concerns were raised over the lack of a reference to confidentiality, the DAC did propose an amendment that would have introduced a mention of confidentiality and privacy in section 81 (which introduces a saving for matters governed by common law). The amendment, however, was not adopted. See Departmental Advisory Committee on Arbitration Law, 'Supplementary Report on the Arbitration Act 1996' (1997) 13(3) Arbitration International 317, para 44; Kyriaki

Accordingly, the significance of the decision by the *Lena Goldfields v. USSR* tribunal to open up the proceedings and publish its award was far from confined to the immediate case with which the tribunal was concerned. Instead, the tribunal's decision eventually came to be viewed by a body formally involved in the legislative process in the place where the award was handed down as having been of precedential value for determining the content of the norms regulating confidentiality and privacy in arbitration. Such normative influence exerted by the tribunal's decision by way of being a representative exception to the principle of privacy in arbitration was accordingly taken into account when that body was deciding on whether to recommend for specific provisions relating to transparency of proceedings – a matter of particular interest in ISA – to be included in new legislation. This extended normative influence of the decision by the *Lena Goldfields v. USSR* tribunal therefore potentially came to affect all parties that could come under the reach of the said legislation, which remains all the more significant when considering that the jurisdiction in which this extended normative influence was felt – the UK – was not only one of the most important jurisdictions for arbitration in general but also for ISA in particular.

5 Conclusions

This Chapter has examined the role of historical ISA in contributing to the development of the normative frameworks that governed, and still govern, investor-state relations. In doing so, it demonstrated that these historical ISA tribunals did not merely exist and operate in pre-determined normative surroundings, but were instead themselves constitutive of them, as they exerted a certain normative influence through which they added to, and developed, the very normative frameworks within which they operated. Equally as important, the Chapter revealed that historical ISA's role in contributing to the development of the law governing investor-state interaction was multi-layered, as it operated on three different planes of generality.

At the narrowest level of generality, this implied that the tribunals were not only applying legal rules to a particular factual matrix in a dispute between two parties, but that they also took active participation in giving those very rules normative content for the purposes of the parties' relationships. As the cluster of arbitrations that arose under the Greek 1925 Concession revealed,

---

Noussia, *Confidentiality in International Commercial Arbitration: A Comparative Analysis of the Position under English, US, German and French Law* (Springer 2010) 58–59.

historical ISA's role in contributing to the development of the norms governing the two disputing parties' relationship was particularly marked when the relationship in question continued beyond the arbitration, since in such instances historical ISA tribunals essentially partook in molding the normative framework pursuant to which that investor-state relationship would be structured going forward. In contrast, at the intermediate level of generality, historical ISA's contribution to developing the law was, through the conduit of either of the parties participating in the arbitration, known to extend also to those disputing parties' investor-state relations that were external to the initial arbitral process. As the in-depth account of the *RCA v. China* arbitration and its ensuing fallout illustrated, this implied that the disputing parties in a historical ISA took a tribunal's decision as an authoritative pronunciation as to the meaning of certain norms that were recurrent in their other investor-state relationships and adjusted their understanding of such norms, as well as their corresponding relationships, accordingly. Crucially, however, it was not only over the investor-state relationships to which they were connected through (at least) one of the disputing parties that decisions by historical ISA tribunals exerted normative influence, but also over those to which they bore no connection whatsoever. Indeed, historical ISA was shown by the Chapter to have eventually cultivated a tendency of contributing also to the development of norms of a general scope of application governing investor-state relationships (regarding both substantive and procedural aspects of the investor-state dynamic).

While examining historical ISA's contribution to developing the law through the prism of these distinct levels of generality has been a useful tool for conveying the breadth of historical ISA's normative influence, it is at the same time important to ensure that doing so does not distort how the phenomenon is perceived. Thus, as much as historical ISA's role in contributing to the development of the law governing investor-state relations may have been observable on various planes of generality, by no means should this be taken to imply that in each particular instance its operation on these planes of generality was to the exclusion of one another. Probably the best illustration of such possible overlap is the *RCA v. China* arbitration, where the tribunal's normative influence was seen to have operated on all three distinguishable planes of generality (as is reflected in the tribunal's activism *vis-à-vis* the normative structure that governed the disputing parties' relations,[324] the RCA's subsequent adjustment of its similar contractual relations,[325] and the influence that the tribunal's decision eventually had on interpreting the rights and obligations of

324 See in particular n 233.
325 See sub-section 3.4.

wholly unrelated parties in *Saudi Arabia v.* ARAMCO).[326] Similarly, while the Chapter has for narration purposes followed a gradation of the tribunals' normative influence along the path from the narrow, through the intermediate, and culminating with the general, in individual instances such progression would hardly have been inevitable. Indeed, the fact that a tribunal had in a particular instance influenced the meaning of norms regulating the concrete relationship of the disputing parties before it was no guarantee that its decision would go on to also influence how norms of a broader generality came to be understood (as appears to have been the case with numerous decisions that have never again been referenced). Nor did the fact that a tribunal's decision had contributed to the development of norms of general application necessarily presuppose that it had previously exerted such normative influence at the intermediate level.

One question that undoubtedly remains to be addressed is the exact extent to which the observations from this Chapter regarding historical ISA's contribution to developing the law are generalisable. This is a complex question that is perhaps as multilayered as this contribution itself; it is also one to which the answer must always remain at least somewhat provisional, as the potential for a decision by a historical ISA tribunal to exert (additional) normative influence may lay dormant for considerable time before eventually materialising (see e.g. sub-section 4.2.2.2). If assessed separately at different levels of generality, historical ISA's contribution to the development of the law governing investor-state interaction would undoubtedly be generalisable to varying degrees. At the narrowest level of generality, what was recounted in this Chapter is certainly capable of being extrapolated with some confidence considering that, as was discussed in Chapter 2, every act of norm-application in historical ISA was to a certain extent also an act of norm-generation. Thus, the type of contribution to developing the law that was discussed in relation to the cluster of cases that arose under the Greek 1925 Concession, affecting the two parties to a particular dispute, would hardly have been unconventional,[327] even if in other instances it might not have been as pronounced. Similarly, while it was undeniably far from ubiquitous for historical ISA tribunals to contribute to the development of norms of a general scope of application,[328] it is equally clear from what was discussed above that such practice was sufficiently prevalent so as not to merely constitute the occasional exception. The situation admittedly may have been somewhat different when it comes to historical ISA's

326 See sub-section 4.2.1.

327 Indeed, see only n 233 or the Peace Treaty railway cases discussed in ch 4.

328 See nn 286–287.

contribution to developing the law at the intermediate level of generality, as there as of yet appears to be a dearth of evidence that the type of normative influence that was recounted in sub-section 3.4 in relation to the *RCA v. China* arbitration was particularly widespread, although this may also partially be because evidence of such normative influence likely would have often been contained in a parties' direct correspondence and thus more scarcely obtainable.[329] What is in any event far more important than how generalisable historical ISA's propensity to contribute to the development of the law governing the investor-state dynamic may have been at each of the different levels of generality that have been discussed is that, when such practice is viewed in its totality across these different levels of generality, it unmistakably invites the conclusion that historical ISA as such was a habitual contributor to the development of the normative structures that governed investor-state relations.

Crucially, this contribution was all the more important when accounting for the fact that it concerned norms that governed relationships that were more often than not characterised by a state appearing in its official capacity. This, as has been a constant theme throughout this Chapter, in turn implied that the types of norms to whose development historical ISA contributed included norms that determined how public authority was to be exercised by those states and how such exercise of public authority was going to be assessed. Notably, as the previous sections have demonstrated, whether it was norms affecting worker rights in inter-war Greece, norms regulating how telecommunications services were to be offered in countries across the globe, norms relevant for how the rights and obligations under a major Middle Eastern concession were to be understood, or even norms determining the procedure pursuant to which investor-state disputes were to be resolved, this was a feature that was consistent and that cut across all of the different levels of generality at which historical ISA exerted normative influence. It is consequently critical to properly appreciate the fact that historical ISA not only contributed to the development of the law that governed investor-state relations, but that it did so specifically with respect to normative structures that regulated, *inter alia*, the behaviour of states in their exercise of official functions.

329 It does nonetheless appear that this type of practice was at least not unheard of. For example, in the context of the Peace Treaty railway disputes discussed in ch 4, Austria had, in relation to a dispute with one railway company, informed the Secretary General of the League of Nations that it would, before taking any further decision, be preferable to wait for the tribunal's award regarding 'a claim of a similar nature' in its dispute with another railway company. See Letter from the Austrian Government to the Secretary General of the League of Nations (22 February 1929) (United Nations Archives at Geneva: R2568/9D/5295/5295).

In fact, it is precisely because of the confluence of these two elements that this Chapter furthers the narrative of historical ISA's role in governance that has been advanced in the preceding parts of this book. Within this context, historical ISA's role in contributing to the development of the normative framework that prescribed how governance was to be exercised indeed serves to complement the earlier discussion of its role in determining the cost of governance (Chapter 3) and in directing state conduct (Chapter 4). By capturing this aspect of historical ISA, this Chapter thus, if not exhausts, then certainly further accentuates the reasons for which historical ISA should not be perceived as merely having been a by-party mode of dispute resolution, but rather also as a mode of governance. That being so, the implications that follow from this conclusion are further elaborated upon in the next, concluding, chapter.

CHAPTER 6

Historical Investor-State Arbitration as a Mode of Governance

1 A Recapitulation of Investor-State Arbitration's Historical Role in Governance

All histories are unique and all require to be told in their own way, depending on what story the relevant source material may inspire. Allowing the source material to steer the story, rather than the other way around, is perhaps one of the most crucial aspects of historical research. When telling histories, it is indeed often the conscious effort to make them interesting – the pursuit of a captivating narrative – that makes it all too inviting to fixate on certain distinct aspects of the past that would best catch the reader's attention and allow for the construction of the most compelling story possible. As the preceding pages have shown, the rich yet mostly forgotten past of investor-state arbitration (ISA) is certainly not lacking in such attention-catching detail – detail that could serve as fertile ground for fascinating narratives about the discipline. This includes, to name but a few examples, the accidental origins of the Permanent Court of Arbitration's (PCA) involvement in administering ISA, the existence of ISAs that were based on international treaties that preceded the advent of the bilateral investment treaty (BIT) by half a century or so, the deep involvement with historical ISA by imposing political figures such as Winston Churchill and William Howard Taft, as well as early 20th century debates in the Canadian parliament regarding the appropriateness of resorting to arbitration in order to settle disputes between states and private enterprises. As interesting as these various individual aspects of ISA's past may be, however, they nonetheless remain exactly that – individual fragments of the past that, while certainly not mere curiosities whose relevance is exhausted in providing colour to the overarching narrative, can hardly in and of themselves explain what historical ISA was and how it developed.

Indeed, the overall narrative about ISA's past that emerges from the historical accounts that this book has told is hardly reducible to a few grandiose isolated moments in time, crucial junctures or seminal cases that are responsible for the 'origin' of ISA or that can be said to have entirely altered the course of the discipline. Bearing in mind the richness of ISA's past that the preceding pages have aimed to help chronicle, yet which they have admittedly only barely

 | DOI:10.1163/9789004733824_007

begun to tap into, not only would such narratives that centre on a momentous event or few be extremely simplistic and distortive, but they would effectively in fact contribute to the forgetting of the very past that they purport to help uncover. The picture that is formed from the preceding pages is thus in a sense much more pointillistic – the topography of historical ISA is one that was shaped, not through a few identifiable major tectonic shifts that were brought about by either chance or planned intervention, but rather through the steady process of accretion over time caused by a constant, and seemingly ever increasing, stream of historical ISAs. This does not, of course, imply that there were no historical instances or events that stand out, sometimes markedly so, in terms of their influence on the future course of the development of ISA and its various aspects; indeed, many of them have been highlighted throughout this book. However, ultimately and at its core, the story of what historical ISA was and how it developed simply is not reducible to a few, even if carefully chosen and aimed to be representative, singular events or cases.

That this may be so, however, in no way makes ISA's past any less interesting. In fact, quite to the contrary, it is exactly this non-susceptibility to a grandiose origins or conscious construction narrative that not only makes the story of ISA's past captivating, but all the more salient. There is indeed something sobering in being confronted with the fact that ISA was not at a relatively recent point in time crafted out of thin air with a simple stroke of a pen, or at least moulded from an ephemeral phenomenon into something that is essentially of a ubiquitous presence; instead, for at least a century and a half (but probably more) – ISA simply was, existing in its various iterations, time periods and geographic localities. In fact, the single most important takeaway that can be had from this book is that ISA had a deeply rooted and widespread historical presence, both temporally and geographically; its various historical manifestations thus cannot simply be glossed over as an occasional anomaly, explained away through one particular event or series of events, nor can its 'origin' be easily pinpointed. Indeed, as can be deduced from the cases that were discussed over the course of this book, any expedition that sets out to try to trace the 'origins' of ISA as such would need to go back in time at least a century and a half (and very likely significantly more), as well as visit numerous socio-legal traditions. In light of the seeming lack of any connection between the various historical ISAs that materialised all over the globe in times when modes of communication, and thus also the possibility of adopting practices from other socio-legal cultures, would have been far less developed than they are today, such an expedition would do so without a guarantee, and perhaps even the likelihood, of ever arriving at the desired destination.

While the (hi)story of ISA may thus be one that very well may not have an identifiable beginning, the discipline certainly does have, as the preceding pages have shown, a demonstrably rich tradition. What is crucial for present purposes, and what has been the underlying theme throughout this book, is that this tradition suggests that historical ISA has been, if not necessarily synonymous with, than at least frequently accompanied by, significant governance implications. Indeed, the cases that have been recounted throughout this book chronicle a tradition of governance through historical ISA that appears almost as widespread and varied as the discipline itself. In other words, much like historical ISA as a discipline, so too did the governance implications that accompanied it show a deeply rooted historical presence. The discussion of this governance role by historical ISA that was had in the preceding chapters invites a number of important observations about this enduring practice.

The first, as was discussed in Chapter 2, is that the preconditions for historical ISA to have been much more than merely a mechanism for resolving disputes of sole interest to the two disputing parties were, if not omnipresent, then at least deeply entrenched within the discipline's core features. Indeed, the interests that were implicated in historical ISA were often, if not as a matter of course, of a broader public importance. Through historical ISA, matters involving such broader societal interests were further decided upon by way of a process that relied upon a normative basis markedly lacking in determinacy; as a result, this process thus essentially necessitated a certain degree of creative input from the relevant, in large part independent and private-actor, decision-makers. What is of particular import in this respect is that such characterisation of the processes underlying the discipline appears to have remained true more or less independently of the considerable variability in terms of the underlying legal or conceptual frameworks within which historical ISA was known (or was perceived) to have operated. In other words, the fact that historical ISA was a discipline that was not reducible to a mere dyadic mechanism of (private) dispute resolution but could have instead been expected to have had governance implications was something that was interwoven into the very fabric of the discipline, and was seemingly not restricted to particular geographical, temporal or socio-legal circumstances.

Second, it would be difficult to overstate just how complex and heterogeneous historical ISA's role in governance was. This is already discernible upon first impression from the different modalities through which historical ISA's role in governance was observed to have manifested itself, which were respectively described in Chapters 3, 4, and 5. Chapter 3 examined the various manners and instances in which historical ISA purported to, and in fact influenced, the cost of states' governance choices. For its part, Chapter 4 then recounted historical ISA's role in directing state conduct, while Chapter 5 explored historical ISA's capacity to contribute to the development of the normative structure governing investor-state relations. Yet, while each of these three modalities were already indicative of the fact that historical ISA's governance role could have differing manifestations, the complexity of this governance role was far from exhausted in their very existence. This is because, as the preceding pages have illustrated, neither of these different modalities could themselves be said to have been entirely homogenous – within each of them, one could instead distinguish further sub-modalities, variations or iterations. Indeed, Chapter 3 discussed how historical ISA imposed cost on governance by deciding on matters relating to public debt, by determining the cost of state appropriation of the property of private enterprises or by imposing liability for states' failure to comply with their obligations; Chapter 4 examined the capacity of historical ISA to direct state conduct by either reviewing state or state entity conduct, or by acting as a primary decision-maker in determining the course of such conduct; and Chapter 5 explored historical ISA's contribution to developing the law governing investor-state relations at three different levels of generality.[1]

Crucially, these distinctions are hardly of merely academic interest – that historical ISA's governance role was so variegated is not without important implications for how it is to be viewed and understood. Indeed, each of the different modalities or sub-modalities through which historical ISA's role in governance was observed to have manifested itself would have potentially given rise to very different problems and questions, in particular from the perspective of their perceived (il)legitimacy. This applies equally across the three different modalities of governance through historical ISA that have been described in Chapters 3, 4, and 5, as it does in between their various sub-modalities. For example, the fact that decisions by historical ISA tribunals influenced the cost of certain governance decisions (Chapter 3) would have likely raised wholly different potential concerns from them taking upon themselves to direct the conduct of the particular disputing parties before them, states included (Chapter 4), or from their contributing to the development of the normative

1 Notably, these categorisations are provided primarily for illustrative purposes and should not be understood as being exclusive of one another. Indeed, singular acts by historical ISA tribunals were very much capable of falling under more than one of these modalities or sub-modalities. This would, for example, be the case if a decision that purports to direct state conduct or determine the cost of governance in the process also simultaneously contributes to developing the law on a certain point.

architecture that governed investor-state relations (Chapter 5). Equally as contrasting would have been the potential implications that might have accompanied the fact that historical ISA tribunals directed governmental conduct by reviewing its legality to those that might have arisen from them doing so by acting as primary decision-makers (Chapter 4); the same applies to concerns that might have been raised by the fact that historical ISA tribunals contributed to the development of the normative framework that governs the relationship of the particular disputing parties before them as opposed to them doing so *vis-à-vis* the normative framework that governs investor-state relations of unrelated third parties (Chapter 5). This book stops short of engaging in an in-depth discussion of whether such exercise of governance through historical ISA in any singular instance could have been considered (il)legitimate as it appears difficult, if not inherently impossible, to attain the requisite tools to, from the present-day, assess in any meaningful manner what would have been considered legitimate at any relevant day and age in the distant past. That being so, based on the aforesaid, it nonetheless appears impossible not to observe that any such assessment would by necessity need to be a nuanced one that parallels the complexities of historical ISA's governance role.

Third, neither historical ISA nor its role in governance can be said to have been obscure phenomena that were kept clandestine or that took place entirely away from the public eye. Indeed, already the award from the earliest historical ISA that falls within the time period analysed by this book – the mid-19th century arbitration between the Suez Canal Company and Egypt – was contemporaneously published in the British and Foreign State Papers and the French newspaper *Moniteur*.[2] A similar approach was taken regarding the award handed down in *Peru v. Peruvian Corporation* some half a century later, which was published in the bulletin of Peru's Ministry of Foreign Affairs.[3] Other subsequent historical ISA's were likewise made public through various fora. Thus, in addition to the famous printing of the better part of the *Lena Goldfields v. USSR* award in the London *Times* in 1930,[4] numerous historical ISA awards from the inter-war period were published by specialised journals

2 See Foreign Office, *British and Foreign State Papers: 1864–1865*, vol LV (William Ridgway 1870) 970–1021; Jason Webb Yackee, 'The First Investor-State Arbitration: *The Suez Canal Company v Egypt* (1864)' (2016) 17 The Journal of World Investment and Trade 401, 448.

3 *Government of Peru v The Peruvian Corporation Limited* (1913) 50 Boletin del Ministerio de Relaciones Exteriores (Peru) 144.

4 See Arthur Nussbaum, 'The Arbitration between Lena Goldfields Ltd and the Soviet Government' (1950) 36 Cornell Law Quarterly 31; VV Veeder, 'The *Lena Goldfields* Arbitration: The Historical Roots of Three Ideas' (1998) 47 ICLQ 747, 754.

or collections of arbitral awards such as the American Journal of International Law,[5] the United Nations Reports of International Arbitral Awards,[6] the Recueil des Décisions des Tribunaux Arbitraux Mixtes Institués par les Traités de Paix[7] and/or the League of Nations Official Journal;[8] yet other awards were included in the publicly available documents from the proceedings before the Permanent Court of International Justice (PCIJ).[9] After World War II, the practice of making awards handed down in historical ISA public hardly subsided.[10] In addition to such an established record of making historical ISA awards public,

---

5 See eg *The Administration of Posts and Telegraphs of the Republic of Czechoslovakia v The Radio Corporation of America* (1936) 30 AJIL 523; *Sopron-Köszeg Local Railway Company v Austria and Hungary* (1930) 24(1) AJIL 164; *Barcs-Pakrac Railway Company, Ltd v Hungary and Yugoslavia* (1935) 29(3) AJIL 523.

6 See eg *Radio Corporation of America v The National Government of the Republic of China* (1935) 3 RIAA 1621; *Sopron-Köszeg Local Railway Company v Austria and Hungary* (1929) 2 RIAA 961; *Barcs-Pakrac Railway Company, Ltd v Hungary and Yugoslavia* (1934) 3 RIAA 1569; *Zeltweg-Wolfsberg and Unterdrauburg-Woellan Railway Company v Austria and Yugoslavia* (1933–1938) 3 RIAA 1795.

7 See eg *La Societe Rialet v The Government of Ethiopia* (1929) 8 Recueil des Décisions des Tribunaux Arbitraux Mixtes Institués par les Traités de Paix 742.

8 See eg *Barcs-Pakrac Railway Company, Ltd v Hungary and Yugoslavia* [1934] League of Nations Official Journal 1679; *Zeltweg-Wolfsberg and Unterdrauburg-Woellan Railway Company v Austria and Yugoslavia* [1934] League of Nations Official Journal 84 (*Zeltweg-Wolfsberg I*); *Zeltweg-Wolfsberg and Unterdrauburg-Woellan Railway Company v Austria and Yugoslavia* [1934] League of Nations Official Journal 1005 (*Zeltweg-Wolfsberg II*); *Zeltweg-Wolfsberg and Unterdrauburg-Woellan Railway Company v Austria and Yugoslavia* [1934] League of Nations Official Journal 1007 (*Zeltweg-Wolfsberg III*); *Zeltweg-Wolfsberg and Unterdrauburg-Woellan Railway Company v Austria and Yugoslavia* [1938] League of Nations Official Journal 1172 (*Zeltweg-Wolfsberg IV*).

9 *Losinger & cie SA and 'Kompass' Allgemeine Kredit- und Garantie-Bank v The Kingdom of Yugoslavia*, Award (31 October 1934) (*Losinger I*), reproduced in *The Losinger & Co Case (Switzerland v Yugoslavia)* PCIJ Rep Series C No 78 at 54; *Losinger & cie SA v Kingdom of Yugoslavia*, Preliminary Award (11 October 1935) (*Losinger II*), reproduced in *The Losinger & Co Case (Switzerland v Yugoslavia)* PCIJ Rep Series C No 78 at 105; *The Government of Greece v Sociéte Commerciale de Belgique (Socobelge)*, Award (3 January 1936) (*Socobelge I*), reproduced in *The 'Société commerciale de Belgique' (Belgium v Greece)* PCIJ Rep Series C No 87 at 36; *The Government of Greece v Sociéte Commerciale de Belgique (Socobelge)*, Award (25 July 1936) (*Socobelge II*), reproduced in *The 'Société commerciale de Belgique' (Belgium v Greece)* PCIJ Rep Series C No 87 at 44.

10 See only the many awards from the Middle Eastern oil arbitrations that were published (in whole or in part): *Petroleum Development (Qatar) Ltd v Ruler of Qatar* (1951) 18 ILR 161; *Petroleum Development Ltd v The Sheikh of Abu Dhabi* (1951) 18 ILR 144; *Ruler of Qatar v International Marine Oil Company, Ltd* (1953) 20 ILR 534; *Saudi Arabia v ARAMCO* (1963) 27 ILR 117; *Sapphire International Petroleums Limited v National Iranian Oil Co (NIOC)* (1967) 35 ILR 136; *BP Exploration Company (Libya) Limited v The Government of the Libyan Arab Republic* (1979) 53 ILR 297; *Texaco Overseas Petroleum Company and California Asiatic Oil*

the involvement of some of the most prominent international institutions and/or its personnel (including the League of Nations, the PCIJ, the PCA, and the International Labour Office (ILO)) in the historical ISAs implied that, irrespective of whether awards were to be published, professional circles in two of the capitals of international law, The Hague and Geneva, would certainly have been well acquainted with the practice and its implications. Finally, and perhaps most importantly, information about what took place in these historical ISAs was made available not only to those with specialised academic or practical knowledge about international dispute resolution, but also to the public at large. Thus, many historical ISAs received extensive coverage in the media,[11] while some, as has already been mentioned, were even debated in parliament.[12] Accordingly, it appears difficult to escape the conclusion that the fact that these historical ISAs existed, what they were about and what the arbitrators had decided was not something that was unknowable either to those with specialised knowledge or to the general public.

Fourth, it is important not to overlook by whom decisions with governance implications were being taken in historical ISA. Undoubtedly, the profiles of the arbitrators who had sat in the historical ISAs discussed in the preceding pages show considerable diversity of background; despite the seeming diversity in profile, one frequent yet all important common trait is nonetheless noticeable – these were in large part individuals who would not have been out of their comfort zone in making important policy-related decisions. Thus, among the many who had acted as arbitrators in historical ISAs were, *inter alia*, individuals who were at the time, had previously been, or would in the future become, supreme court justices,[13] judges on prominent international courts such as

Company v The Government of the Libyan Arab Republic (1978) 17 ILM 1; *Libyan American Oil Company* (*LIAMCO*) *v The Government of the Libyan Arab Republic* (1981) 20(1) ILM 1.

11 The contemporaneous media coverage of historical ISA is too profuse to exhaustively reference. As illustrative examples, see only the extensive reporting on *Lena Goldfields v USSR* mentioned in Veeder (n 4) 754, on *Suez v Egypt* referenced in Yackee, 'The First Investor-State Arbitration' (n 2) 426–427 and 448, and the various references to media reports in ch 3 regarding the dispute between the Duff Development Company and Kelantan or the *Grand Trunk Railway Arbitration*.

12 See eg the discussion of the *Grand Trunk Railway Arbitration* in ch 3.

13 Thus, several sitting, former, or to be judges of the Swiss Federal Tribunal sat as arbitrators in historical ISAs: Henri Thelin in *Losinger v Yugoslavia*, Louis Python in *Alsing v Greece*, Pierre Cavin in *Sapphire v NIOC*, Andre Panchaud in *SEEE v Yugoslavia*, and Emil Kirchhofer and Carlo Pometta in disputes arising out of the Greek public utility concession discussed in ch 5. In addition, the *Peru v Peruvian Corporation* case was decided by the first president of the French Court of Cassation, Alexis Ballot-Beaupré (see ch 3), Norwegian Chief Supreme Court Justice Paal Berg acted as arbitrator in the Greek concession

the PCIJ[14] and the European Court of Human Rights,[15] heads of international organisations,[16] as well as individuals who had held the highest national political office – whether as heads of state,[17] as part of the legislature,[18] or as part of the executive.[19] For many of these individuals, historical ISA would have indeed been but only one of the many avenues through which they would have been engaged in governance. Although not exclusively, the decision-makers in historical ISA, then, were frequently individuals to whom taking decisions with governance implications would have almost been second nature.

Fifth and final, it is crucial to contextualise what took place in historical ISA against the broader backdrop of how contemporaneous governance in relation to investor-state relations operated, as historical ISA would have hardly been the only institution that dealt with investor-state relations that would have carried with itself such governance implications. In fact, there were a number of other mechanisms that would have dealt with a comparable *problematique* within the sphere of investor-state interaction as did historical ISA and whose

---

cases discussed in ch 5, while William Howard Taft was an arbitrator in the *Grand Trunk Railway Arbitration* (see ch 3).

14 For example, Judge José Gustavo Guerrero was an arbitrator in the Peace Treaty railway arbitrations discussed in ch 4, BCJ Loder presided over *Rialet v Ethiopia* (see ch 4), while PCIJ Deputy-Judge Frederik Valdemar Nikolai Beichmann chaired *The Jaffa-Jerusalem Railway Arbitration* (see ch 3).

15 Thus, long tenured judge and eventual court president GJ Wiarda had years prior chaired the *Lebanon and the Municipality of Beyrouth v The Beyrouth Water Company* arbitration, while Swedish nominee to the court Gunnar Lagergren had previous to his appointment sat as arbitrator in several historical ISAs (see ch 2). See European Court of Human Rights, 'Judges of the Court Since 1959' <https://www.echr.coe.int/Documents/List_judges_since_1959_BIL.pdf> accessed 27 September 2024.

16 As discussed in ch 5, while Director of the International Labour Office, Albert Thomas had presided over several ISAs that arose out of a Greek public utility concession. Likewise, the aforementioned Judge Guerrero (see n 14) had prior to his appointment to the PCIJ been president of the Assembly of the League of Nations.

17 The *Suez v Egypt* arbitration was decided by Napoleon III (see Yackee, 'The First Investor-State Arbitration' (n 2) 402), while former US president Taft was an arbitrator in the *Grand Trunk Railway Arbitration* (see ch 3).

18 This was the case, for example, with Sir Thomas White, who was an arbitrator in the *Grand Trunk Railway Arbitration* (see ch 3), with Andre Zakkas, who served as arbitrator in multiple Greek concession cases discussed in ch 5, and with Sir Walter Monckton, who was an 'arbitrator-advocate' in *Petroleum Development (Qatar) Ltd v Ruler of Qatar*. Regarding the latter, see 'Sir Walter Monckton' <https://api.parliament.uk/historic-hansard/people/sir-walter-monckton/index.html> accessed 27 September 2024.

19 Thus, several arbitrators who had sat in historical ISAs had at one time or another held ministerial posts, including: Sir Thomas White (see ch 3), Andre Zakkas (see ch 5), Judge Guerrero (see ch 4), Rene Mayer (see ch 4), Cesar Borja (see ch 2), Sir Walter Monckton (see n 18), and Paal Berg.

decisions would have carried similar implications for investor-state relations. A particularly illustrative example in this respect is the Arbitral Tribunal of Upper Silesia,[20] which was established in the aftermath of World War I under a 1922 convention concluded between Poland and Germany in order to facilitate between them the partitioning of Upper Silesia.[21] The tribunal, whose decisions were not only final and executory like national court decisions, but were also capable of holding formally binding precedential value,[22] had a mandate that encompassed claims brought by individuals against the two concerned governments.[23] In the words of the tribunal's only ever president, matters that could within this sphere be submitted to the tribunal ranged 'as well over *public, administrative* and industrial law as over private and commercial law';[24] *inter alia*, this included claims regarding compensation owed for the suppression or diminution of vested rights, questions of nationality, of rights of option, the right of residence or circulation permits, as well as disputes relating to water supplies.[25] In practice, such a broad competence for the tribunal translated to, to name but a few examples, cases revolving around an alleged loss of business because of the introduction of state monopolies, claims of compensation due to alleged legislative infringements of mining privileges, alleged injury caused to minority groups through introduced legislation, social security and labour disputes, the expulsion of individuals on grounds of national security, and questions of acquisition and loss of nationality.[26] In other words, thus, seemingly as a matter of course, the Arbitral Tribunal of Upper Silesia had been tasked with deciding matters (and even creating law) in areas of

20 On the Arbitral Tribunal of Upper Silesia, see G Kaeckenbeeck, 'The Character and Work of the Arbitral Tribunal of Upper Silesia' (1935) 21 Transactions of the Grotius Society: Problems of Peace and War, Papers Read Before the Society in the Year 1935 27; Gerard Conway, 'The Arbitral Tribunal for Upper Silesia: An Early Success in International Adjudication' in Ignacio de la Rasilla and Jorge E Viñuales (eds), *Experiments in International Adjudication: Historical Accounts* (CUP 2019) 98; Michel Erpelding, 'Local International Adjudication: The Groundbreaking "Experiment" of the Arbitral Tribunal for Upper Silesia' in Michel Erpelding, Burkhard Hess and Hélène Ruiz Fabri (eds), *Peace Through Law: The Versailles Peace Treaty and Dispute Settlement After World War I* (Nomos 2019) 277.

21 Convention between Germany and Poland Relating to Upper Silesia (signed 15 May 1922) 9 LNTS 465. The convention is reproduced in Georges Kaeckenbeeck, *The International Experiment of Upper Silesia: A Study in the Working of the Upper Silesian Settlement 1922–1937* (OUP 1942) 567.

22 Kaeckenbeeck, 'The Character and Work of the Arbitral Tribunal of Upper Silesia' (n 20) 33.

23 Ibid 28.

24 Ibid. Emphasis added.

25 Ibid 28–29.

26 Ibid 35 and 38; Conway (n 20) 110–115.

social interaction that pitted individuals and private enterprises against the concerned states' regulatory authority.

Other institutions that could, much like the Arbitral Tribunal of Upper Silesia, be said to have had a role comparable to that of historical ISA (save for, in some instances, the direct involvement of private investors in the relevant processes) include, but are certainly not limited to, the PCIJ and its successor the International Court of Justice,[27] claims commissions and post-World War I Mixed Arbitral Tribunals,[28] state-to-state arbitrations over espoused claims arising out of investment disputes,[29] international organisations such as the ILO (which has from its inception been characterised by a process – 'tripartism' – that reserves a prominent role for private enterprises in the adoption of regulation),[30] as well as of course the various relevant national authorities. The crucial implication that necessarily follows from this is that historical ISA's role in governance hardly appears to have been exceptional – it was but one of many mechanisms, and in particular dispute resolution mechanisms, through which investor-state relations of the time were governed. Moreover, although it is difficult to say with any exactitude to which extent these other mechanisms overlapped in their governance imprint with historical ISA, it is evident that some overlap did in fact exist, not least because some of the very individuals who participated in historical ISA also partook in some of these other mechanisms of investor-state

---

27 See eg only *Case Concerning the Payment of Various Serbian Loans Issued in France* (*France v Kingdom of the Serbs, Croats and Slovenes*) PCIJ Rep Series A No 20; *Case Concerning the Payment in Gold of the Brazilian Federal Loans Issued in France* (*France v Brazil*) PCIJ Rep Series A No 21; *The 'Société Commerciale de Belgique'* (*Belgium v Greece*) PCIJ Rep Series A/B No 78; *The Oscar Chinn Case* (*UK v Belgium*) PCIJ Rep Series A/B No 63; *Anglo-Iranian Oil Co Case* (*United Kingdom v Iran*) (Preliminary Objection) [1952] ICJ Rep 93; *Case Concerning the Barcelona Traction, Light and Power Company, Limited* (*Belgium v Spain*) (*New Application: 1962*) (*Second Phase*) [1970] ICJ Rep 3.

28 On claims commissions and Mixed Arbitral Tribunals, see Rudolf Dolzer, 'Mixed Claims Commissions', *Max Planck Encyclopedia of Public International Law* (article last updated May 2011) <https://opil.ouplaw.com/view/10.1093/law:epil/9780199231690/law-9780199231690-e64> accessed 27 September 2024; Frédéric Mégret, 'Mixed Claim Commissions and the Once Centrality of the Protection of Aliens' in de la Rasilla and Viñuales (n 20) 127; Marta Requejo Isidro and Burkhard Hess, 'International Adjudication of Private Rights: The Mixed Arbitral Tribunals in the Peace Treaties of 1919–1922' in Erpelding, Hess and Ruiz Fabri (n 20) 239.

29 See only *Canevaro Claim* (*Italy v Peru*) (1912) 11 RIAA 397; *Delagoa Bay Railway Arbitration* (*Great Britain and United States v Portugal*) (1898) 2 Moore Int Arb 1865.

30 See eg Guy Fiti Sinclair, 'Managing the "Workers Threat": Preventing Revolution Through the International Labour Organization' in Erpelding, Hess and Ruiz Fabri (n 20) 159, 168–169.

governance.[31] Thus, rather than having been an isolated island that governed investor-state relations, historical ISA would instead better be understood as having been, however loosely so, part and parcel of a much broader 'web of governance' that cut across both the national and the international, through which investor-state relations were governed.

Overall, then, historical ISA leaves one with the impression of a discipline that was not only extremely varied and well established, but also almost intrinsically accompanied by significant governance implications. This coupling between historical ISA and governance does not appear to have been merely circumstantial, but was instead present irrespective of the specific underlying circumstances. The manner in which historical ISA's role in governance manifested itself, meanwhile, was extremely complex, taking on different modalities and revealing various sub-variants. Further, this was not something that merely operated in the background, away from the public eye, but was instead, to a greater or lesser extent, knowable to both those with the relevant specialised knowledge and to the general public. Finally, governance through historical ISA was in large part exercised by individuals who were in other walks of public life accustomed to making decisions with governance implications and it formed part, together with other institutions that had a comparable reach, of a broader 'web of governance' through which investor-state relations of the time were governed.

2 With an Eye to the Future: Toward a Comprehensive Understanding of Investor-State Arbitration's Role as a Mode of Governance

While this book has provided a detailed account of ISA's historical governance role, which is to the best of my knowledge at the same time also the most detailed historical account of the discipline in general, it has equally helped reveal just how much work still remains to be done in learning about and understanding ISA's past. Indeed, as mentioned in Chapter 1, there should be little doubt that ISA's past has only begun to be charted. Accordingly, the book

31 See only nn 13-19. This, of course, hardly exhausts such overlap; thus, as but further illustrative example, Joost Adriaan van Hamel, who presided over *Radio Corporation of America v China*, had served as the High Commissioner of the League of Nations in the Free City of Danzig and as a neutral judge on the Hungaro-Yugoslav Mixed Arbitral Tribunal (see ch 5), while Gunnar Lagergren (see n 15) had, in the *Rann of Kutch Arbitration*, presided over the tribunal that determined a disputed boundary between India and Pakistan. See *The Indo-Pakistan Western Boundary (Rann of Kutch) between India and Pakistan (India v Pakistan)* (1968) 17 RIAA 1.

should serve as a catalyst that will spark further interest into the many aspects of ISA's past that have as of yet remained underexplored.

At the same time – and this is crucial – the book's findings do not only point to a need for additional research regarding the past of ISA, but also in relation to its present. Namely, as the book has demonstrated, the novelty narrative that has almost invariably accompanied investment-treaty arbitration's governance role (see Chapter 1) appears to have significantly overstated the extent to which this practice represents an innovation that considerably departs from previous practice. Indeed, the realisation that investment-treaty arbitration allows tribunals consisting of private actors to take on a role in governance by, *inter alia*, reviewing acts of public law, would best be characterised, not so much as a recognition of a recent paradigm shift in international adjudication, as it would as the scholarly gaining of broader awareness over a deeply-rooted phenomenon that goes back at least a century and a half. This, to be sure, in no way detracts from the significance of the fact that this long overdue observation is increasingly made in scholarship, nor does it in and of itself negate the criticism of investment-treaty arbitration that has in most cases accompanied the observation of its governance role. Similarly, the fact that ISA tribunals have for at least a century and a half been engaged in governance does not imply that the advent of investment-treaty arbitration is not an important milestone that has in many ways significantly transformed how governance takes place through ISA; indeed, there should be little doubt that the introduction of investment-treaty arbitration has in fact added many important new facets to this equation.[32] It is merely the case that the change that has been introduced

---

32 For example, as Van Harten rightfully emphasises, investment-treaty arbitration is distinguishable on account of how states give their consent to arbitrate, since in investment treaties such consent is typically prospective and general in scope (in that it applies to an unidentifiable number of potential foreign investors). See Gus Van Harten, *Investment Treaty Arbitration and Public Law* (OUP 2007) 63–68. The closest historical parallel to the type of general consent given through investment treaties would most probably be the aforementioned arbitration provisions contained in the World War I Peace Treaties (see ch 4). In those instances, however, although companies had through international treaties been accorded the right to arbitrate their disputes with states, this pertained to a yet unknown, but nonetheless identifiable, number of potential future disputes. The reach of these provisions, therefore, was more circumscribed in nature – while the disputes were indeed future disputes in the sense that they had at the time when the treaties were concluded not yet fully crystallised, the relationships from which such disputes could have possibly arisen were limited to a specific historical situation. This (and some other similar exceptions, such as the Franco-Algerian agreements arising out of Algerian independence that offered companies in the hydrocarbons sector direct arbitral recourse against the Algerian state) notwithstanding, historically consent to arbitrate was nonetheless by and large most often individualised and contained in a specific instrument concluded

in terms of the governance role of ISA tribunals can most probably better be described not as a change in kind but as a change in degree. With this in mind, the historical governance role of ISA chronicled by this book thus suggests that blanket characterisations as to the supposedly revolutionary nature of investment-treaty arbitration's governance role are not particularly useful, and need instead to be replaced with a meticulous analysis that will try to distil and better understand the novel governance aspects that have accompanied the rise of investment-treaty arbitration. While this type of analysis is far too demanding and nuanced to be conducted here, there should be little doubt that it carries with itself the potential to significantly influence how this, not new, but rather for the most part *newly observed*, phenomenon is to be understood.

The conclusion that the governance role of investment-treaty arbitration is not nearly as revolutionary as has commonly been presumed, which follows from the preceding pages, in turn further points to the need to look more extensively into whether, and to which extent, such practice is at the present taking place beyond investment-treaty arbitration. Indeed, because the exercise of governance through ISA did not start with investment-treaty arbitration, there would seem to be little reason to think that, the ISAs that are based on investment treaties notwithstanding, such practice has subsided since the days of the arbitrations analysed in this book; quite to the contrary, it can be expected that it has, much like arbitration in general, continued to grow. This expectation does in fact appear to be borne out by the anecdotal evidence that is available on those present-day non-treaty-based ISAs that have come into the public domain. Indeed, such anecdotal evidence indicates that, not only historically but also today, cases that are centred on decidedly public-law issues such as expropriation, fallouts from legislative or administrative action, and licensing or taxation powers, are not merely outliers outside of the investment-treaty arbitration realm. Thus, virtually all leading international arbitral institutions are known to administer non-treaty based ISA cases of this profile, including the International Chamber of Commerce (ICC) International Court of Arbitration,[33] the Arbitration Institute of the Stockholm Chamber of

---

between an investor and a state. By considerably expanding the domain within which ISA tribunals could operate, the introduction of general prospective consent through investment treaties was thus undoubtedly a development that changed the manner in which their governance role could manifest itself.

33 See only Luke Eric Peterson, 'As Hydro v Albania BIT Case Plays Out at ICSID, Albania Announces Victory in Related ICC Contract Case; Claimant Says it has Filed a Second ICC Claim for Expropriation' (*Investment Arbitration Reporter*, 26 January 2018) <https://www.iareporter.com/articles/as-hydro-v-albania-bit-case-plays-out-at-icsid-albania-announces-victory-in-related-icc-contract-case-claimant-says-it-has-filed-a-second-icc

Commerce,[34] the London Court of International Arbitration,[35] the PCA,[36] and the Singapore International Arbitration Centre.[37] It goes without saying that

-claim-for-expropriation/> accessed 27 September 2024; Damien Charlotin, 'ICC Tribunal Finds in Favour of Energy Consortium in Billion Dollar Tax Dispute with Philippines' (*Investment Arbitration Reporter*, 25 April 2019) <https://www.iareporter.com/articles/icc-tribunal-finds-in-favour-of-energy-consortium-in-tax-dispute-with-philippines/> accessed 27 September 2024; Lisa Bohmer, 'Divided ICC Tribunal Orders Argentina to Pay +$67 million (US), after Majority Derives Consent from a Draft Arbitration Agreement' (*Investment Arbitration Reporter*, 27 August 2019) <https://www.iareporter.com/articles/divided-icc-tribunal-orders-argentina-to-pay-67-million-us-after-majority-derives-consent-from-a-draft-arbitration-agreement/> accessed 27 September 2024.

34 See Ridhi Kabra, 'Details Surface of Russian Power Company' Claims against Georgia; Complaints Include Government's Refusal to Adjust Electricity Tariff and to Compensate for Currency Depreciation' (*Investment Arbitration Reporter*, 29 June 2017) <https://www.iareporter.com/articles/details-surface-of-russian-power-company-claims-against-georgia-complaints-include-governments-refusal-to-adjust-electricity-tariff-and-to-compensate-for-currency-depreciation/> accessed 27 September 2024.

35 See eg Luke Eric Peterson, 'LCIA Award at Center of Caribbean Court Proceedings had Deemed Tax Waivers to be Valid Despite their having been Kept Out of Public Eye' (*Investment Arbitration Reporter*, 30 April 2013) <https://www.iareporter.com/articles/lcia-award-at-center-of-caribbean-court-proceedings-had-deemed-tax-waivers-to-be-valid-despite-their-having-been-kept-out-of-public-eye/> accessed 27 September 2024; Zoe Williams, 'Dubai-Owned Company Alleges Expropriation of its Port Investment in Djibouti, and Files a New Claim against the State' (*Investment Arbitration Reporter*, 22 February 2018) <https://www.iareporter.com/articles/dubai-owned-company-alleges-expropriation-of-its-port-investment-in-djibouti-and-files-a-new-claim-against-the-state/> accessed 27 September 2024.

36 See eg Damien Charlotin, 'In Now-Public Award, Arbitrators Interpret Ghana's Constitution and Disagree with Supreme Court's Reading of Key Provision; Gov't is Estopped from Arguing that Contract is Invalid due to Lack of Parliamentary Approval' (*Investment Arbitration Reporter*, 2 April 2017) <https://www.iareporter.com/articles/in-now-public-award-arbitrators-interpret-ghanas-constitution-and-disagree-with-supreme-courts-reading-of-key-provision-govt-is-estopped-from-arguing-that-contract-is-invalid-due-to-lack-of-pa/> accessed 27 September 2024; Clovis Trevino, 'Ecuador in Midst of UNCITRAL Arbitration Following Spurning by Petrobras and Partners of Migration to "Service Agreements"' (*Investment Arbitration Reporter*, 4 May 2015) <https://www.iareporter.com/articles/ecuador-in-midst-of-uncitral-arbitration-following-spurning-by-petrobras-and-partners-of-migration-to-service-agreements/> accessed 27 September 2024; Zoe Williams, 'Centerra Goes Back to Arbitration with Kyrgyzstan over Contentious Kumtor Gold Project' (*Investment Arbitration Reporter*, 1 June 2016) <https://www.iareporter.com/articles/centerra-goes-back-to-arbitration-with-kyrgyzstan-over-troubled-kumtor-gold-project/> accessed 27 September 2024.

37 See Luke Eric Peterson, 'East Timor Launches Arbitration against Australia, as Separate Tax Dispute with US Investor Plays Out at Singapore International Arbitration Centre' (*Investment Arbitration Reporter*, 7 May 2013) <https://www.iareporter.com/articles/east-timor-launches-arbitration-against-australia-as-separate-tax-dispute-with-u-s-investor-plays-out-at-singapore-international-arbitration-centre/> accessed 27 September 2024.

the contract-based ICSID claims, which by default need to arise out of an 'investment' in order to satisfy the jurisdictional requirements under the ICSID Convention,[38] largely fall into this same category.

With this in mind, the inference appears ineluctable that, even beyond investment-treaty arbitration, present-day ISA tribunals to some extent exercise a governance role that is similar to that of the historical ISA tribunals. Exactly how deep this practice runs still remains to be determined, due primarily to the fact that, unlike investment-treaty arbitration, which has made large strides in terms of transparency in the last decade or so, the rest of ISA is yet to catch up on this front and is therefore in most part still not observable to the public eye. There is thus a need to undertake in-depth research that will try to better ascertain how deeply intertwined the non-treaty-based segment of ISA is with governance. The need for such research is particularly pressing in light of the fact that investment-treaty arbitration is, precisely in large part because of its perceived role in governance, currently engulfed in extensive legitimacy and reform debates. It is thus essential to have, sooner rather than later, an informed discussion on whether it is necessary to expand the governance discourse that is currently overwhelmingly centred on investment-treaty arbitration so as to also include the remainder of ISA. At least at face value, it would certainly appear that the governance implications of this less visible segment of ISA, the non-treaty-based cases, are not insignificant. From this, one can deduce that it is highly likely that the concerns that are recognised to exist with respect to investment-treaty arbitration, but which are in actuality most probably of considerably broader scope, can truly begin to be addressed only through a fully exhaustive approach – an approach that will centre on the entirety of ISA, rather than just on its investment-treaty variant.

---

38 Convention on the Settlement of Investment Disputes between States and Nationals of Other States (opened for signature 18 March 1965, entered into force 14 October 1966) 575 UNTS 159 art 25.

Bibliography

Archival Materials Consulted

The National Archives of the UK

CO 1071/220

CO 1073/133

CO 717/53/12

CO 717/73/16

CO 827/1

FCO 141/15915

FCO 141/16701

FCO 141/16702

FCO 141/16703

FCO 141/16704

FCO 141/16705

FCO 141/16706

FCO 141/16707

FCO 141/16708

FCO 141/16709

FCO 141/16710

FCO 141/16711

FCO 141/16712

FCO 141/16713

FCO 141/16714

FCO 141/16715

FCO 141/16840

FCO 39/505

FCO 39/710

FO 286/1120/190

FO 286/1123/190

FO 286/1127/99

FO 286/992

FO 32/674

FO 32/675

FO 32/756

FO 371/82082

FO 371/87759

TS 27/143

TS 27/144
TS 36/216

The Commonwealth Office Pamphlet Collection at the University of Manchester Library Special Collections

Eastern 10936.111
Eastern 10936.138
Eastern 10936.232
Eastern 10936.286

Foyle Special Collections Library at King's College London

FCDO Historical Coll, FOL DS598.K3 DUF

University College London Special Collections

PERUCORP B3/2
PERUCORP B4/1
PERUCORP C2/39
PERUCORP C2/65A
PERUCORP C2/65B/1
PERUCORP C2/65B/2-3
PERUCORP C2/65C/1-2

The National Archives of the Netherlands

Arrondissementsrechtbank Den Haag 1960–1979, access number 3.03.79, inventory number 4903

Collection 179 JA van Hamel, 1632–1964, access number 2.21.081, inventory number 61–62

Collection 341 Prof mr dr GWJ Bruins, Supplement 1981, 1929–1939, access number 2.21.191.02, inventory number 1–8

The Hagley Museum and Library

Records of MCI International, Inc, call number 2225, Series XV, boxes 581 and 583
Box 581, files:

- China: Chinese Arbitration Legal Documents
- China: Chinese Arbitration Correspondence (1 of 13)
- China: Chinese Arbitration Correspondence (2 of 13)
- China: Chinese Arbitration Correspondence (3 of 13)
- China: Chinese Arbitration Correspondence (4 of 13)
- China: Chinese Arbitration Correspondence (5 of 13)
- China: Chinese Arbitration Correspondence (6 of 13)

- China: Chinese Arbitration Correspondence (7 of 13)
- China: Chinese Arbitration Correspondence (8 of 13)
- China: Chinese Arbitration Correspondence (9 of 13)
- China: Chinese Arbitration Correspondence (10 of 13)
- China: Chinese Arbitration Correspondence (11 of 13)
- China: Chinese Arbitration Correspondence (12 of 13)
- China: Chinese Arbitration Correspondence (13 of 13)
- China: Correspondence (RCA)
- China: Traffic Agreements
- China: Correspondence (1 of 6)

Box 583, files:
- Czechoslovakia: Correspondence and Agreements (1 of 6)
- Czechoslovakia: Correspondence and Agreements (2 of 6)
- Czechoslovakia: Correspondence and Agreements (3 of 6)
- Czechoslovakia: Correspondence and Agreements (4 of 6)
- Czechoslovakia: Correspondence and Agreements (5 of 6)
- Czechoslovakia: Correspondence and Agreements (6 of 6)
- Czechoslovakia: Arbitration (1 of 3)
- Czechoslovakia: Arbitration (2 of 3)
- Czechoslovakia: Arbitration (3 of 3)

The United Nations Archives at Geneva

CRID134/343/160/2
CRID134/343/162
CRID134/343/163/1
CRID134/343/163/2
CRID134/343/163/4
CRID134/343/163/5
R1178/14/60292/60292
R2564/9D/1243/1243
R2564/9D/1496/1496
R2564/9D/1497/1497
R2565/9D/1500/1500
R2567/9D/3423/3422
R2568/9D/5295/5295
R2568/9D/5295/5295
R2569/9D/11479/11479
R2569/9D/11480/11480
R2570/9D/13823/13823
R2570/9D/13870/13870

R2570/9D/13898/13898
R2570/9D/16211/16211
R2571/9D/30174/30174
R2571/9D/39786/39786
R4277/9D/1199/309/Jacket1
R4278/9D/1199/309/Jacket3
R4278/9D/3801/309
R4279/9D/3801/309/Jacket4-7
R4280/9D/10963/309
R4280/9D/11351/309
R4280/9D/15670/309
R4280/9D/3801/309/Jacket8
R4280/9D/6225/309
R4585/10C/27028/2055
S492/11/6

The International Labour Office Archives

AR 1–26
AR 1–26–1
AR 1–26–1–1
AR 1–26–2
AR 1–26–3
AR 1–26–4
AR 1–26–4–1
AR 1–26–5
AR 1–26–6
AR 1–26–7
AR 1–26–8
AR 1–26–9
AR 1–26–10
AR 1–26–17
AR 1–26–18
AR 1–26–19
AR 1–26–307
AR 1/26
AR 1/26/0
AR 1/26/0/1
AR 1/26/1
AR 1/26/2
AR 1/26/2/1

AR 1/26/3/1
AR 1/26/4/1
AR 1/26/5
AR 1/26/5/1
AR 1/26/6
AR 1/26/6/1
AR 1/26/7
AR 1/26/8
AR 1/26/9
AR 1/26/10
AR 1/26/10/1
AR 1/26/11
AR 1/26/11/1
AR 1/26/12
AR 1/26/12/1
AR 1/26/13
AR 1/26/14
AR 1/26/14/1
AR 1/26/15
AR 1/26/15/1
CAT 5–37–2

The Archives of the Graduate Institute of International and Development Studies in Geneva

1.7.5.HEI 2198
1.7.5.HEI 2446
1.7.5.HEI 2447
1.7.5.HEI 2448
1.7.5.HEI 2449
1.7.5.HEI 2477

The Archives of Yugoslavia

70-255-460
70-285-531
70-288-535
70-288-536
70-292-542
70-463-761
125-218 (1936–1943)
125-234-364

125-483 (1933–1941)
138-6-32
151-47-71
334-28-69
338-33 (1931–1938)
338-45 (1935–1936)
338-45 (1935–1936)
395-28-270
780-F10 (1971)
780-F12 (1971)
780-F13 (1963–1965)
780-F17 (1976–1977)
780-F8 (1954)
780-F9 (1971)

The Diplomatic Archive of the Ministry of Foreign Affairs of the Republic of Serbia

Fund PA, fascicle 25, dossier 16
Fund PA, fascicle 29, dossier 331

Books, Monographs, Articles and Case Reports

——'Gut Dam Case (Canada/United State of America)' in Cairo AR Robb (ed), *International Environmental Law Reports, Volume 1: Early Decisions* (CUP 1999) 386

——'Percy Horsfall: A Scholar in the City' (1965) 55 The Round Table 207

——'Sudan v Turriff Construction Company' in P Hamilton and others (eds), *The Permanent Court of Arbitration: International Arbitration and Dispute Resolution: Summaries of Awards, Settlement Agreements and Reports* (Kluwer 1999) 164

——*Ministere du Commerce et des Travaux Publics – Chemins de fer Orientaux: Arbitrage de 1903* (*Compromis, Proces-Verbaux, Sentences et Avis Separes*) (H Matteosian 1904)

——*Papers Relating to the Foreign Relations of the United States, With the Annual Message of the President Transmitted to Congress December 8, 1908* (US Government Printing Office 1912)

——*Papers Relating to the Foreign Relations of the United States, With the Annual Message of the President Transmitted to Congress December 3, 1907, (In two parts), Part I* (US Government Printing Office 1910)

Abdalla El Sheikh FER, *The Legal Regime of Foreign Private Investment in Sudan and Saudi Arabia* (2nd ed, CUP 2003)

Alter K, *The New Terrain of International Law: Courts, Politics, Rights* (Princeton University Press 2014)

Alter K, Helfer LR and Madsen MR, 'How Context Shapes the Authority of International Courts' in Karen J Alter, Laurence R Helfer and Mikael Rask Madsen (eds), *International Court Authority* (OUP 2018)

Alvarez JE, 'What are International Judges for? The Main Functions of International Adjudication' in Cesare PR Romano, Karen Alter and Yuval Shany (eds), *The Oxford Handbook of International Adjudication* (OUP 2013) 158

Alvik I, *Contracting with Sovereignty: State Contracts and International Arbitration* (Hart Publishing 2011)

Alvik I, 'Protection of Private Property in the Early Law of Nations' (2018) 20 Journal of the History of International Law 217

Archer GL, *History of Radio to 1926* (The American Historical Society 1938)

Archer GL, *Big Business and Radio* (The American Historical Society 1939)

Armitage D, 'What's the Big Idea? Intellectual History and the Longue Durée' (2012) 38(4) History of European Ideas 493

Armitage D and Guldi J, 'The Return of the Longue Durée: An Anglo-American Perspective' (2015) 70(2) Annales HSS (English edn) 219

Baillargeon D, '"Imperium in Imperio": The Corporation, Mining, and Governance in British Southeast Asia, 1900–1930' (2022) 23(2) Enterprise & Society 325

Baker RS, *Woodrow Wilson: Life and Letters: President 1913–1914* (First Greenwood Printing 1968, vol IV)

Bandera VN, 'The New Economic Policy (NEP) as an Economic System' (1963) 71(3) Journal of Political Economy 265

Batsele F, 'The Unknown Innovator: Switzerland and the Beginning of the Investment Treaty Regime' (2024) 34 Swiss Rev Int'l & Eur L 181

Bean JJ, 'Nikolai Bukharin and the New Economic Policy: *A Middle Way?*' (1997) 2(1) The Independent Review 79

Bentwich N, 'Mandated Territories: Palestine and Mesopotamia (Iraq)' (1921–1922) 2 Brit YBIL 48

Bevir M, 'Objectivity in History' (1994) 33(3) History and Theory 328

Bevir M, 'The Contextual Approach' in George Klosko (ed), *The Oxford Handbook of the History of Political Philosophy* (OUP 2011)

Boue JC, 'Much More than a Footnote (or Three): Frank C Hendryx and an Untold Story of Petroleum Concessions and the Genesis of ICSID' (2022) 13(1) Journal of International Dispute Settlement 1

Blackaby N and others, *Redfern and Hunter on International Arbitration* (6th edn, OUP 2015)

Blandford AC, 'The History of Fair and Equitable Treatment before the Second World War' (2017) 32(2) ICSID Review – Foreign Investment Law Journal 287

Blejan E, Costache B and Aloman A, 'The National Bank of Romania during The Great Depression: 1929–1933' (Fourth Conference of Southeast Europe Monetary History Network (SEEMHN), Belgrade, 27–28 March 2009) <https://www.nbs.rs/export/sites/NBS_site/documents/publikacije/konferencije/seemhn_conf/SEEMHN_14_Rumunija.pdf> accessed 27 September 2024

Blejan E, Costache B and Iarovici A, 'International Reserves of the National Bank of Romania 1920–1944' (December 2006) 9 <https://www.bnr.ro/Studies-3215.aspx> accessed 27 September 2024

Böckstiegel KH, 'Arbitration of Disputes Between States and Private Enterprises in the International Chamber of Commerce' (1965) 59 AJIL 579

Böckstiegel KH, *Der Staat als Vertragspartner ausländischer Privatunternehmen* (Athenäum Verlag 1971)

Böckstiegel KH, *Arbitration and State Enterprises: A Survey on the National and International State of Law and Practice* (Kluwer 1984)

Bohmer L, 'Divided ICC Tribunal Orders Argentina to Pay +$67 million (US), after Majority Derives Consent from a Draft Arbitration Agreement' (*Investment Arbitration Reporter*, 27 August 2019) <https://www.iareporter.com/articles/divided-icc-tribunal-orders-argentina-to-pay-67-million-us-after-majority-derives-consent-from-a-draft-arbitration-agreement/> accessed 27 September 2024

Borchard E, *State Insolvency and Foreign Bondholders: General Principles*, vol 1 (Beard Books 2000)

Born GB, *International Arbitration: Law and Practice* (Kluwer 2012)

Born GB, *International Commercial Arbitration* (2nd edn, Kluwer 2014, vol 1)

Born GB, 'The 1933 Directives on Arbitration of the German Reich: Echoes of the Past?' (2021) 38(4) Journal of International Arbitration 417

Braudel F, 'History and the Social Sciences: The *Longue Durée*' in Fernand Braudel, *On History* (Sarah Matthews tr, University of Chicago Press 1980)

Bray HL, 'Understanding Change: Evolution from International Claims Commissions to Investment Treaty Arbitration' in Stephan W Schill, Christian J Tams and Rainer Hofmann (eds), *International Investment Law and History: Towards a Historiographical Turn* (Edward Elgar Publishing 2018) 102

Brekoulakis S, 'International Arbitration Scholarship and the Concept of Arbitration Law' (2013) 36(4) Fordham International Law Journal 745

Brower CN and Schill SW, 'Is Arbitration a Threat or a Boon to the Legitimacy of International Investment Law?' (2009) 9(2) Chicago Journal of International Law 471

Cantegreil J, 'The Audacity of the Texaco/Calasiatic Award: René-Jean Dupuy and the Internationalization of Foreign Investment Law' (2011) 22(2) EJIL 441

Caron DD, 'The Nature of the Iran-United States Claims Tribunal and the Evolving Structure of International Dispute Resolution' (1990) 84 AJIL 104

Caron DD, 'Towards a Political Theory of International Courts and Tribunals' (2006) 24 Berkeley J Int'l Law 401

Casasempere García A and Pérez Yuste A, 'The Role of the White House in the Establishment of a Governmental Radio Monopoly in the United States. The Case of the Radio Corporation of America' (2010 Second Region 8 IEEE Conference on the History of Communications, Madrid, 3–5 November 2010) 1 <https://ieeexplore.ieee.org/document/5735292> accessed 27 September 2024

Cerna S, 'Romanian Stabilisation in the 1920s and the Missing Gold Reserves' (conference titled Facing the Crisis and Depression Discussions on Economic Policy and Reforms in Europe during the Interwar Period, Amiens, 21–22 September 2017) 12 <https://www.researchgate.net/publication/320077223_Romanian_Stabilization_at_the_20thies_and_the_missing_gold_reserves_Conferinta_Facing_the_Crisis_and_Depression_Discussions_on_Economic_Policcy_and_Reforms_in_Europe_during_the_Interwar_period_Unversi> accessed 27 September 2024

Charlotin D, 'In Now-Public Award, Arbitrators Interpret Ghana's Constitution and Disagree with Supreme Court's Reading of Key Provision; Gov't is Estopped from Arguing that Contract is Invalid due to Lack of Parliamentary Approval' (*Investment Arbitration Reporter*, 2 April 2017) <https://www.iareporter.com/articles/in-now-public-award-arbitrators-interpret-ghanas-constitution-and-disagree-with-supreme-courts-reading-of-key-provision-govt-is-estopped-from-arguing-that-contract-is-invalid-due-to-lack-of-pa/> accessed 27 September 2024

Charlotin D, 'ICC Tribunal Finds in Favour of Energy Consortium in Billion Dollar Tax Dispute with Philippines' (*Investment Arbitration Reporter*, 25 April 2019) <https://www.iareporter.com/articles/icc-tribunal-finds-in-favour-of-energy-consortium-in-tax-dispute-with-philippines/> accessed 27 September 2024

Chernykh Y, 'The Gust of Wind: The Unknown Role of Sir Elihu Lauterpacht in the Drafting of the Abs-Shawcross Draft Convention' in Stephan W Schill, Christian J Tams and Rainer Hofmann (eds), *International Investment Law and History: Towards a Historiographical Turn* (Edward Elgar Publishing 2018) 241

Chiappini R and others, 'Romania's Unsustainable Stabilization: 1929–1933' (66th Annual Congress of the French Economic Association, Nice, 19–21 June 2017) 3–4 <https://afse2017.sciencesconf.org/143369/chiappini_costache_torre_tosi_20feb.pdf> accessed 27 September 2024

Chisholm AHT, *The First Kuwait Oil Concession Agreement: A Record of the Negotiations 1911–1934* (Frank Cass 1975)

Choudhury B, 'Recapturing Public Power: Is Investment Arbitration's Engagement of the Public Interest Contributing to the Democratic Deficit?' (2008) 41 Vand J Transnat'l L 775

Clayton RJB, *Kelantan Administration Report for the Year 1927* (Government Printing Office Singapore 1928)

Collier J and Lowe V, *The Settlement of Disputes in International Law: Institutions and Procedures* (OUP 1999)

Collins L, 'Captain Duff, the Sultan of Kelantan and Their Legacy in the Law of State Immunity and International Arbitration' (2021) 37 Arbitration International 463

Conway G, 'The Arbitral Tribunal for Upper Silesia: An Early Success in International Adjudication' in Ignacio de la Rasilla and Jorge E Viñuales (eds), *Experiments in International Adjudication: Historical Accounts* (CUP 2019) 98

Corporation of Foreign Bondholders, 'Twelfth Annual General Report of the Council of the Corporation of Foreign Bondholders' (Wertheimer, Lea & Co 1885)

Corporation of Foreign Bondholders, 'Twenty-Eight Annual General Report of the Council of the Corporation of Foreign Bondholders' (Wertheimer, Lea & Co 1901)

Corporation of Foreign Bondholders, 'Thirtieth Annual General Report of the Council of the Corporation of Foreign Bondholders' (Wertheimer, Lea & Co 1903)

Corporation of Foreign Bondholders, 'Fifty-Fourth Annual General Report of the Council of the Corporation of Foreign Bondholders' (Williams, Lea & Co)

Craven M, 'Theorizing the Turn to History in International Law' in Anne Orford and Florian Hoffmann (eds), *The Oxford Handbook of the Theory of International Law* (OUP 2016) 21

Craven M, Fitzmaurice M and Vogiatzi M (eds), *Time, History and International Law* (Martinus Nijhoff 2007)

Crawford J, 'The Permanent Court of Arbitration and Mixed Arbitration' (Celebration of the Centenary of the PCA, The Hague, 18 October 2007) 1–2 <https://docs.pca-cpa.org/2016/01/Reflections-on-the-Current-Relevance-of-the-PCA-Presentation-by-Professor-James-Crawford-SC.pdf> accessed 27 September 2024

Currie AW, *The Grand Trunk Railway of Canada* (University of Toronto Press 1957)

de Blois M, 'The Unique Character of the Mandate for Palestine' (2016) 49 Isr L Rev 365

De Luca A, 'Non-Pecuniary Remedies Under the Energy Charter Treaty' (2015) Energy Charter Secretariat Knowledge Centre Occasional Paper, 2 <https://ssrn.com/abstract=2589428> accessed 27 September 2024

Delaume GR, 'Jurisdiction of Courts and International Loans: A Study of Lenders' Practice' (1957) 6 The American Journal of Comparative Law 189

Delaume GR, 'State Contracts and Transnational Arbitration' (1981) 75(4) AJIL 784

Delaume GR, 'SEEE v Yugoslavia: Epitaph or Interlude?' (1987) 4(3) Journal of International Arbitration 25

Denza E and Poulsen LNS, 'The Euro – Arab Investment Treaty That Nearly Was' (2020) 69 ICLQ 267

Diggelmann O, 'The Periodization of the History of International Law' in Bardo Fassbender and Anne Peters (eds), *The Oxford Handbook of the History of International Law* (OUP 2012) 997

Dimolitsa A, 'Arbitration Agreements and Foreign Investments – The Greek State between Contractual Commitment and Sovereign Intervention' (1988) 5(4) Journal of International Arbitration 17

Dolzer R, 'Mixed Claims Commissions', *Max Planck Encyclopedia of Public International Law* (article last updated May 2011) <https://opil.ouplaw.com/view/10.1093/law:epil/9780199231690/law-9780199231690-e64> accessed 27 September 2024

Dolzer R, Kriebaum U and Schreuer C, *Principles of International Investment Law* (3rd edn, OUP 2022)

Domke M, 'The Settlement of International Investment Disputes' (1956–1957) 12 The Business Lawyer 264

Domke M, 'Foreign Nationalizations: Some Aspects of Contemporary International Law' (1961) 55 AJIL 585

Douglas Z, *The International Law of Investment Claims* (CUP 2009)

Dritsas M, 'Foreign Capital and Greek Development in a Historical Perspective' (1993) Uppsala Papers in Economic History – Working Paper No 10 <https://www.diva-portal.org/smash/get/diva2:128582/FULLTEXT01.pdf> accessed 27 September 2024

Dugan CF and others, *Investor-State Arbitration* (OUP 2008)

Dupuy PM and Chetail V (eds), *The Roots of International Law/Les fondements du droit international: Liber Amicorum Peter Haggenmacher* (Brill 2014)

Eagle JA, 'Monopoly or Competition: the Nationalization of the Grand Trunk Railway' (1981) 62(1) The Canadian Historical Review 3

Eastman LE, 'Nationalist China During the Nanking Decade 1927–1937' in John K Fairbank and Albert Feuerwerker (eds), *The Cambridge History of China*, vol XIII (CUP 1986) 116

Erades L, 'The Sudan Arbitration' (1970) 17(2) Netherlands International Law Review 200

Erpelding M, 'Local International Adjudication: The Groundbreaking "Experiment" of the Arbitral Tribunal for Upper Silesia' in Michel Erpelding, Burkhard Hess and Hélène Ruiz Fabri (eds), *Peace Through Law: The Versailles Peace Treaty and Dispute Settlement After World War I* (Nomos 2019) 277

Falada D, 'Codification of Private Law in the Czech Republic' (2009) 15(1) Fundamina: A Journal of Legal History 38

Farmanfarma A, 'The Oil Agreement Between Iran and the International Oil Consortium: the Law Controlling' (1955–1956) 34 Tex L Rev 259

Farrer RJ, *Kelantan Administration Report for the Year 1916* (Federated Malay States Government Printing Office 1917)

Fasolt C, *The Limits of History* (University of Chicago Press 2004)

Fassbender B and Peters A, 'Introduction: Towards a Global History of International Law' in Bardo Fassbender and Anne Peters (eds), *The Oxford Handbook of the History of International Law* (OUP 2012) 1

Fassbender B and Peters A (eds), *The Oxford Handbook of the History of International Law* (OUP 2012)

Fatouros AA, 'International Law and the Internationalized Contract' (1980) 74(1) AJIL 134

Ferrell RH, 'The Mukden Incident: September 18–19, 1931' (1955) 27(1) The Journal of Modern History 66

Ferrier RW, *The History of the British Petroleum Company: Volume I, the Developing Years 1901–1932* (CUP 1982)

Fischer P (ed), *A Collection of International Concessions and Related Instruments*, vol I (Oceana 1976)

Fischer P (ed), *A Collection of International Concessions and Related Instruments*, vol III (Oceana 1976)

Fischer P (ed), *A Collection of International Concessions and Related Instruments*, vol VIII (Oceana 1979)

Fitch SD, 'The Harriman Manganese Concession in the Soviet Union: Lessons for Today' (1991) 9 Int'l Tax & Bus Law 209

Flaherty MS, 'History "Lite" in Modern American Constitutionalism' (1995) 95 Colum L Rev 523

Fleming RB, *Railway King of Canada: Sir William MacKenzie, 1849–1923* (UBC Press 1991)

Ford AW, *The Anglo-Iranian Oil Dispute of 1951–1952: A Study of the Role of Law in the Relations of States* (University of California Press 1954)

Foreign Office, *British and Foreign State Papers: 1864–1865*, vol LV (William Ridgway 1870)

Franck SD, 'The Legitimacy Crisis in Investment Treaty Arbitration: Privatizing Public International Law Through Inconsistent Decisions' (2005) 73 Fordham Law Review 1521

Franck T, 'Legitimacy in the International System' (1988) 82 AJIL 705

Freyer DH and Gharavi HG, 'Finality and Enforceability of Foreign Arbitral Awards: From "Double Exequatur" to the Enforcement of Annulled Awards: A Suggested Path to Uniformity Amidst Diversity' (1998) 13(1) ICSID Review – Foreign Investment Law Journal 101

Fuller JV (ed), *Papers Relating to the Foreign Relations of the United States, With the Annual Message of the President Transmitted to Congress December 3, 1912* (US Government Printing Office 1919)

Fuller JV (ed), *Papers Relating to the Foreign Relations of the United States, With the Address of the President to Congress December 2, 1913* (US Government Printing Office 1920)

Fuller JV (ed), *Papers Relating to the Foreign Relations of the United States, With the Address of the President to Congress December 8, 1914* (US Government Printing Office 1922)

Fuller JV (ed), *Papers Relating to the Foreign Relations of the United States, With the Address of the President to Congress December 4, 1917* (US Government Printing Office 1926)

Fuller JV (ed), *Papers Relating to the Foreign Relations of the United States, 1918* (US Government Printing Office 1930)

Fuller JV (ed), *Papers Relating to the Foreign Relations of the United States, 1919* (US Government Printing Office 1934, vol II)

Gaillard E, *Legal Theory of International Arbitration* (Martinus Nijhoff 2010)

Galindo GRB, 'Martti Koskenniemi and the Historiographical Turn in International Law' (2005) 16 European Journal of International Law 539

Gatrell P, 'Economic and Demographic Change: Russia's Age of Economic Extremes' in Ronald Grigor Suny (ed), *The Cambridge History of Russia*, vol III (CUP 2006) 383

Gélinas F, 'Arbitration as Transnational Governance by Contract' (2016) 7(2) Transnational Legal Theory 181

Glazebrook GPT, *A History of Transportation in Canada* (originally published by Ryerson Press 1938, Greenwood Press 1969)

Gottschalk L, *Understanding History: A Primer of Historical Method* (Alfred A Knopf 1956)

Graham WA, *Kelantan: A State of The Malay Peninsula: A Handbook of Information* (James Maclehose and Sons 1908)

Graves R, *Storm Centres of the Near East: Personal Memories, 1879–1929* (Hutchinson and Company Ltd 1933)

Greenman K, *State Responsibility and Rebels: The History and Legacy of Protecting Investment Against Revolution* (CUP 2021)

Grigg S, 'Archival Practice and the Foundations of Historical Method' (1991) 78 Journal of American History 228

Grunwald K, *Turkenhirsch: A Study of Baron Maurice de Hirsch, Entrepreneur and Philanthropist* (Israel Program for Scientific Translations 1966)

Hamilton P and others (eds), *The Permanent Court of Arbitration: International Arbitration and Dispute Resolution: Summaries of Awards, Settlement Agreements and Reports* (Kluwer 1999)

Happ R, 'Why Investment Arbitration Contributes to the Rule of Law: Without Knowing Where We Came from We Cannot Know Where We Are Heading' (2016) 1 EILA Rev 278

Harris B, 'Report on the Arbitration Act 1996' (2007) 23(3) Arbitration International 437

Harrison M, 'Why Did NEP Fail?' (1980) 16(2) Economics of Planning 57

Hausman WJ, Hertner P and Wilkins M, *Global Electrification: Multinational Enterprise and International Finance in the History of Light and Power, 1878–2007* (CUP 2008)

Hepburn J and others, 'Investment Law before Arbitration' (2020) 23 JIEL 929

Ho J, *State Responsibility for Breaches of Investment Contracts* (CUP 2018)

Hueck IJ, 'The Discipline of the History of International Law: New Trends and Methods on the History of International Law' (2001) 3 Journal of the History of International Law 194

Hughes O, 'Does Governance Exist?' in Stephen P Osborne (ed), *The New Public Governance: Emerging Perspectives on the Theory and Practice of Public Governance* (Routledge 2010) 87

Indlekofer M, *International Arbitration and the Permanent Court of Arbitration* (Kluwer 2013)

Iriye A, 'Japanese Aggression and China's International Position 1931–1949' in John K Fairbank and Albert Feuerwerker (eds), *The Cambridge History of China*, vol XIII (CUP 1986) 492

Johnson OT and Gimblett J, 'From Gunboats to BITs: the Evolution of Modern International Investment Law' in Karl P Sauvant (ed), *Yearbook on International Investment Law and Policy 2010–2011* (OUP 2012) 649

Kabra R, 'Details Surface of Russian Power Company' Claims against Georgia; Complaints Include Government's Refusal to Adjust Electricity Tariff and to Compensate for Currency Depreciation' (*Investment Arbitration Reporter*, 29 June 2017) <https://www.iareporter.com/articles/details-surface-of-russian-power-company-claims-against-georgia-complaints-include-governments-refusal-to-adjust-electricity-tariff-and-to-compensate-for-currency-depreciation/> accessed 27 September 2024

Kaeckenbeeck G, 'The Character and Work of the Arbitral Tribunal of Upper Silesia' (1935) 21 Transactions of the Grotius Society: Problems of Peace and War, Papers Read Before the Society in the Year 1935 27

Kaeckenbeeck G, *The International Experiment of Upper Silesia: A Study in the Working of the Upper Silesian Settlement 1922–1937* (OUP 1942)

Kaur A, *Bridge and Barrier: Transport and Communications in Colonial Malaya 1870–1957* (OUP 1985)

Kaushal A, 'Revisiting History: How the Past Matters for the Present Backlash against the Foreign Investment Regime' (2009) 50 Harvard International Law Journal 491

Kingsbury B and Schill S, 'Investor-State Arbitration as Governance: Fair and Equitable Treatment, Proportionality, and the Emerging Global Administrative Law' in Albert Jan van den Berg (ed), *50 Years of the New York Convention* (Kluwer 2009) 5

Knickerbocker HR, 'The Soviet Five-Year Plan' (1931) 10(4) International Affairs (Royal Institute of International Affairs 1931–1939) 433

Kooiman J and Jentoft S, 'Meta-Governance: Values, Norms and Principles, and the Making of Hard Choices' (2009) 87(4) Public Administration 818

Koskenniemi M, *The Gentle Civilizer of Nations: The Rise and Fall of International Law 1870–1960* (CUP 2001)

Koskenniemi M, 'Why History of International Law Today?' (2004) 4 Rechtsgeschichte 61

Koskenniemi M, 'Histories of International Law: Significance and Problems for a Critical View' (2013) 27(2) Temple Int'l & Comp LJ 215

Kramer LD, 'When Lawyers Do History' (2003) 72 The George Washington Law Review 387

Krysko MA, *American Radio in China: International Encounters with Technology and Communications, 1919–41* (Palgrave Macmillan 2011)

Kulick A, 'Narrating Narratives of International Investment Law: History and Epistemic Forces' in Stephan W Schill, Christian J Tams and Rainer Hofmann (eds), *International Investment Law and History: Towards a Historiographical Turn* (Edward Elgar Publishing 2018) 41

Lake WT and Tucker Dana J, 'Judicial Review of Awards of the Iran-United States Claims Tribunal: Are the Tribunal's Awards Dutch' (1984) 16 Law & Pol'y Int'l Bus 755

Langham-Carter W, *Kelantan Administration Report for the Year 1912* (FMS Government Printing Office 1913)

Legum B, 'The Innovation of Investor-State Arbitration Under NAFTA' (2002) 43 Harv Int'l LJ 531

Leiter A, *Making the World Safe for Investment: The Protection of Foreign Property 1922–1959* (CUP 2023)

Lesaffer R, 'International Law and its History: The Story of an Unrequited Love' in Matthew Craven, Malgosia Fitzmaurice and Maria Vogiatzi (eds), *Time, History and International Law* (Martinus Nijhoff 2007) 34

LeVos E, 'Robert W Duff: a British Seigneur in Kelantan, 1892–1932' (1997) 70(1) Journal of the Malaysian Branch of the Royal Asiatic Society 1

Lobban M, 'Introduction: The Tools and the Tasks of the Legal Historian' in Andrew Lewis and Michael Lobban (eds), *Law and History: Current Legal Issues 2003 Volume 6* (OUP 2004) 3

Lundesgaard J and Tevlina VV, 'Profit under the Soviets: Timber Concessions, Western Interests and the Monetary Reforms under NEP' (2021) 34(1) Revolutionary Russia 71

MacMurray JVA (ed), *Treaties and Agreements With and Concerning China: 1894–1919* (OUP 1921, vol I)

Makarczyk J, *Principles of a New International Economic Order: A Study of International Law in the Making* (Springer 1988)

Marisi Flavia, *Rethinking Investor-State Arbitration* (Springer 2023)

Matheson C, 'Weber and the Classification of Forms of Legitimacy' 1987 (38) The British Journal of Sociology 199

Mattli W and Dietz T (eds), *International Arbitration and Global Governance: Contending Theories and Evidence* (OUP 2014)

Maugham F, *At the End of the Day* (Heinemann 1954)

McKay JP, 'Foreign Enterprise in Russian and Soviet Industry: A Long Term Perspective' (1974) 48(3) The Business History Review 336

McNair A, 'Sir Cecil James Barrington Hurst, GCMG, KCB, QC, LLD' (1962) 38 Brit YBIL 400

Mégret F, 'Mixed Claim Commissions and the Once Centrality of the Protection of Aliens' in Ignacio de la Rasilla and Jorge E Viñuales (eds), *Experiments in International Adjudication: Historical Accounts* (CUP 2019) 127

Miles K, *The Origins of International Investment Law: Empire, Environment and the Safeguarding of Capital* (CUP 2013)

Miller R, 'The Making of the Grace Contract: British Bondholders and the Peruvian Government, 1885–1890' (1976) 8(1) Journal of Latin American Studies 73

Miller R, 'The Grace Contract, the Peruvian Corporation, and Peruvian History' (1983) 9 Ibero-amerikanisches Archiv 319

Millington WM, *Kelantan Administration Report for the Year 1926* (Government Printing Office Singapore 1927)

Montt S, *State Liability in Investment Treaty Arbitration: Global Constitutionalism and Administrative Law in the BIT Generation* (Hart Publishing 2009)

Muchlinski P, 'The Diplomatic Protection of Foreign Investors: A Tale of Judicial Caution' in Christina Binder and others (eds), *International Investment Law for the 21st Century: Essays in Honour of Christoph Schreuer* (OUP 2009)

Mustill MJ, 'Foreword: Sources for the History of Arbitration' (1998) 14(3) Arbitration International 235

Nappert S, 'International Arbitration as a Tool of Global Governance: The Use (and Abuse) of Discretion' in Eric Brousseau, Jean-Michel Glachant and Jérôme Sgard (eds), *The Oxford Handbook of Institutions of International Economic Governance and Market Regulation* (online edn, Oxford Academic 2019) <https://doi.org/10.1093/oxfordhb/9780190900571.013.23> accessed 27 September 2024

Nelson TG, '"History Ain't Changed": Why Investor-State Arbitration Will Survive the "New Revolution"' in Michael Waibel and others (eds), *The Backlash against Investment Arbitration: Perceptions and Reality* (Kluwer 2010) 555

Nelson WE, 'Standards of Criticism' (1982) 60 Tex L Rev 447

Newcombe A and Paradell L, *Law and Practice of Investment Treaties: Standards of Treatment* (Kluwer 2009)

North RC, 'The NEP and the New Democracy' (1951) 24(1) Pacific Affairs 52

Norton P, 'A Law of the Future or a Law of the Past? Modern Tribunals and the International Law of Expropriation' (1991) 85 AJIL 474

Nötel R, 'International Capital Movements and Finance in Eastern Europe 1919–1949' (1974) 61(1) VSWG: Vierteljahrschrift für Sozial- und Wirtschaftsgeschichte 65

Notter H, *The Origins of the Foreign Policy of Woodrow Wilson* (Johns Hopkins Press 1937) 244

Noussia K, *Confidentiality in International Commercial Arbitration: A Comparative Analysis of the Position under English, US, German and French Law* (Springer 2010)

Nussbaum A, 'Comparative and International Aspects of American Gold Clause Abrogation' (1934) 44(1) The Yale Law Journal 53

Nussbaum A, 'The Arbitration between Lena Goldfields Ltd and the Soviet Government' (1950) 36 Cornell Law Quarterly 31

Obregón L, 'The Third World Judges: Neutrality, Bias or Activism at the Permanent Court of International Justice and International Court of Justice?' in William A Schabas and Shannonbrooke Murphy (eds), *Research Handbook on International Courts and Tribunals* (Edward Elgar Publishing 2017) 181

Oosterlinck K and Ureche-Rangau L, 'Interwar Romanian Sovereign Bonds: the Impact of Diplomacy, Politics and the Economy' (2012) 19(2) Financial History Review 219

Orakhelashvili A (ed), *Research Handbook on the Theory and History of International Law* (Edward Elgar Publishing 2011)

Orford A, 'On International Legal Method' (2013) 1 London Review of International Law 167

Paparinskis M, *The International Minimum Standard and Fair and Equitable Treatment* (OUP 2013)

Parra AR, *The History of ICSID* (2nd ed, OUP 2017)

Paulsson J, 'Arbitration Without Privity' (1995) 10 ICSID Review – Foreign Investment Law Journal 232

Paulsson J, *Denial of Justice in International Law* (CUP 2005)

Paulsson J, 'Public Interest in International Arbitration' (2012) 106 Proceedings of the Annual Meeting (American Society of International Law) 300

Paulsson J, *The Idea of Arbitration* (OUP 2013)

Pauwelyn J, 'At the Edge of Chaos? Foreign Investment Law as a Complex Adaptive System, How It Emerged and How It Can Be Reformed' (2014) 29(2) ICSID Review – Foreign Investment Law Journal 372

Pepelasis Minoglou I, 'The Greek State and The International Financial Community, 1922–1932: Demystifying the "Foreign Factor"' (PhD thesis, London School of Economics and Political Science 1993) <http://etheses.lse.ac.uk/2590/> accessed 27 September 2024

Perrone NM, *Investment Treaties and the Legal Imagination: How Foreign Investors Play By Their Own Rules* (OUP 2021)

Peterson LE, 'East Timor Launches Arbitration against Australia, as Separate Tax Dispute with US Investor Plays Out at Singapore International Arbitration Centre' (*Investment Arbitration Reporter*, 7 May 2013) <https://www.iareporter.com/articles/east-timor-launches-arbitration-against-australia-as-separate-tax-dispute-with-u-s-investor-plays-out-at-singapore-international-arbitration-centre/> accessed 27 September 2024

Peterson LE, 'LCIA Award at Center of Caribbean Court Proceedings had Deemed Tax Waivers to be Valid Despite their having been Kept Out of Public Eye' (*Invest-*

ment Arbitration Reporter, 30 April 2013) <https://www.iareporter.com/articles/lcia-award-at-center-of-caribbean-court-proceedings-had-deemed-tax-waivers-to-be-valid-despite-their-having-been-kept-out-of-public-eye/> accessed 27 September 2024

Peterson LE, 'As Hydro v Albania BIT Case Plays Out at ICSID, Albania Announces Victory in Related ICC Contract Case; Claimant Says it has Filed a Second ICC Claim for Expropriation' (*Investment Arbitration Reporter*, 26 January 2018) <https://www.iareporter.com/articles/as-hydro-v-albania-bit-case-plays-out-at-icsid-albania-announces-victory-in-related-icc-contract-case-claimant-says-it-has-filed-a-second-icc-claim-for-expropriation/> accessed 27 September 2024

Pinchis-Paulsen M, 'Resolving Challenges to Historical Research: Developing a Project to Define Fair and Equitable Treatment' in Stephan W Schill, Christian J Tams and Rainer Hofmann (eds), *International Investment Law and History: Towards a Historiographical Turn* (Edward Elgar Publishing 2018) 179

Pineo R, *Ecuador and the United States: Useful Strangers* (University of Georgia Press 2007)

Polanco R, *The Return of the Home State to Investor-State Disputes: Bringing Back Diplomatic Protection?* (CUP 2019)

Poulsen LNS, *Bounded Rationality and Economic Diplomacy: The Politics of Investment Treaties in Developing Countries* (CUP 2015)

Radi Y, *Rules and Practices of International Investment Law and Arbitration* (CUP 2020)

Rashba ES, 'Settlement of Disputes in Commercial Dealings with the Soviet Union' (1945) 45(4) Columbia Law Review 530

Ratnasingam Robert L, 'The Duff Syndicate in Kelantan 1900–1902' (1972) 45(1) Journal of the Malaysian Branch of the Royal Asiatic Society 81

Redfern A and others, *Law and Practice of International Commercial Arbitration* (4th edn, Sweet & Maxwell 2004)

Requejo Isidro M and Hess B, 'International Adjudication of Private Rights: The Mixed Arbitral Tribunals in the Peace Treaties of 1919–1922' in Michel Erpelding, Burkhard Hess and Hélène Ruiz Fabri (eds), *Peace Through Law: The Versailles Peace Treaty and Dispute Settlement After World War I* (Nomos 2019) 239

Reynolds M, 'The Jaffa Jerusalem Railway Company Arbitration 1922' (1991) 6 Arab Law Quarterly 215

Roberts A, 'Clash of Paradigms: Actors and Analogies Shaping the Investment Treaty System' (2013) 107 AJIL 45

Rose J, 'Musing on Clio and Legal History: Why Study the Past, History, and Legal History' (2009) U Texas Law School Tarlton Library Legal History Series, 2009 <https://papers.ssrn.com/sol3/papers.cfm?abstract_id=1411875> accessed 27 September 2024

Rosenne S, 'The Jaffa-Jerusalem Railway Arbitration (1922)' in Shabtai Rosenne, *Essays on International Law and Practice* (Martinus Nijhoff 2007) 295

Rubin AP, *Piracy, Paramountcy and Protectorates* (Penerbit Universiti Malaya 1974)

Schill SW, 'Crafting the International Economic Order: The Public Function of Investment Treaty Arbitration and Its Significance for the Role of the Arbitrator' (2010) 23 Leiden Journal of International Law 401

Schill SW, 'International Investment Law and Comparative Public Law – an Introduction' in Stephan W Schill (ed), *International Investment Law and Comparative Public Law* (OUP 2010)

Schill SW, 'Conceptions of Legitimacy of International Arbitration' in David D Caron and others (eds), *Practising Virtue: Inside International Arbitration* (OUP 2015) 106

Schill SW, Christian J Tams and Rainer Hofmann, 'International Investment Law and History: An Introduction' in Stephan W Schill, Christian J Tams and Rainer Hofmann (eds), *International Investment Law and History: Towards a Historiographical Turn* (Edward Elgar Publishing 2018) 3

Schwebel SM, 'The Alsing Case' (1959) 8 ICLQ 320

Shapiro M, *Courts: A Comparative and Political Analysis* (University of Chicago Press 1981)

Shaw GE, *Kelantan Administration Report for the Year 1925* (Government Printing Office Singapore 1926)

Shaw MN, *International Law* (6th edn, CUP 2008)

Shearer DR, 'Stalinism, 1928–1940' in Ronald Grigor Suny (ed), *The Cambridge History of Russia*, vol III (CUP 2006) 192

Sheridan JE, 'The Warlord Era: Politics and Militarism Under the Peking Government, 1916–28' in John K Fairbank (ed), *The Cambridge History of China*, vol XII (CUP 1983) 284

Sinclair GF, 'Managing the "Workers Threat": Preventing Revolution Through the International Labour Organization' in Michel Erpelding, Burkhard Hess and Hélène Ruiz Fabri (eds), *Peace Through Law: The Versailles Peace Treaty and Dispute Settlement After World War I* (Nomos 2019) 159

Skinner Q, 'Meaning and Understanding in the History of Ideas' 8 History and Theory (1969) 3

Snyder E, 'Foreign Investment Protection: Is Institutional Arbitration an Answer?' (1961–1962) 40 NC L Rev 665

Snyder E, 'Foreign Investment Protection: A Proposed Arbitration Convention' 1962 11 J Pub L 191

Snyder E, 'Foreign Investment Protection: The Dispute Solving Aspect' (1963–1964) 3 Colum J Transnat'l L 127

Sobel R, *ITT: The Management of Opportunity* (Truman Talley Books 1982)

Sobel R, *RCA* (Stein and Day 1986)

Somerville H, 'The Soviet Five Year Plan' (1930) 19 Studies: An Irish Quarterly Review 624

Sornarajah M, *The International Law on Foreign Investment* (3rd edn, CUP 2010)

St John T, *The Rise of Investor-State Arbitration: Politics, Law, and Unintended Consequences* (OUP 2018)

Stanivuković M and Đajić S, 'From *Losinger* to *ATA v Jordan*: Retroactive Application of National Law to Arbitration Agreements' in Marianne Roth and Michael Geistlinger (eds), *Yearbook on International Arbitration and ADR* (Neuer Wissenschaftlicher Verlag 2019) 149

Stanivuković M and Đajić S, 'Hommage jednom zastupniku pred međunarodnim sudovima – profesor dr Slavko Stojković' (2020) 2(2) Revija Kopaoničke škole prirodnog prava 197

Stoenescu GV and others, 'Foreign Exchange Regime in Romania between 1929 and 1939' in Peter Mooslechner and Ernest Gnan (eds), *Proceedings of OeNB Workshops No 13: The Experience of Exchange Rate Regimes in Southeastern Europe in a Historical and Comparative Perspective: Second Conference of the South-Eastern European Monetary History Network* (Oesterreichische Nationalbank 2008) 244

Stone Sweet A, 'The New Lex Mercatoria and Transnational Governance' (2006) 13(5) Journal of European Public Policy 627

Stone Sweet A, and Grisel F, *The Evolution of International Arbitration: Judicialization, Governance, Legitimacy* (OUP 2017)

Stuyt AM, 'Dr Erades, Chairman of Two International Arbitral Tribunals' in TMC Asser Instituut, *Essays on International & Comparative Law* (Springer 1983) 178

Stuyt AM, (ed) *Survey of International Arbitrations: 1794–1989* (Martinus Nijhoff 1990)

Suwannathat-Pian K, 'The 1902 Siamese-Kelantan Treaty: An End to the Traditional Relations' (1984) 72 Journal of the Siam Society 95

Talib S, *History of Kelantan: 1890–1940* (The Malaysian Branch of the Royal Asiatic Society 1995)

The Royal Institute of International Affairs, 'The National Economy of the USSR: the Five-Year Plan' (1930) 7(4) Bulletin of International News 3

Torre D and Tosi E, 'Charles Rist and the French Missions in Romania 1929–1933: Why the "Money Doctors" Failed?' (Fourth Conference of Southeast Europe Monetary History Network (SEEMHN), Belgrade, 27–28 March 2009) 3–5 <https://www.nbs.rs/export/sites/NBS_site/documents/publikacije/konferencije/seemhn_conf/SEEMHN_5_Torre_Tosi.pdf> accessed 27 September 2024

Tosh J, *The Pursuit of History: Aims, Methods and New Directions in the Study of Modern History* (5th edn, Pearson 2010)

Tourme-Jouannet E and Peters A, 'The Journal of the History of International Law: A Forum for New Research' (2014) 16 Journal of the History of International Law 1

Trakman L and Ranieri N, 'Foreign Direct Investment: A Historical Perspective' in Leon Trakman and Nicola Ranieri (eds), *Regionalism in International Investment Law* (OUP 2013)

Trevino C, 'Ecuador in Midst of UNCITRAL Arbitration Following Spurning by Petrobras and Partners of Migration to "Service Agreements"' (*Investment Arbitration*

Reporter, 4 May 2015) <https://www.iareporter.com/articles/ecuador-in-midst-of-uncitral-arbitration-following-spurning-by-petrobras-and-partners-of-migration-to-service-agreements/> accessed 27 September 2024

Vadi V, 'Global Cultural Governance by Investment Arbitral Tribunals: The Making of a *Lex Administrativa Culturalis*' (2015) 33 Boston University International Law Journal 101

Vadi V, and Gruszczynski L, 'Standards of Review in International Investment Law and Arbitration: Multilevel Governance and the Commonweal' (2013) 16(3) Journal of International Economic Law 613

Van Harten G, 'Private Authority and Transnational Governance: The Contours of the International System of Investor Protection' (2005) 12(4) Review of International Political Economy 600

Van Harten G, *Investment Treaty Arbitration and Public Law* (OUP 2007)

Van Harten G, and Loughlin M, 'Investment Treaty Arbitration as a Species of Global Administrative Law' (2006) 17(1) EJIL 121

Vandevelde KJ, 'A Brief History of International Investment Agreements' (2005) 12 UC-Davis Journal of International Law & Policy 157

Vandevelde KJ, *The First Bilateral Investment Treaties: US Postwar Friendship, Commerce, and Navigation Treaties* (OUP 2017)

Veeder VV, 'The *Lena Goldfields* Arbitration: The Historical Roots of Three Ideas' (1998) 47 ICLQ 747

Veeder VV, 'Lloyd George, Lenin and Cannibals: The Harriman Arbitration – The 1999 Freshfields Lecture' (2000) 16 Arbitration International 115

Veeder VV, 'Chancellor Wirth and the Mologales Concession 1923–1927: The German-Speaking Origins of the 1965 ICSID Convention' in Christina Binder and others (eds), *International Investment Law for the 21st Century: Essays in Honour of Christoph Schreuer* (OUP 2009) 387

Venzke I, *How Interpretation Makes International Law: On Semantic Change and Normative Twists* (OUP 2012)

Venzke I, 'Investor-State Dispute Settlement in TTIP from the Perspective of a Public Law Theory of International Adjudication' (2016) 17 JWIT 274

Venzke I, and Philipp Günther, 'International Investment Protection Made in Germany? On the Domestic and Foreign Policy Dynamics behind the First BITs' (2022) 33(4) EJIL 1183

Vizcarra C, 'Guano, Credible Commitments, and Sovereign Debt Repayment in Nineteenth-Century Peru' (2009) 69(2) The Journal of Economic History 358

von Bogdandy A and Venzke I, *In Whose Name?* (OUP 2014)

von Mehren RB and Kourides PN, 'International Arbitrations between States and Foreign Private Parties: The Libyan Nationalization Cases' (1981) 75 AJIL 476

Waibel M, *Sovereign Defaults before International Courts and Tribunals* (CUP 2011)

Wallace-Bruce NL, *The Settlement of International Disputes: The Contribution of Australia and New Zealand* (Martinus Nijhoff 1998)

Warner JC, 'A History of Radio Corporation of America – The Years to 1938' (1957) 3(1) RCA Engineer 3

Weber M, *Economy and Society: A New Translation* (Keith Tribe ed and tr, Harvard University Press 2019)

Weidemaier WMC, 'Contracting for State Intervention: The Origins of Sovereign Debt Arbitration' (2010) 73 Law & Contemp Probs 335

Weiler T, *The Interpretation of International Investment Law: Equality, Discrimination and Minimum Standards of Treatment in Historical Context* (Martinus Nijhoff 2013)

Wetter JG and Schwebel SM, 'Some Little-Known Cases on Concessions' (1964) 40 Brit YBIL 183

White RCA, 'Expropriation of the Libyan Oil Concessions: Two Conflicting International Arbitrations' (1981) 30(1) The International and Comparative Law Quarterly 1

Whytock CA, 'Private-Public Interaction in Global Governance: The Case of Transnational Commercial Arbitration' (2010) 12(3) Business and Politics 1

Wikander U, *Kreuger's Match Monopolies, 1925–1930: Case Studies in Market Control through Public Monopolies* (Julie Sundquist tr, LiberFörlag 1979)

Wilbur CM, 'The Nationalist Revolution: from Canton to Nanking, 1923–28' in John K Fairbank (ed), *The Cambridge History of China*, vol XII (CUP 1983) 527

Williams Z, 'Centerra Goes Back to Arbitration with Kyrgyzstan over Contentious Kumtor Gold Project' (*Investment Arbitration Reporter*, 1 June 2016) <https://www.iareporter.com/articles/centerra-goes-back-to-arbitration-with-kyrgyzstan-over-troubled-kumtor-gold-project/> accessed 27 September 2024

Williams Z, 'Dubai-Owned Company Alleges Expropriation of its Port Investment in Djibouti, and Files a New Claim against the State' (*Investment Arbitration Reporter*, 22 February 2018) <https://www.iareporter.com/articles/dubai-owned-company-alleges-expropriation-of-its-port-investment-in-djibouti-and-files-a-new-claim-against-the-state/> accessed 27 September 2024

Williamson SH and Cain LP, 'Defining Measures of Worth: Most are Better than the CPI' (*MeasuringWorth*, 2022) <www.measuringworth.com/defining_measures_of_worth.php> accessed 27 September 2024

Womack B, 'Warlordism and Military Regionalism in China' in Richard H Yang and others (eds), *Chinese Regionalism: The Security Dimension* (Westview Press 1994)

Yackee JW, 'Do We Really Need BITs – Toward a Return to Contract in International Investment Law' (2008) 3 Asian Journal of WTO and International Health Law and Policy 121

Yackee JW, 'Pacta Sunt Servanda and State Promises to Foreign Investors before Bilateral Investment Treaties: Myth and Reality' (2008–2009) 32 Fordham Int'l LJ 1550

Yackee JW, 'Do Bilateral Investment Treaties Promote Foreign Direct Investment? Some Hints from Alternative Evidence' (2011) 51 Virginia Journal of International Law 397

Yackee JW, 'Controlling the International Investment Law Agency' (2012) 53(2) Harvard International Law Journal 391

Yackee JW, 'The First Investor-State Arbitration: *The Suez Canal Company v Egypt* (1864)' (2016) 17 The Journal of World Investment and Trade 401

Yackee JW, 'The First Investor-State Arbitration? The Suez Canal Dispute of 1864 and Some Reflections on the Historiography of International Investment Law' in Stephan W Schill, Christian J Tams and Rainer Hofmann (eds), *International Investment Law and History: Towards a Historiographical Turn* (Edward Elgar Publishing 2018) 70

Yackee JW, 'Investor-State Dispute Settlement at the Dawn of International Investment Law: France, Mauritania, and the Nationalization of the MIFERMA Iron Ore Operations' (2019) 59(1) American Journal of Legal History 71

Yackee JW, 'The First French BIT' (2024) 35(3) EJIL 623

Živković V, 'ISDS and Nazis or History Without Context: A Reply to Gary Born' (2022) 39(4) Journal of International Arbitration 575

Cases

Investor-State Arbitrations

Asian Agricultural Products Ltd (AAPL) v Democratic Socialist Republic of Sri Lanka, ICSID Case No ARB/87/3, Award (27 June 1990)

Barcs-Pakrac Railway Company, Ltd v Hungary and Yugoslavia (1935) 29(3) AJIL 523

BP Exploration Company (Libya) Limited v The Government of the Libyan Arab Republic (1979) 53 ILR 297

Colombia v Cauca Company, Award (22 October 1897)

Compagnie du Katanga v The Colony of the Belgian Congo, Award (11 December 1931), reported in Wetter JG and Schwebel SM, 'Some Little-Known Cases on Concessions' (1964) 40 Brit YBIL 183, 184

Dominion of Canada v The Grand Trunk Railway Company of Canada, Award (7 September 1921)

Electric Transport Company Ltd and Athens-Piraeus Electricity Company Ltd v Greece, Award (1 March 1933)

Government of Greece v Hellenic Electric Railways Ltd and Electric Transport Company Ltd, Award (5 June 1930), reported in Wetter JG and Schwebel SM, 'Some Little-Known Cases on Concessions' (1964) 40 Brit YBIL 183, 204

Government of Peru v The Peruvian Corporation Limited (1913) 50 Boletin del Ministerio de Relaciones Exteriores (Peru) 144

Government of the Republic of the Sudan v Turriff Construction (Sudan) Limited, Award (23 April 1970)

Greek Telephone Company v The Government of Greece, Award (3 January 1935), reported in Wetter JG and Schwebel SM, 'Some Little-Known Cases on Concessions' (1964) 40 Brit YBIL 183, 216

Greek Transport Company Ltd v The Greek State (17 May 1956)

Hambros Bank Limited and Lazard Brothers and Co Limited v Kingdom of Roumania Monopolies Institute, Award (10 June 1937)

Hellenic Electric Railways Ltd v The Greek State, Award (23 December 1933)

Hellenic Electric Railways Ltd v The Greek State, Award (31 August 1935)

International Thunderbird Gaming Corporation v United Mexican States, UNCITRAL, Separate Opinion of Thomas Wälde (1 December 2005)

La Société de Construction des Batignolles v Yugoslavia, Award (5 February 1938) (*Batignolles v Yugoslavia I*)

La Société de Construction des Batignolles v Yugoslavia, Award (8 July 1938) (*Batignolles v Yugoslavia II*)

La Société Européenne d'Etudes et d'Entreprises (SEEE) v The Popular Federative Republic of Yugoslavia (1959) 86 Journal du Droit International 1075

La Societe Rialet v The Government of Ethiopia (1929) 8 Recueil des Décisions des Tribunaux Arbitraux Mixtes Institués par les Traités de Paix 742

Lena Goldfields, Ltd v USSR, Award (2 September 1930), reproduced in Nussbaum A, 'The Arbitration between Lena Goldfields Ltd and the Soviet Government' (1950) 36 Cornell Law Quarterly 31, 42

Libyan American Oil Company (LIAMCO) v The Government of the Libyan Arab Republic (1981) 20(1) ILM 1

Losinger & cie SA and 'Kompass' Allgemeine Kredit- und Garantie-Bank v The Kingdom of Yugoslavia, Award (31 October 1934) (*Losinger I*), reproduced in *The Losinger & Co Case (Switzerland v Yugoslavia)* PCIJ Rep Series C No 78 at 54

Losinger & cie SA v Kingdom of Yugoslavia, Preliminary Award (11 October 1935) (*Losinger II*), reproduced in *The Losinger & Co Case (Switzerland v Yugoslavia)* PCIJ Rep Series C No 78 at 105

Martin Cowley Railway Construction Co, Limited and Alderton Construction (Westminster) Limited v The Higher Committee for the Recommissioning of the Hedjaz Railway Line, Award (22 September 1972)

Methanex Corporation v United States of America, UNCITRAL (NAFTA), Decision of the Tribunal on Petitions from Third Persons to Intervene as 'amici curiae' (15 January 2001)

Petroleum Development (Qatar) Ltd v Ruler of Qatar (1951) 18 ILR 161

Petroleum Development Ltd v The Sheikh of Abu Dhabi (1951) 18 ILR 144

Radio Corporation of America v The National Government of the Republic of China (1935) 3 RIAA 1621

Ruler of Qatar v International Marine Oil Company, Ltd (1953) 20 ILR 534

Sapphire International Petroleums Limited v National Iranian Oil Co (*NIOC*) (1967) 35 ILR 136

Saudi Arabia v ARAMCO (1963) 27 ILR 117

Société des Grands Travaux de Marseille v East Pakistan Industrial Development Corporation (1984) 65 ILR 445

Societe des Quais de Smyrna v Greek Government (1930) 37 Revue Générale de Droit International Public 335

Societe du Chemin de Fer Ottoman de Jaffa a Jerusalem et Prolongements v His Britannic Majesty's Government, Preliminary Decision (29 May 1922), reproduced in Shabtai Rosenne, 'The Jaffa-Jerusalem Railway Arbitration (1922)' in Shabtai Rosenne, *Essays on International Law and Practice* (Martinus Nijhoff 2007) 295, 327

Societe du Chemin de Fer Ottoman de Jaffa a Jerusalem et Prolongements v His Britannic Majesty's Government, Award (4 October 1922), reproduced in Shabtai Rosenne, 'The Jaffa-Jerusalem Railway Arbitration (1922)' in Shabtai Rosenne, *Essays on International Law and Practice* (Martinus Nijhoff 2007) 295, 313

Societe generale Hellinique SA, Societe d'Electricite Athenes-Le Piree and Societe Electrique des Transports SA v The Greek State (1951) 4 Revue Hellénique de Droit International 373

Suez Canal Company v Egypt, Award (6 July 1864), reproduced in Foreign Office, *British and Foreign State Papers: 1864–1865*, vol LV (William Ridgway 1870) 1004

Texaco Overseas Petroleum Company and California Asiatic Oil Company v The Government of the Libyan Arab Republic (1978) 17 ILM 1

The Administration of Posts and Telegraphs of the Republic of Czechoslovakia v The Radio Corporation of America (1936) 30 AJIL 523

The Alsing Trading Company, Ltd and Svenska Tändsticks Aktiebolaget v Greece (1956) 23 ILR 633

The Ditta Luigi Gallotti v The Somali Government (1970) 40 ILR 158

The Duff Development Company Limited v The Government of Kelantan, Award (31 March 1916) (*Duff v Kelantan I*)

The Duff Development Company, Ltd v The Government of Kelantan, Award (17 November 1921) (*Duff v Kelantan II*)

The Government of Greece v Sociéte Commerciale de Belgique (*Socobelge*), Award (25 July 1936) (*Socobelge II*), reproduced in *The 'Société commerciale de Belgique' (Belgium v Greece)* PCIJ Rep Series C No 87 at 44

The Government of Greece v Sociéte Commerciale de Belgique (*Socobelge*), Award (3 January 1936) (*Socobelge I*), reproduced in *The 'Société commerciale de Belgique' (Belgium v Greece)* PCIJ Rep Series C No 87 at 36

The Government of the State of Kuwait v The American Independent Oil Company (*AMINOIL*) (1982) 21(5) ILM 976

The Greek State v Hellenic Electric Railways Ltd, Award (18 March 1930)
The Greek State v Hellenic Electric Railways Ltd, Award (6 March 1928)
The Greek State v The Hellenic Electric Railways Company, Award (10 February 1930)
The Sopron-Köszeg Local Railway Company v Austria and Hungary (1930) 24(1) AJIL 164
The State of Lebanon and the Municipality of Beyrouth v La Compagnie des Eaux de Beyrouth, Award (3 November 1953)
Zeltweg-Wolfsberg and Unterdrauburg-Woellan Railway Company v Austria and Yugoslavia [1934] League of Nations Official Journal 84 (*Zeltweg-Wolfsberg I*)
Zeltweg-Wolfsberg and Unterdrauburg-Woellan Railway Company v Austria and Yugoslavia [1934] League of Nations Official Journal 1005 (*Zeltweg-Wolfsberg II*)
Zeltweg-Wolfsberg and Unterdrauburg-Woellan Railway Company v Austria and Yugoslavia [1934] League of Nations Official Journal 1007 (*Zeltweg-Wolfsberg III*)
Zeltweg-Wolfsberg and Unterdrauburg-Woellan Railway Company v Austria and Yugoslavia [1938] League of Nations Official Journal 1172 (*Zeltweg-Wolfsberg IV*)

Other International Cases

'Électricité de Beyrouth' Company Case (France v Lebanon) ICJ Pleadings
Anglo-Iranian Oil Co Case (United Kingdom v Iran) (Preliminary Objection) [1952] ICJ Rep 93
Canevaro Claim (Italy v Peru) (1912) 11 RIAA 397
Case Concerning the Barcelona Traction, Light and Power Company, Limited (Belgium v Spain) (New Application: 1962) (Second Phase) [1970] ICJ Rep 3
Case Concerning the Payment in Gold of the Brazilian Federal Loans Issued in France (France v Brazil) PCIJ Rep Series A No 21;
Case Concerning the Payment of Various Serbian Loans Issued in France (France v Kingdom of the Serbs, Croats and Slovenes) PCIJ Rep Series A No 20
Delagoa Bay Railway Arbitration (Great Britain and United States v Portugal) (1898) 2 Moore Int Arb 1865
The 'Societe Commerciale de Belgique' (Belgium v Greece) PCIJ Rep Series A/B No 78
The Greco-Bulgarian 'Communities' (Advisory Opinion) PCIJ Series B No 17
The Indo-Pakistan Western Boundary (Rann of Kutch) between India and Pakistan (India v Pakistan) (1968) 17 RIAA 1
The Oscar Chinn Case (UK v Belgium) PCIJ Rep Series A/B No 63

Domestic Court Cases

Colombia v Cauca Co, 106 Fed 337 (DW Va 1901)
Colombia v Cauca Co, 190 US 524 (1903)
Duff Development Co Ltd v Government of Kelantan [1924] AC 797 (HL)
Kelantan Government v Duff Development Company, Limited [1922–1923] 39 Times L Rep 337 (HL)

The Barcs-Pakrac Railway Company v Estate of the Kingdom of Yugoslavia, Decision of the Table of Seven (at the time the highest court instance for Croatia, then part of Yugoslavia) of 19 November 1937
The Grand Trunk Railway Company of Canada v The King [1923] AC 150
The Sapphire, 78 US 164 (1870)

Other International Documents

— 'Advisory and Technical Committee for Communications and Transit' [1928] League of Nations Official Journal 720
— 'Annex 1065: Dispute Concerning the Sopron-Köszeg Local Railway' [1928] League of Nations Official Journal 1609
— 'Annex 1065a: Dispute Concerning the Sopron-Köszeg Local Railway' [1928] League of Nations Official Journal 1614
— 'Annex 1076: Dispute Concerning the Boldva Valley Local Railway' [1928] League of Nations Official Journal 1763
— 'Annex 1487: Petition from the Barcs-Pakrac Railway Company, Limited, Budapest' [1934] League of Nations Official Journal 183
— 'Annex 1488: Petition from the Radkersburg-Luttenberg Railway Company Limited Vienna' [1934] League of Nations Official Journal 185
— 'Annex 1510: Petition of the Radkersburg-Luttenberg Railway Company, Ltd., Vienna' [1934] League of Nations Official Journal 1397
— 'Annex 1512: Appointment of a Trustee for the Priority Bonds Fund of the Zeltweg-Wolfsberg and Unterdrauburg-Woellan Railway Company' [1934] League of Nations Official Journal 1411
— 'Annex 1603: Constitution, Procedure and Practice of Committees of the League of Nations' [1936] League of Nations Official Journal 725
— 'Annex 1683: Petition by the Zeltweg-Wolfsberg and Unterdrauburg Woellan Railway Company, Vienna' [1937] League of Nations Official Journal 1273
— 'Communications and Transit' [1930] League of Nations Official Journal 324
— 'Communications and Transit' [1932] League of Nations Official Journal 1493
— 'Minutes of the Eighty-Sixth Session of the Council: Second Meeting (Private, Then Public)' [1935] League of Nations Official Journal 599
— 'Minutes of the Fifty-First Session of the Council: Seventh Meeting (Public, Then Private)' [1928] League of Nations Official Journal 1483
— 'Minutes of the Fifty-Fourth Session of the Council: First Meeting (Private, Then Public)' [1929] League of Nations Official Journal 502
— 'Minutes of the Fifty-Fourth Session of the Council: Seventh Meeting (Public, Then Private)' [1929] League of Nations Official Journal 553

—— 'Minutes of the Fifty-Ninth Session of the Council: First Meeting (Private, Then Public)' [1930] League of Nations Official Journal 496

—— 'Minutes of the Fifty-Second Session of the Council: Sixth Meeting (Public, Then Private)' [1928] League of Nations Official Journal 1664

—— 'Minutes of the Fifty-Sixth Session of the Council: First Meeting (Private, Then Public)' [1929] League of Nations Official Journal 1442

—— 'Minutes of the Forty-Fourth Session of the Council: Third Meeting (Public)' [1927] League of Nations Official Journal 373

—— 'Minutes of the Forty-Third Session of the Council: First Meeting (Private, Then Public)' [1927] League of Nations Official Journal 114

—— 'Minutes of the Forty-Third Session of the Council: Sixth Meeting (Private, Then Public)' [1927] League of Nations Official Journal 160

—— 'Minutes of the Ninety-Fourth Session of the Council: Fourth Meeting (Private)' [1936] League of Nations Official Journal 1194

—— 'Minutes of the Ninety-Ninth Session of the Council: First Meeting (Private, Then Public)' [1937] League of Nations Official Journal 922

—— 'Minutes of the Seventieth Session of the Council: First Meeting (Private, Then Public)' [1933] League of Nations Official Journal 180

—— 'Minutes of the Seventy-Eighth Session of the Council (Part I): Second Meeting (Private, Then Public)' [1934] League of Nations Official Journal 111

—— 'Minutes of the Seventy-Sixth Session of the Council (Part I): First Meeting (Private, Then Public)' [1933] League of Nations Official Journal 1300

—— 'Minutes of the Seventy-Third Session of the Council (Part I): First Meeting (Private, Then Public)' [1933] League of Nations Official Journal 798

—— 'Minutes of the Seventy-Third Session of the Council (Part I): Fourth Meeting (Private, Then Public)' [1933] League of Nations Official Journal 823

—— 'Minutes of the Seventy-Third Session of the Council (Part I): Sixth Meeting (Public)' [1933] League of Nations Official Journal 838

—— 'Minutes of the Sixty-Eighth Session of the Council: Third Meeting (Public)' [1932] League of Nations Official Journal 1736

—— 'Minutes of the Sixty-Second Session of the Council: Sixth Meeting (Public, Then Private)' [1931] League of Nations Official Journal 194

—— 'Minutes of the Sixty-Sixth Session of the Council: First Meeting (Private, Then Public)' [1932] League of Nations Official Journal 438

—— 'Minutes of the Thirty-Fifth Session of the Council: Seventeenth Meeting (Public and Then Private)' [1925] League of Nations Official Journal 1395

'The Proposed Convention to Protect Private Foreign Investment – Introduction' (1960) 9 J Pub L 115

Agreement between France, Great Britain, Italy, Roumania, Czechoslovakia and Yugoslavia Concerning the Constitution of a Special Fund Entitled 'Fund B' (signed 28 April 1930) (1931) 30 UKTS Cmd 3910

Agreement between Great Britain and Kelantan respecting Administration (signed 22 October 1910) (1910) 212 CTS 276

Agreement Between the Republic of Austria, the Kingdom of Hungary, the Kingdom of Italy, the Kingdom of the Serbs, Croats and Slovenes and the Southern Railway Company (Sudbahn), Drawn Up with the Concurrence of the Committee Representing the Holders of Bonds Issued by the Above Company with a View to the Administrative and Technical Re-organisation of the Southern Railway Company's System (Signed 29 March 1923) 23 LNTS 336

Agreement on Arbitration of Disputes between Algeria and France Regarding Exploitation of the Saharan Subsoil (signed 26 June 1963) (1963) 2 ILM 1025

Agreement on economic cooperation (Netherlands-Indonesia) (signed 7 July 1968, entered into force 17 July 1971).

Agreement Regarding the Final Discharge of the Financial Obligations of Austria (signed 20 January 1930, entered into force 28 June 1930) 104 LNTS 413

Agreements Relating to Algerian Independence (Algeria-France) (signed 18 March 1962) (1962) 1 ILM 214

Algeria-France Oil Accord (signed 29 July 1965) (1965) 4 ILM 809

Convention between Germany and Poland Relating to Upper Silesia (signed 15 May 1922) 9 LNTS 465

Convention for the Pacific Settlement of International Disputes (adopted 18 October 1907; entered into force 26 January 1910) (1907) 205 CTS 233

Convention on the Recognition and Enforcement of Foreign Arbitral Awards (opened for signature 10 June 1958, entered into force 7 June 1959) 330 UNTS 38

Convention on the Settlement of Investment Disputes between States and Nationals of Other States (opened for signature 18 March 1965, entered into force 14 October 1966) 575 UNTS 159

European Convention on International Commercial Arbitration (opened for signature 21 April 1961, entered into force 7 January 1964) 484 UNTS 349

International Convention for the Pacific Settlement of International Disputes (adopted 29 July 1899, entered into force 4 September 1900) (1899) 187 CTS 410

International Law Commission, 'Fragmentation of International Law: Difficulties arising from the Diversification and Expansion of International Law – Report of the Study Group of the International Law Commission, finalized by Mr Martti Koskenniemi' (13 April 2006) UN Doc A/CN4/L682

League of Nations Advisory and Technical Committee for Communications and Transit, 'Records of the Work of the Seventeenth Session, Held at Geneva from June 1st to 4th, 1932 (Annex 7: Report of the Committee of Experts Appointed to Study a Question Connected with the Petition Submitted to the Council by the Zeltweg-Wolfsberg and Unterdrauburg-Wöllan Railway Company, Vienna)' (23 June 1932) Official No C.531.M.265.1932.VIII

League of Nations Financial Committee, 'Report to the Council on the Work of the Fifty-Fifth Session of the Committee (*Geneva, September 3rd-10th, 1934*)' (10 September 1934) Official No C.393.M.177.1934.II.A.

League of Nations, 'Report of the Committee for the Study of International Loan Contracts' (12 May 1939) Official No C.145.M.93.1939.II.A.

Permanent Court of Arbitration, 'Circular Note of the Secretary General' (1960) 54 AJIL 933

Permanent Court of Arbitration, 'Rules of Arbitration and Conciliation for Settlement of International Disputes Between Two Parties of Which Only One is a State' (1963) 57(2) AJIL 500

Secretariat of the League of Nations, 'Memorandum on the Different Questions Arising in Connection with the Establishment of the Permanent Court of International Justice' in PCIJ Advisory Committee of Jurists, *Documents Presented to the Committee Relating to Existing Plans for the Establishment of a Permanent Court of International Justice* (HM Stationery Office Press 1920)

Treaty and Notes between Great Britain and Siam regarding the Cession and Boundaries of the Siamese Malay States, the Jurisdiction of the Siamese Courts and the Non-cession etc of Siamese Territory (signed 10 March 1909) (1909) 208 CTS 367

Treaty between the Federal Republic of Germany and Pakistan for the Promotion and Protection of Investments (signed 25 November 1959, entered into force 28 April 1962)

Treaty of Peace between the Allied and Associated Powers and Austria (signed 10 September 1919, entered into force 16 July 1920) (1919) 11 UKTS Cmd 400

Treaty of Peace between the Allied and Associated Powers and Germany (signed 28 June 1919, entered into force 10 January 1920) (1919) 225 CTS 188

Treaty of Peace between the Allied and Associated Powers and Hungary (signed 4 June 1920, entered into force 26 July 1921) (1920) 10 UKTS Cmd 896

Treaty of Peace between the Allied and Associated Powers and Turkey (signed 10 August 1920, never entered into force) (1921) 15 AJIL Supp 179

UN General Assembly Resolution 1761 (XVII) (6 November 1962) UN Doc A/RES/1761(XVII)

UNCITRAL Arbitration Rules (1976) 15 ILM 701

UNCITRAL Model Law on International Commercial Arbitration (1985) 24 ILM 1302

UNSC 'Report by the Secretary-General in Pursuance of the Resolution Adopted by the Security Council at its 1056th Meeting on 7 August 1963 (S/5386)' (11 October 1963) UN Doc S/5438

UNSC 'Report of the Special Committee on the Policies of Apartheid of the Government of the Republic of South Africa' (26 September 1963) UN Doc S/5426/Add 1

Domestic Legislation

An Act providing for the acquisition by His Majesty of the capital stock of the Canadian Northern Railway Company, SC 1916–17, ch 24 (Canada)

An Act to confirm the Agreement dated the eighth day of March, 1920, between His Majesty The King and the Grand Trunk Railway Company of Canada for the acquisition by His Majesty of the capital stock of the said Grand Trunk Railway Company, except the four per cent guaranteed stock, SC 1920, ch 13 (Canada)

Arbitration Act 1996 (UK)

The Grand Trunk Railway Acquisition Act, 1919, SC 1919 (3d Sess), ch 17 (Canada)

Newspaper articles

––'Birkenhead Explains Grand Trunk Award: He Upholds the Majority Arbitrators' Decision, to Which Justice Taft Dissented' *The New York Times* (New York, 11 November 1922) 6

––'Canada Asks Taft to Represent Her' *The New York Times* (New York, 15 June 1920) 1

––'Company Meetings: Duff Development Company' *The Times* (London, 22 October 1926) 25

––'Decree Dissolving Radio Group Under Anti-Trust Law' *The New York Times* (New York, 22 November 1932) 17

––'Duff Development Co: Arbitrator's Decree Against Kelantan Government' *The Straits Times* (Singapore, 29 November 1921) 12

––'Ex-President Taft Succeeds White as Chief Justice' *The New York Times* (New York, 1 July 1921) 1

––'Grand Trunk Names Taft: Appoints Him on Board to Fix Price to be Paid by the Dominion' *The New York Times* (New York, 13 July 1920) 14

––'Grand Trunk Stocks Tumble in London as Arbitrators Declare Them Valueless' *The New York Times* (New York, 9 September 1921) 1

––'GTR Paid Taft $75,000: Canadian Railway Shareholders Bore Charge for Arbitration' *The New York Times* (New York, 16 March 1923) 31

––'L de Brouckere, Belgian Socialist: Member of Council of State Dies at 81' *The New York Times* (New York, 5 June 1951) 31

––'Lake Copais Company' *The Times* (London, 27 October 1926) 23

––'RCA Units Enjoined on Foreign Claims' *The New York Times* (New York, 3 July 1935) 23

––'The Cauca Company's Claim: Arbitrators Make Their Award, Fixing the Amount Colombia Must Pay at $452,048.93' *The New York Times* (New York, 24 October 1897) 5

——'The Duff Development Company, Limited: Kelantan Government's Breach of Contract: Important Bearing of Arbitrator's Award' *The Times* (London, 21 December 1921) 20

——'The Grace Contract: The Peruvian Bondholders Claims against Chili' *The New York Times* (New York, 14 January 1890) 2

Miscellaneous

——'Albert Thomas: Director of the International Labour Organization, 1919–1932' <https://www.ilo.org/global/about-the-ilo/how-the-ilo-works/ilo-director-general/former-directors-general/WCMS_192645/lang--en/index.htm> accessed 27 September 2024

——'Churchill's Political Offices, 1906–1955' (14 October 2008) <https://winstonchurchill.org/resources/reference/churchills-political-offices-1906-1955/> accessed 27 September 2024

——'History of the ILO' <https://www.ilo.org/global/about-the-ilo/history/lang--en/index.htm> accessed 27 September 2024

——'Mater André' (*Comité des travaux historiques et scientifiques*, 21 January 2009) <https://cths.fr/an/savant.php?id=100895> accessed 27 September 2024

——'Mayer, René (1895–1972)' <https://www.siv.archives-nationales.culture.gouv.fr/siv/rechercheconsultation/consultation/producteur/consultationProducteur.action?notProdId=FRAN_NP_050262> accessed 27 September 2024

——'Rapport du Conseil Administratif de la Cour Permanente d'Arbitrage sur les travaux de la Cour, sur le fonctionnement des services administratifs et sur les depenses de l'exercice 1970' (Bureau International de la Cour Permanente d'Arbitrage 1971)

——'René Besnard: 1879–1952' <https://www2.assemblee-nationale.fr/sycomore/fiche/(num_dept)/749> accessed 27 September 2024

——'Sir Walter Monckton' <https://api.parliament.uk/historic-hansard/people/sir-walter-monckton/index.html> accessed 27 September 2024

——'The Right Hon Sir William Thomas White, PC, KCMG, MP' <https://lop.parl.ca/sites/ParlInfo/default/en_CA/People/Profile?personId=1380> accessed 27 September 2024

——'Transnational Private-Public Arbitration as Global Regulatory Governance: Charting and Codifying the Lex Mercatoria Publica' (headed by Prof Dr Stephan Schill) <https://acil.uva.nl/content/research-projects/current-research-projects/lexmercpub-kopie-2.html> accessed 27 September 2024

——'Ζάκκας Ανδρέας: 1892–1971' <https://greek-parliament-members.anavathmis.eu/%CE%B6%CE%AC%CE%BA%CE%BA%CE%B1%CF%82-%CE%B1%CE%BD%CE%B4%CF%81%CE%AD%CE%B1%CF%82/> accessed 22 August 2022

Agreement between the National Iranian Oil Company and La Societe AGIP Mineraria (24 August 1957) (available at Columbia University Library)

Agreement between the National Iranian Oil Company and Sapphire Developments, Ltd (16 June 1958) (available at Columbia University Library)

Agreement between the National Iranian Oil Company and the Pan American Petroleum Corporation (24 April 1958) (available at Columbia University Library)

Canada. Parliament. House of Commons. Debates, 13th Parliament, 3rd Session, 1919, vol 140 (Ottawa: J de Labroquerie Taché 1920)

Canada. Parliament. House of Commons. Debates, 13th Parliament, 3rd Session, 1919, vol 139 (Ottawa: J de Labroquerie Taché 1920)

CG Roelofsen, 'Hamel, Joost Adriaan van (1880–1964)' (*Biografisch Woordenboek van Nederland*, 12 November 2013) <http://resources.huygens.knaw.nl/bwn1880-2000/lemmata/bwn1/hamelja> accessed 27 September 2024

Dag Michalsen, 'Frederik Beichmann' (*Norsk huygsk leksikon*) <https://nbl.snl.no/Frederik_Beichmann> accessed 27 September 2024

Departmental Advisory Committee on Arbitration Law, '1996 Report on the Arbitration Bill' (1997) 13(3) Arbitration International 275

Departmental Advisory Committee on Arbitration Law, 'Supplementary Report on the Arbitration Act 1996' (1997) 13(3) Arbitration International 317

European Court of Human Rights, 'Judges of the Court Since 1959' <https://www.echr.coe.int/Documents/List_judges_since_1959_BIL.pdf> accessed 27 September 2024

International Court of Justice, 'Tribute to José Gustavo Guerrero, first President of the International Court of Justice' (23 October 2018) 2 <https://www.icj-cij.org/public/files/press-releases/0/000-20181023-PRE-01-00-EN.pdf> accessed 27 September 2024

NobelPrize.org, 'Nomination Archive: José Gustavo Guerrero' <https://www.nobelprize.org/nomination/archive/show_people.php?id=3703> accessed 27 September 2024

NobelPrize.org, 'Nomination Archive' <https://www.nobelprize.org/nomination/archive/show.php?id=7391> accessed 27 September 2024

NobelPrize.org, 'Nomination Archive: Permanent Court of International Justice (Cour permanente de justice internat.)' <https://www.nobelprize.org/nomination/archive/show_people.php?id=7124> accessed 27 September 2024

Oil Concession Granted by the Shaikh of Qatar to the Anglo-Persian Oil Co, Ltd (17 May 1935) (available as part of the Qatar Digital Library at <https://www.qdl.qa/en/archive/81055/vdc_100000000833.0x000006> accessed 27 September 2024)

Saudi Arabia v Arabian American Oil Company (*ARAMCO*), Arbitration Agreement (1963) 27 ILR 229

Sociedad Colombiana de Ingenieros, 'Historia' <https://sci.org.co/historia/> accessed 29 September 2024

Supreme Court of the United States, 'Justices 1789 to Present' <https://www.supremecourt.gov/about/members_text.aspx> accessed 27 September 2024

Index

AAPL v Sri Lanka 23
Abs-Shawcross Draft Convention 23
Abu Dhabi 51
  See also *Petroleum Development v Abu Dhabi*
abuse of rights 237
acquiescence 51*n*69, 155, 208, 321
acquired rights 256–264, 280, 355
  limit to 261
administrative
  law 46, 50, 76*n*152, 80, 236 (*see also* contract, nature of: administrative)
  rights 42
agreement to arbitrate 23*n*82, 32–33, 35, 70–71, 105–106, 113, 115*n*134, 134, 198, 232
  arbitration clause in 33–35, 41*n*25, 59*n*101, 60–61, 72, 77, 91, 113, 142, 150, 153*n*296, 175, 235*n*255, 252, 337
  compromis in 33, 35–36, 96, 105, 133–134*n*222, 153, 235, 255
  international treaty in 23, 32–33*n*1, 70–71, 198, 201–202, 232, 358*n*32
Algeria 33*n*1, 70, 242, 358*n*32
Allied Power(s) 132
Alsing v Greece 41, 79*n*163, 353*n*13
Alvarez, Alejandro 135
American Arbitration Association 339
American Journal of International Law 352
amiables compositeurs 52
amicable settlement
  See settlement
amicus curiae 341*n*319
anational (arbitration)
  See transnational (arbitration)
anti-trust
  issues, arbitrability of 300*n*199
  law(s) 45*n*50, 187, 300
  suit 174, 177, 194, 317*n*249, 319–323
apartheid 45, 154
appellate body 262
applicable law 49–51, 76, 98–99, 100, 102, 175, 236, 239, 252, 285, 305, 313, 323, 324, 328, 334, 335
appointing authority 60, 145, 153, 198–199, 252, 253*n*17
appropriation of investor property, cost of 109–110, 117–118, 130, 131, 138, 163
  See also expropriation
arbitrariness 261, 262
arbitration
  ad hoc 5
  apprehension of 125, 130, 150, 151, 177, 178, 292–293
  commercial 11, 13–14*n*40, 155, 157, 341
  consent to (*see* agreement to arbitrate)
  control over 55–56
  damages phase 148
  defence of 122
  definition 11
  dispute resolution as 11, 25
  function of 25–26
  independent of party will 221
  institutional 5
  internationalisation of 70, 71*n*140
  multiparty 198
  seat of 69*n*128, 73–74
  threat of 56, 204*n*146
  withdrawal from 62*n*115, 153–156
arbitration clause (*see under* agreement to arbitrate)
Arbitration Institute of the Stockholm Chamber of Commerce 359–360
arbitrator(s)
  sole 58–59, 60*n*102–104, 63, 66, 142*n*255, 208
  presiding (*see* tribunal: president)
  party-appointed 63–65, 66*n*124, 126, 181–182*n*75, 263–264*n*49, 301, 302*n*204
  neutrality 59–66, 182, 295
  nationality 62–63, 125–126, 296–297
  replacement 55*n*89, 64*n*118, 115*n*134, 153, 214*n*186
  resignation 55*n*89, 115, 117, 153, 155*n*308
  bias 55*n*89, 63–64, 181–182*n*75, 301
  independence 59–66, 113–114, 125–126, 145*n*269, 182*n*75, 301
  impartiality 59–66, 123, 126, 180–181

arbitrator(s) (*cont.*)
holding public office 63–64*n*118, 66*n*124, 126
withdrawal 86
designation by name 123
compensation 125
communication with parties during proceedings 64*n*118, 181*n*75, 301*n*204
profiles 353–354
arbitrator appointment
considerations 59–66, 180–181, 204–205*n*147, 208, 256*n*28, 294–295
deferral of 213
failure 265–267
home state by 55–56*n*89
objection to 62*n*115, 207, 213, 295
repeat 113*n*127, 204, 264–265, 269*n*68, 272, 277, 294–295
revocation 155
See also appointing authority
Arendt, Otto 180*n*72
assurance 178, 260, 288
AT&T 172
Austria 4, 70, 200, 345*n*329
Austrian Railways 211
South Austrian Railway Company 201, 225, 227, 228, 229
See also Austro-Hungary; *Sopron-Köszeg Local Railway Company v Austria and Hungary*; *Zeltweg-Wolfsberg and Unterdrauburg-Woellan Railway Company v Austria and Yugoslavia*
Austro-Hungary 29, 198, 200–202
award (arbitral)
adverse, anticipation of 144–145, 151, 162
antedating of 302
authentic interpretation of 223
bindingness 11, 53, 246, 315
costs on 147*n*278, 148
dispositif 149*n*282, 192, 262–264, 311, 320
enforcement 16, 57, 69*n*130, 74, 140*n*246, 147*n*278, 148, 199*n*133, 222, 230, 231
finality 53, 105, 128*n*198, 314, 315
inoperative (part of) 221*n*211
majority by 114, 117, 123–124, 128, 187, 263*n*49, 303 (*see also* dissenting opinion)
monetary 56, 84, 90, 138, 149, 156, 157–163, 167, 230, 242
nationality of 69*n*130, 71–74
precedential value of (*see* precedent)
preliminary objections on (*inter alia*) 114, 136–138, 156, 213–219
publication of 17, 152, 253*n*18, 340–342, 351–352
registration 71
review by parliament 121*n*164
self-executory 70*n*135, 242
unanimous 128, 240*n*268
unreasoned 115, 143, 325, 326–327
award, compliance with 101, 157*n*315, 195–196, 245, 314
inability of 149, 159–161, 163*n*337, 164–165
refusal of 157*n*315, 222, 230, 231*n*245
reputational costs due to failure of 163*n*337
award, recourse against 53, 74, 121–122*n*164
annulment 71–72, 116–117, 148
appeal 128
standard of review 53, 116–117, 128–129

balancing competing (private and public) interests 54, 233, 261, 270, 279
Ballot-Beaupré, Alexis 106–108, 353*n*13
Bank of International Settlements 221*n*211
Baquerizo Moreno, Alfredo 64*n*118
Barcs-Pakrac Railway Company v Hungary and Yugoslavia 74*n*147, 205*n*147, 224–232
Batignolles v Yugoslavia 4*n*8, 69*n*128, 71*n*140
Beichmann, Frederik Valdemar Nikolai 60*n*104, 135, 354*n*14
Belgium 182
beneficial ownership 154*n*302
Bentsi-Enchill, Kwamena 154
Berg, Paal 60*n*104, 353*n*13, 354*n*19
Besnard, Rene 265, 269*n*68
bilateral investment treaty
See BIT
BIT 8, 23, 347
Germany-Pakistan 23
with investor-state dispute settlement 23, 70

bona fide
See good faith
bond 93, 95, 97, 99, 100, 103, 104, 121
bondholders 95, 98, 99, 100, 103–108, 115*n*133, 201, 219–223
as holders of independent rights from company 223
Borja, Cesar 63*n*118, 354*n*19
BP v Libya 48*n*63, 50*n*68, 69*n*130, 73, 79, 167–168, 243, 328
Bruins, Gijsbert Weijer Jan 60*n*103, 96–102

Calvo clause 113*n*123
Calvo doctrine 113
Cameron, Charles A 153
Canada
Canadian National Railway 129
Canadian Northern Railway 118–119, 121, 126
Exchequer Court of 63*n*116, 123
nationalisation of railway industry 47, 119*n*149–150, 120, 126, 130
Nova Scotia supreme court 119
Ontario chief justice 119
Parliament 121–123, 125–127, 129–130, 164, 347, 353
Supreme Court 128*n*198
War Measures Act 120, 126
Case Concerning the Collection of a Pension Fund Charge 276–278
Cassels, Walter 63*n*116, 123, 124, 125, 126, 127
Cavin, Pierre 60*n*102, 353*n*13
chartered company 42
Cherry, James L 110, 111*n*112
Chile 103, 105, 106, 107
China
Manchuria 284, 286–287 (*see also* Japan: Manchukuo)
Ministry of Communications 291, 292*n*156, 295*n*169
Mukden incident 286–287
Mukden Traffic Agreement 284–289
National Council of Reconstruction 285
Nationalist Party of 284
North Eastern Radio and Long Distance Telephone Administration 284
Northern Expedition 284
Shanghai Traffic Agreement 285–286, 288–289, 292–293, 313, 332
warlord era 283
See also *Radio Corporation of America v China*
choice of law clause
See applicable law
chose jugée
See *res judicata*
Churchill, Winston 71*n*139, 131, 135, 140*n*246, 347
civil law
See contract, nature of: private law
civil procedure rules 69*n*, 128
claims commissions 328*n*283, 356
Clarke, Orme 136–137
coercion 120
Colombia
chargé d'affaires 114
congress 110–113
courts 113
president 113*n*124
See also *Colombia v Cauca Company*
Colombia v Cauca Company 46, 47*n*59, 110–118, 130, 138, 159, 164
commercial
arbitration 11, 13–14*n*40, 155, 157, 341
dispute 155
law 80, 355
policy 186
transactions 41, 299
See also under arbitration
commissioners, distinction from arbitrators 112*n*121
common law 304, 341
common sense 54*n*86
community for mutual profit
See joint (ad)venture
community interest 261
compensation
actual costs for 155
based on equitable considerations 52*n*80, 132, 233
calculation 230*n*244
cancellation of public law contract for 189*n*109, 240*n*268
contractual breach for 139*n*244, 148–149, 156
contractual payments for 155
expropriation for 110*n*107, 112, 131, 212, 220, 222
full 240
just 52*n*80, 112

compensation (*cont.*)
  lack of 86, 109, 129
  legislative change for 274, 277*n*101, 279
  nominal 146
  reasonable 240
  repudiation of contract for 155
  unjust enrichment for 335
competence-competence
  See *Kompetenz-Kompetenz*
compromis
  See under agreement to arbitrate
concession
  assignment 110–111
  breach 87–88, 139*n*244, 148, 166, 168, 235–237, 274, 331
  continuation following territorial change 44, 209–211, 214–215, 217, 221, 227
  expropriation of 45
  forfeiture 110–113
  interpretation 255, 258, 260, 266, 275, 279, 329, 331–334 (*see also* contract, interpretation)
  nature of 80, 236, 334–335
  ratification of 41*n*25, 47*n*59, 61, 110, 140*n*246, 157*n*314, 250–251, 252*n*12, 254, 255, 259
  termination 44, 137, 237
  unilateral changes to 79, 259, 272, 274, 279
  validity 207, 209, 210, 221, 229*n*239
confidentiality in arbitration 15 (*see also* privacy in arbitration, exception to; transparency)
  exception to 340–342
conflict of laws 49*n*65, 98, 99, 102
congress
  See parliament
consent decree 174, 194, 319*n*255, 320–321
contract
  (un)enforceability 155, 209, 210, 211, 224, 227
  ambiguity 239, 264, 268, 270, 305
  cancellation of 44, 78, 112–113, 139, 142, 150, 153, 190, 237
  inoperable 239
  intention 99, 147, 260, 300, 306–307
  model 318
  modification of 79, 142, 189*n*109, 190, 194–195, 210, 226–228, 251, 252*n*12, 272, 274, 279, 292
  negotiations 48, 59*n*101, 60–61, 103, 147, 193, 255, 304
  unequal 239
  validity of 143–144, 156, 189*n*109, 209–210, 211, 221, 228
  voidability of 154–155
contract, interpretation 35, 54*n*86, 108, 176, 279
  circumstances at the time of conclusion and 147
  contracts affecting the public interest of 77, 304–306
  good faith in 279
  restrictive (of state contracts) 269, 332–334
  textual 183–184, 268, 307, 308*n*226
  textual differences and 309, 315
  See also concession: interpretation
contract, nature of
  administrative 76, 79, 80, 186 (*see also* administrative: law)
  private law 79, 186, 188–191, 197, 236–237, 274, 313
  public law 50, 51–52, 78–80, 186, 188–191, 236, 274, 313 (*see also* compensation: cancellation of public law contract for; public law)
  sui generis 185
contrat administratif
  See under contract, nature of: administrative
Convention on the Settlement of Investment Disputes between States and Nationals of Other States
  See international treaties: ICSID Convention
counsel 55, 56*n*90, 62*n*115, 67
  acting as arbitrator (*see* double-hatting)
  nationality 63*n*117, 296–297
counter-measure 57*n*96
currency devaluation 95, 97
Czechoslovakia
  See *The Administration of Posts and Telegraphs of the Republic of Czechoslovakia v Radio Corporation of America*

damages
  See compensation
Davis, Manton 183, 194, 300–302
de Brouckere, Louis 241, 277, 278*n*102

decision-maker
primary as 169–170, 197, 199, 210, 212, 234, 244, 350, 351
private actors as 54–67, 78, 80, 82, 349
secondary as 169, 197, 244, 350, 351
decision-making
discretionary and/or creative 37, 48–54, 74, 75, 78–79, 80, 81–82, 102, 108, 129–130, 164, 233, 250, 253, 266, 269, 270, 279, 310*n*233, 311, 339–340, 349
externalisation of 58–66, 82
deference 78, 164
diplomatic correspondence 133*n*222
diplomatic protection 8, 55, 65, 91, 111, 113, 116*n*137, 251*n*11, 356
diplomatic relations 16, 57
direct state (entity) conduct, capacity by tribunals to
impact on state behaviour and 195–196, 198, 245
modalities 169–170
primary decision maker as 199, 208, 210–212, 219–220, 224, 226, 229–230, 231, 234, 244
pursuant to international treaty 242
recurrence 235–243, 244
through arbitral review, as a secondary decision-maker 188, 192–193, 196–197, 244
dispute resolution clause 71*n*140, 216
See also agreement to arbitrate: arbitration clause in
dissenting opinion 47, 114, 124, 128, 187*n*103, 263–264*n*49
practical relevance of 128
Ditta Luigi Gallotti v Somalia 52*n*80, 54*n*85, 69*n*128, 110*n*107
domestic courts
Canada 119, 122*n*164, 123, 128*n*198
Colombia 113
Denmark 69*n*130
France 57, 74*n*147
Netherlands 152
oversight by 69, 72*n*142, 74
Switzerland 71, 73
UK 53*n*84, 128–130, 140*n*246, 147, 148
US 46, 53*n*84, 65*n*119, 99, 111*n*112, 112*n*121, 115*n*133–134, 116–118, 128, 130, 293*n*164
Yugoslavia 74*n*147, 231
double exequatur 57*n*93
double-hatting 63*n*118
Duff Development Company 141
concession in Kelantan 40*n*16, 42, 141–142
See also *Duff v Kelantan*; Duff, Robert W
Duff v Kelantan 4*n*8, 56*n*91–92, 69*n*128, 140–151, 159–162, 165, 242*n*276, 245*n*277, 353*n*11
Duff, Robert W 42, 141
Duke Henry II of Bavaria 4
Dupuy, René-Jean 56*n*91, 73, 79, 166–169, 235, 243

ECtHR 354
Ecuador
dispute with Guayaquil and Quito Railway Company 46*n*59, 55*n*89, 63–64*n*118, 65, 71*n*140
Minister of Foreign Affairs 65
president 46*n*59
Effendi, Youssouf Navon 131
Egypt 161*n*332
See also *Suez v Egypt*
Einstein, Albert 61
El Salvador 205
employee rights
See worker rights
equitable treatment 219
equity 52, 65, 130*n*203, 132, 133, 233, 275–279
court of 116*n*137
suit in 116
See also general principle(s): justice and equity of
Erades, Lambertus 60*n*103, 153
Erwerbsgesellschaft
See joint (ad)venture
espousal of claims
See diplomatic protection
Ethiopia
administrative law, absence of 50, 236
alcohol monopoly 41, 235, 236
State Liquor Board 235–237
See also *Rialet v Ethiopia*
European Court of Human Rights
See ECtHR
European public law 51, 236

evidence, admissibility of 124, 136
exceptions, restrictive interpretation of 217
excise duties 235, 237
exclusivity
- agreements of 177, 194, 305, 309, 318, 321
- rights of 141, 142, 236, 331–334

expert 67
expert committee 204*n*145, 213
expert report 67*n*126, 136*n*234
expropriation 29, 43, 199, 201, 218, 224, 237, 244
- ordering of 211–212, 219–220, 230, 231
- prohibition of 226, 229–230

fairness 52, 129
Federated Malay States 149–150, 161
- High Commissioner 149*n*282, 161
- Railways 150

financial consequences (for states)
- award of 149, 151, 159–161, 164–165
- capacity to govern, impact on 161–163, 165

fiscal
- benefits 43, 251
- immunity 275

forum (absence of) 102
Fox, Williams C 64*n*118
France 16, 57, 71*n*139, 72*n*142, 133–134
- *Conseil d'État* 206
- Court of Cassation 105, 106, 353*n*13
- *See also* Franco-Algerian agreements on Algerian independence

Franck, Louis 235*n*256
Franco-Algerian agreements on Algerian independence 33*n*1, 70, 242, 358*n*32
Furrer, Reinhold 182, 187*n*103, 295

General Electric Company 172
general principle(s) 73, 264*n*49
- conflict of laws of 49*n*65, 99, 102
- justice and equity of 51, 52*n*80
- law of 49, 51, 167*n*7, 327, 335
- public law of 51–52, 239, 240*n*268, 257, 263
- *See also* general rule(s) of law; generally accepted principles of law; ordinary principles of law; principle(s) of (public) international law; principles of right

general public 251, 353, 357
general rule(s) of law 51, 239
- *See also* general principle(s)

generally accepted principles of law 236*n*257
Geneva 206, 353
gold basis 97–101, 225, 226
gold clause 98, 100
- (in)validity of 99, 100

gold standard, abandonment of 45*n*50, 95
gold value 95
gold value clause 98
good faith 79, 274, 279
governance
- adjustment of manner in which it is carried out due to historical ISA 56, 144–145, 151, 162, 165, 198, 245
- beyond present day investment-treaty arbitration 361
- capacity to exercise 158, 162–163, 165
- cost of 84, 88–89, 92, 101–102, 108–110, 114, 118, 127, 129–130, 136, 138–140, 149, 157–158, 162–165, 350
- definition 26–27
- heterogeneity 26–27, 349–350, 357
- ISA's historical tradition in 349, 357
- modalities of 28–30, 349–350, 357
- present day investment-treaty arbitration and 12–13, 358–359, 361
- the novelty narrative and 13, 358

governing law
- *See* applicable law

government
- policy (*see* policy; public policy)
- interference with investor rights 44, 58–59, 86, 258–261, 263*n*49, 269

Grace, Michael P 104
Grand Trunk Railway Arbitration 4*n*8, 47, 118–131, 136, 138, 164, 353*n*11–12, 354*n*13, 354*n*17–18
Greco-Bulgarian 'Communities' 296
Greece
- applicability of legislation to concessionaire(s) 257, 258, 259, 262, 263, 272–273, 275, 278

Greece (*cont.*)
  arbitrations under Power and Traction concession 241, 252–281
  legislation providing for investor-state arbitration 281
  Minister of Communications 255, 269
  Ministry of Agriculture, Trade and Industry 271
  Ministry of Communications 254, 255, 256, 261, 262, 263*n*47, 263–264*n*49, 272
  Ministry of Economy 272
  Ministry of Labour 265
  parliament 251
  Power and Traction public utilities concession 250–251
  tradition of arbitration 281*n*109
  See also *Alsing v Greece*; *Greece v Socobelge*; *Greek Telephone Company Case*; *Hellenic Electric Railways v Greece* (1935); *Safety and Control Regulations Case*; *Staff Regulations Case*; *Ten Lepta Charge Case*; *Truncated Tribunal Case*
Greece v Socobelge 41*n*20, 63*n*118, 67*n*126, 91, 159
Greek Telephone Company Case 238–240
guarantee 222, 250*n*2, 251*n*11
  hypothecary 222
  letter of 291
Guayaquil and Quito Railway Company
  See under Ecuador
Guerrero, José Gustavo 205–206, 208*n*167, 213–214*n*186, 221–222*n*213, 232, 354*n*14, 354*n*16, 354*n*19
Guillemard, Laurence 161

Hague, The 206, 353
Hambros and Lazard v Romanian Monopolies Institute 45*n*50, 49*n*65, 92–102, 108, 164
Harris, Robert E 119
Haupt, Lewis M 114
head of state 354
Hedjaz Railway Arbitration 65*n*119, 73*n*145, 79*n*163
Hellenic Electric Railways v Greece (1935) 241 (see also *Safety and Control Regulations Case*; *Staff Regulations Case*; *Ten Lepta Charge Case*; *Truncated Tribunal Case*)
historical research
  anachronism and 19–22
  contextualism and 20*n*73, 24*n*94
  informational indeterminacy and 19
  limitations of 19–22
  longue durée and 24
  periodisation and 22–25
home state 33*n*1, 55, 57, 91
  See also diplomatic protection
Horsfall, Percy 63*n*118, 256, 257*n*30, 263*n*49
host state 8, 33*n*1, 57
Huber, Max 135
Hubert, Auguste 181*n*75, 294–295, 297, 301–302, 338
Hungary 70, 200 (*see also* Austro-Hungary; *Barcs-Pakrac Railway Company v Hungary and Yugoslavia*; *Sopron-Köszeg Local Railway Company v Austria and Hungary*)
Hurst, Cecil 131, 134*n*222
hydrocarbons 70, 242, 281, 358*n*32 (*see also* natural resources)

ICC International Court of Arbitration 5, 23*n*92, 359
ICJ 60, 135, 153, 205, 356
ICSID 6, 167, 361
ICSID Convention
  See international treaties: ICSID Convention
Idelson, Vladimir 62*n*115
illegality 78, 196, 303
imperium in imperio 142
indemnification
  See compensation
inducement, to enter into agreement 121, 144, 154-155*n*305
infrastructure (public) 38, 41, 44, 91, 109, 149
  See also public utilities; railways
injunctive relief 70*n*135, 242, 293*n*164
Institute of International Law 135, 235*n*256
International Centre for Settlement of Investment Disputes
  See ICSID

International Chamber of Commerce International Court of Arbitration
See ICC International Court of Arbitration
International Court of Justice
See ICJ
international judge 70*n*133, 216
International Labour Office 267, 278, 280, 353, 356
administering institution as 253*n*17
appointing authority as 252, 253*n*17, 256*n*28, 265, 267
Director of 252, 256, 264, 265–266, 267*n*60, 272, 275, 280, 354*n*16
international law
See public international law
International Law Commission 73
international organisation 252–253, 354, 356
See also International Labour Office; League of Nations; PCA; United Nations
international treaties
Agreement Regarding the Final Discharge of the Financial Obligations of Austria (Hague Agreement) 215, 218, 219
European Convention on International Commercial Arbitration 23
ICSID Convention 23, 361
multilateral 198, 201*n*136
New York Convention 23, 57*n*93, 74
providing for investor access to arbitration against state(s) 23, 32–33*n*1, 70–71, 198, 201–202, 232, 358*n*32
Rome Agreement (1923) 225–229, 231
Treaty of Ancon 103, 105, 106, 107
Treaty of Saint-Germain 49*n*64, 200–201, 207, 209, 213–219, 224, 234
Treaty of Sevres 132–133, 134*n*222, 201*n*136, 233*n*252
Treaty of Trianon 49*n*64, 200–201, 209, 227, 234
See also BIT: Germany-Pakistan
investment protection, substantive standards of 6
investment-treaty arbitration
novelty narrative and 12, 358
criticism of 358–359
advent of 23, 347, 358
transparency of 15, 17, 361
governance as 12–13, 358–359, 361
investor
administrative and financial independence 254–255, 257–260, 263, 264*n*49, 269
animosity towards 281
contributory fault 148
control over awards 57
fraud 154
liability 138–139*n*241
misrepresentation 155*n*305
obligation to participate in social security scheme 241
protests against 251–252
public perception 252
risk 58–59
standing to bring and control over claim 8, 55–58, 355
treaty protection of investor rights 214–215
treaty right to arbitrate disputes with states (*see* agreement to arbitrate: international treaty in)
investor-state arbitration
democratic approval of 130–131, 164
historiographical turn 10
treaty-based (*see* agreement to arbitrate: international treaty in; investment-treaty arbitration)
means of structuring continuing investor-state relations as 253
backlash against, absence of 281
incentive to investment as 281
governance implications and 349, 353–354, 356–357, 358–361
social importance 278, 280–281
origins narrative 6, 22, 347–348
historical tradition 3–5, 348–349
Islamic law 80
IT&T 173, 176, 179*n*64, 302*n*206
Italian Civil Code 69*n*128

Jaffa-Jerusalem Railway Arbitration 49*n*64, 56*n*89, 65, 71*n*139, 131–138, 159
Janes, Henry L 55*n*89, 64*n*118
Japan
Manchukuo 287–290 (*see also* China: Manchuria)
Mukden incident 286–287

Jeze, Gaston 76*n*152, 98*n*55
joint (ad)venture 185, 187, 191–192, 298, 306–307, 313
jurisdiction
- court of 116, 129
- tribunal of 216–217, 224

Kalff, Jacob Adriaan 206*n*155, 208*n*167, 213–214*n*186
Katold of Harroz 4
Kelantan
- compliance with Duff arbitration award 149, 151, 245*n*277
- Duff concession in 40*n*16, 42, 141–142
- Rajah 42
- sovereign status of 140*n*246
- supreme court 150*n*290
- See also *Duff v Kelantan*

Kelsen, Hans 48, 189
Kirchhofer, Emil 353*n*13
Kompetenz-Kompetenz 114, 117, 118*n*141, 216, 224, 232*n*249
Kreuger, Ivar 41*n*20
Kucera, Otto 316–317

labour
- conditions 256, 259
- disputes 355
- standards 276

Lagergren, Gunnar 60*n*104, 69*n*130, 73, 79, 167*n*7, 168, 243, 328, 354*n*15, 357*n*31
Lake Copais Company 39*n*15, 67*n*126
land and water resources, ownership of 44
Lascelles, Alfred George 143–146
Lausanne Conference 230
Lauterpacht, Elihu 67*n*126
law of nations
- *See* public international law

law of nature 51
law, development by tribunals
- between a disputing party and a third party as 282, 312–323
- between the disputing parties as 249–282
- general application of 323–342
- generalisability 344–345
- institutional endorsement 339–340
- levels of generality 247–249, 342–344

law, domestic
- American 98–100, 102, 185, 313*n*239
- Austrian 189, 190*n*110
- Canton of Vaud 72
- Chinese 298, 306, 313*n*239
- Colombian 113
- Czechoslovakian 50, 175, 185, 186, 190, 313*n*239
- English 51, 98–101, 341
- Ethiopian 50–51, 236
- Hungarian 210, 211
- Libyan 49, 50
- New York 50, 65*n*122, 175
- Saudi Arabia 334*n*298
- Yugoslav 222

LCIA 360
League of Nations 64*n*118, 70, 132, 199*n*133, 222, 232, 353
- Advisory and Technical Committee for Communications and Transit 204*n*145, 205, 213
- Assembly 205, 354*n*16
- Council 70*n*134, 133, 199, 201–204, 207–209, 212–214, 217, 223–225, 232, 234
- delegate to 241, 277
- Financial Committee 221*n*211
- High Commissioner in the Free City of Danzig 296, 357*n*31
- Official Journal 352
- Permanent Committee on Transport by Rail of the Communications and Transit Committee 204*n*145, 205
- Permanent Legal Committee of the Communications and Transit Committee 39, 208, 223
- Secretariat 296
- Secretary General 345*n*329

Lebanon and the Municipality of Beyrouth v The Beyrouth Water Company 39*n*13, 354*n*15
legal costs 115*n*133, 160, 194, 208, 291
legal framework (procedural) 68–76
- a-/transnational 71–72
- diversity of 68, 72
- international law 69–71
- national 69

legal indeterminacy
- *See under* legal norms

legal norms
  application to facts 48, 54, 233, 246
  assessing procedural conditions for investor-state arbitration for 336–342
  assessing substantive state conduct for 330–336
  character of 249, 330, 345
  indeterminacy of 37, 48–54, 75, 81, 246, 250, 279, 342, 349
  interpretation of 48, 247, 324
legislation
  applicability, scope of 257, 258, 263, 272–273, 275, 278
  exemption from 259, 262, 263, 275
legislative
  acts of general application 45, 79, 263, 272, 274
  change 86 (*see also* policy: change in)
  changes due to award 273, 276, 278, 279
  infringement of rights 274, 279, 355
  processes, formal 246
  sovereignty 79, 274
  veto 141*n*251
legitimacy 14*n*41, 250, 350–351, 361
Lena Goldfields 86–88
  concession 34, 61
  expropriation 86
  See also *Lena Goldfields v USSR*
Lena Goldfields v USSR 7, 16–17, 59*n*99, 62*n*115, 86–88, 117–118*n*141, 139, 159, 161*n*332, 327, 335, 340–342, 351, 353*n*11
lex loci solutionis 99
liability
  investors of 138–139*n*241
  non-compliance with obligations for 138–157, 163
LIAMCO v Libya 73, 79, 110*n*107, 159, 167
Libyan oil arbitrations 49, 51*n*74, 243–244, 327, 329
  See also *BP v Libya*; *LIAMCO v Libya*; Middle Eastern oil arbitrations; *Texaco v Libya*
licensing 359
litigation funding 291
loan
  agreement 100
  contract 98–100, 102
  guarantee 97, 103
  repayment 44, 97, 101
Loder, BCJ 60*n*103, 235, 296, 354*n*14
logic 54*n*86
London Court of International Arbitration *See* LCIA
London stock exchange 99*n*59, 128*n*195
Lord Asquith of Bishopstone 51, 326–327
Lord Radcliffe 326
Losinger 61–62
Losinger v Yugoslavia 41*n*20, 61–62, 91
Lyon-Caen, Charles 236*n*256

Mackay Radio and Telegraph Company 173
  traffic agreement with China 289–293, 303, 310*n*233
  traffic agreement with The Czechoslovakian Administration of Post and Telegraphs 176–178, 192, 195, 317*n*249
Mahmassani, Sobhi 73*n*145, 79
Maison, M 269*n*68
Mance, Henry Osborne 66*n*123, 136
mandatory norms 45, 98, 102
Mantas, Georges 241*n*270
Marconi Wireless Telegraph
  American 171–172
  British 171–172
Mater, Andre 277
Mayer, Ferdinand 136
Mayer, Rene 206, 208*n*167, 214*n*186, 354*n*19
media coverage 19, 46*n*59, 340–341, 353
Meighen, Arthur 121, 122*n*164, 122*n*166, 123, 127, 129, 130*n*203
Meredith, William 119
Methanex v Mexico 341*n*319
Middle Eastern oil arbitrations 7*n*20, 40, 327, 328, 352*n*10
  See also Libyan oil arbitrations; *Petroleum Development (Qatar) v Ruler of Qatar*; *Petroleum Development v Abu Dhabi*; *Ruler of Qatar v International Marine Oil Company*; *Saudi Arabia v ARAMCO*
military service 255, 256, 258*n*33
minister
  communications of 255, 269, 290, 291
  finance of 123, 126

minister (*cont.*)
  foreign affairs of 65, 205
  interior of 121
  plenipotentiary 63–64*n*118
  public instruction of 63*n*118
  public works of 111
  water management of 206*n*155
ministry
  agriculture, trade and industry of 271
  communications of 254, 255, 256, 261, 262, 263*n*47, 263–264*n*49, 272, 291, 292*n*156, 295*n*169
  economy of 272
  finance of 63*n*118
  foreign affairs of 206, 351
  interior of 46*n*59
  labour of 265
Mixed Arbitral Tribunals 203*n*139, 230*n*245, 296, 356, 357*n*31
Modderman, HAE 296, 297*n*180
Möller, Julius 60*n*104, 182, 183
Monckton, Walter 354*n*18–19
monetary policy 99, 102
monopoly 177, 187, 195, 299, 300, 320, 355
  See also anti-trust
monopoly, state 38, 41, 44–45, 93, 235–237
moratorium 74*n*147, 230, 232
Mudawi, Sayed Mohammed Yussif 153, 155*n*308
multifunctionality 25

Napoleon III 63*n*116, 67, 354*n*17
national security 172, 259*n*37, 355
nationalisation 72, 110*n*107, 166–167
  See also expropriation
nationality
  acquisition and loss of 355
  See also under arbitrator(s)
natural resources 40, 44
  exploitation of, interference with 44, 86
  gold 40*n*16
  mining 40*n*16, 60, 86, 148*n*281, 355
  oil 40, 72, 331, 335 (*see also* Middle Eastern oil arbitrations)
negotiation history 260
  See also contract: negotiations
Nesbitt, Wallace 119
Netherlands, the 60, 182, 206
Nobel Peace Prize 135, 206
normative influence, definition 247
  direct 246
  extended 247–249
  See also law, development by tribunals
notification
  arbitration of 180
  assignment of 110, 111*n*112
  dispute of 267–268

obligation
  explicit 87, 145–146, 148, 191, 196, 236, 259, 269–270, 279, 303–306, 308, 332–333
  failure to perform 87, 138–139, 145, 148–149, 151, 152, 156–157, 163, 230, 235, 237, 240, 330, 350 (*see also* concession: breach)
  implied 87, 146–148, 151, 191, 303–304
occupation, impact on concessions 44
Onassis, Aristotle 331
oral hearings 98, 123, 183, 253*n*17, 297
  open to the media 340–341
Order of St. John of Jerusalem 4
ordinary principles of law 51*n*74
  See also general principle(s)
Oriental Railways Company v The Ottoman Empire 4*n*8, 139*n*241
Ottoman Debt Council 92*n*23
Ottoman Empire 131, 139*n*241
  See also *Oriental Railways Company v The Ottoman Empire*; Turkey
ownership, indirect 154*n*302

pacta sunt servanda 78, 80, 189
  specifically in public law 78, 189
Palestine 131–132
  civil administration 132
  mandate 132
  military administration 132
  See also *Jaffa-Jerusalem Railway Arbitration*
Panchaud, Andre 353*n*13
Pangalos, Theodoros 250–251
Paris Peace Conference 132*n*218, 207
Parker, Roger J 153
parliament
  Canada of 121–123, 125–127, 129–130, 164, 347
  Colombia of 110–113
  debate 121–123, 126–127, 129–130, 164, 251, 347, 353

parliament (*cont.*)
  Greece of 251
  member of 126*n*185
  opposition to arbitration 121, 122*n*166, 130, 164
  ratification 41*n*25, 47*n*59, 110, 121*n*164, 122, 250–251, 252*n*12, 254, 255, 259
partnership
  See joint (ad)venture
PCA 5, 6, 135, 353
  Administrative Council 338
  appointing authority as 60
  first ever investor-state arbitration at 16, 152, 170
  introduction of investor-state arbitration at 16, 170, 296, 337–340, 347, 360
  member of 135
  Rules of Arbitration and Conciliation for Settlement of International Disputes Between Two Parties of Which Only One is a State 5*n*10, 23, 339
  Secretary General 338–339
PCIJ 135, 296, 340*n*315, 352, 353, 356
  appointing authority as 60
  deputy-judge 135
  inviolability against Nazi intrusion 206
  judge 131, 135–136, 182, 205–206, 208*n*167, 232, 235, 353–354
  president 131, 205, 213-214*n*186, 235, 296
  vice-president 213–214*n*186
Peace Palace
  hearings at 98, 297
  defence during Nazi invasion of Netherlands 206
Peace Treaty railway arbitrations
  See under World War I Peace Treaties
Peña, Manuel H 113, 114
pension fund 241, 271–272
Permanent Court of Arbitration
  See PCA
Permanent Court of International Justice
  See PCIJ
Peru
  Grace Contract 103–108
  Iglesias debt 105–108
  Lobos Islands 105–107
  Ministry of Foreign Affairs 351
  See also *Peru v Peruvian Corporation*
Peru v Peruvian Corporation 102–109, 164, 351
Petroleum Development (Qatar) v Ruler of Qatar 326, 354*n*18
Petroleum Development v Abu Dhabi 51, 326, 327, 333
policy 139, 154–155, 157, 353
  change in 84–88
  choice 83, 84, 88, 109, 119, 140, 149
  implementation 45, 126, 129, 138
  See also public policy
politician 241, 256, 265, 277
Politis, Athanase 206*n*155, 214*n*186
Politis, N 269*n*68
Politis, Nikolaos 235–236*n*256
Pometta, Carlo 353*n*13
Power and Traction Company 250, 252*n*13
  See also under Greece
precedent
  formally binding 355
  implicit reference to 217–218, 326
  increased reliance on 326–327
  no reference to 324–325, 329
  not formally binding 246, 323, 335
  persuasive value 257, 272, 275, 282, 312–319, 323–324, 326–328, 333–335, 341*n*319, 343
  references to other ISAs 324–330
  specific value of investor-state awards 328–329
preliminary objection 156, 157, 213–219
preliminary issue 114, 136–138, 213–219
prime minister
  Canada of 121
  France of 206
principles of right 51, 105, 108
  See also general principle(s)
principle(s) of (public) international law 49, 217, 243
  See also general principle(s)
privacy in arbitration, exception to 340–342
  See also confidentiality in arbitration; transparency
private international law
  See conflict of laws
private law 37, 76–80, 188–191, 196*n*131, 197, 236, 274, 283, 355
private party
  See investor

procedural rights, (in)separability from substantive rights 218, 224
profit 124–125, 136–137, 185, 192, 306
proper law of contract
 See applicable law
public authority 42, 58, 59, 189–190, 259, 264, 305, 336, 345
 abuse of 237, 261
 general principle of 259–260
 See also sovereignty, limitations upon states' freedom of exercise; sovereignty, states' freedom of exercise
public criticism 150*n*288
public debt 40
 arbitration clauses and 90–91
 default on 101, 103, 162
 investor-state arbitration and 90–109
 suspension of payments 95, 101
 See also loan
public function 41, 43–44, 46, 56, 58, 81, 151, 158, 166, 304
public good 289
public institution 186, 192
public interest 17, 38, 39, 40, 46, 47*n*59, 76, 77, 80, 90, 94, 101, 117, 118, 132, 136, 186, 189, 190, 192, 197, 214, 251, 258*n*33, 270, 274, 280, 289, 304, 307, 341, 349
public international law 8, 11, 49–51, 68–71, 73, 74, 75*n*150, 167, 168, 208, 209, 216, 217, 232, 243, 304–305, 329
public law 23*n*82, 37, 76–80, 186, 188–191, 196, 197, 236, 239, 240*n*268, 257, 258, 263, 283, 311, 355, 358, 359
 See also administrative: law; contract, nature of: administrative; contract, nature of: public law; European public law
public loan
 See public debt
public office 63–64*n*118, 66*n*124, 126
public official
 conduct 138
 testimony 155
public order 259*n*37, 261
public policy 45, 54, 67, 100, 102, 152, 155, 157
public purpose 272, 274
public purse
 See treasury
public utilities 38–39, 244, 328
 electrification 39, 162*n*335, 250
 gas supply 39
 public transport 39, 44, 241*n*271, 250 (*see also* railways)
 telecommunications 39, 44, 78, 171–175, 193, 197, 240, 285, 289, 304, 306, 323, 345
 telegraphy (radio) 44, 77–78, 171–176, 178, 186–193, 195–196, 198, 245, 283–285, 289, 298–300, 303–308, 314, 318, 319, 322, 335
 water 39, 44, 355
 See also Greece: arbitrations under Power and Traction concession; Greece: Power and Traction public utilities concession
Python, Louis 60*n*102, 353*n*13

quasi-governmental powers 42
 See also sovereignty, limitations upon states' freedom of exercise

racial discrimination
 See apartheid
Radio Corporation of America
 anti-trust suit 174, 177, 194, 317*n*249, 319–323
 Czechoslovakian Traffic Agreement 50, 174–175, 179, 180, 194–195, 313, 315, 332
 emergence as independent company 174
 incorporation of 171–172
 Mukden Traffic Agreement 284–289
 Shanghai Traffic Agreement 285–286, 288–289, 292–293, 313, 332
 See also *Radio Corporation of America v China; The Administration of Posts and Telegraphs of the Republic of Czechoslovakia v Radio Corporation of America*
Radio Corporation of America v China 16, 77–78, 196, 282–323, 332–335, 337–340, 343, 345
 See also China; Radio Corporation of America; *The Administration of Posts and Telegraphs of the Republic of Czechoslovakia v Radio Corporation of America*

railways 38–39
  expropriation of 201, 211–212, 219–220, 224, 226, 229–230
  nationalisation 119–120, 126, 130
  reorganisation (administrative and technical) 198, 200–201, 207, 209–211, 219, 225–226, 228–229, 233, 244
Rann of Kutch Arbitration 357*n*31
ratification
  arbitral award of 121*n*164
  concessions of 41*n*25, 47*n*59, 61, 110, 140*n*246, 157*n*314, 250–251, 252*n*12, 254, 255, 259
Reber, Samuel 177*n*55
Recueil des Décisions des Tribunaux Arbitraux Mixtes Institués par les Traités de Paix 352
reform debates 361
regulate, right to 46, 270, 276, 279, 299, 355–356
  limitations upon 43*n*30
  limitations, explicit 269–270
  relinquishment, lack of explicit 259
regulation, government 157*n*314, 235, 236
regulatory disputes 13*n*40
remedy
  monetary damages (*see* award (arbitral): monetary; compensation)
  recision of state action 242
  specific performance/*restitutio in integrum* 56*n*91, 79*n*162, 167–169
reparations 230, 231*n*245
representations (by government) 143–144
requisitioning 132
  See also appropriation of investor property, cost of; expropriation
res judicata 105, 272, 312
residence, right of 355
retroactivity 226
Rialet v Ethiopia 41, 50, 235–238
Ripert, Georges 236*n*256
Romania
  Government 93
  Monopolies Institute 93, 96–97
  National Bank 94, 96
  Stabilisation Loan of 1929 93–94, 96–97
  See also *Hambros and Lazard v Romanian Monopolies Institute*
royalties 228–229
Ruler of Qatar v International Marine Oil Company 327
rules of procedure 183, 337

Safety and Control Regulations Case 268–270
safety regulations 44, 252, 269, 270, 280
San Remo Conference 132*n*218
Sapphire v National Iranian Oil Company 139, 159, 327*n*280, 336
Sarnoff, David 174*n*36, 181*n*75, 302*n*206
Saudi Arabia v ARAMCO 46, 54*n*86, 59*n*101, 70, 80, 157*n*314, 242*n*276, 245*n*277, 327, 329, 331-335
Sauser-Hall, Georges 60*n*102
SCC
  See Arbitration Institute of the Stockholm Chamber of Commerce
Schinas, Demetrios 257, 263–264*n*49
Schrame, Christian F 114
Schuloff, Heinrich 302, 303*n*209, 310*n*233, 311*n*234, 338
Scott, Leslie 296*n*172
secret police 59*n*99, 86
Secretan, Jacques 280, 281
SEEE v Yugoslavia 16, 41*n*20, 52, 57, 64*n*118, 71–72, 73–74, 91
separate opinion
  See dissenting opinion
set-off 107
settlement
  between investor and state 16, 112, 131, 136, 139*n*244, 142, 149, 157*n*315, 202, 203–204, 213, 231
  inter-state 57, 101*n*69
Shecklen, George 288
SIAC 360
Siemens & Halske AG 238
  See also *Greek Telephone Company Case*
Singapore International Arbitration Centre
  See SIAC
Slaughter and May 98*n*55
social contribution(s) 270, 272, 274, 278
social insurance 275–276, 278*n*101
social security 241, 244, 275, 276, 278, 280, 355
Société de Banque Suisse 221*n*211
Société du Chemin de Fer Ottoman de Jaffa à Jérusalem et Prolongements 132

See also *Jaffa-Jerusalem Railway Arbitration*
Solidarity 275
Somalia
See *Ditta Luigi Gallotti v Somalia*
Sopron-Köszeg Local Railway Company v Austria and Hungary 207–212, 217, 218, 220, 224, 326*n*272
South Africa 154–156
Siam 140*n*246
sovereign
debt (*see* public debt)
risk 58–59

sovereignty, limitations upon states' freedom of exercise 42–43, 78, 167, 245, 329, 331–332, 334, 335
explicit 78, 196, 236, 303, 305, 306, 308
implicit 303–304
no presumption 298, 304–307, 332
See also direct state (entity) conduct, capacity by tribunals to
sovereignty, states' freedom of exercise 44, 237, 298, 304
legislative 79, 274 (*see also* regulate, right to)
See also public authority
Speed, Edwin Arney 145, 147–149, 160
stabilisation clause 43
staff council 255, 258*n*33, 261, 264*n*49
staff regulation(s) 255–256, 258–264
Staff Regulations Case 254–264, 272, 275
stakeholders 37, 38, 41, 47, 81
stare decisis 323
See also precedent
state contract(s)
internationalisation 336
interpretation (*see* contract, interpretation: restrictive (of state contracts))
motivation for concluding 192, 306–307
status of 189–190
See also concession; contract; contract, nature of
state succession, impact on concessions 44, 209–211, 214–215, 217, 221, 227
state-state disputes 4*n*8, 46, 201*n*136, 328*n*283–284, 332, 334, 337, 356
Stojković, Slavko 62*n*115, 64*n*118
Straits Settlements 149, 150, 161
Governor 149*n*282, 161
Legislative Council 161
Sudan
1963 South Africa Boycott Act 154*n*303
policy towards South African apartheid 154–156
See also *Sudan v Turriff*
Sudan v Turriff 51*n*72, 152–157, 159–160, 162, 163*n*337, 164–165
Südbahn
See Austria: South Austrian Railway Company
Suez Canal 38, 39*n*9
See also *Suez v Egypt*
Suez v Egypt 4*n*6, 35, 52*n*80, 63*n*116, 67, 72*n*142, 139, 159, 161*n*332, 351, 354*n*17
supreme court 150*n*290
Canada 128*n*198
US 46, 112*n*121, 115*n*134, 116–118, 124, 128, 130
supreme court judge 119, 353
Switzerland 353*n*13
US 123
Swiss Federal Tribunal
judge of 353*n*13
president of 60, 62
Switzerland 60

Taft, William Howard 47, 123–125, 127–128, 347, 354*n*13, 354*n*17
taxation 241, 252, 271, 273, 280, 281*n*111, 359
benefits 43, 44, 271
changes 229
distinction from other social charges 272–274, 277*n*101
rights 141*n*251
strict interpretation of exemptions 277
Ten Lepta Charge Case 79, 270–278
territorial changes (*see under* concession; state succession, impact on concessions)
Texaco v Libya 56*n*91, 70, 73, 79, 166–170, 235, 243, 336

The Administration of Posts and Telegraphs of the Republic of Czechoslovakia v Radio Corporation of America 77–79, 170–199, 234, 235, 242–245, 299, 303, 309, 312–315, 332–335, 337
  See also Radio Corporation of America; *Radio Corporation of America v China*
Thelin, Henri 60*n*102, 62, 353*n*13
third-party funding
  See litigation funding
third-party intervention 223–224, 232*n*249
Thomas, Albert 256, 263*n*49, 264, 272, 275, 280, 354*n*16
transnational (arbitration) 71, 72*n*142, 73, 74, 75*n*150
transparency 15, 16, 17, 340–342, 361
  See also under confidentiality in arbitration; investment-treaty arbitration; privacy in arbitration, exception to
treasury 47, 84, 162–164, 250*n*2, 251, 273
treaty interpretation 216–217, 224, 233, 326*n*272, 329
treaty-making practice 6
tribunal
  decisions, constitutive nature of 54, 164, 342
  deliberation 115*n*134, 301–302
  overlapping constitution 206, 216, 219, 224, 231, 232–233, 272
  president 58–63, 66, 123, 127, 221, 222*n*213, 295–297
  reappointment 222–223
  reconstitution of 115*n*134, 153
  secretary 280, 338
  truncated 86, 115, 117, 118*n*141
  umpire 58–59, 60*n*102, 61–64
  vacancy on 153
tribunal, mandate 32–36, 45, 70*n*135, 74, 83, 86, 114, 117–118, 125, 130, 188, 209, 223, 224, 233, 242, 265, 269
  arbitrators' understanding of 115, 188, 209–210, 211, 212, 216, 218, 219–220, 224, 226, 227, 232, 233, 238, 257, 269
  expiry of 115*n*134
  going beyond the strict confines of 115, 263–264, 275, 277–278, 310, 311
Truncated Tribunal Case 264–268, 272
trustee 221, 222*n*213
Turkey 132
  See also Ottoman Empire

UNCITRAL
  Arbitration Rules 23
  Model Law 23
unforeseen circumstances 211, 221, 223, 226, 227, 228
United Fruit Company 172
United Kingdom
  Ambassador in Khartoum 154, 160, 162
  Arbitration Act 1189 69*n*128, 142*n*255
  Arbitration Act 1996 17, 341
  Colonial Office 135*n*224, 140*n*246
  Court of Appeal 147
  Departmental Advisory Committee on Arbitration Law 341
  Foreign Office 131
  House of Lords 147*n*278, 148
  Privy Council 128–130
  Report on the Arbitration Bill 341
  Secretary of State for the Colonies 131, 140*n*246, 142*n*255
United Nations
  General Assembly 154
  Reports of International Arbitral Awards 352
United Nations Commission on International Trade Law
  See UNCITRAL
United States
  Congress 100, 102
  Constitution 116*n*137
  Department of Justice 320
  Government 64*n*118, 95, 172, 174, 177, 194, 317*n*249, 319–323
  President 47, 65, 123, 124
  Secretary of State 114
  Senate Interstate Commerce Commission 177
  Supreme Court 46, 112*n*121, 115*n*134, 116–118, 124, 128, 130
unjust enrichment 335
UNRIAA
  See under United Nations
Upper Silesia, Arbitral Tribunal of 355
Urquhart, Leslie 59*n*101, 60–61
use of force 59

USSR
  capitalism and 84, 86–87
  First Five Year Plan 84–88
  market economy and 84, 88
  New Economic Policy 84–88
  October Revolution 86
  socialism and 84, 88
  See also *Lena Goldfields v* USSR

valuation 47, 54*n*85, 117, 118, 121, 125, 127, 129, 136
valuation, basis for 129
  earning capacity 123, 136
  market value 128
  reproductive value 124, 136–137
van Hamel, Joost Adriaan 18*n*54, 60*n*103, 296–297, 305, 337–338, 339–340*n*315, 357*n*31
Veeder, VV 61*n*111, 88, 117–118*n*141, 161*n*332, 340–341
vested rights
  See acquired rights
Viscount Maugham 148*n*280

waiver 215
Wamwetzos, Alexandre 63*n*118, 241*n*270
War of the Pacific 103
Westinghouse Electric & Manufacturing Company 172
Whitmore, GS 181*n*75, 182, 294, 295*n*170
Wiarda, GJ 60*n*103, 354*n*15
Winterbottom, William 181*n*75, 194
withdrawal, of claims 223
worker rights 44, 255, 256–264, 272–273, 275, 280, 345
worker visas 45
World War I 132, 200, 355
World War I Peace Treaties
  applicability of 207–208, 214–215
  arbitration provisions 32*n*1, 70, 198, 201–202, 232, 358*n*32
  arbitrations held pursuant to (see *Barcs-Pakrac Railway Company v Hungary and Yugoslavia*; *Sopron-Köszeg Local Railway Company v Austria and Hungary*; *Zeltweg-Wolfsberg and Unterdrauburg-Woellan Railway Company v Austria and Yugoslavia*)
  purpose of provisions on arbitration 209, 214, 217
  See also international treaties: Treaty of Saint-Germain; international treaties: Treaty of Trianon
World War II 4, 95, 101, 206, 326

Yugoslavia
  See *Barcs-Pakrac Railway Company v Hungary and Yugoslavia*; *Batignolles v Yugoslavia*; *Losinger v Yugoslavia*; *SEEE v Yugoslavia*; *Zeltweg-Wolfsberg and Unterdrauburg-Woellan Railway Company v Austria and Yugoslavia*

Zakkas, Andre 265, 277, 354*nn*18–19
Zeltweg-Wolfsberg and Unterdrauburg-Woellan Railway Company v Austria and Yugoslavia 4*n*8, 38*n*7, 212–224, 326*n*272
Zhang Xueliang 285
Zhang Zuolin 284–285

www.ingramcontent.com/pod-product-compliance
Lightning Source LLC
LaVergne TN
LVHW020653300926
849161LV00004B/926